The Information System Consultant's Handbook

Systems Analysis and Design

The Information System Consultant's Handbook

Systems Analysis and Design

William S. Davis
Miami University

and

David C. Yen
Miami University

CRC Press
Taylor & Francis Group
Boca Raton London New York

CRC Press is an imprint of the
Taylor & Francis Group, an **informa** business

CRC Press
Taylor & Francis Group
6000 Broken Sound Parkway NW, Suite 300
Boca Raton, FL 33487-2742

First issued in hardback 2019

© 1999 by Taylor & Francis Group, LLC
CRC Press is an imprint of Taylor & Francis Group, an Informa business

No claim to original U.S. Government works

ISBN 13: 978-0-8493-7001-4 (hbk)

Visit the Taylor & Francis Web site at
http://www.taylorandfrancis.com

and the CRC Press Web site at
http://www.crcpress.com

Library of Congress Cataloging-in-Publication Data

Davis, William S., 1943-
    The information system consultant's handbook : systems analysis and design / by William S. Davis and David C. Yen.
        p.   cm.
    Includes index.
    ISBN 0-8493-7001-9 (alk. paper)
    1. System analysis--Handbooks, manuals, etc. 2. System design--Handbooks, manuals, etc. 3. Management information systems--Handbooks, manuals, etc. I. Yen, David C. II. Title.
T57.6.D378 1998
004.2'1--dc21

                                                    98-28765
                                                    CIP

Library of Congress Card Number 98-28765

Preface

Purpose

As the title implies, *The Information System Consultant's Handbook: Systems Analysis and Design,* was written for professional systems analysts, system designers, and information system consultants.

The premise is simple. If you are an information system professional, you often work with existing documentation and are frequently assigned to a new system development project in midstream, after considerable work has already been done. In both cases you are likely to encounter unfamiliar documentation, tools, techniques, and methodologies. The schedule is (always) tight, so you must quickly get "up to speed" and begin contributing. This book is written to help you quickly get up to speed.

Assumed background

The Information System Consultant's Handbook: Systems Analysis and Design assumes that you have a firm grasp of basic information processing technology and that you have had some experience analyzing and designing information systems. Consequently, you understand the underlying principles. The material contained in this book builds on those principles.

Content

The book is organized into eight parts:

- Principles
- Information gathering and problem definition
- Project planning and project management
- Systems analysis
- Identifying alternatives

- Component design
- Testing and implementation
- Operation and maintenance

Except for Part I, which reviews basic underlying principles, the parts correspond to the primary stages in the system development life cycle.

Each of the 82 chapters covers a single tool, technique, set of principles, or methodology and contains the following major topics:

- *Contents* — A list of the chapter's key topics.
- *Purpose* — A brief, single-paragraph statement of the chapter's purpose and content.
- *Strengths, weaknesses, and limitations.*
- *Inputs and related ideas* — Things you must know before using the tool; links to other related chapters in this book.
- *Concepts* — Explanations, in-context definitions, examples, and so on.
- *Key terms* — An alphabetized list of the chapter's key words with definitions.
- *Software* — A list of programs and other software resources that support the tool or technique.
- *References* — Citations, web pages, and suggestions for additional reading.

Clearly, it is impossible to fully cover every detail of 82 different systems analysis and design tools, techniques, principles, and methodologies in a single volume; complete books have been written on virtually every topic in this book. In selecting the material to cover, we relied on Pareto's law (Chapter 11), sometimes called the 80 : 20 rule. For most tools, techniques, principles, and methodologies, knowledge of a relatively small subset (perhaps 20 percent) of the underlying concepts and terminology is sufficient to understand the lion's share (perhaps 80 percent) of the topic's functionality. Our objective was to identify and clearly explain that crucial 20 percent.

Features

The reference value of the book is enhanced by several features, including:

- *Contents in brief* — A list of chapter titles.
- *Detailed contents* — A complete listing of the chapter's contents at the beginning of each chapter.
- *Glossary* — A consolidated list of key terms from all the chapters, with chapter references.

- *Index*
- *Trademarks* — A list of sources for all the software products referenced in this book.
- *Chapter cross-references* — Each chapter contains hyperlink-like references to other related chapters.
- *References* — The end-of-chapter references suggest sources for further in-depth study of the topic.

Note that the chapters are written to stand on their own, so, except perhaps for the specific topics mentioned in *Inputs and related ideas,* you can go directly to the material you actually need.

We enjoyed preparing this book. We hope you find it useful.

Authors/editors

William S. Davis   Professor of Decision Sciences and Management Information Systems, Miami University, Oxford, OH. Professor Davis is the author of thirty textbooks on various computer-related topics.

Dr. David C. Yen   Department Chair and Professor of Decision Sciences and Management Information Systems, Miami University, Oxford, OH. Dr. Yen is an experienced researcher and the author of numerous professional journal articles.

Acknowledgements

Jerry Papke was responsible for signing this project. Enjoy your retirement, Jerry. Suzanne Lassandro and Sue Zeitz managed the production process, and Jane Stark was our marketing manager. Additionally, we would like to acknowledge the contributions of the rest of the editorial, production, and marketing staff at CRC Press.

Portions of this book were derived from or based on three titles previously published by William Davis:

- *Business Systems Analysis and Design,* Wadsworth, Belmont, CA, 1994.
- *Systems Analysis and Design: A Structured Approach,* Addison-Wesley, Reading, MA, 1983.
- *Tools and Techniques for Structured Systems Analysis and Design,* Addison-Wesley, Reading, MA, 1983.

Finally, we would like to thank the contributors, who are listed on a separate page.

William S. Davis

David C. Yen

Contributors

Dr. John "Skip" Benamati
Department of Decision Sciences
  and Management Information Systems
Miami University
Oxford, Ohio

Dr. Bruce L. Bowerman
Department of Decision Sciences
  and Management Information Systems
Miami University
Oxford, Ohio

Dr. Michael S. Broida
Department of Decision Sciences
  and Management Information Systems
Miami University
Oxford, Ohio

Dr. David C. Haddad
Professor and Dean
School of Applied Sciences
Miami University
Oxford, Ohio

Dr. Timothy C. Krehbiel
Department of Decision Sciences
  and Management Information Systems
Miami University
Oxford, Ohio

Dr. Neil B. Marks
Department of Decision Sciences
  and Management Information Systems
Miami University
Oxford, Ohio

Richard T. O'Connell
Department of Decision Sciences
  and Management Information Systems
Miami University
Oxford, Ohio

Dr. Eleni Pratsini
Department of Decision Sciences
  and Management Information Systems
Miami University
Oxford, Ohio

Dr. T. M. Rajkumar
Department of Decision Sciences
  and Management Information Systems
Miami University
Oxford, Ohio

Maria Scott
Software Architects
Columbus, Ohio

Dan Michael Terrio
Director
P&G Center and SBA Technologies
Richard T. Farmer
  School of Business Administration
Miami University
Oxford, Ohio

Contents

part one

Principles

chapter one

The systems development life cycle

William S. Davis

Contents

1.1 Purpose

The purpose of a methodology is to specify a set of well-defined steps or phases, coupled with a set of clear, measurable exit criteria, for solving a complex problem (such as developing an information system). The system development life cycle (SDLC) is a set of steps that serves as the basis for most systems analysis and design methodologies.

1.2 Strengths, weaknesses, and limitations

A methodology (such as the system development life cycle) acts as a memory aid by imposing discipline, thus reducing the risk that key details will be

0-8493-7001-9/99/$0.00+$.50
©1999 by CRC Press LLC

overlooked. Communication is enhanced because the methodology imposes a consistent set of documentation standards. The steps in the methodology enhance management control, providing a framework for scheduling, budgeting, and project management. The tools associated with a good methodology make it easier to solve the problem. Finally, a good methodology increases the likelihood that significant errors are detected early.

There are dangers associated with using a methodology, however. Some people become so bogged down in the mechanics of following the steps and completing the exit criteria that they fail to solve the real problem. (There is a fine line between discipline and rigidity.) Additionally, no matter what methodology is chosen, there will be problems for which that methodology is (at best) inappropriate, and it is a mistake to try to force the application to fit the tool.

There is always a concern that the system developed may not accurately reflect the current business environment. The elapsed time between the initial proposal and system completion can be quite lengthy (often one or more years). Many methodologies require that specifications be "frozen" as work progresses from one step to the next, and user requirements do change over time. Given the fast pace of technology, this problem is particularly acute with hardware and/or software selected early in the process.

The traditional methodologies are not optimal for developing some types of information systems, such as expert systems and real-time processing systems. Additionally, fourth-generation, fifth-generation, and objected-oriented languages require modifications to the traditional approach.

Sometimes management is tempted to believe (or hope) that technology can replace technical experts. A good methodology makes a competent analyst more productive, but no methodology can convert an unskilled, untrained person into a competent analyst.

1.3 *Inputs and related ideas*

The system development life cycle provides a framework or structure for virtually all the tools and techniques discussed in this book.

The system development life cycle implies a phased approach, with complex tasks decomposed into smaller phases (stages, steps) that are easier to achieve, control, and manage. Many traditional methodologies, such as Martin's information engineering (Chapter 2) and Orr's structured requirements definition (Chapter 4), emphasize the phased approach, with clearly defined entrance and exit criteria for each individual phase. Practicing analysts often deviate from the rigidly phased approach defined by the methodology, however.

The project management life cycle is similar to the system development life cycle, with stages or phases defining a schedule and triggering resource allocations. Note, however, that a given project might encompass several related systems, and a given system might be divided into several sequential or concurrent projects.

1.4   Concepts

A system (Figure 1.1) is a set of interrelated components that function together in a meaningful way. A system is delimited from its environment (its suprasystem) by a boundary. A system accepts inputs at its boundaries. Outputs flow back across the boundaries. A process is an activity that changes the system in some way. Of particular interest are the interfaces, the points at which the various systemcomponents communicate or interact. As a general rule, the more interfaces a system contains, the more complex the system.

In addition to inputs, processes, interfaces, and outputs, the system also includes control and feedback mechanisms that together allow the system to determine if it is achieving its purpose. Feedback is the return of a portion of the system's output to its input. If the feedback suggests a deviation from the expected value (the control), the system reacts by attempting to adjust itself.

1.4.1   Information systems

This book is concerned with the analysis and design of information systems. An information system is a set of hardware, software, data, human, and

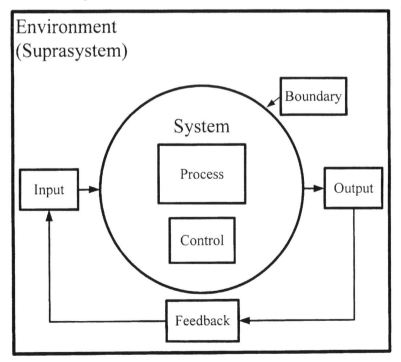

Figure 1.1   A system.

procedural components intended to provide the right data and information to the right person at the right time.

1.4.2   The system life cycle

Every system has a life cycle (Figure 1.2). An information system is "born" when a problem is recognized. After the system is developed, it grows until

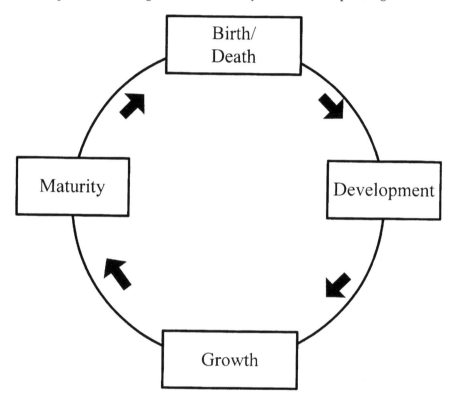

Figure 1.2   The system life cycle.

it reaches maturity. Eventually, a change in the nature of the problem or increasing maintenance costs degrade the value of the system, so it "dies" and a new or replacement system is born to take its place.

1.4.3   Methodologies

A methodology is a body of practices, procedures, and rules used by those who work in a discipline or engage in an inquiry. Often, a methodology is implemented as a set of well-defined steps or phases, each of which ends with a clear, measurable set of exit criteria. A key purpose of a methodology is ensuring that nothing is overlooked in the process of solving a complex problem (such as developing a complex information system).

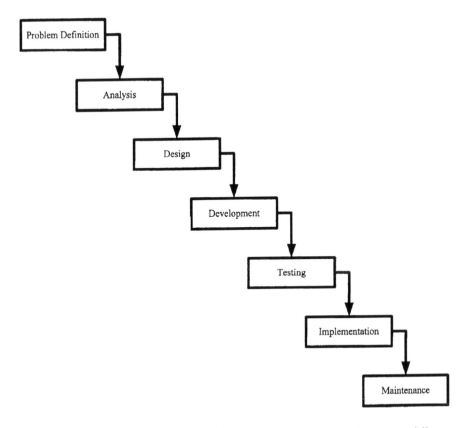

Figure 1.3 The system development life cycle is sometimes called the waterfall method.

1.4.4 The waterfall method

The basis for most systems analysis and design methodologies is the system development life cycle or SDLC (Figure 1.3). It is sometimes called the waterfall method because the model visually suggests work cascading from step to step like a series of waterfalls. (*Note:* In reality, there is considerable feedback between the various steps or phases.)

The first step is problem definition. The intent is to identify the problem, determine its cause, and outline a strategy for solving it.

Given a clear problem definition, analysis begins. The objective of analysis is to determine exactly *what* must be done to solve the problem. Typically, the system's *logical* elements (its boundaries, processes, and data) are defined during analysis.

The objective of design is to determine *how* the problem will be solved. During design the analyst's focus shifts from the logical to the *physical*. Processes are converted to manual procedures or computer programs. Data elements are grouped to form physical data structures, screens, reports, files, and databases. The hardware components that support the programs and the data are defined.

The system is created during development. (*Note:* Because the entire process is called the system *development* life cycle, some experts prefer to use other labels, such as system creation, for this stage.) Programs are coded, debugged, documented, and tested. New hardware is selected and ordered. Procedures are written and tested. End-user documentation is prepared. Databases and files are initialized. Users are trained.

Once the system is developed, it is tested to ensure that it does what it was designed to do. After the system passes its final test and any remaining problems are corrected, the system is implemented and released to the user. After the system is released, maintenance begins. The objective of maintenance is to keep the system functioning at an acceptable level.

1.5   Key terms

Analysis — To attack a problem by breaking it into sub-problems. The second step in the system development life cycle (following problem definition) during which the responsible people determine exactly what must be done to solve the problem.

Boundary — An entity that serves to delimit or separate a system from its environment.

Control — An expected value that can be compared with feedback. If the feedback suggests a deviation from the expected value (the control), the system reacts by attempting to adjust itself.

Design — The third step in the system development life cycle (following analysis and preceding development) during which the responsible people determine how the problem will be solved by specifying the system's physical components.

Development — The fourth step in the system development life cycle (following design and preceding testing) during which the system is created.

Feedback — The return of a portion of the system's output to its input.

Implementation — The sixth step in the system development life cycle (following testing and preceding maintenance) during which the system is installed and released to the user.

Information system — A set of hardware, software, data, human, and procedural components intended to provide the right data and information to the right person at the right time.

Interface — A mechanism or point of interaction between two or more system components.

Maintenance — The final step in the system development life cycle (following implementation) intended to keep the system functioning at an acceptable level.

Methodology — A body of practices, procedures, and rules used by those who work in a discipline or engage in an inquiry. Often implemented as a set of well-defined steps or phases, each of which ends with a clear, measurable set of exit criteria.

Problem definition — The first step in the system development life cycle during which the problem is identified, its cause determined, and a strategy for solving it developed.

Process — An activity that changes a system in some way.

Suprasystem — A system's environment.

System — A set of interrelated components that function together in a meaningful way.

System development life cycle (SDLC) — A set of steps for solving information system problems; the basis for most systems analysis and design methodologies.

System life cycle — A model that stresses the stages of system usefulness. The stages are birth, development, growth, maturity, and death.

Testing — The fifth step in the system development life cycle (following development and preceding implementation) intended to ensure that the system does what it was designed to do.

1.6   Software

Not applicable.

1.7   References

1. Davis, W. S., *Business Systems Analysis and Design,* Wadsworth Publishing, Belmont, CA, 1994.
2. Fertuck, L., *System Analysis and Design with CASE Tools,* William C. Brown Publishing, Dubuque, IA, 1992.
3. Kendall, K. E. and Kendall, J. E., *Systems Analysis and Design,* Prentice-Hall, Englewood Cliffs, NJ, 1992.
4. Laudon, K. C. and Laudon, J. P., *Managing Information Systems: A Contemporary Perspectives,* 2nd ed., Macmillan, New York, 1991.
5. Modell, M. E., *A Professional's Guide to Systems Analysis,* McGraw-Hill, New York, 1996.
6. Whitten, J. L., Bentley, L. D., and Dittman, K. C., *Systems Analysis and Design Methods,* Richard D. Irwin, New York, 1997.

chapter two

Information engineering

David C. Yen and William S. Davis

Contents

2.1 Purpose

Initially proposed by James Martin and Clive Finkelstein, the purpose of the information engineering methodology is to investigate the data and data relationships among different disciplines, and then organize those data to match the *corporation's* goals and objectives. A user-driven system is then developed using a top-down approach.

2.2   Strengths, weaknesses, and limitations

The information engineering methodology relates well to the corporate mission. The analyst is expected to relate *all* the essential information system components and match those functions to corporate objectives before performing data analysis. The link to the corporation's goals and objectives adds a high-level, executive, strategic perspective to the methodology. The methodology has a strong data orientation, leading to clearly-defined and documented data and data relationships. It enforces data normalization, which greatly reduces data redundancy and, hence, increases the accuracy and reliability of the database.

Information engineering is not a good candidate for designing real-time systems or systems in which the data have a strong time dimension because the methodology is based on a static data model.

2.3   Inputs and related ideas

The information engineering methodology can be viewed as a special case of the system development life cycle introduced in Chapter 1. Relevant tools are covered in problem analysis paradigms (Chapter 15), systems analysis (Part IV), and component design (Part VI).

2.4   Concepts

The steps in the information engineering methodology are summarized in Figure 2.1.

2.4.1   Strategic requirements analysis

During the strategic requirements analysis stage, the responsible personnel study the corporation's objectives, access the corporation's industry and competitive environment, and examine the corporate-wide impact of the proposed system. Key tools and techniques are covered in problem analysis paradigms (Chapter 15) and systems analysis (Part IV).

2.4.2   Information analysis

During the information analysis stage, a data model is created. The analyst begins by analyzing (organizationally and/or functionally) the information gathered during the first stage and further defining the system objectives. Next, the system's data requirements are defined, the necessary entities, related attributes, and keys are identified, and the appropriate data characteristics (length, type, alias, etc.), structure (name, address, etc.), and relationships are documented in the data dictionary. Given the data dictionary entries, the data are partitioned and normalized. Finally, the results are compared with the predetermined system objectives.

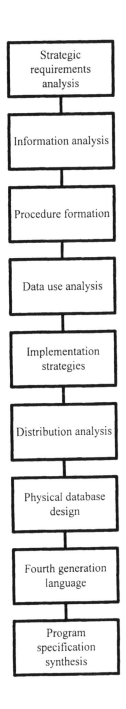

Figure 2.1   The steps in the information engineering methodology.

Many of the tools and techniques covered in Part IV can be used to perform information analysis, particularly, data flow diagrams (Chapter 24), data dictionary (Chapter 25), entity-relationship models (Chapter 26), and data normalization (Chapter 28).

2.4.3   Procedure formulation

During this stage, the analyst determines the operational procedures (add, delete, update, read, write, etc.) implied by data identified in the previous step. Additionally, physical file attributes (read-only, read-write, etc.) are identified for the subsequent physical database design step.

2.4.4   Data use analysis

During this stage, such data requirements as throughput, turnaround time, file size, and the number of records in each file are defined.

2.4.5   Implementation strategies

Such key decisions as the testing philosophy, hardware and software specifications, development strategy, software make-or-buy decisions, outsourcing/reengineering decisions, and so on are made during this stage.

2.4.6   Distribution analysis

Such factors as the management philosophy (centralized versus distributed), network analysis and design, the need for remote access, and the use of the Internet are considered during this stage. Such tools as network models (Chapter 52) and location connectivity models (Chapter 53) are commonly used.

2.4.7   Physical database design

As the name implies, the database is designed during this stage (Chapter 45). Other major concerns include screen design and output design (Chapters 46 through 51).

2.4.8   Fourth-generation language

The information engineering methodology recommends that non-procedural, fourth-generation languages (CASE generators, screen generators, report generators, object-oriented language, html, Java, etc.) be used to develop the system.

2.4.9 Program specifications synthesis

During the final stage, such details as output specifications (query versus report), the physical relationships among the various files, and the precise structure of the menus (icon, abbreviated, and traditional) are defined.

2.5 Key terms

Data model — A logical model that emphasizes or is driven by a system's data.

Data normalization — A formal technique for designing easy-to-maintain, efficient logical data structures.

Data redundancy — The state that occurs when the same data are stored in two or more different files.

Fourth-generation language — A programming language that allows the programmer to describe (in some way) the logical procedure and then let the language translator determine how to implement it; also called a *nonprocedural language.*

Generator — A program that starts with information in graphical, narrative, list, or some other logical form and outputs the appropriate source code; also called an *application generator, code generator* or *a program generator.*

Information systems strategy — High-level information system goals and objectives, often derived from or compatible with corporate goals and objectives.

Logical model — A model that exists on paper or in an analyst's mind. Logical models are easily manipulated; contrast with *physical.*

Make-or-buy decision — A decision to purchase or build internally software (or some other component).

Outsourcing — Subcontracting work outside the organization.

Physical — Real; actual, operational hardware, software, or data; contrast with *logical.*

Procedure — Guidelines, rules, or instructions for performing a task.

Reengineering — Rethinking and redesigning business processes.

Throughput — The amount of work flowing through a process, a component, or a system.

Turnaround time — The time between a request for a service and the completion of that service.

2.6 Software

Not applicable.

2.7 References

1. Connor, D., *Information System Specification and Design Road Map*, Prentice-Hall, Englewood Cliffs, NJ, 1985.
2. Inmon, W. H., *Information Engineering for the Practitioner, Putting Theory Into Practice*, Prentice-Hall, Englewood Cliffs, NJ, 1988.
3. Martin, J., *Information Engineering: Introduction*, Vol. I, Prentice-Hall, Englewood Cliffs, NJ, 1990.
4. Martin, J., *Information Engineering: Planning and Analysis*, Vol. II, Prentice-Hall, Englewood Cliffs, NJ, 1990.
5. Martin, J., *Information Engineering: Design and Construction*, Vol. III, Prentice-Hall, Englewood Cliffs, NJ, 1990.
6. Martin, J., *An Information Systems Manifesto*, Prentice-Hall, Englewood Cliffs, NJ, 1984.
7. Martin, J. and Leben, J., *Strategic Information Planning Methodologies*, Prentice-Hall, Englewood Cliffs, NJ, 1989.

chapter three

Structured analysis and design

William S. Davis and David C. Yen

Contents

0-8493-7001-9/99/$0.00+$.50
©1999 by CRC Press LLC

3.1   Purpose

"Structured Analysis and Design" is divided into two components: structured analysis as defined by DeMarco[2] and structured design as defined by Yourdon and Constantine[4]. Structured analysis is a front-end methodology that allows users and/or systems analysts to convert a real-world problem into a pictorial diagram or other logical representation that can subsequently be used by the systems developers and/or programmers to design an information system. Structured design is concerned with physical design based on the results of structured analysis. More generally, structured analysis transforms the abstract problem into a feasible logical design, while structured design concentrates on converting the logical design into a physical information system.

3.2   Strengths, weaknesses, and limitations

Structured analysis and design may be the best known analysis and design methodology. It features a top-down, hierarchical approach that tends to generate well-organized systems. Its step-by-step approach (parallel to the system development life cycle described in Chapter 1) simplifies project management, risk management, and resource management. Additionally, this methodology's tools and techniques can all be used to support other methodologies.

Managing and/or controlling the amount of data created by the structured analysis and design methodology can be time-consuming. Maintaining, updating, and documenting a complete set of data flow diagrams and a complete data dictionary are significant data management tasks in their own right. The step-by-step design philosophy makes this methodology inflexible. System and data requirements must be frozen at the beginning of the life cycle, so the actual systems developed may not reflect the current data and system requirements. Compared with other methodologies, structured analysis and design is not very user-friendly.

3.3   Inputs and related ideas

The structured analysis and design methodology can be viewed as a special case of the system development life cycle introduced in Chapter 1. Relevant tools include data flow diagrams (Chapter 24), data dictionaries (Chapter 25), decision trees (Chapter 57), decision tables (Chapter 58), structured English (Chapter 60), and structure charts (Chapter 63). Structured program design (Chapter 62) discusses the structured design process.

3.4   Concepts

Structured analysis and design is divided into two components: structured analysis as defined by DeMarco and structured design as defined by Yourdon and Constantine.

3.4.1 Structured analysis

The major steps in structured analysis are outlined in Figure 3.1.

3.4.1.1 Study the current business environment

The purpose of the first step is to study the old system, perform a market analysis to analyze the current business environment, perform a functional end-user analysis to determine the new data requirements, and perform a needs analysis to determine if a new system is necessary. Many of the tools and techniques described in Part II are used.

3.4.1.2 Model the old logical system

The objective of this step is to construct a logical model that captures the essence of the current environment by eliminating operational and physical details. Typically, the logical model consists of a data flow diagram (Chapter 24), a data dictionary (Chapter 25), and other models as appropriate.

3.4.1.3 Model the new logical system

Based on the old system model, a new, improved logical model is created. New user requirements are added, redundant requirements are eliminated and consolidated, and existing data requirements are updated. Complex primitives are decomposed into simpler primitives and/or more thoroughly documented. Finally, the data flows are verified.

3.4.1.4 Model the new physical environment

In this step, the necessary physical details are added back to the new logical design created in the previous steps. As appropriate, design options (hardware, software, platform, and interface) are identified for each of the primitives.

3.4.1.5 Evaluate alternatives

During this step, a cost estimate, a schedule, an estimate of resource requirements, a cost/benefit analysis, and similar parameters are prepared for each design option using the tools described in Part V.

3.4.1.6 Select the best design

The best alternative is selected using the tools described in Part V.

3.4.1.7 Create the structured specification

The purpose of the step is to prepare a recommendation for management's approval and to provide documentation for structured design.

3.4.2 Structured design

The major steps in structured design are outlined in Figure 3.2. See structured program design (Chapter 62) for additional depth on many of the topics overviewed in this section.

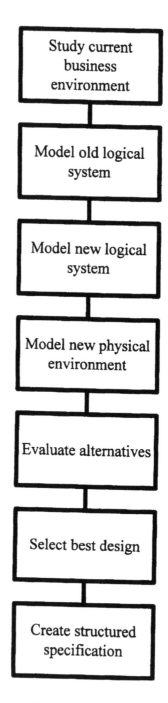

Figure 3.1 The major steps in the structured analysis process.

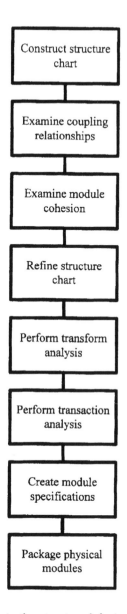

Figure 3.2 The major steps in the structured design process.

3.4.2.1 Construct a structure chart

As the name implies, the purpose of this step is to construct a structure chart (Chapter 63) that shows the hierarchical relationship and structure of all the data flows identified during structured analysis. In addition, control flows are added to the model to facilitate subsequent systems development.

3.4.2.2 Examine the coupling (interdependency) relationships

A key objective of structured design is to define loosely coupled, independent modules. Generally, a module's degree of independence is inversely proportional to the number of data elements (or composites) that flow between the module and the rest of the system. Consequently, the focus of this step is to increase module independence by identifying and restructuring modules with excessive data flows.

3.4.2.3 Examine module cohesion

A second objective of structured design is to define cohesive modules that perform a single, complete function. The focus of this step is on combining modules that perform common functions, consolidating functions to reduce the number of interfaces, and relocating modules to increase system efficiency.

3.4.2.4 Refine the structure chart

Using the results of the previous two steps, a final version of the structure chart is prepared.

3.4.2.5 Perform transform analysis

The purpose of transform analysis is to group together the modules (or processes) that manipulate a particular set of data or a particular data structure. For example, the processes that accept inventory transaction data, modify inventory levels, and update the master inventory data are probably related. The afferent (input), efferent (output), transform (data modification), and coordinate (controlling) modules are identified first. Grouping the modules to form a control structure might involve designating one module as the master (promoting a boss) or creating a new master (hiring a new boss). The subordinate modules are called slaves.

3.4.2.6 Perform transaction analysis

The purpose of transaction analysis is to group all modules (or processes) triggered by the same transaction to form a transaction center. For example, all the tasks performed in response to the arrival of an order from a supplier are related. Often, the control center serves as a control module.

3.4.2.7 Create module specifications

The primitives defined in the data flow diagram are defined in terms of logical sequence, selection, and repetition blocks.

3.4.2.8 Package the physical modules

The key purpose of this step is to ensure that the parent-child relationships between the modules are preserved when the procedures are grouped to form physical load modules for efficient execution on a computer. Often, a procedural analysis is performed to determine which procedures must be grouped within the same load module to avoid severe execution and/or testing errors.

3.5 Key terms

Cohesion — A measure of a module's completeness.

Control flow — The transfer of control into or out from a module.

Coupling — A measure of a module's independence; fewer parameters flowing into or out from a module imply looser coupling.

Data dictionary — A collection of data about a system's data.

Data flow — Data in motion; the transfer of data into or out from a module.

Data flow diagram — A logical model of the flow of data through a system.

Load module — The unit of program logic that is physically loaded and executed on a computer.

Logical model — A model that exists on paper or in an analyst's mind; logical models are easily manipulated; contrast with *physical*.

Module — A portion of a larger program that performs a specific task.

Physical — Real; actual, operational hardware, software, or data; contrast with *logical*.

Primitive — A process (or transform) that requires no further decomposition.

Process — An activity that changes, moves, or manipulates data.

Requirement — An element (process, data, etc.) that must be part of a system.

Structure chart — A hierarchy chart on which the data flows and control flows between modules are traced.

Structured analysis — A set of tools and techniques intended to transform an abstract problem into a feasible logical design.

Structured design — A set of tools and techniques intended to convert a logical design into a concrete information system.

Transaction — Typically, one occurrence of a business activity; for example, a single customer order or a single shipment from a supplier; an event.

Transaction analysis — The act of grouping all modules (or processes) triggered by the same transaction to form a transaction center.

Transform analysis — The act of grouping together the modules (or processes) that manipulate a particular set of data or a particular data structure.

3.6 Software

Not applicable.

3.7   References

1. Aktas, A. Z., *Structured Analysis and Design of Information Systems,* Prentice-Hall, Englewood Cliffs, NJ, 1987.
2. DeMarco, T., *Structured Analysis and System Specification,* Prentice-Hall, Englewood Cliffs, NJ, 1979.
3. Martin, J. and McClure, C., *Structured Techniques: The Basis for CASE,* Prentice-Hall, Englewood Cliffs, NJ, 1988.
4. Yourdon, E. and Constantine, L. L., *Structured Design. Fundamentals of a Discipline of Computer Program and Systems Design,* Prentice-Hall, Englewood Cliffs, NJ, 1979.
5. Yourdon E., *Modern Structured Analysis,* Prentice-Hall, Englewood Cliffs, NJ, 1989.
6. Yourdon, E., *Techniques of Program Structure and Design,* Prentice-Hall, Englewood Cliffs, NJ, 1989.

chapter four

Structured requirements definition

David C. Yen and William S. Davis

Contents

4.1   Purpose

Structured requirements specification, a data driven, output-oriented, bottom-up methodology, was initially proposed by Orr[2] and builds on the work of Warnier.[4,5] The focus of this methodology is designing a system to provide the right outputs to satisfy the user's needs.

4.2   Strengths, weaknesses, and limitations

The methodology's output orientation gives it a strong user focus; the objective is to provide the users with exact data they need to perform their jobs. The bottom-up approach tends to reinforce the output orientation because the methodology starts by investigating the necessary outputs, uses those outputs to determine the data and data structures, and then uses the data structures to suggest the necessary functions and/or modules. The methodology's tools and techniques, such as Wanier-Orr diagrams (Chapter 33), can be used to support other systems analysis and design methodologies.

In part because of the bottom-up orientation, data redundancy is a concern. The methodology's report and/or output orientation can lead the analyst to overlook such significant design criteria as the business environment, corporate policy and goals, and upper management philosophy. Also, this methodology lacks a strategic perspective.

4.3   Inputs and related ideas

The structured requirements definition methodology can be viewed as a special case of the system development life cycle introduced in Chapter 1. Relevant tools include entity-relationship diagrams (Chapter 26) and Warnier-Orr diagrams (Chapter 33).

4.4   Concepts

Structured requirements specification, a data driven, output-oriented, bottom-up methodology, was initially proposed by Orr and builds on the work of Warnier.

4.4.1   System outputs

The methodology is output oriented. It focuses on the system outputs, the exact data the users need to perform their jobs. More specifically, the analyst's objective is to define:

1. The layouts, formats, volumes, frequencies, and response times of the system outputs.
2. The risks, costs, and benefits associated with the system outputs.
3. The assumptions, constraints, and limitations that restrict and/or impact the system outputs.
4. The definitions, attributes, descriptions, and relationships of the data and the data structures needed to generate the system outputs.

4.4.2   The logical definition phase

The analyst begins by analyzing and designing a logical system and then specifying the system's logical requirements. The steps in the logical design phase are outlined in Figure 4.1.

4.4.2.1   Define the application context

The first task is to define a separate entity diagram for each major user. An entity diagram is a simplified entity-relationship diagram (Chapter 26) that identifies a major user's primary data entities (the things about which data are stored) and shows how those entities are related without regard for cardinality.

Next, the individual user entity diagrams are combined to form a merged entity diagram and eventually an application entity diagram. The application entity diagram can be viewed as an initial entity-relationship diagram that does not detail the attributes associated with each entity or specify the cardinality of the relationships.

Key objectives of this first phase include establishing a clear boundary for the proposed application or system and identifying the application's internal and external entities. Next, the system's major functions (the tasks or processes the system must perform) are defined and translated into measurable system objectives. The *major* functions produce the desired system outputs. Note that the objectives are stated in terms of the required system outputs.

4.4.2.2   Define the application functions

The entities and relationships (the interactions between the entities) are defined in the entity diagram, but the process details are not yet known. Thus, the next step is to add process information to the functions implied by the entity diagram by identifying the mainline functional flow (the primary logical path) through the system.

After studying the interrelationship between various entities in the application entity diagram, the analyst prepares a mainline functional flow diagram (analogous to an assembly line) to sequentially link all the processes in the proposed system (Figure 4.2). Key data entities are shown inside document symbols, with the related processes listed below. Note (in Figure 4.2) that once the *Customer order* is completed, the processes that generate a *Reorder* can be performed concurrently with the processes that generate a *Delivery* document.

After the mainline functional flow diagram is completed, the inputs, outputs, and processes are analyzed and the time frame factor (or execution frequency) is added to the diagram, yielding a sense of the system's scope, or magnitude. (In this methodology, scope refers to input, processing, and output time, not cost, although the methodology does not exclude estimating system size or cost.) For example, billing is a monthly, process, delivery occurs daily (or on demand), and so on.

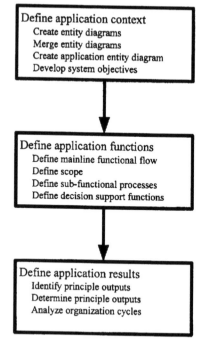

Figure 4.1   The steps in the logical design phase.

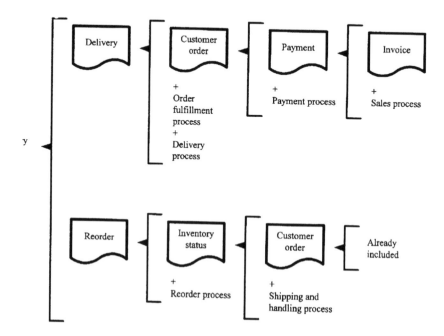

Figure 4.2   A mainline functional flow diagram.

Given a sense of the mainline functional flow, the complex functions and/or processes are decomposed into feasible, simple sub-functions. Decomposition continues until the sub-functions at the lowest level accomplish a single task. As part of this process, the logical data structures associated with the key data entities are defined. The detailed data structures are further defined in the next stage (Section 4.4.2.3).

Finally, such factors as user needs (output data and form), system objectives (query versus report), and the constraints and/or requirements placed on the results are used to define the system's decision support (decision-making) functions. These less tangible factors are significant when the logical data structures developed previously are converted into physical data structures.

4.4.2.3 Define the application results

For each process, a Warnier-Orr in-out diagram (Chapter 33) is prepared and all the required inputs and outputs are generated. Data layouts for each output are determined, samples of the various output forms (including such specific data as heading, title, date, page number, etc.) are prepared, the output structures are defined, and the logical structures (sequence, selection, and repetition) implied by the data structures are identified. The data items are documented in the data dictionary. Finally, during the organizational cycle analysis step, the report frequency (annually, quarterly, monthly, weekly, daily, hourly, on demand, and interactive) is defined.

4.4.3 The physical design phase

The physical design phase converts the detailed requirements determined by the logical design phase into a physical specification for developing the system. The steps are outlined in Figure 4.3.

4.4.3.1 Determine the constraints

During this step, system performance requirements (throughput, response time, and turnaround time) are set; system features such as security, locking, authentication, control, and audit are specified; and operating/execution requirements (processing speed and storage space) are defined.

4.4.3.2 Identify alternatives

Several alternatives for implementing the system are identified and documented.

4.4.3.3 Perform cost/benefit and risk analysis

Tangible and/or intangible benefits, costs, and associated risks are identified for each alternative. Cost/benefit and risk analyses are then performed for each alternative using the tools and techniques described in Part V.

Figure 4.3 The steps in the physical design phase.

4.4.3.4 Select and recommend the best alternative
The best alternative is selected and recommended.

4.4.3.5 Prepare requirements definition document
A final report containing all analysis and design documents is prepared.

4.5 Key terms

Application entity diagram — An entity diagram that combines all the user entity diagrams and merged entity diagrams for the entire application.

Bottom-up — A methodology that starts with the details and works upward.

Cardinality — A measure of the relative number of occurrences of two entities.

Data dictionary — A collection of data about a system's data.

Data-driven — A methodology or tool that starts with the data and derives the processes.

Data structure — A set of related data elements.

Decision support function — A function or operation that supports managerial decision making, often based on responding to "what-if" questions.

Entity — A thing about which data are stored.

Entity diagram — A simplified entity-relationship diagram that uses bubbles instead of rectangles and ignores cardinality.

Entity-relationship diagram — A model of a system's data that shows how the primary data entities are related.

Function — A meaningful operation or process that produces a desired result for a proposed system; similar to a process.

Logical data structure — A set of related data elements that ignores how the data are physically stored.

Logical design phase — The phase in the structured requirements definition methodology during which the system's logical requirements are defined.

Mainline functional flow diagram — A diagram that sequentially links all the processes in a proposed system.

Merged entity diagram — An entity diagram that combines the lower-level entity diagrams from two or more major users.

Output oriented — A methodology or tool that works backward from the output, through the processes, to the input.

Physical data structure — A set of related data elements as they are physically stored.

Physical design phase — The phase in the structured requirements definition methodology during which the detailed requirements determined by the logical design phase are converted into physical specifications for developing the system.

Process — An activity that changes, moves, or manipulates data.

Scope — In the structured requirements definition methodology, an estimate of input, processing, and output time; more generally, size or magnitude; often, a preliminary estimate of the size or cost of an information system.

System objective — A desired function of and/or operation performed by a proposed system.

System outputs — The exact data the users need to perform their jobs.

Time frame factor — A processing cycle; e.g., annually, monthly, daily, hourly, on demand, and so on.

4.6   Software

The diagrams in this chapter were prepared using Visio. Other charting programs (such as Micrografx's Flowcharter and SPSS's allCLEAR) and most paint programs can be used to create Warnier-Orr and related diagrams. Some CASE tools support this methodology.

4.7   References

1. Connor, D., *Information Systems Specification and Design Road Map*, Prentice-Hall, Englewood Cliffs, NJ, 1985.
2. Orr, K. T., *Structured Requirements Definition*, Ken Orr and Associates, Inc., Topeka, KS, 1981.
3. Orr, K. T., *Structured Systems Development*, Yourdon, Inc., New York, 1977.
4. Warnier, J.-D., *The Logical Construction of Programs*, Van Nostrand Reinhold, New York, 1976.
5. Warnier, J.-D., *Program Modification*, Martinus Nijhoff, London, 1978.

chapter five

CASE

T. M. Rajkumar
Miami University

Contents

0-8493-7001-9/99/$0.00+$.50
©1999 by CRC Press LLC

5.1   Purpose

The analysis, design, development, testing, and maintenance of software are complex processes that must be managed and controlled. Computer aided software engineering (CASE) is a technology that aids in this process. CASE can be broadly defined as a set of automated tools that assist in the entire software engineering process. Properly used, CASE tools help improve productivity during the development process and the quality of the resulting system.

5.2   Strengths, weaknesses, and limitations

The major benefit attributed to CASE is improved productivity. When used properly, CASE significantly reduces development time. A major reason is automation. CASE replaces many tedious manual procedures with automated tools.

Another major benefit of CASE is improved quality. CASE tools help enforce style conventions, validate syntax, perform consistency checks across models, generate highly maintainable code, and improve quality. CASE can also be used to track the progress of a project and maintain traceability from analysis, through design and implementation.

CASE aids in managing the ripple effects that result from a change to a model. In response to a change, CASE makes the necessary changes in all affected models, so the analyst does not have to redraw the diagrams. Consequently, the analyst is more likely to try more alternatives and develop better solutions.

A secondary benefit of CASE is better documentation because the system makes it easy to create, assemble, and maintain high quality documentation. Because of improved system quality and better documentation, using CASE often results in reduced software maintenance costs. Also, CASE documentation provides a new form of corporate memory that survives staff changes and the limits of paper documentation.

Some CASE tools are based on a specific methodology or do not support the modeling conventions required by a given project. As a result, they sometimes force the users to adopt and use the approach imposed by the CASE tool. It is the analyst's responsibility to choose the right tool for the application. The application should not be forced to fit the tool.

While most research indicates that CASE helps in the development process and improves productivity, various studies have shown that CASE is often not used uniformly across the organization, is used by only one group, or is never used.[5] A possible reason is that the perceived complexity outweighs the advantages of using the CASE tool. Given proper training, if users perceive that CASE tools provide them a relative advantage they are likely to use them voluntarily. Also, management commitment and support is essential.

The benefits of using CASE are rarely achieved unless the CASE tools are implemented correctly and managed carefully. CASE is not an end in itself. The real goal is not a successful CASE implementation, but the improvement of the software development process. Without continuous improvement in the software development process, CASE may be more detrimental than beneficial.[2]

Successfully implementing CASE tools requires that a structured or object-oriented systems methodology be in place. The CASE tool is used to facilitate the chosen business methodology, not to replace it. Unless the organization realigns its CASE technology goals with its business goals, the results are likely to be disappointing.

5.3   Inputs and related ideas

CASE incorporates and integrates many of the tools described in Parts III, IV, V, and VI. CASE tools are sometimes used during the information gathering and problem definition stage, particularly to support conducting a feasibility study (Chapter 13) or a JAD session (Chapter 14).

Unlike CASE, a programming environment supports programming activities and provides little or no support for analysis and design.

5.4   Concepts

CASE is a mechanism for automating system development methodologies. CASE tools typically:

- Support the notation conventions of a specific development method and enforce the method's rules.
- Support teams of analysts and designers working together on a project.
- Allow the user to navigate freely between different models and support automatic transformations from one stage to the next where appropriate.
- Support activities across the life cycle, from requirements to code.
- Support maintenance of traceability and configuration management information to help management control the development process.
- Support checking and testing the internal consistency of models.
- Support testing to ensure that a model is consistent with the real-world problem it represents.

5.4.1   CASE architecture

CASE is an environment that supports the software engineering process. The environment usually consists of distinct tools, such as editing tools, programming tools, verification and validation tools, configuration management tools,

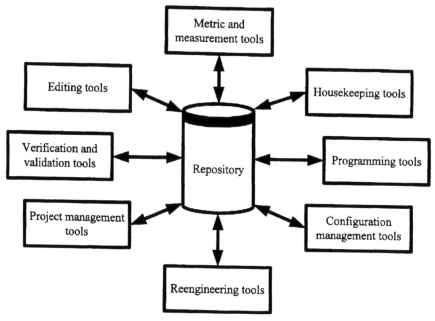

Figure 5.1   A standard CASE architecture.

metrics and measurement tools, project management tools, housekeeping tools, reengineering tools, and miscellaneous tools.[3] These tools are linked via the central repository, the most critical component in a CASE environment. Figure 5.1 shows a standard CASE architecture.

5.4.1.1   Editing tools
Editing tools include traditional tools (such as word-processing and programming editors) that help in creating documentation and diagramming tools that provide graphical capabilities such as drawing a data flow diagram (Chapter 24), entity-relationship diagram (Chapter 26), or class-structure diagram (Chapter 29).

5.4.1.2   Programming tools
Coding and debugging tools are the standard tools used to compile (or interpret), run, and debug a program. Code generators are tools that write code from a high-level specification of an application. For example, in an object-oriented application a code generator might write the code for the class given the object-class diagrams. In a visual programming environment, a code generator might write the code for the underlying interface given a user interface. Restructuring tools help in analyzing and reformatting existing code by removing unnecessary go-to statements or other unreachable portions of code.

5.4.1.3   Verification and validation tools

Verifiers ensure that the syntax is correct. Validation tools ensure that the requirements are correct and the product functions are the functions desired or requested by the customer.

Within this classification is a variety of tools. Static analyzers generate cross-references, check for syntax, and enforce standards on a program without executing the code. Dynamic analyzers, such as tracers and profilers, monitor program execution. Comparators check for differences or similarities between files; they are used for checking test output and expected program results. Correctness proof assistants support formal techniques to help prove mathematically the correctness of the code and evaluate the consistency between the code and the specification. Test management tools (Part VII) include test case generators that generate a variety of input test data based on the test criteria and the program's input data structures. They also include tools to manage the results, verify checklists, and run regression checking.

5.4.1.4   Configuration management tools

Configuration management tools help coordinate and manage software development. Version management tools help maintain the various versions of code and ensure that the correct copy of the code is incorporated in subsequent work. Librarians control the checkin and checkout of software from the repository.

Building an application involves preprocessing, compiling, and linking a variety of software components. Configuration builders ensure that the correct version of each component or piece of software is included in the finished product. These tools become critical when the same product is being built for different target platforms such as Unix or Windows because they keep track of the components used for each target platform.

When changes are made to one software component, other components are affected. If a given component is used in multiple software projects or by multiple designers or developers, then the changes must be synchronized across all developers and projects to ensure that all products continue to work correctly. Change control monitors help with this synchronization.

5.4.1.5   Project estimation and management

Developers and planners have expressed concern over their inability to accurately predict costs and estimate efforts, human resource requirements, and project duration. CASE provides modules that can help in the estimation process. For example, the COCOMO model (constructive cost model)[1] is integrated into some CASE software. Function point models are common, too. The scope of the necessary effort can be estimated by counting the number of business activities called function points. The basic idea is to determine problem complexity, code complexity, and data complexity so that a reasonable estimate can be derived.

Typical project management tools enable managers to create and use detailed work plans for resource allocation, identify and track task dependency relationships, implement project tracking, maintain charge-back allocations, and create PERT (Chapter 21) and Gantt (Chapter 20) charts.

A third sub-class of project management tools (email, bulletin boards, shared whiteboards) supports group work and may include tools to record various decisions taken during the system development process.

5.4.1.6   Reengineering tools

Legacy code (for example, old programs that must be modified for Year 2000 compliance) often lack structure, and in some cases, the source code may not even exist. Reengineering is the process of revising application software using a CASE tool. With reverse engineering, the existing application software is studied to understand its design. Forward engineering involves a complete redesign of the system to take advantage of new technologies such as client server computing.

CASE provides several tools to support reverse engineering. Documenters read the program code and generate high-level information about the system, such as cross-referencing information. Restructurers change the unstructured code into something more structured. Analyzers evaluate the strength and weaknesses of the system. Diagrammers read database code and generate such graphical tools as hierarchy diagrams (Chapters 62, 63, and 64) or entity-relationship diagrams (Chapter 26). To support forward engineering, CASE provides standard software development life cycle tools for redesigning the existing system.

5.4.1.7   Metric tools

Metric tools collect data on programs and program execution; for example, evaluating a set of code based on such metrics as McCabe statistics. Other tools are used to gather program run-time statistics.

5.4.1.8   Housekeeping tools

Housekeeping tools generate user accounts, generate and control repository access privileges, implement backup and recovery, and perform other housekeeping functions.

5.4.1.9   The repository

All the tools are integrated via the repository. The repository is a holding area for storing and integrating diagrams, descriptions, specifications, test data, and other items relevant to the development process. The repository allows users and developers to share information, supports team-based developmental activities, provides a mechanism for integrating a diverse set of CASE tools, and maintains a secure source of storage for software resources.

Additionally, the repository maintains information about the interrelationships between the various (logical and physical) models, and even with models related to implementations outside the repository (such as within programs). For example, if a logical definition of a process is related to its implementations, a repository can search for and retrieve all the implementations (programs, etc.) of that process in the MIS application environment.

Repository models must be open and extensible (in other words, they must accommodate other vendors' tools). The market is currently moving toward standardization, and CASE vendors are starting to provide hooks to allow their models to be stored in other vendors' repositories. For example, Rational's CASE tool allows the import and export of their models to Microsoft's repository product. Vendors are also starting to provide access to the data in their repositories via the World Wide Web.

Typically a separate repository is maintained for each project and a central repository maintains the details for all projects. Version control software is used to check in and check out the various project repositories from the central repository.

5.4.2   Workbenches

Integration in a CASE environment takes place along four dimensions[4]. Data integration ensures that the data are managed in a consistent manner across the entire environment. Control integration allows for combining the various tools and functions according to the needs of the project and the environment it supports. Presentation integration allows the users to see a consistent interface across the entire tool spectrum. Process integration ensures that tools interact effectively in support of a specific process.

Workbenches provide integration for only a portion of the system development life cycle. Upper CASE tools support the earlier phases (problem definition, analysis, and design), but provide little or no support for the back end (code generation, implementation, etc.). Lower CASE tools support the design, implementation, testing, and maintenance phases of the system development life cycle (in general the back end). Typical lower CASE tools include application generators for dialogue design, screen painting, code generation, etc. They provide little or no support for the earlier phases of the development life cycle. Both upper and lower CASE tools work in conjunction with implementational or programming workbenches (editors, compilers, debuggers, test tools, etc.).

5.4.3   Object-oriented CASE tools

Object-oriented CASE tools[6] support diagramming techniques for such basic object-oriented concepts as classes, inheritance, etc. (Chapter 6). Code generation and integration with other repositories and tools is also essential. Many CASE tools support the unified modified language (UML) notation

(Chapter 29). The UML, a standard approved by the Object Management Group, integrates the notation used in various object-oriented methods such as Booch, OMT, or Objectory (Chapters 29 and/or 66) into a single object-oriented modeling language.

An object orientation requires changes in the way CASE tools operate, however. For example, a CASE code generator must not only generate object-oriented code in languages such as C++ or Java, but also allow for modification of such code by the programmer. Any programmer modifications must be synchronized with the underlying diagrams, so the CASE tool must have the ability to maintain bi-directional synchronization between the graphical models and the generated code. In other words, the code, whether generated by the CASE tool or the programmer, must be integrated with the CASE tool.

Object-oriented CASE tools must support consistency checks and provide error checking capabilities. If the CASE tool is to perform error checking, it must support encapsulation, inheritance, message passing, and other object-oriented characteristics (Chapter 6), and users must be able to view an object on screen, and not rely simply on the diagramming techniques.

Browsing capabilities and the need to hide and reveal portions of the model are unique to object-oriented CASE tools. Browsing is essential because object-oriented development stresses reuse, which means the designer must find potentially reusable classes rather than reinventing the wheel. Reuse librarian software (a library of components and query retrieval mechanisms) helps retrieve software components for reuse.

Much of this browsing does not fit such standard techniques as searching by keyword. Various object-oriented CASE tools are intended to help the analyst or designer visualize and understand the abstraction and specialization process during class definition and classification. For example, the analyst might browse through a hierarchy or might wish to determine all classes that use a specific class or all the component classes in a given class.

To make the browsing process more effective, the analyst might want to hide or expand certain details. For example,[6] the analyst may require that the CASE tool support hiding or revealing the attributes or operations in an object class, the relationships between object classes, parameters of messages between object classes, or sequences of messages between a specified group of collaborating object classes

5.4.4   *CASE environments*

The term environment is reserved for the complete set of automated facilities (such as the operating framework) required to support all the activities in the systems development life cycle, including facilities that allow users to switch easily from one activity to another. An environment must support reusability of tool components, ease of tool integration, prototyping, and support for system development life cycle activities in big multi-user, multi-project software environments.

An environment must be extensible. New tools are likely to emerge during the lifetime of the CASE product, and the environment must be capable of augmenting its tool capabilities and integrating the new tools easily. Extensibility is more easily achieved when the environment is open. An environment must also support interconnectivity, the smooth integration and maintenance of multiple users working on various projects over a network. The infrastructure needed to provide extensibility and interconnectivity exceeds the capabilities of the base operating system.

Examples of environments include IBM's AD/Cycle and Digital Equipment Corporation's Cohesion. These two environments provide basic tools, workbenches, and an integrating platform that lets other companies enrich the environment with additional products or tools.

5.5   Key terms

CASE (computer-aided software engineering) — A set of automated tools that assist in the entire software engineering process.

Environment — A collection of tools and workbenches that support the entire software process.

Forward engineering — Completely redesigning a system to take advantage of new technologies such as client server computing.

Lower CASE — A set of tools that support the design, implementation, testing, and maintenance phases of the system development life cycle (in general the back end).

McCabe statistics — A complexity metric based on a count of the number of decisions in a program. An indicator of the testability and maintainability of software.

Reengineering — The process of revising application software using a CASE tool.

Repository — An integrated holding area where diagrams, descriptions, specifications, test data, and other items are stored and integrated. The repository is the most critical component in a CASE environment.

Reverse engineering — The process of studying the existing application software to understand its design.

Tool — Software that supports a specific task in the software development process.

Upper CASE — A set of tools that support the earlier phases (problem definition, analysis, and design) of the system development life cycle.

Workbench — A single application that integrates several tools, providing a consistent user interface, consistent invocation of tools and tool-sets, and access to a common data set from a repository (data integration).

5.6   Software

Several software companies and their CASE products are listed in Table 5.1. This list is by no means comprehensive nor does it represent the author's

Table 5.1 A Representative List of CASE Products

Company	Products
Microsoft	Visual Modeler, Visual Source Safe
Rational	Rational Rose
Digital Equipment Corp.	Cohesion
Intersolv	Excelerator II, PVCS
Andersen Consulting	Foundation
Sterling Software	Composer
Popkin Software	System Architect
Hewlett Packard	Softbench
Oracle	Designer
PowerSoft	Power-Designer
LogicWorks	ERWIN, BPWIN, OOWIN
IBM	CMVC, AD/Cycle

recommendations. For a more up-to-date list, please visit one of the following World Wide Web sites:

1. http://www.qucis.queensu.ca/Software-Engineering/vendor.html
2. http://www.yahoo.com/Business_and_Economy/Companies/ Computers/Software/Programming_Tools/Computer_Aided_ Software_Engineering__CASE/

Note: In the second URL, there are two underline characters (__) between *Engineering* and *CASE*.

5.7   References

1. Boehm, B. W., *Software Engineering Economics,* Prentice-Hall, Englewood Cliffs, NJ, 1981.
2. Boone, G., Establishing the context of continuous improvement for technology transfer, in *The Impact of CASE Technology on Software Process,* Cooke, D. E., Ed., World Scientific, Singapore, 1994, 215.
3. Fuggetta, A., A classification of CASE technology, *IEEE Comput,* 26(12), 25, 1993.
4. Thomas, I. and Nemjeh, B. A., Definition of tool integration for environments, *IEEE Soft,* 9(2), 29 1992.
5. Tuhari, I., Why are CASE tools not used?, *Commun. ACM,* 30(10), 94, 1996.
6. Yourdon, E., Whitehead, K., Thomann, J., Oppel, K., and Nevermann, P., *Mainstream Objects: An Analysis and Design Approach for Business,* Yourdon Press, Upper Saddle River, NJ, 1995, 101.

chapter six

Object-oriented concepts

William S. Davis

Contents

6.1 Purpose

The objective of the object-oriented approach to software development is to support creating software that is easier to change, debug, and maintain than is traditional software. Today, object-oriented principles are also applied to system development.

6.2 Strengths, weaknesses, and limitations

The object-oriented approach offers many advantages over traditional software (and system) development. Object-oriented software and systems are intuitive. Objects are things that really exist, events are things that really happen, and real-world objects really do respond to something like signals.

Object-oriented software and systems are easier to change, debug, and maintain than are traditional structured software and systems because they are highly modular. Because the modules reflect natural classifications, they tend to be more independent and more stable than the somewhat arbitrary modules suggested by traditional structured techniques. Because data and methods are grouped in the same object, ripple effects are isolated and thus easier to trace.

The object-oriented approach to software development supports reusable code. The principle of reusability is imbedded in the theory that underlies object-oriented software.

Object-oriented software is often less efficient than structured software on traditional single-processor computers. Note, however, that object-oriented software may actually be *more* efficient on the parallel systems that are evolving.

More significantly, relatively few programmers are trained in the object-oriented approach, leading to personnel shortages, and adding to software development expense. Current academic curricula are beginning to stress object-oriented software, however, so this problem may grow less severe given time.

6.3   Inputs and related ideas

Object-oriented analysis is discussed in Chapter 29. Object-oriented software design is discussed in Chapter 66.

6.4   Concepts

An object is a thing about which data are stored and manipulated. It might be a physical thing such as a person, a customer, a book, or an item in inventory. It might be an abstract thing such as a model, a concept, or a process. Unlike many technical terms, the word *object* means what people intuitively think it means.

6.4.1   Objects and object types

To avoid being swamped by the sheer number of objects, similar objects are grouped to form classes or object types. Classifying or grouping objects makes it easier to track them.

An individual object is a single instance (or occurrence) of an object class (or object type). For example, a given computer (the object itself) has a unique serial number. That particular computer is but one instance of a given model. Moving up the classification hierarchy, a store might distinguish between tower, desktop, laptop, and hand-held computers. Finally, computers, printers, boards, software, supplies, books, and services clearly represent different categories.

6.4.2   Encapsulation

Both data (attributes) and methods (processes) are associated with an object. For example, an item in inventory might be described by listing such attributes as its product code, a brief description, its selling price, and so on. A method is a process that accesses an object. For example, associated with a given product in inventory are methods for placing it in inventory, changing one of more of its attributes, removing it from inventory, and so on. Methods define how the object's data are manipulated.

In an object-oriented program, an object's data and methods are bundled so that the only way to access the data is through the object's own methods. Hiding implementation details in this way is called encapsulation. The only way other objects can obtain a given object's data is through one of that object's own methods.

6.4.3   Signals

Because the objects in a well-designed object-oriented system are encapsulated, they are isolated from each other and changes to one object cannot inadvertently affect others. Objects do not exist in a vacuum, however. They interact with other objects by transmitting and responding to signals.

Signals are generated by events. An event occurs when an object's state changes. A change in state usually implies a change in the value of one of the object's attributes. The only way to change an attribute is through one of the object's own methods, so events imply methods.

An operation is an external view of an object that can be accessed by other objects. An operation is implemented by one of more methods. In effect, an operation is a method (or methods) that responds to or generates external signals.

Note that a given event does not direct its signal to a specific target object. Instead, the initiating event simply broadcasts the signal. Other objects might respond to the signal or ignore it, but the source object neither knows nor cares. In this case, indifference implies independence.

6.4.4   Inheritance

A Mazda Miata can be described as a small, sporty, two-seat automobile. Because it is a *type* (subclass) of automobile, all the attributes the Miata shares with other automobiles (four wheels, an engine, a cooling system, methods for propulsion, steering, and stopping) can be assumed.

Moving down another level, a specific Mazda Miata (an object) can be described in terms of the attributes that make *it* unique (red, convertible top, serial number), and the attributes it shares with other Miatas (small, two seats, sporty) can be assumed. In effect, each subclass borrows (or inherits) attributes and methods from its superclass. This concept is called inheritance.

6.4.5 Polymorphism

A given operation or method is considered polymorphic if it produces similar results in different objects or at different levels. For example, a customer sale, a customer return, the arrival of a shipment, and the completion of a physical inventory are all events that can change the value of the inventory stock-on-hand for a given object type. The general structure of the inventory update method might be inherited from the highest-level class, and then customized for each of these special cases.

6.5 Key terms

Class (object type) — A group of similar objects.

Encapsulation — Hiding implementation details by bundling an object's data and its methods so that the only way to access the data is through the object's own methods.

Event — An occurrence that generates a signal.

Inheritance — The principle that allows an object to get attributes and methods from its superclass.

Method — A process that accesses an object.

Object — A thing about which data are stored and manipulated.

Object type (class) — A group of similar objects.

Operation — An external view of an object that can be accessed by other objects.

Polymorphism — The property of an operation or method that allows it to produce similar results in different objects or at different levels.

Signal — A message that allows objects to interact with other objects.

State — A set of attribute values for an object.

6.6 Software

Not applicable.

6.7 References

1. Budd, T., *An Introduction to Object-Oriented Programming*, Addison-Wesley, Reading, MA, 1991.
2. Davis, W. S., *Business Systems Analysis and Design*, Wadsworth, Belmont, CA, 1994.
3. Martin, J. and Odell, J. J., *Object-Oriented Analysis and Design*, Prentice-Hall, Englewood Cliffs, NJ, 1992.
4. Winblad, A. L., et al., *Object Oriented Software*, Addison-Wesley, Reading, MA, 1990.

chapter seven

Expert system analysis and design

David C. Yen and William S. Davis

Contents

7.1   Purpose

An expert system (or knowledge-based system) is a computer program that emulates the thought process of a human expert. This chapter defines several key terms and examines the process of creating an expert system.

0-8493-7001-9/99/$0.00+$.50
©1999 by CRC Press LLC

7.2   Strengths, weaknesses, and limitations

Expert systems differ in important ways from both conventional information systems and systems developed in other branches of artificial intelligence. Among the characteristics that make expert systems distinctive are
symbolic representation, symbolic reasoning, natural language processing,
heuristics search, and reasoning processing capabilities.

Expert systems are valuable in applications that call for judgment and
inference based on incomplete data. They are particularly good at extracting
the best alternatives from a long list of options. Over time, as users interact
with an expert system, the system senses patterns in those interactions,
incorporates the new knowledge into its knowledge base, and, in effect,
learns.

Perhaps most importantly, an expert system captures and stores expertise in a permanent, consistent, affordable, well-documented, easily transferred form. In contrast with artificial expertise, human expertise is perish-
able, difficult to transfer and document, unpredictable, and expensive.

In the medical field, expert systems are used to screen patients, provide
second opinions, and check the accuracy of a diagnosis. Geologists use
expert systems to help locate oil and mineral deposits. Business expert
systems support such tasks as training, capital resource planning, loan
application analysis, and strategic planning. Telephone companies use
expert systems to route telephone traffic during peak hours and to suggest
the best type of phone service for their business customers. Computer manufacturers use expert systems to help configure computer systems. "Smart"
bombs are guided by expert systems.

Generally, expert systems should be considered only when the need for
judgment and/or the lack of complete data make traditional algorithm-
based systems unacceptable. Expert systems are difficult to create.
Identifying the necessary inference rules depends on the cooperation of an
expert, and even experts sometimes behave as they *should* (rather than as
they normally do) while under observation. Creating an expert system is an
open-ended process that is difficult to manage using such traditional tools
as budgets and schedules. Additionally, expert systems can be expensive to
operate and maintain.

7.3   Inputs and related ideas

The process of creating an expert system parallels the system development
life cycle introduced in Chapter 1. Developing an expert system implies
developing a prototype (Chapter 31). Selected knowledge engineering and
problem solving tools are discussed in Chapter 34. Knowledge representation is discussed in Chapter 67. Prototyping techniques (Chapter 31) are
often used to develop an expert system.

7.4 Concepts

An expert system (or knowledge-based system) is a computer program that emulates the thought process of a human expert.

7.4.1 Expert system components

An expert system (Figure 7.1) is built around a rule base that incorporates knowledge, algorithms, and heuristic rules. The process of creating a rule base begins with a human expert whose expertise is captured, encoded by a knowledge engineer, and entered through a knowledge acquisition facility. In addition to the rule base, most expert systems also incorporate a database, a model base, and a graph base.

A user accesses the system through a user interface called the expert system shell and enters the parameters of a problem to an inference engine. Often, the expert system shell incorporates natural language processing. The inference engine uses the input parameters to access the rule base, the database, the model base, and the graph base. Based on the available information and its reasoning capability, the inference engine reaches a conclusion and offers expert advice. Most expert systems also contain an explanation facility that reproduces the logic the inference engine followed to reach its conclusion.

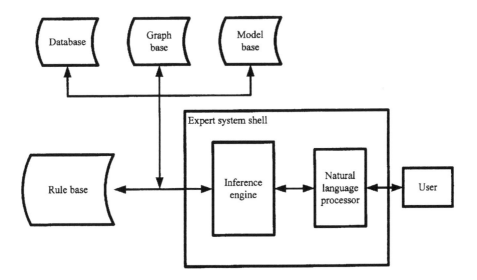

Figure 7.1 The components of an expert system.

7.4.2   Creating an expert system

The steps in a typical expert systems analysis and design methodology are summarized in Figure 7.2.

7.4.2.1   Identification phase

The first step in the identification phase, *Identify problem,* is similar to the problem definition phase in the traditional systems development life cycle. The objective is to identify, characterize, and define the problems the system will be expected to solve and then partition the problem into appropriate sub-tasks.

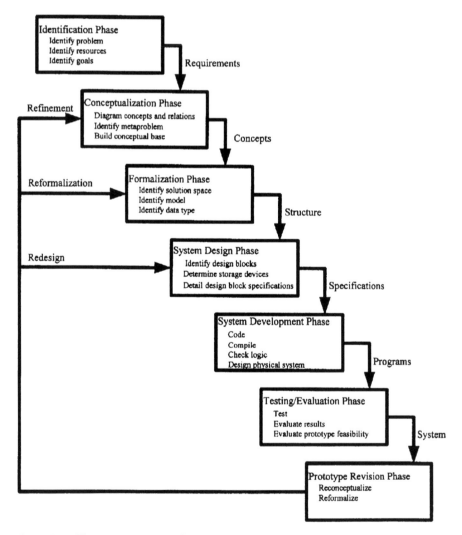

Figure 7.2   The steps in a typical expert systems analysis and design methodology.

Once the problem is defined, the resources necessary for acquiring knowledge, implementing the system, and testing the system are identified. Typical resources include knowledge, time, computing facilities, and money. Because expert systems are expensive and creating one takes considerable time, a feasibility study (Chapter 13) is often conducted before work progresses beyond this point.

In addition to identifying resources, the expert system analysts and/or designers also identify the system's goals and objectives. It is helpful to identify and explicitly document the goals because certain design approaches, such as heuristic search, breadth search, depth search, and reasoning are goal-driven.

7.4.2.2 Conceptualization phase

The central task of the conceptualization phase is to diagram the system's key concepts and relations to define a conceptual base for a prototype system. Key objectives include separating the inference engine from the problem domain, factoring (analyzing) the problem into meta-problems, identifying the system's key concepts and relations, and testing those concepts and relations by challenging them (with specific examples of problem-solving activities) to ensure that they cover every general case. Many of the tools and techniques described in Part II are used in this phase.

7.4.2.3 Formalization Phase

The formalization phase involves mapping key concepts, sub-problems, and information flow characteristics isolated during conceptualization into more formal representations based on various knowledge engineering and problem solving tools (Chapter 34) and knowledge representation frameworks (Chapter 67). The key objectives are to identify the solution space (a domain with a collection of all possible solutions), the hypothesis space (the hypothetical solution space), the underlying model, and the characteristics of the data.

To define the structure of the hypothesis space, the systems analysts or designers must formalize the concepts (knowledge in an abstract format that can be used to guide a searching or reasoning process) and determine how they are joined to form a hypothesis. The concepts provide clues about the nature of the space such as if it is finite, if a hierarchy must to be considered, if certain levels of abstraction can be applied, and if a specific class of the concept must be generated. Such searching techniques as blind search, heuristic search, and abstracting the solution space (Chapter 34) are often used. Reasoning techniques such as assumption building, justification building, and the constraints and goal technique (Chapter 34) help to identify the underlying model of the process used to generate solutions in the domain.

7.4.2.4 System design phase

During the system design phase (sometimes called the logical design phase) the analyst and/or designer specifies how the system will meet the requirements identified during the previous three phases. Typically, the reports and other outputs the systems must produce are defined first. This phase is similar to the design stage in the traditional systems development life cycle. Note, however, that the representation schemes used to describe knowledge (Chapter 67) differ from traditional methodologies.

7.4.2.5 System development phase

A prototype (Chapter 31) expert system is created during the system development (or physical design) stage. This stage is similar to the development stage in the traditional system development life cycle.

7.4.2.6 Testing and evaluation phase

During this phase, the prototype system is evaluated. This phase parallels the testing stage in the traditional system development life cycle. However, in addition to the testing tools and techniques described in Part VII, expert systems utilize a dynamic testing technique to verify the reasoning and/or inference process.

7.4.2.7 Prototype revision phase

An expert system evolves over time, calling for almost constant revision, a trait expert systems share with most prototypes. Based on the results of the testing/evaluation phase, concepts and relations are refined, the solution space, the model, and the data characteristics are reformalized, and the system is redesigned.

7.5 Key terms

Breadth search — A searching technique that investigates all the nodes at a given level before moving down to the next level.

Concept — Knowledge in an abstract format that can be used to guide a searching or reasoning process.

Depth search — A searching technique that investigates all lower-level nodes before considering the next node at the same level.

Domain — A possible problem space in which searching or reasoning techniques can be applied.

Expert system (knowledge-based system) — A computer program that emulates the thought process of a human expert.

Expert system shell — The user interface to an expert system.

Explanation facility — An expert system component that reproduces the logic the inference engine followed to reach its conclusion.

Factoring — A technique for grouping several sub-problems into a meta-problem.

Graph base — A database with a collection of graphs or graphing tools; for example, most graphic software implements a graph base of customized symbols or pictures.

Heuristic rule — A specific rule of thumb or common sense that can be used to restrict a search to a subset of a problem domain.

Heuristic search — A search technique that applies heuristics to reduce the size of a problem domain.

Heuristics — General rules derived from experience, common sense, inferences, and intelligent trial and error.

Hypothesis space — A mathematical term for a space that is defined abstractly; generally, the subset of a solution space to be considered.

Inference engine — The component of an expert system that uses input parameters to access the knowledge base, reach a conclusion, and offer expert advice.

Knowledge acquisition facility — A set of software tools for capturing and encoding a human expert's expertise and creating a knowledge base.

Knowledge base — A collection of data, algorithms, and heuristic rules that forms the core of an expert system.

Knowledge engineer — A person who captures and encodes a human expert's expertise and creates a knowledge base.

Machine learning — The capacity of a machine (or an expert system) to "learn" from experience.

Meta-problem — A problem that is synthesized or generalized from several lower level sub-problems.

Model base — A collection of models that support decision making and/or data analysis; an example is a collection of different forecasting models.

Natural language processing — Hardware and/or software that allows people to communicate with computers in much the same way they communicate with other people.

Partition — To decompose a large problem into several smaller problems.

Prototype — A reasonably complete, working model of a system.

Reasoning — The act of using inference to lead to a conclusion based on existing knowledge and/or data.

Reasoning capability — An inference engine feature that reaches a conclusion by applying the rules in the rule base.

Relation — An association or link between two objects or entities.

Rule — A formal specification or description of a unit of knowledge.

Rule base — A collection of executable rules; the rule base is accessed by the inference engine to support reasoning.

Solution space (problem space) — A mathematical term for the set of all possible solutions.

Symbolic reasoning — A technique for performing reasoning or inference with symbolic data such as graph, image, and/or picture.

Symbolic representation — A technique for representing symbolic data or knowledge.

7.6   Software

LISP (list programming language) and PROLOG (programming logic language) are popular expert system programming languages. Variations include common LISP, Franz LISP, CProlog, Knowledge Workbench, Quintus Prolog, Prolog-2, Arity Prolog, UNSW Prolog, and Turbo Prolog.

Popular systems building products include Expert-Ease, ADVISE, RULEMASTER, SEEK, and RULE WRITER. Other relevant products include KEE, KMS, RLL, SRL, SRL+ (frame-based), APES and HSRL (logic based), ROSS, SMALLTALK, and KBS (object oriented), INTERLISP and PSL (procedure-oriented), and ARS, ART, EXPERT, EXPERT-II, OPS5, RITA, and ROSIE (rule-based).

7.7   References

1. Connor, D., *Information Systems Specification & Design Road Map*, Prentice-Hall, Englewood Cliffs, NJ, 1985.
2. Harmon, P. and King, D., *Expert Systems: Artificial Intelligence in Business*, John Wiley & Sons, Inc., New York, 1985.
3. Hayes-Roth, F., Waterman, D. A., and Lenat, D. B., *Building Expert Systems*, Addison-Wesley, Reading, MA, 1983.
4. Waterman, D. A., *A Guide to Expert Systems*, Addison-Wesley, Reading, MA, 1986.

part two

Information gathering and problem definition

chapter eight

Interviewing

William S. Davis

Contents

8.1   Purpose

During the problem definition, feasibility study, and analysis stages, interviewing is one of the analyst's most important sources of information about the present system and the user's requirements. The purpose of this brief introduction is to provide some suggestions for planning and conducting an interview.

8.2   Strengths, weaknesses, and limitations

Written documentation often provides a one-dimensional view of the problem. Interviews, in contrast, give the analyst the opportunity to sit down face to face with the affected people, investigate their opinions, feelings, and goals (as well as the facts), observe nonverbal behavior, and probe for additional feedback. An interview can serve as an effective entry point to the problem definition and analysis stages, identifying relevant personnel and specific topics that must be investigated in more depth. Interviews are excellent tools for achieving user involvement in the system development process and for verifying information collected using other tools.

Interviewing is time consuming and costly. Its effectiveness is a function of the interviewer's skill. Not all subjects are comfortable being interviewed, and many people react negatively or defensively to an interviewer's questions. Interviewing is not particularly effective for uncovering technical or operational details.

8.3   Inputs and related ideas

Interviews can be used in virtually any stage of the system development life cycle. Interviewing is often one of the first tasks performed during the information gathering and problem definition stage. Interviews are often performed as part of conducting a survey (Chapter 17).

8.4   Concepts

During the problem definition, feasibility study, and analysis stages, interviewing is one of the analyst's most important sources of information about the present system and the user's requirements. The purpose of this brief introduction is to provide some suggestions for planning and conducting an interview.

8.4.1   Preparing for the interview

People resent interviewers who waste their time, so do your homework. Good interviewers do not just "wing it." Effective interviewing requires careful preparation.

Study the user's environment. Identify the people responsible for the problem area. Study the organization chart and learn what those people do. Familiarize yourself with the available reports, documents, and procedures, note unanswered questions, missing pieces, and ambiguities, and develop a specific set of objectives for the interview. Unless you know what you want to learn (more accurately, unless you know what you do *not* know), you cannot ask intelligent questions.

Given a set of objectives, the next step is to select the person (or the group) to be interviewed. The organization chart is a good starting point. Interview the responsible manager first, get an overview of the problem, request the names of the people who know the details, and request permission to interview them. Failing to obtain appropriate authorizations for an interview is usually a mistake.

8.4.2   Scheduling the interview

Interviews should be scheduled; do not simply drop in unannounced and expect cooperation. Remember that you are the one who needs information and that you are asking another person to give up his or her time to help you achieve *your* goals, so you must be willing to meet at the subject's convenience. Also, limit the length of the interview to no more than an hour; half an hour is better.

Before you meet the subject, prepare a list of questions you hope to answer. The purpose of the list is to help you remember your objectives and to help you prevent the interviewee from dragging the interview off topic. Interviewees *will* talk about the details of their jobs, and it is easy to become distracted.

8.4.3   The Interview Itself

A well-conducted interview has four parts: an opening, a body, a closing, and follow-up.

8.4.3.1   The opening

Be on time. If you know you are going to be late, call and give the subject the option to reschedule.

The point of the opening is to establish rapport and to encourage the subject to respond freely. Identify yourself, the topic to be discussed, the purpose of the interview, and how long you expect the interview to last. Tell the subject why he or she was selected for the interview. Where appropriate, identify the manager or managers who authorized the interview.

In an attempt to establish a relaxed atmosphere, many good interviewers begin with a period of small talk. While this technique can be effective, it can also backfire. Avoid wasting the subject's time. When in doubt, get to the point.

8.4.3.2   The body

You are conducting the interview, so you are responsible for getting things going. Have your first question prepared. Many interviewers like to start with an open-ended question, such as:

> When I read the documentation for this system, I had
> some trouble with (mention the part or section). Can
> you explain it to me?

Consider asking the subject how his or her job relates to the project. Another good opener is to ask the subject to walk you through some process or to explain how he or she uses the data in a report.

Listen to the answer. A good technique is to say something like, "Let me see if I understand what you're saying," and then offer a brief summary. If you are wrong, the subject will probably tell you. If you can paraphrase correctly, you establish that communication is taking place.

Check your list of questions occasionally. As the subject responds to an open-ended question, he or she will answer some of them before they are asked. Unanswered questions tell you what to ask next. Use follow-up questions, such as, "Why?" or "Can you give me an example?" to probe for additional details. Listen for the answers to questions you did not include on your list, too.

One advantage of starting with an open-ended question is that (almost by definition) the subject knows more about the topic than you do. Consequently, your prepared questions might focus on the wrong issues or force the subject to cover key points in the wrong order. If you can get the subject to tell you what you *should* know, you can learn a great deal very quickly. '

Not all interviewers are comfortable with open-ended questions, however, and the interviewee might be nervous or even hostile. In such cases, it might be better to start with closed-ended questions that can be answered with a few words. (A forced-choice survey is an extreme example.) The answers to those questions, in turn, might suggest more open follow-up questions.

Generally, skilled interviewers start with open-ended questions for their initial interviews, particularly with higher-level managers. As they learn more about the system and begin to hone in on specific issues, the questions become more closed and specific. Beginners, on the other hand, should consider preparing (perhaps with the help of an experienced interviewer) a list of closed questions, and let the responses suggest follow-up questions.

During the interview, be careful not to concentrate so intently on your next question that you miss the answer to the current one. (This is a common beginner's mistake.) Your list of prepared questions should be used as a guide or as a memory jog, not as a script.

Listen to the answers. Delete questions that seem unimportant. Skip questions you know your subject cannot or will not answer. Bypass questions that have already been answered. Avoid needlessly complex or multi-part questions; ask one clear question at a time. Be flexible. Try to stick to the subject, and do not allow the interviewee to drag the interview off topic, but do allow a certain amount of spontaneity. You might learn something.

Avoid technical jargon; take the time to learn the subject's application-specific language. An interview is not a trial. Ask probing questions, but do not conduct a cross-examination. Finally, avoid attacking the subject's credibility or implying that you know more about the topic than the inter-viewee. (If the assumption is true, why conduct the interview?) You will sit through an occasional useless interview. An early closing might be in order, but always act professionally in spite of your disappointment.

Unless you have an incredible memory, take notes. One suggestion is to leave space for notes on your list of questions or your interview outline. Do not take dictation, however. When you try to write down every word, you miss the speaker's meaning, and you cannot ask probing follow-up questions if your attention is focused on a piece of paper. Be honest with yourself. If you feel compelled to take dictation, request permission to tape the interview or bring a secretary with you.

8.4.3.3   The closing

Pay attention to the time. If the interview runs longer than expected, ask permission to continue and offer to reschedule a follow-up interview.

When you have the information you need, ask if there is anything you missed. (At this point, let the subject take the lead.) When the interview ends, thank the subject for cooperating and offer to make your written summary available for review. If you anticipate a follow-up or subsequent interview, say so.

Some interviewers like to "wind down" with a brief period of casual conversation. If you feel comfortable with this approach, use it. Do not force it, though. Remember: avoid wasting the subject's time.

8.4.4   Follow-up

As soon as possible after the interview, transcribe your notes. Ideally, they should identify key points; use your memory to fill in the details. (Don't wait too long, you might forget something important.) If you recorded the interview, listen to the tape and compile a set of selective notes. If appropriate, prepare a transcript.

Type the summary. Identify the person, the date, the place, and the primary topic. Offer to share your summary with the subject; it is good public relations and it provides an excellent opportunity for correcting misunderstandings and errors. Also, the subject might add something you forgot.

One or more follow-up interviews might be necessary. Consider using e-mail or the telephone to ask a question or two. If you need more than five minutes, schedule an appointment.

8.5   Key terms

Interview — A face-to-face meeting between two (or more) people in which one person obtains information from another by asking questions.

8.6   Software

Not applicable.

8.7   References

1. Barone, J. T. and Switzer, J. Y., *Interviewing Art and Skill,* Allyn & Bacon, Needham Heights, MA, 1995.
2. Brady, J. J., *The Craft of Interviewing,* Random House, New York, 1977.
3. Hickman, L., *Case Method: Business Interviewing,* Addison-Wesley, Reading, MA, 1995.
4. Stewart, C. J. and Cash, W. B., *Interviewing Principles and Practices,* 7th ed., McGraw-Hill (Brown & Benchmark), New York, 1993.

chapter nine

Sampling

Michael S. Broida
Miami University

Contents

9.1 Purpose

Sampling is a technique for obtaining an estimate from a population by studying, measuring, or interviewing a subset (or sample) of that population. This chapter discusses basic sampling concepts.

0-8493-7001-9/99/$0.00+$.50
©1999 by CRC Press LLC

9.2   Strengths, weaknesses, and limitations

A well-selected sample yields an estimate of the target parameters in much less time and at much less cost than studying, measuring, or interviewing the entire population (conducting a census). It is often impossible to achieve 100 percent response because some of the entities to be studied, measured, or interviewed are unavailable or do not respond. A sample is sometimes more accurate than a census because obtaining numerous measurements introduces errors owing to fatigue, inaccurate or inconsistent data entry, and the use of less qualified personnel.

The sample answer, called an estimate, is almost never exactly the same as the corresponding population value. (This difference is called *error.*) Additionally, before a statistically valid sample can be selected, a great deal of information about the population must be available.

9.3   Input and related ideas

Before conducting a sample, it is necessary to define the specific information being sought and the population from which the sample will be drawn. For example, if an analyst needs information about perceived weaknesses in the existing sales order tracking system, the population would consist of all the people who utilize the existing system.

Sampling can be used to select the subset of a population to be interviewed (Chapter 8), the members of a JAD team (Chapter 14), or the members of an inspection team (Chapter 23). Sampling is an effective way to study an existing system by selecting the entities, transactions, occurrences, or personnel to be observed and measured. Sampling is an effective tool for estimating population characteristics when using such mathematical tools as simulation (Chapter 19) and queuing theory (Chapter 79). During the testing phase of the system development life cycle (Part VII), sampling is used to generate test data and select the specific events to be monitored. During the operation and maintenance phase (Part VIII), sampling is an effective tool for evaluating and monitoring performance and for implementing system controls (Chapter 77). For example, quality control is often implemented by taking random samples of a process. Sometimes the estimates generated by sampling a process are plotted on a control chart (Chapter 10) to determine if the process is in control.

9.4   Concepts

Sampling is a technique for obtaining an estimate from a population by studying, measuring, or interviewing a subset (or sample) of the population. This chapter discusses basic sampling concepts.

9.4.1   Why sample?

Every year, *Consumer Reports* magazine conducts tests on new automobiles and reports its findings to its readers. Given the (literally) millions of automobiles that roll off the assembly lines every year, testing the entire population would be incredibly time consuming, prohibitively expensive, and practically impossible, so the test results are based on a sample.

In many cases, testing a sample is actually more accurate than testing the entire population. A tester's reactions and perceptions are likely to change between the first car and the tenth car, if only because of fatigue. Multiple tests mean considerable data, and data entry errors are inevitable. Multiple tests also imply multiple testers, not all of whom are equally skilled. Finally, the test conditions and criteria will almost certainly change over time. For example, if enough cars are crashed into a barrier, the barrier will eventually be deformed, thus changing the test conditions.

If the sample is drawn properly, it is reasonable to assume that the sample estimate reflects the population. The balance of this chapter discusses the process of drawing a good sample.

9.4.2 *Sample size and sampling error*

The difference between the sample estimate and the true population value is called error. As a general rule, the sampling error decreases as the sample size increases. For example, assuming a 95 percent confidence interval, a sample of 1,000 voters might predict the outcome of an election with an error of slightly more than plus or minus 3 percent. Increase the sample size to 4,000, and the error drops to plus or minus 1.5 percent, while a sample size of 10,000 reduces the error to less than plus or minus 1 percent.

A useful formula for computing the sample size is:

$$n = (z^2\sigma^2) / E^2, \tag{9.1}$$

where z is a number from the normal distribution table that corresponds to the desired confidence interval, σ is the standard deviation of the population as estimated by the sample standard deviation, and E is the maximum acceptable error between the sample mean and the actual population mean. For a 95 percent confidence interval, use $z = 1.96$. For a 99 percent confidence interval, use $z = 2.575$. As a practical matter, one-fifth the sample range can be used as an estimate of the standard deviation.

For example, suppose you want to estimate the average amount of money a state university student spends on food and beverages in an average week. The maximum acceptable error is $2. Based on a preliminary sample, σ is estimated to be $8. The desired confidence interval is 95 percent. Plugging those numbers into Equation (9.1) suggests a sample size of:

$$n = [(1.96^2)(8^2)] / 2^2 = 62.426$$

or 63 students. (It is impossible to sample a fractional student, and rounding up yields a confidence interval slightly higher than 95 percent.) Assuming the students answer truthfully, averaging the weekly food expenditures of 63 randomly selected university students will yield a value that is within $2 of the population average with 95 percent confidence. To put it another way, there is a 0.95 probability that the sample mean will lie within $2 of the true mean. (*Note:* A real statistician would probably argue that the last statement is not *technically* correct, but in most cases it is a reasonable way to visualize a confidence interval.)

9.4.3   Bias

Simply selecting the right sample size is not enough, however. For example, a sample taken outside an expensive restaurant and a sample taken outside a food bank will almost certainly yield two very different (and equally invalid) estimates of the weekly food expenditures of university students because those samples are likely to be biased. A biased sample systematically favors some members of the population over others. To cite another example, if a telephone book is used to select a sample, people with unlisted numbers, people who have recently moved into that telephone market, and people with no telephone are automatically excluded from the sample.

Non-response bias occurs when one or more members of the selected group are not included in the sample. A survey that includes information only from people who answer their telephones at a certain time of day excludes one subset of the population. Dismissing or excluding people who refuse to answer certain questions is another source of non-response bias. Be aware of non-response bias. Before taking a sample, study the sampling process, identify subsets of the population that might be excluded or choose not to participate, and adjust the sampling process as necessary.

9.4.4   Random sampling

One relatively easy way to avoid introducing bias is to sample randomly. A sample is considered random if each member of the population has the same chance of being selected. Random samples yield unbiased estimates. Generally, an unbiased estimate is high about half the time and low about half the time.

There are two commonly used techniques for selecting a random sample. If the population is small, the members (or slips of paper representing each member) can be mixed thoroughly and the sample selected directly (like bingo markers or lottery tickets). For larger populations, assign each member a number and use a random number generator or a table of random numbers to select the sample.

9.4.5   Random-like samples

In cases where it is impossible or inconvenient to select a true random sample, the objective is to generate estimates that behave as though they were based on a random sample. The key to successful, *almost random* sampling is to avoid introducing bias. For example, imagine a grocer inspecting a shipment of fruit. An estimate based on a sample taken from a single box or even from the tops of several boxes is unlikely to accurately reflect the quality of all the fruit. However, if the grocer selects several boxes and then selects fruit from the top, the middle, and the bottom of each, the sample is likely to be random-like.

On an assembly line, selecting every tenth, hundredth, or thousandth item (generally, every nth item) as it flows by might be an effective way to select a random-like sample. An option is to select every $m \pm n$th item), where n is a random number (for example, every 100 ± 5th item.

Avoid predictability when sampling human beings, however, because it often introduces bias. For example, if the boss walks through the work area every hour on the hour, he or she is likely to find everyone hard at work. If another boss were to use a random number table to define the times for random visits to the work area, he or she is likely to gain a more accurate picture of the employees' work habits.

9.4.6   Stratified random sampling

With stratified random sampling, a population of size N is divided into m subgroups. Each subgroup is called a stratum, and each member of the population must lie in exactly one stratum. For example, dividing a group of people by sex yields two strata (male and female); dividing a group of voters into Democrat, Republican, Independent, and Socialist yields four strata; and comparing the products produced on the first, second, and third shifts calls for three strata. Samples are taken randomly within each stratum.

Stratified random sampling is important if the different strata have different means and/or different levels of variability. For example, suppose the newer, relatively inexperienced employees who work the third shift produce markedly more errors than the people who work the other two shifts. In such cases, stratified sampling tends to yield more accurate estimates than simple random sampling.

9.4.6.1   Proportional allocation

One technique for distributing a sample across several strata is called proportional allocation. If 200 employees are distributed over three shifts with 100 on first shift, 60 on second shift, and 40 on third shift, a reasonable sample distribution might be 50 percent first shift, 30 percent second shift, and 20 percent third shift.

9.4.6.2   Optimal allocation

If one stratum exhibits significantly more variability than the others, proportionally more samples should be taken from the inconsistent stratum. Also, if one stratum is more costly to measure or interview than another, proportionally fewer samples should be taken from the expensive stratum.

Optimal allocation is a technique for distributing a sample across several strata that considers variability and cost. The optimum allocation formula is:

$$(n_i/ n) = [W_i\sigma_i/ (C_i^{1/2})] / \Sigma [W_i\sigma_i / (C_i^{1/2})], \qquad (9.2)$$

where n_i is the number of samples in stratum i, n is the total sample size, W_i is the percentage of the population in stratum i, σ_i is the standard deviation of stratum i, and C_i is the cost to sample stratum i. The formula calculates a relatively larger sample size for a given stratum if its variability (measured by σ_i) is higher than average or if the cost of sampling from that stratum is lower than average.

For example, suppose n, the total sample size, is 500. The population is divided among three strata, with costs to sample of $3, $4, and $5 per item for strata 1, 2, and 3 respectively (C_1 = $3, C_2 = $4, and C_3 = $5). Stratum 1 contains 50 percent of the population (W_1 = 0.5), stratum 2 contains 30 percent of the population (W_2 = 0.3), and stratum 3 contains 20 percent of the population (W_3 = 0.2). Finally, the estimated standard deviations for the three strata are σ_1 = 1.5, σ_2 = 2, and σ_3 = 2.5.

First calculate

$$\Sigma(W_i\sigma_i/(C_i^{1/2})) = [W_1\sigma_1/(C_1^{1/2})] + [W_2 \sigma_2/(C_2^{1/2})] + [W_3\sigma_3/(C_3^{1/2})]$$

$$= [0.5(1.5) / (3^{1/2})] + [0.3(2) / (4^{1/2})] + [0.2(2.5) / (5^{1/2})]$$

$$\approx 0.433 + 0.300 + 0.224 = 0.957.$$

Next, compute

$$n_1/n = 0.433/0.957 = 0.452$$

$$n_2/n = 0.300/0.957 = 0.314$$

$$n_3/n = 0.224/0.957 = 0.234.$$

Those numbers suggest that n_1 (the stratum 1 sample size) should be 45.2 percent (or 226 units) of the total sample size (500 items), n_2 should be 31.4 percent (or 157 units), and n_3 should be 23.4 percent (or 167 units).

9.5 Key terms

Bias — Any factor that systematically favors some members of the population over others when a sample is drawn.

Census — A set of measurements (or interviews) for every element of a population.

Confidence interval — A range of numbers around an estimate that contains the corresponding population parameter with the stated probability. For example, a 95 percent confidence interval for an estimate of the population mean is a range of numbers that contains the population mean with 95 percent certainty.

Error — The difference between the value of a parameter as estimated by a sample and the actual value of that parameter for the entire population.

Estimate — A value of a parameter determined by a sample.

Mean — An arithmetic average; the sum of all the observations divided by the number of observations.

Non-response bias — A form of bias that occurs when one or more members of the selected group are not included or choose not to participate in the sample.

Population — The entire set of relevant entities or measurements.

Random sample — A sample in which each item in the population has the same chance of being selected.

Range — The difference between the highest value and the lowest value in a set of measurements.

Sample — A selected subset of a population.

Standard deviation — The square root of the variance.

Strata — The set of subgroups in a stratified random sample.

Stratified random sampling — A random sampling technique in which the population is divided into subgroups called strata such that each element of the population lies in exactly one stratum; samples are taken randomly within each stratum.

Stratum — A single subgroup in a stratified random sample.

Unbiased estimate — An estimate that is high about half the time and low about half the time.

Variance — The average of the squared differences between the individual population values and the population mean.

9.6 Software

Random number tables are found in many statistics textbooks and/or in the software packages that accompany those books. Random number functions are found in most spreadsheet programs. SAS users can generate random observations from a binomial distribution (RANDBIN), an exponential distribution (RANEXP), a normal distribution (RANNOR), a Poisson distribution (RANPOI), or a uniform distribution (RANUNI). Minitab for Windows users should check the RANDOM DATA sub-window on the CALC pull down window.

9.7 References

1. Aczel, A. D., *Complete Business Statistics*, Irwin, Homewood, IL, 1989, chap. 16.
2. Badarinathi, R., *Introduction to SAS*, Dryden Press, New York, 1992, 21.
3. Bowerman, B. L. and O'Connell, R. T., *Applied Statistics. Improving Business Processes*, Irwin, Chicago, 1997.

chapter ten

Control charts

Timothy C. Krehbiel
Miami University

Contents

10.1   Purpose

Information systems contain interrelated processes. Control charts are proactive management tools that can be used to help control, predict, and improve the processes found in information systems as well as processes in general. A control chart allows an analyst to categorize a process as either stable or unstable. The output from a stable process is predictable and consistent over time, while an unstable process is chaotic and produces unpredictable output. To truly judge the capability or usefulness of a process, it must be stable, i.e., predictable. When encountering an unstable process, the process must first be brought into a stable state before assessing its usefulness to the overall system. Control charts are also useful in monitoring stable processes and notifying the analyst if and when a given process moves to an unstable state.

10.2   Strengths, weaknesses, and limitations

Control charts have been proven effective in a wide range of diverse applications. Wherever business activity can be characterized as a process, control charts can be applied to monitor, predict, and ultimately help improve the output from those processes. The managerial implications associated with control charts are enormous. Perhaps the most important is that it allows managers to distinguish between common causes of variation and assignable causes of variation. Quality guru Deming[1] often stressed that the failure to identify and distinguish these two types of variation was the most common mistake in modern management practice.

Control charts are used to distinguish common cause variation from assignable cause variation, not to determine whether or not the output from a process meets certain specifications. In general, it is incorrect to compare a control limit from a control chart to a specification limit.

The calculation of the control limits may seem difficult and unintuitive to someone untrained in statistics. The use of a statistical package should avoid calculation problems. When an analyst is constructing control charts from a spreadsheet or graphing package that does not have control chart procedures built in, extreme care must be taken to insure that the correct formulas are used.

Effective setup and analysis of control charts requires a certain amount of statistical sophistication. Although initial training in control chart techniques may be necessary, the long-term economic benefits should greatly outweigh the short term costs of training.

10.3   Inputs and related ideas

The use of control charts is a central part of the TQM movement as espoused by Deming[1] and other quality gurus. In general, the seven tools for quality improvement (Pareto diagram, cause-and-effect diagram, control chart, process flow diagram, checksheet, scatter diagram, and histogram) serve as a complimentary tool set that has been proven to be effective in improving many systems. Errors or out of control conditions suggested by control charts are commonly used to identify possible errors during the problem definition stage (Part II) of the system development life cycle. Pareto diagrams are discussed in Chapter 11. During the operational stage (Part VIII), control charts are commonly used to support system controls (Chapter 77) and performance analysis (Chapter 78).

10.4   Concepts

A process is the transformation of inputs to outputs. Control charts are statistical tools that help analysts determine whether the output from a process is predictable or unpredictable. Control charts are also used to monitor a process to detect changes in the process and, therefore, changes in the outputs from the process. The basic philosophy behind control charting is that if the process can be controlled, then the output from the process can be controlled. Used correctly, control charts can detect changes in a process before those changes produce undesirable output.

In this chapter, we will consider the operation of a local area network (LAN) from a process perspective. A quality characteristic of the network operation is application turnaround time. To monitor this, a benchmark program will be run every hour and the time required to complete the program recorded.

10.4.1   Run charts

In this section a run chart is constructed and analyzed. A run chart plots individual observations versus the time the observations are taken. In Figure 10.1, the times required to complete a benchmark program on a LAN are plotted. The horizontal axis indicates that one observation was taken per hour. The times are recorded in microseconds, thus observation one indicates that the benchmark time for the first hour was approximately 625,000 ms. The slowest time recorded was observation 14 at approximately 670,000 ms. The figure illustrates the variability in the time to run the benchmark program. If the LAN was consistently slowing down or speeding up, a noticeable trend would have appeared on the run chart. For this example, there are no trends, but observation 14 appears to be quite a bit slower than the others. Is this slow time due to inherent variability in the design of the LAN, or is it due to an outside effect that comes and goes periodically? In other words, is it a time we should expect to see when the LAN is operating correctly, or is it an abnormally slow time? A run chart cannot answer this question.

10.4.2   Types of variation

Variation in the output of a process is owing to either common cause variation or assignable cause variation. Common cause variation is inherent to the process, e.g., it is the variation that is owing to the machines, methods, materials, and so on, that constitute the process itself. In other words, common cause variation is owing to the process design and, therefore, can affect all the outputs from the process. All processes exhibit common cause variation.

Run Chart for Benchmark Times

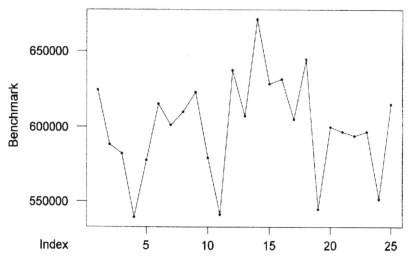

Figure 10.1   Run chart produced by Minitab for Windows.

Assignable cause variation is owing to sources outside of the process. A process experiencing assignable cause variation is operating in a fashion different than would be expected from the process design. By definition, assignable cause variation can only affect a subset of output. Possible reasons for assignable cause variation include a hardware malfunction, a power surge, or operator error.

10.4.3   Constructing a control chart

A control chart plots statistics on the vertical axis while the horizontal axis represents time, like a run chart. Unlike a run chart, a control chart also contains a centerline, a lower control limit and an upper control limit. When points are plotted within the control limits, the process is said to be stable. If points lie outside the control limits, the process is said to be unstable. See Section 10.4.4 for more details on analysis.

Figure 10.2 presents a control chart for the benchmark program example discussed earlier. The centerline for a control chart is the mean of the statistic being plotted. The mean may be a known value or it may be an estimated value of the mean. In this example, the mean of the benchmark times is assumed to be 600,000. The control limits are placed three standard deviations away from the mean. The standard deviation for the benchmark times is assumed to be 30,000; thus the control limits are drawn at 510,000 and 690,000. The reason for using three standard deviations is that most observations should lie within three standard deviations of the mean. Any points plotted outside these limits would be unusual observations.

Control Chart for Stable Benchmark Times

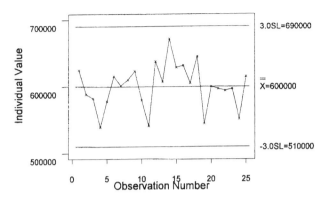

Figure 10.2 Individuals chart produced by Minitab for Windows illustrating a stable process.

10.4.4 Analyzing a control chart

A process is said to be unstable if a point plotted on a control chart is outside the control limits. A point outside a control limit indicates that the cause of the unusually low or high number must be owing not to common cause variation, but to assignable cause variation. In Figure 10.2 all the points are contained within the control limits and the process is said to be stable. Thus, although observation 14 is higher than the other benchmark times, it is an observation that is consistent with the way that the process is currently operating. In contrast, in Figure 10.3, a point is outside the control limits and the process is said to be unstable.

Control Chart for Unstable Benchmark Times

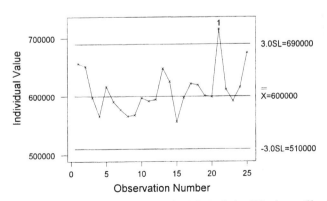

Figure 10.3 Individuals chart produced by Minitab for Windows illustrating an unstable process.

If a process is stable and is producing output that is acceptable to management, then the process should be allowed to continue on its normal path. The stable process should continue to be control charted so that if at a later date it becomes unstable, the analysts will be quickly notified of the change in the process.

A stable process is not necessarily a good process, it simply means that the process is consistent, and the output is known and predictable. If the output from a stable process is unacceptable, then the process itself must be changed. In other words, the process is stable but owing to a large amount of common cause variation, the process is consistently producing output that is unacceptable. In Figure 10.2, the control chart indicates that the process is stable and, therefore, the variation in the benchmark times is consistent and predictable. If the times being observed are acceptable to the analyst, then the LAN (i.e., the process) as it is currently designed is sufficient. If the times are too slow, then a fundamental change in the LAN must occur in order for the LAN to operate at an acceptable level.

When encountering an unstable process, the analyst must determine the sources of the assignable cause variation. The reason for the assignable cause must be investigated and in most cases eliminated. The actual capability of the process cannot be determined until the process actually performs as it was designed, i.e., until all assignable cause variation is removed. In some cases, the assignable cause variation may actually improve the output and in this case the process needs to be redesigned to include the newly discovered improvement. In Figure 10.3 an unstable point is observed and, therefore, the network at time period 21 must be investigated. At this time, an assignable cause is responsible for the slow benchmark time; i.e., a root cause outside of the design process must have been affecting the output. The analyst must identify the source and then institute change that will not allow this type of output to reappear at a later time.

More sophisticated rules than the "single point outside a control limit" have been developed to help identify unstable processes. This rule, however, is the most important and is often the only one used. For a discussion of these additional rules, the reader is referred to Montgomery[2].

10.4.5   *Types of control charts*

In the above example, the statistic being plotted is an individual measurement and the control chart is known as an individuals chart. It is the simplest type of control chart. An individuals chart is appropriate when the data are collected one at a time and are distributed, or approximately distributed, as a normal random variable. Other common types of control charts are listed below.

1. *C chart*   For use when the data appear to come from a Poisson distribution; for example, the number of network crashes in a day.

2. *P chart*   For use with binomial data; for example, the proportion of time a network server is active.
3. *X-bar and R charts*   For use with normal, or approximately normal, data which are collected in samples of size two or more; for example, every hour we could run a benchmark program ten times and calculate the mean, *X*-bar, and the range, *R*, for those ten measurements. In general, the *X*-bar and *R* charts are more sensitive to changes in a process than an individuals chart.

10.4.6   Rational subgrouping

The individuals control charts discussed in this chapter require the simplest sampling scheme of any control charts. As noted above, only one observation per time period is collected. In many cases, to set up a control chart repeated process samples of size two or more must be collected. For example, it is common to use samples of size four or five when using *X*-bar and *R* charts. A *P* chart typically requires rational subgroups of size 30 or more. Process samples taken for the purpose of constructing control charts are called rational subgroups.

A rational subgroup should be a sample collected in such a manner as to maximize the probability that the sample captures common cause variability and that any possible assignable cause variability occurs between rational subgroups. If a rational subgroup is too small, the sample will not be subject to all the common cause variability in the process. This will lead to control limits that are too narrow and may ultimately result in labeling a stable process as unstable, which is referred to as a false alarm. If a rational subgroup is too large, the sample may contain common cause and assignable cause variation. This will result in control limits that are too wide and may result in unstable processes going undetected.

10.4.7   Estimating limits

In many instances the mean and standard deviation of the statistic being plotted will not be known. The analyst must then estimate these parameters using the data contained in the chart. The reader is referred to Montgomery[2] for details on proper estimation procedures.

10.5   Key terms

Assignable cause variation — Variation that is not part of the design of the process; the sources or factors producing assignable cause variation can, by definition, only affect a subset of the output from that process. Assignable cause variation is sometimes referred to as special cause variation.

Common cause variation — Variation that is inherent to a process; common cause variation has the ability to affect all output from a process. All processes are subject to this form of variation.

Control limits — The upper and lower boundary lines of a control chart; the control limits are typically placed three standard deviations above and below the centerline. The centerline is usually the mean of the statistic being charted.

Rational subgroup — A sample of measurements taken from a process in such a manner that will maximize the probability that the sample captures common cause variability and that any possible assignable cause variability will occur between rational subgroups. In other words, the variation in the rational subgroup should be the result of common causes of variation only.

Stable process — A process that only exhibits common cause variation. In other words, the output from a stable process produces a population of items which has a constant mean and a constant variance. A stable process is predictable and, therefore the output from a stable process is predictable. If a stable process is generating output that is undesirable, then the process itself must be redesigned. A stable process is sometimes called an in-control process. If a process is not stable, it is said to be unstable.

Unstable process — A process that exhibits common cause and assignable cause variation; an unstable process is unpredictable and, therefore, the output from such processes cannot be predicted. Thus, before the true capability of a process can be determined, all assignable causes of variation must be eliminated from the process, i.e., the process must become stable. An unstable process is sometimes called an out-of-control process.

10.6   Software

Most statistical software packages have the ability to produce control charts. The control charts in this chapter were made using Minitab for Windows. In SAS, the most commonly used control charts are in the Shewhart procedure. Spreadsheet packages like Excel require add-in packages to construct the charts automatically, however, the charts can be easily constructed from any spreadsheet package assuming a book of statistical tables and formulas is available.

10.7   References

10.7.1   Citations

1. Deming, W. E., *Out of the Crisis*, MIT Center for Advanced Engineering Study, Cambridge, MA, 1986, chap. 11.
2. Montgomery, D. C., *Statistical Quality Control*, 3rd ed., John Wiley & Sons, Inc., New York, 1996.

10.7.2   Suggestions for additional reading

1. Gitlow, H., Oppenheim, A., and Oppenheim, R., *Quality Management: Tools and Methods for Improvement*, 2nd ed., Irwin, Burr Ridge, IL, 1995, chap. 9.
2. Ozeki, K. and Asaka, T., *Handbook of Quality Tools: The Japanese Approach*, Productivity Press, Cambridge, MA, 1990, chap. 12.

chapter eleven

Pareto Diagrams

Timothy C. Krehbiel
Miami University

Contents

11.1 Purpose

In most systems, quality related problems are owing to numerous factors, but the vast majority of the problems are the result of only a small subset of those factors. A Pareto diagram is used to separate the few significant factors from the trivial many. Identification of the most important sources of problems can help managers to prioritize and allocate resources.

11.2 Strengths, weaknesses, and limitations

The Pareto diagram has proven to be a very quick and easy graphical method to identify when the Pareto principle holds, and to identify the significant factor or factors at play. When used correctly, the Pareto diagram is an important tool in quality improvement efforts because of its ability to help focus attention on the area or areas where attention is

0-8493-7001-9/99/$0.00+$.50
©1999 by CRC Press LLC

warranted. Practice has shown that the Pareto principle holds in many different situations, thus the Pareto diagram can be quite useful in a large range of applications.

The most common mistake when constructing Pareto diagrams is not categorizing the data correctly. If categories are defined too broadly, then too few categories are present in the diagram. If categories are defined too narrowly, then too many categories are present. In both cases, little or nothing is learned by constructing the diagram. The process of collecting data and constructing the diagram can often lead to better definitions. At any time during the process, one can redefine the categories and then reclassify the data. If the diagrams are being constructed by hand or with software not specifically tailored to produce Pareto diagrams, a common mistake is not to rank order the categories from left to right. The resulting diagrams are misleading and not of great interest.

The greatest weakness of the Pareto diagram is the subjectivity inherent in using categorical data. In many situations, the definitions of the categories are quite subjective and the measurement process of placing observations into the correct category is subjective as well. Furthermore, like all graphical methods, the information relayed by a Pareto diagram is subject to personal interpretation.

11.3   Inputs and related ideas

Brainstorming is a useful tool when developing a list of categories to be used in a Pareto diagram. Once the Pareto diagram is drawn, it is often helpful to use cause-and-effect diagrams (Chapter 18) to study the cause-and-effect relationships associated with the significant factors. In general, the seven tools for quality improvement (Pareto diagram, cause-and-effect diagram, control chart, process flow diagram, check sheet, scatter diagram, and histogram) serve as a complimentary tool set that has been proven to be effective in improving many systems.

11.4   Concepts

In most systems, quality related problems are due to numerous factors, but the vast majority of the problems are the result of only a small subset of those factors. This phenomenon is called the Pareto principle. The concept is named after the Italian economist Alfredo Pareto who recognized that a large proportion of the wealth in Italy was in the hands of a small number of people. A Pareto diagram is used to separate the few significant factors from the trivial many. Identification of the most important sources of problems can help managers to prioritize and allocate resources.

A Pareto diagram can help to identify the important factors leading to a specific event. For example, consider a systems analyst interested in evaluating the causes of downed servers. The first step in the construction

Table 11.1 Six Factors Causing a Downed Server

Factor	Count	Percent
Server out of memory	28	47.5
Server software	24	40.7
Power failure	3	5.1
Physical connection	2	3.4
Server hardware	1	1.7
Inadequate bandwidth	1	1.7

of the diagram is to collect data pertaining to past episodes of downed servers, and then categorizing the factor responsible for each event. Categories must be selected so that each observation of the downed server is in one and only one category. For example, Table 11.1 lists six factors causing a downed server and the count associated with each. Count simply refers to the number of times, or frequency, a particular factor is deemed responsible. The table also lists the percent of times a certain factor is responsible for a downed server.

A Pareto diagram is a specialized bar chart. The horizontal axis lists the categories of interest, the left-hand vertical axis represents counts, and the right-hand vertical axis represents percent. Note that the categories must be rank ordered left to right according to the count for each category. As you can see in Figure 11.1, the most common factor associated with a downed server is that the server is out of memory.

Across the top of the bars in Figure 11.1 is a line (the cum-line) identifying the cumulative count and the cumulative percentage. In our example, over 88 percent of the time a server went down the cause was an error with the server software or a lack of server memory. All of the other factors leading to a downed server resulted in less than 12 percent of the problems. Thus the Pareto principle holds and the systems analyst should focus attention on the two significant factors identified in the diagram. Note that in situations where the Pareto principle holds, the cum-line will have a very pronounced bend between the few significant factors and the trivial many. In situations where the principle does not hold, the cum-line will take on the appearance of a piece-wise arc. In all cases, the cum-line will reach 100 percent in the final category.

Selecting the appropriate number of categories to include in the diagram is critical. In general, at least five categories should be used. In cases where there are a large number of factors, the maximum number of categories actually charted is usually determined by when the cumulative percent reaches 95 percent. At this point, all the remaining categories are typically combined together in an "other" category.

In some situations it is helpful to use multiple levels of Pareto diagrams. In our example it might be helpful to produce two more diagrams, one

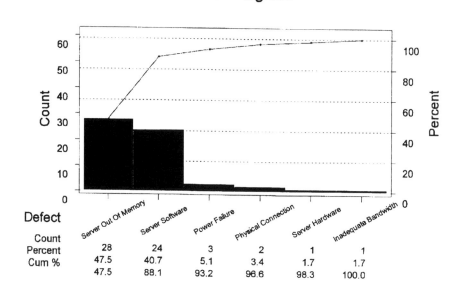

Figure 11.1   A Pareto diagram produced by Minitab for Windows.

addressed at server software problems and one addressed to the memory problems. Consider the server memory problems. The systems analyst will need to critically examine all of the 28 cases categorized as out of memory problems. A new Pareto diagram and analysis can then take place with the event of interest being memory problems and the factors being the underlying reasons for the memory shortages. It may very well be that even though there are many possible factors leading to memory errors, the vast majority of those errors can be traced to a few significant factors.

11.5   Key terms

Count — The number of observations in a category.

Cumulative count — The total number of observations in all the categories up to and including the category of interest; for example, the cumulative count corresponding to the third category is the sum of the counts for categories one, two, and three.

Cumulative percent — The combined percentages of all the categories up to and including the category of interest; the cumulative percent for the last category will always be 100 percent.

Pareto principle — In many different situations, the majority of outcomes are the result of a few significant factors. The remainder of the outcomes is owing to a large number of less important factors. This concept is named after the Italian economist Alfredo Pareto who recognized that a large proportion of the wealth in Italy was in the hands of a small number of people.

11.6   Software

Most statistical or quality improvement software has the ability to produce Pareto diagrams. Construction of Pareto diagrams using Minitab for Windows is very easy and flexible. In SAS, use the Pareto procedure. Statistical add-ins for Excel and Lotus are available which have the capability to produce Pareto diagrams. By not including the cumulative frequency line, a simplified version of a Pareto diagram can be easily produced in spreadsheet packages by constructing a bar chart.

11.7   References

1.   Gitlow, H., Oppenheim, A., and Oppenheim, R., *Quality Management: Tools and Methods for Improvement,* 2nd ed., Irwin, Burr Ridge, Illinois, 1995, chap. 9.
2.   Ozeki, K. and Asaka, T., *Handbook of Quality Tools: The Japanese Approach,* Productivity Press, Cambridge, MA, 1990, chap. 11.

chapter twelve

The problem statement

William S. Davis

Contents

12.1 Purpose

A good problem statement lists symptoms, suggests the problem's likely causes, and estimates the resources needed to solve the problem. It serves to communicate to the user, to management, and to the technical people the analyst's understanding of the nature of the problem and an initial sense of the problem's resource implications.

12.2 Strengths, weaknesses, and limitations

A well-written problem statement is an effective means of communicating the analyst's understanding of the problem and its causes to the user, technical personnel, and management, thus helping to ensure that the right problem is solved. The focus on symptoms, objectives, *and* scope supports high level verification.

0-8493-7001-9/99/$0.00+$.50
©1999 by CRC Press LLC

The problem statement is, by its very nature, preliminary. By itself, it does not represent a sufficient base for selecting, designing, or implementing a specific physical system. In particular, the scope should be viewed as a ballpark or order of magnitude cost estimate. Common mistakes include suggesting possible physical solutions to the problem rather than logical objectives for solving the problem, treating the preliminary estimate of system scope as a serious cost estimate, and writing a problem statement that includes too much *technical* detail.

12.3   Inputs and related ideas

The problem statement often serves as a "charter," or formal authorization for the information gathering and problem definition phase (Part II). The problem statement is often based on a limited number of preliminary interviews (Chapter 8) or observations. The detailed system requirements defined at the end of the analysis stage (Part IV) often reference the objectives in the initial problem statement. Detailed cost estimates, schedules, and budgets are typically based on the requirements and prepared before the design stage begins.

12.4   Concepts

Once a problem is defined, a sense of its causes and its likely resource implications must be communicated to the user, to management, and to technical personnel. Generally, this communication takes the form of a written problem statement, sometimes called a statement of scope and objectives, a user needs assessment, an operations concept document, or a mission statement.

12.4.1   Problem statement components

The precise form of the problem statement varies from organization to organization. The ideal length varies from project to project. No matter what format is used, however, a good problem statement includes the following elements (Table 12.1):

- A list of observed symptoms (the things that are wrong) stated in measurable form. The more specific the symptoms, the more likely it is that the problem will be solved.
- A list of suspected causes stated as measurable business (or application) objectives. The objectives, if met, are likely to contribute to solving the problem (or fixing the symptoms).
- A preliminary estimate of the problem's resource implications, or scope, typically (but not always) stated in financial terms. The scope represents the analyst's sense of the problem's magnitude.

Table 12.1   The Contents of a Good Problem Statement

A. The problem	A list of measurable symptoms.
Examples:	Inventory value is $100,000 too high.
	Our competitor can process an order in one day but we need three.
B. The objectives	The likely cause or causes, usually stated as measurable objectives that, if achieved, are likely to contribute to solving the problem.
Examples:	Reduce average stock time by two days.
	Reduce inventory cost by $100,000 by eliminating obsolete inventory.
	Reduce inventory cost by $100,000 by reducing safety stock to a level sufficient to cover expected reorder time plus five days.
	Reduce sales order processing time by one day by improving paperwork flow.
C. The scope	A sense of the problem's magnitude, often stated as a preliminary cost estimate.
Examples:	The estimated cost of this system is $10,000 plus or minus 25 percent.
	Preliminary estimates suggest that a team of three analyst/programmers will need six months to solve this problem.

12.4.2   Verification

The first step in verifying the problem statement is to compare the symptoms to the objectives. Each symptom should be addressed by one or more objectives, because orphan symptoms are not likely to be corrected. Each objective should address one or more symptoms, because orphan objectives suggest overlooked symptoms or superfluous features.

Comparing the scope to the symptoms allows the user to judge if solving the problem is worth the cost. Comparing the scope to the objectives allows the technical personnel to judge if they can achieve the objectives given the scope. The scope, by itself, allows management to determine if adequate resources are available. The combination of the symptoms, the scope, *and* the objectives allows users, management, and technical personnel to independently determine if the problem is worth solving.

12.5   Key terms

Objective — A measurable goal which, if met, is likely to contribute to solving the problem.

Problem statement — A written statement that defines a problem by listing its symptoms, identifying a set of objectives for solving the problem, and indicating the problem's scope.

Scope — A sense of the problem's magnitude; often, a preliminary estimate of the problem's resource implications or cost.

12.6   Software

Not applicable.

12.7   References

1. Blanchard, K. and Johnson, *The One Minute Manager,* William Morrow, New York, 1982.
2. Davis, W. S., *Business Systems Analysis and Design,* Wadsworth Publishing, Belmont, CA, 1994.
3. Gause, D. C. and Weinberg, *Are your Lights On? How to Figure Out What the Problem REALLY Is,* Dorset House Publishing, New York, 1990.
4. Paulos, J. A., *Innumercy,* Vintage Books, New York, 1988.

chapter thirteen

The feasibility study

William S. Davis

Contents

13.1 Purpose

A feasibility study is a compressed, capsule version the analysis phase of the system development life cycle aimed at determining quickly and at a reasonable cost if the problem can be solved and if it is worth solving. A feasibility study can also be viewed as an in-depth problem definition.

13.2 Strengths, weaknesses, and limitations

A well-conducted feasibility study provides a sense of the likelihood of success and of the expected cost of solving the problem, and gives management a basis for making resource allocation decisions. In many organizations, the feasibility study reports for all pending projects are submitted to a steering committee where some are rejected and others accepted and prioritized.

Because the feasibility study occurs near the beginning of the system development life cycle, the discovery process often uncovers unexpected problems or parameters that can significantly change the expected system scope. It is useful to discover such issues before significant funds have been expended. However, such surprises make it difficult to plan, schedule, and budget for the feasibility study itself, and close management control is needed to ensure that the cost does not balloon out of control. The purpose of a feasibility study is to determine, *at a reasonable cost*, if the problem is worth solving.

It is important to remember that the feasibility study is preliminary. The point is to determine if the resources should be allocated to solve the problem, not to actually solve the problem. Conducting a feasibility study is time consuming and costly. For essential or obvious projects, it sometimes makes sense to skip the feasibility study.

13.3   Inputs and related ideas

The feasibility study begins with the problem description (Chapter 12) prepared early in the problem definition phase of the system development life cycle. Often, the feasibility study report is the primary input to the steering committee that authorizes further work on the project.

The feasibility study is, in essence, a preliminary version of the analysis phase of the system development life cycle. Depending on the nature of the problem, the analyst uses various tools from Parts II, IV, and V. The information collected during the feasibility study is used during project planning to prepare schedules, budgets, and other project management documents using the tools described in Part III. Prototypes (Chapter 31) and simulation models (Chapter 19) are sometimes used to demonstrate technical feasibility. Economic feasibility is typically demonstrated using cost/benefit analysis (Chapter 38).

13.4   Concepts

Developing a new system is a form of investment. Any investment carries risk, and it makes sense to investigate the likelihood of success before committing resources. Thus, problem definition is often followed by a feasibility study, a capsule version of the analysis phase of the system development life cycle aimed at determining quickly and at a reasonable cost if the problem can be solved and if it is worth solving.

Note that the feasibility study is *optional*. On some small or obvious projects it is a waste of time. Other jobs simply *must* be done. For example, if federal income tax rates change, a firm has no choice but to update its payroll system. Fixing a bug in a critical program is another example. There is little point trying to prove feasibility when the problem *must be* solved (although the analyst might want to investigate the relative feasibility of alternative approaches). However, doing a feasibility study should be the default, and the burden of proof should be on skipping this step.

13.4.1   The cost of a feasibility study

The point of the feasibility study is to determine, at a reasonable cost, if the problem is worth solving. Thus the cost of the feasibility study should represent a small fraction of the estimated cost of developing the system, perhaps five or ten percent of the scope.

13.4.2   Types of feasibility

Four types of feasibility are considered:

- *Technical feasibility*—Is it possible to solve the problem using existing technology? Typically, the analyst proves technical feasibility by citing existing solutions to comparable problems. Prototypes (Chapter 31), physical models, and analytical techniques [such as simulation (Chapter 19)] are also effective.
- *Economic feasibility*—Do the benefits outweigh the cost of solving the problem? The analyst demonstrates economic feasibility through cost/benefit analysis (Chapter 38).
- *Operational feasibility*—Can the system be implemented in the user's environment? Perhaps a union agreement or a government regulation constrains the analyst. There might be ethical considerations. Maybe the boss suffers from computer phobia. Such intangible factors can cause a system to fail just as surely as technology or economics. Some analysts call this criterion *political* feasibility.
- *Organizational feasibility*—Is the system consistent with the organization's strategic objectives? If the answer is no, funds might be better spent on some other project.

Note that not all organizations consider all four types of feasibility.

13.4.3   The steps in a typical feasibility study

The steps in a typical feasibility study are summarized in Figure 13.1.

Starting with the initial problem description (Chapter 12), the system's scope and objectives are more precisely defined. The existing system is studied, and a high-level logical model of the proposed system is developed using one or more of the analysis tools described in Part IV. The problem is then redefined in the light of new knowledge, and these first four steps are repeated until an acceptable level of understanding emerges.

Given an acceptable understanding of the problem, several possible alternative solutions are identified and evaluated for technical, economic, operational, and organizational feasibility. The responsible analyst then decides if the project should be continued or dropped, roughs out a development plan (including a schedule, a cost estimate, likely resource needs, and a cost/benefit analysis), writes a feasibility study report, and presents the results to management and to the user.

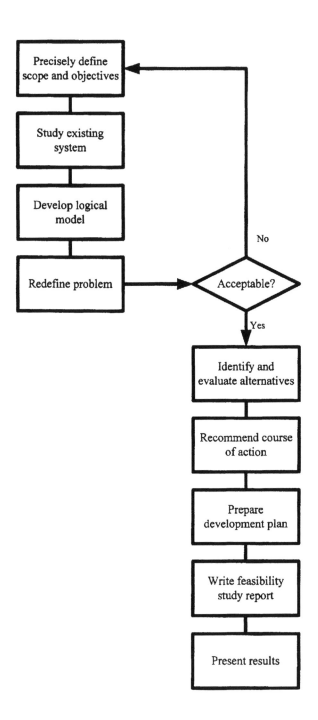

Figure 13.1   The steps in a typical feasibility study.

13.4.4   *The feasibility study report*

Assuming that one or more feasible solutions exist, the analyst prepares a feasibility study report that identifies several alternatives and recommends a course of action. Table 13.1 shows a typical feasibility report outline.

Table 13.1   An Outline of a Typical Feasibility Study.

1. **Title page**—Project name, report title, author(s), date.

2. **Contents**—A list of report sections with page numbers.

3. **Problem definition**—A clear, concise, one-page description of the problem.

4. **Executive summary**—A clear, concise, one-page summary of the feasibility study, the results, and the recommendations. Include necessary authorizations, key sources of information, alternatives considered, and alternatives rejected. Highlight the costs, benefits, constraints, and time schedule associated with the recommended alternative.

5. **Method of study**—A description of the approach and procedures used in conducting the feasibility study. Mention sources and references; identify key people; and briefly describe the existing system (if appropriate). Much of the detail belongs in the appendix; include only those facts directly relevant to the study or to your conclusions.

6. **Analysis**—A high-level analysis of the proposed logical system. Include an expanded statement of the system objectives, constraints, and scope; include a logical model (data flow diagram, and entity-relationship model) and perhaps a preliminary data dictionary for the proposed system; and identify key interrelationships with other systems.

7. **Alternatives considered**—For each alternative seriously considered, include a statement of its technical, economic, operational, and organizational feasibility, a rough implementation schedule, and a high-level system flow diagram or other system description. *Note:* Much of the detail belongs in the appendix.

8. **Recommendations**—Clearly state the recommended course of action. Provide material to support and justify your recommendation. In particular, provide a cost/benefit analysis.

9. **Development plan**—Include a projected schedule and projected costs for each step in the system life cycle, assuming that the recommended course of action is followed. Provide detailed time and cost estimates for the analysis step.

10. **Appendix**—Charts, graphs, statistics, interview lists, selected interview summaries, diagrams, memos, notes, references, key contacts, acknowledgements, and so on; in short, the details that support the study.

13.5   Key terms

Economic feasibility — Proof that the likely benefits outweigh the cost of solving the problem; generally demonstrated by a cost/benefit analysis.

Feasibility study — A compressed, capsule version of the analysis phase of the system development life cycle aimed at determining quickly and at a reasonable cost if the problem can be solved and if it is worth solving.

Operational feasibility — Proof that the problem can be solved in the user's environment.

Organizational feasibility — Proof that the proposed system is consistent with the organization's strategic objectives.

Steering committee — A committee consisting of representatives from various user groups that accepts, rejects, and prioritizes information system proposals.

Technical feasibility — Proof that the problem can be solved using existing technology

13.6   Software

Not applicable.

13.7   References

1. Clifton, D. S. and Fyffe, *Project Feasibility Analysis: A Guide to Profitable New Ventures*, John Wiley & Sons, New York, 1977.
2. Davis, W. S., *Business Systems Analysis and Design*, Wadsworth Publishing, Belmont, CA, 1994.
3. Fitzgerald, J., Fitzgerald, and Stallings, *Fundamentals of Systems Analysis*, 2nd ed., John Wiley & Sons, New York, 1981.

chapter fourteen

Joint application design (JAD)

David C. Yen and William S. Davis

Contents

14.1 Purpose

IBM coined the term joint application design (JAD) in 1970, but some experts prefer joint application *development*. The key idea to organize a team consisting of major users, managers, and systems analysts (or

0-8493-7001-9/99/$0.00+$.50

information consultants) and to charge that team with quickly determining, in an intensive session, the requirements for a proposed new or replacement information system.

14.2   Strengths, weaknesses, and limitations

The cost and time associated with data collection, analysis, and requirements definition can be significantly reduced by using the JAD technique. The input from numerous people provides different perspectives on the desired system and often generates creative ideas. Because all interested parties are represented on the JAD team, conflicts and discrepancies can be identified and resolved during the problem definition stage. Because they are involved in system planning, the participants feel a sense of system ownership. JAD is particularly suited to projects that face tight time and scheduling constraints, and it is an excellent choice for developing a system from scratch.

Sometimes, so many ideas are generated that additional sessions and meetings are needed to resolve the conflicts. Strong or influential users can easily dominate a session, leading to a skewed sense of the users' needs. JAD is not a good technique for systems with relatively few inputs and outputs or for highly computational, process-oriented systems.

14.3   Inputs and related ideas

JAD is used to determine the system requirements during the problem definition (or information gathering) phase of the system development life cycle. Often, a preliminary problem definition (Chapter 12 and other Part II tools) precedes the JAD session. JAD can also be used to perform feasibility analysis (Chapter 13), cost/benefit analysis (Chapter 38), and risk analysis. Often, such design specifications as data flow diagrams (Chapter 24), entity relationship diagrams (Chapter 26), and system flow diagrams (Chapter 37) are generated during the JAD session.

14.4   Concepts

Joint application design (JAD), also know as joint application development, is a technique for quickly determining system requirements by obtaining input from a representative cross section of interested parties. An ad hoc team composed of major users, managers, and systems analysts (or information consultants) is assembled. The team then meets in an intensive session to gather data, brainstorm, discuss ideas, reconcile differences, identify and prioritize requirements, and generate desirable alternative solutions. The primary steps in a JAD session are summarized in Figure 14.1.

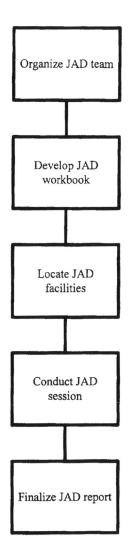

Figure 14.1 The primary steps in a JAD session.

14.4.1 *Organize the JAD team*

The members of a JAD team consist of end users from the relevant business functional areas, managers from those same functional areas, systems analysts or information consultants, and appropriate systems specialists. The moderator or session leader is usually the senior systems analyst or information consultant. A scribe takes notes, records all discussions, and organizes and compiles the necessary documents.

14.4.2   Develop the JAD workbook

The JAD workbook consists of a management definition guide, information relevant to the project, any special criteria or constraints, any assumptions, an overview of existing technology and standards, a statement of the system's scope and objectives (Chapter 12), and information about the existing system and/or relevant new technology. The purpose of the workbook is to help the team members understand the proposed project. The design of the workbook should facilitate note taking.

14.4.3   Locate the JAD facilities

As a minimum, a conference room large enough to accommodate all the team members and equipped with whiteboards or chalkboards, an overhead projector, and a slide projector must be available. With the emergence of the electronic meeting systems (EMS), group decision support systems (GDSS), and computer aided software engineering (CASE) tools, additional requirements might include computers for conducting an electronic meeting, teleconferencing facilities, and a master station equipped with CASE software.

14.4.4   Conduct the JAD session

A JAD session is an intensive (typically) two- or three-day meeting of the complete JAD team. Team members are expected to give the JAD session their complete attention, scheduling no other conflicting activities.

14.4.4.1   Preparation

Before the JAD session begins, the responsible systems analysts or information consultants must:

- Define the system scope.
- Identify the problems, limitations, and constraints.
- Estimate the resource needs (time, budget, personnel) for developing the system.
- Identify preliminary costs, benefits, risks, and impacts of the project.
- Identify the nature and major attributes of the project, the project dependencies, and the project interrelationships.
- Identify appropriate sub-projects. (The project is sometimes, decomposed into several sub-projects owing to the timing and/or budgetary constraints.)
- Perform the background analysis necessary to define such key parameters as the number of users, the size of the database, the required throughput, and the minimum acceptable response times.
- Plan the JAD session.

In performing these tasks, the responsible analysts utilize many of the tools and techniques described in Part II.

14.4.4.2   *The session*
A JAD session begins with an overview of the material collected during the preparation stage. Once the participants understand the problem, the process of identifying the problem's dimensions, possible causes, requirements, and alternative solutions begins.

During a JAD session, it is the moderator's responsibility to effectively manage session time, to ensure that the team stays focused on the agenda items, to encourage all team members to participate, and to resolve any conflicts generated during the session. Because the team is composed largely of non-technical personnel, it is important that the systems analysts or information consultants minimize the use of technical terms.

14.4.4.3   *Brainstorming*
The process of soliciting ideas often involves brainstorming. A specific question is raised; for example, the moderator might ask the JAD team to suggest possible causes of a specific problem or sub-problem. The participants are then invited to suggest ideas, and as suggestions are made they are posted for all to see. Ideally, at some point in the brainstorming session, a synergy begins to emerge, with one participant's contribution eliciting new and creative suggestions from other participants.

The time allocated to a brainstorming session is limited to (perhaps) half an hour, and the time limit is announced to all participants before the session begins. The focus is on soliciting and listing ideas, not on attacking, defending, or investigating those ideas. Often, targets are set; for example, a brainstorming group might be challenged to list 25 possible (direct or contributing) causes of the problem under study. Sometimes, the JAD team is divided into several brainstorming sub-teams, and a friendly competition is launched to see which sub-team can list the most ideas.

14.4.4.4   *Investigation, consolidation, resolution, and tabulation*
Following a brainstorming session, the JAD team divides into sub-groups to investigate the ideas on the various lists. Vague or unclear ideas are refined and rephrased. Similar or redundant ideas are categorized and consolidated, and the resulting meta-ideas are reconciled.

Meanwhile, other sub-groups might conduct additional brainstorming and/or discussion sessions to consider other sub-problems or identify and resolve conflicts within and between the meta-ideas until, eventually, a consensus is reached. The consensus ideas are then tabulated and distributed to the JAD team members for feedback. The session ends with a presentation of the final results.

14.4.5   Finalize the JAD report

After the JAD session is concluded the responsible systems analysts or information consultants update the necessary documents and prepare a final report that summarizes all discussions, facts, findings, and conclusions. They then construct a plan for action and a schedule for developing the system. If follow-up sessions are required, they collect the required additional information.

There is no standard format for a JAD report, although the feasibility study report outline (Table 13.1) suggested in Chapter 13 is a good model.

14. 5   Key terms

Brainstorming — A small-group technique for soliciting and consolidating ideas and thoughts about a problem, a problem's possible causes, system requirements, alternative solutions, and similar issues.

JAD workbook — A workbook designed to provide JAD team members with necessary information about the project and to facilitate note taking.

Joint Application Design (JAD) — A technique for quickly determining system requirements in an intensive session attended by a team consisting of major users, managers, and systems analysts.

Management definition guide — A portion of the JAD workbook that lists and defines technical terms related to computing platforms, computer technology, and other elements relevant to the problem under study.

Moderator — The person responsible for conducting a JAD session.

Project dependency — A dependency relationship between two or more sub-projects. For example, the input(s) to one sub-project are typically output from another sub-project.

Project interrelationship — A link or relationship between two or more sub-projects. For example, the successful completion of one sub-project might be a prerequisite for several other sub-projects.

Scope — A sense of a problem's magnitude; often, a preliminary estimate of the problem's resource implications or cost.

Scribe — During a JAD session, the person responsible for taking notes, recording all discussions, and organizing and compiling the necessary documents.

14.6   Software

There is no software specifically designed to support a JAD session. However, certain groupware, such as Lotus Notes, supports limited computer mediated conferencing.

14.7   References

1. Hoffer, J. A., George, J. F., and Valacich, J. S., *Modern Systems Analysis and Design*, Benjamin/Cummings, Redwood City, CA, 1996.
2. Whitten, J. L., Bentley, L. D., and Dittman, K. C., *Systems Analysis and Design Methods*, Richard D. Irwin (McGraw-Hill), New York, 1997.
3. Wood, J. and Silver, D., *Joint Application Development*, John Wiley & Sons, New York, 1995.
4. Yen, D. C., Case study: Armco Steel Company, L.P., General Electric Foundation Case Study, Miami University, Oxford, OH, 1989.

chapter fifteen

Problem analysis paradigms

David C. Yen and William S. Davis

Contents

15.1   Purpose

This chapter introduces several paradigms for locating, pinpointing, and identifying a problem or an opportunity, including decomposition, factoring, synthesis, and generate and test. These paradigms can also be applied to problem solving.

15.2   Strengths, weaknesses, and limitations

The strengths and weaknesses of each paradigm will be noted in context.

0-8493-7001-9/99/$0.00+$.50
©1999 by CRC Press LLC

15.3   Inputs and related ideas

These paradigms serve as the philosophical basis for numerous tools, techniques, and methodologies. Significant links will be noted in context.

15.4   Concepts

This chapter introduces several paradigms for locating, pinpointing, and identifying a problem or an opportunity. These paradigms serve as the philosophical basis for numerous problem-solving tools, techniques, and methodologies.

15.4.1   Decomposition

Decomposition is a top-down, goal-oriented approach that is used when the problem is too complex or too abstract to study directly. The idea is to divide (or decompose) the problem into logically consistent, more manageable sub-problems, and then to attack the sub-problems. Much as a book can be broken into chapters, sections, and then paragraphs, the decomposition approach divides a large, abstract problem into several small, concrete sub-problems, each with clear goals or specific tasks to perform.

For example, imagine that a firm requires seven days to process an order and deliver the merchandise to a customer, but a competitor needs only three days to perform the same service. Rather than trying to solve the excessive turnaround time problem directly, it might be more effective to decompose the problem into order taking, order entry, order authorization, order filling, and shipping components, and then independently study those sub-problems.

The primary weakness of decomposition is that it can be difficult to track the interrelationships between the sub-problems. Additionally, independently solving a number of sub-problems can be time consuming. Determining acceptable criteria for decomposing the main problem can also be a difficult task.

Decomposition is used throughout the information engineering (Chapter 2) and structured analysis and design (Chapter 3) methodologies and plays an important role in such tools and techniques as data flow diagrams (Chapter 24), data normalization (Chapter 28), functional decomposition (Chapter 62), and HIPO (Chapter 64). Although this paradigm might be applied to selected sub-problems, decomposition is not as effective for bottom-up, data-oriented, or output-oriented tools and techniques. The decomposition paradigm is widely used in database design and is sometimes called normalization.

15.4.2   Factoring

The essential idea of factoring is to merge several small, isolated, overlapping, or related problems to form a meta-problem. Generally, a problem can be reformulated by identifying those sub-problems that share similar characteristics, and then grouping the related sub-problems.

For example, a system analyst investigating low profits might identify several possible causes, including excess warehouse personnel, sales floor understaffing, high stock expenses, poor quality control, poor sales effort, inadequate advertising, product shortages, excessive rework, and so on. With so many possible causes to consider, it is difficult to distinguish the trivial from the significant. Consequently, the analyst might begin studying the low profit problem by factoring the sub-problems to form the following meta-problems:

- High production costs resulting from poor quality control and excessive rework.
- Low sales resulting from poor sales effort, inadequate advertising, and sales floor understaffing.
- High shipping and handling costs resulting from high stock expenses, product shortages, and excess warehouse personnel.

Focusing on the meta-problems is likely to be more efficient than attempting to independently analyze the sub-problems.

The factoring process calls for judgment. Often, a given problem can be factored in several different ways, and individual systems analysts or information system consultants might reasonably view the same problem differently. Consequently, it is essential that agreement on the sub-problems, the factoring criteria, and the meta-problems be reached early in the process.

Factoring is a bottom-up approach that lends itself to data-oriented methodologies and tools, such as the structured requirements specification methodology (Chapter 4) and Warnier-Orr diagrams (Chapter 33). Additionally, this method is widely used by expert systems (Chapter 7) to perform reasoning.

15.4.3 Synthesis

Synthesis is an evolutionary paradigm. It starts with a major or influential user's viewpoint and expands (perhaps with revisions and/or modifications to the original problem description) by incorporating other users' perspectives until all relevant viewpoints are included. It is useful when the core problem is well-defined and well-structured and the sub-problems are simple add-on functions that use the core as a base.

Inventory is a good example of a core problem. The starting viewpoint might be that of the functional group in charge of the warehouse. Once an effective inventory control system is implemented and a stable inventory database is established, other viewpoints can be considered. For example, the system might be enhanced to incorporate time-to-ship commitments for the sales department, on-demand inventory status reports and queries for the purchasing department, a just-in-time inventory system for production, such applications as inventory aging, continuous physical inventory, and inventory shrinkage analyses for accounting, and so on. Note that the sub-problems cannot be solved until the core problem (inventory control) is solved.

The major concern with synthesis is correctly identifying the core problem. Also, comprehensive testing is difficult because of the evolutionary nature of the paradigm. However, once the core problem is identified and solved, it becomes relatively easy to identify and solve the sub-problems. Prototyping (Chapter 31) is particularly effective for problems that fit the synthesis paradigm.

15.4.4   Generate and test

Generate and test is a hierarchical, test-oriented paradigm that is used in expert systems to define a solution that meets certain criteria or constraints. The technique starts at the top of a hierarchy with the main problem and continues down the hierarchy through the sub-problems, conducting tests of the appropriate criteria and constraints at each level until the bottom is reached and no more testing is necessary.

For example, imagine that an analyst has identified three problems, all of which contribute to lower than expected profits (the main problem):

- Production costs are too high.
- Sales revenues are too low.
- Inventory costs are too high.

Management is concerned about the lower than expected profits and expects to see results within one month (a time constraint).

An initial study suggests that high production costs are probably the result of poor quality control, excessive rework, and frequent shortages of essential raw materials. Solving the first two sub-problems (quality control and rework) will require the purchase of new inspection equipment. Delivery time on that equipment is two months, which clearly exceeds management's time constraint. Raw material shortages result from poor production planning and inadequate coordination between the production and the warehouse. Consequently, the raw material shortage problem must be solved in concert with certain warehousing problems.

The likely causes of low sales revenue appear to include poor sales effort, inadequate advertising, and understaffing in the sales department. The solutions to these three sub-problems might include better management and the reallocation of resources, and those solutions can be implemented within management's one-month target.

High warehousing and distribution costs result from poor materials handling procedures and poor inventory management. Preliminary analysis suggests that solving the materials handling sub-problem will require a lengthy study of the existing materials handling procedures followed by the purchase of new materials handling equipment and several weeks of employee retraining. Total elapsed time to complete these tasks is expected to be three to four months. The inventory management sub-problem appears to be related to production's raw material shortage sub-problem, so a one-month study of the relationship between production and inventory will be needed before the true scope of the problem can even be determined.

The initial low profit problem can now be viewed as five sub-problems:

1. Poor quality control and excessive rework.
2. Raw material shortages.
3. Poor sales effort, inadequate advertising, and understaffing in the sales department.
4. Poor materials handling procedures.
5. Poor inventory management.

Solving sub-problem 1 or sub-problem 4 will exceed management's time constraint. Sub-problems 2 and 5 are interrelated, and the need to study inventory management for a month before the true scope of the problem can be estimated means that it, too, will exceed management's constraint. Consequently, in the short run the analyst should start by attacking sub-problem 3 (poor sales effort, inadequate advertising, and understaffing in the sales department) because it is the only sub-problem that has a chance of yielding results within the time constraint imposed by management.

The generate and test paradigm can be used to pinpoint the correct sub-problem to be solved, particularly for complex (large domain) problems with time and budgetary constraints and additional constraints on specific sub-problems. Perhaps the most important strength of the generate-and-test paradigm is its focus on real world constraints. Note, however, that other paradigms may be needed to identify the main problem and the sub-problems. Also, selecting a small set of sub-problems based on artificial constraints can lead to sub-optimization and may increase the time and cost to solve the main problem.

15.5   Key terms

Bottom-up — An approach to problem solving that starts with the details and works upward.

Data-oriented — A tool or technique that starts with the data and derives the necessary processes.

Decomposition — A problem analysis paradigm that calls for breaking a problem into more manageable sub-problems and then attacking the sub-problems.

Factoring — Merging several small, isolated, overlapping, or related problems to form a meta-problem.

Generate and test — A hierarchical, test-oriented paradigm that starts at the top of a hierarchy with a main problem and continues down the hierarchy through the sub-problems, conducting tests of the appropriate criteria and constraints at each level until the bottom is reached and no more testing is necessary.

Goal-oriented — A method or technique which searches through a process until a predefined goal is accomplished.

Meta-problem — A large problem defined by combining several smaller problems.

Sub-problem — A problem that is part of a larger problem.

Synthesis — An evolutionary paradigm that starts with a major or influential user's viewpoint and incorporates other users' perspectives until all relevant viewpoints are included.

Top-down — An approach to problem solving that starts with the high-level control structures and works down to the details.

15.6   Software

Not applicable.

15.7   References

1. Awad, E. W., *Building Expert Systems: Principles, Procedures, and Applications*, West, Minneapolis/St. Paul, MN, 1996.
2. Buchanan, B. G., and Shortliffe, E. H., *Rule-Based Expert Systems: The MYCIN Experiments of the Standard Heuristic Programming Project*, Addison-Wesley, Reading, MA, 1984.
3. Connor, D., *Information Systems Specification & Design Road Map*, Prentice-Hall, Englewood Cliffs, NJ, 1985.
4. Hayes-Roth, F., Waterman, D. A., and Lenat, D. B., *Building Expert Systems*, Addison-Wesley, Reading, MA, 1983.
5. Holsapple, C. W., and Whinston, A. B., *Business Expert Systems*, Irwin, Homewood, IL, 1987.
6. Liebowitz, J., and De Salvo, D. A., *Structured Expert Systems: Domain, Design, and Development*, Prentice-Hall, Englewood Cliffs, NJ, 1989.
7. Waterman, D. A., *A Guide to Expert Systems*, Addison-Wesley, Reading, MA, 1986.
8. Zahedi F., *Intelligent Systems for Business: Expert Systems with Neural Networks*, Wadsworth, Belmont, CA, 1993.

chapter sixteen

Requirements analysis paradigms

David C. Yen and William S. Davis

Contents

16.1 Purpose

This chapter introduces several paradigms used to identify and prioritize potential information system problems and opportunities and to establish certain high-level criteria for performing requirements analysis.

16.2 Strengths, weaknesses, and limitations

The strengths and weaknesses of each paradigm will be noted in context.

0-8493-7001-9/99/$0.00+$.50
©1999 by CRC Press LLC

16.3   Inputs and related ideas

Not applicable.

16.4   Concepts

This chapter introduces several requirement analysis paradigms.

16.4.1   The behavior-oriented paradigm

The basic idea of the behavior-oriented approach is to study the behavior, the decision-making style, and the data utilized by the responsible executives, and to use the resulting information to provide a crucial strategic-level framework for defining system requirements. After performing the background analysis needed to understand a specific problem (or opportunity), the analyst uses case study techniques to study how the responsible executives have historically dealt with similar problems. The top executives are then interviewed to determine the main causes of the new problem before detailed information about the problem is gathered and summarized.

Matching system development with the problem-solving and decision-making styles of the responsible executives tends to produce systems that are consistent with the organization's strategic direction. This approach is particularly valuable when developing executive information systems or top-level decision-support systems. Care must be taken to avoid overlooking the needs or middle managers, supervisors, and operational personnel, however, because they are usually the primary users of an information system. Additionally, executive behavior is difficult to quantify, and a lack of concrete, systemic data can lead to misunderstandings during the analysis and design stages.

16.4.2   The information-oriented paradigm

The focus of the information-oriented approach is on the information system products actually used by supervisory and middle managers. Studying management's information needs gives the analyst a baseline against which to prioritize or assess the requirements associated with a new problem or opportunity.

Because this approach focuses on how the major users actually utilize information system technology, it tends to produce functionally useful system. However, the information-oriented paradigm largely ignores organizational, environmental, and strategic issues, and the "existing system" orientation tends to encourage gradual modifications to the old system and to discourage creative new approaches. Finally, the middle management and supervisory focus ignores the needs of operational personnel.

16.4.3   The industry analysis paradigm

The industry analysis paradigm rests on an assumption: To survive in the marketplace, a firm needs information systems that are at least comparable to its competitors' systems. Information about competitors' information system spending (personnel, hardware, software), new information system product development, and improvements in existing information services is obtained from such sources as industry associations, trade magazines, newspapers, professional journals, hardware and software vendors, and consultants. Comparing a firm's own internal figures to the industry norms suggests relative strengths and weaknesses and provides a basis for defining the requirements for a proposed system or opportunity.

Comparing a firm to its competitors stresses real-world marketplace problems and can yield solid, quantitative data that suggest specific, concrete actions. Information technology evolves more quickly than such data suggest, however. Different companies have different information structures and operating environments, and it is not always possible to generalize industry trends to a given firm. Collecting appropriate data for a new industry can be particularly difficult. Finally, applying industry-wide data to a specific development project is at best tricky.

16.4.4   The project-oriented paradigm

The project-oriented paradigm starts by studying the requirements of a particular information system's end users. The idea is to establish a group of users who represent all the affected functional areas and work through those users to study the existing system, identify new needs or opportunities, and define the new system's requirements. Such techniques as JAD (Chapter 14) and RAD (Chapter 32) are good examples of this paradigm.

The project-oriented approach is the most responsive to end user needs and often produces a more user-friendly system. However, end users typically lack an organizational and/or strategic perspective and cannot be expected to have the broad vision needed to implement a global information system or a company-wide network. Also, information systems often cut across functional boundaries, and it can be difficult to resolve the conflicts that arise from conflicting functional objectives.

16.4.5   The critical success factors paradigm

The critical success factors paradigm starts by identifying and prioritizing corporate-level information system goals and objectives. Based on these goals and objectives, critical success factors are then defined for each major functional group within the organization. These critical success factors subsequently suggest, prioritize, and shape the requirements associated with specific information system projects.

Focusing on critical success factors helps to encourage a strategic perspective and ensure that information system development is consistent with the corporation's mission, goals, and objectives. However, it is difficult to define quantitative, measurable critical success factors, to resolve the conflicts between inconsistent critical success factors, and to prioritize critical success factors. Additionally, local, divisional, and organizational critical success factors can conflict, and that can lead to confusion.

16.5   Key terms

Behavior-oriented paradigm — An approach to requirements analysis in which the analyst observes and investigates the problem from the strategic level by focusing on executive decision-making and problem-solving styles.

Critical success factor — A target that must be met or an event that must occur if an organization is to accomplish its strategic goals and objectives.

Critical success factors paradigm — An approach to requirements analysis that starts by identifying and prioritizing corporate-level management information systems goals and objectives and then defining critical success factors for each major functional group within the organization.

Industry analysis paradigm — An approach to requirements analysis in which the responsible analysts study competitors' information systems and use the resulting information as a primary factor in defining internal information system requirements.

Information-oriented paradigm — An approach to requirements analysis that focuses on the information system products actually used by supervisory and middle managers.

Project-oriented paradigm — An approach to requirements analysis that focuses on end user requirements.

16.6   Software

Not applicable.

16.7   References

1. Cash, J. I., Jr., McFarlan, W. F., McKenney, J. L., and Vitale, M. R., *Corporate Information Systems Management: Text and Cases,* Irwin, Chicago, 2nd ed., 1988.
2. Laudon, K. C. and Laudon, J.P., *Managing Information Systems: A Contemporary Perspective,* 2nd ed., Macmillan, New York, 1991.
3. McFarlan, W. F., ed., *The Information Systems Research Challenge,* Harvard Business School Press, Boston, MA, 1985.

4. Panko, R. R., *End User Computing: Management, Applications, & Technology,* John Wiley & Sons, New York, 1988.
5. Rockart, J. F., Chief executives define their own data needs, *Harv. Bus. Rev.,* 57(2), 81, 1979.
6. Rockart, J. F. and Treacy, M. E., The CEO goes on line, *Harv. Bus. Rev.,* 60(1), 82, 1982.
7. Shank, M. E., Boynton, A. C., and Zmud, R. W., Critical success factor analysis as a methodology for MIS planning, *MIS Q.,* 9(2), 121, 1985.

chapter seventeen

Survey planning and questionnaire design

Bruce L. Bowerman and Richard T. O'Connell
Miami University

Contents

17.1 Purpose

Surveys and questionnaires are among the analyst's most important sources of information about user problems, user requirements, user satisfaction, and similar system parameters. In this chapter, we briefly discuss sample surveys and questionnaire design.

0-8493-7001-9/99/$0.00+$.50
©1999 by CRC Press LLC

17.2   Strengths, weaknesses, and limitations

A sample survey is taken when it is not practical or convenient to conduct a census of an entire population. A sample survey is less expensive and less time consuming than a census. Moreover, the use of an appropriate sampling design allows the analyst to make valid statistical inferences about the population. In fact, survey results based on a proper sampling plan can be more accurate than the results of a census of an entire population. This can happen because a survey can often be conducted by a small number of highly trained field workers who are far less apt to make mistakes than are the possibly large number of field workers who would be needed to conduct a census.

On the other hand, errors can occur when a sample survey is employed. Sampling error occurs because we do not examine the entire population when we conduct a sample survey. Thus, a survey result is likely to be less accurate than the result of an accurate census. Other errors of non-observation can occur when certain segments of the population are not represented in the sample. Errors of observation can occur when the information obtained from a survey is not the truth. However, it is possible to minimize the impact of such errors by intelligently designing the survey instrument or questionnaire.

17.3   Inputs and related ideas

Sample surveys and questionnaires might be used in any stage of the system development life cycle, but they are particularly valuable during the information gathering and problem definition stage (Part II). Sampling techniques are discussed in Chapter 9.

17.4   Concepts

The purpose of this chapter is to give a brief overview of how to plan a survey and of how to design a questionnaire. For additional details, see Scheaffer et al[5].

17.4.1   Planning a survey

In their discussion of survey sampling, Scheaffer et al[5] present a checklist containing eleven items that need to be considered when planning a survey (Table 17.1). In much of the remainder of this chapter, we will concentrate on the measurement instrument; more particularly, we will discuss how to design a useful questionnaire.

17.4.2   Errors in survey sampling

There are several common sources of error that are encountered when conducting a sample survey. These errors can be divided into two categories: errors of non-observation and errors of observation.

Table 17.1 A checklist of items to be considered when planning a survey.[5]

1. Statement of objectives	A set of simple objectives must be clearly stated and must be understood by everyone working on the survey.
2. Target population	The population to be sampled must be clearly defined using terminology that everyone understands. The population must be defined clearly enough so that a sample can be selected from the population.
3. The frame	The frame is a list of sampling units from which the sample will be selected. The frame must be defined so that it closely agrees with the target population.
4. Sample design	The sample design must be chosen so that the sample will provide enough information to fulfill the survey objectives. Several sample designs (for instance, the *simple random sample*) are briefly discussed in Chapter 9.
5. Method of measurement	Several different measurement methods, such as interviews, questionnaires, direct observation, etc., are available, and the method to be used for the survey must be chosen. Interviews are discussed in Chapter 8. Questionnaires are discussed in this chapter.
6. Measurement instrument	The survey instrument (for instance, the questionnaire or script of questions to be asked in an interview) must be carefully designed in order to minimize bias in the survey results.
7. Selection and training of field workers	The field workers actually collect the data. For instance, they administer questionnaires, conduct interviews, and so forth. These people must be carefully trained so that how they do their job does not have a detrimental effect on the survey results.
8. The pretest	In a pretest the measurement instrument is field tested on a small preliminary sample of respondents. Changes suggested by the pretest results are made before full-scale sampling is done.
9. Organization of fieldwork	Carefully plan and organize how the field workers will do their jobs and clearly define who has the authority in various situations.
10. Organization of data	Carefully plan how the survey data will be processed, managed, and analyzed at all stages of the survey process.
11. Data analysis	Specify in detail exactly how the data will be analyzed and carefully plan what information is to be included in the final survey report.

Errors of non-observation occur because the elements in a sample are only some (not all) of the elements in the target population. Such errors can be due to sampling, coverage, or non-response. Sampling error refers to the difference between an estimate based on a sample and the true value of the population parameter being estimated. This type of error will always exist because a sample is being taken instead of a census. Errors of coverage occur when the sampling frame is not identical to the target population. For instance, a list of local businesses obtained through the Chamber of Commerce will not be completely up to date and, therefore, a sample randomly selected from the Chamber of Commerce list is not a random sample of all businesses in the locality. Non-response occurs when a sampled element (person, business, etc.) cannot be contacted, when a respondent is not able to answer a question, or when a respondent refuses to answer.

Errors of observation occur when the survey data that has been collected is different from the truth. Such errors can be caused by the data collector (the interviewer), the survey instrument, the respondent, or the data collection process. For instance, the manner in which a question is asked can influence the response. Or, the order in which questions appear on a questionnaire can have an influence on the responses. Or, the data collection method (telephone interview, questionnaire, personal interview, or direct observation) can influence the survey results.

17.4.3　Questionnaire design

One of the best ways to reduce error when conducting a sample survey is to carefully design the questionnaire to be used. There are several important considerations that must be kept in mind when designing a questionnaire.

17.4.3.1　Question ordering

The order in which questions are asked can affect the responses to the questions. One reason for this is that respondents try to answer questions in a consistent fashion. As an example, we consider an example originally discussed in Schuman and Presser[6]. An experiment involved asking two questions:

1. *Do you think the United States should let Communist newspaper reporters from other countries come in here and send back to their papers the news as they see it?*
2. *Do you think a Communist country like Russia should let American newspaper reporters come in and send back to America the news as they see it?*

In surveys conducted in 1980, when question 1 was asked first, 54.7 percent of respondents answered yes to question 1 and 63.7 percent answered yes to question 2. When question 2 was asked first, 74.6 percent answered yes to question 1 and 81.9 percent answered yes to question 2. Evidently, the respondents' sense of fair play led more respondents to approve of Communist reporters being allowed to report news in the United States as they see it when they had first approved of U.S. reporters doing the same in Communist countries.

We should also point out that a respondent's reaction to a question can be set by asking preliminary questions dealing with the same topic and that the first question asked is often thought of differently from questions that follow. For instance, the responses to a question about government spending might be very favorable to increased government spending if the question is preceded by several questions emphasizing useful services provided by the government. In contrast, the responses might be opposed to increased government spending if the question is preceded by several questions emphasizing government waste and inefficiency.

As an example of how the first question asked can be thought of differently from the questions that follow, when questions ask the respondent to supply ratings, the first question tends to be given the most extreme rating. For instance, when people are asked to rate the appeal of resort hotels based on descriptive materials, if the first hotel seems appealing it would likely be rated higher than other appealing hotels that are subsequently rated. On the other hand, if the first hotel is not appealing, it would likely be rated lower than other equally unappealing hotels that are subsequently rated.

In addition, the ordering of question *responses* can also influence survey results. Often, the first choice (or first several choices) in a list of choices are more likely to be selected than are later choices. Moreover, if a choice is long, complicated, or difficult to understand or interpret, the choice that precedes the difficult choice is likely to be selected.

In order to reduce the impact of question ordering and response ordering, one strategy is to vary the orders of questions and/or responses presented to different respondents. Another approach is to carefully describe the context in which each survey question was asked in the analysis of the survey results.

17.4.3.2 Open questions and closed questions

When an open question is posed, the respondent is allowed to formulate any answer that he or she wishes. On the other hand, a closed question requires one of several predetermined choices (such as a, b, c, or d) or requires a single numerical response (such as the number of years a respondent has spent in his or her current job position). Closed questions are advantageous because it is easy to summarize and analyze the responses to such questions (especially when a computer is used). On the other hand, open questions allow the respondent to express ideas and nuances that the designer of the questionnaire may not have considered. However, it might be very difficult to summarize and interpret the responses to open questions because the responses cannot be easily quantified.

For instance, in a market research study we might ask the open question:

What do you like most about this product?

This question would elicit a wide variety of responses, while a closed question such as:

What I like most about this product is its:
(a) price   (b) quality   (c) design   (d) styling

would produce responses that are more easily summarized but might force a respondent to choose a response that would not be his or her best response. As a compromise, a questionnaire will often contain a few open questions in addition to a number of closed questions. If only closed questions are to be employed, a good strategy is to use open questions on a preliminary survey to develop the responses for the closed questions to be asked.

17.4.3.3   *Response options and screening questions*

When a question is posed, sometimes the respondent would like to answer by stating that he or she has no opinion or does not know how to answer. Therefore, when constructing a questionnaire, one must decide whether a *no opinion* option will be included among the responses to the various questions. Generally, *no opinion* responses provide little useful information, and, therefore, such responses are often not allowed. On the other hand, it does not seem reasonable to require a response when the respondent may not have the information needed to intelligently formulate a response.

As a general rule, when a question requests an opinion about a subject that everyone (or almost everyone) is familiar with, a *no opinion* option is not allowed. For instance, a question about whether federal income taxes are too high might be posed without a *no opinion* option. On the other hand, a question whose answer requires a specialized background or very specific knowledge might be posed with a *no opinion* option. For example, a question about a little known and seldom used tax provision would probably include a *no opinion* option.

A common strategy is to use screening questions. Such questions are posed in order to determine whether or not a respondent has enough knowledge or information to answer the main question. If a respondent does not know enough to answer the main question, the main question is skipped. If a respondent does have the needed background, he or she is asked to answer the main question and this main question is posed without a *no opinion* option.

Besides deciding whether to include a *no opinion* option, one must decide how many options will be employed. Because middle ground responses often give respondents an easy out, questions are often posed without a middle ground or neutral option. For instance, the question:

In your opinion, are taxes in the United States too high or too low?

attempts to elicit a response on one side of the taxation issue or the other with no neutral response allowed. If we believe that it will be too difficult for many respondents to choose one side or the other, then more response options should be included. In general, however, it is a good idea to keep the number of response options as small as possible.

17.4.3.4   Wording of questions

The language and phrasing used in constructing questions is also an important consideration. In the book *Essentials of Marketing Research,* Dillon et al.[2] present seven basic principles of question construction. Their principles are summarized in Table 17.2.

Table 17.2   Seven basic principles of question construction.[2]

1. Be clear and precise.	A question must be understandable and must elicit a precise answer. For instance, the question *How many cola drinks do you consume?* is too vague. A better version would be: *Here is a 16 ounce bottle of a cola drink. If all of the cola you drink came in 16 ounce bottles, how many would you consume in a week? State a number.*
2. Response choices should not overlap and should be exhaustive.	The response choices should not overlap and should cover all relevant possibilities.
3. Use natural and familiar language.	Questions should be phrased using words and expressions that respondents will understand. For instance, the question, *Do you think that every public building should be equipped with a bubbler?*, will be understood in Wisconsin because in that state a water fountain is called a bubbler, but this question will not be understood elsewhere in the United States.
4. Do not use words or phrases that show bias.	Do not use wordings that suggest what the answer to a question should be (that is, do not use *loaded questions*). In addition, questions should be asked in a balanced way. For instance, the question, *Do you favor the death penalty?* should be asked in the more balanced form, *Do you favor or oppose the death penalty?*
5. Avoid double-barreled questions.	Double-barreled questions are questions that ask the respondent to answer two questions at the same time.

6. State explicit alternatives.

For instance, the question, *Do you feel that major league baseball games are too slow paced and are too expensive?*, contains two questions. They should be separated.

For instance, if we wish to investigate the desirability of DSS satellite systems, the question, *Would you purchase a DSS satellite system?*, does not supply as much information as the question, *If you currently subscribe to cable television and DSS satellite television were available to you, would you:*

1. *subscribe to cable only,*

2. *purchase a DSS satellite system only,*

3. *subscribe to cable and purchase a DSS satellite system.*

7. Questions should meet criteria of validity and reliability.

Questions must measure what the researcher is trying to measure (validity) and responses should be able to be replicated by other researchers (reliability).

When designing questions one must keep in mind that people do not remember facts very well. Also, people do not determine frequencies by counting. Rather, they determine a rate for a shorter period and then multiply (for instance, I consume 3 cases of soft drinks per month, which when multiplied by 12 gives a yearly consumption of 36 cases). Finally, people *telescope* easily remembered events so that they believe that they occurred in a shorter period of time than they actually did. On the other hand, events that are difficult to remember are believed to have occurred longer ago than they actually did.

17.5   Key terms

Census — A set of measurements (or interviews) for every element of a population.

Closed question — A question that requires one of several predetermined choices or that requires a single numerical response.

Double barreled question — A question that asks the respondent to answer two questions.

Errors of coverage — Errors owing to the sampling frame differing from the target population.

Errors of non-observation — Errors that occur because the elements in the sample are not all of the elements in the target population.

Errors of observation — Errors that occur when the survey data is different from the truth.

Frame — A list of sampling units from which the sample will be selected.

Loaded question — A question whose wording suggests what the answer should be.

Non-response — A type of sampling error that occurs when a sampled element (person, business, etc.) cannot be contacted, when a respondent is not able to answer a question, or when a respondent refuses to answer.

Open question — A question for which the respondent is allowed to formulate any answer he or she wishes.

Population — A set of units that we wish to study.

Sample — A subset of the units in a population.

Sampling error — The difference between an estimate based on a sample and the true value of the population parameter being estimated.

Screening questions — Questions posed in order to determine whether or not a respondent should answer the main question.

17.6 Software

Not applicable.

17.7 References

1. Dillman, D. A., *Mail and Telephone Surveys : The Total Method,* John Wiley & Sons, New York, 1978.
2. Dillon, W. R., Madden, T. J., and Firtle, N. H., *Essentials of Marketing Research,* Richard D. Irwin, Homewood, IL, 1993, 304.
3. Gallup, G., *The Sophisticated Poll Watchers Guide,* Princeton Opinion Press, Princeton, NJ, 1972.
4. Groves, R. M., *Survey Errors and Survey Costs,* John Wiley & Sons, New York, 1989.
5. Scheaffer, R. L., Mendenhall, W., and Ott, R. L., *Elementary Survey Sampling,* 5th ed., Duxbury Press, Belmont, CA, 1996, 68.
6. Schuman, H. and Presser, S., *Questions and Answers in Attitude Surveys,* Academic Press, New York, 1981.

chapter eighteen

Cause-and-effect diagrams

John "Skip" Benamati and Timothy C. Krehbiel
Miami University

Contents

18.1   Purpose

A cause-and-effect diagram is a graphical representation of the cause and effect relationships present in an information system or a system in general. The diagram can be used to conduct a root cause analysis, to help design or redesign systems, and to help create or redefine operation standards. The diagrams are sometimes referred to fishbone diagrams, because of their appearance, or Ishikawa diagrams in reference to the quality expert Kaoru Ishikawa who championed their use.

18.2   Strengths, weaknesses, and limitations

A correctly constructed cause-and-effect diagram will lead to a better understanding of the system of interest. The underlying causal relationships among the subsystems and processes comprising the system should become clear to the people constructing the diagrams and the people interpreting them. The diagram can then be used as an effective tool for identifying the root cause of an undesirable system effect. The diagram is also helpful in facilitating a wide range of discussions concerning the system and efforts to improve the system. Moreover, a detailed cause-and-effect diagram can be used as a technical source for a wide range of purposes including the development and revision of technical, operating, and inspection standards.

The effectiveness of the cause-and effect diagram is directly related to the quality of the work that goes into developing the diagram. Everyone involved with the system must participate in the construction process by offering their input concerning all the factors involved in the problem. These factors must be placed into categories that are relevant and properly defined. The relationships among the categories must also be correctly identified. If possible, causal relationships should be verified with regression analysis or other statistical techniques.

Three common mistakes in constructing cause-and-effect diagrams are not clearly defining the categories, improper verification of the causal relationships, and not having enough detail in the diagram. Teamwork and dedication to detail should overcome these problems.

18.3   Inputs and related ideas

Cause-and-effect diagrams are useful tools for identifying the likely causes of a problem during the problem definition stage (Part II) of the system development life cycle. Brainstorming (Chapter 14, Section 14.4.4.3) is a valuable tool when developing a list of possible activities to be used in a cause-and-effect diagram. Once the cause-and-effect diagram is drawn, it is often helpful to use it in conjunction with a Pareto diagram (Chapter 11) to help prioritize and allocate resources. In general, the seven tools for quality improvement (Pareto diagram, cause-and-effect diagram, control chart, process flow diagram, check sheet, scatter diagram, and histogram) serve as a complimentary tool set which has been proven to be effective in improving many systems.

18.4   Concepts

A cause-and-effect diagram is a graphical representation of the causal relationships inherent in a system. Constructing a cause-and-effect diagram requires a team composed of people knowledgeable about the system of interest. In the following example, a cause-and-effect diagram for evaluating client server application failures is presented.

18.4.1   Constructing the diagram

The first step in constructing a cause-and-effect diagram is to develop a clear definition of the effect or outcome of interest. Then all possible causes leading to that outcome are brainstormed. It is important in the brainstorming period to consider all possibilities so that no important factors are overlooked. Unimportant causes can be dropped later.

In our example a *client server application failure* is the system event of interest and is placed in the box on the right side (the effect side) of the diagram, as shown in Figure 18.1. Next, the main arrow pointing into the effect box (the trunk) is drawn.The trunk is in the left side of the diagram (the causal side).

Four to six branches are then selected to represent the main causes of the main effect. The branches represent cause-and-effect relationships with the main effect of interest. Leading into the big branches, are medium branches which are used to represent the next layer of causal relationships. Note that the cause-and-effect relationships should move in the direction of the arrows in the figure. For example, a software bug leads to a middleware problem, which leads to the client server application failure. Or, a broken physical connection can lead to a network problem, which results in the client server application failure.

A cause-and-effect diagram can contain as many different levels of branches as necessary. Typically two to five levels are used. If four or five levels are used, it is often helpful to produce the diagram in pieces. Note that in Figure 18.1 the big and medium branches are displayed, while in Figure 18.2 the small and tiny branches attached to the *Client hardware failure* medium branch (a horizontal arrow near the lower right of Figure 18.1)

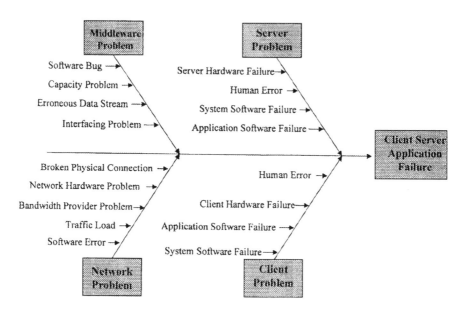

Figure 18.1   The main portion of the cause-and-effect diagram for the client server application failure.

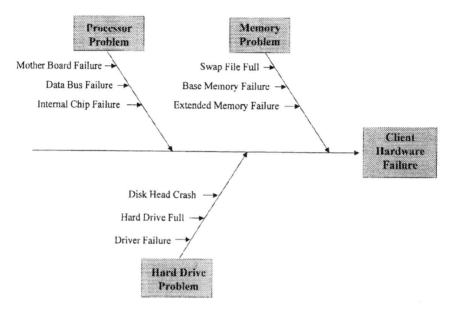

Figure 18.2   The detailed portion of the cause-and-effect diagram associated with client hardware failure.

are displayed. Three small branches are used to identify the main causes for this type of failure, and sub-categories within the small branches are displayed in the tiny branches. For illustrative purposes, only one of the medium branches in Figure 18.1 is expanded, but in practice any or all of the medium branches could be broken down and illustrated in detail.

18.4.2   Root cause analysis

A correctly constructed cause-and-effect diagram is very useful for conducting a root cause analysis. For example, suppose that a client server application failure has occurred. The cause-and-effect diagram shown in Figure 18.1 suggests that the cause is one of the following four factors: middleware, server, network, or client. Assuming that the problem is determined to be with the client, we now investigate the possible sources within the client, listed in Figure 18.1 as human error, client hardware failure, application software failure, and system software failure.

Suppose that the problem was determined to be with the client hardware. Next, we turn our attention to Figure 18.2 and try to determine if the client hardware failure was owing to a processor problem, a memory problem, or a hard drive problem. Assuming that it was a hard drive problem, the cause-and-effect diagram gives three possibilities for such an event: disk head crash, hard drive full, and driver failure. Answering this question leads to the root cause of the client server application failure. Suppose that the hard drive was found to be full. The full hard drive is said to be the root cause of the client server application failure. Reaching the root cause required a series of four questions each probing a causal relationship one step further.

A root cause analysis is only possible when the causal relationships in a cause-and-effect diagram are valid. An analyst should verify the structure of the branches and the direction of the arrows beginning with all tiny branches before using the diagram. For instance, tracing the logic presented above, the analysts should have previously verified that a full hard drive can lead to a hard drive problem, which can lead to a client hardware failure, which can lead to a client problem, which can lead to the client server application failure. If possible, these paths should be verified with data and statistical models.

18.5   Key terms

Branches — The factors causing the effect of interest; branches are sub-divided into big, medium, small, and tiny branches. When the term fishbone diagram is used, branches are referred to as bones.

Effect of interest — A characteristic or event of a system that the cause-and-effect diagram is meant to study; typically, a problem or undesirable event.

Root cause analysis — Identification of the initial factor resulting in an effect of interest; the root cause is usually found in a tiny branch. This initial factor starts a chain reaction of cause and effect situations, moving from a tiny branch to a small branch to a medium branch to a big branch, and ultimately resulting in the effect of interest.

Sources of variability — Many different things can affect the outcomes from systems, including the effects of workers, machines, materials, methods, measurements, and the environment. These six sources of variation are sometimes used as the big branches on a cause-and-effect diagram.

Trunk — The trunk is the central part of the diagram to which the big branches are attached. When using the term fishbone diagram, the trunk is referred to as the spine.

18.6   Software

Most graphing packages have the ability to produce cause-and-effect diagrams. For example, the chapter figures were produced with Microsoft PowerPoint.

Many statistical or quality improvement software packages can be used to produce cause-and-effect diagrams. Construction of cause-and-effect diagrams using Minitab for Windows is easy, but not very flexible. In SAS, use the Ishikawa procedure.

18.7 References

1. Gitlow, H., Oppenheim, A., and Oppenheim, R., *Quality Management: Tools and Methods for Improvement*, 2nd ed., Irwin, Burr Ridge, IL, 1995, chap. 9.
2. Ozeki, K. and Asaka, T., *Handbook of Quality Tools: The Japanese Approach*, Productivity Press, Cambridge, MA, 1990, chap. 12.

chapter nineteen

Simulation

Eleni Pratsini
Miami University

Contents

19.1 Purpose

Simulation is the use of a mathematical model that behaves in the same manner as the system under study. The purpose of a simulation model is to give management an insight into the behavior of the system and to give information about possible alternative actions. By changing parameter values and testing different proposed solutions to a problem, simulation can provide an insight on how the system behaves under various conditions and help management evaluate the available options.

19.2 Strengths, weaknesses, and limitations

The information obtained from the simulation model can be used to study the behavior of the system without disturbing the system, or to compare various proposed solutions and actions without actually implementing those actions. It is generally easier to understand a simulation model than an analytical model (although an analytic model, if one exists, is preferable to a simulation model). Furthermore, with the recent technological advances, computer animation can give a visual representation of a model and enable managers to better understand the model. Finally, simulation is very flexible and can be used to represent very complex systems that cannot be otherwise studied.

The quality of results depends on the quality of inputs. Gathering data to generate input values can be time consuming and expensive. Building a model requires time, effort and expertise, and the output can be hard to interpret. Simulation cannot prescribe a solution; it merely describes the behavior of a system under various inputs. Thus, the analysis will not detect the existence of a better action that was not tested.

Note that several simulation trials are necessary before inferences about an output variable can be made. In discrete simulations, multiple runs are necessary, and the mean of the average values obtained from each run serves as the point estimate for the measure of interest.

19.3 Inputs and related ideas

Before building a simulation model, you must:

1. Formulate the problem and identify a clear objective for the model. Identify output variables and specific issues to be addressed. Decide on budget and time restrictions.
2. Define the probability distributions of all stochastic inputs. These input distributions are obtained or estimated from empirical data or through heuristic procedures if no data are available.
3. Obtain a good understanding of the system and determine a level of detail for the model.

Once the model is developed, verify that it is free of any programming mistakes. Throughout the entire simulation process, validate the model to ensure it represents the system under study. Use pilot runs to test the model's behavior to small changes. Use real output data, if available, to evaluate simulated output. After verifying and validating the model, make multiple simulation runs to gather output data. Use statistical techniques to analyze the output and make inferences about the performance of particular designs.

Simulation and queuing theory (Chapter 79) are mathematically-based techniques that can be applied to similar problems. Simulation is often used to support network analysis (Chapter 53) and network routing (Chapter 54).

19.4   Concepts

Simulation models imitate real life systems. The models frequently deal with stochastic rather than deterministic inputs. These inputs have probabilistic components that can be modeled through the use of random numbers. Simulation languages and spreadsheets have built-in probability functions that allow the user to generate values from certain probability distributions.

Simulation models can be categorized into three groups: Monte-Carlo simulations, discrete simulations, and continuous simulations. Discrete and continuous simulations are often called systems simulations. The main difference between Monte-Carlo and systems simulations is the effect of time. In Monte-Carlo simulations time plays no substantive role, while in systems simulations time is an important part of the model. In discrete simulations variables change instantaneously at particular points in time, while in continuous simulations, variables change continuously. Continuous models typically use differential equations and have applications in the engineering field. Thus, they are not discussed in this chapter.

19.4.1   Monte-Carlo simulation

Monte-Carlo simulations have one or more random inputs and the passage of time plays no substantive role. Random numbers are used to generate values from the input distributions. Typically, the output depends on these probabilistic inputs and takes on different values with repeated simulation trials. The outcomes of consecutive simulation trials are independent of each other, and standard statistical methods can be used to analyze the results. Moreover, risk analysis can be performed to evaluate the potential loss resulting from a decision. Most popular spreadsheets have build-in probability functions and allow repeated sampling. Furthermore, spreadsheet add-ins make it much easier to perform simulations and generate important statistical information that facilitates the analysis of the output.

The following example is used to demonstrate the application of Monte-Carlo simulation. Albert's Bakery Store specializes in fruitcakes. Daily demand for cakes is normally distributed with a mean of 12 and a standard deviation of 2. Production cost is $3.10 per cake and the unit selling price is $5. Any cakes not sold at the end of the day are given to the free store. Albert would like to know how many cakes to make at the beginning of the day in order to maximize his profit. Furthermore, he believes that it is important to have a profit of at least $5, and would like to minimize the probability of not meeting this minimum profit.

The unit production cost and the unit selling price are found in cells B3 and B4 of the Excel spreadsheet in Figure 19.1. The decision on daily production is shown in cell B6. Cell B7 generates demand using the normal distribution and rounds the value to the nearest integer. Production cost is in cell B8, revenue is in cell B9, and profit is the difference between revenue and cost as shown in cell B11. It is good practice to have the input values at a designated place in the spreadsheet and refer to them for the calculation of the various costs. That way, sensitivity analysis can be performed by simply changing the values of the input cells (and not the cell formulas).

19.4.1.1   Output analysis

The output variable in this example is profit. Whenever demand changes in cell B7, profit also changes. Furthermore, the daily production value in cell B6 affects profit.

To analyze this problem, multiple simulation trials are necessary for each production value. Using a two-way table in Excel, the profit was generated for 1000 simulation trials and 6 different production values. For each production value, the average, standard deviation, minimum, and maxi-

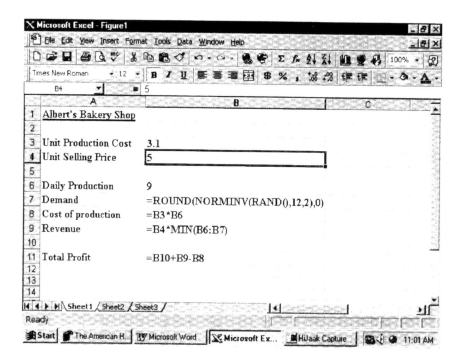

Figure 19.1   Spreadsheet setup for Albert's Bakery Store.

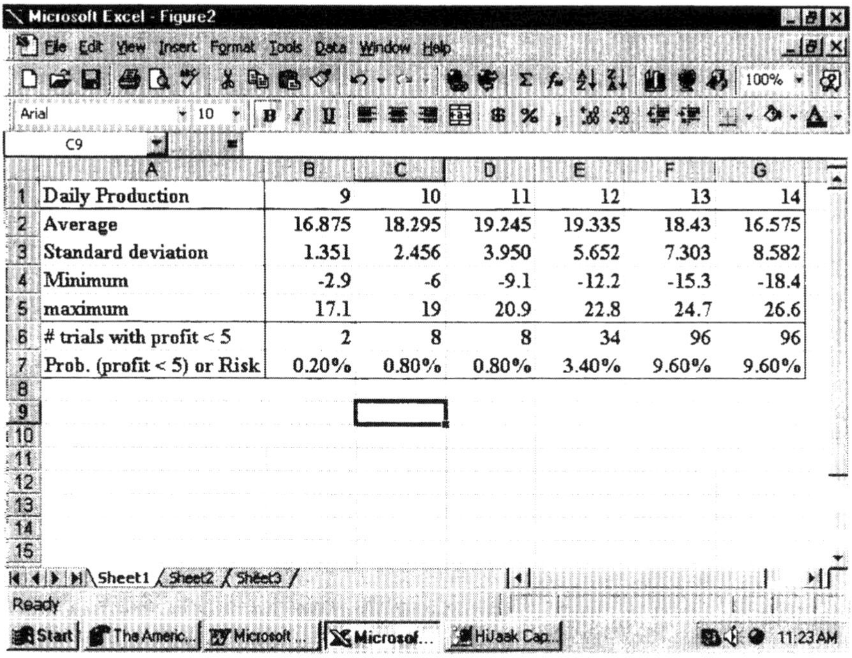

	A	B	C	D	E	F	G
1	Daily Production	9	10	11	12	13	14
2	Average	16.875	18.295	19.245	19.335	18.43	16.575
3	Standard deviation	1.351	2.456	3.950	5.652	7.303	8.582
4	Minimum	-2.9	-6	-9.1	-12.2	-15.3	-18.4
5	maximum	17.1	19	20.9	22.8	24.7	26.6
6	# trials with profit < 5	2	8	8	34	96	96
7	Prob. (profit < 5) or Risk	0.20%	0.80%	0.80%	3.40%	9.60%	9.60%

Figure 19.2 Simulation results for Albert's Bakery Store.

mum profit values were calculated using the =AVERAGE, =STDEV, =MIN, and =MAX functions.

The summary statistics of the simulation trials are shown in Figure 19.2. A daily production value of 12 maximizes average profit at 19.335 with a standard deviation of 5.652. A daily production value of 11 gives an average profit at 19.245 and a standard deviation of 3.95. This option gives a lower profit but has less variability.

The formula for computing a 95 percent confidence interval of the average profit given a specific production value is shown in Table 19.1 (Formula 19.1). $\bar{x}$ is the average profit, s is the standard deviation, n is the number of simulation trials, and $Z_{0.25}$ is 1.96, and is obtained from the standardized normal tables. The 95 percent confidence interval for a daily production value of 11, is $19.245 \pm 1.96(3.95/1000^{1/2})$, or from 19.000 to 19.490. For a daily production value of 12, the 95 percent confidence interval is 18.985 to 19.685. Again, the intervals indicate that a production of 12 has a higher average value but also a higher variability.

Table 19.1 Confidence Intervals

19.1	$\bar{x} \pm Z_{0.25}\,[s/(n^{1/2})]$

Since simulation trials are independent of each other, other statistical methods (for example, hypothesis testing) can be used to analyze and compare the various decisions.

19.4.1.2   Risk analysis

Risk is the potential occurrence of an undesirable outcome when a decision must be taken in the presence of uncertainty. In the Albert's Bakery Store example, the undesirable outcome is a profit less than $5.

For each production value, the number of simulation trials having a profit less than $5 can be obtained using Excel's =COUNTIF(range,"<5") function. This number is divided by the total number of simulation trials (1000) to give the risk or probability of profit being less than $5 (Figure 19.2).

Risk is minimized when daily production is 9, but profit is low at this level. Compare the two production values with the highest average profit. A production quantity of 12 has the highest average profit with a risk of 3.4 percent. A production quantity of 11 has a slightly lower profit with a lower risk at 0.8 percent.

19.4.2   Discrete simulation

Discrete simulations represent systems in which changes occur instantaneously at particular points in time. They model a sequence of events that occur over time and are typically used for inventory, queuing, and manufacturing analyses. Lately, their applications have been extended to the service and public policy sectors among others.

Even though the analysis of such models can be done manually or in spreadsheets, the amount of information that must be kept can be overwhelming and the use of computer simulation languages is recommended.

Queuing applications of discrete simulations abound. In these studies, the characteristics of the system change with the occurrence of two events: arrival of entities and departure (or end of service) of entities. The simulation clock is advanced to the time when the next event takes place, and the changes in the system are recorded. Thus, the models are frequently called next-event simulations.

Consider the example of Harry, the barber (Chapter 79). Customers arrive at Harry's shop at the average rate of 4 per hour, according to a Poisson distribution. Harry's average service rate is 3.2 customers per hour, exponentially distributed. Chapter 79 shows the calculation of performance measures (length of queue, waiting time in queue, etc.) using an analytical approach. In this chapter, the same analysis is performed with the help of a simulation language.

Using SLAM II,[1] the graphical network of the problem is shown in Figure 19.3. The first node in the network creates arrivals at an average rate of one every 0.25 h. The customers are routed to a queue (HARRY) where they wait for service. Average service time is 0.2 h, and after service they leave the system.

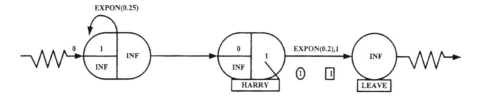

Figure 19.3 SLAM II network for Harry's barbershop.

The simulation was run for 4000 h and statistics were cleared after 1000 h in order to eliminate any effects of transient state. The output statistics in Figure 19.4 represent steady state statistics for one run. Average length of the queue is 3.189 and average waiting time is 0.795 h or 47.7 min. These values can be found under "FILE STATISTICS" and are in agreement with the analytical values (Chapter 79) of 3.2 and 48 min.

Consider the same example with the following extension: There is a 50 percent chance that an arriving customer will balk if there are more than 4 customers waiting. The new network in Figure 19.5 shows conditional as well as probabilistic branching. Variable NNQ(1) refers to the number of customers waiting for service. The condition and probabilities on the branches indicate that 50 percent of the arriving customers leave if the line is greater than 4. As expected, the average length of the queue decreased to 1.692, and average waiting time is 0.444 h or 26.64 min (Figure 19.6). Furthermore, the output indicates that during the 3000 simulated hours, 722 customers left the system without receiving service (regular activity statistics) while 11,443 customers received service (service activity statistics).

```
SIMULATION PROJECT HARRY'S BARBER SHOP        BY PRATSINI
     DATE   1/ 1/1998                         RUN NUMBER    1 OF    1

     CURRENT TIME    0.4000E+04
     STATISTICAL ARRAYS CLEARED AT TIME   0.1000E+04


                **FILE STATISTICS**

     FILE                   AVERAGE   STANDARD   MAXIMUM   CURRENT AVERAGE
     NUMBER   LABEL/TYPE    LENGTH    DEVIATION  LENGTH    LENGTH  WAIT TIME

        1        QUEUE       3.189      4.252       28        9      0.795
        2       CALENDAR     1.797      0.402        3        2      0.118


                **SERVICE ACTIVITY STATISTICS**

     ACT ACT LABEL OR   SER AVERAGE    STD   CUR AVERAGE MAX IDL MAX BSY  ENT
     NUM START NODE      CAP  UTIL     DEV   UTIL BLOCK  TME/SER TME/SER  CNT

        1      QUEUE       1   0.797   0.40    1   0.00    2.49   69.38 12023
```

Figure 19.4 SLAM II output for Harry's barbershop.

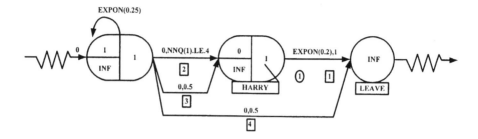

Figure 19.5   SLAM II network for Harry's barbershop with probabilistic balking.

```
SIMULATION PROJECT HARRY'S BARBER SHOP        BY PRATSINI
   DATE  1/ 1/1998                           RUN NUMBER    1 OF    1

   CURRENT TIME   0.4000E+04
   STATISTICAL ARRAYS CLEARED AT TIME   0.1000E+04


              **FILE STATISTICS**
```

FILE NUMBER	LABEL/TYPE	AVERAGE LENGTH	STANDARD DEVIATION	MAXIMUM LENGTH	CURRENT LENGTH	AVERAGE WAIT TIME
1	HARR QUEUE	1.692	1.998	12	5	0.444
2	CALENDAR	1.768	0.422	3	2	0.119

```
              **REGULAR ACTIVITY STATISTICS**
```

ACTIVITY INDEX/LABEL	AVERAGE UTILIZATION	STANDARD DEVIATION	MAXIMUM UTIL	CURRENT UTIL	ENTITY COUNT
2	0.0000	0.0000	1	0	10731
3	0.0000	0.0000	1	0	717
4	0.0000	0.0000	1	0	722

```
              **SERVICE ACTIVITY STATISTICS**
```

ACT NUM	ACT LABEL OR START NODE	SER CAP	AVERAGE UTIL	STD DEV	CUR UTIL	AVERAGE BLOCK	MAX IDL TME/SER	MAX BSY TME/SER	ENT CNT
1	HARR QUEUE	1	0.768	0.42	1	0.00	2.26	14.95	11443

Figure 19.6   SLAM II output for Harry's barbershop with probabilistic balking.

19.4.2.1 Stopping rules

In the preceding example, the model was run for a fixed amount of time. The simulation lasted 4000 h and the statistics were cleared after 1000 h in order to eliminate transient state effects. If the transient state is of interest, then statistics are collected over the initial stages of the simulation.

Other stopping rules for discrete simulations can depend on the number of entities that go through the system. It is possible to generate only 100 customers for Harry's barbershop, and end the simulation when the last customer leaves the system. Alternatively, it is possible to keep generating customers, but end the simulation when the 100th customer leaves the system. In the first example, the system is empty when the simulation terminates, while in the latter example, there can be customers in the system at the end of simulation. The performance measures of the two scenarios will probably be different.

19.4.2.2 Output analysis

Statistical analysis of discrete simulations is not as straightforward as in Monte-Carlo simulations because observations are not independent. For example, the waiting time in queue for the 10th customer is correlated with the waiting time of the 9th customer. If customer 9 was in line for a long time, most probably, customer 10 will be in line for a long time. Multiple simulation runs are necessary, with each run lasting a reasonable amount of time or processing a large number of entities. If the transient state is not of interest, statistics should be collected after the steady state has been reached. A popular technique for collecting statistics is the batch means approach. One long simulation run is used instead of many shorter ones. Statistics are cleared after the warm-up period in order to eliminate the transient state. The remaining length of the simulation is divided into the desired number of batches. Statistics are collected at the end of each batch and then cleared in order to start collection for the next batch. For each batch, the average value of a performance measure is calculated. The 95 percent confidence interval for a performance measure is given by Formula 19.2 in Table 19.2. $\bar{x}$ is the mean of all batch averages, n is the number of batches (which is typically small), $t_{0.25}$ has $n-1$ degrees of freedom and is obtained from the t-tables, and s is the standard deviation of the average values, given by Formula 19.3, where x_i is the average value of the ith batch.

Table 19.2 Discrete Simulation Output Analysis

19.2	$\bar{x} \pm t_{0.25} [s/(n^{1/2})]$
19.3	$\sqrt{[\Sigma_i (x_i - \bar{x})^2/(n-1)]}$

The simulation model for Harry's shop with probabilistic balking (Figure 19.5) was run for 16,000 h; statistics were cleared after the first 1000 h, and then collected, and subsequently cleared at 3000 h intervals. The average queue-lengths for the five batches are: 1.692, 1.507, 1.715, 1.633, and 1.585. The mean, $\bar{x}$, is 1.6264 and the standard deviation, s, is 0.0839. The 95 percent confidence interval for the length of the queue is $1.6264 \pm 2.776(0.0839/5^{1/2})$ or 1.522 to 1.730. In other words, there is a 95 percent chance that the length of the queue is between 1.522 and 1.730.

19.5   Key terms

Analytic model — A mathematical equation(s) that will give the value of an output when an input value is specified.

Balking — The act of walking away from a queue; usually occurs when the queue is either too long or at maximum capacity.

Continuous simulation — A simulation model of a system in which changes occur continuously.

Deterministic model — A model having all inputs fixed and known (or assumed known).

Discrete simulation — A simulation model of a system in which changes occur instantaneously at particular points in time.

Entities — Units such as people, parts, jobs, etc., that flow through a system.

Monte-Carlo simulation — A simulation with one or more random variables where the passage of time plays no substantive role. Random numbers are used to generate values from probability distributions.

Risk analysis — An analysis of the potential occurrence of an undesirable outcome when a decision must be taken in the presence of uncertainty.

Simulation — The use of a mathematical model that behaves in the same manner as the system under study.

Steady state — The end of transient state as the system reaches normal operations.

Stochastic or probabilistic model — A model having some data described by probability distributions.

System — A set of components (entities, machines, etc.) that interact to perform an operation that is of interest to the modeler.

Transient state   The beginning or warm-up period of a model as activity builds up.

19.6   Software

Most standard spreadsheet programs are sufficient for Monte-Carlo simulations. Build-in probability functions give the analyst the capability to sample from certain distributions. However, the number of available distributions is limited. Furthermore, it can become cumbersome to generate thousands of trials of a simulation model. Spreadsheet add-ins (@RISK Crystal Ball, etc.) provide a wide variety of probability distributions, and make it much easier to perform multiple trials, and generate important statistical information to facilitate the analysis of the output.

Both general-purpose languages (C, C++, Fortran, etc.) and simulation languages (SLAM II, SIMSCRIPT, GPSS, Extend, etc.) can be used for discrete simulation. Even though general-purpose languages offer greater flexibility, simulation languages can be more efficient as far as computing time and effort. Simulation languages provide most of the features required in a simulation model and are easier to change.

For a comprehensive survey of available simulation software see Swaim.[2]

19.7   References

19.7.1   Citations

1.   Pritsker, A. B., *Introduction to Simulation and SLAM II*, 3rd ed., Halsted Press (John Wiley & Sons), New York, 1986.
2.   Swaim, J. J., Simulation goes mainstream, *OR/MS Today,* 24(5), 35, 1997.

19.7.2   Suggestions for additional reading

1.   Law, A. M. and Kelton, W. D., *Simulation Modeling & Analysis,* 2nd ed., McGraw-Hill, New York, 1991.
2.   Winston, W. L., *Simulation Modeling Using @RISK,* Duxbury Press, Belmont, CA, 1996.

part three

---

*Project planning and
project management*

chapter twenty

Gantt charts

William S. Davis

Contents

20.1 Purpose

A Gantt chart is a tool for graphically depicting a schedule. Gantt charts can be used to plan, record, and document the schedule, and to track actual results against the schedule.

20.2 Strengths, weaknesses, and limitations

Gantt charts are easy to create and easy to understand. They are particularly useful for planning relatively small projects because they can often show the entire schedule at a glance.

A Gantt chart is primarily a planning tool. Gantt charts are not as useful for project control because the percent completion depicted by a bar is based on subjective judgment. Also, a Gantt chart does not show the precedence relationships between the tasks. Consequently, project networks (Chapter 21), PERT, and CPM are better for larger projects.

20.3   Inputs and related ideas

Before preparing a Gantt chart the tasks or activities to be performed must be identified and each activity's duration, start time, and end time estimated. A project network (Chapter 21) is a better tool for scheduling a large project.

20.4   Concepts

On a Gantt chart (Figure 20.1), the activities (or tasks) are listed at the left and time progresses from left to right across the top. In this example, time is shown in days.

Each activity is represented by a horizontal bar. The bar's left edge indicates when the activity begins, its length corresponds to the activity's duration, and its right edge shows when the activity ends. Typically, a vertical line identifies the current day. Often, the bars that represent the plan are shown in one color and the actual results are shown in a contrasting color. The result is an easily visualized comparison between the plan and actual performance.

The Gantt chart in Figure 20.1 assumes that all work will be done by one programmer/analyst and one data entry clerk, with the bulk of the work beginning after the customer's new computer is installed. Figure 20.2 shows a different Gantt chart for the same project. On this schedule, design work begins as soon as the new computer is ordered and a programmer writes the necessary code. Note that the work is completed in significantly less time because more tasks are done in parallel.

ID	Task Name	Start Date	End Date	Duration	February	March
1	Select/order hardware and software	2/9/98	2/10/98	2d	▬	
2	Shipping time	2/11/98	2/17/98	5d	▬▬	
3	Prepare site and install	2/18/98	2/18/98	1d	▪	
4	Clarify manual procedures	2/17/98	2/17/98	1d	▪	
5	Design files	2/19/98	2/24/98	4d	▬▬	
6	Design record shipment program	2/25/98	2/25/98	1d	▪	
7	Write record shipment program	2/26/98	2/26/98	1d	▪	
8	Design and write sales data entry program	2/27/98	2/27/98	1d	▪	
9	Customize reports	3/2/98	3/2/98	1d		▪
10	Train clerical personnel	3/3/98	3/3/98	1d		▪
11	Train sales clerks	3/4/98	3/5/98	2d		▬
12	Train inventory manager	3/6/98	3/6/98	1d		▪
13	Train store manager	3/9/98	3/9/98	1d		▪
14	Initialize vendor file	2/25/98	2/25/98	1d	▪	
15	Initialize customer file	2/26/98	2/27/98	2d	▬	
16	Initialize inventory file	3/2/98	3/6/98	5d		▬▬
17	Perform system test	3/10/98	3/10/98	1d		▪

Figure 20.1   A Gantt chart shows the schedule for all a project's activities at a glance.

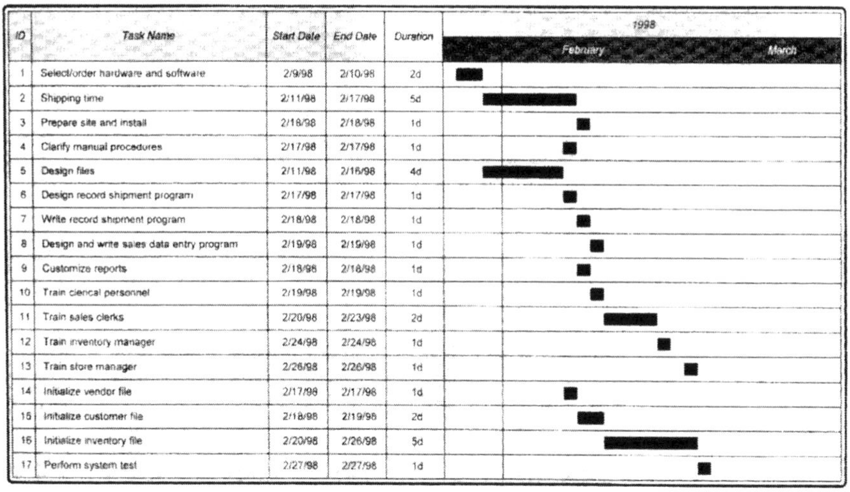

ID	Task Name	Start Date	End Date	Duration	1998 February	March
1	Select/order hardware and software	2/9/98	2/10/98	2d		
2	Shipping time	2/11/98	2/17/98	5d		
3	Prepare site and install	2/18/98	2/18/98	1d		
4	Clarify manual procedures	2/17/98	2/17/98	1d		
5	Design files	2/11/98	2/16/98	4d		
6	Design record shipment program	2/17/98	2/17/98	1d		
7	Write record shipment program	2/18/98	2/18/98	1d		
8	Design and write sales data entry program	2/19/98	2/19/98	1d		
9	Customize reports	2/18/98	2/18/98	1d		
10	Train clerical personnel	2/19/98	2/19/98	1d		
11	Train sales clerks	2/20/98	2/23/98	2d		
12	Train inventory manager	2/24/98	2/24/98	1d		
13	Train store manager	2/26/98	2/26/98	1d		
14	Initialize vendor file	2/17/98	2/17/98	1d		
15	Initialize customer file	2/18/98	2/19/98	2d		
16	Initialize inventory file	2/20/98	2/26/98	5d		
17	Perform system test	2/27/98	2/27/98	1d		

Figure 20.2 On this Gantt chart, several activities are performed in parallel.

20.5 Key terms

Activity — A task to be completed.

Duration — The elapsed time required to complete an activity.

Gantt chart — A chart that shows a project schedule as a series of horizontal lines or bars.

Schedule — A series of events or activities with estimated completion times or target dates.

20.6 Software

The Gantt charts in this chapter were created using the Visio Timeline Wizard. Most project management software tools (such as Microsoft Project, Primavera's Suretrack Project Manager, and CA-SuperProject) support Gantt charts.

You can also create a Gantt chart using spreadsheet software such as Excel, Lotus 1-2-3, or Quattro Pro. List the activities in column A, their start times (in days, weeks, months, or other time units from the beginning of the project) in column B, and each activity's duration in Column C. Plot the data as a horizontal, stacked bar chart and select attributes that make the first bar (the start times) invisible.

20.7 References

1. Badiru, A. B. and Whitehouse, *Computer Tools, Models and Techniques for Project Management*, TAB Books, Blue Ridge Summit, PA, 1989.
2. Davis, W. S., *Business Systems Analysis and Design*, Wadsworth, Belmont, CA, 1994.

3. Humphrey, W. S., *Managing the Software Process*, Addison-Wesley, Reading, MA, 1989.
4. Roetzheim, W. H., *Structured Computer Project Management*, Prentice-Hall, Englewood Cliffs, NJ, 1988.
5. Weinberg, G. M. and Weinberg, D., *General Principles of Systems Design*, Dorset House, New York, 1988.

chapter twenty-one

Project networks, PERT, and CPM

William S. Davis

Contents

21.1   Purpose

A project network chart is a tool for graphically depicting a schedule and serves as a basis for PERT and CPM. Project networks can be used to plan, record, and document a schedule and to track actual results against the schedule.

21.2   Strengths, weaknesses, and limitations

Project networks are excellent tools for planning, tracking, and managing large projects. They are not particularly useful for small projects, however.

PERT (Program Evaluation and Review Technique) is useful in research and development projects where the times required to complete the various activities are uncertain. The critical path is the primary focus of management control, and monitoring the critical events provides an early warning if estimates are inaccurate.

CPM (Critical Path Method) is used to help solve scheduling problems when the activity times are known more precisely. Only by shortening the critical path can the project completion time be improved. Consequently, the critical path defines those activities into which additional resources might be poured to accelerate the schedule.

Creating a project network is a complex undertaking. The computations are straightforward, but non-trivial. Without appropriate software tools, maintaining or changing a project network can be difficult.

The accuracy of the project network is no better than the estimated duration of each of the activities. The lack of a relationship between an activity's duration and the length of the arrow that represents the activity can lead to misunderstandings. Errors in computing earliest event times, latest event times, and slack times are not always apparent, so all computations should be checked carefully.

21.3   Inputs and related ideas

Before preparing a project network, the tasks or activities to be performed must be identified and each activity's duration (the time required to complete the activity) estimated. Additionally, the sequential relationships between activities must be known. The necessary information is typically collected during the problem definition and information gathering stages of the system development life cycle (Part II).

A Gantt chart (Chapter 20) may be a better tool for scheduling a small project. The project network is the basis for crash mode scheduling (Chapter 22).

21.4   Concepts

A project network chart is a tool for graphically depicting a schedule and serves as a basis for PERT and CPM. Project networks can be used to plan, record, and document a schedule and to track actual results against the schedule.

The examples in this chapter are based on the activities listed in Table 21.1. Figure 21.1 is a project network for these activities.

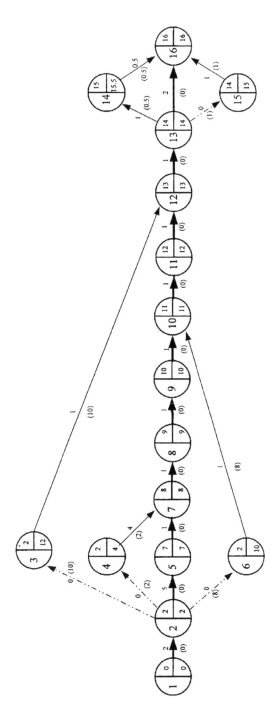

Figure 21.1 A project network for an inventory system.

Table 21.1   A List of the Activities Associated
with an Inventory System

Description	Duration	Activity
Order hardware and software	2	1-2
Shipment time	5	2-5
Clarify manual procedures	1	3-12
Design files	4	4-7
Prepare site and install	1	5-7
Design record shipment program	1	6-10
Initialize vendor file	1	7-8
Initialize customer file	1	8-9
Initialize inventory file	1	9-10
Write record shipment program	1	10-11
Customize reports	1	11-12
System test	1	12-13
Train inventory manager	1	13-14
Train sales clerks	2	13-16
Train clerical personnel	0.5	14-16
Train store manager	1	15-16

21.4.1   Events and activities

Each activity (a line or an arrow) in the project network begins and ends
with an event (a circle or a bubble). The events are numbered (the numbers
do not necessarily imply sequence), and a given activity is identified by the
numbers associated with its beginning and ending events. *Order hardware
and software* is activity 1-2. *Shipment time* (activity 2-5) begins with event 2
and ends with event 5. Note that events are points in time, while activities
consume both time and (usually) resources.

Each activity's duration is shown just above its arrow. Note that there is
no relationship between the length of an arrow and the duration of the
activity. The arrows identify dependency relationships; all activities that
enter a given event must be completed before that event occurs.

21.4.2   Precedence

The project network defines event precedence. For example, to the right of
Figure 21.1, event 13 must occur before activity 13-14 or activity 13-15 can
begin, and event 16 does not occur until activities 13-16, 14-16, and 15-16 are
all completed. Activities on parallel paths can be performed in parallel.

The path through a project network is said to diverge when a single-line
path splits into multiple paths. For example, a single path (activity 12-13)
enters event 13, and three paths (13-14, 13-15, and 13-16) leave event 13.
Paths are said to merge when multiple input paths lead to a single output.
For example, activities 3-12 and 11-12 both end at event 12, and only activity 12-13 leaves event 12.

21.4.3 Dummy activities

Some of the activities in Figure 21.1 are shown as dashed lines. These dummy activities link parallel events and consume neither time nor resources. They show dependency relationships that are not associated with activities.

21.4.4 The earliest event time

The project network defines the dependency relationships between the events. Given a clear sense of the order in which events must occur, the analyst can prepare a schedule.

The first step is to compute the earliest event time (EET) for each event. The EET is the earliest time the event can possibly begin. By convention it is zero for the first event. To compute the earliest event time for all the other events, work from left to right and follow these three rules:

1. Select all activities that *enter* the event.
2. For each entering activity, sum the activity's duration and the EET of its *initial* event.
3. Select the *highest* computed EET and record it in the upper right quadrant of the event circle.

An event occurs when *all* the activities that enter it are completed. That is why the *highest* computed EET is selected.

In Figure 21.1 the earliest event times are shown at the upper right quadrant of each circle. For example, consider event 2. There is only one entering activity, 1-2. Activity 1-2's initial event is 1. Event 1's EET is 0 and activity 1-2's duration is 2 d, so the earliest event 2 can possibly occur is 2 d after the project begins.

Next, consider event 10. It has two entering activities (6-10 and 9-10), so two computations are needed. Event 6's EET is 2 and activity 6-10's duration is 1 d, so the computed EET is 3 d. Event 9's EET is 10 and activity 9-10's duration is 1 d, so the second EET is 11 d. The highest computed EET for event 10 is 11 d, so record 11 at the top right of the bubble that represents event 10.

21.4.5 The latest event time

The latest event time (LET) is the latest time an event can occur without impacting the project schedule. By convention, the LET of the last or terminal event is equal to its earliest event time, so 16 d is both the EET and the LET for event 16 (Figure 21.1). To compute the latest event time for all the other events, work from right to left and follow these three rules:

1. Consider all activities that *leave* an event.
2. Subtract each activity's duration from the LET of its *terminal* event.
3. Select the *smallest* computed LET and record it in the lower right quadrant of the event circle.

For example, consider event 13. Three activities (13-14, 13-15, and 13-16) leave event 13. Event 14 has a latest event time of 15.5 d and activity 13-14 has a duration of 1 d, so event 13's first computed LET is 14.5 d. Event 15 has a latest event time of 15 and activity 13-15 has a duration of 0 d (it is a dummy activity), so the second candidate LET is 15 d. The computation for activity 13-16 yields 14 d. Because the smallest computed LET is 14 d, the latest event time for event 13 is 14 d.

Why pick the *smallest* LET? The idea is to allow enough time for the most lengthy activity or series of activities. If event 13 actually occurs at time 15.5, event 14 cannot possibly occur before day 16.5 because activity 13-14 takes 1 full day to complete. That would impact the schedule.

Next, consider event 12. Only one activity (12-13) leaves it. The LET for event 13 is 14 d and the duration of activity 12-13 is 1 d, so event 12's LET is 13 d.

21.4.6   The critical path

Note that the earliest and latest event times are the same for several events (Figure 21.1). Those events define the critical path, which is marked by a heavy black line. If the project is to be completed on time, the critical events must begin on time and the critical activities must require no more than their estimated duration.

21.4.7   Slack time

Activities not on the critical path can (to a point) start late or exceed their estimated duration without affecting the schedule. The extra time associated with an activity, called slack or float, is computed by subtracting from the latest event time of its *terminal* event both the activity's duration and the earliest event time of its *initial* event:

$$\text{Total slack} = (\text{LET})_t - (\text{EET})_i - \text{duration.} \qquad (21.1)$$

Slack time is enclosed in parentheses and recorded below the activity arrow (Figure 21.1). Note that critical path slack times are all 0.

For example, consider activity 6-10. The LET of its terminal event (10) is 11 d, the EET of its initial event (6) is 2 d, and its duration is 1 d. Plug those numbers into the equation and you get a slack time of 8 d.

Slack represents the maximum time the activity can slip without affecting the project schedule. If an activity begins late, of course, its available slack is reduced.

21.4.8   PERT and CPM

The project network is the foundation of both PERT and CPM.

PERT gained prominence during the late 1950s when it proved invaluable in scheduling and controlling the Polaris missile program. It is particularly useful in research and development projects where the times to complete the various activities are uncertain. The critical path is the primary focus of management control, and monitoring the critical events provides an early warning if estimates are inaccurate.

Industry developed CPM (Critical Path Method) to help solve scheduling problems when the activity times are known more precisely. Only by shortening the critical path can the project completion time be improved. Consequently, the critical path defines those activities into which additional resources might be poured to accelerate the schedule. An application of the critical path method to crash mode development is illustrated in Chapter 22.

21.5   Key terms

Activity — A task to be completed.

CPM (Critical Path Method) — A project management technique based on a project network; the focus of CPM is project planning, with the critical path defining those activities into which additional resources might be poured to accelerate the schedule.

Critical path — The path through a project network that links the critical events that must begin on time and the critical activities that must require no more than their estimated duration if the project is to be completed on time.

Diverge — To split a single input path into multiple paths.

Dummy activity — An activity that links parallel events, but consumes neither time nor resources.

Duration — The elapsed time required to complete an activity.

Earliest event time (EET) — The earliest time the event can possibly begin.

Event — The beginning or end of an activity.

Latest event time (LET) — The latest time an event can occur without impacting the project schedule.

Merge — To combine two or more input paths into a single output path.

PERT (Program Evaluation and Review Technique) — A project management technique based on a project network; with PERT, the critical path is the primary focus of management control and monitoring the critical events provides an early warning if estimates are inaccurate.

Project network — A bubble chart that graphically depicts activities, their starting and completion times, and their interrelationships.

Slack — The maximum time an activity can slip without affecting the project schedule.

21.6 Software

Such project management software products as Microsoft Project, Primavera Suretrack Project Manager, SuperProject from Computer Associates, Harvard Project Manager from Software Publishing Company, and Project Management Workbench from Applied Business Technology support project networks, PERT, CPM, and related techniques. Such charting or drawing tools as Visio and Flowcharter by Micrografx can be used to create a project network, although the project management tools are much more effective.

21.7 References

1. Badiru, A. B. and Whitehouse, *Computer Tools, Models and Techniques for Project Management,* TAB Books, Blue Ridge Summit, PA, 1989.
2. Davis, W. S., *Business Systems Analysis and Design,* Wadsworth, Belmont, CA, 1994.
2a. Humphrey, W. S., *Managing the Software Process,* Addison-Wesley, Reading, MA, 1989.
3. PERT Coord. Group, *PERT: Guide for Management Use,* U.S. Government Printing Office, publication number 0-6980452, Washington, D.C., 1963.
4. Roetzheim, W. H., *Structured Computer Project Management,* Prentice-Hall, Englewood Cliffs, NJ, 1988.
5. Weinberg, G. M. and Weinberg, D., *General Principles of Systems Design,* Dorset House, New York, 1988.

chapter twenty-two

Crash mode analysis

David C. Yen and William S. Davis

Contents

22.1 Purpose

A project network is a tool for graphically depicting a schedule. This chapter discusses the use of project networks and the critical path method to evaluate options for developing a system in crash mode.

22.2 Strengths, weaknesses, and limitations

CPM (Critical Path Method) is used to help plan and monitor a project schedule when the activity times are known with reasonable precision. Only by shortening the critical path can the project completion time be improved. Consequently, the critical path defines those activities into which additional resources might be poured to accelerate the schedule.

Creating a project network and performing crash mode analysis are complex undertakings. The computations are straightforward but non-trivial. Errors in computing earliest event times, latest event times, and slack times are not always apparent, so all computations should be checked carefully. Finally, the accuracy of the project network is no better than the activity duration estimates, and the accuracy of the cost computations is no better than the cost estimates.

22.3   Inputs and related ideas

This chapter assumes that the reader understands the concepts and techniques introduced in Chapters 20 (Gantt charts) and 21 (project networks). Before preparing a project network, the tasks or activities to be performed must be identified and each activity's duration (the time required to complete the activity) and cost must be estimated. Additionally, the precedence relationships between activities must be known. The necessary information is typically collected during the problem definition and information gathering stage of the system development life cycle (Part II).

22.4   Concepts

This chapter discusses the use of project networks and the critical path method to evaluate options for developing a system in crash mode. Often, it is possible to expedite a project by pouring additional resources (personnel, computing power, etc.) into one or more critical path activities, essentially trading cost for time. Crash mode analysis is a technique for studying the cost/time tradeoff by manipulating the project network (Chapter 21).

Table 22.1 lists the activities associated with a generic system development project. The initial project network is shown as Figure 22.1. The time to complete each activity is shown above the activity arrow. The earliest event time and latest event time for each event are noted to the right of the event circle. Note that there are two critical paths, 1-2-3-7-8 and 1-2-3-4-7-8.

Table 22.2 provides additional information about the completion times and costs for each of the activities. For example, the normal completion time for activity 1-2 is 2 weeks, but the crash mode time (the shortest possible

Table 22.1   The Activities Associated with
the Chapter Example

Activity	Description	Duration (Weeks)
1-2	Study the old system	2
2-3	Interview users	6
2-4	Determine user needs	4
2-5	Examine old system requirements	2
3-7	Analyze interview results	4
4-7	Define new system objectives	5
3-6	Resolve conflicts	3
7-8	Determine new systems specifications	2

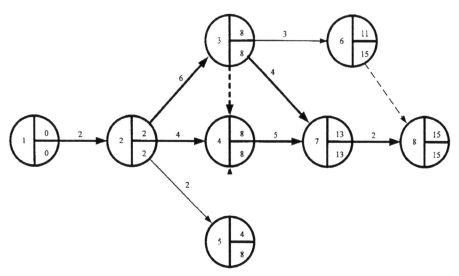

Figure 22.1 The initial project network for the chapter example.

time for completing the activity) is only 1 week. Saving that week is expensive, however. Normally, activity 1-2 is expected to cost $5000, but operating in crash mode will increase the cost by $3000 to $8000. Thus, the cost per week saved (the cost increase divided by the number of weeks saved) is $3000.

Read through Table 22.2. The time and cost columns are estimates. Cost per week is computed by dividing the extra cost for crash mode by the number of time periods (in this example, weeks) saved.

Given the data in Table 22.2, the project network can be modified (Figure 22.2) to show crash time (next to the normal time, in parentheses) and the cost per week (below the activity line) for each activity. The next step is to investigate the impact of performing one or more of the activities on the critical path in crash mode. Generally, those activities with a smaller

Table 22.2 Normal and Crash Mode Activity Times and Costs

| Activity | Time (weeks) | | | Cost ($) | | Cost | Cost |
	Normal	Crash	Saved	Normal	Crash	increase	week
1-2	2	1	1	5,000	8,000	3,000	3,000
2-3	6	4	2	14,000	20,000	6,000	3,000
2-4	4	3	1	8,000	10,000	2,000	2,000
2-5	2	1	1	4,000	6,000	2,000	2,000
3-7	4	3	1	5,000	10,000	5,000	5,000
4-7	5	3	2	9,000	15,000	6,000	3,000
3-6	3	2	1	4,000	6,000	2,000	2,000
7-8	2	1	1	3,000	4,000	1,000	1,000
Total				52,000	79,000		

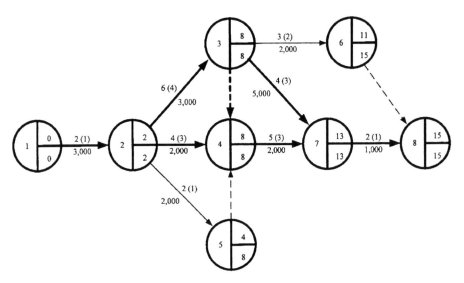

Figure 22.2   The project network with crash times and crash costs per week saved.

cost per week saved promise a greater return (time saved per dollar spent). Obviously, those activities with the greatest difference between normal and crash mode time have the greatest potential for shortening the schedule.

For example, suppose the system designer decides to crash those activities that promise to save the greatest amount of time (2-3 and 4-7). Figure 22.3 shows the new project network; note that activities 2-3 and 4-7 use the crash mode time estimates while the other activities use the normal time estimate. Changing some of the activity times changes the computed earliest and latest event times which, in turn, (potentially) changes the critical path. The new project network has a single critical path (1-2-3-7-12). The total elapsed time is 12 weeks, a saving of 3 weeks. From Table 22.2, the extra cost associated with activity 2-3 is $6,000, and the extra cost associated with 4-7 is $6,000, so the total project cost is $64,000, an increase of $12,000 over performing all activities in normal mode.

Additional alternatives can be considered. For example, Figure 22.4 shows the project network for performing only activity 2-3 in crash mode. Once again there are two critical paths. The total elapsed time is 13 weeks and the total system cost is $58,000, an increase of $6,000 over performing all activities in normal mode.

Table 22.3 summarizes the elapsed times and total system costs for several alternatives, including performing all activities on the critical path in crash mode. Clearly, the option of crashing 4-7 (14 weeks, $58,000) can be eliminated because crashing 2-3 (13 weeks, $58,000) saves an extra week for the same cost. Note that crashing activity 7-8 (14 weeks, $53,000) saves one

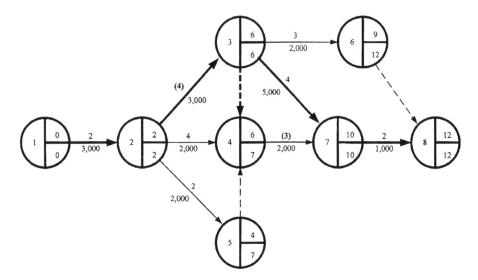

Figure 22.3 The project network with activities 2-3 and 4-7 performed in crash mode.

week at a cost of only $1,000, an outcome consistent with the cost per week saved computations in Table 22.2. Although the optimal solution is not obvious, the cost/time tradeoff is clearly defined, giving the responsible managers the information they need to make a decision.

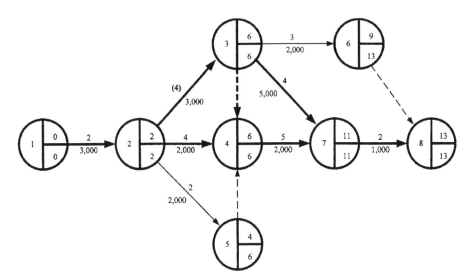

Figure 22.4 The project network with only activity 2-3 performed in crash mode.

Table 22.3 Several Alternatives

Crash	Total Time	Total Cost
None	15 weeks	$52,000
2-3, 4-7	12 weeks	$64,000
2-3	13 weeks	$58,000
4-7	14 weeks	$58,000
7-8	14 weeks	$53,000
All	10 weeks	$68,000

22.5 Key terms

Activity — A task to be completed.

CPM (Critical Path Method) — A project management technique based on a project network; the focus of CPM is project planning, with the critical path defining those activities into which additional resources might be poured to accelerate the schedule.

Crash mode — Pouring additional resources into an activity in order to complete the activity in the shortest possible time.

Crash mode analysis — An analysis technique that involves modifying a project network to study time and cost tradeoffs.

Critical path — The path through a project network that links the critical events that must begin on time and the critical activities that must require no more than their estimated duration if the project is to be completed on time.

Duration — The elapsed time required to complete an activity.

Earliest event time (EET) — The earliest time the event can possibly begin.

Event — The beginning or end of an activity.

Latest event time (LET) — The latest time an event can occur without impacting the project schedule.

Project network — A bubble chart that graphically depicts activities, their starting and completion times, and their interrelationships.

22.6 Software

Such project management software products as Microsoft Project, Primavera Suretrack Project Manager, SuperProject from Computer Associates, Harvard Project Manager from Software Publishing Company, and Project Management Workbench from Applied Business Technology support project networks, PERT, CPM, and related techniques. Such charting or drawing tools as Visio and Flowcharter by Micrografx can be used to create a project network, although the project management tools are much more effective.

22.7   References

1. Burch, J. G., *Systems Analysis, Design, and Implementation*, Boyd & Fraser, Boston, MA, 1992.
2. Dewitz, S. D., *Systems Analysis and Design and The Transition to Objects*, McGraw-Hill, New York, 1996.
3. Eppen, G. D., Gould, F. J., and Schmidt, C. P., *Introductory Management Science*, 4th ed., Prentice-Hall, Englewood Cliffs, NJ, 1993.
4. Gibson, M. L., and Hughes C. T., *Systems Analysis and Design: A Comprehensive Methodology with CASE*, Boyd & Fraser, Boston, MA, 1994.
5. Hoffer, J. A., George, J. F., and Valacich, J. S., *Modern Systems Analysis and Design*, Benjamin/Cummings, Redwood City, CA, 1996.
6. PERT Coordinating Group, *PERT: Guide for Management Use*, Publ. No. 0-6980452, U.S. Government Printing Office, Washington, D.C., 1963.
7. Power, M. J., Cheney, P. H., and Crow, G., *Structured Systems Development: Analysis, Design, Implementation*, 2nd ed., Boyd & Fraser, Boston, MA, 1990.

chapter twenty-three

Inspections and walkthroughs

William S. Davis

Contents

23.1 Purpose

An inspection is a formal review of a set of documentation conducted by technical personnel. The intent is to determine the technical accuracy of the documentation. When a set of documentation passes an inspection, it is reasonable to assume that the work is both technically acceptable and consistent with the system's objectives. An inspection often marks the completion of a stage or activity in a larger project. In some companies, an inspection is a prerequisite to a management review.

A walkthrough is an informal inspection. Although valuable at any stage in the system development life cycle, walkthroughs are particularly useful during the implementation stage as a means of checking the accuracy of the code.

23.2   Strengths, weaknesses, and limitations

Because an inspection is a *formal* review of the exit criteria conducted by *technical* personnel, it is an excellent quality control tool. Passing an inspection can be viewed as an event that marks completion of a life cycle phase or an activity.

The formal nature of the process puts pressure on both the creators and the inspectors. Meeting objectives "to the letter" does not necessary guarantee quality, particularly when requirements and/or technology change. An inspection is performed by human beings, and people sometimes find it difficult to maintain objectivity.

Excessive management involvement can blunt the effectiveness of the inspection process. A manager's comments tend to take on added significance simply because they come from a manager. Misusing the error reports generated during the inspection session is a particularly significant problem. People naturally fear that an error report will in some way be used against them and that error rates will eventually creep into personnel evaluations.

A walkthrough is, in effect, a "dry run" inspection without the formality. Consequently, walkthroughs provide many of the benefits with few of the problems. However, because they lack formality, walkthroughs cannot serve as dependable quality control mechanisms.

Inspections and walkthroughs are time consuming and, as is the case with any product, it is impossible to inspect quality into a set of documentation.

23.3   Inputs and related ideas

Inspections and walkthroughs can be conducted on the exit criteria from virtually any stage or any activity in the system development life cycle. Inspections are sometimes used as a part of the testing process (Chapter 74) and to support certain system controls (Chapter 77).

23.4   Concepts

An inspection is conducted by a team consisting of technical personnel and/or skilled-users. An inspection team normally consists of four individuals: the moderator, the author, and two inspectors.

23.4.1 The inspection team

The moderator runs the inspection, scheduling all meetings, distributing all necessary documentation, conducting all sessions, and making certain that the inspection is both thorough and fair. The ideal moderator enjoys the respect of his or her technical peers and is unbiased, with no direct involvement in the project. Without management's authority, the moderator must perform several management-like functions, so management's support is essential.

The author is usually the person (or the project leader) who prepared the documentation being inspected. The author's primary responsibility is to answer technical questions and to avoid defending the work.

The inspectors are technical professionals or skilled users who, while not directly involved in preparing the documentation, have a stake in the outcome; e.g., the individual responsible for the previous step or a member of the group that will perform a subsequent step. Normally, two inspectors are assigned, but the team can be larger or smaller.

23.4.2 The inspection process

As soon as the documentation for a given step is completed, the author contacts the moderator and asks that the inspection process begin. The steps in the inspection process are summarized in Figure 23.1.

23.4.2.1 Planning

The first task is to select an inspection team. In many organizations, the moderator selects the team; in others, management assumes this responsibility. Once the team has been named, the moderator distributes all relevant documentation and schedules the inspection meeting or meetings.

23.4.2.2 Overview

If a project is particularly extensive or involves a number of concepts or techniques that are not apparent to the inspectors, the author might be asked to present a brief technical overview of the project and the documentation. Note that the overview is optional.

The objective of the overview session is to save the moderator and the inspectors some time. The author's presentation should stick to the facts, stressing what and how, not why. Only later, after the other members of the team have had an opportunity to review and understand the documentation, should the reasons behind the technical decisions be considered.

23.4.2.3 Preparation

The preparation step calls for individual work on the part of each of the participants. The moderator and the inspectors read the documentation and note any questions or potential problems. In some organizations, contact

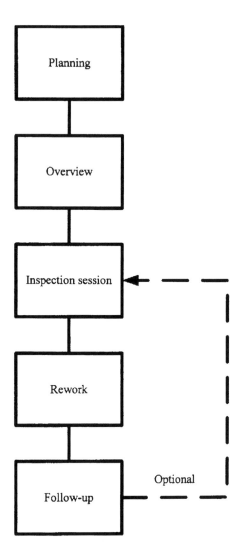

Figure 23.1 The steps in the inspection process.

between the inspectors and the author during the preparation step is officially prohibited, but such rules are difficult to enforce. At the very least the participants should be aware of the potential for bias, and should avoid non-essential contact with the author.

23.4.2.4 *The inspection session*

The moderator conducts the inspection session. One of the inspectors (not the author) serves as the reader and reads aloud or paraphrases the documentation. During the inspection session, the author's primary responsibility is to answer technical questions and to avoid defending his or her work.

The inspection session should be limited to perhaps 90 min, and all participants should be aware of the time limit. The objective is to find errors. All participants, including the moderator, the author, and the reader, are encouraged to identify errors. Note, however, that the inspection team should not suggest corrections. That is the author's job.

During the inspection session, the moderator maintains an error log, noting each error and estimating its severity (trivial, moderate, significant, severe, or fatal). Estimating the severity of errors is a common point of contention. The author may see an error as trivial, while an inspector may consider it severe. The result could well be a protracted argument. After a reasonable discussion, the moderator must break in, arbitrarily assign a severity level to the error, and move on. The important thing is that the error be detected; its classification is secondary.

Several problems can occur during the inspection session. Rather than inspecting the work, the author might act as a proponent or defender and attempt to discredit the errors identified by the other committee members. One or more inspectors might conduct a "witch hunt" rather than an inspection. An individual inspector might dominate the inspection by force of personality. It is the moderator's job to avoid or minimize the impact of these problems.

Inspecting incomplete or sloppy documentation is a waste of time, so if excessive errors are encountered the moderator has the authority to terminate and reschedule the inspection session. Finally, the moderator can, if necessary, schedule a reinspection after rework has been completed.

23.4.2.5   Rework
Following the inspection, the moderator and the author meet to discuss the results. The focus of this meeting is the error list compiled during the inspection session. Each error is discussed, and the rework time estimated.

The responsibility for actually doing the rework rests with the author. As each error is corrected, the author notes the actual rework time. Often, estimated and actual rework times are entered into an inspection database and combined with other historical data to help improve the estimation process.

23.4.2.6   Follow-up
When the rework is completed, the author and the moderator meet once again to review the results. If the moderator is satisfied with the rework, the inspection process ends. If not, the moderator may request additional rework and another follow-up session, or even schedule a reinspection. If a reinspection is necessary, the inspection team is reconvened, and the inspection session, rework, and follow-up steps are repeated. In some organizations, a reinspection is a formal part of the process, and the moderator is given the authority to cancel this step if appropriate.

23.4.3   The management review

Following the successful completion of an inspection, the moderator formally notifies management that the project has been technically reviewed and found acceptable by (depending on the organization) writing a memo, completing a standard form, or signing the error list (complete with rework notations). In the subsequent management review, technical aspects of the system can be assumed valid and management can concentrate on costs, benefits, and the schedule.

23.5   Key terms

Author — In an inspection, the person (or the team leader) who prepared the documentation or the code being inspected.

Inspection — A formal review of a set of exit criteria conducted by technical personnel.

Inspector — A technical professional or a skilled user who participates in an inspection.

Moderator — The individual who runs an inspection, scheduling all meetings, distributing all necessary documentation, conducting all sessions, and making certain that the inspection is both thorough and fair.

Walkthrough — An informal inspection.

23.6   Software

Not applicable.

23.7   References

1. Freedman, D. P. and Weinberg, G. M., *Handbook of Walkthroughs, Inspections, and Technical Reviews*, Little, Brown, Boston, 1982.
2. IBM Corporation, *Inspections in Application Development Introduction and Implementation Guidelines*, IBM Pub. No. GC20-2000, White Plains, NY, 1977.

part four

Systems analysis

chapter twenty-four

Data flow diagrams

William S. Davis

Contents

0-8493-7001-9/99/$0.00+$.50
©1999 by CRC Press LLC

24.1   Purpose

A data flow diagram is a logical model of the flow of data through a system that shows how the system's boundaries, processes, and data entities are logically related.

24.2   Strengths, weaknesses, and limitations

A data flow diagram is an excellent tool for summarizing and organizing detailed information about a system's boundaries, processes, and data entities, providing the analyst with a logical map of the system. Documenting the system's boundaries by drawing a context diagram helps the analyst, the user, and the responsible managers visualize alternative high-level logical system designs. The elements of a data flow diagram lead directly into physical design, with processes suggesting programs and procedures, data flows suggesting composites, and data stores suggesting data entities, files, and databases.

Creating a data flow diagram is a process driven task. Consequently, it is relatively easy to overlook key data elements and composites. Balancing a data flow diagram verifies the model's *internal* consistency, but does not necessarily reveal missing elements. Attempting to balance a significant logical model without appropriate software (such as CASE software) is at best difficult and can be misleading. Beginners and users often confuse data flow diagrams with process flowcharts.

24.3   Inputs and related ideas

The first step in creating a data flow diagram is to prepare a list of the system's boundaries, data, and processes using the tools covered in Part II. Data flow diagrams are a significant part of the structured analysis and design methodology (Chapter 3). A data flow diagram is sometimes created in conjunction with an entity-relationship diagram (Chapter 26) or data normalization (Chapter 28). Processes are documented using one or more of the process description tools in Part VI (Chapters 55 through 60). The data elements and data composites are documented in the data dictionary (Chapter 25). The data flow diagram is sometimes included in the requirements specification (Chapter 35). A completed data flow is required by the automation boundaries technique described in Chapter 36.

24.4   Concepts

A data flow diagram is a logical model that shows the flow of data through a system.

24.4.1   Data flow diagram symbols

Using Gane and Sarson's notation,[4] four primary symbols are used to create a data flow diagram (Figure 24.1). A source or destination (sink) is represented by a (shaded) square. Sources and destinations define the system's boundaries; each one represents a person, organization, or other system that supplies data to the system, gets data from the system, or both. A process, or transform, (a round-cornered rectangle) identifies an activity that changes, moves, or otherwise transforms data. A data store (an open-ended, horizontal rectangle) represents data at rest and implies that the data are held (for some logical reason) between processes. A data flow (an arrow)

Figure 24.1   These four symbols are used to construct a data flow diagram.

represents data in motion. Additionally, Gane and Sarson use thick arrows to show physical or material flows.

Using Yourdon[7] and DeMarco's[2] notation, sources and sinks are represented as rectangles, processes as circles, and data stores as horizontal rectangles open at both ends (two parallel horizontal lines). Data flows are shown as arrows. There is no symbol for a material flow.

24.4.2   Conventions

The following conventions are used.

24.4.2.1   Legal and illegal data flows

All data flows must begin and/or end with a process (Figure 24.2). Data cannot legally flow directly from a source to a destination or between a source/destination and a data store unless they pass through an intermediate process.

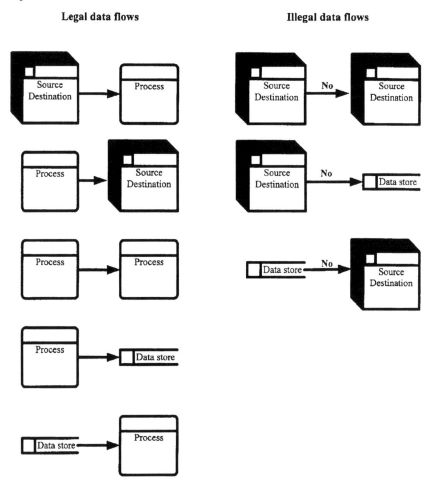

Figure 24.2   All data flows must begin and/or end with a process.

24.4.2.2   Data flow lines

Multiple data flows between two components can be shown by two data flow lines or by a two-headed arrow. Some analysts use two flow lines when the input and output data flows are different and a single two-headed arrow when they are the same. For example, a process that gets data from a store, updates the data, and then sends the same data elements back to the store calls for a two-headed arrow.

24.4.2.3   Naming

A process name consists of a verb followed by a noun. By convention, the names of the sources, destinations, and data stores are capitalized, while process names and data flows are shown mixed case.

24.4.2.4   Numbering

By convention, the processes in a level 1 data flow diagram are numbered 1, 2, 3, and so on. The numbers do not imply sequence; they are for reference only.

The sub-processes in an exploded data flow diagram are assigned numbers starting with the parent process's number. For example, level 1 process 4 might be exploded into level 2 processes 4.1, 4.2, 4.3, and so on, while level 2 process 4.3 might be decomposed into level 3 processes 4.3.1, 4.3.2, 4.3.3, and so on.

Many analysts use the letter D followed by a number to identify the data stores. For example, in an inventory system, INVENTORY might be D1, SALES might be D2, and so on. Some analysts identify the sources and destinations as well.

24.4.2.5   Duplicate symbols

Symbols can be repeated if doing so makes the diagram easier to read. For example, duplicating a symbol might be clearer than drawing lengthy or crossing data flows. Duplicate symbols are usually marked in some way; for example, source/destinations might be marked with a slash in the lower-left corner and data stores might be marked with an extra vertical line.

24.4.3   Underlying principles

Two general principles guide the creation of a data flow diagram: the principle of data conservation and the principle of iteration.

24.4.3.1   The principle of data conservation

There are no miracles, and there are no black holes. A given process can neither lose nor create data. Any data that flow into a process must be used by or output by that process. Any data output by a process must be input to or created by an algorithm within that process. Except for constants, any data used by an algorithm within a process must first flow into the process. Finally, any data created by an algorithm must either be used by another algorithm within the same process or output by the process.

24.4.3.2   *The principle of iteration*

High-level processes are decomposed into lower-level processes. At the lowest level are primitive processes that perform a single function (or algorithm). Note that a lower-level process gets its data from its higher-level parent.

24.4.4   *The context (level 0) diagram*

A context (level 0) diagram documents the system's boundaries by highlighting its sources and destinations. Documenting the system's boundaries by drawing a context diagram helps the analyst, the user, and the responsible managers visualize alternative high-level logical system designs.

For example, Figure 24.3 shows a context diagram for a typical inventory system. The system itself is shown as a single process. It provides data to the FINANCIAL SYSTEM. It both provides data to and gets data from MANAGER, SUPPLIER, and CUSTOMER. Note that the data flows are labeled with (at this level) composite names.

Moving the boundaries significantly changes the system, and the ability to visualize the implications of different boundary assumptions is a pow-

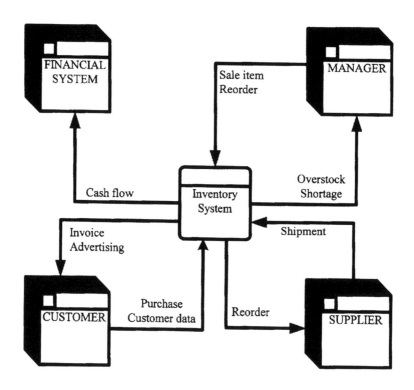

Figure 24.3   A context diagram.

erful reason for creating a context diagram. For example, in Figure 24.3 the financial system and the inventory system are independent. An alternative logical design might move the financial system inside the inventory system (or vice versa), effectively integrating them. The result would be a somewhat more complex (but perhaps more efficient) system.

24.4.5   The level 1 data flow diagram

A level 1 data flow diagram shows the system's *primary* processes, data stores, sources, and destinations linked by data flows. Generally, a system's primary processes are independent, and thus, separated from each other by intermediate data stores that suggest the data are held in some way between processes.

For example, Figure 24.4 shows a level 1 data flow diagram for an inventory system. Start at the upper left with source/destination FINAN-CIAL SYSTEM. Data flow to FINANCIAL SYSTEM from process 9, *Report cash flow.* Data enter process 9 from data store D1, SALES. Data enter D1 from process 2, *Sell appliance.* Process 2 gets its data from CUSTOMER and from data stores D1, D3, D5, and D6, and so on. Note how intermediate data stores serve to insulate the primary processes from each other and thus promote process independence.

A level 1 process is a composite item that might incorporate related programs, routines, manual procedures, hardware-based procedures, and other activities. For example, process 2, *Sell appliance* might imply (in one alternative) a set of sales associate's guidelines, while another alternative might include a point-of-sale terminal equipped with a bar code scanner and necessary support software. In effect, the level 1 process *Sell appliance* represents all the hardware, software, and procedures associated with selling an appliance. As the data flow diagram is decomposed, the various sub-processes are eventually isolated and defined.

24.4.6   Documenting the model

The data flow diagram shows the data flows between the system's sources, destinations, processes, and data stores.

24.4.6.1   The data dictionary

The data elements are recorded in the data dictionary (Chapter 25). As work progresses, the data elements that occupy the same data store or share a data flow form composite items or data structures that are also documented in the data dictionary. For example, *Supplier name, Supplier address, Description, Reorder quantity* and other data elements flow to SUPPLIER from process 4 and form a data structure that might be called *Reorder.*

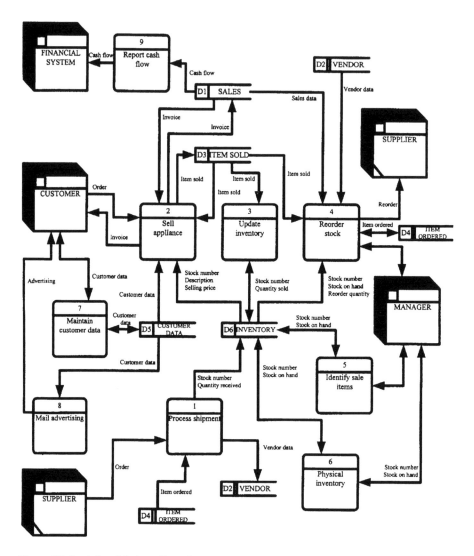

Figure 24.4   A level 1 data flow diagram.

24.4.6.2   *Process descriptions*

Each process is defined in a process description that notes its input and output data elements and composites and briefly describes the tasks or activities it performs. (Process description tools are described in Part VI.) Process (or data transform) descriptions are sometimes recorded in the data dictionary.

24.4.6.3   *The CASE repository*

In most CASE products (Chapter 5), the data descriptions and process descriptions are stored in the CASE repository.

24.4.7 Verifying the model

The point of verification is to ensure that the model is complete and internally consistent.

24.4.7.1 Syntax checking

Every data flow must begin and/or end with a process and have at least one arrowhead to define the direction of data movement. Every process and every data store must have at least one input data flow and at least one output data flow. If the inflow is missing, the source of the data is unknown. If the outflow is missing, that process or store acts like a black hole. In either case, something is wrong.

Other syntax checks involve judgement. Process names should imply their function. Component names should be unique because redundant names are confusing.

24.4.7.2 Tracing data elements

Following the principle of data conservation, each data element in a level 1 data flow diagram must be rigorously traced from its destination, through the model, back to its source. If the source of *every* data element is accounted for, the data flow diagram is internally consistent.

24.4.7.3 Cross referencing

On the data flow diagram, each data element, data store, and data flow must appear in the data dictionary, and each process must have a matching process description.

In the data dictionary, each logical data structure must match a data flow or a data store, and each data element must appear at least once on the data flow diagram. Additionally, each data element and each logical data structure must appear in the input or output list of at least one process description. There are two possible explanations for unused data elements: Either they are not needed by the system, or the analyst overlooked them.

Each process description must match a process on the data flow diagram, and the input and output lists must match the data flows. Every data element entering or leaving a process must appear in the data dictionary. Unused processes may have been overlooked when the data flow diagram was created. If not, they are unnecessary.

24.4.7.4 Tracing objectives

Note that if a significant feature of the system was overlooked, verification will not necessarily find the error. Consequently, the logical model should always be checked against the system objectives and the process or processes that contribute to meeting each one identified. If an objective cannot be matched with at least one process, that objective may have been overlooked. If a process cannot be matched with at least one objective, that process might be unnecessary.

24.4.8   Exploding the processes

A level 1 data flow diagram is a high-level logical map of the system. It shows the key relationships but hides most of the details. Consequently, the next step is to explode the processes by taking advantage of the principle of iteration. The act of exploding a data flow diagram is sometimes called functional decomposition.

24.4.8.1   Level 2

Each level 1 process consists of several sub-processes that are listed on the process description. To explode the data flow diagram, the analyst creates an independent level 2 data flow diagram for each level 1 process.

For example, Figure 24.5 shows a level 2 data flow diagram for process 4, *Reorder stock* (Figure 24.4). Note the numbering scheme. Processes 4.1, 4.2, 4.3, 4.4, and 4.5 are sub-processes of level 1 process 4.

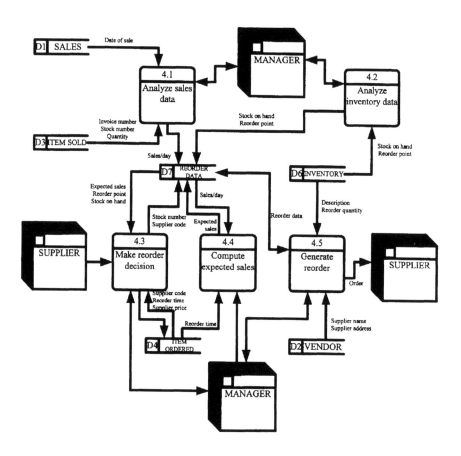

Figure 24.5   A level 2 data flow diagram for process 4.

24.4.8.2 Local and global data

Global data are shared by two or more higher level processes. Local data are known only within one part of the system; intermediate computations are a good example. For example, in Figure 24.5, the data elements in data store D7, REORDER DATA are known only within the level 2 explosion of process 4 (and its sub-processes).

Mistakes made while working with local data tend to be limited in scope, but global data errors can ripple throughout the system. Local data elements should be recorded in the data dictionary and identified as local. If they already exist, they might not be local; perhaps a global data element was overlooked.

24.4.8.3 Balancing the level 2 explosion

An exploded data flow diagram must be balanced by accounting for each input from the parent level and each output to the parent level. Checking to ensure that an explosion is balanced is similar to tracing data elements from their destination (output) back to their source (input). The only difference is that the higher-level process's outputs are traced back to the higher-level process's inputs through the exploded data flow diagram.

Every global data element (or composite) input to the lower level must be used by at least one lower-level sub-process. Every global data element (or composite) output to the higher level must either be input to the lower level or generated by an algorithm within a lower-level sub-process. Each data element or composite input to or used by an exploded process must be defined in the higher-level process.

Note that a higher-level composite might be decomposed into data elements or sub-composites at the lower level. Local data (by definition) are neither input to nor output from the explosion.

24.4.9 Functional primitives

A functional primitive is a process (or transform) that requires no further decomposition. The process description for a functional primitive is sometimes called a mini-spec. The system's discrete physical components lie one step below a functional primitive.

24.4.10 The configuration item level

The functional primitives and the data stores that appear at the lowest level of decomposition are called configuration items. A configuration item is a composite rather than a specific physical component; for example, a composite item might represent a program and the computer on which it runs, or a database and the device on which it resides. In a complete logical model, all the processes are decomposed down to the configuration item level, an imaginary line that links the system's configuration items.

24.4.11   The complete logical model

A logical model consists of a complete set of balanced data flow diagrams, a data dictionary, and one process description for each process at each level down to the configuration item level. Note that some processes will be exploded only to level 2, others to level 3, and so on, so the configuration item level does not necessarily correspond to a single, consistent data flow diagram level.

The documentation package for a large system can be quite lengthy. Processes above the configuration item level are purely logical; their process descriptions consist of little more than lists of sub-processes. Those sub-processes can be obtained from the exploded data flow diagram, so some organizations exclude them from the finished model process descriptions above the configuration item level.

The configuration item level processes will decompose into the system's programs and procedures. The data stores will map into files and databases. The data flows will become reports, screens, forms, and dialogues. Above the configuration item level, the logical relationships between the components support planning, coordination, and control.

24.4.12   Logical and physical data flow diagrams

A logical data flow diagram's symbols are used to describe *logical* not physical entities. A process might eventually be implemented as a computer program, a subroutine, or a manual procedure. A data store might represent a database, a file, a book, a folder in a filing cabinet, or even notes on a sheet of paper. Data flows show how the data move between the system's components, but they do *not* show the flow of control. The idea is to create a logical model that focuses on *what* the system does while disregarding the physical details of how it works.

A physical data flow diagram uses data flow diagram symbols to represent the system's physical processes (programs, manual procedures) and physical data stores (files, databases, reports, screens, etc.) and shows how the system works. Some analysts like to start the analysis process by preparing a physical data flow diagram of the present system. Following the analysis stage, physical data flow diagrams can be used to document alternative solutions.

24.5   Key terms

Balance — A characteristic of an exploded data flow diagram in which each input from and output to the parent level is accounted for.

Composite — A set of related data elements; a data structure.

Configuration item — A functional primitive that appears at the lowest level of decomposition.

Configuration item level — An imaginary line that links the system's configuration items.

Context diagram (level 0 data flow diagram) — A data flow diagram that documents the system's boundaries by highlighting its sources and destinations.

Data flow — Data in motion.

Data flow diagram — A logical model of the flow of data through a system.

Data store — Data at rest; implies that the data are held between processes.

Data structure — A set of related data elements; a composite.

Destination (sink) — A person, organization, or other system that gets data from the target system; a destination defines a system boundary.

Explode — To decompose a process in a data flow diagram to a lower level.

Functional decomposition — The act of exploding a data flow diagram.

Functional primitive — A process (or transform) that requires no further decomposition.

Global data — Data elements or composites that are shared by two or more processes.

Level 1 data flow diagram — A data flow diagram that shows the system's primary processes, data stores, sources, and destinations linked by data flows.

Level 2 data flow diagram — An explosion of a level 1 process.

Local data — Data elements or composites that are known only within one part of the system.

Logical data flow diagram — A data flow diagram that does not suggest physical references but shows the system's components as logical entities.

Mini-spec — The process description for a functional primitive.

Physical data flow diagram — A data flow diagram that identifies the system's physical processes and physical data stores.

Process (transform) — An activity that changes, moves, or otherwise transforms data.

Source — A person, organization, or other system that supplies data to the target system; a source defines a system boundary.

24.6   Software

Many CASE products support creating, modifying, maintaining, and balancing data flow diagrams. Charting programs, such as Visio and Micrografx's Flowcharter can be used to create data flow diagrams. The data flow diagrams in this chapter were created using Visio.

24.7 References

1. Davis, W. S., *Business Systems Analysis and Design,* Wadsworth, Belmont, CA, 1994.
2. DeMarco, T., *Structured Analysis and System Specification,* Yourdon, New York, 1978.
3. Gane, C., *Rapid System Development,* Rapid System Development, New York, 1987.
4. Gane, C. and Sarson, T., *Structured Systems Analysis: Tools and Techniques,* Prentice-Hall, Englewood Cliffs, NJ, 1979.
5. Martin, J. and McClure, C., *Diagramming Techniques for Analysts and Programmers,* Prentice-Hall, Englewood Cliffs, NJ, 1985.
6. Thayer, R. H. and Dorfman, M., *System and Software Requirements Engineering,* IEEE Computer Society Press, Los Alamitos, CA, 1990.
7. Yourdon, E. and Constantine, L. L., *Structured Design,* Prentice-Hall, Englewood Cliffs, NJ, 1979.

chapter twenty-five

The data dictionary

William S. Davis

Contents

25.1   Purpose

A data dictionary is a collection of data about the data. Its purpose is to rigorously define each and every data element, data structure, and data transform.

25.2   Strengths, weaknesses, and limitations

A data dictionary helps to improve communication between analysts and users and between technical personnel by establishing a set of consistent data definitions. If programmers develop data descriptions from a common data dictionary, several potentially serious module interface problems can be avoided. At a higher level, different systems must often be linked or interfaced, and a common set of data definitions helps to minimize misunderstandings.

By highlighting already existing data elements, a data dictionary helps the analyst avoid data redundancy. If all programs using a given data element are cross-referenced in the data dictionary, assessing the ripple effects of a change in the data is simplified.

25.3   Inputs and related ideas

The first step in creating a data dictionary is to identify the system's data elements and composites, a key objective of the information gathering phase of the system development life cycle (Part II). The data dictionary is an important adjunct to several analysis tools, such as data flow diagrams (Chapter 24), entity-relationship diagrams (Chapter 26), and data normalization (Chapter 28). Creating a data dictionary is an important step in designing and developing traditional files (Chapter 44) or a database (Chapter 45). The data dictionary often serves as a foundation for the requirements specification (Chapter 35). Data structures are described in Chapter 43. Inverted-L charts (Chapter 27) and Warnier-Orr diagrams (Chapter 33) are useful for visualizing a data structure.

25.4   Concepts

A data dictionary is a collection of data about the data in which each and every data element, data structure, and data transform is rigorously defined.

25.4.1   Data elements

The data dictionary defines each data element, assigns it a meaningful name, specifies both its logical and physical characteristics, and records information concerning how it is used. Table 25.1 summarizes the type of information that might be recorded in the data dictionary. Figure 25.1 shows a few partial (generic) data dictionary entries.

25.4.1.1   Data names
It is important to follow a consistent standard when assigning data names. For example, an organization might use the rules imposed by its primary programming language, database management system, data dictionary software, or CASE product.

Some data elements are known by two or more names. This often happens when different groups use the same data for different purposes or when several analysts work concurrently on the system. Rather than creating redundant data dictionary entries, resolve any differences in the definitions of the equivalent data elements, merge them, and record the alias name on the primary description.

Table 25.1 Information That Might Be Recorded for Each Data Element in a Data Dictionary*

General	Usage characteristics
Data element name	Range of values
Aliases or synonyms	Frequency of use
Definition	Input/output/local
	Conditional values
Format	Limits
Data type	
Length	**Relationships**
Picture	Parent structures
Units (meters, pounds, etc.)	Child structures
Composite description	File or database
	Key
Control Information	Data flows
Source	Processes
Change authorizations	Reports
Access authorizations	Forms
Security information	Screens
Authorized users	
Date of origin	

Note that not every entry is relevant to every data element.

If two clearly different data elements have similar names, change at least one of them because similar names can be confusing.

25.4.1.2 Definitions

A good definition precisely indicates the data element's purpose and clearly distinguishes it from the system's other data elements. Examples are useful, particularly for identifying exceptions to a general rule.

25.4.2 Data structures or composites

Data structures (Chapter 43), also called group or composite data items, are defined by showing the data elements and substructures that comprise them. The symbols depicted in Table 25.2 (or their equivalents) are sometimes used to document (or partition) composite items. Figure 25.2 shows how the data on a sales receipt might be defined using the symbols. Inverted-L charts (Chapter 27) and Warnier-Orr diagrams (Chapter 33) are other tools for visualizing a data structure.

Note that a data structure can contain both composite items and data elements. In the data dictionary, composite items are decomposed or partitioned down to the data element level, and each data element is fully defined (as described earlier).

25.4.3 Keys and relationships

In a database, an entity is a thing about which data are stored and an occurrence is a single instance of an entity composed of data elements (or attributes).

Stock number

Alias:	UPC, Product ID, Product code
Definition:	A key field that uniquely identifies an item of merchandise.
Type:	Character. Picture X(10)
Relationships:	

Product description

Alias:	Description
Definition:	A brief verbal description of a product. For example, "Zenith 21-inch color TV" or "GE 19-cubic-foot refrigerator."
Type:	Character. Picture X(40)

Unit price

Alias:	Retail price, Customer price, Selling price, Your price
Definition:	The amount of money a customer pays for a single unit of merchandise.
Type:	Numeric. Picture 9,999.99
Relationships:	

Figure 25.1   Some typical data dictionary entries.

Table 25.2   These Symbols Can Be Used to
Document a Data Structure

Symbol	Meaning
=	Contains, or is composed of
+	And
[ ]	Selection
		Separator
( )	Optional
{ }	Repetition

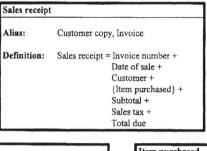

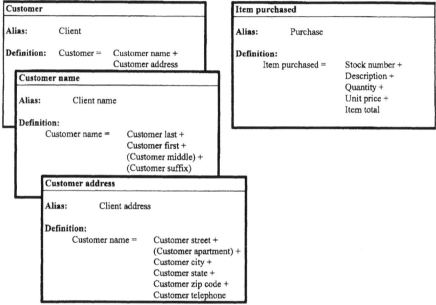

Figure 25.2   Documenting a data structure.

Physically, entities map to files, occurrences map to records, and attributes map to fields.

Occurrences (records) are composite data structures. In addition to the attributes that make up the composite, the key (the attribute or group of attributes that uniquely distinguishes one occurrence of the entity) is documented in the data dictionary.

A database is composed of a set of related files (or entities). Typically, the files are linked (or related) by storing an entity's key in the related entity. These relationships are also documented in the data dictionary.

25.4.4   Transforms

A transform is a process or operation that modifies data. Many data dictionary systems allow the analyst to name, define, and record data about the transforms in the data dictionary.

25.5   Key terms

Alias — An alternate name for a data element.
Attribute — A property of an entity.
Composite — A set of related data elements.
Data dictionary — A collection of data about the data.
Data element — An attribute that cannot be logically decomposed.
Data structure — A set of related data elements.
Database — A set of related files.
Entity — An object (a person, group, place, thing, or activity) about which data are stored.
Field — A data element physically stored on some medium.
File — A set of related records.
Foreign key — A key to some other entity stored with the target entity.
Key — The attribute or group of attributes that uniquely distinguishes one occurrence of an entity.
Meta-data — The contents of the data dictionary.
Occurrence — A single instance of an entity.
Record — The set of fields associated with an occurrence of an entity.
Relationship — A link between two data structures.
Transform — A process or operation that modifies data.

25.6   Software

Numerous data dictionary software packages are commercially available. Some are associated with a specific database management system; others are more general. Most provide data entry support. Some can prepare at least part of the entry from programmer source code or generate source code directly from the data dictionary. Data usage reports and queries are common features. Additionally, CASE software (Chapter 5) often incorporates a data dictionary within the CASE repository.

25.7   References

1. Atre, S., *Data Base: Structured Techniques for Design, Performance, and Management*, John Wiley & Sons, New York, 1980.
2. Davis, W. S., *Business Systems Analysis and Design*, Wadsworth, Belmont, CA, 1994.
3. Kroenke, *Database Processing*, SRA, Chicago, 1977.
4. Lomax, J. D., *Data Dictionary Systems*, NCC Publications, Rochelle Park, NJ, 1977.

chapter twenty-six

Entity-relationship diagrams

William S. Davis and David C. Yen

Contents

26.1 Purpose

Entity-relationship diagrams were first proposed as a means of quickly obtaining, with minimum effort, a good sense of the structure of a database. They are used to plan and design a database and to model a system's data.

0-8493-7001-9/99/$0.00+$.50
©1999 by CRC Press LLC

26.2   Strengths, weaknesses, and limitations

An entity-relationship diagram is an excellent tool for planning and designing a database, particularly when used in conjunction with data normalization. The entity-relationship model starts with the entities, data normalization starts with the attributes, and the two tools tend to verify each other. The entity-relationship model's entities, attributes, and relationships map smoothly to a physical database.

During the systems analysis phase, an entity-relationship diagram gives the analyst a clear, high-level view of the data. Used in conjunction with data flow diagrams, an entity-relationship model gives the analyst an alternative logical view of the system. If a great deal is known about the data but not much about the processes, an entity-relationship diagram is an excellent starting point for modeling the system.

An entity-relationship model is data driven. The model implies processes but does not clarify the processes. Non-technical people find entity-relationship models difficult to understand and the nature of a relationship (one, many) confusing, and numerous notational variations sometimes make it difficult for even an experienced person to quickly grasp a particular diagram.

26.3   Inputs and related ideas

Before creating an entity-relationship diagram, the analyst must have at least a preliminary sense of the system's logical entities, attributes, and data structures. The necessary information is obtained during the information gathering and problem definition stage (Part II). Data structures are discussed in Chapter 43. Other key data concepts are found in Chapters 25, 44, and 45. Entity-relationship diagrams are important tools in the structured requirements methodology (Chapter 4) and in database design (Chapter 45). They are often used in conjunction with data flow diagrams (Chapter 24) and data normalization (Chapter 28).

26.4   Concepts

Entity-relationship diagrams are used to plan and design a database and to model a system's data.

26.4.1   Entities and relationships

An entity is an object (a person, group, place, thing, or activity) about which data are stored. A relationship links two entities and is shown by drawing a line between them (Figure 26.1).

Logically, a relationship can be stated in the form of a sentence with a verb linking the two entities, for example,

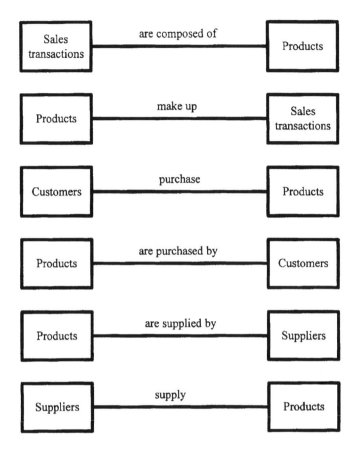

Figure 26.1 A relationship between two entities is shown by drawing a line between them.

Sales transactions are composed of products.

or

Products make up sales transactions.

The act of creating such sentences is a good test of the relationship's validity. In cases where the relationship is unclear, the sentence might be written alongside the relationship line as shown in Figure 26.1. A given relationship can be mandatory (shown by a solid line) or optional (a broken line).

26.4.2 Cardinality

For a variety of reasons, some relationships are more stable and easier to maintain than others. (A detailed discussion of the underlying database theory is beyond the scope of this book.) Cardinality, a measure of the related entities' relative number of occurrences, is an important predictor of the strength of the relationship.

26.4.2.1   One-to-one relationships

In a one-to-one relationship, each occurrence of entity A is associated with one and only one occurrence of entity B, and each occurrence of entity B is associated with one and only one occurrence of entity A.

For example, imagine that an instructor maintains examination grades for each student in his or her class. There are two entities in this example: *Students* and *Exams*. For each *Student* there is one and only one *Exam*, and for each *Exam* there is one and only one *Student*.

Graphically, a one-to-one relationship is described by drawing short crossing lines at both ends of the line that links the two entities (Figure 26.2). However, some practitioners simply show the relationship line with no embellishment, and other symbols are used as well.

26.4.2.2   One-to-many relationships

In a one-to-many relationship, each occurrence of entity A is associated with one or more occurrences of entity B, but each occurrence of entity B is associated with only one occurrence of entity A.

For example, a student's grade in most courses is based on numerous grade factors (such as exams, papers, and projects). A given *Student* has several different *Grade factors*, but a given *Grade factor* is associated with one and only one *Student*.

Graphically, a one-to-many relationship is shown by drawing a short crossing line (or no extra marking) at the "one-end" and a small triangle (sometimes called a crow's foot) at the "many-end" of the relationship line (Figure 26.3). Some practitioners use other symbols, however.

26.4.2.3   Many-to-many relationships

In a many-to-many relationship, each occurrence of entity A is associated with one or more occurrences of entity B, and each occurrence of entity B is

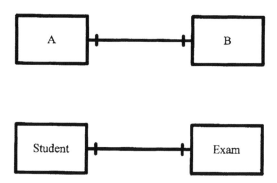

Figure 26.2   In a one-to-one relationship, each occurrence of entity A is associated with one and only one occurrence of entity B, and each occurrence of entity B is associated with one and only one occurrence of entity A.

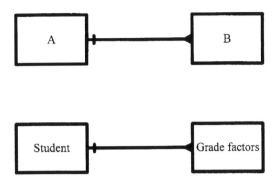

Figure 26.3 In a one-to-many relationship, each occurrence of entity A is associated with one or more occurrences of entity B, but each occurrence of entity B is associated with only one occurrence of entity A.

associated with one or more occurrences of entity A. For example, a student's end-of-term *Grade report* can list several *Courses*, and a given *Course* can appear on many students' *Grade reports*.

Graphically, a many-to-many relationship is shown by drawing a crow's foot at both ends of the relationship line (Figure 26.4). Some practitioners use other symbols, however.

26.4.2.4   *Other relationships*

Although this chapter will focus on one-to-one, one-to-many, and many-to-many relationships, other types of relationships are possible. Sometimes entities are mutually exclusive, with A linked to either B or C, but not both. In a mutually *inclusive* relationship, if A is linked to B it must also be linked to C. Zero cardinality implies that an occurrence of A means *no* occurrence of B. Crosslinks and loops can exist, too. A recursive relationship is shown by drawing a semicircle from the entity back to itself.

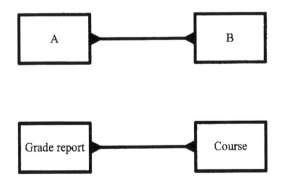

Figure 26.4 In a many-to-many relationship, each occurrence of entity A is associated with one or more occurrences of entity B, and each occurrence of entity B is associated with one or more occurrences of entity A.

26.4.3 Analyzing relationships

For a variety of reasons, one-to-many relationships tend to be the most stable. Consequently, a primary objective of entity-relationship modeling is to convert one-to-one and many-to-many relationships into one-to-many relationships.

26.4.3.1 Resolving one-to-one relationships

One-to-one relationships can often be merged. Generally, entities that share a one-to-one relationship are really the same entity and should be merged unless there is a good reason to keep them separate.

Note that not all one-to-one relationships can be merged, however. For example, imagine a relationship between athletes and drug tests. There is one *Drug test* per *Athlete* and one *Athlete* per *Drug test*, so the relationship is clearly one-to-one. In this case, however, because merging the entities would probably violate security requirements (and possibly the law), there is a good logical reason to maintain separate entities.

26.4.3.2 Resolving many-to-many relationships

Many-to-many relationships can cause maintenance problems. For example, Figure 26.5 shows a many-to-many relationship between *Inventory* and *Supplier*. Each product in *Inventory* can have more than one *Supplier,* and each *Supplier* can carry more than one product. If a list of suppliers were stored in *Inventory,* adding or deleting a supplier might mean updating several *Inventory* occurrences. Likewise, listing products in *Supplier* could mean changing several *Supplier* occurrences if a single product were added or deleted.

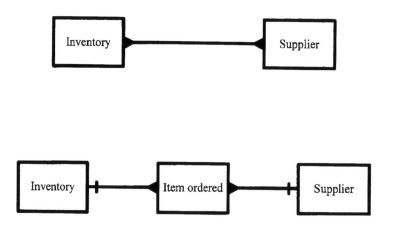

Figure 26.5 A many-to-many relationship can often be converted to two one-to-many relationships.

One solution is to create a new entity that has a one-to-many relationship with both original entities. For example, imagine a new entity called *Item ordered* (Figure 26.5). Given such a design, a given product in *Inventory* can appear on several active *Items ordered*, but each *Item ordered* is for one and only one product. Likewise, a given supplier can appear on several active *Items ordered*, but each *Item ordered* lists one and only supplier. Note that a given *Item ordered* links a specific product in *Inventory* with a specific occurrence of *Supplier*. The many-to-many relationship has been converted to two one-to-many relationships.

26.4.4 Creating an entity-relationship diagram

Assume a preliminary analysis of a retail sales application suggests four primary entities: *customer, sales, inventory,* and *supplier.*

The *Sales, Customer,* and *Inventory* entities are related as follows:

Customer initiates Sales.
Sales are drawn from Inventory.

The first relationship is one-to-many (Figure 26.6); a given *Customer* can have many *Sales* transactions, but a given *Sale* is associated with one and only one *Customer.* However, the second relationship is many-to-many because a given *Sale* can include several products from *Inventory* and a given product in *Inventory* can appear in many *Sales.*

To resolve the many-to-many relationship, create a new entity, *Item sold,* that has a one-to-many relationship with both *Sales* and *Inventory* (Figure 26.7). A given *Sales* transaction can list many *Items sold,* but a given *Item sold* is associated with one and only one *Sales* transaction. A given product in *Inventory* can appear in many *Items sold,* but a given *Item sold* lists one and only one product. (Think of an *Item sold* as one line in a list of products purchased on a sales invoice.)

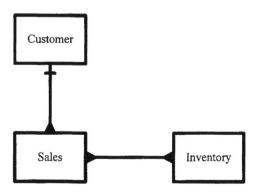

Figure 26.6 *Customer* has a one-to-many relationship with *sales*. The relationship between *sales* and *inventory* is many-to-many.

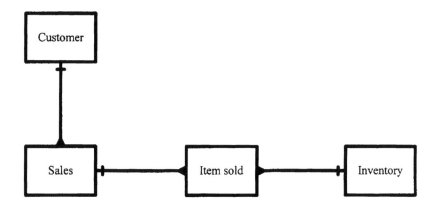

Figure 26.7   Resolving the many-to-many relationship calls for a new entity.

There is one possible source of confusion about the *Inventory* entity that might need clarification. A specific 19-inch color television set is an example of a single occurrence of that entity, but *Inventory* might hold numerous virtually identical television sets. For inventory control purposes, tracking television sets (a *class* of occurrences) is probably good enough. However, the *Customer* purchases a *specific* television set (identified, perhaps, by concatenating the serial number to the stock number). Thus a given *Item sold* lists one and only one occurrence of *Inventory*.

The relationship between *Inventory* and *Supplier* (Figure 26.8) is many-to-many because a given product can have many suppliers and a given supplier can supply many different products. Many-to-many relationships must be resolved, so add a new entity called *Item ordered* to the model, yielding two one-to-many relationships.

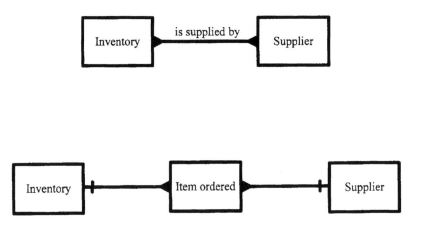

Figure 26.8   The many-to-many relationship between *supplier* and *inventory* can be resolved by creating a new entity called *item ordered*.

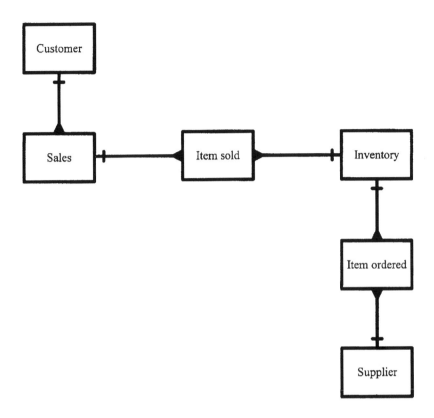

Figure 26.9 The finished entity-relationship model.

Finally, the *Inventory* entity is related to both *Item sold* and *Item ordered*, so combine the two partial diagrams to form a single entity-relationship model (Figure 26.9).

26.4.5 Documenting composites and attributes

After the entities have been identified, each one is recorded in the data dictionary (Chapter 25) as a data composite and the attributes (or data elements) it contains are defined. Many analysts prepare inverted-L charts (Chapter 27) to graphically represent the entities' contents.

26.5 Key terms

Attribute — A property of an entity.
Cardinality — A measure of the relative number of occurrences of two entities.
Composite — A set of related data elements.

Data element — An attribute that cannot be logically decomposed.

Data structure — A set of related data elements; a composite.

Entity — An object (a person, group, place, thing, or activity) about which data are stored.

Entity-relationship diagram — A diagram that shows how a system's primary data entities are related.

Many-to-many relationship — A relationship in which each occurrence of entity A is associated with one or more occurrences of entity B, and each occurrence of entity B is associated with one or more occurrences of entity A.

Occurrence — A single instance of an entity.

One-to-many relationship — A relationship in which each occurrence of entity A is associated with one or more occurrences of entity B, but each occurrence of entity B is associated with only one occurrence of entity A.

One-to-one relationship — A relationship in which each occurrence of entity A is associated with one occurrence of entity B and each occurrence of entity B is associated with one occurrence of entity A.

Relationship — A link between two data structures.

26.6 Software

The entity-relationship diagrams in this chapter were prepared using Visio. Other graphing tools, such as Micrografx's Flowcharter provide comparable support. Additionally, many CASE products support entity-relationship models.

26.7 References

1. Barker, R., *Case Method: Entity Relationship Modelling,* Addison-Wesley, Reading, MA, 1990.
2. Chen, P., The entity-relationship model—towards a unified view of data, *ACM Trans. Data. Syst.,* 1(1), 9, 1976.
3. Date, C. J., *An Introduction to Database Systems,* vol. 1, 6th ed., Addison-Wesley, Reading, MA, 1994.
4. Davis, W. S., *Business Systems Analysis and Design,* Wadsworth, Belmont, CA, 1994.
5. Dutka, A. F. and Hanson, *Fundamentals of Data Normalization,* Addison-Wesley, Reading, MA, 1989.
6. Martin, J. and McClure, C., *Structured Techniques: The Basis for CASE,* Prentice-Hall, Englewood Cliffs, NJ, 1988.
7. McDermid, D. C., *Software Engineering for Information Systems,* Blackwell Scientific Publications, Oxford, U.K., 1990.

chapter twenty-seven

Inverted-L charts

William S. Davis and David C. Yen

Contents

27.1   Purpose

An inverted-L chart is a tool for graphically representing a data structure. Inverted-L charts are often used with entity-relationship diagrams to document the attributes that make up an entity. The completed inverted-L charts represent a preliminary set of logical data structures.

27.2   Strengths, weaknesses, and limitations

An inverted-L chart is a clear, easy-to-visualize, graphical model of a data structure. The inverted-L model lacks many of the necessary details that must be recorded in the data dictionary, however.

27.3   Inputs and related ideas

Before an inverted-L chart can be constructed, the data elements (or attributes) that make up the data structure or entity must be known (Part II). If an

0-8493-7001-9/99/$0.00+$.50
©1999 by CRC Press LLC

inverted-L chart is prepared in conjunction with an entity-relationship model, the entity-relationship model (Chapter 26) is generally prepared first.

Alternatives for documenting data structures include the data dictionary (Chapter 25) and Warnier-Orr diagrams (Chapter 33). Data concepts are discussed in Chapters 43, 44, and 45.

27.4   Concepts

An inverted-L chart is a tool for graphically representing a data structure. Inverted-L charts are often used with entity-relationship diagrams to document the attributes that make up an entity. The completed inverted-L charts represent a preliminary set of logical data structures.

Figure 27.1 shows two examples of inverted-L diagrams. The entity name (or data structure name) appears at the top of the imaginary upside-down letter L. Attributes are listed under the entity name, and some analysts like to include the data type or a picture clause for each attribute. Note that the key field (or fields) is clearly marked.

The entity's links (or relationships) are listed below the attributes. For example, note the link *Supplied by supplier* under *Inventory.* Move down to the second inverted-L chart and find the link that reads *Supplies inventory.* The same link appearing in inverse form under two entities defines the relationship between them. Some analysts add cardinality limits to the links; the greater than (>) symbol implies a "many to" relationship.

27.5   Key terms

Attribute — A property of an entity.

Cardinality — A measure of the relative number of occurrences of two entities.

Data element — An attribute that cannot be logically decomposed.

Data structure — A set of related data elements; a composite.

Entity — An object (a person, group, place, thing, or activity) about which data are stored.

Entity-relationship diagram — A diagram that shows how a system's primary data entities are related.

Inverted-L chart — A tool for graphically representing a data structure.

Key — The attribute or group of attributes that uniquely distinguishes one occurrence of an entity.

Relationship — A link between two entities or data structures.

27.6   Software

The inverted-L diagrams in this chapter were prepared using Visio. Other graphing tools, such as Micrografx's Flowcharter provide comparable support. Additionally, many tools for creating entity-relationship models also support inverted-L charts.

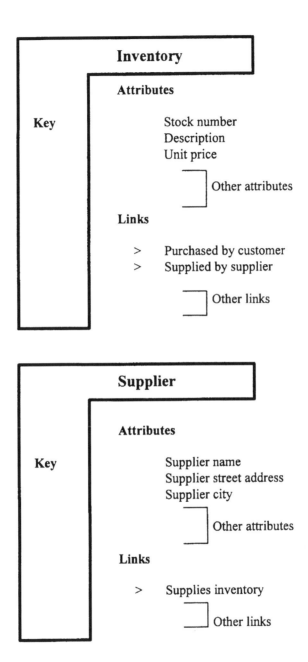

Figure 27.1   Two inverted-L diagrams.

27.7   References

1. Barker, R., *Case Method: Entity Relationship Modelling*, Addison-Wesley, Reading, MA, 1990.
2. Davis, W. S., *Business Systems Analysis and Design*, Wadsworth, Belmont, CA, 1994.
3. McDermid, D. C., *Software Engineering for Information Systems*, Blackwell Scientific, Oxford, U.K., 1990.

chapter twenty-eight

Data normalization

William S. Davis and David C. Yen

Contents

28.1 Purpose

Data normalization is a formal technique for converting preliminary data structures into easy to maintain, efficient data structures.

28.2 Strengths, weaknesses, and limitations

Data normalization is a rigorous, formal technique for defining efficient data structures. The resulting normalized data structures serve as a useful starting point for file and database design. Normalized data tend to be relatively easy to maintain. Additionally, data normalization helps to reduce data redundancy, ensure that all non-key attributes are dependent on the key, eliminate unnecessary dependency relationships within a database file, and facilitate database design using a data definition language.

Data normalization is derived from the relational database model. Consequently, the normalized data structures may not be optimal for other database models or for traditional files. Also, when the data are physically stored it is often necessary to modify the normalized data structures to gain processing efficiencies.

28.3   Inputs and related ideas

Before a set of data structures can be normalized, the logical data structures must first be defined. The necessary logical data structures might be derived from a data flow diagram (Chapter 24), an entity-relationship model (Chapter 26), a set of inverted-L diagrams (Chapter 27), a set of Warnier-Orr models (Chapter 33), or a similar tool. Generally, the composites and attributes are documented in the data dictionary (Chapter 25).

Data normalization is often performed as a preliminary step to file design (Chapter 44) or database design (Chapter 45). Relevant data concepts are discussed in Chapters 25, 43, and 44.

28.4   Concepts

Data normalization is a formal technique for converting preliminary data structures into easy to maintain, efficient data structures.

28.4.1   First normal form (1NF)

The first step is to transform the preliminary data structures into first normal form by removing any repeating sets of data elements. Data in first normal form can be represented as one or more two-dimensional flat files that resemble simple spreadsheets. Each column holds one attribute and each row holds a single occurrence of the entity.

For example, assume that Table 28.1 is a list of the data elements associated with entity *Sales*. (*Invoice number* is the key attribute.) A customer can purchase more than one item in a single transaction, so the set of data elements that describe an item sold might be repeated several times. To convert the sales data to first normal form, the repeating substructure must be moved to a new entity (Table 28.2).

Note that the key to the new entity, *Item sold*, is made up of two attributes, *Invoice number* and *Stock number*. (In other words, it has a concatenated key.) The first half of the key links the item sold to the invoice and the second half points to an item on that invoice, so the concatenated key uniquely identifies a specific item on a specific invoice.

Table 28.1 The *Sales* Entity Contains These
Data Elements

Sales
*Invoice number
Date-of-sale
Customer code
Customer name
Customer address
Item purchased (one or more)
Stock number
Description
Quantity
Unit price
Item total
Subtotal
Sales tax
Total due

An asterisk marks the key field, *Invoice number.*

Table 28.2 To Put Data into First Normal
Form, Move Repeating Substructures to New
Data Structures

Sales	Item sold
*Invoice number	*Invoice number
Date-of-sale	*Stock number
Customer code	Description
Customer name	Quantity
Customer address	Unit price
Subtotal	Item total
Sales tax	
Total due	

28.4.2   Second normal form (2NF)

A data structure in first normal form can still cause maintenance problems if one or more data elements depend on only *part* of the key. To convert data in first normal form to second normal form, concentrate on those records with concatenated keys, check each non-key attribute to see if it depends on the *entire* key, and move to a new entity any data element that depends on only part of the key.

For example, consider the data structures in Table 28.3. The first entity, *Inventory*, has a single-attribute key, *Stock number*, so it is already in second normal form. However, the second entity (*Supplier*) has a concatenated key (*Stock number* and *Supplier code*).

Two of the *Supplier* data structure's attributes, *Reorder time* and *Supplier price*, depend on both keys. They are both attributes of a given product, and

Table 28.3   The *Inventory* Data in
First Normal Form

Inventory	Supplier
* Stock number	*Stock number
Description	*Supplier code
Stock-on-hand	Suppler name
Reorder quantity	Supplier address
Reorder point	Reorder time
Unit price	Supplier price

Table 28.4   The *Inventory* Data in
Second Normal Form

Inventory	Item ordered	Supplier
*Stock number	*Stock number	*Supplier code
Description	*Supplier code	Supplier name
Stock-on-hand	Reorder time	Supplier address
Reorder quantity	Supplier price	
Reorder point		
Unit price		

the *Reorder time* and *Supplier price* for a given item might vary from supplier to supplier, so they depend on *Supplier code*, too.

The other two attributes, *Supplier name* and *Supplier address*, depend only on the *Supplier code*, however, because *Stock number* does not uniquely define the supplier. A supplier might sell numerous products. If a given supplier moves to a new address, several different product/supplier records would have to be changed, and that creates a maintenance problem. Consequently, the *Supplier* data must be separated from the *Item ordered* data (Table 28.4).

28.4.3   Third normal form (3NF)

To be in third normal form, each data element in the structure must be a function of *the key, the whole key, and nothing but the key*. That definition lacks rigor, but it is easy to remember, and it expresses the essence of third normal form.

More formally, to reach third normal form (3NF), all transitive dependencies must be removed from a second normal form (2NF) data structure. A transitive dependency occurs when a non-key attribute is determined by the key and by another non-key attribute. For example, consider the data in Table 28.5 and look at the first entity, *Sales*. *Customer name* and *Customer address* both depend directly on the *Invoice number* (the key), but they also depend on the *Customer code* which, in turn, depends on the *Invoice number*.

The process to reach a third normal form is simple: Review the structure's non-key data elements, identify any that depend on an attribute other

Table 28.5   The *Sales* Data in Second
Normal Form

Sales	Item sold	Inventory
Invoice number	*Invoice number*	*Stock number*
Date-of-sale	*Stock number*	Description
Customer code	Quantity	Unit price
Customer name	Item total	
Customer address		
Subtotal		
Sales tax		
Total due		

Note that the third data structure holds *Inventory* data.

than the key, and move them to a new entity. Table 28.6 shows all the data in third normal form. The fact that the *Customer code* appears in both *Sales* (as a foreign key) and *Customer* links a given sales transaction to a specific customer.

28.4.4   Boyce-Codd normal form (BCNF)

A relation is in Boyce-Codd normal form if and only if every determinant is a candidate key. Boyce-Codd normal form is a special type of third normal form. A relation in BCNF is also in 3NF, but a relation in 3NF may not be in BCNF.

For example, a car has such attributes as license number, engine number, color, make, type (2-door, 4-door), and description (minivan, pickup, 4×4, sedan). Both the license number and the engine number are sufficiently unique to be candidate keys.

Table 28.6   The Data in Third Normal Form

Sales	Customer	Item sold
Invoice number	*Customer code*	*Invoice number*
Customer code	Customer name	*Stock number*
Date-of-sale	Customer address	Quantity
Subtotal		Item total
Sales tax		
Total due		

Inventory	Item ordered	Supplier
Stock number	*Stock number*	*Supplier code*
Description	*Supplier code*	Suppler name
Stock-on-hand	Reorder time	Supplier address
Reorder quantity	Supplier price	
Reorder point		
Unit price		

Note that *Description* and *Unit price* are associated with *Inventory* data.

Table 28.7 Boyce-Codd Normal Form

License relation	Vehicle relation
License number	*Engine number*
Engine number	Color
	Make
	Type
	Description

This relation can be expressed in Boyce-Codd normal form by breaking it into two groups (Table 28.7). The first group holds both candidate keys, the license number (the key) and the engine number. The second group holds the engine number (the key) and all the other attributes (color, make, type, and description). Note that each group holds only a single candidate key.

28.4.5 Fourth normal form (4NF)

Fourth normal form emerged from third normal form to deal with the issue of multi-value dependency. A multi-value dependency exists when one attribute multi-determines (or is multi-determined by) the other attribute(s). For example, in Table 28.8 three attributes (dealer, manufacturer, and make) are associated with automobiles. Note that the manufacturer and the dealer both determine the car make. Also, a manufacturer (GM) can produce several makes (Chevrolet, Buick, Pontiac, Oldsmobile) and a dealer can sell several makes from GM (Pontiac, Buick) and several makes from Chrysler (Plymouth, Dodge). Within this relation are multi-value dependencies between dealers and makes and between manufacturers and makes.

A relation is in fourth normal form if and only if all existing multi-value dependencies are converted into regular functional dependencies. In Table 28.8 three attributes (dealer, manufacturer, and make) are associated with automobiles. To remove the multi-value dependencies described in the previous paragraph, this relation should be separated into two sub-relations (Table 28.9), one with dealers and manufacturers and the other with manufacturers and makes. In sub-relation A, manufacture and dealer together form a composite key. In sub-relation B, manufacturer and make form the composite key.

Table 28.8 A Relation between Automobile
Dealers, Manufacturers, and Makes

Dealer	Manufacturer	Make
Bill's Auto	GM	Chevrolet
Bill's Auto	GM	Pontiac
Dave's Auto	GM	Chevrolet
Dave's Auto	Chrysler	Plymouth
Dave's Auto	Chrysler	Dodge
Dan's Auto	GM	Buick
Dan's Auto	GM	Pontiac

Table 28.9   Fourth Normal Form

Sub-relation A		Sub-relation B	
Manufacturer	Dealer	Manufacturer	Make
GM	Bill's Auto	GM	Chevrolet
GM	Dave's Auto	GM	Buick
GM	Dan's Auto	GM	Pontiac
Chrysler	Dave's Auto	Chrysler	Plymouth
		Chrysler	Dodge

Table 28.10   Fifth Normal Form

1. The original relation

Author	Book	School
A1	B1	S1
A1	B2	S2
A2	B1	S2

2. After projection

Author	Book	Book	School	Author	School
A1	B1	B1	S1	A1	S1
A1	B2	B2	S2	A1	S2
A2	B1	B1	S2	A2	S1

3. After the first two relations are joined

Author	Book	School	
A1	B1	S1	
A1	B1	S2	*Spurious*
A1	B2	S2	
A2	B1	S1	
A2	B1	S2	*Spurious*

4. The data in fifth normal form

Author	Book	School
A1	B1	S1
A1	B2	S2
A2	B1	S2

28.4.6   Fifth normal form (5NF)

Fifth normal form is sometimes called projection-join normal form (PJNF). Projection is the process of separating one relation into sub-relations. Join is the process of consolidating sub-relations into one relation. Sometimes, join and projection operations produce spurious values called join dependencies.

The key objective of fifth normal form is to remove any join dependencies. For example, consider Table 28.10. The original relation between authors, books, and school can be projected to form three sub-relations (authors and books, books and schools, and authors and schools). If the first two sub-relations are joined by (or joined over) book, the result is a spurious value; note that A2-B1-S2 did not exist in the original relation. Fifth normal form is reached after the join dependency is removed. In this example, joining the third sub-relation with the already-joined sub-relation yields the original relation.

28.5 Key terms

Attribute — A property of an entity.

Boyce-Codd normal form — A relation is in Boyce-Codd normal form (BCNF) if and only if every determinant is a candidate key.

Candidate key — A possible key; an attribute or group of attributes that uniquely distinguishes one occurrence of an entity. Note that a given entity can have more than one candidate key.

Composite — A set of related data elements.

Data element — An attribute that cannot be logically decomposed.

Data normalization — A formal technique for designing easy to maintain, efficient logical data structures (or relations).

Data structure — A set of related data elements.

Determinant — Usually, a key; the value of the key determines the values of all the non-key attributes because the key defines a unique occurrence of the entity (a unique set of attributes).

Entity — An object (a person, group, place, thing, or activity) about which data are stored.

Fifth normal form — A fourth normal form relation with all join dependencies removed.

First normal form — A logical data structure that contains no repeating sets of data elements.

Foreign key — A key to some other entity stored with the target entity.

Fourth normal form — A relation is in fourth normal form (4NF) if and only if all existing multi-value dependencies are converted into regular functional dependencies.

Functional dependency — A situation that exists when a non-key attribute is fully dependent on the key.

Join — The process of consolidating sub-relations into one relation.

Join dependency — A type of dependency that is created as a result of a projection or join process.

Key — The attribute or group of attributes that uniquely distinguishes one occurrence if an entity.

Multi-determine — Determined (or defined) by more than one attribute; for example, a value that is determined by the key and by some other attribute is multi-determined.

Multi-value dependency — A situation that exists when one attribute multi-determines (or is multi-determined by) another attribute or attributes.

Occurrence — A single instance of an entity.

Projection — The process of separating one relation into sub-relations.

Relation — An entity in tabular form, with attributes (fields) stored in columns and tuples (records or occurrences of the entity) stored in rows.

Relationship — A link between two data structures (or relations).

Second normal form — A first normal form relation from which any data elements that depend on only part of a concatenated key have been removed to a separate entity.

Third normal form — A relation in which each data element in the relation is a function of the key, the whole key, and nothing but the key. To reach third normal form, all transitive dependencies must be removed from a second normal form relation.

Transitive dependency — A non-key attribute that depends indirectly (via a third attribute) on the key attribute.

Tuple — A row in a relation that holds one occurrence of the entity (or one record).

28.6   Software

Many CASE products include data normalization algorithms that operate on the information in the data dictionary or the repository.

28.7   References

1.   Date, C. J., *An Introduction to Database Systems,* vol. 1, 6th ed., Addison-Wesley, Reading, MA, 1994.

2.   Dutka, A. F. and Hanson, *Fundamentals of Data Normalization*, Addison-Wesley, Reading, MA, 1989.

3.   Elmasris, R. and Navathe, S. B., *Fundamental of Database Systems*, 2nd ed., Benjamin/Cummings, Redwood City, CA, 1994.

4.   Martin, J. and McClure, C., *Structured Techniques: The Basis for CASE*, Prentice-Hall, Englewood Cliffs, NJ, 1988.

5.   McDermid, D. C., *Software Engineering for Information Systems*, Blackwell Scientific, Oxford, U.K., 1990.

6.   Ullman, J. D., *Principles of Database and Knowledge-Based Systems*, vol. I, Computer Science Press, Rockville, MD, 1988.

7.   Ullman, J. D., *Principles of Database and Knowledge-Based Systems*, vol. II, *The New Technologies*, Computer Science Press, Rockville, MD, 1989.

chapter twenty-nine

Object-oriented methods

T. M. Rajkumar
Miami University

Contents

29.1 Purpose

This chapter describes object-oriented analysis. The purpose of object-oriented analysis is to find and describe the business objects and to identify the relationships between the objects via a conceptual model.

29.2 Strengths, weaknesses, and limitations

Presently, the dominant mode of analysis and design is the structured analysis and design technique. Despite its dominance, this approach has limitations in that it is not able to deliver robust systems on time or within budget and is often not able to meet the complete needs of new client/server and distributed systems. Increasingly, the industry is looking to object-oriented analysis and design.

The architectures of object-oriented systems consist of networks of interconnected subsystems, with each subsystem encapsulating data and providing methods. Because the subsystems reflect natural classifications, they tend to be independent and stable. The subsystems communicate via messages and object-oriented analysis and design encourages platform independent designs, leading to more reliable distributed systems.

Developer productivity is enhanced because objects and code can be reused. Developers have a library of reusable classes and can create specialized subclasses from them by using inheritance. This reduces coding and maintenance costs because the library of classes has been debugged prior to inclusion in the system.

Object-oriented analysis and design leads to quicker development because of the increased use of prototyping. Prototyping and reuse go together because it is easier to prototype if there is a library of reusable classes.

In addition, there is a closer association between the real world object and the system object. Business users tend to see the world in terms of objects, so a program developed to reflect those objects is easier to communicate to the user. The object models lead to a more natural representation because data and programs are stored together. In addition, a hierarchical model structure is possible, with each layer showing greater levels of detail. All these lead to object models that are easier to understand and use.

Programmer training is a problem. Most practicing programmers were trained on structured programming techniques and on languages such as COBOL. Writing object-oriented programs or designing object-oriented systems requires learning new languages and new ways to conceptualize logic. This is a challenge.

Reuse is also difficult to achieve. Significant management, cultural, and organizational issues must be tackled prior to achieving reuse. Management commitment must be obtained before object technology provides any benefits. In addition, a sizeable number of employees must be trained in object-oriented techniques and technologies. Control issues also need to be handled such as: Should everyone be forced to use the standard version?

Should adaptations be allowed? Who decides? Should designs, specifications, and architectures also be reused? Akin to the capability maturity model, reuse maturity models exist that can guide organizations in their implementations of the reuse process.

While objects are easier to communicate with users, it is naïve to expect that system objects that mirror real world objects will result in software that is easily maintainable, reusable and makes efficient use of resources.[1] A study of design patterns and modifying the system design to effectively utilize true and tried methods in object-oriented design would, in general, improve the quality of software that is developed, however.

In addition, the message passing mechanism used for communication between objects does not always accurately reflect the way events occur in the real world. For example, when two cars bump into each other, it cannot be assumed that one car sent a *bump ( )* message. Instead, an event has taken place in which each car is a reluctant participant. Because of this, object-oriented analysis and design approaches introduce messages late in the design process.

29.3   Inputs and related ideas

Structured analysis and design pictures a software system as a collection of data that are processed by functions (processes) external to the data. Analysts and designers use data flow diagrams (Chapter 24), data dictionaries (Chapter 25), and structure charts (Chapter 63) to develop systems. Entity relationship diagrams (Chapter 26) stress the data and show how a system's primary data entities are related. These tools are appropriate for data-rich systems (for example, systems that incorporate relational databases).

An object is a concept or thing about which information is stored. An object consists of a set of related methods and attributes. Object-oriented concepts are covered in Chapter 6. Object-oriented design is covered in Chapter 66.

29.4   Concepts

In general, divide and conquer is the strategy used to deal with software project complexity in both structured analysis and design and object-oriented analysis and design (OOAD). In structured analysis and design, the decomposition is performed via function or process, resulting in a hierarchical breakdown of processes made up of other subprocesses. In OOAD, the decomposition is by objects rather than by processes or functions. OOAD emphasizes considering the problem and its logical solution from the perspective of objects (things, concepts, entities).

The object-oriented life cycle can be broadly thought of as including analysis, design, and a construction phase. Analysis is the investigation of a problem rather than a solution. Design emphasizes a logical solution and the design of a system that fulfills the requirements. Construction is developing code, debugging, and testing the application.

In object-oriented analysis, the analyst finds and describes the objects. For example, if we consider a student registration system at an university or college, some objects of interest would be students, courses, and faculty. During the design phase, the analyst defines software objects that ultimately will be implemented in an object-oriented language. These objects have properties (attributes) and methods. For example, a course may have number, title, time, instructor and a *print class rolls* method. During construction the design objects are implemented in an object-oriented language such as C++, Java, or Visual Basic.

During the object-oriented analysis stage, the analyst defines the problem statement (the requirements), defines use cases both at a high level and an expanded level, develops a conceptual model, and records the terms in a glossary.

29.4.1   Requirements

Requirements are used to specify the overall goals, system functions, and attributes. For example, imagine that the goals for an appliance store inventory system are to reduce inventory by providing accurate, daily inventory status data to support reorder and sale item decisions and to maintain the new inventory levels into the future.

System functions identify what the system is supposed to do. Some system functions implied by the inventory system goals include recording all transactions, maintaining inventory of all items in some persistent storage, reporting items to reorder, updating inventory when items are received, and identifying items with excess stock.

System attributes are non-functional qualities such as operating system and platform, response time, and interface (windows, GUI, etc.). Requirements also include evaluating project feasibility (Chapter 13), recording a list of key contacts, and documenting any constraints (such as the maximum cost of the project).

29.4.2   Use case modeling

Use case modeling is a technique used to identify and define the business objects. The objectives of use case modeling include identifying user requirements in a manner that can be clearly communicated to the user and developers, enabling the finding of objects in the real world, enabling the discovery of properties and methods for each object, and establishing a basis for developing a test plan and user manuals.

A use case corresponds to a specific kind of system use. Use cases describe the behavior of a system from a user's point of view. A use case begins with an actor (a person or entity external to the system) initiating some business task. The system responds with a dialogue to which the user

Table 29.1 A High-Level Use Case

Use case	Buy appliance
Actors	Customer, Sales representative
Description	A customer talks to a sales representative about appliances that he/she is interested in buying, and picks the item in consultation with the sales representative. The sales representative then prepares the bill, and the customer makes the payment.
Type	Primary

responds and so on. The use case describes this sequence of events. Use cases are not functional requirements per se but imply the requirements. Use case modeling breaks down the entire scope of system functionalities by specifying all the relevant ways of using the system.

29.4.2.1   High level use case

High-level use cases tersely describe the functionality required and are useful to obtain a quick understanding of the overall processes in the system. Table 29.1 describes a typical high level use case. It contains a title, the actors involved in the use case (including the one who initiates), a brief description of the case, and whether the use case represents a fairly important (primary) business process or is of secondary importance.

29.4.2.2   Expanded use case

Expanded use cases are used to obtain an in-depth understanding of the processes and requirements. In an expanded use case, in addition to the high-level description, the purpose, and a typical or normal sequence of actions are recorded. For example, Table 29.2 is an expanded description for the high-level use case in Table 29.1.

Alternative courses (a cash payment, a disapproved credit card transaction) are generally not included in the use case because the objective is understanding the basic requirements, not the details. It is easier to read the standard use case without being distracted by unusual cases, and the developer should focus more on the most common case. The alternate courses are delineated and described later.

An assumptions section can also be added to the use case to deal with important issues such as security and performance that do not fit the use case scenario. For example, assumptions might state that no manufacturer's rebate coupons will be accepted, or no security or password is required for the sales representative to enter the information into the system.

Table 29.2   An Expanded-Level Use Case

Use case	Buy appliance
Actors	Customer (initiator), Sales representative
Purpose	Record the sale of an appliance to a customer
Description	A customer, talks to a sales representative about appliances that he/she is interested in buying, and picks the item in consultation with the sales representative. The sales representative then prepares the bill, and the customer makes the payment.
Type	Primary
Normal course of events	1. Customer walks up to a sales representative and discusses items to buy. 2. In consultation, customer decides on item to buy. 3. Sales representative enters the appliance identifier and the quantity desired into the system. 4. System responds with the price, and verifies that the appliance is in stock. (Not in stock is not a normal course of events.) 5. If additional items are to be entered, sales representative does so, and steps 3 and 4 are repeated. 6. System adds the amounts, calculates tax, and presents the total. 7. Sales representative informs the customer of the total.* 8. Customer runs his/her credit card through the verification system. 9. System receives credit approval and presents credit card transaction form. 10. Customer signs the credit card transaction form. 11. System logs the details of the transaction, including sales representative, customer, and item information. 12. System updates the inventory and closes the transaction. 13. System generates the receipt. 14. Receipt is handed by sales representative to customer. 15. Customer leaves the premises with appliance. *Alternative courses:* Note errors that can occur and how they are handled can be described here.

*Assumption: the normal event is a credit card purchase. Cash purchases are described separately.

29.4.2.3   Identifying use cases

One method for identifying use cases is to start by identifying the actors and then identifying the business processes each actor initiates or participates in.

Actors are generally external to the system, so the system context diagram (Chapter 24) may be a good place to start. Defining everything each actor is able to do enables the analyst to document the complete functionality of the system. Jacobson[2] recommends that the analyst consider:

1. The main tasks of the actor,
2. The type of access to system information (read or update) the actor requires,
3. The information about changes in the world outside the system the actor is to send to the system,
4. The information the system is to send to the actor about changes of which the system is aware.

Note that the use cases should describe real processes (such as processing a sale) and not trivial events (such as printing the receipt for the customer). In this example, the real process is the sale.

29.4.2.4   Use case diagrams
Use case diagrams depict:

1. A set of use cases for a system,
2. The actors,
3. The relations between the actors and the use cases.

The purpose of the use case diagram is to present a context diagram. By understanding the use case diagram, one can understand the actors external to the system and the many ways in which the system is used by the actors. In the unified modeling language (UML) notation,[3] ovals represent use cases and stick figures represent actors. For example, Figure 29.1 shows a sample use case diagram for the appliance store.

29.4.2.5   Developing use cases
Use cases can be categorized as primary and secondary. Primary use cases depict processes commonly seen in the business. Secondary use cases depict processes used less often (such as deciding to order a new category of appliance).

Use cases are typically ranked using some sort of priority. For example, the analyst might give priority to use cases that represent the primary functions of the business, those that impact the design, those that enable easy identification of objects, those that impact the architecture of the system (database requirements, network requirements), those that implement complex functions, and so on.

Once they are ranked, the more critical use cases are developed iteratively using a time boxed approach. For example, the *Buy appliance* use case may first be written with just the typical course of events. In the second iteration, the use case may be developed for handling credit refusals and cash

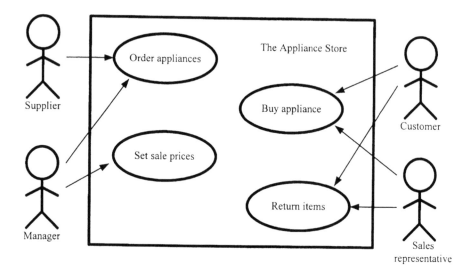

Figure 29.1   A use case diagram for an appliance store.

payments. In the third iteration, handling check payments may be added to the use case, and so on. Each assumption or simplification of the scenario must be noted in the use case model at each stage.

Use cases are not object oriented. The objective is to create a first-cut model from a business process or system perspective. The completed use case diagram gives the analyst a view of the system and provides the tools to identify the objects and build a conceptual model.

29.4.3   *The conceptual model*

In the conceptual model, the real world concepts (i.e., the objects) are explicitly identified, their attributes are documented, and the associations among the objects are specified. Creating a conceptual model is the most important object-oriented analysis activity.

In the unified modeling language, conceptual models are shown using static diagrams. Static diagrams describe the different kinds of objects that can exist in the system and the possible ways in which the objects can be linked to each other. Typically, no methods or responsibilities are shown, as static models do not contain information about how a system behaves. The most important type of static diagram is the class-structure diagram. The class-structure diagram defines the groups or classes the objects fall into and defines the structural relationships between the groups.

It should be emphasized that during the analysis phase, the conceptual model represents the real-world entities, not the software components. It shows information on objects (concepts) in the application, how the objects are associated with each other, and the attributes of each object. Figure 29.2 shows the UML notation for an object.

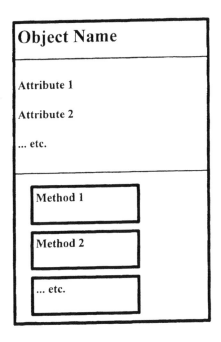

Figure 29.2 Object representation in UML.

29.4.3.1 *Identifying objects*

Objects are identified by extracting nouns (candidate classes/objects) from a problem statement or from the expanded use case. A few of these noun phrases may be candidate concepts; others may be attributes.

For example, the use case statements for an inventory application might suggest such concepts (objects) as customer, sales representative, appliance item, stock, payment, credit card, verification system, inventory, price, quantity, total, transaction, receipt, and so on. A similar analysis is done for all use cases, and a candidate list of objects is drawn up. Once this is done, the candidate list is cleaned up by looking for synonyms (inventory and stock), concepts outside the scope of the system (the verification system), nouns that are attributes (price), and so on. The reasons for keeping some nouns and removing others from the list must be documented.

Once the key objects are identified, the next step is to group them to form object classes. Certain objects, for example, objects that share attributes, seem to naturally fit together. For example, the object *appliance item* clearly belongs to a more general concept called *inventory,* and the data associated with a *receipt* have a great deal in common with a *sale.*

29.4.3.2 *Identifying associations*

An association is a relationship between concepts that indicates some meaningful and interesting connection. Much as objects correspond to nouns, associations correspond to verbs.

For each association, the analyst must decide if the association is useful by checking if information about the association must be stored. For example, consider the association between the sales representative and the actual sale. If the store pays its sales representatives on a commission basis, then the system must keep track of this association. However, if the appliance store pays its sales representatives an hourly wage, the association may not be needed. All necessary associations are assigned a name that clearly reflects the purpose of the association.

Once the association (relationship) has been identified, the multiplicity that governs the relationship must also be defined. Multiplicity defines the minimum and maximum number of occurrences of one conceptual object for a single occurrence of the other; the concept is similar to cardinality (Chapter 26.) Since associations are bidirectional, multiplicity must be defined in both directions for the association.

An example of an association and its multiplicities is shown in Figure 29.3. The association is *customer purchases from inventory.* The relationship is many to many because a customer is associated with (may purchase) many items in inventory and a given item in inventory may be purchased by many different customers. Figure 29.4 summarizes several unified modeling language multiplicity notations.

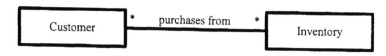

Figure 29.3   Association in UML.

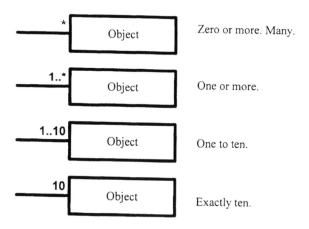

Figure 29.4   Representing multiplicity in UML.

Two objects can have more than one association. When several associations exist between two objects, then role names specified on either side of the association are used to clarify the relationship. Role names are typically nouns. For example, in Figure 29.5, the graduate student has two roles, one as a student taking a course from the faculty member and the second as a research assistant working for the faculty member.

29.4.3.3   Aggregation

An aggregation association depicts a complex object that is composed of other objects. In general it models a whole-part relationship between objects. An aggregation is used to express "part-of" associations between objects. For example, a sale is composed of multiple sales line items, so a sale can be modeled as an aggregation of sales line items. Figure 29.6 (top) depicts this aggregation which is actually a composition. A composition is a stronger form of aggregation, with the multiplicity at the composite end being at most one (signified by a filled diamond).

A hollow diamond indicates a shared aggregation, and the composite end may be more than one. For example, the second association in Figure 29.6 depicts an asymmetrical relationship where the parent takes care of the children as a shared aggregation. An asymmetrical relationship is one in

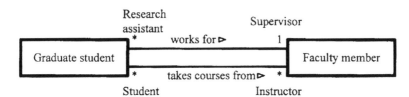

Figure 29.5   Roles in UML.

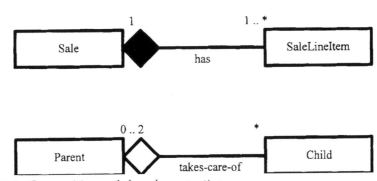

Figure 29.6   Composition and shared aggregation.

which one end plays a more significant role. Here, the parent object plays a more significant role than the children. Note that a child can have at most two (0 . . . 2) parents.

Booch[4] suggests the following tests to determine whether a relationship is an aggregation:

1. Is a part-of phrase used to describe it?
2. Are some operations of the whole applied automatically to the parts?
3. Are some attribute values propagated from the whole to the parts?
4. Is one object class subordinate to the other?

29.4.3.4 *Generalization and specialization*

Class hierarchies enable us to manage complexity by ordering objects within trees of classes with increasing levels of abstraction. Generalization and specialization are points of view that are based on class hierarchies. Generalization consists of factoring out the common elements (attributes and methods) from a set of classes into a more general class called a parent class. The most general level is at the top, with the more specific object types shown as children. The parent's attributes and methods are then inherited by the children. Generalization and specialization hierarchies describe systems that should be implemented using inheritance in an object-oriented language.

Figure 29.7 depicts a common occurrence of a generalization/specialization in the real world. An employee can be either a salaried worker or an hourly worker. A salaried worker may be a manager or a non-manager. In the appliance sales example, payment has a hierarchy with sub-types credit payment and cash payment.

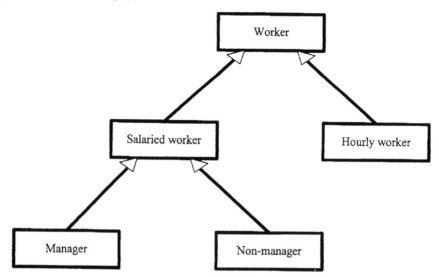

Figure 29.7 Generalization/specialization.

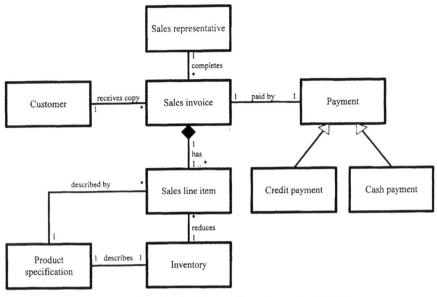

Figure 29.8   A conceptual model for the appliance inventory system.

A conceptual model for the appliance store inventory project that integrates the various objects is shown in Figure 29.8.

29.4.4   Glossary

A glossary is a document that defines terms. Conceptually, it resembles a data dictionary (Chapter 25). The glossary lists and defines all the terms that must be clarified. The objective is to reduce misinterpretation of the terms by various analysts and to enhance communication by providing consistent meanings for the various terms.

29.5   Key terms

Actor — A person or entity external to the system.

Aggregation — A description of part-of relationships among objects; the higher-level objects are completely described by all of their components.

Association — A relationship between objects that indicates some meaningful and interesting connection.

Capability maturity model — A comprehensive framework for describing and evaluating the software development capability of an organization.

Class structure diagram — A diagram that defines the groups or classes the objects fall into and defines the structural relationships between the groups.

Composition — A stronger form of aggregation, with the multiplicity at the composite end being at most one.

Concept — An object.

Conceptual model — A model in which the real-world concepts (i.e., the objects) are explicitly identified, their attributes are documented, and the associations among the objects are specified.

Expanded use case — A description of the step-by-step events in a process; an expanded use case is more detailed than a high-level use case.

Generalization — A technique wherein commonality among concepts is identified and a general concept or super-type is defined. Subtypes depict "type-of" relationships.

High-level use case — A brief, two, or three sentence description of a process.

Multiplicity — The minimum and maximum number of occurrences of one conceptual object for a single occurrence.

Object-oriented analysis — The investigation of a problem by identifying and describing the objects.

Object-oriented design — The logical solution of a problem through a set of interacting objects.

Reuse maturity model — A comprehensive model that measures the extent of reuse of software components, architecture, and processes in an organization.

Specialization — The creation of a subtype from a super-type by refining the super-type; the opposite of generalization.

Static diagram — A model that describes the different kinds of objects that can exist in the system and the possible ways in which the objects can be linked to each other; no methods or responsibilities are shown because static models do not contain information about how a system behaves.

Timed box approach — A project management approach that divides the set of all requirements for a system into subsets, each of which is implemented as a version of the system; the delivery of each new version of the system in a regular and timely fashion is guaranteed by this approach.

Unified modeling language — The universal language for object-oriented modeling; its notation forms an object-oriented modeling language and can replace the notation of various object-oriented analysis methods.

Use case — The behaviorally related sequence of transactions that a user performs in a dialogue with the system when he or she uses the system.

Use case diagram — A diagram that depicts the set of use cases for a system, the actors, and the relation between the actors and the use cases.

29.6   Software

CASE (Chapter 5) tools exist to help the analyst develop use cases, draw class diagrams and enter terms in a data dictionary.

29.7   References

29.7.1   Citations

1. Priestley, M., *Practical Object Oriented Design*, McGraw-Hill, London, 1997.
2. Jacobson, I., Christerson, M., Jonsson, P., and Overgaard, G., *Object Oriented Software Engineering: A Use Case Driven Approach*, ACM Press, Reading, MA, 1992.
3. UML 1.1 Specification (Rational Software), *http://www.rational.com/uml/*.
4. Booch, G., *Object Oriented Design with Applications*, Benjamin/Cummings, Redwood City, CA, 1991.

29.7.2   Suggestions for additional reading

1. Brown, D., *An Introduction to Object Oriented Analysis: Objects in Plain English*, John Wiley & Sons, New York, 1997.
2. Larman, C., *Applying UML and Patterns: An Introduction to Object Oriented Analysis and Design*, Prentice-Hall, Upper Saddle River, NJ, 1997.
3. Fowler, M., *Analysis Patterns: Reusable Object Models*, Addison-Wesley, Reading, MA, 1997.
4. Muller, P. A., *Instant UML*, Wrox Press, Olton, Canada,1997.
5. Rumbaugh, J., Blaha, M., Premerlani, W., Eddy, F., and Lorenson, W., *Object Oriented Modeling and Design*, Prentice-Hall, Englewood Cliffs, NJ, 1991.
6. Yourdon, E., Whitehead, K., Thomann, J., Oppel, K., and Nevermann, P., *Mainstream Objects: An Analysis and Design Approach for Business*, Yourdon Press, Upper Saddle River, NJ, 1995.

.

chapter thirty

State transition diagrams

David C. Yen and William S. Davis

Contents

30.1 Purpose

The purpose of a state transition diagram is to represent a system as a series of states and related activities, display the interrelationships among the states, show how the system moves from state to state, and document the sequence and priority of the states. State transition diagrams were initially developed to help design compilers. Systems analysts and information system consultants use state transition diagrams to analyze and design real-time and object-oriented systems.

0-8493-7001-9/99/$0.00+$.50
©1999 by CRC Press LLC

30.2   Strengths, weaknesses, and limitations

State transition diagrams are excellent tools for representing the precedence relationships between a system's processes and states and for representing recursive and feedback structures. They are particularly useful when a system exhibits multiple changes of state or requires synchronization. A state transition diagram is easily converted into object-oriented code.

State transition diagrams are used primarily in real-time and/or object-oriented systems analysis and design and to support such computer science applications as compiler design. They are not generally useful for designing or documenting batch processing systems. Also, because they are not considered standard tools in the traditional systems analysis and design methodologies, many systems analysts and information system consultants are unfamiliar with them.

30.3   Inputs and related ideas

State transition diagrams are used primarily for analyzing and designing real-time (Chapter 73) and object-oriented (Chapters 6, 29, and 66) systems. They are sometimes used to support prototyping (Chapter 31) and rapid application development (Chapter 32).

30.4   Concepts

A state transition diagram is used to represent a system as a series of states and related activities, display the interrelationships among the states, show how the system moves from state to state, and document the sequence and priority of the states.

30.4.1   Basic elements

Figure 30.1 shows the basic elements of a state transition diagram. The various states (or nodes) are shown as circles. State 0 is the initial (starting) state. Arrows representing functions or activities link a state to its accepting (or following) states. An arrow that originates and returns to the same state represents a recursive loop. The initial and final states are shown as double circles.

On a non-deterministic state transition diagram, a given input function is associated with more than one transition from the state. A deterministic state transition diagram, in contrast, can have at most one transition from a given state for any given input. Deterministic is a special case of non-deterministic.

30.4.2   An example

Figure 30.2 shows, for example, an entity relationship diagram for a real-time system for producing grape jam. State 0 is the initial state. During

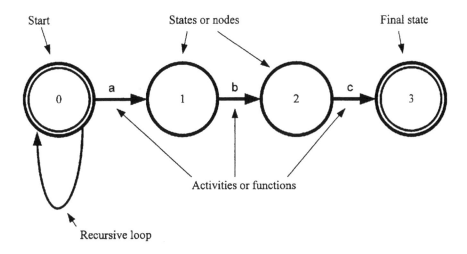

Figure 30.1 The basic elements of a state transition diagram.

activity A, the initial mix of raw materials is prepared and the production process begins.

State 1 is a target temperature. The production process cannot move on to the next state until the target temperature is achieved, so activity B is a recursive loop during which the temperature of the mix is constantly monitored and adjusted.

After the mix reaches the appropriate temperature, it moves on (activity C) to the next state. State 2 is the target acidity ratio which must be rechecked and balanced after each succeeding state is completed. Activity D

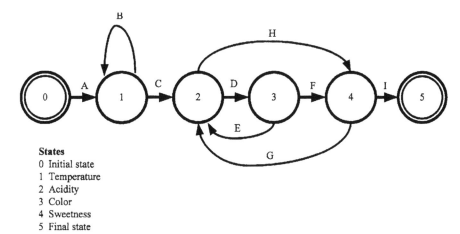

States
0 Initial state
1 Temperature
2 Acidity
3 Color
4 Sweetness
5 Final state

Figure 30.2 A state transition diagram for a real-time production system.

adds artificial color to the mix. State 3 is the target color. Activity E is a feedback loop to state 2, where acidity is rechecked.

When both acidity (state 2) and color (state 3) are in balance, sugar is
added to the mix (activity F) until the desired level of sweetness is reached
(state 4). Activity G is another feedback loop to state 2. Activity H returns the
process to state 4, where sweetness is rechecked. When the mix reaches the
desired acidity, color, and sweetness, it moves on to the packaging stage
(activity I), and the production process ends (state 5).

30.4.3   Fence diagrams

A state transition diagram can also be prepared in the form of a fence
diagram. On a fence diagram, the states are shown as vertical lines and the
activities that move the system from one state to another are shown as horizontal arrows.

For example, Figure 30.3 shows a fence diagram of the life cycle of a
single object in inventory. Starting at the left, the object is ordered, received,
inspected, and either accepted or returned to the supplier (the left-pointing
arrow).

Once the object is accepted, it is stored in the warehouse. From the warehouse, the object can be transferred to the showroom or returned to the supplier. Objects in the showroom can be sold and delivered to a customer. If the
customer accepts the object, it is deleted from inventory records. If the customer rejects the object, it is returned to the showroom where it can be resold
or returned to the warehouse.

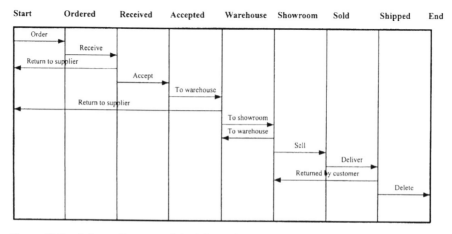

Figure 30.3   A fence diagram of the life cycle of a single object in inventory.

30.5   Key terms

Activity (function) — A process or event that moves a system from one state to another.

Deterministic state transition diagram — A state transition diagram in which a given input function is associated with at most one transition from a given state.

Feedback — The return of a portion of a system's output to its input; on a state transition diagram, a feedback loop returns the system to a previous state.

Fence diagram — A state transition diagram on which the states are shown as vertical lines and the activities are shown as horizontal arrows.

Node — A symbol (usually a circle) on a state transition diagram that represents a state.

Non-deterministic state transition diagram — A state transition diagram in which a given input function is associated with more than one transition from the state.

Real-time system — A system designed to respond immediately to real-world events.

Recursion — The ability of a subroutine to call itself.

State — A condition or mode of being, particularly with regard to phase, form, composition, or structure.

Transition — A movement or shift from one state to another.

30.6   Software

The state transition and fence diagrams in this chapter were prepared using Visio. Other graphing tools, such as Micrografx's Flowcharter provide comparable support. Additionally, many CASE products support state transition models.

30.7   References

1. Aho, A., Sethi, R., and Ullman J., *Compilers: Principles, Techniques, and Tools,* Addison-Wesley, Reading, MA, 1986.
2. Davis, W. S., *Business Systems Analysis and Design,* Wadsworth, Belmont, CA, 1994.
3. Martin, J. and McClure, C., *Diagramming Techniques for Analysts and Programmers,* Prentice-Hall, Englewood Cliffs, NJ, 1985.

chapter thirty-one

Prototyping

William S. Davis and David C. Yen

Contents

31.1 Purpose

A prototype is a working physical model of a system or a subsystem. Generally, the analyst's (or information consultant's) objective is to gather information about the user's requirements from the bottom up by allowing the user to interact with the prototype. In effect, the prototype serves as a preliminary version of the system or component from which requirements are extracted and on which subsequent versions are based.

31.2 Strengths, weaknesses, and limitations

A prototype is an excellent tool for analyzing and designing an interactive application and/or a user interface and to support object-oriented system development. During the analysis stage, prototyping can be used to replace or supplement logical modeling, particularly when the users are uncomfortable with abstract models. Prototyping is valuable on projects with long development times because the user gets to see something physical. Prototyping is an excellent tool when the requirements are highly uncertain or too abstract to specify, or when no comparable system has been previously developed. Generally, if reaching a solution calls for simulation, experimentation, or incremental evaluation, prototyping might be a reasonable choice.

Creating a large, complex system from the bottom up can be very difficult, and integrating subsystem prototypes can prove almost impossible because there is no clear way (short of a parallel top-down logical or data model) to visualize subsystem relationships. Prototyping is not a good choice for algorithm-driven projects that involve heavy calculation.

Prototyping can bias the systems analysis process in subtle ways. Because the prototype is developed on a computer, the system will almost certainly be implemented on a computer and manual alternatives are unlikely to be considered. Because it is a working model, people will inevitably think of the prototype as *the* solution. A related danger is that the system will never be developed properly because the prototype seems too good.

Prototypes generally lack security, auditing, and other controls (Chapter 77), and data integrity may be difficult to ensure. Additionally, prototypes are often inefficient and difficult to maintain. For example, it is difficult to trace the ripple effects that result from modifying a prototype, and that affects maintainability. Economy of scale is another problem; prototypes that test well sometimes fail when the number of users is dramatically increased.

31.3   Inputs and related ideas

Before creating a prototype, it is necessary to at least partially define the problem and gather preliminary information (Part II). Also, it may be necessary to perform a preliminary analysis (Part IV) and/or create logical models to help plan and (later) to supplement the prototype. A prototype is an excellent tool for analyzing and designing an interactive application and/or a user interface (Chapter 48) and to support object-oriented system development (Chapters 29 and 66). During the analysis stage, prototyping can be used to replace or supplement logical modeling (Chapters 24, 26, and 28). Variations on the standard prototyping approach include evolutionary prototyping, incremental prototyping, and middle-out prototyping (Chapter 72).

31.4   Concepts

Prototyping is a powerful, bottom up alternative or supplement to logical modeling. The basic idea is to build a reasonably complete, working, *physical* model (or prototype) of the system. As a minimum, the analyst can use screen painters, menu builders, and report generators to prepare a "slide show" of sample screens (Chapter 46), dialogues (Chapter 49), and reports (Chapter 47). In a more complete prototype, preliminary working versions of the system's programs are created using a fourth-generation language, spreadsheets, database software, or a similar end-user tool.

31.4.1   The prototyping process

The prototyping process can be viewed as a loop (Figure 31.1). Following problem definition and preliminary analysis, a first draft of the prototype is created. The user then interacts with the prototype and identifies its strengths and weaknesses. Assuming that the first draft is less than totally acceptable, the prototype is modified to reflect the user's suggestions and the user interacts with the new, improved version. The refine-and-test cycle continues until the user is satisfied that the prototype meets his or her requirements.

During the refine-and-test cycle, the emphasis is on quick turnaround, with changes made on the spot or within at most a few days. Instead of conceptualizing needs, the users work with and react to the prototype and the analyst observes and interprets their reactions. To many people, manipulating a working model seems more natural than answering questions in an interview or trying to link an abstract model to reality.

Sometimes, the prototyping process continues until a finished system emerges. Usually, however, the purpose of the prototype is to clarify the system's requirements. The tasks and queries performed by the prototype demonstrate what the system must do and translate into processes. Screens, dialogues, menus, reports, files, and databases map to the required logical data structures. Once the requirements are defined (Chapter 35), design begins and the prototype is discarded.

Variations on the standard prototyping approach include evolutionary prototyping, incremental prototyping, and middle-out prototyping (Chapter 73).

31.4.2   Prototyping vs. conventional approaches

Conventional systems analysis and design relies on various models of the system, and the logical analysis and physical design stages are clearly distinguished. Prototypes, in contrast, are generally created using a fourth-generation language or an application generator using a mix of programming and systems analysis skills because analysis, design, and programming activities are often intermixed and difficult to distinguish.

Prototyping is (by its very nature) iterative. The process starts with a set of partial requirements, and new or expanded requirements are continuously incorporated into the system based on user feedback. Consequently,

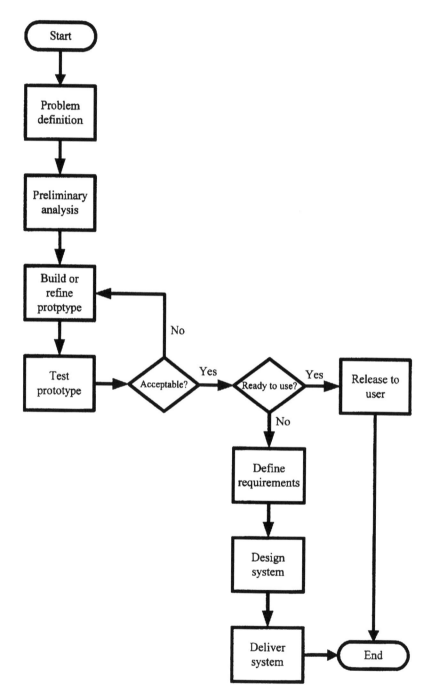

Figure 31.1   Prototyping is a cyclic process.

the requirements can be viewed as floating, or dynamic. In contrast, conventional systems analysis and design calls for a full and complete set of requirements, and the requirements are typically frozen at the end of each stage in the system development life cycle.

31.5   Key terms

Application generator (generator, program generator) — A program that starts with information in graphical, narrative, list, or some other logical form and generates the appropriate source or executable code.

Fourth-generation language — A non-procedural language that generates the appropriate source or executable code from a programmer's definition or description of a logical operation.

Prototype — A preliminary, working, physical model of a system, a subsystem, or a program.

Prototyping — The act of creating a prototype.

31.6   Software

Many CASE products support prototyping. Screen painters, menu builders, report generators, fourth-generation languages, executable specification languages, spreadsheets, and database management programs are popular prototyping tools.

31.7   References

1. Boar, B., *Application Prototyping. A Requirements Strategy for the 80s*, John Wiley & Sons, New York, 1984.
2. Brathwaite, K. S., *Applications Development Using CASE Tools*, Academic Press, San Diego, CA, 1990.
3. Davis, W. S., *Business Systems Analysis and Design,* Wadsworth, Belmont, CA, 1994.

chapter thirty-two

Rapid application development (RAD)

David C. Yen and William S. Davis

Contents

32.1 Purpose

Rapid application development (RAD) is a system development methodology that employs joint application design (to obtain user input), prototyping, CASE technology, application generators, and similar tools to expedite the design process.

32.2   Strengths, weaknesses, and limitations

Rapid application development promotes fast, efficient, accurate program and/or system development and delivery. Compared to other methodologies, RAD generally improves user/designer communication, user cooperation, and user commitment, and promotes better documentation.

Because rapid application development adopts prototyping and joint application design, RAD inherits their strengths and their weaknesses. More specifically, RAD is not suitable for mathematical or computationally-oriented applications. Because rapid application development stresses speed, quality indicators such as consistency, standardization, reusability, and reliability are easily overlooked.

32.3   Inputs and related ideas

Rapid application development is an alternative to the traditional system development life cycle (Chapter 1). The RAD methodology incorporates joint application design (Chapter 14) and prototyping (Chapter 31). CASE technology (Chapter 5) is often used to speed the development process.

32.4   Concepts

Rapid application development (RAD) is a system development methodology that employs joint application design (to obtain user input), prototyping, CASE technology, application generators, and similar tools to expedite the design process. Initially suggested by James Martin, this methodology gained support during the 1980s because of the wide availability of such powerful computer software as fourth-generation languages, application generators, and CASE tools, and the need to develop information systems more quickly. The primary objectives include high quality, fast development, and low cost.

32.4.1   Components

Rapid application development focuses on four major components: tools, people, methodology, and management. Current, powerful computing technology is essential to support such tools as application generators, screen/form generators, report generators, fourth-generation languages, relational or object-oriented database tools, and CASE tools. People include users and the development team. The methodology stresses prototyping and joint application design.

A strong management commitment is essential. Before implementing rapid application development, the organization should establish appropriate project management and formal user sign-off procedures. Additionally, standards should be established for the organization's data resources, applications, systems, and hardware platforms.

32.4.2   Phases

Martin suggests four phases to implement rapid application development: requirements planning, user design, construction, and cutover.

Requirements planning is much like traditional problem definition and systems analysis. RAD relies heavily on joint application design (JAD) sessions to determine the new system requirements.

During the user design phase, the JAD team examines the requirements and transforms them into logical descriptions. CASE tools are used extensively during this phase. The system design can be planned as a series of iterative steps or allowed to evolve (Chapter 72).

During the construction phase, a prototype is built using the software tools described earlier. The JAD team then exercises the prototype and provides feedback that is used to refine the prototype. The feedback and modification cycle continues until a final, acceptable version of the system emerges. In some cases, the initial prototype consists of screens, forms, reports, and other elements of the user interface, and the underlying logic is added to the prototype only after the user interface is stabilized.

The cutover phase is similar to the traditional implementation phase (Chapter 76). Key activities include training the users, converting or installing the system, and completing the necessary documentation.

32.4.3   Variations

There are several variations and/or extensions to the rapid application development methodology.

Courbon et al.[4] defines an evolutionary approach in which "progressive designs" go through "multiple, minimum-length cycles" in which "successive versions of the system under construction are utilized by the end user." Courbon's evolutionary approach[5] is also called middleout, breadboarding, and the iterative design approach.

The essence of the evolutionary approach is to have the user (or the manager) and the builder agree on a small but significant subproblem, and then to design and develop an initial system to support that immediate need. After a short period of use (a few weeks for instance), the system is evaluated, modified, and incrementally expanded. This cycle is repeated three to six times over the course of a few months until a relatively stable system that supports a cluster of related tasks evolves. The word *relatively* is important because, although the frequency and extent of system change will decrease or even cease, the system will never be truly stable. In effect, constant change is a conscious strategy.

Note that the evolutionary approach requires an unusual level of user (or management) participation. The user is actually the designer, and the system analyst merely implements required changes or modifications. Note also that this approach differs from traditional prototyping because the initial system is real, live, and usable, not just a pilot test.

Sprague[6,7] and Carlson's[1,2] quick-hit approach is designed to take advantage of recognized high payoff application tasks for which a system can be built very quickly. The basic idea is to gain user cooperation and confidence by rapidly developing a highly usable system. For example, imagine that a company is losing market share to a rival. Imagine further that a preliminary study suggests that the primary factors contributing to the problem are product quality, after-sale service, and brand recognition. Perhaps a simulation model that focuses on those factors can be designed and constructed quickly, yielding information that can help management correct the problem. Note that the system is designed quickly to hit the main points; hence the name *quick hit approach*. According to Sprague, the quick-hit approach is low risk and has a high potential short run payoff.

32.5   Key terms

Application generator (generator, program generator) — A program that starts with information in graphical, narrative, list, or some other logical form and generates the appropriate source or executable code.

CASE (computer-aided software engineering) — A set of automated tools that assist in the entire software engineering process.

Construction phase — The rapid application development phase during which a prototype is built, exercised, and modified based on user feedback.

Cutover phase — The rapid application development phase during which the system is finalized and released to the user.

Evolutionary approach — An approach to rapid application development in which progressive designs go through multiple, minimum-length cycles in which successive versions of the system under construction are utilized by the end user.

Fourth-generation language — A non-procedural language that generates the appropriate source or executable code from a programmer's definition or description of a logical operation.

Joint application design (JAD) — A technique for quickly determining system requirements in an intensive session attended by a team consisting of major users, managers, and systems analysts.

Prototype — A preliminary, working, physical model of a system, a subsystem, or a program.

Prototyping — The act of creating a prototype.

Quick-hit approach — An approach to rapid application development that takes advantage of recognized high payoff applications for which a system can be built very quickly.

Rapid application development (RAD) — A system development methodology that employs joint application design, prototyping, CASE technology, application generators, and similar tools to expedite the design process.

Requirements planning — The rapid application development phase during which the system requirements are defined using joint application design and other tools and techniques; this phase is similar to traditional problem definition and systems analysis.

User design phase — The rapid application development phase during which the joint application design team examines the requirements and transforms them into logical descriptions.

32.6   Software

Many CASE products support prototyping. Screen painters, menu builders, report generators, fourth-generation languages, executable specification languages, spreadsheets, and database management programs are popular prototyping tools. There is no software specifically designed to support a JAD session. However, certain groupware, such as Lotus Notes, supports limited computer mediated conferencing.

32.7   References

32.7.1   Citations

1. Carslon, E. D., An approach for designing decision support systems, *Data Base*, 3, 1979.
2. Carlson, E. D., Bennett, J., Griddings, G., and Mantey, P., The design and evaluation of an interactive geo-data analysis and display systems, *Inf. Process.*, 74, 1974.
3. Carlson E. D., Grace B. F., and Sutton, J. A., Case studies for interactive problem solving systems, *MIS Q.*, 1(1), 51, 1977.
4. Courbon, J. C., Drageof, J., and Jose, T., L'approache evolutive, *Inf. Gest.*, 103, 51, 1979.
5. Courbon, J. C., Grajew, J. and Tolovi, J., Design and Implementation of Interactive Decision Support System: An Evolutive Approach, Unpublished working paper, France, 1978.
6. Sprague, R. H., Jr., Decision support systems—implications for the systems analysts, in *Systems Analysis and Design: A Foundation for the 1980's*, Elsevier, New York, 1980.
7. Sprague, R. H., Jr., A framework for the development of decision support systems, *MIS Q.*, 1, 1980.
8. Sprague, R. H., Jr. and Watson, H. J., Bit by bit: toward decision support system, *Calif. Manage. Rev.*, 22(4), 60, 1979.
9. Sprague, R. H., Jr. and Watson, H. J., A decision support systems for banks, *OMEGA*, 4(6), 657, 1976.
10. Sprague, R. H., Jr., and Watson, H. J., MIS concepts—Part II, *J. Syst. Manage.*, 26(2), 35, 1975.
11. Sprague, R. H., Jr. and Watson, H. J., MIS concepts—Part I, *J. Syst. Manage.*, 26(1), 34, 1975.

12. Sprague, R. H., Jr. and Watson, H. J., Model management in MIS, *Proceedings, 7th Annual DSI*, Cincinnati, OH, 1975, 213.

32.7.2 Suggestions for additional reading

1. Burch, J. G., *Systems Analysis, Design, and Implementation*, Boyd & Fraser, Boston, MA, 1992.
2. Dewitz, S. D., *Systems Analysis and Design and The Transition to Objects*, McGraw-Hill, New York, 1996.
3. Hoffer, J. A., George, J. F., and Valacich, J. S., *Modern Systems Analysis and Design*, Benjamin/Cummings, Reading, MA, 1996.
4. Keen, P. G. W. and Scott-Morton, M. S., *Decision Support Systems: An Organizational Perspective*, Addison-Wesley, Reading, MA, 1978.
5. Martin, J., *Rapid Application Development*, Macmillan, New York, 1991.
6. McConnell, S., *Rapid Development: Taming Wild Software Schedules*, Microsoft Press, Redmond, WA, 1996.
7. Mullin, M., *Rapid Prototyping for Object-Oriented Systems*, Addison-Wesley, Reading, MA, 1990.
8. Power, M. J., Cheney, P .H., and Crow, G., *Structured Systems Development: Analysis, Design, Implementation*, 2nd ed., Boyd & Fraser, Boston, MA, 1990.
9. Sarna, D. E. Y. and Febish, G. J., *PC Magazine Windows Rapid Application Development/Book and Disk*, Ziff Davis Press, Indianapolis, IN, 1992.
10. Sprague, R. H., Jr. and Carlson, E. D., *Building Effective Decision Support Systems*, Prentice-Hall, Englewood Cliffs, NJ, 1980.

chapter thirty-three

Warnier-Orr diagrams

David C. Haddad and William S. Davis
Miami University

Contents

33.1 Purpose

A Warnier-Orr diagram, a graphical representation of a horizontal hierarchy with brackets separating the levels, is used to plan or document a data structure, a set of detailed logic, a program, or a system.

33.2 Strengths, weaknesses, and limitations

Warnier-Orr diagrams are excellent tools for describing, planning, or documenting data structures. They can show a data structure or a logical structure at a glance. Because only a limited number of symbols are required, specialized software is unnecessary and diagrams can be created quickly by hand. The basic elements of the technique are easy to learn and easy to explain. Warnier-Orr diagrams map well to structured code.

The structured requirements definition methodology (Chapter 4) and, by extension, Warnier-Orr diagrams are not as well known as other methodologies or tools. Consequently, there are relatively few software tools to create and/or maintain Warnier-Orr diagrams and relatively few systems analysts or information system consultants who are proficient with them.

33.3   Inputs and related ideas

Before a Warnier-Orr diagram is created, the system's primary data entities and major tasks must be known. The necessary information is collected during the problem definition and information gathering stage (Part II). A Warnier-Orr diagram is an important tool in the structured requirements definition methodology (Chapter 4). See Chapters 25 and 43 for explanations of key data-related concepts. Entity-relationship diagrams (Chapter 26) and data normalization (Chapter 28) are useful tools for planning data structures. See Chapter 62 for more on software design and program structures.

33.4   Concepts

The Warnier-Orr design methodology, also known as the structured requirements definition methodology (Chapter 4), was developed in the early 1970s by Warnier and extended to system design by Orr. The first step in the methodology is to create entity diagrams (simplified entity-relationship diagrams, Chapter 26) for each major user. The entity diagrams are then merged to create a system entity diagram, and the major tasks that must be performed are derived from the system's data requirements.

33.4.1   In-out diagrams

A Warnier-Orr diagram shows a data structure or a logical structure as a horizontal hierarchy with brackets separating the levels. Once the major tasks are identified, the systems analyst or information system consultant prepares an in-out Warnier-Orr diagram to document the application's primary inputs and outputs.

For example, Figure 33.1 shows an in-out diagram for a batch inventory update application. Start at the left (the top of the hierarchy). The large bracket shows that the program, *Update Inventory*, performs five primary processes ranging from *Get Transaction* at the top to *Write Reorder* at the bottom. The letter N in parentheses under *Update Inventory* means that the program is repeated many (1 or more) times. The digit 1 in parentheses under *Get Transaction* (and the next three processes) means the process is performed once. The (0, 1) under *Write Reorder* means the process is repeated 0 or 1

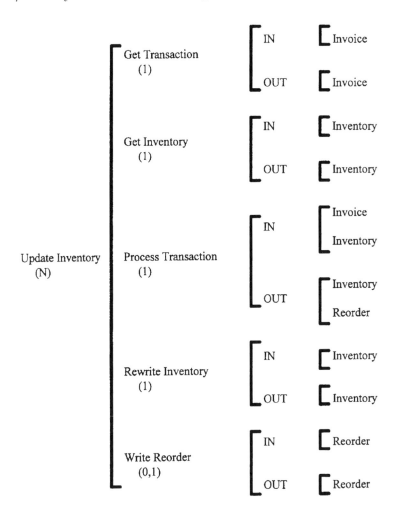

Figure 33.1 An in-out Warnier-Orr diagram.

times, depending on a run-time condition. (Stock may or may not be reordered as a result of any given transaction.)

Data flow into and out from every process. The process inputs and outputs are identified to the right of the in-out diagram. For example, the *Get Transaction* process reads an *Invoice* and passes it to a subsequent process. The last column is a list of the program's primary input and output data structures. Note how the brackets indicate the hierarchical levels.

33.4.2 Data structures

After the in-out diagram is prepared, the data structures are documented. For example, Figure 31.2 shows the data structure for an invoice.

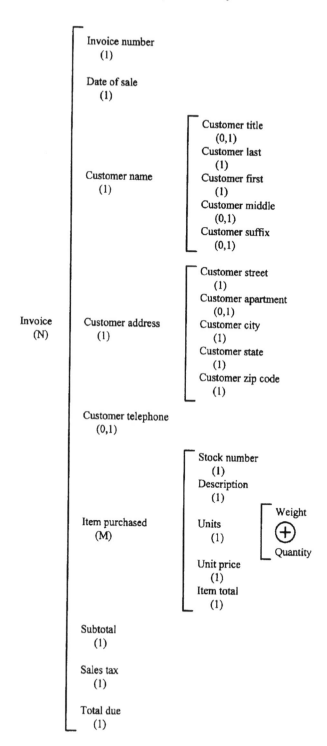

Figure 33.2 A Warnier-Orr diagram of the *Invoice* data structure.

The highest level composite, *Invoice*, is noted at the left. The *N* in parentheses under the data name means that there are many (one or more) invoices. Moving to the right of the first bracket are the components that make up an invoice. *Invoice number, Date-of-sale, Customer telephone, Subtotal, Sales tax,* and *Total due* are data elements, while *Customer name, Customer address,* and *Item purchased* are composite items that are further decomposed.

Consider the composite item *Customer name*. The composite name appears at the left separated from its lower-level data elements by a bracket. Three of the data elements that make up *Customer name* are conditional; *Customer title* (Dr, Mr., Ms.), *Customer middle* (not everyone has a middle name), and *Customer suffix* (Sr., Jr., III) may or may not be present on a given *Invoice*. The entry (0, 1) under a data element name indicates that it occurs 0 or 1 times.

A given sales transaction might include several different products, so *Item purchased* is a repetitive data structure that consists of one or more sets of the data elements *Stock number, Description, Units, Unit price,* and *Item total*. The letter *M* in parenthesis under *Item purchased* indicates that the substructure is repeated an unknown number of times. (*Note: M* and *N* are different values.) The composite item, *Units*, can hold either *Weight* or *Quantity*, but not both. The "plus sign in a circle" is an exclusive or symbol.

33.4.3   Program (logic) structures

A key principle of the Warnier-Orr methodology is that the structure of a well-written program is tied to the structure of its data. For example, because the number of invoices is unknown, the primary structure of an inventory update program designed to process the data described in Figure 33.2 will be a repetitive loop. At the second level, the number of items purchased is unknown, suggesting another loop structure to compute and accumulate the item costs. Finally, the exclusive or and the conditional items at the data element level suggest selection logic.

33.5   Key terms

Composite — A set of related data elements.
Data element — An attribute that cannot be logically decomposed.
Data structure — A set of related data elements.
Entity — An object (a person, group, place, thing, or activity) about which data are stored.
Entity diagram — A simplified entity-relationship diagram that uses bubbles instead of rectangles and ignores cardinality.
Entity-relationship diagram — A model of a system's data that shows how the primary data entities are related.
In-out diagram — A Warnier-Orr diagram that documents the application's primary inputs and outputs.

Warnier-Orr diagram — A diagramming technique that shows a data structure or a logical structure as a horizontal hierarchy with brackets separating the levels.

33.6 Software

The Warnier-Orr diagrams in this chapter were prepared using Visio. Other graphing tools, such as Micrografx's Flowcharter provide comparable support. Most popular paint or drawing programs incorporate text and brackets and thus can be used to create Warnier-Orr diagrams. Some CASE products support Warnier-Orr diagrams.

33.7 References

1. Davis, W. S., *Business Systems Analysis and Design*, Wadsworth, Belmont, CA, 1994.
2. Davis, W. S., *Systems Analysis and Design: A Structured Approach*, Addison-Wesley, Reading, MA, 1983.
3. Orr, K. T., *Structured Requirements Definition*, Ken Orr and Associates, Topeka, KS, 1981.
4. Orr, K. T., *Structured Systems Development*, Yourdon, New York, 1977.
5. Warnier, J. D., *The Logical Construction of Programs*, Van Nostrand Reinhold, New York, 1976.
6. Warnier, J. D., *Program Modification*, Martinus Nijhoff, London, 1978.

chapter thirty-four

Expert system problem-solving analysis

David C. Yen and William S. Davis

Contents

34.1   Purpose

This chapter describes several problem-solving tools and techniques that are used to analyze and design an expert system or, more generally, an information system with a rule (knowledge) base.

0-8493-7001-9/99/$0.00+$.50
©1999 by CRC Press LLC

34.2   Strengths, weaknesses, and limitations

Several inference-oriented, search-oriented, and reasoning-oriented problem-solving tools and techniques will be explored in this chapter. Strengths and weaknesses will be discussed in context.

34.3   Inputs and related ideas

Expert systems are introduced in Chapter 7. Knowledge representation is covered in Chapter 67. The input information required by these tools is collected during the problem definition and information gathering stage using many of the tools described in Part II. Any specific input needed by a particular tool or technique will be discussed in context.

34.4   Concepts

During the analysis phase of an expert system or rule-based system development project, the system's data, knowledge, and rules are determined. A rule is a formal specification or description of a unit of knowledge. Public knowledge is from published literature. Common sense knowledge consists largely of rules of thumb or heuristics.

34.4.1   Inference-oriented techniques

Inference-oriented techniques use inference to lead to a solution. The basic idea (Figure 34.1) is to build a set of facts (a database) based on user input,

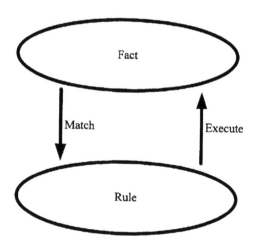

Figure 34.1   Inference-oriented techniques match facts to rules.

match the facts with the rules in the rule base, execute the appropriate rule to determine the solution, and continue the loop until the solution satisfies the goal.

34.4.1.1   Forward-chaining inference

Forward chaining is a data-oriented approach that searches the solution space from an initial state to a final goal state. Facts in the database are matched with rules in the rule base, the appropriate rule(s) are executed, and the resulting new fact(s) are added to the original database. This process continues until the desired solution (or goal) is reached.

For example, consider Figure 34.2. As the forward-chaining process begins (top left), facts F1, F2, F5, F6 are known. In the first step, F1 and F2 are matched to the rule base and, because F1 and F2 lead to (or imply) F7, F7 is added to the database. Next, F5 and F6 are matched to the rule base. F5 leads to F4, so F4 is added to the database, and F6 leads to F3, so F3 is added to the database. Next, F8 is added by using the results from the previous step and applying the rules F3 and F4 lead to F8. Finally, F9 is obtained by applying the rules F7 and F8 lead to F9.

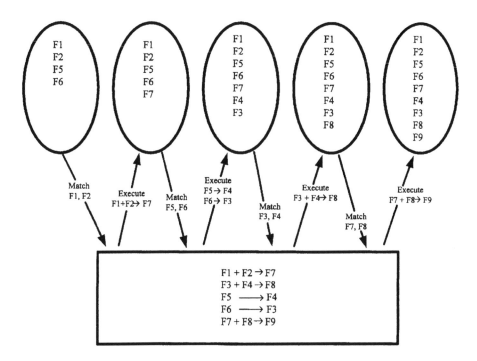

Figure 34.2   Forward chaining.

34.4.1.2 Backward-chaining inference

Backward chaining is a goal-oriented search technique that starts with the desired goal state and works backward to the initial state by applying the inverse operator.

For example, consider Figure 34.3. Once again, F1, F2, F5, F6 are known as the process begins (upper left). The desired goal state is F9. According to the rule base, F7 and F8 lead to F9, so F7 and F8 are needed. The next step focuses on F7. The rule says F1 and F2 lead to F7. F1 and F2 are already known, so F7 can be added to the database. F8 is needed next. The relevant rule is F3 and F4 lead to F8. Neither F3 nor F4 is known, so the rule base is checked for F3. The relevant rule is F6 leads to F3, and F6 is known, so F3 can be added to the database (lower left). The process continues until all the relevant facts are known.

34.4.2 Search-oriented techniques

Search-oriented techniques focus on systematically searching the solution space. Basically, the goals (the desired solutions) are identified, the initial state (the source point for starting the search) is defined, and the problem search space (a set of possible steps that lead to the completion of the goal) is determined.

34.4.2.1 Blind search

A depth-first blind search is a search process that considers successive nodes in the search space before considering alternatives at the same level. For example, in Figure 34.4, path A-B-E-F-C-G-H-D describes a depth-first search.

In contrast, a breadth-first blind search considers alternatives at the same level first and then works down the hierarchy level by level until all the nodes are exhausted. In Figure 34.4, path A-B-C-D-E-F-G-H describes a breadth-first search. Generally, a depth-first search travels deeply into the search tree and a breadth-first search descends uniformly across all nodes at the same level.

Forward chaining, backward chaining, and bi-directional blind searches are possible. The bi-directional approach is a combination of forward chaining and backward chaining, with searches conducted concurrently from both ends (the initial state and the goal state) of the search space and meeting somewhere in the middle.

Blind search techniques are time consuming and require considerable memory or storage space. Blind search is not practical for large problems because too many nodes must be visited before a solution is found. Writing the code to implement a blind search is difficult because the logic calls for complex, multiple-level logical structures.

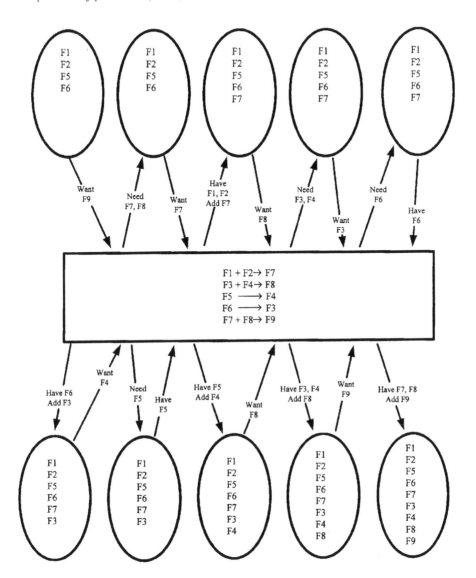

Figure 34.3 Backward chaining.

34.4.2.2 Heuristic search

Blind searches are orderly search approaches that assure a given solution path is followed no more than once. For many applications, it is possible to use specific problem-related information and rules of thumb (heuristic information) to focus the search process on the most likely branches. The process of using heuristics is called heuristic search.

For example, consider the problem of finding a route from Cincinnati, Ohio to Washington, D.C. An appropriate heuristic rule is "head for the

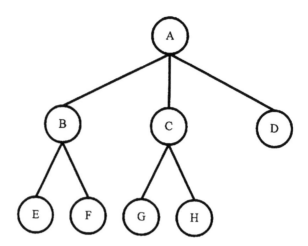

Figure 34.4   A solution space to illustrate blind search techniques.

rising sun" because Washington is east of Cincinnati. By applying this heuristic, all alternative paths that head north, south, or west are disregarded.

34.4.2.3   Abstracting the solution space

The basic idea of abstracting the solution space is to make the heuristic search process faster and more efficient by focusing on a relatively small feasible solution space. This technique reduces complexity, provides a clearer and simpler picture of the problem, and makes it easier to represent the problem in the rule base. Often, the original problem is broken into smaller problems by applying heuristic principles to generate intermediate levels of abstraction.

For example, consider the problem of finding the shortest route from Cincinnati, Ohio to Los Angeles, California. The solution space can be visualized as a search process that starts at Cincinnati, follows each local street in turn, and enumerates paths from town to town until the fastest route to Los Angeles is found.

The problem is that there are thousand of towns between Cincinnati and Los Angeles, each of which has many streets and roads, so the search space is huge. Such heuristic rules as "head south and west" can help reduce the search space to perhaps one-fourth its original size, but even that reduced space is much too large. Instead, the driver is likely to ignore the detailed street maps of all the intermediate towns and start with a map of the interstate highway system. Using such an abstracted map of the search space provides an efficient solution to the problem.

34.4.3 Reasoning-oriented techniques

Reasoning-oriented problem-solving techniques focus on accumulating information until a solution is reached. Dependable data or knowledge (hard facts) and unreliable data or guesses (soft facts) are both used to support reasoning. The basic idea is to continuously draw conclusions (based on data and common sense knowledge) until the desired solution is reached.

Reasoning-oriented problem solving techniques have tremendous potential in information systems analysis and design. The difficulties include locating the pertinent common-sense knowledge, measuring the accuracy of that common-sense knowledge, representing and interpreting the common-sense knowledge correctly and accurately, and verifying the justifications inferred by the reasoning process.

34.4.3.1 Assumption building

Information system researchers have discovered that common sense (which is virtually taken for granted in human beings) is extremely difficult to model. Common sense is, however, essential to the reasoning process. Real-world decision makers often must act immediately despite a lack of facts, knowledge, experience, supporting evidence, and time. Under these conditions, the decision maker must draw conclusions from partial information by applying common sense. Generally, common-sense reasoning requires that a system be capable of revising its beliefs in light of new knowledge it receives or derives.

Clearly, people are willing to accept plausible conclusions for which they have no proof.[2] For example, an automobile traveler is likely to check the gasoline, the battery, and the tire pressure before taking a trip. During the trip, the traveler will probably glance at the fuel gauge frequently, but is unlikely to recheck the battery and the tire pressure. Why? Because a shortage of gasoline is a plausible risk, but the battery seldom malfunctions without warning and the tire pressure is almost certainly within acceptable limits unless the car begins handling erratically. The assumptions that underlie this brief scenario were built or derived from common sense and certain contingent conditions.

34.4.3.2 Justification building

Before a problem solver revises a belief in response to new knowledge, he or she must reason, weighing dependable variables against a current set of beliefs. One common reasoning technique is called backtracking.[3] Backtracking means reviewing or checking what has already been done in an attempt to find another path or another way to accomplish the goal(s). For example, when a search fails, the system might track back through all actions and inferences since the most recent choice point and then continue with the next alternative for that choice.

One way to justify a reasoning process is to apply formal logic. For example, suppose a reasoning system has the following two beliefs:

A. Rain is likely if the dew point is higher than the air temperature.
B. Rain becomes snow if the air temperature is low.

Given these two beliefs and applying the basic rules of logic, it is reasonable to infer that:

C. Snow is likely if the dew point is higher than the air temperature and the air temperature is low.

In this case, the result (belief C) is supported by beliefs A and B, and (logically) if A and B are both true, then C must be true. Backtracking might be used to check temperature readings or request additional weather information (such as air pressure and storm movement) to either reinforce belief C or generate new conclusions (frozen rain or sleet).

Note how the combination of assumptions (the beliefs) and justification (the logical reasoning process) combine to support the inference or reasoning process. Both assumptions and justifications are necessary.

34.5   Key terms

Backtracking — Reviewing or checking what has already been done and attempting to find another path or another way to accomplish the goal(s).

Backward chaining — A goal-oriented search technique that starts with the desired goal state and works backward to the initial state by applying the inverse operator.

Blind search — A search technique that visits every node in the search space while following a given solution path no more than once.

Breadth search — A blind searching technique that investigates all the nodes at a given level before moving down to the next level.

Depth search — A blind searching technique that investigates all lower-level nodes before considering the next node at the same level.

Expert system (knowledge-based system) — A computer program that emulates the thought process of a human expert.

Forward chaining — A data-oriented approach that searches the solution space from an initial state to a final goal state.

Goal — An objective.

Heuristic rule — A specific rule of thumb or common sense that can be used to restrict a search to a subset of a problem domain.

Heuristic search — A search technique that applies heuristics to reduce the size of a search space.

Heuristics — General rules derived from experience, common sense, inferences, and intelligent trial and error.

Inference — The act or process of deriving logical conclusions from premises known or assumed to be true.

Inverse operator — An operator that works backward from the solution and facts to return to the original state.

Justification — Proofs, facts, or reasons/rationales for assumptions.

Knowledge — The sum or range of what has been perceived, discovered, or learned; specific information about something.

Knowledge base — A collection of data, algorithms, and heuristic rules that forms the core of an expert system.

Problem domain — A collection of all types of knowledge (including common sense and informed guesses), facts, and/or data related to a defined problem.

Reasoning — The act of using inference to lead to a conclusion based on existing knowledge and/or data.

Rule — A formal specification or description of a unit of knowledge.

Rule base — A collection of executable rules.

Search space (problem search space) — In a search-oriented problem-solving technique, a domain with all possible sets of steps and/or alternatives to support comprehensive searching for the completion of a goal or goals.

Solution space — A mathematical term for the set of all possible solutions. Solution space is a special type of search space. A desired solution can be obtained by searching all possible problem-solving alternatives in the space.

34.6 Software

Auto-intelligence 1.26, Level 5 supports backward chaining. OPS83 and ART-IM support forward chaining. Advisor-2, Crystal, ESP advisor, EXSYS Professional KnowledgePro, Level 5 Object, and Nexpert Object support both techniques.

34.7 References

1. Awad, E. M., *Building Expert Systems: Principles, Procedures, and Applications*, West Publishing, Minneapolis/St. Paul, MN, 1996.
2. Harmon, P. and King, D., *Expert Systems: Artificial Intelligence in Business*, John Wiley & Sons, New York, 1985.
3. Hayes-Roth, F., Waterman, D., and Lenat, D., *Building Expert Systems*, Addison-Wesley, Reading, MA, 1983.
4. Waterman D., *A Guide to Expert Systems*, Addison-Wesley, Reading, MA, 1986.

chapter thirty-five

The requirements specification

William S. Davis

Contents

0-8493-7001-9/99/$0.00+$.50
©1999 by CRC Press LLC

35.1   Purpose

The requirements specification is a document that clearly and precisely defines the customer's logical requirements (or needs) in such a way that it is possible to test the finished system to verify that those needs have actually been met. The point is to ensure that the customer's needs are correctly defined before time, money, and resources are wasted working on the wrong solution. Typically, writing a formal requirements specification is the final step in the analysis phase of the system development life cycle.

35.2   Strengths, weaknesses, and limitations

The logical models and prototypes prepared during analysis are often less than adequate as a foundation for system design. The requirements specification builds on the logical models, providing an unambiguous, precise definition of the user's needs. If work is outsourced or subcontracted, the requirements specification can be added to the contract to define the deliverables.

Although a few pages might be enough to define a simple system's requirements, a complete requirements specification for a significant system can be quite lengthy, and preparing one is both time consuming and expensive. Requirements can change over time, and the requirements specification must be flexible enough to change with them. Often, this is not the case.

35.3   Inputs and related ideas

Writing a formal requirements specification is the final step in the analysis phase of the system development life cycle (Part IV). The system requirements are typically verified against the goals and objectives identified during the problem definition and information gathering process (Part II). The requirements are the basis for the subsequent design stage (Part VI) and suggest test criteria (Chapter 74) and test data (Chapter 75). The sample requirements in this chapter correspond to specification levels defined in the U.S. Department of Defense competitive procurement process (Chapter 41).

35.4   Concepts

A requirement is something that must be present in the system. The requirements specification is a document that clearly and precisely defines the customer's logical requirements (or needs) in such a way that it is possible to test the finished system to verify that those needs have actually been met. The point is to ensure that the customer's needs are correctly defined before time, money, and resources are wasted working on the wrong solution.

35.4.1 Types of requirements

A behavioral requirement defines something the system does, such as an input, an output, or an algorithm. Under this category, a functional requirement identifies a task that the system or component must perform, and an interface requirement identifies a link to another system component.

Non-behavioral requirements define attributes of the system. For example, performance requirements specify such characteristics as speed, frequency, response time, accuracy, and precision. Other non-behavioral requirements might define such parameters as portability, reliability, security, and maintainability.

Such constraints as physical size and weight, environmental factors, ergonomic standards, and the like are listed in design requirements or constraint requirements. Quality requirements, often stated as an acceptable error rate, the mean time between failures, or the mean time to repair, are sometimes grouped with performance requirements, but many organizations list them separately. Firms that have adopted total quality management often include additional measures of quality.

Economic requirements specify such things as performance penalties, limits on development and operating costs, the implementation schedule, and resource restrictions. They are more common in Europe than in the United States. Occasionally, marketing and political requirements are added.

35.4.2 Characteristics of a good requirement

A good requirement is unambiguous, testable (or verifiable), consistent with other requirements, correct (every listed requirement must actually *be* a requirement), understandable, modifiable (requirements can change), and traceable to both higher-level (parent) and lower-level (child) requirements.

35.4.3 Writing requirements

The examples shown below illustrate the types of requirements that might be written at three key specification levels. Note that the data dictionary and (perhaps) one or more logical models are often included in the requirements specification as an appendix to provide clear definitions for the data elements, data structures, processes, and algorithms.

35.4.3.1 The high-level system/segment specifications

The high-level system/segment specifications identify the system and its major segments at a conceptual level. Typically they define key terms and identify broad, system-wide objectives and constraints down to the configuration item level. They are logical, describing what the system must do, not how the system must work.

For example, imagine that the objective for an inventory system (as defined during the problem definition phase) is:

> *To reduce inventory cost by 10 percent by providing accurate, daily inventory status data to support reorder and sale item decisions.*

What exactly does it mean to *reduce inventory cost by 10 percent?* Ten percent of what? What exactly does *providing accurate, daily inventory status data* mean? How accurate must the data be? What data must be provided? The point of the system/segment specifications is to answer precisely these kinds of questions.

Table 35.1 shows a (partial) set of high-level system/segment specifications for the objective listed above. Note that subspecifications (not shown) are used to provide additional details. For example, the supervisory-level managers responsible for making reorder and sale item decisions will almost certainly be listed under specification 2.1. A well-written set of system/segment specifications leaves no unanswered logical questions.

Table 35.1   High-Level System/Segment Specifications

The system must:

1. Reduce inventory cost by 10 percent.

   1.1 The 10 percent target represents a reduction from inventory levels as determined by the physical inventory completed on March 30, 1999.

   1.2 A unique item in inventory is defined by a UPC code or by the item's manufacturer code plus its model code.

   1.3 Stock-on-hand is defined for each item in inventory as the sum of the number of units in the warehouse plus the number of units on the showroom floor.

   1.4 Inventory cost is computed by multiplying the stock-on-hand by the supplier invoice cost for each item in inventory and then adding those products.

   1.5 . . .

2. Provide accurate, daily inventory status data.

   2.1 Inventory status reports must be available to the appropriate supervisory-level managers no later than 7:30 a.m. on each working day.

   2.2 A given day's inventory status report shall reflect the status of inventory as of 12 midnight on the previous day.

   2.3 For each item in inventory (1.2), the inventory status report will list the item's unique identifier, description, stock-on-hand (1.3), the number of units in the warehouse, and the number of units on the showroom floor.

   2.4 . . .

And so on.

35.4.3.2   *The lower-level system/segment specifications*

The system/segment specifications form a hierarchy that logically defines the system from the high-level objectives down to the configuration item level. At the bottom of this hierarchy, one system/segment design document is prepared for each configuration item.

For example, Table 35.2 shows several logical requirements for a configuration item named reorder stock. Note that the requirements are logical; they specify what must be done but they do not specify or suggest a physical implementation. Note also that the requirements are *not* independent. For example, it might be possible for a team of three or four clerks to manually generate up to 50 reorders per week, including up to five emergency reorders per day, but only if all those clerks and all their equipment can fit into a relatively small room. If a given solution violates any single requirement, that solution is unacceptable.

35.4.3.3   *The system/segment design documents*

A low-level system/segment specification (Table 35.2) lists requirements that help the analyst decide if the procedure should be performed manually or on a computer. Once that decision has been made, system/segment design documents specify the high-level requirements for each physical component implied by the decision.

For example, if the analyst decides to implement the reorder stock process on a computer, both hardware and software are required. One system/segment design document (Table 35.3) identifies the high-level requirements for writing the software but not for selecting the hardware. A

Table 35.2   System/Segment Specifications for a Configuration
Item Level Process Named *Reorder Stock*

2.1.1 The system must support the store manager's stock reorder decisions.

1. Reorder decisions are made by the store manager based on sales and inventory data.
2. All reorders identified during a business week must be ready to send to the supplier no later than 3:00 p.m. on the last business day of that week.
3. The system must be able to prepare an emergency reorder ready to send to a supplier within 1 h of the time the need is identified.
4. The system must be able to generate at least 50 reorders per week, including emergency reorders.
5. The system must be able to generate as many as five emergency reorders on any given business day.
6. The space available for performing the reorder stock process is limited to a 6 × 8 ft room.

Table 35.3 Some Examples of System/Segment Functional Requirements

2.1.1.1 A program will be written to support the store manager's stock reorder decisions.

1. To minimize the risk of redundant reorders, the system must track reorders that have been issued, but have not yet arrived.
2. The store manager must approve all reorders before they are sent to the supplier.
3. The store manager must be able to modify the supplier name, the reorder quantity, or any other reorder parameters before approving the reorder.
4. Reorders must be prepared using the parent chain's standard reorder form.

separate system/segment design document identifies requirements that are relevant to selecting the hardware but not to writing the software.

System/segment design documents are prepared for each physical component at (or immediately below) the configuration item level. They define black-box level requirements. For example, a system/segment design document might be prepared for a program, but the routines that make up the program are below the configuration item level and thus are not defined in a system/segment design document.

35.4.3.4 The software requirement and prime item development specifications

The high-level design requirements associated with each system/segment design document are defined in prime item development specifications (hardware) or software requirements specifications (software). They define *how* the solution will be implemented. For example, the software requirements specification for a reorder program might specify key algorithms, file formats, input and output data structures, a programming language, a database management system, or a high-level control structure. In short, the software requirements specification contains enough information for a programmer to start writing the program or for an analyst to select the appropriate commercial software.

35.4.3.5 The flowdown principle

Within the requirements specification, the flowdown principle states that each lower level requirement must be linked to a single higher level parent. Note that parent requirements can be distributed downward to several different children, but each child requirement can have only one parent. Tracing requirements is a form of verification.

35.5 Key terms

Behavioral requirement — A requirement that defines something the system does, such as an input, an output, or an algorithm.

Black box — A routine, module, or component whose inputs and outputs are known, but whose contents are hidden.

Child — A related, lower-level requirement.

Configuration item — A composite entity that decomposes into specific hardware and software components; in a data flow diagram, a functional primitive that appears at the lowest level of decomposition.

Configuration item level — An imaginary line that links the system's configuration items; a system's physical components lie just below the configuration item level.

Design or constraint requirement — A requirement that specifies such constraints as physical size and weight, environmental factors, ergonomic standards, and the like.

Economic requirement — A requirement that specifies such things as performance penalties, limits on development and operating costs, the implementation schedule, and resource restrictions.

Flowdown — A principle that requires each lower-level requirement to be linked to a single higher-level parent.

Functional primitive — A process (or transform) that requires no further decomposition.

Functional requirement — A requirement that identifies a task that the system or component must perform.

Interface requirement — A requirement that identifies a link to another system component.

Non-behavioral requirement — A requirement that defines an attribute of the system, such as speed, frequency, response time, accuracy, precision, portability, reliability, security, or maintainability.

Parent — A related, higher-level requirement.

Performance requirement — A requirement that specifies such characteristics as speed, frequency, response time, accuracy, precision, portability, reliability, security, and maintainability.

Prime item development specification — A set of high-level design requirements associated with each hardware component defined in (or implied by) a parent system/segment design document.

Quality requirement — A requirement that specifies a measure of quality, such as an acceptable error rate, the mean time between failures, or the mean time to repair.

Requirement — Something that must be present in the system; a user need.

Requirements specification — A document that clearly and precisely defines the customer's logical requirements (or needs) in such a way that it is possible to test the finished system to verify that those needs have actually been met.

Software requirements specification — A set of high-level design requirements associated with each software component defined in (or implied by) a parent system/segment design document.

System/segment design document — A black-box specification defined for each physical component at (or directly below) the configuration item level.

System/segment specifications — A hierarchy of requirements specifications that logically defines the system from its high-level objectives down to the configuration item level.

35.6   Software

The information stored in the CASE repository is an invaluable aid to creating a requirements specification. Functional and performance requirements can often be taken directly from the repository, and logical models suggest interface requirements. Perhaps most important is the ability of the CASE software to trace requirements and thus automate flowdown.

35.7   References

1. Davis, A. M., *Software Requirements: Analysis and Specification,* Prentice-Hall, Englewood Cliffs, NJ, 1990.
2. Gause, D. C. and Weinberg, G. M., *Exploring Requirements: Quality Before Design,* Dorset House, New York, 1989.
3. Martin, C. F., *User-Centered Requirements Analysis,* Prentice-Hall, Englewood Cliffs, NJ, 1988.
4. Thayer, R. H. and Dorfman, M., *System and Software Requirements Engineering,* IEEE Computer Society Press, Los Alamitos, CA, 1990.
5. **Anon.,** *Military Standard, Defense System Software Development,* (DoD-STD-2167A), U.S. Department of Defense, Washington, D.C.

part five

Identifying alternatives

chapter thirty-six

Automation boundaries

William S. Davis

Contents

36.1   Purpose

Defining automation boundaries is a technique for generating alternative, high-level, physical system designs.

36.2   Strengths, weaknesses, and limitations

Because the automation boundary technique builds on the logical models developed during the analysis stage, the suggested alternatives are likely to be logically consistent. A single set of automation boundaries defines a family of related alternatives, so this technique can be used to identify numerous options (which can be viewed both as an advantage and a disadvantage). Using automation boundaries to identify alternatives requires expertise in data flow diagrams.

36.3   Inputs and related ideas

The techniques described in this chapter require a complete logical model consisting of a set of balanced data flow diagrams and supporting documentation (Chapter 24). Additionally, various system parameters identified during the problem definition and information gathering stage (Part II) and the analysis stage (Part IV) and documented in the requirements specifications (Chapter 35) are used to help identify feasible alternatives. Typically, a few of the best alternatives are further documented using such tools as system flow diagrams (Chapter 37), and a cost/benefit analysis (Chapter 38) is performed for these options. The selected physical alternative forms the basis for component design (Part VI).

36.4   Concepts

A logical model consisting of a data flow diagram (Figure 36.1) and associated documentation (Chapter 24) is the starting point for generating alternatives using automation boundaries.

36.4.1   Trigger events

The trigger event is the event that activates the process. For example, in Table 36.1, *Process shipment* is triggered by the arrival of a shipment and the activities associated with *Sell appliance, Update appliance,* and *Reorder stock* are all triggered by a sales transaction. Because the manager will almost certainly need a week's summary of sales to make decisions on sale items, *Identify sale item* is a scheduled (batch) end-of-week activity, and so on.

36.4.2   Response time

Response time is the maximum allowable time to complete a process once the trigger event has occurred. For example, in Table 36.1, *Sell appliance* is an interactive task that must be completed while the customer is in the store, so its response time is measured in minutes. The other processes in this system can all be performed in batch mode, so their response time requirements are identified as end of day, end of week, and so on. Note that the *maximum* allowable response time is listed. For example, it would be perfectly acceptable to update inventory within minutes of a sales transaction, but it would *not* be acceptable to put off selling appliances until the end of the day.

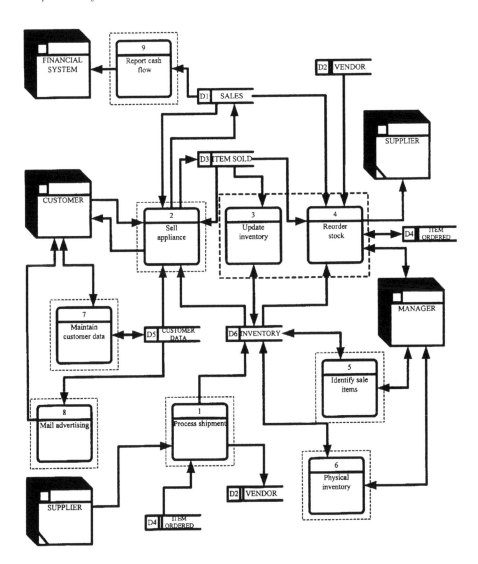

Figure 36.1 In this example, processes 3 and 4 are inside the same automation boundary. Note that the data flows are not labeled to more clearly show the automation boundaries.

36.4.3 Defining automation boundaries

Given the trigger events and response time requirements for each process, alternatives are generated by superimposing automation boundaries on the data flow diagram. An automation boundary is simply a line drawn around one or more processes. The idea is to group the processes enclosed by an automation boundary to form a single program or procedure. Note that a set of automation boundaries defines a family of alternative solutions.

Table 36.1 The Trigger Events and Response Time Requirements for Each of the Processes on the Data Flow Diagram Pictured in Figure 36.1

Process	Trigger event	Response time
1. Process shipment	Shipment arrival	End of day
2. Sell appliance	Sales transaction	Minutes
3. Update inventory	Sales transaction	End of day
4. Reorder stock	Sales transaction	End of week
5. Identify sale items	End of week	End of week
6. Physical inventory	End of quarter	End of quarter
7. Maintain customer	Sales transaction	End of day
8. Mail advertising	End of month	End of month
9. Report case flow	End of day	End of day

One possibility is to enclose each process within its own automation boundary. In this family of alternatives (not illustrated, but refer to Figure 36.1), each process is implemented as an independent program or procedure. A manual system might incorporate procedures to *Process shipment, Sell appliance, Update inventory,* and so on. A second alternative might include nine programs, one for each process. A third alternative might call for a *Process shipment* program, a *Sell appliance* manual procedure, programs to *Update inventory* and *Perform physical inventory,* and manual procedures to perform the other tasks. Additional alternatives might be suggested by studying the associated level 2 data flow diagrams.

Changing the automation boundaries yields a new family of alternatives. For example, Figure 36.1 includes an automation boundary that encloses processes 3 and 4. Because all the processes within a given boundary are implemented in a single physical component or set of components (e.g., a program and the computer on which it runs), the alternatives in this family contain a single program or procedure that performs all the functions associated with *Update inventory* and *Reorder stock.*

When two or more processes are merged, the shortest response time applies to the new process. For example, Table 36.1 shows that inventory must be updated *at least* daily and reorders must be issued *at least* weekly. Daily reorders are fine, but weekly inventory updates are unacceptable, so if processes 3 and 4 are merged, the resulting program or procedure must be executed at least daily.

Processes 2, 3, and 4 are all triggered by a sales transaction (Table 36.1), so it might make sense to define a new family of automation boundaries that groups them (Figure 36.2). One possible physical alternative within this family features a program to perform the functions associated with *Sell appliance, Update inventory,* and *Reorder stock.* Stock might be reordered weekly and inventory might be updated daily, but appliances are sold continuously as customers arrive. Because the tightest response time rules, the program would have to run continuously and respond to sales transactions in minutes. That, in turn, implies an on-line, interactive program.

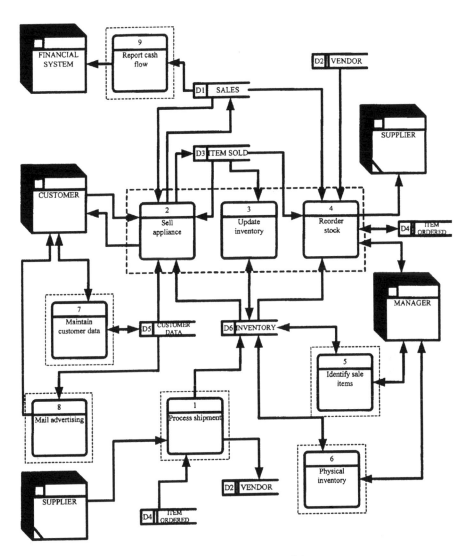

Figure 36.2 This example groups processes 2, 3, and 4.

36.4.4 A strategy

Follow a systematic procedure to generate alternatives. Start by drawing a separate automation boundary around each process. Then try grouping processes by drawing a boundary around 1 and 2, then 1 and 3, and so on. Next, try sets of two processes each; for example, group 1 and 2 within one automation boundary and 3 and 4 within another. Gradually, move up to groups of three, then groups of four, and so on, until every possible combination has been considered. The limit is a single automation boundary containing all the processes and suggesting (perhaps) an on-line, interactive program that does everything.

Another option is to focus on grouping processes that have the same response time requirement or trigger event or that share a common data store. Processes calling for similar response times can often be merged to form a single program or procedure. Processes that occur in response to the same trigger event can often be performed concurrently. Processes that manipulate the same data often belong together.

Given even a small data flow diagram, an amazing number of alternative solutions can be generated. Some, of course, will make no logical sense and thus can be eliminated quickly; for example, because physical inventory is performed quarterly, it would make no sense to combine processes *Sell appliance* and *Physical inventory*. The scope is another useful screen. If the cost of an alternative significantly exceeds the scope, that alternative is not economically feasible. The idea is to identify two or three reasonable alternatives that are worthy of further study.

36.5   Key terms

Automation boundary — A line drawn around one or more processes on a data flow diagram, thus grouping them to form a single program or procedure; a set of automation boundaries defines a family of alternative solutions.

Data flow diagram — A logical model of the flow of data through a system.

Level 1 data flow diagram — A data flow diagram that shows the system's primary processes, data stores, sources, and destinations linked by data flows.

Level 2 data flow diagram — An explosion of a level 1 process.

Response time — The maximum allowable time to complete a process once its trigger event has occurred.

Trigger event — The event that activates the process.

36.6   Software

Many CASE products include routines that allow a user to graphically define automation boundaries on a data flow diagram. The examples in this chapter were prepared using Visio.

36.7   References

1. Davis, W. S., *Business Systems Analysis and Design*, Wadsworth, Belmont, CA, 1994.
2. Gane, C. and Sarson, T., *Structured Systems Analysis: Tools and Techniques*, Prentice-Hall, Englewood Cliffs, NJ, 1979.

chapter thirty-seven

System flowcharts

William S. Davis

Contents

37.1 Purpose

A system flowchart is a concrete, physical model that documents, in an easily visualized, graphical form, the system's discrete physical components (its programs, procedures, files, reports, screens, etc.).

37.2 Strengths, weaknesses, and limitations

A system flowchart is a valuable presentation aid because it shows how the system's major components fit together and interact. In effect, it serves as a system roadmap. During the information gathering stage, a system flowchart is an excellent tool for summarizing a great deal of technical information about the existing system. A system flowchart can also be used to map a hardware system.

System flowcharts are valuable as project planning and project management aids. Using the system flowchart as a guide, discrete units of work (such as writing a program or installing a new printer) can be identified, cost estimated, and scheduled. On large projects, the components suggest how the work might be divided into subsystems.

Historically, some analysts used system flowcharts to help develop job control language specifications. For example, IBM's System/370 job control language requires an EXEC statement for each program and a DD statement for each device or file linked to each program. Consequently, each program symbol on the system flowchart represents an EXEC statement and each file or peripheral device symbol linked to a program by a flowline implies a need for one DD statement. Working backward, preparing a system flowchart from a JCL listing is good way to identify a program's linkages.

A system flowchart's symbols represent *physical* components, and the mere act of drawing one implies a physical decision. Consequently, system flowcharts are poor analysis tools because the appropriate time for making physical decisions is *after* analysis has been completed.

A system flowchart can be misleading. For example, an on-line storage symbol might represent a diskette, a hard disk, a CD-ROM, or some combination of secondary storage devices. Given such ambiguity, two experts looking at the same flowchart might reasonably envision two different physical systems. Consequently, the analyst's intent must be clearly documented in an attached set of notes.

37.3   Inputs and related ideas

The first step in drawing a system flowchart is to identify the system's physical components by using such tools as automation boundaries (Chapter 36). Some analysts prefer to use physical data flow diagrams (Chapter 24) to document physical alternatives. A completed system flowchart is sometimes used to support the project planning stage (Part III). During the design stage (Part VI), a system flowchart serves as a high-level map of the system.

37.4   Concepts

A system flowchart (or system flow diagram) is a concrete, physical model that documents, in an easily visualized, graphical form, the system's discrete physical components (its programs, procedures, files, reports, screens, etc.).

37.4.1   Flowcharting symbols and conventions

On a system flowchart, each component is represented by a symbol that visually suggests its function (Figure 37.1). The symbols are linked by

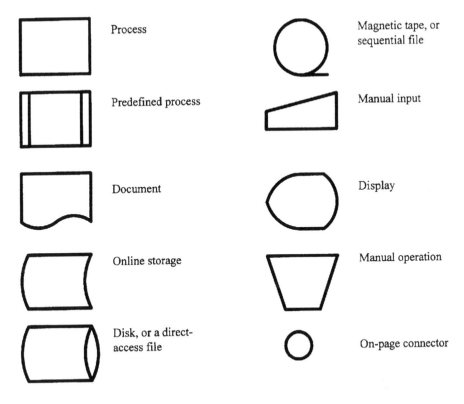

Figure 37.1   System flowcharting symbols.

flowlines. A given flowline might represent a data flow, a control flow, and/or a hardware interface. By convention, the direction of flow is from the top left to the bottom right, and arrowheads must be used when that convention is not followed. Arrowheads are recommended even when the convention is followed because they help to clarify the documentation.

The symbols in Figure 37.1 conform to the International Organization for Standards (ISO) recommendation R1028 and to the American National Standards Institute (ANSI) Standard X3.5-1970, but other symbols are used, too. A given organization might define a unique internal standard, and some analysts substitute icons (or clip art images of physical components) for the symbols.

37.4.2   Predefined processes

The flowchart for a complex system can be quite large. An off-page connector symbol (resembling a small home plate) can be used to continue the flowchart on a subsequent page, but multiple-page flowcharts are difficult to read. When faced with a complex system, a good approach is to draw a high-level flowchart showing key functions as predefined processes and

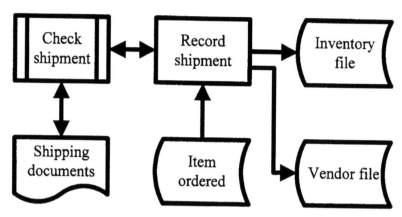

Figure 37.2 Use predefined processes to simplify a complex system flowchart.

then explode those predefined processes to the appropriate level on subsequent pages. Predefined processes are similar to subroutines.

For example, Figure 37.2 shows a system flowchart for processing a just-arrived shipment into inventory. Note that the shipment is checked (in a predefined process) against the *Shipping documents* (the printer symbol) and recorded (the rectangle) in both the *Inventory file* and the *Vendor file* using data from the *Item ordered* file.

Figure 37.3 is a flowchart of the predefined process named *Check shipment*. When a shipment arrives, it is inspected manually and either rejected or tentatively accepted. The appropriate data are then input via a keyboard/display unit to the *Record shipment* program (the link to Figure 37.2). Unless the program finds something wrong with the shipment, the newly arrived stock is released to the warehouse. If the shipment is rejected for any reason, the *Shipping documents* are marked and sent to the reorder process.

37.4.3   Flowcharting a system

Figure 37.4 shows one physical alternative for implementing an inventory system. At the top left, a *Sales receipt* is prepared as output from the *Sell appliance* predefined process. The data from the *Sales receipt* are then input to the *Inventory program*. Subsequently, a printed *Cash flow* report goes to the *Financial system*. Below the symbols that represent the system files are procedures to send advertising to customers, perform a physical inventory, process incoming shipments from suppliers, and reorder stock. Except for the predefined processes, each symbol represents one of the system's discrete components at a black-box level.

Figure 37.5 shows a different alternative for the inventory system. In this one, much of the system's logic is incorporated in a single *Manage inventory* program. Sales transactions, incoming shipments, and advertising still require manual procedures, but clerical personnel access the *Manage inventory* program to enter data and obtain information.

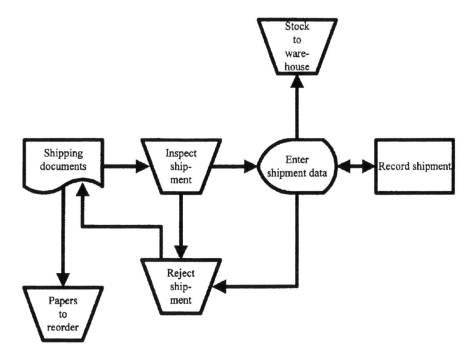

Figure 37.3 A system flowchart for the predefined process named *Check shipment.*

37.4.4 Supporting documentation

Note that each symbol on a system flowchart represents a discrete hardware component *and* either software or data. A process symbol (a rectangle) can represent a computer, a program, or both. An on-line storage symbol represents a disk drive, a file, or both. A printer symbol stands for a printer, a report, or both. A display screen represents a display unit, the data displayed on the screen, or both. A given flowline represents a hardware interface and a control or data flow. To further complicate matters, a given symbol might represent multiple components. For example, an on-line storage symbol might imply one or more hard disks, one or more CD-ROMs, or one or more diskettes.

Consequently, it is easy to misinterpret a system flowchart. Detailed notes are often attached to the diagram to clearly explain the creator's intent.

37.5 Key terms

Predefined process — On a system flowchart, a high-level process that is more fully documented in a separate, lower-level flowchart.

System flowchart — A tool for documenting a physical system in which each component is represented by a symbol that visually suggests its function.

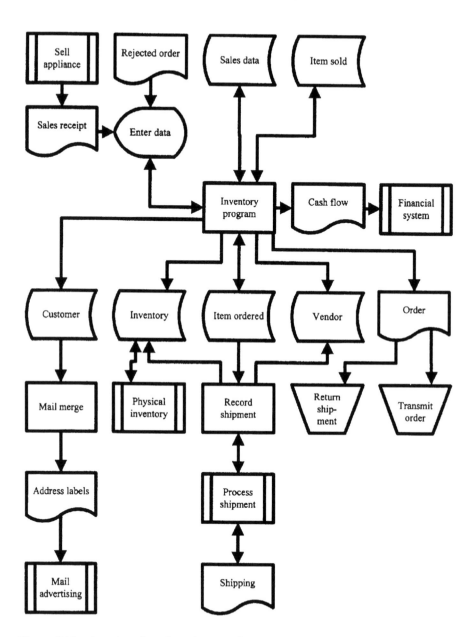

Figure 37.4   A system flowchart for one alternative inventory system.

37.6   *Software*

The system flowcharts in this chapter were prepared using Visio. Numerous flowcharting programs are available, including Micrografx's Flowcharter and allCLEAR from SPSS.

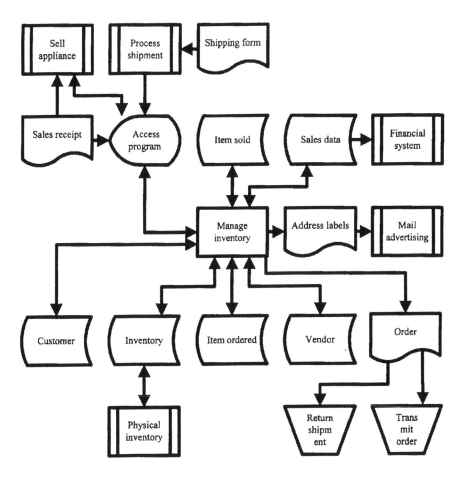

Figure 37.5 A second alternative inventory system.

37.7 References

1. Boillot, M. H., Gleason, and Horn, *Essentials of Flowcharting,* 4th ed., William C. Brown Company, Dubuque, IA, 1985.
2. Davis, W. S., *Business Systems Analysis and Design,* Wadsworth, Belmont, CA, 1994.
3. Gane, C. and Sarson, T., *Structured Systems Analysis: Tools and Techniques,* Prentice-Hall, Englewood Cliffs, NJ, 1979.
4. Gore, M. and Stubbe, *Elements of Systems Analysis,* 4th ed., William C. Brown Company, Dubuque, IA, 1988.
5. Weinberg, G. M. and Weinberg, D., *General Principles of System Design,* Dorset House, New York, 1988.

chapter thirty-eight

Cost/benefit analysis

William S. Davis

Contents

38.1 Purpose

Developing a system is a form of investment. The purpose of cost/benefit analysis is to give management a reasonable picture of the costs, benefits, and risks associated with a given system development project so they can compare it to other investment opportunities. Cost/benefit analysis is the de facto standard for demonstrating economic feasibility and for comparing and selecting among investment opportunities.

0-8493-7001-9/99/$0.00+$.50
©1999 by CRC Press LLC

38.2   Strengths, weaknesses, and limitations

The values generated by cost/benefit analysis resemble standard accounting and financial measures. Consequently, they are meaningful to management and non-technical personnel, and can be used to compare a system
development project to other types of investment opportunities.

The accuracy of a cost/benefit analysis can be no better than the accuracy of the underlying cost and benefit estimates. The standard cost/benefit
models consider only tangible benefits. Using the tools described in this
chapter to compare investment opportunities of substantially different
duration can yield misleading results.

38.3   Inputs and related ideas

Before performing a cost/benefit analysis, the analyst must generate or
otherwise obtain estimates of system development costs, tangible benefits
by time period, and operating costs by time period. The discount rate varies
from organization to organization and from time to time. It might reflect the
prime rate, a business concern's typical profit rate, and/or perceived risk.
Additionally, many organizations specify a standard system or project life;
five years is common.

Cost/benefit analysis is the de facto standard for demonstrating
economic feasibility in a feasibility study (Chapter 13) and is an important
element in project planning and project management (Part III).

38.4   Concepts

The purpose of cost/benefit analysis is to give management a reasonable
picture of the costs, benefits, and risks associated with a given system
development project so they can compare it to other investment opportunities. Cost/benefit analysis is the de facto standard for demonstrating economic feasibility and for comparing and selecting among investment
opportunities.

38.4.1   Costs and benefits

An investment opportunity represents a string of cash flows that occur over
time. Development costs are one-time costs that occur before the system is
released to the user. They include the personnel, hardware, and software
costs accumulated from the time the project is initially approved until the
system is released to the user. Benefits are advantages generated by or
derived from the system after it is released. Some systems reduce operating
costs. Others generate new revenues. The net benefit for any given time
period is computed by subtracting the new costs associated with achieving
the benefits from the related cost savings or new revenues.

38.4.2   *Discounting*

Because money has time value, the best way to compare cash flows that occur at different times is to convert all those cash flows to their present values. Most cost/benefit models assume that interest is compounded. The future value (*FV*) of a sum of money invested today (the present value, or *PV*) at a fixed interest rate (*i*) for a known number of time periods (*n*) is:

$$FV = PV(1+i)^n. \tag{38.1}$$

To compute the present value of a future sum of money, solve that equation for the present value:

$$PV = FV/(1+i)^n. \tag{38.2}$$

Computing the present value of a future sum of money is called discounting. The interest rate is called the discount rate.

When performing interest computations, unless otherwise stated always assume that the interest rate is expressed in annual terms. Also, make sure the interest rate and the time period are consistent. For example, if time is measured in months, divide the annual interest rate by 12 to get the equivalent monthly interest rate.

38.4.3   *Payback period*

The payback period is a measure of the time it takes for accumulated benefits to exactly match the development cost. The process of computing the payback period is best shown by example.

In the Excel worksheet reproduced as Figure 38.1, the development cost ($100,000) is shown as a negative cash flow occurring at time zero and a series of annual benefits are shown as positive cash flows. The discount rate is 5 percent.

To compute the payback period, discount the benefits to their present values, compute cumulative discounted costs and benefits, and determine when accumulated benefits exceed the development cost (or when the cumulative cash flow becomes positive). (*Note:* Some organizations compute the payback period without discounting costs or benefits.) In this example, accumulated cash flows total $14,163 at the end of year 4, so payback occurs sometime during year 4.

To compute the point at which the accumulated benefits exactly match development costs, extrapolate. At the end of year 3, accumulated cash flows were $18,745 short of $100,000. During year 4, discounted benefits totaled $32,908. Divide: (18,745)/(32,908) is 0.57, or 57 percent. Payback occurs at a time 57 percent into year 4, so the payback period is 3.57 y.

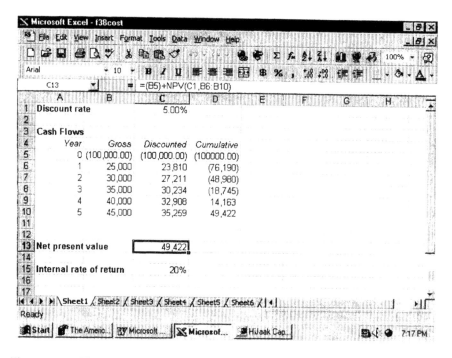

Figure 38.1   This Excel worksheet illustrates payback period and net present value.

38.4.4   *Net present value*

Generally, system development costs (*C*) are assumed to occur at time zero
(0). Annual benefits ($B_1, B_2, B_3, \ldots$) are assumed to occur at the end of year
1, year 2, year 3, and so on, throughout the system's life. To compute the net
present value (*NPV*), those benefits are discounted back to their present
values and added to the development cost (a negative cash flow):

$$NPV = -C + [B_1/(1+i)^1] + [B_2/(1+i)^2] + \ldots + [B_n/(1+i)^n], \quad (38.3)$$

where *n* is the system's life (the last period) and *i* is the discount rate. Note
that the accumulated totals used to illustrate the payback period in Figure
38.1 are equivalent to the net present value at the end of each year.

Most popular spreadsheet programs contain built-in functions to compute net present value. For example, the general form of Excel's net present
value (*NPV*) function is:

=NPV(rate, value1, value2, . . .)

where *rate* is the discount rate and *value1, value2, . . .* represent a series of
future cash flows (negative payments and positive incomes). Note that the
first cash flow (*value1*) occurs one time period from the present, the second
cash flow (*value2*) occurs two time periods from the present, and so on. Note

also that because the first cash flow in the function occurs at time 1, any current (time 0) cash flows must be added to (or subtracted from) the value returned by the NPV function.

In Figure 38.1, the development cost ($100,000) is shown as a negative cash flow occurring at time 0 and a series of annual benefits are shown as positive cash flows. The discount rate is 5 percent.

Look carefully at the formula in the formula bar (just above the column identifiers near the top of Figure 38.1). It reads:

=(B5)+NPV(C1,B6:B10)

B5 is the development cost ($100,000); it is a cash outflow and thus is recorded as a negative number. NPV is the Excel function name. C1 is the discount rate. B6:B10 (B6 to B10) is the range that holds the benefits. Note (in cell C13) that the computed net present value is $49,422, which matches the value in cell D10.

38.4.5   The internal rate of return

Generally, the higher the net present value the better the investment, but comparing the NPVs of projects with significantly different magnitudes can be misleading. Consequently, many organizations use the internal rate of return to rank their investment opportunities.

To compute the internal rate of return (IRR), start with the net present value equation (38.3) and set NPV = 0:

$$0 = -C + [B_1/(1+i)^1] + [B_2/(1+i)^2] + \quad . . . \quad + [B_n/(1+i)^n]. \qquad (38.4)$$

The initial investment cost (C) and the future benefits (B_1, B_2, B_3, . . .) are known. Solve for the internal rate of return (i), the interest rate that yields a zero net present value. Generally, the higher the internal rate of return, the better the investment.

Most popular spreadsheet programs contain built-in functions to compute the internal rate of return. For example, the general form of Excel's internal rate of return (IRR) function is:

=IRR(values,guess)

where *values* is a series of cash flows and *guess* is an initial estimate of the internal rate of return. The list of values must include at least one negative cash flow and at least one positive cash flow. If the initial guess is not coded, 0.1 is assumed.

In Figure 38.2, the development cost ($100,000) is shown as a negative cash flow occurring at time 0 and a series of annual benefits are shown as positive cash flows. The discount rate is 5 percent.

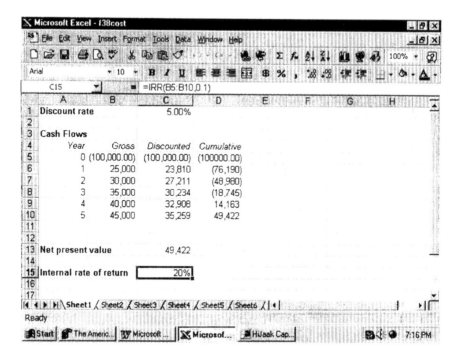

Figure 38.2   This Excel worksheet illustrates internal rate of return.

Look carefully at the formula on the formula bar (just above the column identifiers near the top of Figure 38.2). It reads:

=IRR(B5:B10,0.1)

The range B5:B10 (B5 to B10) holds the series of cash flows. The first cash flow (the negative value in cell B5) is assumed to occur at time 0. The value 0.1 is an initial guess. The computed internal rate of return (cell C15) is 20 percent.

Polynomials such as the formula for computing the internal rate of return have one possible solution for each sign change. If the string of benefits contains one or more negative values in addition to the development cost, the built-in function might return an incorrect answer.

38.5   Key terms

Benefits — Advantages generated by or derived from the system.

Development costs — One-time costs that occur before the system is released to the user; they include the labor, hardware, and software costs accumulated from the time the project is initially approved until the system is released to the user.

Discount rate — The interest rate used to discount a sum of money.

Discounting — The act of computing the present value of a future sum of money.

Future value — The value of a sum of money at some future time.

Intangible benefits — Benefits that cannot be measured in financial terms, such as improved morale or employee safety.

Interest rate — A charge for a loan or a payment for the use of money; usually expressed as a percentage.

Internal rate of return — The interest rate that yields a zero net present value.

Life — The number of time periods (usually years) during which the system is expected to be in use.

Net benefit — Cost savings or new revenues minus the new cost associated with achieving the benefit.

Net present value — The sum of discounted benefits minus the development costs.

Operating costs — Continuing costs that begin after the system is released and last for the life of the system; they include personnel, supplies, maintenance, utilities, insurance, and similar costs.

Payback period — A measure of the time it takes for accumulated benefits to exactly match the development costs.

Present value — The value of a (current or future) sum of money in today's dollars.

Risk — The likelihood that an investment will fail to return the expected benefits.

Tangible benefits — Benefits that can be measured in financial terms, such as reduced operating costs or enhanced revenues.

38.6   Software

The standard cost/benefit criteria are incorporated in most spreadsheet programs as built-in functions. In Excel, the net present value function is = NPV and the internal rate of return function is = IRR. In Lotus 1-2-3, the net present value function is @NPV and the internal rate of return function is @IRR.

38.7   References

1. Boehm, B.W., *Software Engineering Economics*, Prentice-Hall, Englewood Cliffs, New Jersey, 1981.
2. Davis, W. S., *Business Systems Analysis and Design*, Wadsworth, Belmont, CA, 1994.

chapter thirty-nine

Risk-payoff analysis

David C. Yen and William S. Davis

Contents

39.1 Purpose

An organization is often faced with numerous information system development opportunities and inadequate funds to pay for them all. Risk-payoff analysis is widely used to evaluate and prioritize information system projects based on their relative risks (and uncertainties) and their potential payoffs.

39.2 Strengths, weaknesses, and limitations

Risk-payoff analysis is a useful tool for screening out projects that are associated with large risks or uncertainties, thus saving resources for more promising projects. Intangible risks and payoffs are very difficult to quantify, however, and other tools and techniques such as cost/benefit analysis (Chapter 38) must still be used.

39.3   Inputs and related ideas

Before performing a risk-payoff analysis, a given project must be understood in enough depth to reasonably estimate its likely risks, uncertainties, and payoffs. Generally, such estimates cannot be made until near the end of the problem definition stage (Part II), and estimates made after the analysis stage (Part IV) is concluded are likely to be much more accurate. In some organizations, risk-payoff analysis is performed when the feasibility study reports (Chapter 13) for proposed projects are evaluated by a steering committee.

39.4   Concepts

Risk-payoff analysis is widely used to evaluate and prioritize information system projects based on their relative risks (and uncertainties) and their potential payoffs.

39.4.1   Risk and uncertainty

Every information systems project is associated with risk, uncertainty, or both. Risks are possible negative outcomes that can be interpreted, estimated, or quantified by applying past experience. Uncertainties are possible negative outcomes that cannot be interpreted or estimated based on experience because they never happened before. In the discussion that follows, the term risk implies risk, uncertainty, or both. Note, however, that risk-payoff analysis requires that all parameters, including uncertainty, be defined and documented in an easily quantifiable form.

Technological change is perhaps the most obvious risk associated with developing an information system, but there are many others. User or technical personnel might be under-trained, inadequately skilled, or not sufficiently computer literate. A project might be unexpectedly delayed or a given phase might be rushed in an effort to stay on schedule. The need to deal with side issues might slow progress. Poor user or data requirements analysis or incomplete data collection during the problem definition or analysis stages might cause delays during design. Inadequate testing or poor implementation procedures can negatively impact training, maintenance, or user acceptance of the system. The list is endless.

39.4.2   Quantifying risks, uncertainties, and payoffs

The first step in the risk-payoff analysis process is to investigate the possible risks associated with each project and categorize them as tangible or intangible.

The midpoint value associated with each tangible risk is estimated based on such quantifiable parameters as cost, time, resource requirements (people, computers, etc.), and experience. The midpoint is determined by selecting a middle or average value from a range of reasonable estimates. For example, if the cost of a delayed shipment is estimated to lie between $50,000 and 150,000, the midpoint is $100,000.

The midpoint for each intangible risk is estimated using subjective or objective judgment. Often, the informed opinions of several experts are combined to form a range of reasonable values from which the midpoint is selected. The risks (tangible and intangible) associated with a given project are then summed to get a project total.

Quantifying risk is difficult (at best). An analyst might consider such factors as expected failure or error rates, the average elapsed time for new versions of relevant technology to reach the market, estimates of the completeness or quality of significant software, and typical or baseline values associated with a given methodology (e.g., object-oriented, structured) or operating concept (e.g., batch, client-server). Even given such factors, however, there is no way to perfectly quantify risk. Reasonable (or ballpark) estimates can usually be generated, however.

Given estimates of risk, the possible payoffs associated with each project are identified and categorized as tangible or intangible. Once again, the midpoints for each tangible payoff are estimated using quantifiable parameters, the midpoints for the intangible payoffs are estimated using judgment, and the tangible and intangible values are summed.

39.4.3   The risk-payoff matrix

The final step is to construct a risk-payoff matrix (Figure 39.1), with risk on the *x*-axis and payoff on the *y*-axis. The risk and payoff midpoints previously computed for each project are then used as *x* and *y* coordinates to position each project on the matrix.

On the matrix, the average payoff (for all projects) defines a line marking the horizontal midpoint and the average risk defines a line marking the vertical midpoint. Together, those two lines divide the matrix into four quadrants. Area 1 (top right) is the high payoff, high risk quadrant. Area 2 (bottom right) is low payoff and high risk. Area 3 (top left) is high payoff and low risk. Area 4 (bottom left) is low payoff and low risk.

If a given project lies in area 1, the recommended action is to wait until additional analysis reduces the risk. If the project lies in area 2, the recommended action is to stop immediately (abandon the project). If the project lies in area 3, the recommended action is to advance immediately so the project can be completed as quickly as possible. If the project lies in area 4, the recommended action is to do nothing until adequate resources are available or until the expected payoff increases.

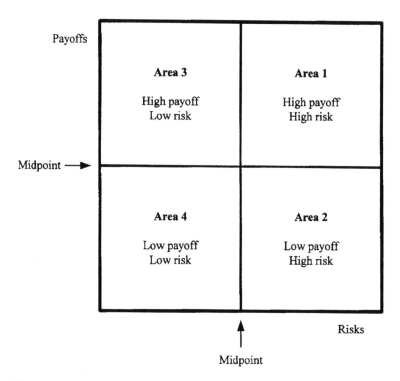

Figure 39.1 A risk-payoff matrix.

39.5 Key terms

Intangible — Difficult to define in concrete, physical (e.g., financial) terms.

Midpoint — The middle or average value from a range of reasonable estimated values for a parameter.

Payoff — A benefit.

Risk — A possible negative outcome that can be interpreted, estimated, or quantified by applying past experience.

Tangible — Easily defined, concrete, physical; for example, payoffs, risks, and uncertainties that can be expressed in financial terms are considered tangible.

Uncertainty — A possible negative outcome that cannot be interpreted or estimated based on experience because it has never happened before.

39.6 Software

Not applicable.

39.7   References

1. Gibson, M. L. and Hughes, C. T., *Systems Analysis and Design: A Comprehensive Methodology with CASE*, Boyd & Fraser, Boston, MA, 1994.
2. Laudon, K. C. and Laudon, J. P., *Managing Information Systems: A Contemporary Perspective*, Macmillan, New York, 1991.

chapter forty

Business function-task analysis

David C. Yen and William S. Davis

Contents

40.1 Purpose

Business function-task analysis was developed by IBM in the 1960s to establish the relationships between an organization's data, processes, and organizational units.

40.2   Strengths, weaknesses, and limitations

Business function-task analysis is particularly valuable when an application or a system development project starts from scratch (no existing system), when a company is faced with a massive reorganization, or when a company's data resources change substantially. Because so many users are involved, it is relatively easy to obtain user buy-in. Once a business function-task analysis is completed, the results can be used to support further system development and/or expansion.

Although the underlying idea is easy to understand, considerable time and effort are required to perform a business function-task analysis. The relevancy of the data collected is not always clear, and no information is collected from the operational level. Finally, this approach is quantitative, and it fails to account for qualitative factors.

40.3   Inputs and related ideas

The results of a business function-task analysis can be used to prioritize information system development projects or as a structure for defining information system strategy.

40.4   Concepts

Business function-task analysis was developed by IBM in the 1960s to establish the relationships between an organization's data, processes, and organizational units. It is also known as the enterprise analysis approach and the business systems planning approach. The basic idea is to analyze the entire organization in terms of organizational units, functions, processes, and data elements.

40.4.1   The focus group

Business function-task analysis is performed by a focus group composed of managers from all the functional units in the entire company. Depending on the scope of an information system project, some functional units might be grouped to form meta-units (e.g., an accounting unit might represent the accounts payable, accounts receivable, and customer credit departments) or divided into smaller subunits.

40.4.2   The 5W analysis

The first step in the process is to survey the focus group by asking the members to answer five key questions (how, where, what, who, and when) about relevant functions, processes, and data elements. This task is sometimes called 5W analysis. Some examples of the kinds of questions that might be asked are listed in Table 40.1.

Table 40.1 Typical 5W Analysis Questions

1. *How?*
   How is the information used?
   How is the information processed and/or stored?
   How are decisions concerning the information made?

2. *Where?*
   Where does the information originate?
   Where is the information delivered?
   Where is the information used and/or modified?

3. *What?*
   What objectives are associated with the information?
   What are the data needs of the participants?

4. *Who?*
   Who creates the data or information?
   Who are the major users of the data?
   Who is authorized to update and/or maintain the data?

5. *When?*
   When and in what form are the data needed?
   When are the data distributed to other branches?

40.4.3   The organizational unit-process matrix

After the 5W analysis survey is completed, an organizational unit-process matrix is constructed (Figure 40.1). The matrix shows the various organizational units along the horizontal axis and the processes the focus group members perform along the vertical axis. Each cell in the matrix is marked with an M (to indicate major involvement) or an S (to indicate some involvement); blank cells indicate no involvement.

The purpose of the organizational unit-process matrix is to identify the relationships between the organizational units and the processes and to determine the degree of involvement of the various units in specific processes. Subsequently, when information systems are developed to perform a given process, the central focus should be placed on those organizational units with major involvement in the process, while organization units with some involvement should receive less attention until adequate resources are available.

40.4.4   The process-data element matrix

The process-data element matrix (Figure 40.2) lists the data elements along the horizontal axis and the processes the focus group members perform

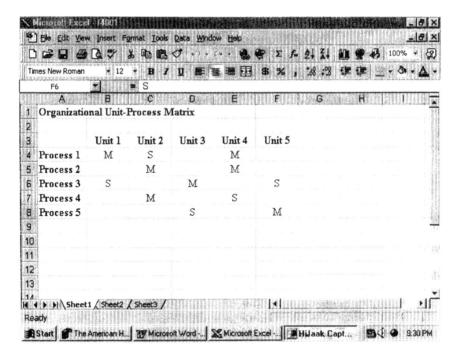

Figure 40.1   An organizational unit-process matrix.

along the vertical axis. Each cell in the matrix is marked with a U (to indicate a user of the data) or a C (to indicate a creator of the data); once again blank cells indicate no involvement. Some organizations further clarify the type of use by coding an M (for modify) or an R (for retrieve or read only). Clusters of letters clearly identify the data required to support related processes.

40.4.5   Data analysis

Analyzing the wealth of information summarized in the unit-process matrix and the process-data element matrix often reveals indirect relationship between the organizational units, the functions, the processes, and the data elements. Additional cross-checks and walk-throughs can help reduce redundancies and resolve conflicts. The final step in the process is to document the specific information requirements of all the functional units and their related processes.

40.5   Key terms

5W analysis — The first step in the business function-task analysis process during which the focus group is asked to answer five key

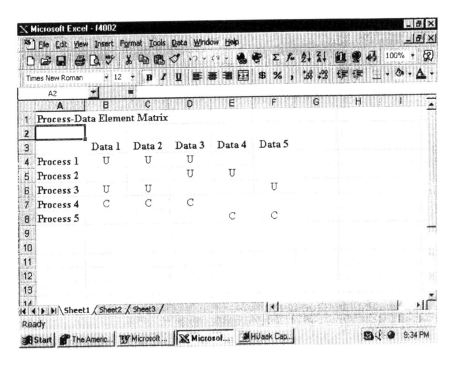

Figure 40.2 A process-data element matrix.

questions (how, where, what, who, and when) about relevant functions, processes, and data elements.

Business function-task analysis — A methodology developed by IBM in the 1960s to establish the relationships between an organization's data, processes, and organizational units.

Focus group — A group composed of managers from all the functional units in the entire company that conducts a business function-task analysis.

Organizational unit-process matrix — A table that identifies the relationships between the organizational units and the processes and shows the degree of involvement of the various units in specific processes.

Process-data element matrix — A table that shows the relationships between the data elements and the processes.

40.6 *Software*

Although no software is specifically designed to support business function-task analysis, spreadsheet software can be used to create and maintain the organizational unit-process matrix and the process-data element matrix. The matrixes in this chapter were created using Excel.

40.7   References

1. Doll, W. J., Avenues for top management involvement in successful MIS development, *MIS Q.*, 1985.
2. Laudon, K. C. and Laudon, J. P., *Management Information Systems: A Contemporary Perspective*, 2nd ed., Macmillan, New York, 1991.
3. Zachman, J. A., Business systems planning and business information control study: a comparison, *IBM Syst. J.*, 21, 1982.

chapter forty-one

Competitive procurement

William S. Davis

Contents

41.1 Purpose

Competitive procurement is a set of procedures for subcontracting work through a bidding process. The intent is to solicit fair, impartial, *competitive* bids.

0-8493-7001-9/99/$0.00+$.50
©1999 by CRC Press LLC

41.2   Strengths, weaknesses, and limitations

Because the contract is typically awarded to the low bidder, the competitive bidding process tends to minimize cost. Multiple bidders bring different viewpoints to the process, and often suggest alternative solutions. The step-by-step nature of the process provides the sponsoring organization with a useful structure for managing subcontracted or outplaced projects.

Preparing specifications and bids is expensive. It is difficult (perhaps impossible) to prespecify every detail of a complex system that will be developed over several years. The competitive bidding process tends to be rigid. Requirements change over time, and procedures for dealing with changes are a major weak point.

Preparing and evaluating the documents submitted by numerous bidders is incredibly time-consuming. In today's economy, firms that cannot react quickly to changing conditions find it difficult to compete, and the delays caused by frequent bidding cycles are intolerable. Consequently, many organizations that subcontract or outsource information system development work use a streamlined version of the competitive bidding process that sacrifices some control to gain time.

Low bids do not always imply high quality. In an effort to improve quality, many organizations have significantly reduced the number of projects that go through the competitive procurement process and have chosen instead to establish long-term relationships with a limited number of subcontractors.

41.3   Inputs and related ideas

Competitive procurement can occur during or immediately after the problem definition (Part II), analysis (Part IV), and design (Part VI) phases of the system development life cycle, and specific subsystems or tasks can be put out for competitive bids at any stage. The requirements specification (Chapter 35) often serves as a basis for competitive procurement.

41.4   Concepts

The competitive procurement process was initially developed by the U.S. Department of Defense as a means to minimize costs and ensure fair access on major military-related projects. Today, the trend toward downsizing and outplacement has led to an increase in the number of firms that subcontract or outplace information system development projects. Many corporate competitive procurement systems are modeled on the Department of Defense standard.

41.4.1   Standards

There are several widely used standards for writing requirements. DoD-STD-2167A[2] defines procedures for defense system software development.

DoD-STD-490 and DoD-STD-499 must be followed on most military contracts. Other standards, such as IEEE STD-729 (a glossary) and IEEE STD-830 are defined by civilian organizations[1] (in this case, by the Institute of Electrical and Electronics Engineers), and many companies have their own internal standards.

41.4.2   Department of Defense Standard 2167A

Figure 41.1 shows a hurricane tracking system that consists of three major subsystems. Outlined below are the key elements of a DoD-STD-2167A requirements specification that might be prepared for such a system.

41.4.2.1   The system/segment specifications

Sometimes called the project or mission requirements, the system/segment specifications (SSS), or A-specs, identify major systems and subsystems at a conceptual level. For example, the highest-level system/segment specification for the system pictured in Figure 41.1 might identify such requirements as:

Locate the position of the hurricane's eye within 500 m every 15 min.

Reproject the hurricane's likely landfalls every 15 min.

Graphically display the hurricane's most current position and likely landfalls in a format acceptable to the television networks.

Note the nature of these requirements. They are logical. They describe what the system must do, not how the system must work. The requirement that a hurricane's position be graphically displayed calls for both hardware and software, making it a hardware/software composite item. Clearly, it specifies more than a single physical component.

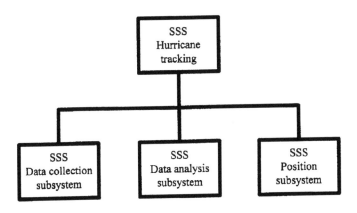

Figure 41.1   A hurricane tracking system that consists of three major subsystems.

The system/segment specifications define the requirements down to, but not including, the configuration item level. (The system's physical components begin to appear at the configuration item level.) A high-level mission requirement might be subdivided into several segments, and those segments might be further subdivided, so there can be several levels of system/segment specifications.

41.4.2.2   The system/segment design documents

The system/segment design documents (SSDD), or B-specs, define, in black-box form, the components that occupy the configuration item level. For example, a system/segment design document might be prepared for a program, but the routines that make up the program are below the configuration item level and so do not appear in the SSDD.

Figure 41.2 shows that the *Data collection subsystem* consists of a *Satellite segment*, an *Observation plane segment*, a *Data preparation segment*, and, perhaps, several other discrete, high-level, physical components. In this example, the *Satellite segment* is hardware and the *Data preparation segment* is software. If controlling the satellite calls for additional software, the appropriate program would appear as a separate segment. One system/segment design document is prepared for each configuration item. These documents summarize high-level design decisions, and they serve as a basis for defining the next lower level of requirements.

Like the system/segment specifications, the system/segment design documents are logical, not physical. Each one describes a discrete physical component, but they specify what that component must do, not how it must work. For example, an SSDD for a microcomputer might specify such things as weight and size limitations, response time requirements, and the number of transactions that must be processed per unit of time, but it will not specify a particular model computer or distinguish between a Dell Dimension system and an Apple Macintosh.

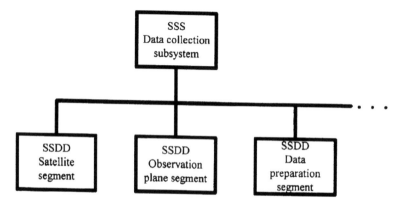

Figure 41.2   The *Data collection subsystem.*

41.4.2.3 The software requirements specifications

Each subsystem that is to be implemented in software is called a computer software configuration item (CSCI) and is documented in a software requirements specification (SRS). These documents consist of program design specifications. They are prepared after key design decisions have been made. Unlike the SSS and SSDD specifications, they define *how* the solution will be implemented.

41.4.2.4 The prime item development specifications

Each subsystem that is to be implemented in hardware is called a hardware configuration item (HWCI) and is documented in a prime item development specification (PIDS). These documents consist of hardware design specifications. They are prepared after key design decisions have been made. Unlike the SSS and SSDD specifications, they define *how* the solution will be implemented.

41.4.3 The procurement process

Figure 41.3 summarizes the competitive procurement process. Note that few organizations seek competitive bids at each stage, so the process is much more flexible than the flow diagram suggests.

The process begins during the problem definition and information gathering stage of the system development life cycle (Part II). Based on a preliminary analysis of the problem, user experts who work for the government agency or the customer organization that is sponsoring the project define a set of needs and write the system/segment specifications (A-specs), which are then released for bids.

On a major system, several firms might be awarded contracts and charged with preparing competitive system/segment design documents (B-specs). The completed SSDDs are submitted to the customer and evaluated. The best set is then selected and once again released for bids. Sometimes, the firm that prepared the system/segment design documents is prohibited from participating in the next round.

Based on the competitive bids, a contract to generate a physical design and prepare a set of specifications based on the system/segment design documents is subsequently awarded to one or (perhaps) two companies. One PIDS (hardware) or SRS (software) is prepared for each SSDD. (In other words, one physical design specification is created for each configuration item.)

At the end of this phase, the PIDS and SRS documents are reviewed and approved. The best design specifications are then released for a final round of competitive procurement, with the winning firm getting a contract to build the system. Clearly, the organization that created the final specifications has an advantage, but there are no guarantees. Sometimes a backup supplier is awarded a portion of the contract.

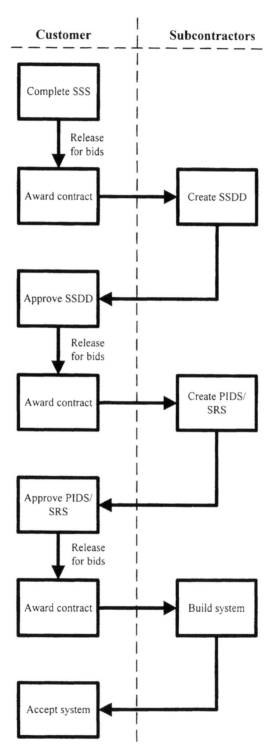

Figure 41.3 The competitive procurement process.

41.5   Key terms

Competitive procurement — A set of procedures for subcontracting work through a bidding process.

Computer software configuration item (CSCI) — A subsystem that is to be implemented in software.

Configuration item — A functional primitive that appears at the lowest level of decomposition.

Configuration item level — An imaginary line that links the system's configuration items.

Hardware configuration item (HWCI) — A subsystem that is to be implemented in hardware.

Prime item development specification (PIDS) — The documentation for a hardware configuration item; a hardware design specification.

Software requirements specification (SRS) — The documentation for a computer software configuration item; a program design specification.

System/segment design documents (SSDD) (B-specs) — A set of specifications that define, in black-box form, the components that occupy the configuration item level.

System/segment specifications (SSS) (A-specs) — A set of specifications that identify major systems and subsystems at a conceptual level; the system/segment specifications define the requirements down to, but not including, the configuration item level; sometimes called the project or mission requirements.

41.6   Software

Not applicable.

41.7   References

1. Thayer, R. H. and Dorfman, M., *System and Software Requirements Engineering*, IEEE Computer Society Press, Los Alamitos, CA, 1990.
2. Anon., *Military Standard, Defense System Software Development*, (DoD-STD-2167A), U.S. Department of Defense, Washington, D.C.

part six

Component design

chapter forty-two

Hardware interface design

David C. Yen and William S. Davis

Contents

42.1   Purpose

Hardware interface design is the process of determining, specifying, evaluating, and acquiring of a set of hardware building blocks and analyzing their relationships with each other.

0-8493-7001-9/99/$0.00+$.50
©1999 by CRC Press LLC

42.2   Strengths, weaknesses, and limitations

This chapter focuses on several issues, techniques, and approaches related to hardware interface design. Consequently, a discussion of specific strengths, weaknesses, and limitations is not relevant.

42.3   Inputs and related ideas

Hardware interface design is the physical backbone that supports input, output, database, and software design (virtually every chapter in Part VI). It also impacts system controls (Chapter 77) and general system design (Chapter 72). Hardware interface design is based on the requirements defined during the analysis stage (Part IV) and documented in the requirements specifications (Chapter 35).

42.4   Concepts

Hardware interface design is the process of determining, specifying, evaluating, and acquiring of a set of hardware building blocks and analyzing their relationships with each other.

42.4.1   Design issues

This section briefly discusses several significant hardware design issues.

42.4.1.1   Choosing a computer

Computers fall roughly into four categories: supercomputers, mainframes, minicomputers, and microcomputers. Given the mix of features available from different vendors, however, these classifications are little more than guidelines. Key factors that must be considered include compatibility with existing systems, adaptability, security, and connectivity. Depending on the organization's management philosophy (centralized, decentralized, or distributed), the available choices range from stand-alone microcomputers; to a centralized supercomputer or mainframe; to a network of microcomputers, terminals, and workstations controlled by a central server; to a cooperative, distributed, peer-to-peer network of sophisticated, co-equal computers.

42.4.1.2   The impact of technological change

The rapidly changing nature of information technology has forced the designer to view the process of evaluating and acquiring hardware from a different perspective. Today, the opinions of the end users are every bit as important as the opinions of the specialists.

For example, hardware interface design was traditionally the first step in the systems design process, and the software, the database, and the other system components were designed in the context of a specific hardware platform. Today, however, the required software or database capabilities and functions are often considered first, and the hardware is subsequently selected to fit the resulting requirements. For example, it is not uncommon for a company to choose Oracle and then identify the hardware needed to implement the tool.

The nature of hardware interface design has itself changed, too. Traditionally, such performance attributes as processing speed and throughput drove the selection of the peripherals, the processor, and secondary storage. Today, however, such factors as user friendliness, flexibility, adaptability, ease of learning, and ease of use are at least as important.

42.4.1.3   The impact of industry standards

Given the popularity of the Internet (and intranets), the system's data communication component has become a crucial consideration in hardware interface design. For example, newly purchased microcomputers often come equipped with a fax modem, communication protocols, and other communication cards or boards. Additionally, sharing such resources as files and network printers and allowing broad access to corporate data are common system requirements. Consequently, conforming to such widely accepted industry standards as open systems interconnection (OSI) has become an important hardware interface design criterion.

In some cases, hardware interface design is considered a subset of a network design. The major network platform and associated capabilities are defined first, and the hardware interface design for a local site or a branch is performed in the context of the network.

42.4.1.4   Environmental issues

Hardware is sensitive to power losses, power surges, and similar power failures. Surge protectors and uninterruptible power supplies (UPS) help to reduce the impact of power failures and are recommended for most systems.

The cables used to connect a system's hardware components must be protected. One option is a raised floor, with load-bearing supports and a grid of cross beams holding removable panels. The cables run under the floor, out of the way, but accessible if connections must be added or removed. A raised floor also helps to protect the hardware from standing water and promotes air movement, thus dissipating heat. Network components are sometimes linked through dedicated cabling conduits, with a central cabling panel on each floor, risers connecting the panels between floors, and distributing cables extending to each room.

Fire protection is essential. This issue is more related to facility design than hardware interface design, but given the electronic nature of computer hardware, such traditional fire control techniques as sprinkler systems can damage the equipment. Some systems rely on fire retardant (but breathable) gasses to control fires in the computer room.

Heat dissipation and moisture prevention are crucial. Adequate ventilation, auxiliary cooling, humidity control, and well-designed cabinets are important elements in hardware interface design.

42.4.1.5 Disaster recovery and planning
The principle of redundancy calls for a second set of important hardware components (a redundant file server, for example) ready to use in the event of a disaster. System reliability is enhanced by redundancy, but the cost can be quite high.

Backup implies creating and storing a second copy of key software, data, the commands needed to perform key operating system procedures and reinstall hardware, and similar system elements. In the event of a disaster, the backup copies are used to restore the affected components. Often, the backup copies are maintained off site so a single disaster cannot destroy both the system and the backup.

42.4.2 Hardware interface design phases

The steps in the hardware interface design process are summarized in Figure 42.1.

42.4.2.1 Planning
The planning stage begins with an element analysis during which the designer identifies the discrete components (processors, monitors, mice, keyboards, secondary memory units, printers, etc.) required by the system. Additionally, such required features as data communication and multimedia capabilities (fax modems, video accelerator cards, sound cards, and the like) are specified.

Configuration analysis deals with system behavior and performance. Key issues include ensuring that the hardware meets response time, performance, and reliability requirements. Sometimes a bottleneck analysis (Chapter 79) is performed. Software issues add to the complexity of configuration analysis. Prototyping (Chapter 31) is an effective tool for pinpointing configuration problems.

42.4.2.2 Evaluation
During the evaluation stage, application analysis is used to study the interactions and relationships between the hardware and software resources. Typically, all the required software is installed on a test system and the behavior of the hardware is evaluated as the applications run. For example, a user evaluating a database application might issue a query, add, update, or delete a record, generate a report, join two or more database files, create a date entry form or screen, and so on.

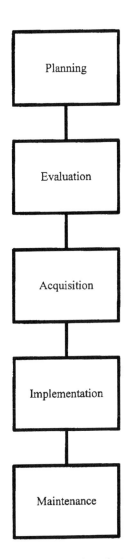

Figure 42.1   The steps in the hardware interface design process.

Resource analysis is used to evaluate the capabilities of the hardware components. For example, data on such factors as mean time between failures, the average number of instructions executed per second, clock speed, multiple processor availability, and expandability might be collected to allow the designer to compare several alternative processors. Demand/utilization analysis focuses on such issues as throughput, average response time, concurrent incoming messages, simultaneous users, maximum data capacity, the component's ability to deal with peak demand, and so on.

Benchmarking is a useful tool for comparing such component parameters as input/output performance, storage capacity, I/O buffer size and speed, searching speed, instruction fetch speed, data transmission speed, and data transmission capacity. Parameter analysis is a useful tool for evaluating such factors as the time required to load a test image, the quality and sharpness of a displayed image, or the maximum number of frames required to store a motion picture or display an animation. Simulation (Chapter 19) and queuing theory (Chapter 79) can be used to study queues and predict such statistics as average waiting time, average processing time, and average queue size.

42.4.2.3   Acquisition

The requirements determined in the previous two steps are reviewed, and additional requirements dealing with such issues as integration with existing hardware and/or software, implementation (e.g., installation support, conversion, and testing), and maintenance (e.g., maintenance contracts, training support, help desk support, and upgrade support) are incorporated. Given a complete set of requirements, a request for proposal (RFP) is released and (often) competitive bids are solicited (Chapter 41). Bids are then evaluated and the hardware is selected. Note that hardware can be leased or purchased.

42.4.2.4   Implementation

During the implementation stage, the hardware is tested (Part VII), necessary conversion tasks are performed, and the hardware is released (Chapter 76).

42.4.4.5   Maintenance

After the hardware is released, it must be maintained (Part VIII) and, as necessary, upgraded.

42.5   Key terms

Adaptability — A measure of the ease of changing or modifying a system, often in response to a technological change.

Application analysis — A study of the interactions and relationships between the hardware and software resources; typically, all the required software is installed on a test system and the behavior of the hardware is evaluated as the applications run.

Backup — A duplicate copy of a set of data, a program, a hardware component, or some other system element that is used to restore the system in the event of failure.

Benchmark — A standard program, procedure, or set of test data used to measure such performance characteristics as a computer's processing speed.

Bottleneck analysis — A study of the waiting lines or queues that develop within a system; the objective is to find choke points, or bottlenecks.

Configuration analysis — A study of such system behavior and performance characteristics as response time and reliability.

Connectivity — In a network, the ability of a given hardware or software component to cooperate with other components supplied by other vendors.

Demand/utilization analysis — A study that focuses on such utilization issues as throughput, average response time, concurrent incoming messages, simultaneous users, maximum data capacity, the component's ability to deal with peak demand, and so on.

Element analysis — The process of identifying discrete hardware components and required features.

Expandability — The ability to add components to a system or features to a component.

Hardware interface design — The process of determining, specifying, evaluating, and acquiring of a set of hardware building blocks and analyzing their relationships with each other.

Open systems interconnection (OSI) — An International Standards Organization network model that specifies seven interconnection layers.

Parameter analysis — A study of such factors as the time required to load a test image, the quality and sharpness of a displayed image, or the maximum number of frames required to store a motion picture or display an animation.

Redundancy — Two (or more) copies of a hardware component. In the event of component failure, the redundant copy provides backup.

Request for proposal (RFP) — A formal (often advertised) request for competitive bids based on a set of requirements.

Resource analysis — An evaluation of such hardware component capabilities as mean time between failures, the average number of instructions executed per second, clock speed, multiple processor availability, and expandability.

Simulation — The use of a mathematical model that behaves in the same manner as the system under study.

Surge protector — A device that protects electronic components against sudden changes in electrical current.

Uninterruptible power supply (UPS) — A device that continues to supply electrical current in the event of a power failure; many uninterruptible power supplies incorporate surge protectors.

42.6   Software

Not applicable.

42.7 References

1. Burch, J. G., *Systems Analysis, Design, and Implementation*, Boyd & Fraser, Boston, MA, 1992.
2. Burd, S. D., *Systems Architecture: Hardware and Software in Business Information Systems*, Boyd & Fraser, Boston, MA, 1994.
3. Pressman, R. S., *Software Engineering: A Practitioner's Approach*, 2nd ed., McGraw-Hill, New York, 1987.

chapter forty-three

Data structures

William S. Davis and David C. Yen

Contents

43.1   Purpose

A data structure is a way of organizing data that considers both the data items and their relationships to each other. Selecting the right data structure

0-8493-7001-9/99/$0.00+$.50
©1999 by CRC Press LLC

can improve memory utilization, improve processing efficiency, and reduce development costs.

43.2   Strengths, weaknesses, and limitations

This chapter introduces several basic principles of data structures. The strengths and weaknesses of individual data structures will be discussed in context.

43.3   Inputs and related ideas

The study of data structures is an essential component of most computer science curricula. Consequently, this chapter is aimed at non-computer science graduates who have not been exposed to formal data structures. The emphasis is on terminology and visualization rather than mathematics and formal logic. Several relevant key terms are introduced in Chapter 25. Files and databases are discussed in Chapters 44 and 45, respectively.

43.4   Concepts

A data structure is a way of organizing multiple data items (usually, data elements or records) that considers both the data items and their relationships to each other. Selecting the right data structure can improve memory utilization, improve processing efficiency, and reduce development costs.

43.4.1   Algorithms and recursion

The study of data structures is tightly linked to algorithms for efficiently creating a structure, inserting data into or deleting data from the structure, finding a specific data item, and traversing the structure. Sort and search algorithms are of particular interest.

A subroutine is considered recursive if it calls itself or if it initiates a circular chain of calls that returns eventually to itself. Many data structures are inherently recursive, so the concept of recursion appears in numerous algorithms and definitions.

43.4.2   Data elements, arrays, and pointers

A data element is the most basic unit of data that has logical meaning. A single data element might hold an integer number, a floating-point number, a character string, a Boolean value (true or false), or any other data type. In this chapter, the term *data item* will be used to designate a data element, a data composite, or a record.

An array is an elementary data structure that resembles a table. A one-dimensional array is sometimes called a vector; a two-dimensional array is sometimes called a matrix. Typically, one data element is stored in each array cell, and the cells are distinguished by subscripts. A transformation or mapping function is used to convert the subscripts to memory addresses. Arrays are supported by most programming languages and, thus, are used to implement several data structures.

A pointer is a link to a data item. Typically, each data item contains the data plus a pointer in the form of the address or the key of the target data item. An access vector is a list of pointers providing access to a set of data items.

43.4.3   Lists

The most basic data structure is a list (Figure 43.1). Each entry in the list is called a node, and each node holds a single data item. In an ordered list, the nodes are stored in data value or key order.

43.4.3.1   Simple lists

The simplest type of list is a set of data items stored in consecutive memory locations. Such lists serve as a basis for comparison for more sophisticated data structures. For example, searching a simple list for a specific data item means, on average, testing half the list's entries. The efficiency of a search algorithm can be measured by comparing the number of tests it needs to find the target data item to the average number of tests required in a simple list.

43.4.3.2   Linked lists

In a simple list, inserting a node means shifting the existing nodes to make room. Similarly, deleting a node means shifting nodes to fill in the freed space. Such data movement is inefficient.

One solution is to create a linked list (Figure 43.2). In a linked list, each node contains data plus a pointer to the next node. Note that the data items need not be stored in adjacent memory locations because the pointers define the list's logical order. To insert a node into a linked list, locate the prior node, change its pointer to the new node, and set the new node's pointer to

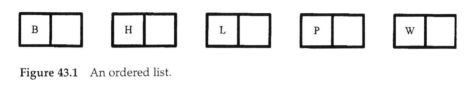

Figure 43.1   An ordered list.

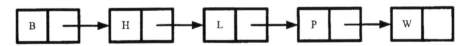

Figure 43.2   A linked list.

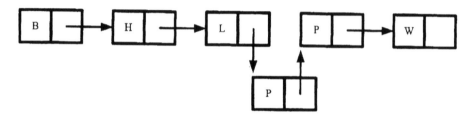

Figure 43.3   Inserting a node into a linked list.

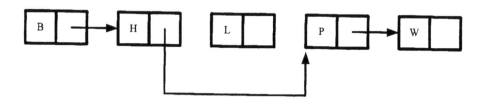

Figure 43.4   Deleting a node from a linked list.

the next node (Figure 43.3). To delete a node from a linked list, change the appropriate pointer to "jump over" the deleted node (Figure 43.4).

In a singly linked list, each node points only to the next node. In a circular linked list, the last node points back to the first node. A doubly linked list contains both forward and backward pointers; in other words, each node points to the previous node and to the next node. In a multi-linked list, each node contains two or more pointers to different data items; for example, a personnel record might contain pointers to a department record and a skills inventory record.

Linked lists are used in a variety of applications. In many operating systems, the set of control blocks that hold the data necessary for dispatching and memory allocation is implemented as a linked list. In MS-DOS, the file allocation table is a linked list of clusters.

43.4.3.3   Stacks
A stack is a special type of linked list in which all insertions and deletions occur at the top. Access to the stack is controlled by a single pointer (Figure 43.5). Adding an entry to the top of the stack is called pushing the stack. Removing an entry from the top is called popping the stack. Because insertions and deletions occur only at the top, the last item added to the stack is the first item removed from the stack (last in, first out). Stacks are used for a variety of applications, including tracking procedure calls to ensure that returns are executed in the proper order, evaluating arithmetic expressions, and parsing.

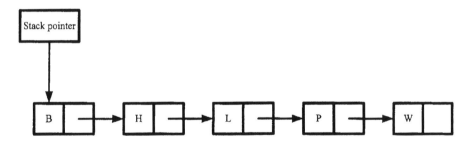

Figure 43.5 Access to a stack is controlled by a single pointer.

43.4.3.4 Queues
A queue is a special type of linked list in which insertions occur at the rear and deletions occur at the front. Access to a queue is controlled by two pointers (Figure 43.6), and the first item added to a queue is the first item removed (first in, first out).

43.4.4 Trees

A list is one-dimensional. A tree is a two-dimensional data structure in which the nodes form a hierarchy (Figure 43.7). Because memory addresses are one-dimensional, implementing a tree requires a mapping function.

43.4.4.1 Terminology
A tree's top (or base) node is called the root node. The root node is the parent to one or more level-2 child nodes, and each of those children is (potentially) a parent to children of its own. A parent of a parent (or the parent of an ancestor) is called an ancestor; a child of a child (or the child of a descendant) is called a descendant. Nodes that share the same level are called siblings. A branch is a link between a parent and a child. A leaf (or leaf node) is a node with no branches. A subtree is a subset of a tree that is itself a tree. A tree can be defined recursively because each node is the root node of a subtree.

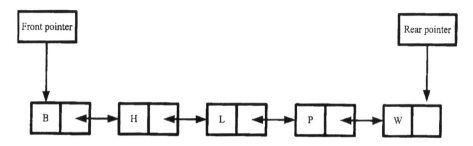

Figure 43.6 Access to a queue is controlled by two pointers.

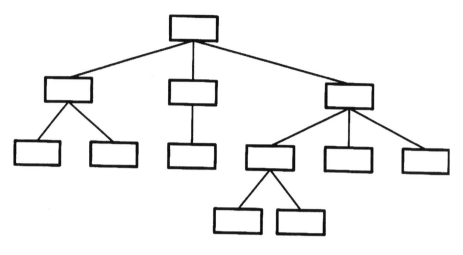

Figure 43.7   A tree.

43.4.4.2   Binary trees

In a binary tree, each node has two branches and holds a data item plus two pointers, left and right (Figure 43.8). Often, the data items are stored in default order, with the left child holding a value less than the parent and the right child holding a value greater than the parent. To search the tree for a particular data item, start at the top of the tree, go left if the search key is less than the node's value, and go right if the search key is greater than the node's value. Then repeat the process at the new node. Insertions are made at the appropriate leaf node. A node is deleted by modifying a pointer.

43.4.4.3   Multi-way trees

In a multi-way tree, each node holds n (two or more) values and can have $(n + 1)$ branches. For example, if the root node holds two values, it can have three branches and thus point to three children (Figure 43.9), each of which can hold up to two values and have up to three branches. All values in the left node are less than the parent node's minimum value. All values in the right node are greater than the parent node's maximum value. All values in the center node lie between the parent node's values.

43.4.4.4   B-trees, or balanced multi-way trees

A B-tree, or balanced multi-way tree is a multi-way tree that has all its leaf nodes at the same level. Balance is achieved by building the tree from the bottom up. New entries are placed in a leaf node if possible. If the target leaf node is full, the leaf is split and the median value is moved up to the parent. B-trees are commonly used to index records on a secondary storage device without overflow.

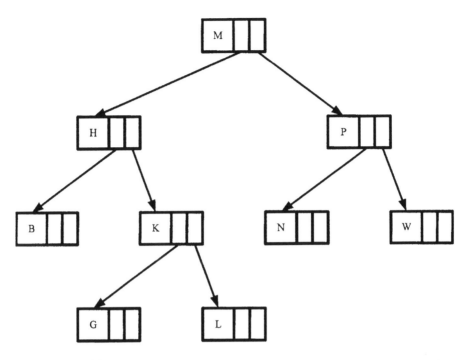

Figure 43.8   A binary tree.

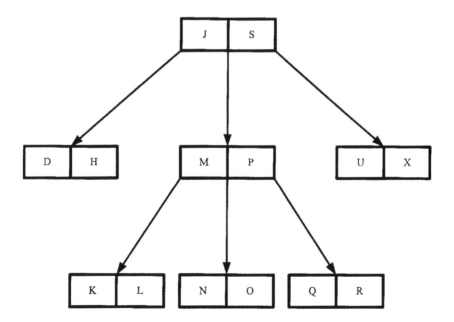

Figure 43.9   A multi-way tree.

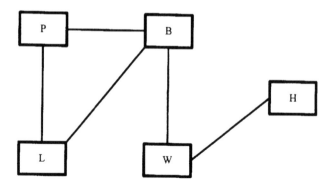

Figure 43.10   An undirected graph.

43.4.5   Graphs and networks

In a tree, the nodes form a hierarchy. Graphs and networks are less restrictive.

A graph is a set of nodes (or vertexes) linked by a set of edges. The edges on an undirected graph have no direction (Figure 43.10); in other words, it is possible to move between two nodes in any direction as long as they are connected by an edge.

On a directed graph, or digraph, each edge (or arc) has a direction (Figure 43.11). A given node's indegree is the number of entering arcs, and its outdegree is the number of exiting arcs. A source is a node of indegree 0, and a sink is a node of outdegree 0.

A path is a sequence of edges that links a set of nodes; on a digraph, the path's direction is significant. A cycle is a path that leads from a node back to the same node. In many operating systems, the set of requests for resources is modeled as a graph, and the graph is evaluated for cycles, which imply deadlock.

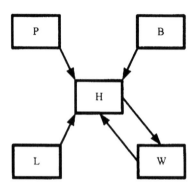

Figure 43.11   A directed graph.

On a network, or weighted graph, the edges have values. For example, a communication network might be modeled as a weighted graph with such values as Baud rate, distance, or cost associated with each edge.

The process of traversing a graph or network involves identifying subtrees or spanning trees within the graph, and then working with the subtrees. A minimum spanning tree is a subtree or spanning tree for which the sum of arc weights is minimal. For example, a project network (Chapter 21) is a network and the critical path is a minimum spanning tree.

43.5 Key terms

Access vector — A list of pointers providing access to a set of data items.

Algorithm — A rule for arriving at an answer in a finite number of steps.

Ancestor — A parent of a parent (or an ancestor).

Arc — An edge on a directed graph.

Array — An elementary data structure that resembles a table; typically, one data element is stored in each array cell and the cells are distinguished by subscripts.

Attribute — A property of an entity.

Binary tree — A special type of tree in which each node has two branches.

Branch — On a tree, a link between a parent and a child.

Child — An immediate lower-level node in a tree.

Circular linked list — A linked list in which the last node points back to the first node.

Cycle — On a graph, a path that leads from a node back to the same node.

Data element — An attribute that cannot be logically decomposed; the most basic unit of data that has logical meaning.

Data structure — A way of organizing data that considers both the data items and their relationships to each other.

Descendant — A child of a child (or a descendant).

Directed graph (digraph) — A graph on which each edge (or arc) has a direction.

Doubly linked list — A linked list in which each node contains both forward and backward pointers.

Edge — On a graph, a link between two nodes.

Entity — An object (a person, group, place, thing, or activity) about which data are stored.

Field — A data element physically stored on some medium.

File — A set of related records.

Graph — A set of nodes (or vertexes) linked by a set of edges.

Indegree — On a directed graph, the number of arcs entering a given node.

Key — The attribute or group of attributes that uniquely distinguishes one occurrence of an entity.

Leaf (leaf node) — On a tree, a node with no branches.

Linked list — A list in which each node contains data plus a pointer to the next node.

List — A series of nodes each of which holds a single data item; the most basic data structure.

Matrix — A two-dimensional array.

Minimum spanning tree — Within a graph, a subtree or spanning tree for which the sum of arc weights is minimal.

Multi-linked list — A linked list in which each node contains two or more pointers, thus providing access to two or more other nodes.

Multi-way tree — A tree in which each node holds n (two or more) values and can have ($n + 1$) branches.

Network (weighted graph) — A graph on which the edges have values.

Node — An entry in a list; often, a single data element or a single record.

Occurrence — A single instance of an entity.

Ordered list — A list in which the nodes are stored in data value or key order.

Outdegree — On a directed graph, the number of arcs exiting from a given node.

Parent — The immediate higher-level node in a tree.

Path — On a graph, a sequence of edges that links a set of nodes; on a digraph, the path's direction is significant.

Pointer — A link to a data item; typically, a key value or an address.

Pop — To remove an entry from the top of a stack.

Push — To add an entry to the top of a stack.

Queue — A special type of linked list in which insertions occur at the rear and deletions occur at the front.

Record — The set of fields associated with an occurrence of an entity.

Recursion — A subroutine calling itself; a subroutine initiating a circular chain of calls that returns eventually to itself.

Root (root node) — A tree's top (or base) node.

Siblings — Two or more nodes that share the same level.

Singly linked list — A linked list in which each node points only to the next node.

Sink — On a directed graph, a node of outdegree 0.

Source — On a directed graph, a node of indegree 0.

Stack — A special type of linked list in which all insertions and deletions occur at the top.

Subtree (spanning tree) — A tree within a graph; a subset of a tree that is itself a tree.

Tree — A two-dimensional, hierarchical data structure; a tree can be defined recursively because each node is the root node of a subtree.

Undirected graph — A graph on which the edges have no direction.

Vector — A one-dimensional array.

43.6   Software

Not applicable.

43.7   References

1. Bamford, C. and Curran, P., *Data Structures, Files and Databases*, MacMillan Education, London, 1987
2. Horowitz, E. and Sahni, S., *Fundamentals of Data Structures in Pascal*, Computer Science Press, Rockville, MD, 1984.
3. Knuth, D. E., *The Art of Computer Programming*, vol. 1. *Fundamental Algorithms*, 2nd. ed., Addison-Wesley, Reading, MA, 1973.
4. Singh, B. and Naps, T. L., *Introduction to Data Structures*, West Publishing, Minneapolis/St. Paul, MN, 1985.

chapter forty-four

Traditional file design

William S. Davis

Contents

0-8493-7001-9/99/$0.00+$.50
©1999 by CRC Press LLC

343

44.1   Purpose

A file is a repository for a set of related data records, a program, a document, a spreadsheet, an image, an object, or some other logical entity. Most information systems create, process, and/or manage data files. This chapter focuses on design options for data files.

44.2   Strengths, weaknesses, and limitations

The strengths and weaknesses of specific file organizations are briefly described in context.

44.3   Inputs and related ideas

A database (Chapter 45) is a set of related files. The individual files that make up a database are defined using the techniques described in this chapter. The first step in designing a data file is to compile the relevant logical data structures using such tools as data flow diagrams (Chapter 24), entity relationship diagrams (Chapter 26), data normalization (Chapter 28), or Warnier-Orr diagrams (Chapter 33). Typically the data elements and composites (the data structures) are documented in the data dictionary (Chapter 25). Data structures are discussed in Chapter 43.

44.4   Concepts

A file can hold data, a program, a document, a spreadsheet, an image, an object, or virtually any imaginable logical entity. This chapter focuses on data files.

44.4.1   The data hierarchy

The data in a file are typically structured using the standard field/ record/file data hierarchy. A field is a data element that cannot be logically decomposed. (A field's individual digits or characters have logical meaning only in aggregate.) Logically related fields are grouped to form records. A file is a set of related records. To put it another way, fields hold attributes, each record holds a single occurrence, and a file holds all the occurrences of an entity. The key field (or key attribute) uniquely identifies a single record (a single occurrence of the entity), distinguishing it from all other records.

44.4.2   File types

A master file holds permanent data that are managed or maintained over time. A transaction file holds data that describe current transactions. Often the data in a transaction file are used to update (or maintain) a master file.

A temporary file holds intermediate results and exists for only a brief time; for example, in a bill processing application a temporary file might be used to hold a set of records between the sorting and processing steps. A backup file is a copy of a master or transaction file used to recover data if disaster strikes. A history file (or archive) holds already processed transactions or non-current master records.

44.4.3   Logical and physical I/O

Logically, a single record is read (input), its fields processed, and the results written (output). Then a new logical input/process/output cycle begins. The physical input/output process is a bit more complex, however.

44.4.3.1   Open and close

When a data file is first created, its name and physical secondary storage location are noted in a directory maintained by the operating system. Subsequently, in response to a user (or application program) command, the operating system opens the file by searching the directory by name, extracting the file's secondary storage address, and (perhaps) transferring all or part of the file into memory. Once a file is opened, its records can be accessed by the application program. The active link to the file is broken by a close command.

44.4.3.2   Physical and logical records

Programmers and users visualize a logical record that holds the set of related fields needed to complete a single input/process/output cycle. A physical record, in contrast, is the unit of data that moves between the peripheral device and main memory. Note that, the logical record and the physical record can be different.

44.4.3.2.1   Blocking   For example, most disks are divided into concentric circles called tracks which, in turn, are divided into fixed-length sectors, and it is the contents of a sector that move between memory and the disk's surface. Assume the sector size is 512 bytes and picture a series of 100-byte logical records. If a single 100-byte logical record is stored in each 512-byte sector, 412 bytes per sector are unused. However, if five of those 100-byte logical records are blocked to form a 500-byte physical record and that physical record is stored in a single sector, only 12 bytes per sector are wasted.

With one *block* per sector, data move between the disk's surface and the computer's memory one block at a time. Software (the database management system, the operating system, a device driver, or an access method) is used to assemble a program's output logical records to form blocks, which are subsequently transferred to disk. The same software disassembles input blocks to get the logical records the program needs.

44.4.3.2.2   Spanned records   On a large file, even a few slack bytes per sector can add up to a great deal of wasted space. Additional space efficiency can be obtained by using spanned records. For example, imagine that five complete 100-byte records plus the first 12 bytes of the sixth record are stored in the first sector. The second sector contains the last 88 bytes of the sixth record, the next four 100-byte records, and the first 24 bytes of record 11, and so on. Spanned records are also used when the logical record length exceeds the sector size.

The problem with spanned records is that two or more physical I/O operations might be required to access a single logical record. In the example above, the first 12 bytes of record number 6 are stored in the first sector and the remaining 88 bytes are stored in the second sector, so the only way to get logical record number 6, is to read both sectors. Because only one sector can be read at a time, two physical I/O operations are needed, and each I/O operation takes time. Using spanned records sacrifices speed for storage efficiency.

44.4.3.3   Primitives

Each peripheral device is controlled by its own set of primitive commands. Consequently, if data are to be transferred between the peripheral device and main memory, the user's logical I/O request must be translated into an appropriate set of primitive commands. For example, physically reading data from a disk is a two-step operation:

1. Move the access mechanism to the target track (seek).
2. Copy (read) the contents of the target sector into memory.

Logically, the user requests a record. Physically, that request is translated into two physical primitives: seek and read (or seek and write). The translation from a logical request to physical I/O commands is typically performed by the operating system, an access method, or a device driver and is transparent to the user.

44.4.4   File organizations

Logically, the data in a file are read and written one record at a time. Consequently, it must be possible to distinguish the individual records. The task of distinguishing the records is greatly simplified if they are stored using a consistent set of rules defined by a file organization. Sequential, random, and indexed sequential are three common file organizations.

44.4.4.1   Sequential files

On a physical sequential file, records are read and written in physical storage order. For example, transactions might be captured, stored on disk or magnetic tape, and subsequently processed in time order. Often, transactions or master file records are sorted on a key field and then processed in key sequence.

Sequential files are excellent for high activity applications in which a large percentage of the records are processed each time the application is launched. Traditional batch processing tasks (such as preparing monthly bills or a weekly payroll) are good examples, and generating a control breaks report (Chapter 47) is an inherently sequential activity. Sequential files should *not* be used if the system requires quick access to specific records, however.

44.4.4.2   *Random or direct access files*

The records on a direct access or random access file can be read or written in any order. Because a program can directly access a specific record, response time is very good. As a general rule, master files that support inter-active or real-time applications should be organized randomly rather than sequentially.

Compared to a sequential file, a random access file has more overhead and thus needs more space to hold the same amount of data. Additionally, average processing time per transaction is higher because it takes longer to process a given number of direct access records than an equivalent number of sequential records. Direct access' response time advantage applies to a specific transaction, not the average of all transactions.

44.4.4.2.1   Indexes   One way to achieve random access is to maintain an index listing of the record key and the associated physical disk address for each record in the file. Depending on the system, the index is maintained by the operating system, by an access method, by the database management system, or by other support software. Often, the index is read when the file is opened and held in storage until the file is closed. When a logical read or write command is issued, the index is searched by key for the record's physical location.

An index can also be used to support logical sequential processing. Logical sequential processing implies key order, but not necessarily physical storage order. For example, the records in a database might be processed in index order even though they are not stored in physical sequential order.

44.4.4.2.2   Relative addressing   Relative addressing is an alternative to maintaining an index. One approach is to assign each record a number indicating its position relative to the beginning of the file; the first record is 0, the second record is 1, the third record is 2, and so on. The record's relative record number might be used as a key, or the record's logical key might be translated to a relative record number using an algorithm (see Section 44.4.4.2.3).

Instead of a relative record number, some systems view the data in a file as a string of bytes or characters and distinguish the records (and fields) by relative byte address. A relative byte (or relative character) address represents the byte's location relative to the beginning of the file; in effect, relative byte addresses resemble main memory address. Relative byte addresses are easily mapped to relative record addresses; for example, if the record length is 100 bytes, records begin at relative byte 0, relative byte 100, and so on.

44.4.4.2.3 Hashing Using a logical key as a relative record number means assigning one physical storage slot for every possible key. For example, using a social security number as a key implies 999,999,999 possible records (there is no social security number 000-00-0000). The result is a significant waste of storage space; for example, a university that enrolls 20,000 students would use only a fraction of the available storage slots to hold student records. Consequently, logical keys are converted into relative addresses using hashing (or scatter storage) algorithms.

Truncation algorithms select a portion of the logical key as the relative address. For example, using the last four digits of a social security number implies a need for only 9,999 record slots. Folding algorithms partition the logical key and add the parts. For example, adding the first three, the middle three, and the last three digits of a social security number generates a number between 0 and 2,997. A variation of the folding technique partitions the logical key, multiplies the parts, and uses the product (or a portion of the product) as a relative record number.

Perhaps the most common type of hashing algorithm is the division/remainder method. Start with a reasonable estimate of the expected number of records to be stored, and divide the logical key by that value. The remainder, a number between 0 and the divisor, becomes the relative record number. Note that the estimated number of records must be odd. Ideally, the divisor is a prime number slightly larger than the estimated number of records.

Using a hashing algorithm generates collisions (two or more logical keys that yield the same relative record number). When collisions occur, a secondary algorithm is used to determine where the new record is stored. Sometimes, the next available storage location is used. Sometimes, the new record is displaced by a constant number of record slots. Sometimes, a second hashing algorithm is used.

44.4.4.2.4 Chaining An alternative to maintaining an index or using a hashing algorithm is to maintain a linked list (Chapter 43) of logical keys. This technique is called chaining.

44.4.4.3 Indexed sequential files
An indexed sequential file is a compromise between sequential and random access. Records are physically stored in key order, so they can be accessed sequentially. Additionally, an index is maintained relating logical keys to physical disk addresses, so the data can be accessed randomly. Examples include IBM's ISAM and VSAM and Control Data's SCOPE.

Problems occur when records are added to or deleted from an indexed sequential file. Rather than moving all the records, new records are stored in an overflow area and the space associated with deleted records is unused. Over time, slack space and overflow data can severely impact the efficiency of both sequential and direct access, so frequent file reorganization is necessary. Do not use indexed sequential files when the data are volatile (in other words, when records are frequently added or deleted).

44.5 Key terms

Attribute — A property of an entity.

Backup file — A file that holds a copy of a master or transaction file; backup files are used to recover data if disaster strikes.

Block — Two or more logical records stored together as part of the same physical record.

Chaining — Maintaining a linked list of the logical keys of the records in a file.

Collision — An event that occurs when two or more logical keys input to a hashing algorithm yield the same relative address.

Data dictionary — A collection of data about the data.

Data element — An attribute that cannot be logically decomposed.

Data structure — A set of related data elements.

Database — A set of related files.

Direct access (random access) — Reading records from or writing records to a file in any order.

Directory — A list of the names and addresses of every file stored on a disk (or other secondary storage device).

Entity — An object (a person, group, place, thing, or activity) about which data are stored.

Field — A data element physically stored on some medium.

File — A set of related records.

File name — A unique logical identifier assigned to a file (usually by the user).

Hashing — Using an algorithm to convert a logical key to a relative address.

History file (archive) — A file that holds already processed transactions or no longer current master records.

Index — A list of the record keys and the associated physical disk addresses for each record in a file.

Indexed sequential file — A file on which records are stored in key order and an index is maintained, thus allowing the records to be accessed sequentially or randomly.

Key — The attribute or group of attributes that uniquely distinguishes one occurrence of an entity.

Logical record — The set of related fields needed to complete a single input/process/output cycle.

Master file — A file that holds permanent data that are accessed over a period of time.

Occurrence — A single instance of an entity.

Physical record — The unit of data that moves between the peripheral device and main memory.

Primitive — A command that tells a peripheral device to perform one of its basic functions.

Random access (direct access) — Reading records from or writing records to a file in any order.

Record — The set of fields associated with an occurrence of an entity.

Relative addressing — Assigning each record (or byte) in a file to an address that represents its position relative to the beginning of the file.

Sequential access — Reading records from or writing records to a file in key and/or physical storage order.

Spanned record — A logical record that extends over two or more physical records.

Temporary file — A file that holds intermediate results and exists for only a brief time.

Transaction file — A file that holds current data; a transaction file is often used to update (or maintain) a master file.

44.6   Software

Most programming languages support the file organizations described in this chapter.

44.7   References

1. Austing, R. F. and Cassel, L. N., *File Organization and Access: From Data to Information*, D. C. Heath, Lexington, MA, 1988.
2. Davis, W. S., *Business Systems Analysis and Design*, Wadsworth, Belmont, CA, 1994.
3. Davis, W. S., *Computers and Information Systems: An Introduction*, West Publishing, Minneapolis/St. Paul, MN, 1997.
4. Davis, W. S., *Systems Analysis and Design: A Structured Approach*, Addison-Wesley, Reading, MA, 1983.

chapter forty-five

Database design

John "Skip" Benamati
Miami University

Contents

45.1   Purpose

Database design is the process of gathering data requirements for an organization, a business process, or a proposed information system, and transforming these requirements into a set of specifications that can be used to create a database.

45.2   Strengths, weaknesses, and limitations

This chapter discusses several database design principles. Relevant strengths, weaknesses, and limitations will be discussed in context.

45.3   Inputs and related ideas

The primary inputs to database design are the user's views of the information as defined during the problem definition (Part II) and analysis (Part IV) stages of the system development life cycle. In addition to the existing views, new information requirements may be included in the system design.

Key data concepts are defined in Chapters 25, 43, and 44. Commonly used database design tools and techniques include data dictionaries (Chapter 25), entity-relationship models (Chapter 26), and data normalization (Chapter 28). Additionally, information concerning the application design is also relevant. In particular, database design influences or is influenced by hardware interface design (Chapter 42) and software design (Chapters 62, 66, 67, and 69).

45.4   Concepts

Database design is the process of gathering data requirements for an organization, a business process, or a proposed information system, and transforming these requirements into a set of specifications that can be used to create a database. The goal of database design is not only to provide the ability to capture all necessary information, but to organize that information in an efficient and usable way. To do so requires knowledge about what the information is and how it will be used, as well as information about the computing environment in which the database will be implemented. The computing environment typically includes a database management system, a network, and the computing platforms upon which the information system will be installed.

45.4.1   Database structures

The simplest database structure is called a flat-file database. All the data in a flat-file database are stored in a single, spreadsheet-like table that is not linked with any other files. The advantage is simplicity. Although technically not databases, flat files are fine for many personal computer applications.

In a hierarchical database, the file links form a hierarchy; for example, Figure 45.1 shows a student name and address file with links or pointers to an academic file, a financial file, and an activity file. In this example, the name and address file is the parent and the other files are its children. Database access starts at the top of the hierarchy and flows downward, so it

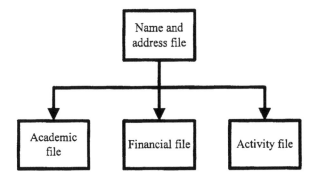

Figure 45.1 A hierarchical database.

is possible to access a student's academic file starting from his or her name and address record, but not vice versa. Note that a parent can have many children, but a child can have only one parent.

In a network database (Figure 45.2), the links or pointers can describe relationships between any two files in any direction, so a child can have many parents. For example, if the name and address file contains a link to the academic file and the academic file also contains a link to the name and address file, a given student's grade report might be prepared starting with *either* file. Because links are relatively easy to add to a data structure, the distinction between hierarchical and network databases has practically disappeared.

The files that form a relational database are best visualized as two-dimensional tables that resemble spreadsheets. In a given file, each column holds values of a single field (or attribute) and each row holds a single

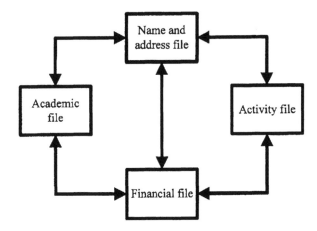

Figure 45.2 A network database.

record (a single occurrence of the entity). Files are linked by pointers or, more generally, relationships. The relational model has become a de facto standard, and data normalization (Chapter 28) suggests logical data structures that are compatible with a relational database.

As the name implies, an object-oriented database holds objects (Chapter 6) and defines the links or relationships between them. An object includes both the data and the procedures to manipulate the data. The objects can be traditional data oriented objects, but often are more complex. For example, an object-oriented database can define and hold such objects as sounds, videos, graphics, and spreadsheets.

45.4.2   Database administration

The responsibility for database design often resides in a database administration group. The database administrators must work closely with the application designers throughout the system design process. Maintaining the integrity of the database is another database administration responsibility. See Chapter 82 for additional details about this group.

45.4.3   Database design methodologies

Many organizations have a formal process for designing application databases. Because database design is a key part of information system design, the database design methodology is generally integrated into the design phase of the organization's application development methodology. Although the specific steps and tools vary considerably from organization to organization (and even across a given organization), the process is generally divided into two primary stages: logical (or conceptual) database design and physical database design.

Changes in the physical database design can affect the logical design. Consequently, these two steps are tightly integrated, with numerous feedback cycles. Note, however, that the application design and the logical database design must be completed before the physical database design can be finalized.

45.4.3.1   Logical database design

Logical or conceptual database design is concerned with defining and documenting the database in user terms. The objective is to formally define the *user's* understanding of the data and how the various data elements and composites are interrelated. This phase is geared to a non-technical audience. From the user's standpoint, it *is* the database design.

The process starts with a study of the user's data views and data uses in the context of the application. Following the organization's standards, data elements and composites are defined, named, and documented in the data dictionary (Chapter 25). Additionally, the relationships between the entities are studied and documented, often using such tools as entity relationship models (Chapter 26) and/or data normalization (Chapter 28). The output of the logical design process is a set of detailed documentation for all the data that will be stored in the database and for the interrelationships between those data.

45.4.3.2 Physical database design

The objective of physical database design is to produce a blueprint for physically implementing the database. (The resulting documentation is intended for a technical audience.) In addition to the logical database design, inputs to this stage also include key elements of the application design. The logical database design defines the data requirements. The application design defines how the data will be used. The goal is to design a physical database that implements the logical design and efficiently provides for all appropriate uses of the data.

The physical database design process starts with transaction analysis, a study of expected usage levels associated with the various application functions. Future users are usually involved in this process because they know how much work they do. The application design identifies points where the application accesses data, and these data interfaces (or transactions) provide a focus for transaction analysis. Generally, statistical information about the level of use is collected for each transaction type.

Based on these usage levels, decisions about how the data will be physically implemented are made. Note that high volume portions of the database receive more attention than those accessed less frequently. One option is to index high volume information for quicker access. Indexes improve performance, but maintaining them adds to system overhead.

Another physical database design requirement is ensuring the integrity of the database. Many database management systems provide features that help ensure database integrity, and integrity enforcement can also be implemented through the application software. The physical database design describes the methods that will be used for enforcing data integrity.

45.4.3.3 Modifying the logical design

Because physical design decisions can affect the logical design, logical and physical database design are not independent. Consequently, logical and physical database design can be viewed collectively as an iterative process with numerous feedback loops.

For example, based on a transaction analysis, it might be necessary (for performance reasons) to store a small percentage of the data redundantly. Altering the logical database design to include the redundant data is called denormalization. Like indexing, denormalization can improve performance, but at the cost of more overhead.

Most applications include information that is calculated from other information in the database; a sales commission (a percentage of sales revenue) is a good example. A choice must be made between physically storing such values in the database or calculating them as needed. This decision is based on how often the computed value is needed and how much information is needed to calculate it. Note that storing the computed value means computing it only once and subsequently reading it on demand. Stored calculated fields must be added to the logical database design.

The application design can also be altered to avoid projected performance problems. For example, it is not unusual for a large, high frequency transaction to provide more information than is needed for most of its invocations. Such transactions might be broken into a primary transaction that accesses only the data needed most of the time and a supplemental transaction that accesses the remaining information only when needed.

45.4.3.4 Schema and subschema

Finally, consider the database's schema and subschema. The database's physical contents are defined in a schema, a general description of the entire database that shows all the record types and their relationships. A large database might contain scores of files, but most users will access only a few of those files. To minimize the risk of a user accidentally accessing confidential data or changing data in an unneeded file, custom subschema that include only those records and relationships needed by a particular user or class of users can be defined. Clearly, the subschema must be consistent with the user's logical view of the data. Consequently, defining the schema and the subschema affects both logical and physical database design.

45.5 Key terms

Child — A lower-level record in a hierarchical database structure.
Composite — A set of related data elements.
Conceptual database design — See *logical database design*.
Data administration — The administrative function charged with the overall responsibility for data resources in an organization.
Data dictionary — A collection of data about the data.
Data element — An attribute that cannot be logically decomposed.
Data structure — A set of related data elements.
Database — A collection of interrelated and shared data of different types organized into a structure that minimizes redundancies and enhances the manipulation of the data; generally, a set of related files.
Database administration — The technical function charged with physically managing an organization's databases, including such issues as backup and recovery, performance, and security enforcement.
Database integrity — The state of a database that is protected against loss or contamination.
Database Management System (DBMS) — A software package that provides the means to define, maintain, control, and administer a

database and its applications; a set of software routines that define the rules for creating, accessing, and maintaining a database.

Denormalization — Altering the logical database design to include redundant data.

Entity — An object (a person, group, place, thing, or activity) about which data are stored.

Filter — A set of logical conditions used to screen records in a query.

Flat-file database — A database (more accurately, a file) in which all the data are stored in a single, spreadsheet-like table that is not linked with any other files.

Hierarchical database — A database in which the file links (or relationships) form a hierarchy.

Index — A list of the keys and physical locations of each record in a file.

Logical database design — The database design stage concerned with defining and documenting the database in user terms.

Network database — A network in which the links or pointers can describe relationships between any two files in any direction, so a child can have many parents.

Parent — A higher-level record in a hierarchical database structure.

Physical database design — The database design stage during which a blueprint for physically implementing the database is produced.

Query — A question; usually, a request for data or information.

Relation — A table (analogous to a file) in a relational database.

Relational database — A database in which the files (or relations) are visualized as two-dimensional tables with each column holding values of a single field (or attribute) and each row holding a single record (a single occurrence of the entity). The files are linked by pointers or, more generally, relationships.

Relationship — A link between two data structures or entities.

Schema — A general description of the entire database that shows all the record types and their relationships.

Subschema — A subset of the schema that includes only those records and relationships needed by a particular user or class of users.

Transaction — The sequence of steps required to carry out an event about which data are recorded or processed; also, a single occurrence of a business activity; for example, a single sale or the receipt of a single order from a supplier.

Transaction analysis — A study of expected usage levels associated with the various application functions.

View — A subset of the database that includes only selected fields from the records that meet a set of conditions defined in a logical filter.

45.6   *Software*

Many CASE products (Chapter 5), such as Texas Instrument's Information Engineering Facility (IEF), include software to provide integrated support for both database and application design. Other tools such as automated data dictionaries (Chapter 25) provide support as well. Access, Paradox, dBase, Filemaker Pro, Approach, 4th Dimension, and Alpha Four are popular microcomputer database management programs. Examples of mainframe database software include DB2, IDMS, and ORACLE.

Most database management systems include a data definition language (DDL) for specifying file structures, relationships, schema, and subschema. Once the database is created, its contents are accessed and maintained using a data manipulation language (DML). Most database management systems incorporate a query language (such as Structured Query Language, or SQL) and a report generator. The database administrator uses a data control language (DCL) to perform such activities as backing up files, keeping track of user names and passwords, and monitoring system performance.

45.7   References

1. Date, C. J., *An Introduction to Database Systems, vol.* 1, 6th ed., Addison-Wesley, Reading, MA, 1994.
2. Hansen, G. W. and Hansen, J. V., *Database Management and Design*, Prentice-Hall, Upper Saddle River, NJ, 1996.
3. Kroenke, D. M., *Database Processing: Fundamentals, Design, and Implementation*, Prentice-Hall, Upper Saddle River, NJ, 1995.
4. McFadden, F. R. and Hoffer, J. A., *Modern Database Management*, Benjamin/ Cummings, Redwood City, CA, 1994.
5. Watson, R. T., *Data Management, an Organizational Perspective*, John Wiley & Sons, New York, 1996.

chapter forty-six

Data entry forms and screens

William S. Davis

Contents

46.1 Purpose

A form is a document (or a simulated document on a screen) that is used to capture data. This chapter discusses several basic form design and screen design principles and identifies some input controls that can be used to screen input data.

46.2   Strengths, weaknesses, and limitations

Paper forms are extremely flexible. They can be carried virtually anywhere and completed using such simple technology as a pen or a pencil. Except for running out of forms or ink, they are not subject to failure. However, the data recorded on a paper form must subsequently be entered into a computer through a keyboard, a scanner, or similar equipment. Because the data capture and data entry steps are separated by time, the data might not be available in a timely fashion, and the process of obtaining the feedback needed to correct errors is lengthy and complex.

Although laptop computers are quite portable, screens generally require the user to stay near a source of electrical power and to avoid certain environments, and a screen can fail. (Field personnel sometimes carry an appropriate set of paper forms as a backup.) However, because a screen is directly linked to a computer, the data can be utilized as soon as they are entered (thus enhancing timeliness) and verified and corrected interactively (thus enhancing data accuracy).

46.3   Inputs and related ideas

Forms and screens are important parts of the user interface (Chapter 48). The contents of a given form or screen can often be derived from the logical data structures identified during the analysis stage of the system development life cycle by using such tools as data flow diagrams (Chapter 24), prototypes (Chapters 31 and 32), and Warnier-Orr diagrams (Chapter 33). The data are typically documented in the data dictionary (Chapter 25), and important form and screen design criteria can often be found in the requirements specification (Chapter 35). At the high-level physical design stage, symbols on the system flowchart (Chapter 37) identify necessary screens and forms. Prototyping (Chapter 31) and rapid application design (Chapter 32) are useful tools for designing forms and screens.

Related concepts include survey instruments (Chapter 17), report design (Chapter 47), user interface design (Chapter 48), dialogue design (Chapter 49), windows design (Chapter 50), web page design and hyperlinks (Chapter 51), and system controls (Chapter 77). The contents of forms and screens are an important source of information about the existing system during the problem definition and information gathering stage (Part II) of a subsequent system development life cycle.

46.4   Concepts

A form is a document (or a simulated document on a screen) that is used to capture data. This chapter discusses several basic form design and screen design principles and identifies some input controls that can be used to screen input data.

46.4.1 Data capture and data entry

As the term implies, data capture is the process of initially capturing source data. Data entry, in contrast, is the process of converting the source data into a machine-readable form and entering the data into a computer.

In a batch environment, data capture and data entry are sometimes viewed as separate steps. First, the data are captured on paper or some other medium and collected over time. Then the data are entered using such equipment as a keyboard, a MICR reader, an optical character recognition (OCR) scanner, a regular scanner with OCR software, a mark sense reader, and so on.

In an on-line or interactive environment, data capture and data entry are combined in a single step. For example, when a customer uses an ATM machine to perform a banking transaction, the data are captured in electronic form and immediately processed, eliminating the need for a subsequent data entry step.

46.4.2 Designing forms

Many applications call for forms; for example, Figure 46.1 shows a sales receipt (or sales invoice) form. Forms are used to capture source data, and

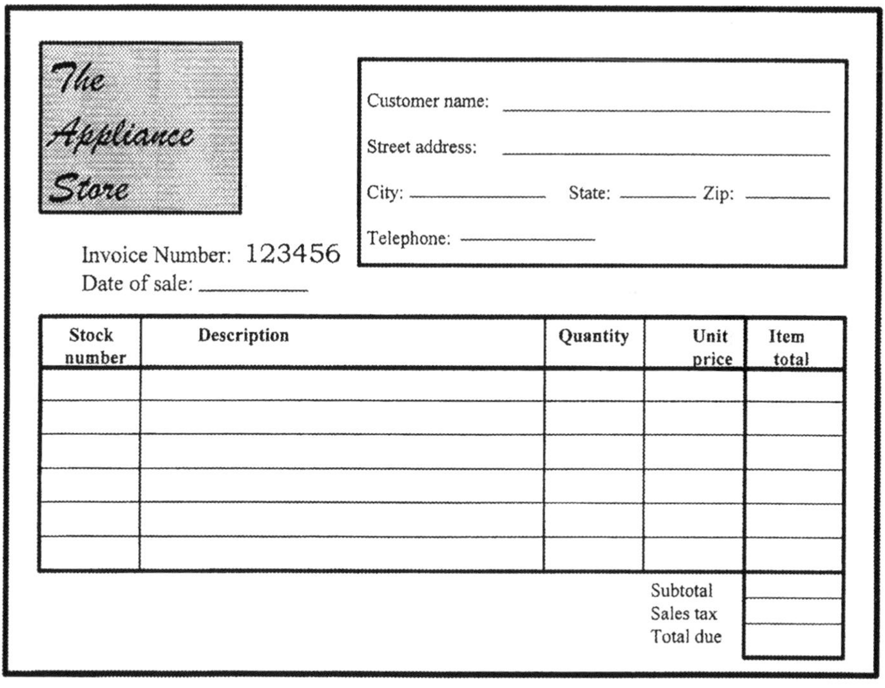
The Appliance Store

Customer name: ______
Street address: ______
City: ______ State: ______ Zip: ______
Telephone: ______

Invoice Number: 123456
Date of sale: ______

Stock number	Description	Quantity	Unit price	Item total

Subtotal
Sales tax
Total due

Figure 46.1 An invoice form.

the forms themselves are sometimes retained in long-term storage. Completed forms can be scanned or the data can be input to a computer through a keyboard. Alternatively, a form image can be displayed on a screen and used as a template for on-line or interactive data entry.

Form design is an art, but a few simple guidelines can help. The starting point is the necessary data. Analyze the appropriate data flow diagrams, data dictionary entries, data structures, requirements, and other analysis documentation and identify *all* the data elements or fields that must appear on the form.

A key consideration in designing a form is anticipating how the user is likely to scan the form. In Western societies, people read from left to right, starting at the top left and preceding down the page. Consequently, users naturally look first at the upper left of a document and follow a left to right and top to bottom pattern from the starting point. A well-designed form takes advantage of that natural tendency. For example, the invoice pictured in Figure 46.1 features a prominent logo at the upper left (the starting point), positions customer information (the first data to be entered) to the right of the logo, and then provides a series of lines for entering the item purchased data. Notice how the lines and boxes tend to guide the eye and suggest the proper order for entering data values.

A second primary objective is to make sure the form itself does not introduce errors. Allow enough space for each field. Although it is tempting to try to avoid the need for a second form, jamming too much information on a single page virtually guarantees that important data will be missed or recorded incorrectly. Clearly distinguish captions, directions, and other supporting information from the data. For example, set the supporting information in a unique font or color that cannot possibly be mistaken for source data. The preprinted invoice number on Figure 46.1 is another good example; note that it is set in a font that clearly distinguishes it from the preprinted captions. Finally, avoid the temptation to overdo fonts, colors, graphics, and special effects. The focus should be on the data, not the form.

A well-designed form can help to enhance data accuracy. For example, related fields should be entered together. Proximity implies association, so use lines, boxes, color, and white space to group related fields and to visually separate the groups. Group fields (or attributes) that are associated with the same entity; for example, the customer's name, address, and telephone number are grouped in a box at the top right of Figure 46.1 and the data associated with sales are grouped in the lower box. Consider the source of each field and group fields from the same source. Anticipate the order in which the user is likely to enter the data and try to follow that natural order (e.g., name first, then street address, then city, etc.).

Provide clear, unambiguous directions and captions, and include examples where appropriate. Some fields call for free-form data recording; the lines for entering customer data on Figure 46.1 are good examples. Sometimes, single-character blocks or (lightly) printed examples or templates show the user exactly where and how to record the values for specific fields. Blocks are particularly useful for fixed length fields (Figure 46.2). Templates are particularly useful for numeric only or character only fields. Check lists are also popular; the available choices are listed on the form and the user selects an entry by marking it in some way or clicking on a box (Figure 46.3, lower right). It is not unusual for a given form to incorporate different data recording techniques for different fields.

Common or "standard" forms can be purchased from most office supply stores, and many form design software packages include libraries of sample forms and form templates that can be customized.

46.4.3   Designing screens

A screen can be used to display a report or to electronically simulate a form, but more dynamic images can be displayed, too. Like form design, screen design is a bit of an art, but once again a few simple guidelines can help.

The principles of form design still apply to screen design. The starting point is the necessary data. People still read a screen from left to right and from top to bottom. The screen itself must not introduce errors, so allow

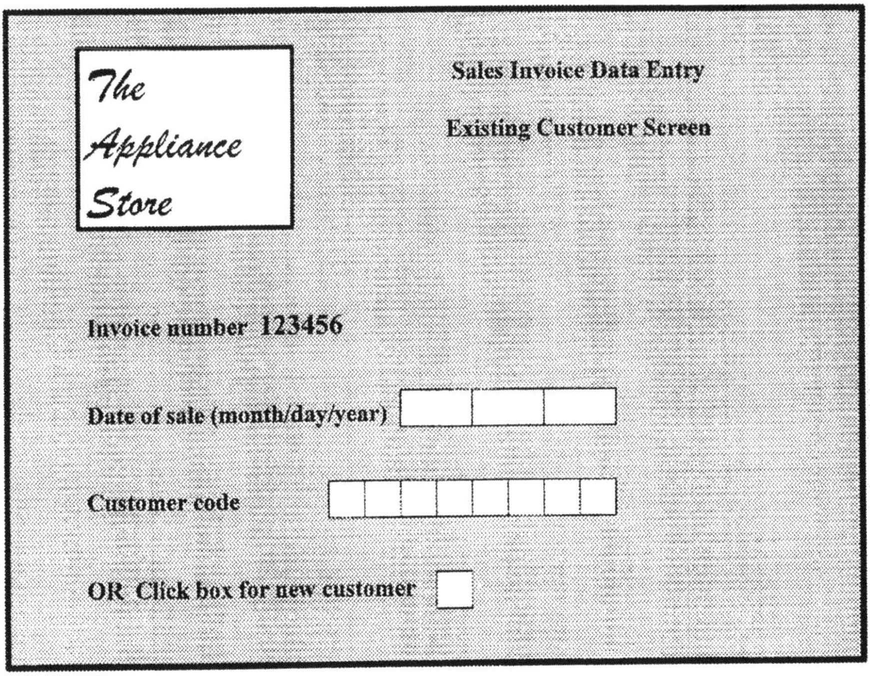

Figure 46.2   A screen for entering a date and a customer code.

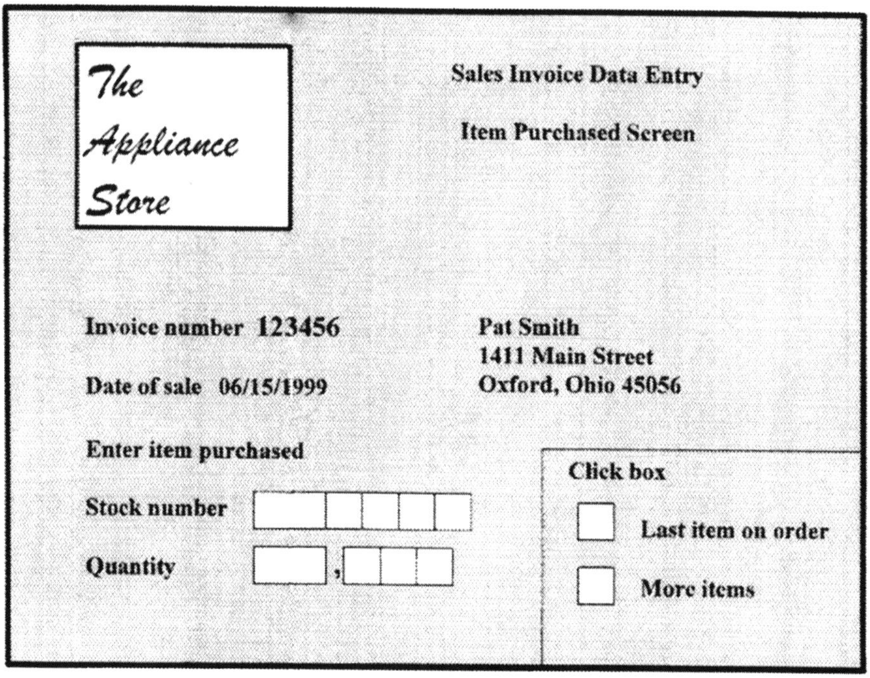

Figure 46.3 A screen for entering an item purchased.

enough space for each field and clearly distinguish captions, directions, and other supporting information from the data. Use lines, boxes, color, and white space to group related fields and to visually separate the groups. Provide clear, unambiguous directions and captions, and provide examples where appropriate.

Design for the user. Get the user involved in the process by prototyping the screens. Take advantage of what the user already knows by simulating existing forms and reports on the screen and by following the conventions of applications the user already knows. Always provide feedback; following any transaction or operation, tell the user what happened. *Never* leave the user hanging. As a minimum, provide features to support easy recovery from errors and to facilitate backward migration. For example, allow the user to back up one screen by pressing the escape key.

Extend the idea of grouping related fields by designing a set of related screens so that each screen supports a complete operation or a complete set of related operations. For example, consider using one screen to collect customer data (Figure 46.2) and another screen to collect item purchased data (Figure 46.3), and so on. When data must be entered through a set of related screens, be consistent. Use the same conventions on all parts of the screen and on all screens.

Unlike paper forms, screens support numerous features (such as color changes, font changes, reverse video, blinking characters, variable lines, boxes, shapes, graphics, and animation) that can be used to dynamically capture the user's attention or communicate information. For example, graying out or ghosting unavailable options can help to avoid confusion, and blinking a field, displaying it in reverse video, or pointing to it with an animated arrow can call the user's attention to a data entry error. (People notice things that move, change, or are different.) Avoid adding special features just because they are technically feasible (or just to show off), however.

Monitor capability is an important factor in determining what can be displayed on a screen. For example, resolution, the level of detail a screen can show, is a function of the number of pixels (or dots) on the screen. A CGA (Color/Graphics Adapter) monitor supports low-resolution (640 × 200 pixels, 2 color or 320 × 200 pixels, 4 color) graphics. The VGA (Video Graphics Array) standard supports higher resolutions (640 × 480, 256 colors), and superVGA (SVGA) increases the resolution to at least 800 × 600 pixels and makes more colors available. An XGA (extended graphics array) monitor supports 1024 × 768 pixels. A detailed discussion of the related hardware concepts is beyond the scope of this book.

Traditionally, screens are used to display output, echoing the characters typed through a keyboard or displaying selected data stored in memory, but new technology makes it possible to use a screen as an input device. Hyperlinked screens are used to support graphic presentation such as a slide show, with the hyperlinks controlling slide sequence. An icon input screen allows the user to trigger the execution of a related routine by clicking on an icon. Finally, a graphic input screen, or touch screen, allows a user to input a command or request information by pointing; the touch screens in shopping mall kiosks are a good example.

Screen design tools are often incorporated in prototyping and CASE software.

46.4.4   Input controls

The objective of input controls is to screen out and (if possible) correct bad data before they enter the system. Validity tests are used to ensure that each input field is the right type (numeric, alphabetic), that the value of a given field is within upper and lower bounds, that fixed length fields (e.g., social security number, telephone number) are the right length, and so on. Exception tests are used to screen such "exceptional" values as a zero in a field that will be used as a divisor. Reasonableness tests are used to screen invalid values (e.g., anything but F or M in a single-character sex or gender field).

Input controls are implemented at data entry time. If the data capture and data entry steps are separated by time, the input controls are used to flag erroneous transactions for subsequent review. In some cases, the bad transactions can be corrected in time for processing with the current batch. In other cases, the flagged transactions are corrected off-line and must wait until the next scheduled batch run. However, if the data collection and data entry steps are combined in an on-line, interactive system, errors can be identified and corrected as they are entered.

46.5   Key terms

Data capture — The process of initially capturing source data.

Data entry — The process of converting source data into a machine-readable form and entering them into a computer.

Exception test — A test used to screen such exceptional values as a zero in a field that will be used as a divisor.

Form — A paper document (or a simulated document on a screen) that is used to capture data.

Graphic input screen (touch screen) — A screen that allows a user to input a command or request information by pointing.

Hyperlinked screens — A set of screens connected by hyperlinks; for example, in a slide show presentation, hyperlinks are used to control slide sequence.

Icon input screen — An input screen that allows the user to trigger the execution of a related routine by clicking on an icon.

Input control — A test or control, designed to screen out and (if possible) correct bad data before they enter the system.

Pixel — A picture element; a dot on a screen.

Reasonableness test — A test used to screen invalid values (e.g., anything but F or M in a single-character sex or gender field).

Resolution — The level of detail a screen can show, a function of the number of pixels (or dots) on the screen.

Screen (display screen) — An output device that resembles a television screen.

Source data — The original data that describe a transaction.

Validity test — A test used to ensure that each input field is the right type (numeric, alphabetic), that the value of a given field is within upper and lower bounds, that fixed length fields (e.g., social security number, telephone number) are the right length, and so on.

White space — Space on a form or a screen that contains no information; empty space.

46.6   Software

Form Designer (The Learning Company), Formtool 97 (International Microcomputer Software, Inc.), Informs (Novell), and Jetform Design (Jetform Corporation) are examples of form design software packages. Screen design tools are often incorporated in prototyping and CASE software.

46.7   References

1. Davis, W. S., *Business Systems Analysis and Design*, Wadsworth, Belmont, CA, 1994.
2. Galitz, W. O., *Handbook of Screen Format Design*, QED Information Systems, Wellesley, MA, 1989.

chapter forty-seven

Report design

William S. Davis

Contents

47.1 Purpose

A report is a formal, organized presentation of data, often in the form of a printed document or a set of screens. Reports are an important part of a system's user interface. This chapter discusses text-only reports.

47.2 Strengths, weaknesses, and limitations

Reports were common long before computers were invented. They are excellent tools for organizing and summarizing large amounts of data.

0-8493-7001-9/99/$0.00+$.50
©1999 by CRC Press LLC

Traditionally, reports were static and often suffered from information overload, but such modern software as report generators and query languages have made it possible to select on demand only the desired data from a file or database.

47.3   Inputs and related ideas

Reports are an important part of a system's user interface (Chapter 48). Before a report can be prepared, the data must exist, usually in the form of one or more files (Chapter 44) or databases (Chapter 45). During the high-level system design phase (Part V), reports are identified as data flows to users. The contents of a report can often be derived from the logical data structures identified during the analysis stage by using such tools as data flow diagrams (Chapter 24), prototypes (Chapters 31 and 32), and Warnier-Orr diagrams (Chapter 33). Reports are an important source of information about the existing system during the problem definition and information gathering stage (Part II).

47.4   Concepts

A report is a formal, organized presentation of data, often in the form of a printed document or a set of screens. This chapter discusses text-only reports.

47.4.1   Report format

Figure 47.1 illustrates the format of a traditional control breaks report. It begins with a report header or a report title that identifies the report. Other identifiers, such as the report date and the person or department responsible for compiling the report, are often included in the report header. Sometimes, a separate title page is printed or displayed. On multiple page reports, the report title is often repeated at the top of each page or screen.

The body of the report is divided into an imaginary grid of columns and rows (or lines). Column headers near the top of each page or screen identify the field displayed in each column. Each row holds a single detail line that displays the appropriate field values from a single input record (e.g., from a single sales receipt) or a single set of related input records.

Note in Figure 47.1 that the stock number and the description are repeated on each detail line for stock number 17593, but the repetitive values are suppressed on the detail lines for the second item, stock number 17594. Suppressing repetitive data makes the report easier to read, but either approach is acceptable.

The data used to generate a report are often sorted or indexed by one or more key fields. (In Figure 47.1, the stock number serves as the key.) Because

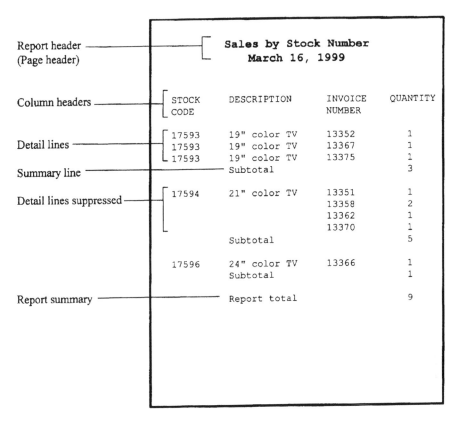

Figure 47.1   The elements of a control breaks report.

the source records are accessed in key order, the detail lines for all records with the same key value are grouped together on the report. For example, all the records for stock number 17593 will be read (and, thus, be printed or displayed) before the first stock number 17594 record is read.

A change in the value of the key field is called a control break. For example, when the first record for stock number 17594 is read, it is reasonable to assume that all the stock number 17593 records have been processed. When a control break occurs, a summary line (Figure 47.1) can (optionally) be printed. Summary lines typically hold a count of the number of records and/or the sums of selected fields in the control group.

Some reports feature multiple control fields, with primary control breaks, secondary control breaks, and so on. If desired, summary lines can be printed at each level control break. In some reports, the detail lines are suppressed and only summary lines are printed.

Most reports end with a report summary line, section, or page. On multiple-page reports, page summaries are common, too. Page numbers and a page header are usually added to lengthy reports.

47.4.2 Types of reports

A detail report lists data for each input record or transaction. As the name suggests, a summary report summarizes data accumulated or derived from several detail records, often showing *only* the summarized data. An exception report lists or summarizes only the data for input records that pass a predefined condition or filter, for example, listing only overdue accounts or only items than have been in inventory for longer than 30 days. An unusual occurrence report lists or summarizes data describing only abnormal or out of the ordinary occurrences.

A scheduled report is prepared at a predetermined time; for example, at the end of the day, the week, the month, the quarter, or the year. A key indicator report is a form of scheduled report that summarizes critical activities, often on a daily basis. A demand report, in contrast, is created on request. Often, end users are given the ability to create their own demand reports using a query language.

47.4.3 Report layout

To lay out a report, start by defining the report title and the page title lines. Be sure to include the report date and page numbers (if necessary).

Then, turn to the body of the report. Any number of lines can be printed or displayed, but the number of characters that can be arrayed across a page or a screen is limited, so width is the primary constraint on report design.

To determine the column width for each of the report fields, start with the column headers. Lengthy, multiple-word headers can be spread over two or more lines, so for each column count the number of characters in the widest header line and record the header widths. Then count the number of characters (including decimal points, commas, plus signs, minus signs, dollar signs, and other punctuation) needed to display the biggest (or smallest) possible value for each field and record the data widths. Finally, working across the report one column at a time, compare the header width and the data width for each column and select the larger value. That number is the column width. Add the widths for each of the columns to get the number of characters needed to display the data.

Next, consider the blank space (or white space) needed to separate the columns. A single space might be enough for closely related columns, but additional column separation normally enhances readability. Add white space to the sum of the column widths to get the report width. If that number is bigger than the paper or screen width, modify or delete one or more columns, use a smaller font, reduce the amount of white space, or change the (printed) report orientation from portrait to landscape. Otherwise, subtract the report width from the paper or screen width to get the number of unused spaces that can be distributed across the line to enhance the balance, symmetry, overall appearance, and readability of the report.

47.4.4   Report design guidelines

Historically, reports were designed on paper using report layout forms. Modern report generators (software) have simplified the task by suggesting a reasonable report layout given only a list of the fields to be included, but the designer may still want to fine-tune the suggested layout to enhance clarity. Report design is a bit of an art, but there are several guidelines that can help.

The first guideline is to include *all* the necessary data, but *only* the necessary data. The temptation is to list every available field. Don't. Be selective. Note that no report generator, no matter how sophisticated, can select the correct fields for the designer.

A second set of guidelines is intended to make the data easy to read. Start by using clear, meaningful, descriptive column headers. Visually distinguish the data from the descriptive information; for example, set column headers in uppercase, italic, or boldface and the data in a basal (regular) font. Group closely related fields in adjacent columns. Use white space to separate loosely related and adjacent positioning to group closely related fields. Avoid using too much white space to separate columns (four or five spaces are usually plenty), because too much separation makes it difficult to visually align the rows. Use a visual clue (such as an asterisk, a different type font, and/or blank lines or horizontal spacing) to identify summary lines.

To clarify the meaning of the data, make sure the headers and the associated data are visually aligned. Generally, left-justify character fields and their headers and right-justify numeric fields and their headers, or center the data under the header. If a numeric field includes digits to the right of the decimal point, make sure all the decimal points are aligned. The easiest way to control decimal point alignment is to display the same number of digits in all the values and to right-justify the numbers.

With some type fonts, it is easy to mistake a dollar sign for the digit 8, so by convention, dollar signs are displayed only on column or row totals and (optionally) on the first value in a column. Negative signs are easy to overlook in a column of numbers, so the negative sign (or other designator, such as DB for debit or CR for credit) is typically printed to the right of the negative number. An option is to enclose negative numbers in parentheses.

Some reports print or display negative numbers in red, but relying strictly on color is dangerous because most standard office copiers show red as black. Also, avoid using light blue. Many office copiers are blind to light blue.

The final rule is a simple one: Be consistent. Changes in rules from column to column, row to row, or page to page are confusing and lead to interpretation errors. The reader should not be expected to learn the formatting rules more than once.

47.5   Key terms

Column header — Documentation at the top of each page or screen that identifies the field displayed in each column.

Control break — A change in the value of a key field.

Demand report — A report that is created on request.

Detail line — A single report row that displays the appropriate field values from a single report file record.

Detail report — A report that lists data for each input record or transaction.

Exception report — A report that lists or summarizes only the data for input records that pass a predefined condition or filter.

Field — A data element; a single, logically meaningful unit of data.

File — A set of related records.

Key indicator report — A form of scheduled report that summarizes critical activities, often on a daily basis.

Record — A set of related fields.

Report — An organized presentation of data, often printed or displayed in text form.

Report header (report title) — A page, screen, or section that (typically) precedes and identifies the report.

Report summary — One or more lines, a section, or a page that summarizes the entire report.

Scheduled report — A report that is prepared at a predetermined time.

Summary line — On a report, a line (or row) that holds summary information, such as counts or sums; summary lines are typically printed or displayed following a control break.

Summary report — A report that summarizes data accumulated or derived from several input records, often showing *only* the summarized data.

47.6   Software

Most programming languages can be used to create a report. Most database management programs and many CASE products, screen design tools, and prototyping tools incorporate a report generator or a report layout facility. Some languages, such as RPG, were specifically designed to create reports.

47.7   References

1. Davis, W. S., *Business Systems Analysis and Design*, Wadsworth, Belmont, CA, 1994.

chapter forty-eight

User interface design

David C. Yen and William S. Davis

Contents

0-8493-7001-9/99/$0.00+$.50
©1999 by CRC Press LLC

48.1   Purpose

A user interface is a point in the system where a human being interacts with a computer. This chapter discusses several different types of direct (human/ computer) interfaces and the interface design process.

48.2   Strengths, weaknesses, and limitations

This chapter introduces some important principles of user interface design. The strengths, weaknesses, and limitations associated with specific inter- faces or interface design techniques are discussed in context.

48.3   Inputs and related ideas

Before designing a user interface, the analyst or designer must first know the user and understand the task to be performed. Much of the necessary information is collected during the problem definition and information gathering (Part II), analysis (Part IV) and high-level design (Part V) stages of the system development life cycle. On a data flow diagram (Chapter 24), processes and data flows from sources and to destinations might suggest a need for user interfaces. The data elements that are input by or output to users are typically documented in the data dictionary (Chapter 25). The requirements specification (Chapter 35) identifies user needs, user charac- teristics (skill, training, etc.), and task requirements. At the high-level phys- ical design stage, symbols on the system flowchart (Chapter 37) identify necessary reports, screens, forms, and keyboard operations. Prototyping (Chapter 31) and rapid application design (Chapter 32) are useful tools for designing a user interface.

   This chapter focuses on certain general principles associated with direct user interface design. The contents of the screens that make up a direct user interface are discussed in Chapter 46 (screen and forms design), Chapter 49 (dialogue design), and Chapter 50 (windows design). Related concepts include report design (Chapter 47), web page design (Chapter 51), and natural language processing (Chapter 68).

48.4   Concepts

A user interface is a point in the system where a human being interacts with a computer. The interface can incorporate hardware, software, procedures, and data. The interaction can be direct; for example, a user might access a computer through a screen and a keyboard. Printed reports and forms designed to capture data for subsequent input are indirect user interfaces. This chapter focuses on direct computer interfaces.

48.4.1 The end user

Generally, the purpose of any information system is to provide the right data and information to the right person at the right time. That "person" is an end user.

An end user is any person who needs the output generated by the computer and/or any person who interacts with the computer at an operational level. Examples include a manager reading a report, a clerk entering data, an engineer using a CAD program to prepare a technical diagram, a production supervisor using software to plan a work schedule, and a technical writer using a word processor to prepare a manual. The end user communicates with the system through the user interface.

48.4.2 Types of user interfaces

There are several different types of direct user interfaces.

48.4.2.1 Command interfaces

Some user interfaces rely on abbreviated commands or acronyms. MS-DOS line commands, the single-letter slash commands used by early spreadsheet programs, and the keyboard shortcuts and function key commands available on many word processors are good examples.

Such cryptic commands save a sophisticated user the time that might otherwise be spent traversing menus or windows. Using cryptic commands also reduces the time needed to design the menus and the screens. Command-based interfaces require considerable user training, however, and it is unreasonable to expect users to memorize all the commands without referencing a command template.

48.4.2.2 Menu interfaces

A menu consists of a list of the options available to the user. Typically, the user selects the desired option by typing the option's letter or number, highlighting the option and pressing enter, or pointing to the option and clicking a mouse button. Often, selecting a given option leads to a second menu listing suboptions, so a set of related screens and windows must be designed and implemented to support a menu-driven interface.

On a well-designed traditional interface, the relevant commands, subcommands, and/or menus should be logically grouped, and the design of the hierarchy should be intuitive to the user. Hidden commands or menus should be avoided. The commands and menus (as well as any related windows or screens) should be easy to access and to terminate.

Compared to cryptic commands, menus are more flexible, easier to use, and easier to learn. Traversing multiple menus can be time consuming, however, and creating a set of linked menus adds to system development time.

Also, on large or complex systems, the menus occupy a great deal of random access memory (RAM).

48.4.2.3   Object-oriented interfaces

Object-oriented interfaces, also called icon-based interfaces or graphic user interfaces (GUIs), have become increasingly common since the introduction of the Apple Macintosh and Microsoft's Windows operating systems. Windows, icons (graphic symbols that represent processing options, files, or executable routines), menus, and pointers are the key elements of an object-oriented interface. (Consequently, they are sometimes called WIMP interfaces.) Generally, the user points to the desired element and clicks a mouse button to trigger the associated action.

On a well-designed object-oriented interface, the meaning of each icon is apparent (almost intuitively obvious) to the user. Embedded or linked objects are clearly defined in the icon's menu structure. Finally, each icon has a single entry and a single exit.

Object-oriented interfaces are easy to understand, learn, and use, and because all the available choices are displayed on the screen, there is no need for the user to memorize anything. They are also easy to maintain because each icon (or window, or menu) is implemented as an independent module. The windows, icons, and menus and the pointer logic consume considerable processor time and a great deal of memory, however.

48.4.2.4   Expert system interfaces

Expert system interfaces utilize natural language processing (NLP) (Chapter 68). Key elements include the ability to parse and comprehend human sentences and paragraphs, voice recognition, and voice data entry. Such hardware as keyboards, pointing devices, and microphones might be used for input. Speakers provide audio output. Natural language processing requires a very powerful computer with a great deal of memory and a fast processor.

48.4.2.5   Web-form interfaces

Web-form interfaces (Chapter 51) follow the metaphor established by the Internet and the World Wide Web. Files and executable routines are viewed as hyperlinked pages. Some of those pages are designed to resemble forms that users either fill in directly or complete by selecting answers from a default list.

On a well-designed web-form interface, the layout of all forms is clear (almost intuitively obvious) and data entry is always verified. Additionally, the data entry process is supported by appropriate and meaningful prompts.

48.4.3   User interface design criteria

In the past, when computers were expensive and people were (relatively) cheap, users were expected to interact with the computer on the machine's terms, but that is no longer true. Given today's technology, a user interface must be designed to allow the user to perform his or her job as effectively as possible. Machine efficiency should, of course, be considered, but only if it does not conflict with the primary objective.

Generally, a good interface is easy to use, easy to maintain, easy to learn, and incorporates readily available on-line help. Also, a good interface never leaves the user hanging, providing (as a minimum) a clear exit path from any operation.

48.4.3.1 System type

The precise nature of the user interface is a function of the type of system to be developed. For example, a typical management information system (MIS) incorporates numerous forms, reports, and access controls. A decision support system (DSS) emphasizes dialogues, windows, and interfaces between a database, a model base, a graph base, and/or a text base. An expert system needs interfaces between a rule base, a database, and/or a natural language processing (NLP) facility. Group decision support systems (GDSS) and/or electronic meeting systems (EMS) need interfaces with facilities that transmit and/or share data, such as the network.

48.4.3.2 The mental model

People tend to form their own mental model of a system. For example, a video card game player visualizes cards on a table, a video golf game player can image actually playing golf, and a flight simulator gives the user a realistic sense of flying an airplane. The mental model helps the user understand how the system works. A good mental model allows the user to predict the system's response to a given stimulus, and the more accurate those predictions, the more intuitive the system appears. When the user understands the system at an intuitive level, the need for training declines, the error rate improves, and the user becomes more efficient.

When designing a user interface, the designer should try to select a mental model that makes sense to the user. For example, if the user filled out a paper form in the old system, that form might be simulated on the screen. If the mental model cannot be based on the user's experience, the user must be trained to understand the new mental model and the designer must be prepared to adjust the model if the user has trouble understanding it. A good approach is to adopt a known metaphor such as the Microsoft Windows desktop. There is no point reinventing the wheel, and time spent on Windows training might simplify training for future applications.

48.4.3.3 Environmental issues

The system environment represents a potential constraint on interface design. For example, it is unreasonable to expect an automobile mechanic whose hands are covered with grease to enter data directly into a computer, and people whose work takes them away from sources of electricity or a system access port require special equipment to capture data electronically. Consider the nature of the end user, too. Such variables as education, training, skill, and handicaps serve to limit what a given person can reasonably be expected to do. The system must fit the user.

Other environmental factors have legal, moral, and ethical (as well as financial) implications. For example, over the past several years researchers have identified a variety of problems associated with video terminal use ranging from repetitive stress injuries, to eyestrain, to the possibility that exposure to low-level radiation might represent a hazard for pregnant women. Such factors must be taken into account when the user interface is designed. Many organizations have adopted explicit ergonomic standards for user interfaces.

Finally, consider legal and auditing requirements. For example, if a company's auditing rules specify that a physical (printed) copy of each sales receipt be retained for a period of one full year, the ability to create, store, and retrieve those copies must be built into the system, perhaps through the user interface. If state law requires that all documents used to compute an employee's pay be retained until six months after the fiscal year ends, and pay is computed in part as a commission on sales, then there is a legal reason to maintain a file of sales receipts. Such details can make the difference between a successful system and an embarrassing failure.

48.4.4   *The user interface design process*

End user involvement is valuable throughout the system development life cycle, but it is *essential* during interface design. By definition, supporting the end user is the ultimate objective of any information system. To the end user, the user interface *is* the system. Consequently, user interface design must be user-centered.

Interface design can be viewed as a complete system analysis and design project in its own right, but given the need for user involvement, prototyping (Chapter 31) and rapid application design (RAD, Chapter 32) are highly recommended. The basic idea is to gradually enhance an initial set of generalized, but inefficient (soft) capabilities until an easy-to-use, efficient, user-friendly system evolves. This soft capability approach allows the interface designer to build on a relatively small set of requirements and contributes to a more bug-free conceptual design. Also, as the system evolves, the soft capabilities are easily replaced by newly available technology, leading to an advanced interface design with greater power at a lower cost.

Figure 48.1 outlines the steps in the interface design process.

48.4.4.1   *Overview and define*

The first step is to identify and define the interface requirements (including the criteria described in Section 48.4.3) in enough detail to begin building a

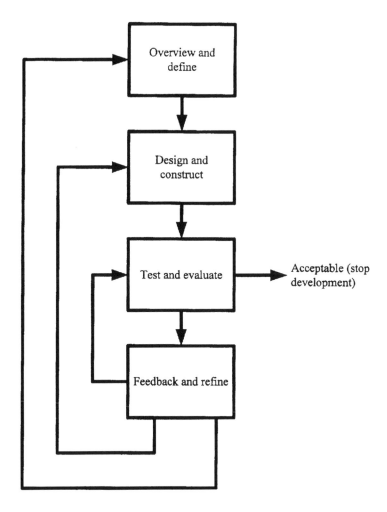

Figure 48.1   The steps in the interface design process.

prototype. The nature of the proposed system must be known, and any important environmental factors must be identified. The nature and characteristics of the user tasks supported by the interface, the user needs implied by the interface, and any links between the interface and the rest of the system must also be known.

This information can usually be obtained from the documentation developed during the problem definition and information gathering (Part II), analysis (Part IV), and high-level design (Part V) stages of the system development life cycle. For example, a properly drawn system flowchart (Chapter 37) shows all the system elements (manual procedures, input documents, output documents, display screens, etc.) that call for user interfaces and the links between those elements and the rest of the system.

48.4.4.2 Design and construct

The key objective of this stage is to construct a prototype based on the available information. Often, the first step in the process is to construct a hierarchy chart that shows the required windows or screens and the paths or links between them. For example, the hierarchy chart in Figure 48.2 shows the relationships between a menu screen and its immediate subscreens. By convention, control flows from top to bottom and back again, and the user can exit the system only from the top.

A hierarchy chart is an excellent tool for evaluating and planning the value, path, and destination associated with each user choice. The value or response associated with a given choice is an input value that activates the choice; for example, a four-choice menu might recognize as valid only choices 1, 2, 3, or 4. Choice 1 follows a path to a single destination (a single lower-level window or a single subscreen). Choice 2 follows a different path to a different destination, and so on.

Related links should be grouped together; for example, in a menu, input options should be grouped to form one subcategory and output options should be grouped to form a different subcategory. A good design leaves room for expansion, too; for example, a given menu might be initially designed to hold only items 1 through 6, leaving items 7 through 9 for new links.

Consistency is a particularly important design criterion. Values must be consistent, for example, a given set of related menus might use alphabetic characters or digits, but not both. Also, certain options (0 for return to main menu, 9 for exit the system) might appear on all menus to provide a consistent set of basic navigating rules. Many organizations impose user interface

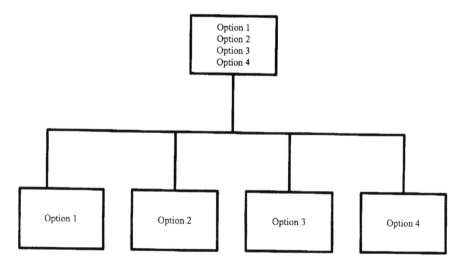

Figure 48.2 This hierarchy chart shows the relationships between a menu screen and its immediate subscreens.

"syntax" rules, often in the form of a standard set of user interface objects, to encourage consistency from application to application and code reusability.

Once the screens and menus are designed, the associated dialogues (Chapter 49) are coded and the prototype is constructed.

48.4.4.3 Test and evaluate

Before the prototype is turned over to the user, its stability must be tested. The basic idea is to trace the top down and bottom up links between the various screens and windows to ensure that elements are called in proper sequence and the necessary parameters are passed between levels. This process helps to correct any inconsistent paths (such as an exit from anything but the top level), eliminate infinite-loops, and fix other problems that might cause the user to lose navigational control. Several CASE tools, fourth-generation languages (4GL), and object-oriented tools contain embedded routines, modules, or functions that allow the designer to run the prototype and test for stability. For example, FOCUS has a feature called *window paint* that tests the prototype's links and connections.

Once the prototype is stable, the user begins to exercise it. The combination of user feedback and designer observation helps to identify unclear or inconsistent elements in the prototype design. Other test criteria include the objectives of the interface, the requirements of any procedures that access or rely on the interface, and such performance factors as error or failure rates, stability, linking sequence, and related systems performance. Essentially, the prototype is compared to the desired and/or expected results. If the prototype interface is acceptable, the next phase is skipped and the interface design is completed.

48.4.4.4 Feedback and refine

If user feedback or other test results suggest a need for reconceptualization, the design process returns to the first phase (overview and define) and the nature of the proposed interface is reevaluated. If user feedback or other test results suggest a need for redevelopment to correct design defects, the design process returns to the second phase (design and construct) and the prototype is modified. If the problems are concerned with the test criteria, test procedures, or test data, the design process returns to the third phase (test and evaluate) for retesting.

48.5   Key terms

Command-based interface — A user interface that relies on cryptic commands and/or specific keystrokes to identify the desired action.

Direct user interface — A user interface through which a user directly accesses a computer (for example, via a screen and a keyboard).

End user — Any person who needs the output generated by the computer and/or who interacts with the computer at an operational level.

Ergonomics — The study of the relationship between human beings and their workplaces.

Expert system interface — A user interface that utilizes natural language processing.

Graphic user interface (GUI) — A user interface that features windows, icons, menus, and pointers; generally, the user points to the desired element and clicks a mouse button to trigger the associated action. The Apple Macintosh and Microsoft Windows interfaces are common examples.

Icon — A graphic symbol that represents a processing option, a file, or an executable routine.

Indirect user interface — A user interface that does not involve direct computer access; for example, a printed report or a form designed to capture data for subsequent input.

Menu interface — A user interface in which the list of the options available to the user is displayed in a table or menu.

Natural language processing — Hardware and/or software that allows people to communicate with a computer in much the same way they communicate with each other; voice recognition is an example.

Object-oriented interface — A user interface that features windows, icons, menus, and pointers; generally, the user points to the desired element and clicks a mouse button to trigger the associated action; also called an icon-based interface, a *graphic user interface*, or a WIMP interface.

Prototype — A working physical model of a system or a subsystem.

User interface — A point in the system where a human being interacts with a computer.

Web-form interface — A user interface that follows the metaphor established by the Internet and the World Wide Web.

48.6   Software

Many CASE products support prototyping. Screen painters, menu builders, report generators, fourth-generation languages, executable specification languages, spreadsheets, and database management programs are popular prototyping tools.

The Apple Macintosh operating system and Microsoft Windows are examples of graphic user interfaces. Dragon Systems' *Naturally Speaking* and IBM's *ViaVoice Gold* are voice recognition software packages that might be used to support an expert system user interface. *Netscape* and Microsoft's *Internet Explorer* define the metaphor for web-form interfaces.

48.7   References

1. Davis, W. S., *Business Systems Analysis and Design*, Wadsworth, Belmont, CA, 1994.

2. Dewitz, S. D., *Systems Analysis and Design and the Transition to Objects*, McGraw-Hill, New York, NY, 1996.

3. Hoffer, J., George, J., and Valacicho, J., *Modern Systems Analysis and Design*, Benjamin/Cummings, Redwood City, CA, 1996.

4. Mayhew, D. J., *Principles and Guidelines in Software User Interface Design*, Prentice-Hall, Englewood Cliffs, NJ, 1992.

5. Powers, M., Cheney, P., and Crow, G., *Structured Systems Development: Analysis, Design, Implementation*, 2nd ed., Boyd & Fraser, Boston, MA, 1990.

6. Rubin, T., *User Interface Design for Computer Systems*, Ellis Horwood, Chichester, England, 1988.

7. Whitten, J. L., Bentley, L. D., and Dittman, K. C., *Systems Analysis and Design Methods*, Richard D. Irwin (McGraw-Hill), New York, 1997.

chapter forty-nine

Dialogue design

David C. Yen and William S. Davis

Contents

49.1   Purpose

A dialogue is the exchange of information between a computer and a user. This chapter discusses several different types of dialogues and the dialogue design process.

49.2   Strengths, weaknesses, and limitations

This chapter introduces some important principles of dialogue design. The strengths, weaknesses, and limitations associated with specific dialogue types and dialogue design techniques are discussed in context.

49.3   Inputs and related ideas

Dialogue design is typically performed in the context of user interface design (Chapter 48). Dialogue design focuses on the contents of specific screens, while interface design is more concerned with defining the structure, the links, and the execution sequence associated with the complete set of screens and windows that defines a user interface. To put it another way, dialogue design is concerned with the data, while user interface design is more action-oriented.

Much of the specific information needed to define the dialogue is collected during the problem definition (Part II) and analysis (Part IV) stages of the system development life cycle. Dialogues often utilize windows (Chapter 50). Data entry concepts are discussed in Chapter 46.

49.4   Concepts

A dialogue (or dialog) is the exchange of information between a computer and a user. Reports, forms, and individual screens are static; think of them as individual slides or still pictures. A dialogue, in contrast, is dynamic and interactive.

Dialogue design is closely linked to user interface design (Chapter 48). During the user interface design process, the designer identifies the necessary screens and defines how those screens are linked. During the dialogue design process, the designer creates the contents of those screens.

49.4.1   Types of dialogue

The purpose of instruction dialogue (sometimes called the systems information interface) is to provide instructions and other information about the system's operations, functions, and structure. The information might be presented in text or graphic form (e.g., a hierarchy chart or a table of menus). The taskbar that shows the open or active programs at the bottom of a Microsoft Windows 95 screen and a detailed Microsoft Word help screen on a particular topic are good examples.

Assistance dialogue is an interactive process intended to help the user find something; the help index and the little character in the corner of a Windows 95 screen are good examples. Note that the detailed explanation displayed at the end of the help process is instruction dialogue. Assistance dialogue normally requires a response of some type; instruction dialogue often does not.

Question-answer dialogue is designed to solicit user input. Action-oriented question-answer dialogue requires only a single keystroke. For example, in many situations, typing Y (for yes) or N (for no) provides the system with enough information to trigger an action, and typing a single letter or digit is often enough to select a choice from a list of options.

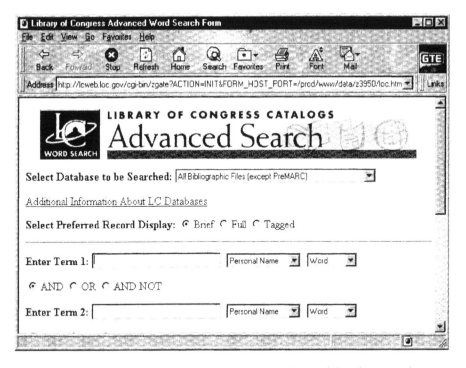

Figure 49.1   A portion of the Library of Congress *Advanced Search* screen showing an example of information-oriented question and answer dialogue.

Information-oriented question-answer dialogue asks the user to provide more information (a sentence, a paragraph, some data), and the input information is generally not used to directly trigger execution. For example, Figure 49.1 shows a portion of the Library of Congress *Advanced Search* screen.

Explanation dialogue is widely used in multi-media and other hyperlinked structures. The supporting material appears in a separate window or screen and provides a sentence or a paragraph of explanation, often for a hot word or hot phrase. In effect, explanation dialogue performs a glossary function. For example, when the mouse is held on a Microsoft Windows 95 icon, a brief description of the icon's function appears in a small dialogue bubble. The status window that appears on some mailers after an e-mail message is sent is another example.

Graphics display dialogue is common in installation or system evaluation routines. For example, the bar chart near the bottom of the FORMAT window in Figure 49.2 gives the user a clear sense of the progress of a format operation. The animated bar chart that shows percent completion while an installation routine runs is another example.

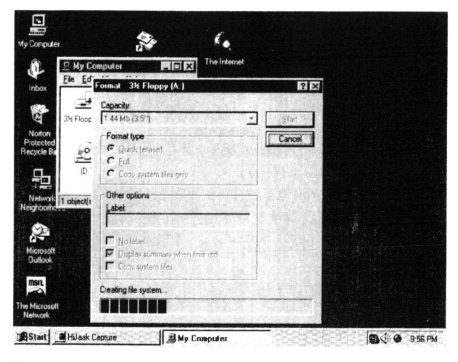

Figure 49.2   A Microsoft Windows 95 FORMAT window.

49.4.2   Dialogue design issues

An ideal dialogue is consistent (in sequence, operation, and/or execution), easy to understand, and easy to use. Each element of the dialogue is built from simple, easy-to-understand, grammatically correct sentences. Computer jargon and abbreviations are used only when absolutely necessary. As a minimum the user is able to exit (or escape) and undo (undelete or cancel) any operation without losing already completed work. The elements of the various dialogues are grouped in a logically consistent manner. When errors must be communicated (for example, through assistance dialogue), all errors are identified and clearly defined, and consistent terminology is used to describe the errors.

Feedback is essential. The user should always be given status information, clear and appropriate prompts and cues, and (when necessary) clear warning messages.

Data entry (Chapter 46) should always be verified. Validity tests are used to ensure that each input field is the right type (numeric, alphabetic), that the value of a given field is within upper and lower bounds, that fixed length fields (e.g., social security number, telephone number) are the right length, and so on. Exception tests are used to screen such "exceptional" values as a zero in a field that will be used as a divisor. Reasonableness tests are used to screen invalid values (e.g., anything but F or M in a single-character sex or gender field). The objective is to screen out and (if possible) correct bad data before they enter the system.

Default or assumed values can help, too. For example, if an input field is empty (or null), a blank space might be assigned to a literal, and the value zero might be assigned to a null numeric field. Sometimes, default values are preassigned to a field or included in a list or menu from which the user can select. Finally, confirmation controls ask users to verify their inputs (often by responding to one or more yes or no questions) before advancing to the next screen or window.

Response time is a very important criterion for a dialogue-driven system. Traditionally, response time is defined as the interval between the instant a command is issued and the instant the response begins to appear on the screen, but that definition ignores the user. A more useful definition of dialogue response time includes the following elements:

1. *System response time*—The traditional definition.
2. *The display rate*—A hardware parameter that determines how quickly the complete screen appears.
3. *User scan/read time*—A measure of how long it takes the user to read and understand the screen.
4. *User think time*—Think time includes a cognitive phase during which the user evaluates the screen and a perceptive phase during which the user decides what to do.
5. *User response time*—User response time includes a motor phase during which the user performs a physical action (press a key, point, and click) and a sensory phase during which the user waits for feedback.
6. *Error time*—The time spent making and recovering from errors; this factor does not occur on all the screens. It is often expressed as an expected value (the time multiplied by the probability of occurrence).

Response time can be estimated or measured for each screen. Transaction response time is the sum of the response times for all the screens in the dialogue.

49.4.3   The dialogue design process

Dialogue design is typically performed in the context of user interface design (Chapter 48), program design, or subsystem design. The user interface design defines the required set of screens and windows and the order of execution for the various dialogue elements. A dialogue is designed and created for each screen or window in the user interface.

Much of the specific information needed to define the dialogue is collected during the problem definition (Part II) and analysis (Part IV) stages of the system development life cycle. Such design requirements as response time and throughput are key criteria, but the dialogue designer's most important task is to study the users, their needs, their interests, and their capabilities. If the dialogue is not meaningful to the user, system performance will be negatively affected.

Once the required dialogue type is defined, the initial draft of the dialogue to support a given screen or window is often prepared using structured English (Chapter 60). After the draft version is desk checked, shared with the user, and approved, the necessary code is incorporated into the user interface prototype, tested, and modified as necessary. When an acceptable user interface prototype (with acceptable dialogues in place) emerges, the dialogues are converted into the finished code using a programming language, a screen generator, or some other tool.

49.5 Key terms

Action-oriented question-answer dialogue — A form of dialogue that requires a single keystroke response to trigger an action.

Assistance dialogue — A form of dialogue designed to provide help with command syntax, error messages, error identification, error symptoms, and so on.

Dialogue — The exchange of information between a computer and a user.

Explanation dialogue — A form of dialogue that performs a glossary function.

Graphics display dialogue — A form of dialogue that shows information in graphical form.

Information-oriented question-answer dialogue — A form of dialogue that asks the user to provide information (a sentence, a paragraph, some data) that is generally not used to directly trigger execution.

Instruction dialogue (systems information interface) — Dialogue that provides instructions and other information about the system's operations, functions, and structure.

Question-answer dialogue — A form of dialogue designed to solicit user input.

Response time — Traditionally, the interval between the instant a command is issued and the instant the response begins to appear on the screen; dialogue response time includes system response time, the display rate, user scan/read time, user think time, user response time, and error time.

Transaction response time — The sum of the response times for all the screens in the dialogue.

User interface — A point in the system where a human being interacts with a computer.

49.6   Software

Many CASE products support dialogue prototyping. Screen painters, menu builders, report generators, fourth-generation languages, and executable specification languages are popular tools for creating dialogues.

49.7   References

1. Dewitz, S. D., *Systems Analysis and Design and the Transition to Objects*, McGraw-Hill, New York, 1996.
2. Hoffer, J., George, J., and Valacicho, J., *Modern Systems Analysis and Design*, Benjamin/Cummings, Redwood City, CA, 1996.
3. Powers, M., Cheney, P., and Crow, G., *Structured Systems Development: Analysis, Design, Implementation*, 2nd ed., Boyd & Fraser, Boston, MA, 1990.
4. Whitten, J. L., Bentley, L. D., and Dittman, K. C., *Systems Analysis and Design Methods*, Richard D. Irwin (McGraw-Hill), New York, 1997.

chapter fifty

Window design

David C. Yen and William S. Davis

Contents

50.1   Purpose

A window is a screen box or a portion of a screen that holds a message, a menu, or some other unit of information. With the growing popularity of Microsoft Windows and the Apple Macintosh platforms, windows have become a de facto user interface standard. This chapter discusses several different types of windows and the windows design process.

0-8493-7001-9/99/$0.00+$.50
©1999 by CRC Press LLC

50.2 Strengths, weaknesses, and limitations

Most users are familiar with the Microsoft Windows and Apple Macintosh interfaces. Consequently, adopting windows as a user interface standard means reduced user learning time because of skill carryover. Key windows design elements exist as standard reusable objects in Visual BASIC and other windows-oriented programming tools, and such reusable code can significantly reduce programming, debugging, and maintenance costs. A windows-based interface requires a great deal of memory and a relatively powerful processor, however.

50.3 Inputs and related ideas

Windows are typically designed in the context of a user interface (Chapter 48). The user interface defines the required set of screens and windows and their order of execution. A dialogue (Chapter 49) is designed and created for each screen or window in the user interface. Windows design provides a template for dialogue design. Much of the specific information needed to define and test the windows is collected during the problem definition (Part II) and analysis (Part IV) stages of the system development life cycle.

50.4 Concepts

A window is a screen box or a portion of a screen that holds a message, a menu, or some other unit of information. With the growing popularity of Microsoft Windows and the Apple Macintosh platforms, windows have become a de facto standard for user interface design.

50.4.1 Types of windows

Menu bars (or command bars) appear at the top of most Microsoft Windows and Apple Macintosh application screens. Major functions (e.g., file, edit, view, help) are displayed on a horizontal menu bar. The subcommands related to a particular function are displayed in a pull-down or drop-down menu when the user clicks or selects the function; for example, *save, save as,* and *print* might be listed under the *file* option. Third and fourth level menus are used to select additional details, such as a data type (percentage, currency, comma) or a font (12-point, Times New Roman).

Button bars usually appear under the command menu bar, but buttons are sometimes displayed at the edge or the bottom of the screen, too. Each button holds a symbol or icon that represents a function and provides a short cut to the function. Generally, there is no hierarchy of subfunctions associated with a button, although pop-up windows are sometimes used to display available options (e.g., a color palette).

Split screens allow the user to divide a screen into several subscreens (or subwindows). For example, most spreadsheet programs allow the user to freeze columns, freeze rows, and define custom windows to simplify working with large spreadsheets. Typically, specific commands or actions allow the user to split the screen, return to the original screen, hide, recall, size, or move a window. The contents of a given window can usually be manipulated (paged, scrolled, etc.) independent of the other windows. Because certain operations are valid only on the active window, a command (or some other mechanism) to transfer control between windows is essential.

Icon windows display multiple icons. Each icon is essentially a shortcut to an executable routine, a file, or an application. The initial (post-startup) Microsoft Windows 95 screen is a good example; note such icons as *My Computer* above the *Start* button.

Some windows are designed to provide feedback. For example, most installation routines display a window that shows an installing message or a bar chart that indicates percentage completion. Consider also the status windows that display loading, searching, or working messages; the FORMAT window shown in Figure 50.1 is a good example.

Other windows provide prompts or cues. For example, the user might be asked to input some data by typing a value (e.g., a social security

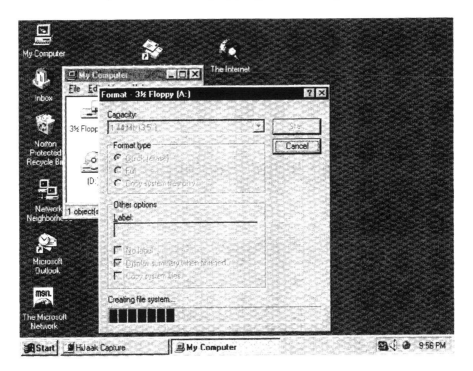

Figure 50.1 A FORMAT window provides feedback.

number or a user name and a password), filling out an electronic form, pressing Y or N, or selecting a choice from a list or a menu.

Windows are also used to provide error messages and warnings. For example, in response to an error, a window might appear showing a symbol (a question mark, a stop sign) followed by a header and an error message, an error code, or a warning number, perhaps accompanied by a button to request additional details. Some error or warning windows give the user a set of options (yes, no, cancel, retry, help, etc.).

Finally, many windows provide help. Help windows can be organized by command and/or syntax (often in alphabetical order), error or warning message number, or by function (e.g., file, view, edit, etc.).

50.4.2   Opening a window

A given window can be opened (activated, triggered, launched) in several different ways. The most common approach is to use a mouse to point to the desired icon or menu choice and then left click (to make a selection), right click (to cancel a selection), or double click (to open an application). An option is to open a specific window in response to pressing a function key. The function key approach is particularly suited to such tasks as switching back and forth between the windows on a split screen.

In some cases, pressing a hot key (usually, a combination of several keys) triggers a response. For example, most of the sample screens that appear throughout this book were captured using a program named HiJaak. To activate HiJaak, the author displayed the screen to be captured and then pressed the hot key combination Ctrl, Shift, and C. Hot keys should be used only for experienced users.

50.4.3   Designing windows

Windows are typically designed in the context of a user interface (Chapter 48). The user interface defines the required set of screens and windows and their order of execution. A dialogue (Chapter 49) is designed and created for each screen or window in the user interface. Windows design provides a template for dialogue design. In effect, the window is the vessel and the dialog is the content.

An ideal windows design incorporates all the parameters associated with an ideal user interface design (Chapter 48) and an ideal dialogue design (Chapter 49). Additionally, a well-designed window is easy to access (maximize, minimize), easy to operate (move, resize, hide, and recall), easy to maintain (modify, add, and/or delete a menu item), and easy to exit.

50.4.3.1   Define window contents

For each window required by the user interface, the designer identifies and documents such parameters as the window name, the window objectives, the window type (Section 50.4.1), the information that must appear in the window, any constraints that affect the window, and additional information about the window as appropriate. Many organizations have standards (often in the form of reusable objects) for each window type.

Menu bar windows require additional planning because they are typically linked to lower-level pull-down menus. Consequently, the designer must study the system objectives, identify the primary functions, determine the relevant subcommands, generate a command hierarchy, and test the design.

Note that sophisticated users and naive users have very different preferences. Consequently, a good understanding of the user is an essential component of windows design. If a given window is not meaningful to the user, system performance will be negatively affected.

50.4.3.2 *Verify window flow and sequence*

The user interface design defines window flow and sequence, but the designer often performs additional tests before beginning detailed design and writing the code to implement the windows.

Window flow analysis is a preexecution analysis technique used to determine if the sequence of calls to and exits from the various windows is correct. Unidirectional flow implies that control is transferred from the top-level (calling) window to a lower level (called) window. Bidirectional flow implies that the called window can transfer control back to the calling window after execution.

Window sequence analysis is particularly important when menus are used. The objective is to ensure that each window is properly linked to the next window during execution. Basically, the designer documents the return value (the value returned when the user selects a particular option) and the goto value (the name of the next menu) for each menu item in the window. For example, Table 50.1 shows the menu options, return values, and goto values for a retail customer transaction. Some designers use such tools as data flow diagrams (Chapter 24) and simple hierarchy charts (Chapters 48 and 62) to support this step.

Table 50.1 The Menu Options, Return Values, and
Goto Values for a Retail Customer Transaction

Menu option	Return	Goto value
Help	0	Main help window
Enter sales transaction	1	Sales transaction window
Enter customer return	2	Customer return window
Enter customer special order	3	Customer special order window
Request special order status	4	Special order status window
Return to main menu	9	Core window

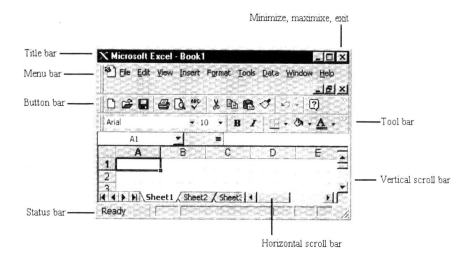

Figure 50.2 A Microsoft Excel screen with several key windows elements identified.

50.4.3.3 *Design each window*

Figure 50.2 shows a Microsoft Excel screen with several key windows elements identified. Each of these elements exists as a standard reusable object in Visual BASIC and other windows-oriented programming tools. Standard objects or templates also exist for other window types. Windows designers are strongly urged to follow the established standards whenever possible.

The detailed content of each window (the specific menu items, the narrative wording, etc.) is defined during the dialogue design process (Chapter 49).

50.4.3.4 *Test each window*

The purpose of this step is to test the paths and execution sequences so any operational errors or difficulties can be identified and corrected before the windows are released to the user. Most fourth-generation languages and CASE packages that support prototyping allow the designer to test the windows, screens, and menus. After the paths and execution sequences are tested, the windows undergo user testing as part of the user interface design process (Chapter 48).

50.5   *Key terms*

Bidirectional flow — A control flow in which the called window can transfer control back to the calling window after execution.

Button bar — A set of buttons that (typically) appears under the menu bar; each button holds a symbol or icon that represents a function and provides a short cut to the function.

Dialogue — The exchange of information between a computer and a user.

Hot key — A key or (more commonly) a combination of keys that triggers a response.

Icon — A graphic symbol that represents a processing option, a file, or an executable routine.

Icon window — A window that displays multiple icons.

Menu bar (command bar) — A window that (typically) appears at the top of the screen and lists such major functions as file, edit, view, and help; the subcommands related to a particular function are displayed in a pull-down or drop-down menu when the user clicks or selects the function.

Pull-down menu (drop-down menu) — A menu of detailed options that appears when the user clicks or selects a major function on a menu bar.

Split screen — A windows technique that allows the user to divide a screen into several subscreens or subwindows.

Unidirectional flow — A transfer of control from the top-level (calling) window to a lower level (called) window.

User interface — A point in the system where a human being interacts with a computer.

Window — A screen box or a portion of a screen that holds a message, a menu, or some other unit of information.

Window flow analysis — A preexecution analysis technique used to verify that the sequence of calls to and exits from the various windows is correct.

Window sequence analysis — An analysis technique intended to ensure that each window is properly linked to the next window during execution.

50.6   Software

Standard window templates exist as reusable objects in Visual BASIC and other windows-oriented programming tools. Windows designers are strongly urged to follow the established standards whenever possible. Most fourth-generation languages and CASE packages that support prototyping allow the designer to design, create, and test windows, screens, and menus.

50.7   References

1. Dewitz, S. D., *Systems Analysis and Design and the Transition to Objects*, McGraw-Hill, New York, 1996.
2. Hoffer, J., George, J., and Valacicho, J., *Modern Systems Analysis and Design*, Benjamin/Cummings, Menlo Park, CA, 1996.
3. Powers, M., Cheney, P., and Crow, G., *Structured Systems Development: Analysis, Design, Implementation*, 2nd ed., Boyd & Fraser, Boston, MA, 1990.
4. Whitten, J. L., Bentley, L. D., and Dittman, K. C., *Systems Analysis and Design Methods*, Richard D. Irwin (McGraw-Hill), New York, 1997.

chapter fifty-one

Web page design

William S. Davis

Contents

0-8493-7001-9/99/$0.00+$.50
©1999 by CRC Press LLC

51.1   Purpose

As web use has grown, the web has become a de facto standard, and designing for World Wide Web compatibility has become an important information system criterion. This chapter discusses several basic web page design concepts and principles.

51.2   Strengths, weaknesses, and limitations

The strengths and weaknesses associated with specific tools and techniques will be discussed in context.

51.3   Inputs and related ideas

The basic principles and guidelines discussed in Chapters 46 (form and screen design), 47 (report design), 48 (user interface design), 49 (dialogue design), and 50 (windows design) pertain to web page design. Prototyping (Chapter 31) and rapid application development (Chapter 32) are useful tools for designing web pages. Network concepts are discussed in Chapters 52, 53, and 54.

51.4   Concepts

Over the past several years, the World Wide Web has become a de facto standard, and designing for web compatibility has become an important information system criterion. This chapter discusses several basic web page design concepts and principles.

51.4.1   The World Wide Web

The World Wide Web is a massive, Internet-based, international collection of hyperlinked pages. The basic structure of the web is designed around a client/server concept. Users (clients) request specific pages through their own computers or workstations. Page requests flow through the Internet to the computer on which the requested page is stored (the server). The requested page is then sent to the client (via the Internet) for display.

51.4.1.1   Web addresses and hyperlinks

Each accessible page on the web is assigned a unique URL (uniform resource locator) address (Figure 51.1); for example, the URL that uniquely identifies the official White House home page (or initial starting page) is

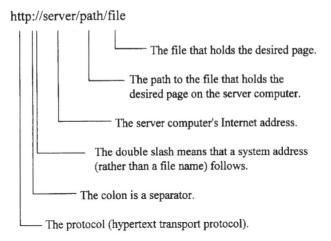

http://server/path/file

The file that holds the desired page.

The path to the file that holds the desired page on the server computer.

The server computer's Internet address.

The double slash means that a system address (rather than a file name) follows.

The colon is a separator.

The protocol (hypertext transport protocol).

Figure 51.1   The structure of a URL.

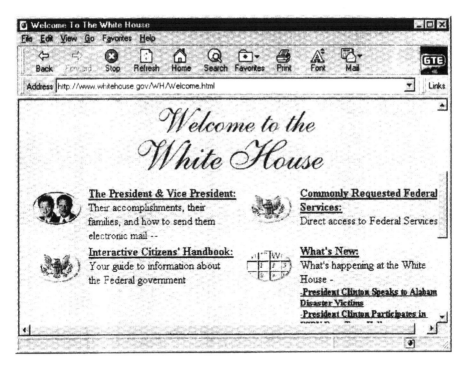

Figure 51.2   The official White House welcome page (after scrolling).

http://www.whitehouse.gov. The addresses of other pages on the White House web site are defined by suffixing server and file information to the home page address; for example, http://www.whitehouse.gov/WH/Welcome.html is the complete URL address of the site's welcome page (Figure 51.2).

Rather than requiring the user to know the URL for each desired page, the World Wide Web relies on symbolic, logical connections called hyperlinks. For example, the White House welcome page contains a set of icons and menus that identify links to the President and the Vice President, an interactive citizen's handbook, commonly requested federal services, and so on. Associated (transparently) with each of those links is the URL of the appropriate web page, and clicking on one of the links initiates a request for the page using the hidden URL. Consequently, a person looking for a specific White House press release can reach the proper page by following a series of logically meaningful key words and icons even if he or she does not know the URL.

51.4.1.2 Browsers

The program that converts hyperlinks into the associated URLs, requests pages from the Internet, and displays those pages is called a browser. Netscape and Microsoft's Internet Explorer are the two best known browsers.

51.4.1.3 Hypertext markup language (html)

A browser relies on hypertext markup language (html) to tell it how to map a page to the screen. When a web page is created, html tags are added to the text, graphics, sounds, and other objects that make up the page. When the browser reads the page, it relies on the html tags to tell it where each object should be placed on the screen, how to format the text, what colors and backgrounds to use, and so on. Table 51.1 summarizes the kinds of tags that can be defined in html.

51.4.1.4 Plug-ins

A plug-in is a program that plays or displays special files that are beyond the capability of a standard browser. Literally hundreds of plug-ins are available, and many can be downloaded free. For example, Adobe Acrobat Reader (Adobe Systems) allows a user to view and print Adobe portable document format (PDF) files. Cosmo Player (Silicon Graphics) is a virtual reality markup language (VRML) viewer popular with game players.

Table 51.1   Html Tags Are Used to Define
These Parameters

Structure	Colors
Formatting	Special characters
Links	Forms
Graphics	Tables
Dividers	Frames
Lists	Java
Backgrounds	Scripts

QuickTime Viewer (Apple) is used to display movies. RealPlayer (RealNetworks) supports video, audio, and animation. Shockwave Player (Macromedia) supports interactive games. Many applications allow the user to download a copy of the appropriate plug-in on request.

51.4.2   Web sites

A web site is a collection of related, hyperlinked pages. For example, the White House web site includes numerous pages pertaining to the President, the Vice President, various federal programs, press releases, and so on.

51.4.2.1   Site structure

Traditionally, the pages that make up a web site are organized in a hierarchy (Figure 51.3), with a high-level home page providing hyperlinks to several secondary pages, each secondary page providing hyperlinks to lower-level pages, and so on. Many modern web sites (sometimes called third-generation sites) add an entry page and (perhaps) an exit page to the core structure (Figure 51.4). Typically, the entry page serves as a hook to catch the visitor's attention, and the site's real content starts with the core page. Some designers add one or more pages to form an entry (and/or exit) tunnel or chimney between the entry page and the core page (or the core page and the exit page). For example, the entry tunnel might invite the visitor to complete a registration form while allowing an already registered repeat visitor to go directly to the core page.

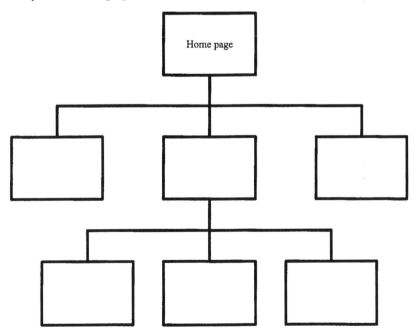

Figure 51.3   A web site's pages are typically organized as a hierarchy.

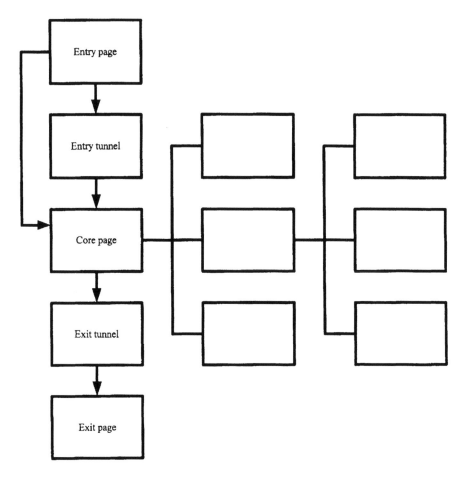

Figure 51.4   Entry page, core page, and exit page structure.

51.4.2.2   *Navigation*

Navigation through a site is controlled by hyperlinks. The standard browsers provide such default navigational links as *Back* (return to the previous screen), *Home* (return to the user's home page, usually on a different web site), vertical and horizontal scroll bars (for on-page navigation), and so on. Additionally, a well-designed site contains its own default internal navigational links designed to move the user quickly to significant pages within the site and/or to specific topics on a page. For example, many web sites display in the same place on every page a navigational bar with links to the site's home page and the most important secondary pages.

51.4.2.3   *Themes and metaphors*

The appearance and ease of navigating a web site can be improved by applying a theme or metaphor. A theme features a consistent use of color, fonts, icons, logos, and sound, a consistent page layout and appearance, and consistent navigational rules. A metaphor relies on a familiar object or a familiar pattern of behavior to suggest how the user might interact with the site. For example, Microsoft Windows and the Apple Macintosh interface use a point-and-click desktop metaphor, and adopting the same metaphor for a web site means that anyone experienced with Windows or a Macintosh already knows the basic operations needed to navigate the site. Many newspaper sites are designed to resemble an electronic version of a newspaper. A library site might present the user with an electronic card catalogue. An on-line shopping service might display a virtual bookshelf to browse, and so on. A well designed, well-implemented metaphor makes navigating a site seem natural, almost intuitive.

51.4.3   Web pages

The basic principles and guidelines discussed in Chapters 46 (form and screen design), 47 (report design), 48 (user interface design), 49 (dialogue design), and 50 (windows design) also pertain to web page design.

51.4.3.1   Html editors
To achieve maximum control over appearance, many web page designers work directly with the html tags to code (or fine tune) their pages. However, such easy to learn html editors as America OnLine's AOLPress (freeware), Trellix Corporation's Trellix, and Microsoft's Front Page do a good job of converting the contents of a WYSIWYG (what you see is what you get) screen into an html document. Additionally, many full-feature word processors (Microsoft Word, WordPerfect, Word Pro), spreadsheets, and other popular programs allow a user to save a document in html format and subsequently display that document as a web page.

51.4.3.2   Objects
On a web page, each physical entity (a block of text, a graphic image, a photograph, an animation, a sound clip, a video clip, a Java applet, etc.) is treated as an object. For example, a designer might use a word processor to create a block of text, a graphics program to create a logo, a scanner to capture a photographic image, and a spreadsheet to create a chart. Each object is physically stored as a separate file. The web page designer surrounds a file reference to each object with the appropriate html tags to control the object's placement on the screen, its size, and so on. Note that the process of downloading a page from the server to the browser involves transferring the contents of a separate file for each object.

51.4.3.3   Frames
Some pages are subdivided into frames (like windows), with each frame holding a separate html document. When frames are used, a frameset

document that defines the relative and/or absolute sizes and positions of each of the windows is sent to the client computer first, followed by the individual html documents and the object files. The client computer's browser then displays each html document in the appropriate window (or frame). For example, one common application is displaying a standard navigation bar in the same relative position (the same frame) on every screen by simply referencing the same navigational html document on each frameset.

Using frames gives the designer considerable control over exactly what is displayed on the client's screen and saves the time needed to redundantly code the html for a common object that appears on several pages. However, because each frame is, in effect, an independent page, frames (unless carefully used) can break the metaphor, leading to user confusion. For example, a print command will print only the contents of the active frame (the one most recently clicked), and not the entire screen as most users (reasonably) assume.

51.4.3.4 *Interactivity*

Because the web page is displayed on the client computer, interactivity implies executing code on the client computer. Downloading executable code is potentially dangerous, so tight security controls are essential. Java (Sun Microsystems), a platform independent, object-oriented programming language that incorporates excellent security features, has become a de facto standard for such applications. JavaScript is a relatively easy to learn, Java-based scripting language that can be used to perform such basic interactive tasks as requesting a choice (yes or no) from a user or supporting the completion and return of a simple form. Each Java or JavaScript applet is viewed as an object in the html stream.

51.4.3.5 *Page design constraints and tradeoffs*

A page designer faces two, often conflicting objectives. The first objective is to catch the user's attention. The second is to provide enough content to satisfy the user's needs.

51.4.3.5.1 Real estate   The user actually sees only one screen at a time, and the available viewing space is further constrained by the browser's button bars, scroll bars, and so on. Technically, a page (or frameset) can be almost any length because the user can scroll through the contents if the page exceeds a single screen, but many potential users are reluctant or unwilling to scroll until after they are hooked. Consequently, particularly on entry or core pages that are designed to quickly capture the viewer's attention, the effective real estate is limited to a single (roughly) fifteen-line window.

51.4.3.5.2 Flash and content   Flash can be defined as everything but content. Examples include animations, sounds, graphic images, photographs, colors, backgrounds, lines, patterns, and other elements intended make the page look neat rather than to deliver real content. A visitor's interest is peaked by flash. Without some flash, a visitor is not likely to bother looking at a site in sufficient detail to assess its content. Return visitors (users) are interested in content, however, so flash without content is useless in the long run. Typically, the designer tries to catch the user's attention on the entry page and the core page. Detailed content is delivered further down the page hierarchy, with the amount of flash diminishing by level.

51.4.3.5.3 Depth and breadth Breadth is a measure of the number of items (for example, menu choices) on a single page. Depth is a measure of the number of levels (the number of mouse clicks) a user must navigate to reach the desired content. Excessive breadth leads to pages that are difficult to understand. Excessive depth implies time lost navigating through multiple intermediate screens. Depth and breadth are tradeoffs. More choices per page (more breadth) mean fewer hierarchical levels (less depth), and more levels (more depth) mean fewer choices per page (less breadth). A common rule of thumb is to include between five and nine choices on a page.

51.4.3.5.4 Page load time Page load time is an important variable because potential users who become frustrated and exit a slow-to-load page are not likely to become repeat visitors. Load time is a function of the number of bits that must be transmitted from the server to the client and the transmission speed of the intermediate lines.

Simple text pages load quickly but contain little to catch the user's attention. Pages that contain sophisticated graphics, sounds, animations, and Java applets are interesting but load slowly because such objects tend to be rather large and each object is stored in a separate file that must be transferred from the server to the client. Somewhere between those two extremes is a mix of flash and content that loads quickly, catches the viewer's attention, and convinces the visitor to investigate the site in more depth.

Compression techniques can help to reduce the number of bits actually transmitted. For example, a bitmap takes up a great deal of memory because it consists of every dot or pixel that makes up an image. The amount of memory space and, hence, transmission time can be substantially reduced if graphic images (lines and shapes) are converted to gif (graphic interchange format) and photographs are converted to jpeg (Joint Photographic Experts Group) format.

51.5   Key terms

Applet — A small application program that performs a single task.

Breadth — A measure of the number of items (for example, menu choices) on a single page.

Browser — A program that converts hyperlinks into the associated URLs, requests pages from the Internet, and displays those pages.

Client/server computing — A form of networked computing in which a computer that needs a service (the client) requests help from a computer that has the ability to provide the service (the server).

Compression — Conserving memory, secondary storage space, and data transmission time by removing repetitive or unnecessary bits from data.

Core page — The highest-level page in a web site's content hierarchy.

Depth — A measure of the number of levels a user must navigate to reach the desired content.

Entry page — The first page a visitor encounters when accessing a web site.

Entry tunnel (entry chimney) — One or more pages between the entry page and the core page.

Exit page — The last page a visitor encounters just before exiting a web site.

Exit tunnel (exit chimney) — One or more pages between the core page and the exit page.

Frame — A window-like unit that holds and displays the contents of a single html document.

Frameset — A document that defines the relative and/or absolute sizes and positions of several related frames. Using the frameset as a guide or framework, the client computer's browser displays each html document in the appropriate frame.

Gif (graphic interchange format) — A popular compression algorithm for graphic images.

Home page — An initial starting page.

Html (hypertext markup language) — A hypertext language used to tell a browser how to map a page to the screen. When a web page is created, html tags are added to the text, graphics, sounds, and other objects that make up the page. When the browser reads the page, it relies on the html tags to tell it where each object should be placed on the screen, how to format the text, what colors and backgrounds to use, and so on.

Hyperlink — On the World Wide Web, a symbolic, logical connection that represents a URL.

Internet — A well-known, widely accessed, international network of computers; the set of continuously connected computers that use Transmission Control Protocol/Internet Protocol (TCP/IP).

Java — A platform independent, object-oriented programming language developed by Sun Microsystems that incorporates excellent security features and has gained wide acceptance on the World Wide Web.

JavaScript — A relatively easy to learn, Java-based scripting language that can be used to perform basic interactive tasks.

Jpeg (Joint Photographic Experts Group) — A popular compression algorithm for photographic images.

Metaphor — A design element that relies on a familiar object or a familiar pattern of behavior to suggest how the user might interact with a web site.

Navigation — The act of moving from page to page through a web site.

Object — A thing about which data are stored.

Page — The basic unit of information transferred between a server and a client on the World Wide Web.

Page load time — A measure of the elapsed time between a request for a page and the display of the complete page on the client computer's screen.

Plug-in — A program that plays or displays special files that are beyond the capability of a standard browser.

Theme — A recurrent idea; on a web page or web site, the consistent use of color, fonts, icons, logos, and sound, a consistent page layout and appearance, and consistent navigational rules.

URL (uniform resource locator) — The address of a page on the World Wide Web.

Web site — A collection of related, hyperlinked pages.

World Wide Web — A massive, Internet-based, international collection of hyperlinked pages.

51.6   Software

Netscape and Microsoft's Internet Explorer are the two best known browsers. America OnLine's AOLPress (freeware), Trellix Corporation's Trellix, and Microsoft's Front Page are examples of html editors. Many full-feature word processors (Microsoft Word, WordPerfect, Word Pro) and other common software tools allow a user to save a document in html format and subsequently display that document as a web page.

Numerous plug-ins are available to supplement the standard browsers. Adobe Acrobat Reader (Adobe Systems) allows a user to view and print Adobe portable document format (PDF) files. Cosmo Player (Silicon Graphics) is a virtual reality markup language (VRML) viewer. QuickTime Viewer (Apple) is used to display movies. RealPlayer (RealNetworks) supports video, audio, and animation. Shockwave Player (Macromedia) supports interactive games.

51.7   References

51.7.1   Web sites

1. *The Bare Bones Guide to html,* http://www.werbach.com/barebones.
2. *The WWW Help Page,* http://www.werbach.com/web/wwwhelp.html.

51.7.2 Suggestions for additional reading

1. Evans, T., *10 Minute Guide to Html 4.0*, Que Education and Training, Indianapolis, IN, 1997.
2. Kidder, G. and Harris, S., *Official Html Publishing for Netscape: Your Complete Guide to Web Page Design & Production*, Ventura Communications Group, Research Triangle Park, NC, 1997.
3. Morris, M. E. S. and Hinrichs, R. J., *Web Page Design: A Different Multimedia*, Prentice-Hall, Englewood Cliffs, NJ, 1996.
4. Siegel, D., *Creating Killer Web Sites*, 2nd ed., Hayden Books, Indianapolis, IN, 1997.
5. Tittel, E. and James, S., *HTML for Dummies*, IDG Books Worldwide, Foster City, CA, 1997.

chapter fifty-two

Network models

David C. Yen and William S. Davis

Contents

52.1   Purpose

Network models are used to determine the physical configuration of the computers and peripherals that form a network or distributed environment. This chapter describes several common network topologies.

Network design is a highly specialized discipline in its own right, and a detailed explanation of network analysis tools and techniques is beyond the scope of this book. This chapter is written for systems analysts and information system consultants who must work with network specialists.

52.2   Strengths, weaknesses, and limitations

The strengths, weaknesses, and limitations of the various topologies will be discussed in context.

52.3   Inputs and related ideas

This chapter is concerned with the overall design of a network or a distributed system. The process of analyzing and design a given network is covered in Chapter 53. Chapter 54 discusses the process of routing messages among a network's nodes. Network design is related to hardware interface design (Chapter 42). The hardware interface is affected by the network topology, and each network node can be viewed as a hardware interface.

Readers who are not familiar with data communications theory and concepts should review the data communications chapter in an introductory management information systems or computer information systems textbook.

52.4   Concepts

Network models are used to determine the physical configuration of the computers and peripherals that form a network or distributed environment. This chapter describes several common network designs, or topologies. The terms *network design* and *topology design* are sometimes used to describe the process of designing a network topology.

A network consists of two or more computers linked by a communication line. The line might consist of coaxial cables, telephone wires, fiber optic cables, microwave signals, satellite signals, or some combination of media.

The computers that form a local area network are usually located in close geographic proximity (for example, within the same building, complex of buildings, or campus) and are generally linked by direct lines. The computers that form a wide area network are usually geographically disbursed and are often linked by common carriers. Each computer in a wide area network is called a host. Each connection point (computer, workstation, peripheral, concentrator, etc.) in the network is called a node.

52.4.1   Star topology

On a star network, all messages must pass through a central computer before they are passed to the destination computer. A simple star network (Figure 52.1) consists of several computers and/or peripherals each linked to a central host computer via a dedicated line. A variation of a simple star network

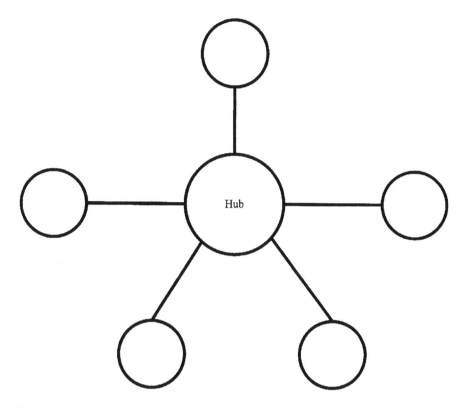

Figure 52.1 A simple star network.

features several computers, terminals, and/or peripherals connected to a cluster controller and sharing a communication link from the controller to the central computer.

Two or more simple star networks can be linked to form a complex star network as shown in Figure 52.2. Generally, one of the hub computers (usually, a powerful mainframe or minicomputer) serves as central boss and controls the network by scheduling, prioritizing, and holding incoming and outgoing messages. For example, in Figure 52.2, hub 2 and hub 3 must communicate with each other through hub 1, the central node or boss. If there is no single, clear, dominant, central node, several hub computers can work together as partners to relay messages.

Because dedicated lines are used to connect the remote nodes to the central node, star topology is the simplest but most expensive topology. The central node makes centralized supervisory and control functions relatively easy to perform. However, the entire network goes down if the central node goes out of service unless funds are spent to provide a reliable backup for both hardware and software. Many telephone company computer systems use star topology.

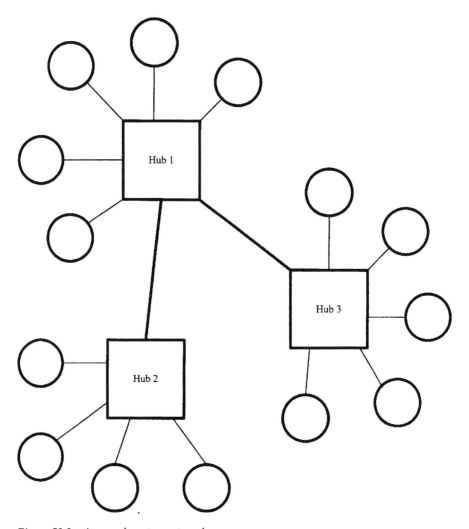

Figure 52.2   A complex star network.

52.4.2   Mesh topology

A mesh network allows any two remote computers to communicate directly, although there may be cases when a third computer relays a message from a source to a destination. In a fully connected mesh network every computer is directly connected to all the other computers in the network (Figure 52.3) In a partially connected mesh network, every computer is connected (either directly or via a relay computer) to at least two other computers in the network by more than one path (Figure 52.4).

Mesh topology is the most reliable and most expensive network topology. Most mesh topology networks belong to the government, the military, or a big corporation that needs a secured path to transmit data.

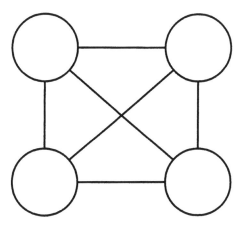

Figure 52.3   A fully connected mesh network.

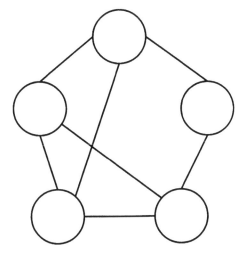

Figure 52.4   A partially connected mesh network.

52.4.3   Bus topology

On a bus network (Figure 52.5), the host computer is located at one end of a common communication line and all the other computers and peripherals in the network are attached to the same line.

A bus network is relatively inexpensive and easy to expand because all the nodes share a common communication path. However, traffic is heavy on the common line, and the network tends to degrade as the number of nodes increases. The location of the host node (relative to certain other nodes) can create an unbalanced network and negatively impact network performance. One host node may not be sufficient to handle all the traffic, and sophisticated equipment and software are needed to control the network.

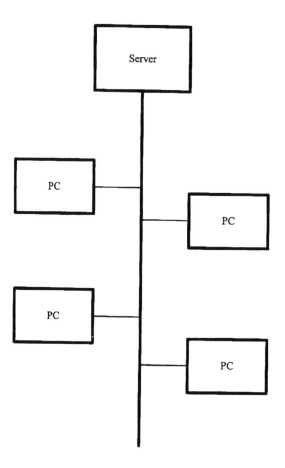

Figure 52.5   A bus network

52.4.4   Tree topology

Tree topology (or hierarchical topology) is a hybrid topology. Generally, two or more star or bus networks are connected to form a tree network. A rooted tree network (Figure 52.6) is a tree network with a clearly defined root node that serves as a base for the entire network. An unrooted tree network (Figure 52.7) has no clearly defined base root. Instead, there are several nodes that act as major hubs to relay messages or perform limited supervisory functions.

Tree topology is easy to implement using gateways, bridges, and/or routers. A major problem is that bottlenecks can develop in the equipment that connects the subnetworks.

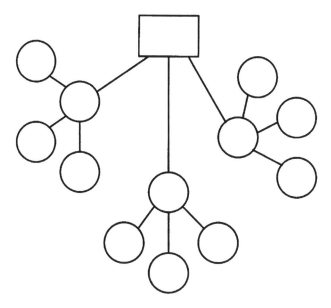

Figure 52.6 A rooted tree network.

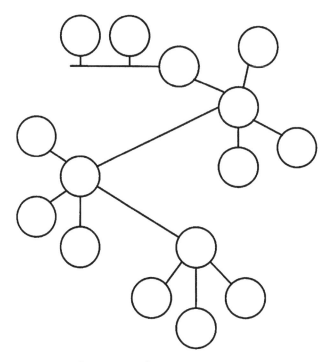

Figure 52.7 An unrooted tree network.

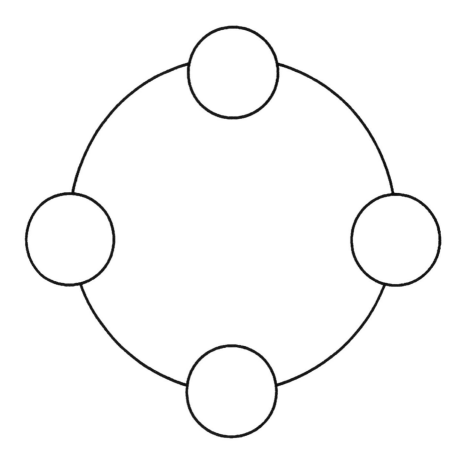

Figure 52.8   A ring network.

52.4.5   Ring topology

A ring network (Figure 52.8) consists of a series of nodes connected to form a ring. Each message is received, repeated, and retransmitted by each node as it works its way around the ring in a predetermined direction. A loop is a variation of a ring network with controlling nodes in the ring.

Because a ring or loop network transmits information in one direction only, transmission speed tends to be faster than with the other topologies. Ring networks are usually implemented using a token-passing protocol, which tends to limit network size, however. (For example, the nodes on a 500-node network can face lengthy delays waiting for the token.) The need for a special token symbol and procedures to enforce the direction of flow adds to the complexity of ring network design.

52.5 Key terms

Bus network — A network in which the host computer is located at one end of a common communication line and all the other computers and peripherals in the network are attached to the same line.

Complex star network — A network that consists of two or more linked simple star networks.

Data communication — The act of transmitting data from one component to another.

Fully connected mesh network — A mesh network in which every computer is directly connected to all the other computers in the network.

Host — A computer in a wide area network.

Local area network (LAN) — A network in which the nodes are located in close geographic proximity and are generally linked by direct lines (such as hard wires).

Mesh network — A network that allows any two remote computers to communicate directly.

Network — Two or more computers linked by a communication line.

Node — A connection point (computer, workstation, peripheral, concentrator, etc.) in a network.

Partially connected mesh network — A mesh network in which every computer is connected (either directly or via a relay computer) to at least two other computers in the network by more than one path.

Ring network — A network that consists of a series of nodes connected to form a ring.

Rooted tree network — A tree network with a clearly defined root node that serves as a base for the entire network.

Simple star network — A network that consists of several computers and/or peripherals, each linked to a central host computer via a dedicated line.

Star network — A network on which all messages must go through a central computer before they are passed to the destination computer.

Token passing — A network management technique in which an electronic token is passed continuously from node to node around the network and a given node can transmit a message only when it holds the token.

Topology — A map of a network; a physical arrangement of the nodes and connections in a network.

Tree topology (hierarchical topology) — A hybrid topology that usually consists of two or more linked star or bus networks.

Unrooted tree network — A tree network with no clearly defined base root; instead, there are several nodes that act as major hubs to relay messages or perform limited supervisory functions.

Wide area network (WAN) — A network in which the nodes are (usually) geographically disbursed and linked by common carriers.

52.6   Software

Not applicable.

52.7   References

1.   Conrad, J. W., *Handbook of Communications Systems Management*, Auerbach, Boston, MA, 1988, 1989, 1990–1991.
2.   Martin, J. and Leben, J., *Principle of Data Communications*, Prentice-Hall, Englewood Cliffs, NJ, 1988.
3.   Martin, J. and Leben, J., *Data Communications Technology*, Prentice-Hall, Englewood Cliffs, NJ, 1988.
4.   Ramos, E., Schroeder, A., and Beheler A., *Computer Networking Concepts*, Prentice-Hall, Englewood Cliffs, NJ, 1996.
5.   Rhodes, P. D., *Building a Network: How to Specify, Design, Procure, and Install a Corporate LAN*, McGraw-Hill, New York, 1995.
6.   Slone, J. P. and Drinan, A., *Handbook of Local Area Networks*, Auerbach, Boston, MA, 1991.
7.   Spohn, D. L., *Data Network Design*, McGraw-Hill, New York, 1997.
8.   Stallings, W., *Business Data Communications*, Macmillan, New York, 1990.
9.   Stallings, W., *Handbook of Computer-Communications Standards: The OSI Model and OSI-Related Standards*, Vol. 1, Macmillan, New York, 1987.
10. Stallings, W., *Handbook of Computer-Communications Standards: Local Network Standards*, vol. 2, Macmillan, New York, 1987.
11. Stallings, W., *Handbook of Computer-Communications Standards: DOD Protocol Standards*, vol. 3, Macmillan, New York, 1988.
12. Taylor, D. E., *The McGraw-Hill Internetworking Handbook*, McGraw-Hill, New York, 1995.

chapter fifty-three

Network analysis

David C. Yen and William S. Davis

Contents

53.1   Purpose

The purpose of this chapter is to overview the key activities in the network analysis and design process. Network analysis is a highly specialized discipline in its own right, and a detailed explanation of network analysis tools and techniques is beyond the scope of this book. This chapter is written for systems analysts and information system consultants who must work with network specialists.

53.2   Strengths, weaknesses, and limitations

Not applicable.

53.3   Inputs and related ideas

Network topologies are discussed in Chapter 52. Location connectivity analysis is covered in Chapter 54. Simulation (Chapter 19) and queuing theory (Chapter 79) are two mathematical tools that are often used to support network analysis. The cost estimating process might include a cost/benefit analysis (Chapter 38). Network consultants often develop detailed cost estimates in response to a competitive procurement opportunity (Chapter 41). The need for a network is established during the analysis (Part IV) and high-level design (Part V) stages of the system development life cycle. Key network design parameters are documented in the requirements specifications (Chapter 35).

53.4   Concepts

The purpose of this chapter is to overview the key activities in the network analysis and design process. A detailed explanation of network analysis tools and techniques is beyond the scope of this book.

53.4.1   Requirements identification

The purpose of requirements identification is to ensure that the network designers have clear definitions and a detailed understanding of the essential network requirements and related network design attributes.

Geographical requirements analysis begins with a careful study of the system's geographical locations (i.e., buildings and areas) and focuses on such issues as topology (Chapter 52) and transmission media (dedicated cable, microwave, satellite, common carrier). Traffic flow pattern analysis is also used to help define the network's topology (Chapter 52) and connections (Chapter 54) as well as message volumes associated with the various data flows.

Traffic load analysis includes such elements as peak load analysis, message duration analysis, and busy hour analysis. Together, they are used to determine the required number of communication lines, the maximum required capacity for each line, the time slots during which the communication lines are likely to be busy, and several related network performance parameters. The purpose of availability requirements analysis is to determine and document the effect of time differences (time zone shifts) between the different geographical areas covered by the network.

As the name implies, response time analysis is concerned with determining the system's response time requirements (e.g., interactive, store and forward, real-time, etc.). Reliability requirements analysis provides information that helps the designer develop a back-up plan or create necessary redundancies.

Hardware analysis is used to define the requirements for the personal computers, workstations, terminals, peripherals, communication interfaces, modems, and other hardware that will be attached to the network. Additionally, such software as the operating system and communication protocols must be specified. Future projection analysis focuses on parameters that affect capacity planning, storage requirements, transmission speed, connections with the Internet, and the highway (or Turnpike) effect.

53.4.2 Network design

Based on the network requirements identified in the previous stage, the network is physically designed.

Topology determination focuses on physically laying out the network using such tools as location connectivity diagrams (Chapter 54). The required line speeds are defined based on such criteria as transmitted characters per day, computer time (input, output, and processing) per message, and the required response time. Concentration point determination is concerned with the system's concentration points (or hubs). Such factors as the number of hubs, the capacities and related requirements for the lines that link the hubs, and the number of clients per server (or per hub) must be weighed against network efficiency.

Bottlenecks (or choke points) are places in the network where message flow exceeds capacity, resulting in delays and even lost messages. Bottleneck analysis (an application of queuing theory, Chapter 79) is a useful, mathematical tool for identifying choke points and for evaluating how various line capacities, transmission speeds, and hardware options (processing speed, storage capacity) affect performance. Queuing theory can also be used to gauge the sensitivity of a network design to such variables (or assumptions) as average message length, message duration, and busy hours. Simulation (Chapter 19) is another useful mathematical tool that can help identify and solve many network design problems. The advantages of using mathematical tools such as queuing theory and simulation include quick feedback, the flexibility to consider numerous variables or assumptions, and low cost.

53.4.3 Cost estimating

Networks are expensive to develop and to operate. Clear, accurate development, and operating cost estimates are essential before the final decision to implement a network is made. The cost estimating process might include a cost/benefit analysis (Chapter 38). Network consultants often develop detailed cost estimates in response to a competitive procurement opportunity (Chapter 41).

53.4.4 Documentation

Once the network analysis is completed, the various design decisions must be carefully documented. Connection diagrams define the topology, connection points, and traffic flows. Key supporting details include the types of transmission media, the desired technology (e.g., T1, ISDN, fiber optics, satellite, microwave), the capacities, speeds, and costs of those media, and a back-up plan. The act of preparing the connection diagrams and supporting documentation is sometimes called logical documentation and preparation.

During the physical documentation and preparation phase, a complete component list is prepared for each node in the network. Key parameters include the brand name, model, speed, and other relevant specifications for such hardware components as the computers, the modems, and related peripherals (printers, scanners, etc.), and the nature and description of all cables and connectors. Sometimes, hierarchy charts (Chapters 48 and 62) are prepared to help document the components that form a subnetwork controlled by a hub.

The network specifications incorporate all the information related to the network. In addition to the documentation described above, routers, bridges, and other message switching equipment or devices must be documented in detail. Finally, such details as floor plans, rising cables, distributing cables, central switch boxes, server locations, telephone jack locations, and power outlets must be documented in a wiring diagram.

53.5 Key terms

Availability requirements analysis — A network analysis process that helps to determine and document the effect of time differences (time zone shifts) between the different geographical areas covered by the network.

Bottleneck (choke point) — A place in the network where message flow exceeds capacity, resulting in delays and even lost messages.

Bridge — A computer that links two networks with similar protocols.

Client — A computer (more generally, a node) that requests a service from a server.

Client/server — A network in which client computers request services from a central server computer.

Concentration point determination — A network analysis process that is concerned with the system's concentration points (or hubs).

Connection diagram — A diagram that shows the topology, connection points, traffic flows, and patterns of a network.

Data communication — The act of transmitting data from one component to another.

Distributing cable — Generally, a cable that links the computers or nodes on a single floor.

Future projection analysis — A network analysis process that focuses on parameters that affect capacity planning, storage requirements, transmission speed, connections with the Internet, and so on.

Gateway — A computer that links two or more networks with different protocols.

Geographical requirements analysis — A preliminary network analysis process that begins with a careful study of the system's geographical locations and focuses on such issues as topology and transmission media.

Hardware analysis — A network analysis process that helps to define the requirements for the personal computers, workstations, terminals, peripherals, communication interfaces, modems, and other hardware that will be attached to the network, and such software as the operating system and communication protocols.

Highway effect (turnpike effect) — The tendency of users to quickly adopt new technology as soon as it proves its usefulness; because of the highway effect, the demands placed on a system often exceed projections. This term was initially coined in the 1950s when the traffic load on the Pennsylvania Turnpike exceeded the designers' long-term, worst-case projections soon after the road opened.

Host — A computer in a wide area network.

Hub — A central controlling device, point, or node in a network.

Local area network (LAN) — A network in which the nodes are located in close geographic proximity and are generally linked by direct lines.

Message switching — The process of routing a message from its source to its destination; note that sometimes messages are decomposed into packets that reach their destination via different transmission paths.

Network — Two or more computers linked by a communication line.

Network topology — A map of a network; a physical arrangement of the nodes and connections in a network.

Node — A connection point (computer, workstation, peripheral, concentrator, etc.) in a network.

Protocol — A set of rules that governs data communication.

Reliability requirements analysis — A network analysis process that helps the designer develop a back-up plan or create necessary redundancies.

Response time analysis — A network analysis process that helps to determine the system's response time requirements (e.g., interactive, store and forward, real-time, etc.).

Rising cable — Generally, a cable that runs between two floors in a building.

Router — An intelligent device that provides network connections and performs such services as protocol conversion and message routing.

Server — A computer that holds centralized resources and provides them to clients on request.

Token passing — A network management technique in which an electronic token is passed continuously from node to node around the network and a given node can transmit a message only when it holds the token.

Topology — A map of a network; a physical arrangement of the nodes and connections in a network.

Topology determination — A network analysis process that focuses on physically laying out the network using such tools as location connectivity diagrams.

Traffic flow pattern analysis — A network analysis process that helps to define the network's topology and connections as well as the message volumes associated with the various data flows.

Traffic load analysis — A network analysis process that helps to determine the required number of communication lines, the maximum required capacity for each line, the time slots during which the communication lines are likely to be busy, and several related network performance parameters.

Wide area network (WAN) — A network in which the nodes are (usually) geographically disbursed and linked by common carriers.

53.6   Software

Not applicable.

53.7   References

1. Conrad, J. W., *Handbook of Communications Systems Management*, Auerbach, Boston, MA, 1988, 1989, 1990–1991.
2. Martin, J. and Leben, J., *Principle of Data Communications*, Prentice-Hall, Englewood Cliffs, NJ, 1988.
3. Martin, J. and Leben, J., *Data Communications Technology*, Prentice-Hall, Englewood Cliffs, NJ, 1988.
4. Ramos, E., Schroeder, A., and Beheler A., *Computer Networking Concepts*, Prentice-Hall, Englewood Cliffs, NJ, 1996.
5. Rhodes, P. D., *Building a Network: How to Specify, Design, Procure, and Install a Corporate LAN*, McGraw-Hill, New York, 1995.
6. Slone, J. P. and Drinan, A., *Handbook of Local Area Networks*, Auerbach, Boston, MA, 1991.
7. Spohn, D. L., *Data Network Design*, McGraw-Hill, New York, 1997.
8. Stallings, W., *Business Data Communications*, Macmillan, New York, 1990.
9. Stallings, W., *Handbook of Computer-Communications Standards: The OSI Model and OSI-Related Standards*, vol. 1, Macmillan, New York, 1987.
10. Stallings, W., *Handbook of Computer-Communications Standards: Local Network Standards*, vol. 2, Macmillan, New York, 1987.
11. Stallings, W., *Handbook of Computer-Communications Standards: DOD Protocol Standards*, vol. 3, Macmillan, New York, 1988.
12. Taylor, D. E., *The McGraw-Hill Internetworking Handbook*, McGraw-Hill, New York, 1995.

chapter fifty-four

Network routing tools and techniques

David C. Yen and William S. Davis

Contents

54.1 Purpose

This chapter focuses on several common network routing techniques (generally, location connectivity analysis). The major objectives of these routing techniques include controlling network data flow, determining the status of the sending and the receiving nodes, identifying the best (sometimes optimal) route to transmit data, reducing transmission delays and related errors, and preventing the overuse of a particular route or node.

0-8493-7001-9/99/$0.00+$.50
©1999 by CRC Press LLC

Network design is a highly specialized discipline, and a detailed explanation of location connectivity analysis tools and techniques is beyond the scope of this book. This chapter is written for systems analysts and information system consultants who must work with network specialists.

54.2   Strengths, weaknesses, and limitations

The techniques described in this chapter are used to estimate and/or predict data flows and minimize data congestion in a distributed information system. Using these techniques can help reduce transmission problems owing to the speed and capacity constraints imposed by the transmission media.

It is difficult to measure the highway effect or to match users needs with emerging computing technology using these techniques. Also, the techniques described in this chapter do not always yield the best route for data transmission.

54.3   Inputs and related ideas

Network topologies are discussed in Chapter 52. Network analysis is covered in Chapter 53. The need for a network is established during the analysis (Part IV) and high-level design (Part V) stages of the system development life cycle. Key network design parameters are documented in the requirements specifications (Chapter 35).

54.4   Concepts

A network consists of a set of nodes (computers, routers, etc.) linked by communication lines. When a source node transmits a message, there are typically several possible paths the message can take from node to node through the network to reach its destination. The specific path selected for a given message is called a route. Location connectivity analysis is used to control network data flow, determine the status of the sending and receiving nodes, identify the best (or optimal) route, reduce transmission delays and related errors, and prevent the overuse of a particular route or node. This chapter focuses on several common routing techniques.

54.4.1   Centralized routing

Centralized routing is used when the distributed network is centrally controlled. The basic idea is to provide the central node with super-authority over all the other nodes. The network routing software installed on the central node can be used to overview the operation of the entire network, locate bottlenecks and underutilized nodes, calculate and recompute the optimal path between a sending node and a receiving node, and adjust the routing path by constructing a new routing table.

Centralized routing provides centralized control, integrated supervision of the network, very good security, and excellent back-up control. The central node is relatively expensive to operate and maintain, however, and the entire network goes down if the central node fails. Some operating inefficiency is possible because the central node must perform all routing calculations. Also, the calculated optimal paths may not reflect the current status of the network if they are based on (even seconds old) historical network information.

54.4.2   Distributed routing

Distributed routing relies on each node to compute its own routing table and build the required connections with its neighbors. Ideally, the network operation, status, and architecture of each node is transparent. Distributed routing is more flexible than centralized routing because each node handles its own routing. The result is often improved system performance.

54.4.2.1   Static routing

Static routing establishes routine paths between sending and receiving nodes based on a data flow analysis of historical data. With static routing, the path is selected from a predefined table, so there is no need to readjust paths or compute the next node. However, if the established link between any pair of nodes fails, static routing cannot adjust. Also, as transmission patterns change, static routing patterns can quickly become inefficient.

Fixed routing always utilizes a predetermined fixed route when transmitting between a specific pair of nodes. Fixed routing is widely used in mesh topology networks, particularly when reliability and security are primary objectives.

With weighted routing, different routing paths are selected for each message based on a predetermined desirable utilization rate. For example, imagine that there are three paths (via node A, B, or C) between the source node and the destination node (Figure 54.1). The objective is to transmit 50 percent of all messages via node A, 30 percent via node B, and the remaining 20 percent via node C. The source node uses a random number generator to select the route based on the predetermined probabilities.

54.4.2.2   Adaptive routing

Adaptive routing, also called dynamic routing, selects the best route based on such criteria as the speed, capacity, or cost of the link, the utilization rate of a particular node, the failure rate of a particular path, the type of data to be transmitted, response time, throughput, and so on. Often, a prioritized list of decision criteria (called a portfolio) is used.

The objective of the quickest route algorithm is to send the message to the next available neighboring node (other than the sending node) as quickly as possible. The advantage is fast transmission, but there is no

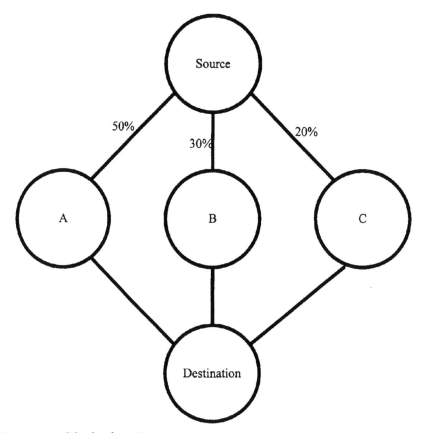

Figure 54.1   Weighted routing.

guarantee that the node selected will be closer to the destination. In some cases, the quickest route algorithm can increase the time required to deliver a message.

The best route algorithm uses such parameters as the type of message, the rate of under-utilization or over-utilization of a particular node, and the number of intermediate nodes between the source and the destination. Such tools as linear programming, goal programming, and similar management science techniques can be used to select and rank the different routing alternatives based on the established criteria.

54.4.2.3   Broadcast routing

With broadcast routing, a header containing the address of the receiving node is added to the message. The message is then transmitted to all the nodes in the network, and the node whose address matches the header reacts to the message. Note that each node must have a list of addresses of all the nodes in the network. Security is a major concern because every node receives a copy of the message. Broadcast routing is popular in collision detection networks.

54.5 Key terms

Adaptive routing — A distributed routing technique that selects the best route based on such criteria as the speed, capacity, or cost of the link, the utilization rate of a particular node, the failure rate of a particular path, the type of data transmitted, response time, throughput, and so on; also known as dynamic routing.

Best route algorithm — An adaptive routing technique that uses such parameters as the type of message, the rate of under-utilization or over-utilization of a particular node, and the number of intermediate nodes between the source and the destination.

Bottleneck (choke point) — A place (usually, a node or a path) in the network where message flow exceeds capacity, resulting in delays, and even lost messages.

Broadcast routing — A routing technique in which a header containing the address of the receiving node is added to the message; the message is then transmitted to all the nodes in the network, and the node whose address matches the header reacts to the message.

Centralized routing — A routing technique in which the central node has super-authority over all the other nodes.

Collision detection — A network management technique in which the nodes are allowed to transmit at any time; if two messages collide, the collision is sensed and the messages are retransmitted.

Distributed database — A database with different subsets of data distributed among several sites that are connected by a network.

Distributed routing — A routing technique that relies on each node to compute its own routing table and build the required connections with its neighbors.

Fixed routing — A static routing technique that always utilizes a predetermined fixed route when transmitting between a specific pair of nodes.

Highway effect (turnpike effect) — The tendency of users to quickly adopt new technology as soon as it proves its usefulness; because of the highway effect, the demands placed on a system often exceed projections. This term was initially coined in the 1950s when the traffic load on the Pennsylvania Turnpike exceeded the designers' long-term, worst-case projections soon after the road opened.

Location connectivity analysis — A network and distributed database design technique used to help control network data flow, determine the status of the sending and receiving nodes, identify the best route to transmit data, reduce transmission delays and related errors, and prevent the overuse of a particular route or node; also known as connectivity analysis or routing analysis.

Network — Two or more computers linked by a communication line.

Node — A connection point (computer, workstation, peripheral, concentrator, etc.) in a network.

Path — A group of connected links that allow the transmission of information from a source to destination(s).

Portfolio — A prioritized list of routing decision criteria.

Protocol — A set of rules that governs data communication.

Quickest route algorithm — An adaptive routing technique that sends the message to the next available neighboring node (other than the sending node) as quickly as possible.

Route — The path(s) or subset used to actually transmit information from a source to a destination(s).

Router — An intelligent device that provides network connections and performs such services as protocol conversion and message routing.

Routing — The process of determining the best available path (or path segment) to transmit a message.

Static routing — A distributed routing technique that establishes routine paths between sending and receiving nodes based on a data flow analysis of historical data.

Token passing — A network management technique in which an electronic token is passed continuously from node to node (following the direction of flow) around the network and a given node can transmit a message only when it holds the token.

Topology — A physical arrangement of the nodes and connections in a network.

Weighted routing — A static routing technique in which different routing paths are selected for each message based on a predetermined desirable utilization rate.

54.6   Software

Not applicable.

54.7   References

1. Conrad, J. W., *Handbook of Communications Systems Management*, Auerbach, Boston, MA, 1988, 1989, 1990–1991.
2. Fitzgerald, J. and Dennis, A., *Business Data Communications and Networking*, John Wiley & Sons, New York, 1996.
3. Martin, J. and Leben, J., *Principle of Data Communications*, Prentice-Hall, Englewood Cliffs, NJ, 1988.
4. Martin, J. and Leben, J., *Data Communications Technology*, Prentice-Hall, Englewood Cliffs, NJ, 1988.
5. Ramos, E., Schroeder, A., and Beheler A., *Computer Networking Concepts*, Prentice-Hall, Englewood Cliffs, NJ, 1996.
6. Rhodes, P. D., *Building a Network: How to Specify, Design, Procure, and Install a Corporate LAN*, McGraw-Hill, New York, 1995.
7. Slone, J. P. and Drinan, A., *Handbook of Local Area Networks*, Auerbach, Boston, MA, 1991.
8. Spohn, D. L., *Data Network Design*, McGraw-Hill, New York, 1997.

9.   Stallings, W., *Business Data Communications*, Macmillan, New York, 1990.
10. Stallings, W., *Handbook of Computer-Communications Standards: Local Network Standards*, vol. 2, Macmillan, New York, 1987.
11. Taylor, D. E., *The McGraw-Hill Internetworking Handbook*, McGraw-Hill, New York, 1995.

chapter fifty-five

Logic (process) flowcharts

William S. Davis

Contents

55.1   Purpose

A logic or process flowchart is a graphical representation of the flow of logic, control, data, or paperwork through a program, a routine, a module, or a process. The flowchart specifies or documents the order in which tasks are performed. Flowcharts are used for documentation and for planning.

55.2   Strengths, weaknesses, and limitations

A properly prepared flowchart can illustrate logical flow at a glance. Flowcharts are useful for describing or planning the logical flow through a relatively small module, routine, or process. A flowchart is a good choice for describing or planning a decision-based algorithm where the number of alternative paths does not exceed three.

Logic flowcharts should not be used for documenting complete programs or large routines. Flowcharts extending over multiple pages are difficult to follow, and flowcharts (of any size) are difficult to maintain. If a flowchart spills beyond a single page (or a single screen), combine several steps to form a subroutine (or predefined process), link to the subroutine from the primary routine, and independently flowchart the subroutine.

Algebra, pseudocode (Chapter 59), and structured English (Chapter 60) may be better choices for describing or planning algebraic algorithms with no decisions. Decision trees (Chapter 57) and decision tables (Chapter 58) may be better for describing or planning complex case structures. Nassi-Shneiderman charts (Chapter 56) are better for planning and documenting structured program logic. Hierarchy charts (Chapter 62) or structure charts (Chapter 63) are better choices for describing or planning the overall logical structure of a program.

55.3   Inputs and related ideas

Before creating a logic or process flowchart, the designer must understand the algorithm or procedure. The necessary information might be compiled from direct observation, extracted from existing documentation, or derived from the information gathered during the problem definition (Part II) and/or systems analysis (Part IV) stages of the system development life cycle.

Other tools for documenting or planning routines or processes include Nassi-Shneiderman charts (Chapter 56), decision trees (Chapter 57), decision tables (Chapter 58), pseudocode (Chapter 59), structured English (Chapter 60), and input/process/output (IPO) charts (Chapter 64). A routine often exists in the context of a larger program. Tools for documenting or planning program structure include structure charts (Chapter 63) and HIPO (Chapter 64).

Logic flowcharts are sometimes confused with system flowcharts (Chapter 37). A system flowchart documents the physical relationships between a system's physical components. A logic flowchart shows the flow of logic, control, or data through a routine or a procedure.

55.4   Concepts

A logic or process flowchart uses seven standard symbols (Figure 55.1). A terminator marks the beginning or end of the flowchart. A process symbol

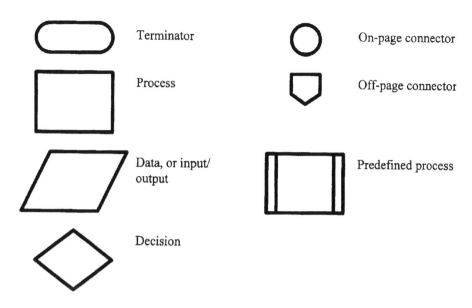

Figure 55.1 Standard flowcharting symbols.

indicates an operation that changes or manipulates data in some way (e.g., arithmetic, move, or copy). A data symbol (a parallelogram) indicates an operation that inputs or outputs data. A diamond indicates a decision. A connector (a small circle) means that the logic is continued at another place on the same page. An off-page connector (home plate) indicates that the logic is continued on another page. A rectangle within a rectangle indicates a predefined process (or subroutine).

The symbols are linked by flowlines that show the sequence and direction of flow. By convention, logic flows from the top down and from left to right, and arrowheads are added to the flowlines to indicate deviations from this standard pattern. Arrowheads make a flowchart easier to read even when the direction of flow follows convention.

55.4.1 Program logic

Flowcharts with multiple entry or exit points are difficult to follow and can easily be misinterpreted. As a general rule, each routine or process should have a single entry point and a single exit point.

Program logic can be expressed as combinations of three basic patterns: sequence, decision, and repetition (Chapter 62). A program is composed of combinations of these three basic structures.

The sequence pattern (Figure 55.2) implies that the logic is executed in simple sequence, one block after another. Note that each block might represent one or more actual instructions.

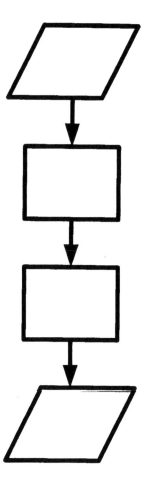

Figure 55.2   Sequence logic.

A decision block implies IF-THEN-ELSE logic (Figure 55.3). A condition (the diamond symbol) is tested. If the condition is true, the logic associated with the THEN branch is executed and the ELSE block is skipped. If the condition is false the ELSE logic is executed and the THEN logic is skipped. Note that the THEN and ELSE blocks might represent one or more actual instructions. Note also that a given THEN or ELSE block might incorporate an additional decision block, yielding nested decision logic.

There are two basic patterns for showing repetitive logic: DO WHILE and DO UNTIL (Figure 55.4). In a DO WHILE block, the test is performed first and the associated instructions are performed only if (while) the test condition is true. In a DO UNTIL block, the associated instructions are executed first and then the exit condition is tested. Note that the logic block

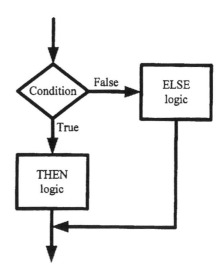

Figure 55.3   Decision logic.

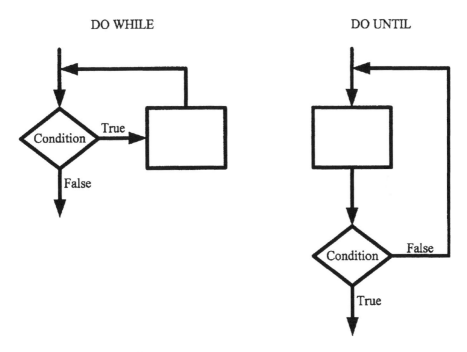

Figure 55.4   Repetitive logic.

associated with a DO WHILE or DO UNTIL might represent one or more actual instructions.

55.4.2   A module flowchart

Figure 55.5 shows a flowchart for computing an average. It begins with sequential logic to initialize a counter and an accumulator and to read the first data value. (Technically, additional logic should be added to this flowchart to ensure that the initial value of X is not negative.) The loop counts and accumulates values of X while X is greater than or equal to zero. The program ends by computing the average and outputting the results.

55.4.3   Predefined processes

Logic flowcharts extending over multiple pages are difficult to follow. If a flowchart spills beyond a single page (or a single screen), combine several steps to form a subroutine (or predefined process), link to the subroutine from the primary routine, and independently flowchart the subroutine.

   For example, Figure 55.6 shows a flowchart for a routine that accepts a transaction and, based on the transaction type calls another routine that adds, deletes, or modifies a record. The predefined process symbols indicate that the detailed logic is flowcharted elsewhere. In effect, using predefined processes allows the designer to decompose the logic.

55.4.4   A process flowchart

Figure 55.7 shows a flowchart for performing a manual procedure: waiting on a customer in a retail store. Note how the logical flow guides the sales clerk's actions. Once again, the predefined processes indicate subprocesses that are flowcharted in more detail elsewhere.

55.4.5   Connectors

Crossing flowlines are very difficult to follow and can easily be misinterpreted. To eliminate crossing flowlines, move one or more symbols or use an on-page connector. Generally, on-page connectors are shown in numbered pairs. For example, if the logic flows into a small circle marked 3, look for another small circle marked 3 with a flowline that rejoins the flowchart at some other point.

   Off-page connectors are used when the logic is continued on another page or another screen. If a flowchart requires multiple off-page connectors, the flowchart is probably too big. One possible solution is to group some of the logic into one or more predefined processes and reduce the number of symbols on the page. Perhaps a better option is to consider using a different tool.

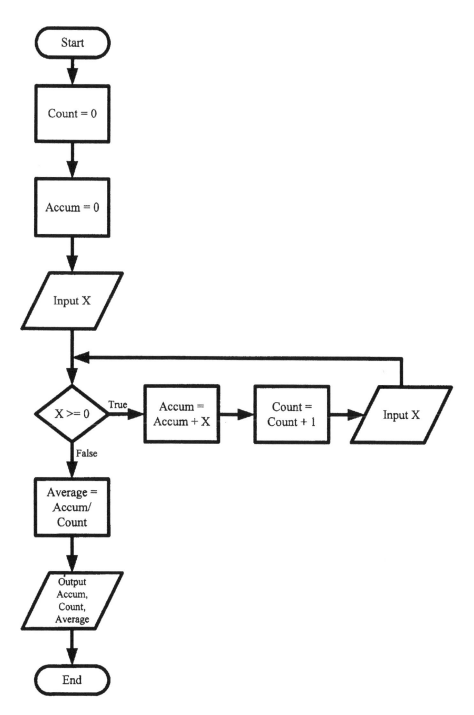

Figure 55.5 A flowchart for computing an arithmetic average.

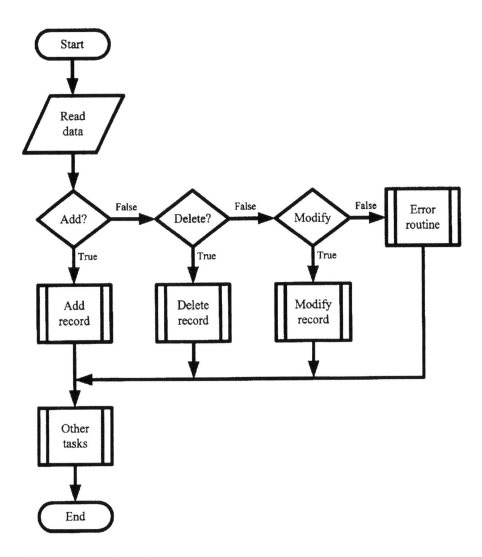

Figure 55.6   A data maintenance routine.

55.5   *Key terms*

Connector — A flowcharting symbol that indicates that the logic is continued at another place on the same page.

Data symbol — A flowcharting symbol that indicates the input or output of data.

Decision — A point in a program where the logical path is determined by a run-time condition.

Flowline — On a flowchart, a line, often terminating in an arrowhead, that indicates the sequence and direction of flow between two symbols.

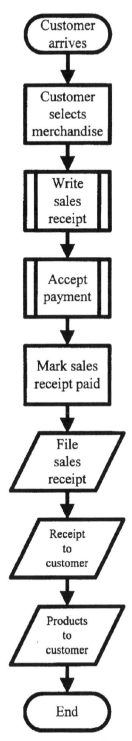

Figure 55.7   A flowchart for a manual procedure.

Logic flowchart (process flowchart) — A graphical representation of the flow of logic, control, data, or paperwork through a program, a routine, a module, or a process.

Module — A portion of a larger program that performs a specific task.

Off-page connector — A flowcharting symbol that indicates that the logic is continued on another page.

Predefined process — A flowcharting symbol that indicates that the logic is flowcharted in more detail elsewhere.

Procedure — Guidelines, rules, and instructions that tell people how to perform a task; often, a *manual* procedure.

Process — A set of steps for performing a task.

Process symbol — A flowcharting symbol that indicates an operation that changes or manipulates data in some way.

Routine — A set of instructions that performs a specific, limited task.

Terminator — A flowcharting symbol that marks the beginning or end of the flowchart.

55.6   Software

ABC Flowcharter (Micrografx.), allCLEAR (SPSS), and Visio (Visio Corporation) are three popular flowcharting programs. The examples in this chapter were created using Visio.

55.7   References

1. Bohl, M., *Flowcharting Techniques*, SRA, Chicago, 1971.
2. Boillot, M. H., Gleason, G. M., and Horn, L. W., *Essentials of Flowcharting*, 5th ed., Business and Educational Technology, Dubuque, IA, 1995.
3. Chapin, N., *Flowcharts*, Auerbach, Princeton, NJ, 1971.
4. Davis, W. S., *Business Systems Analysis and Design*, Wadsworth, Belmont, CA, 1994.
5. Davis, W. S., *Systems Analysis and Design: A Structured Approach*, Addison-Wesley, Reading, MA, 1983.
6. Silver, G. A. and Silver, J. B., *Computer Algorithms and Flowcharting*, McGraw-Hill, New York, 1975.

chapter fifty-six

Nassi-Shneiderman charts

William S. Davis

Contents

56.1   Purpose

Nassi-Shneiderman charts were developed by Nassi and Shneiderman as an alternative to traditional logic flowcharts. Their intent was to provide a structured, hierarchical, graphical view of the flow of logic through a program, a routine, a module, or a process. Nassi-Shneiderman charts are used to document, plan, and design detailed program logic.

56.2   Strengths, weaknesses, and limitations

A properly prepared Nassi-Shneiderman chart can illustrate the flow of logic through a module or routine at a glance. Nassi-Shneiderman charts are

0-8493-7001-9/99/$0.00+$.50
©1999 by CRC Press LLC

useful for describing or planning relatively small modules, routines, or processes. They can be used to clearly show nesting and recursion, and are easily converted to structured code.

Nassi-Shneiderman charts should not be used for documenting complete programs or large routines. As a general rule, Nassi-Shneiderman charts should be limited to a single page with no more than 20 subdivisions. For larger routines, combine several steps to form a subroutine, link to the subroutine, and independently chart the subroutine.

Traditional logic flowcharts (Chapter 55) are more familiar to most users and information system professionals. Algebra, pseudocode (Chapter 59), and structured English (Chapter 60) may be better choices for describing or planning algebraic algorithms with no decisions. Decision trees (Chapter 57) and decision tables (Chapter 58) may be better for describing or planning complex case structures. Hierarchy charts (Chapter 62) or structure charts (Chapter 63) are better choices for describing or planning the overall logical structure of a program.

56.3   Inputs and related ideas

Before creating a Nassi-Shneiderman chart, the designer must understand the algorithm or procedure. The necessary information might be compiled from direct observation, extracted from existing documentation, or derived from the problem definition (Part II) and/or analysis (Part IV) stages of the system development life cycle.

Other tools for documenting or planning routines or processes include logic flowcharts (Chapter 55), decision trees (Chapter 57), decision tables (Chapter 58), pseudocode (Chapter 59), structured English (Chapter 60), and input/process/output (IPO) charts (Chapter 64). A routine usually exists in the context of a larger program. Tools for documenting or planning program structure include structure charts (Chapter 63) and HIPO (Chapter 64).

56.4   Concepts

A Nassi-Shneiderman chart describes within a single rectangular box the flow of logic through a module or a routine. Control enters at the top, drops through the box, and exits at the bottom, yielding a single entry point and a single exit point. No branch instructions are permitted.

56.4.1   Program logic

Within a Nassi-Shneiderman chart, sequential, selection, and repetitive logic (Chapter 62) are shown as a set of stacked, horizontal subdivisions. Each sequence logic step occupies a single subdivision or line (Figure 56.1). Note that a sequential logic block might represent one or more actual instructions or a reference to a subroutine.

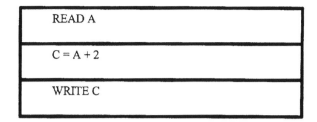

Figure 56.1 Sequence logic.

A selection (or decision) block implies IF/THEN/ELSE logic (Figure 56.2) and is documented in two parts. The top part is divided into three triangles showing, the condition (top), the path to be taken if the condition is true (left), and the path to be taken if the condition is false (right). The THEN logic is entered below the "true" triangle, and the ELSE logic is entered below the "false" triangle. Nested selection logic is documented by showing another IF/THEN/ELSE block on the appropriate path (Figure 56.3). Case structures (Figure 56.4) are documented by showing a separate path for each case.

There are two patterns for showing repetitive logic: DO WHILE and DO UNTIL (Figure 56.5). In a DO WHILE block, the test is performed first and the associated instructions are performed only if (while) the test condition is true. In a DO UNTIL block, the associated instructions are executed first and then the exit condition is tested. Note that the logic block associated with a DO WHILE or DO UNTIL might represent one or more actual instructions.

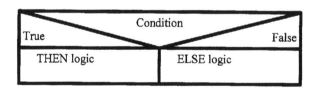

Figure 56.2 Selection logic.

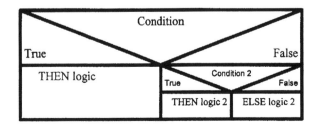

Figure 56.3 Nested selection logic.

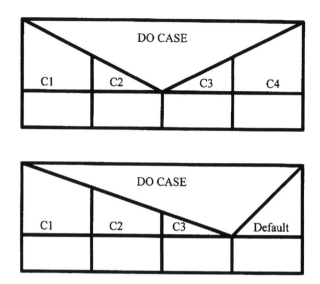

Figure 56.4   A case structure.

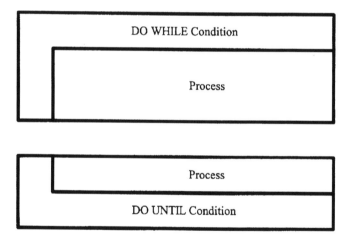

Figure 56.5   Repetitive logic.

56.4.2   *Some examples*

Figure 56.6 shows a Nassi-Shneiderman chart for computing an average. Figure 56.7 shows a Nassi-Shneiderman chart for a routine that accepts a transaction and, based on the transaction type, calls another routine that adds, deletes, or modifies a record.

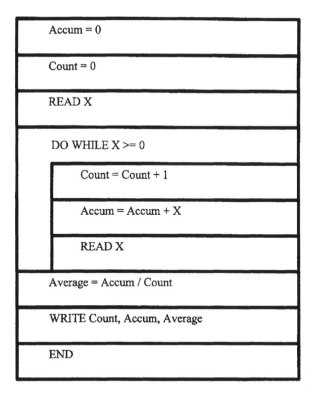

Figure 56.6   A Nassi-Shneiderman chart for computing an arithmetic average.

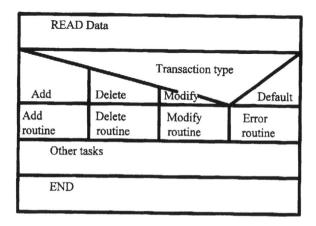

Figure 56.7   A data maintenance routine.

56.5   Key terms

Module — A portion of a larger program that performs a specific task.

Nassi-Shneiderman chart — An alternative to traditional logic flowcharts that provides a structured, hierarchical, graphical view of the flow of logic through a program, a routine, a module, or a process.

Process — A set of steps for performing a task.

Routine — A set of instructions that performs a specific, limited task.

56.6   Software

The examples in this chapter were prepared using Visio. Other charting programs (such as Micrografx's Flowcharter) can also be used.

56.7   References

1. Martin, J. and McClure, C., *Diagramming Techniques for Analysts and Programmers*, Prentice-Hall, Englewood Cliffs, NJ, 1985.
2. Nassi, I. and Shneiderman, B., Flowchart techniques for structured programming, *ACM SIGPLAN Notices*, 8(8), 12, 1973.

chapter fifty-seven

Decision trees

William S. Davis

Contents

57.1   Purpose

A decision tree is a two-dimensional graphic representation of the decisions, events, and consequences associated with a problem. Decision trees are decision science tools typically used to determine probabilities and/or expected values and to illustrate alternative system strategies. They can also be used to plan or document all possible paths through a series of nested decisions.

57.2   Strengths, weaknesses, and limitations

When an algorithm involves more than two or three nested decisions, a decision tree gives a clear and concise picture of the logic. Such algorithms are difficult to describe using logic flowcharts (Chapter 55), Nassi-Shneiderman charts (Chapter 56), pseudocode (Chapter 59), or structured English (Chapter 60).

Decision trees are not useful for planning or documenting non-decision algorithms. Many technical people are unfamiliar with decision science, so a decision tree might not be an effective communication tool.

57.3   Inputs and related ideas

Before creating a decision tree, the designer must understand the algorithm or procedure. The necessary information might be compiled from direct observation, extracted from existing documentation, or derived from the problem definition (Part II) and/or analysis (Part IV) stages of the system development life cycle.

Other tools for documenting or planning routines or processes include logic flowcharts (Chapter 55), Nassi-Shneiderman charts (Chapter 56), decision tables (Chapter 58), pseudocode (Chapter 59), structured English (Chapter 60), and input/process/output (IPO) charts (Chapter 64). A routine usually exists in the context of a larger program. Tools for documenting or planning program structure include structure charts (Chapter 63) and HIPO (Chapter 64).

57.4   Concepts

Decision trees are decision science tools that can be used to plan or document nested decision logic.

57.4.1   Decisions, events, and outcomes

Imagine a company has an opportunity to purchase for $500,000 exclusive rights to market a new product. If the product succeeds, the company stands to make $1,000,000. On the other hand, if the product fails, the company loses its entire investment.

The decision tree pictured in Figure 57.1 graphically represents the problem. The tree starts (on the left) with an act fork (a small box) that indicates a decision. Emanating from it are two branches representing the two choices: *buy* or *do not buy* the rights.

Move along the *buy* branch. The circle represents an event fork. An event is an occurrence that is not entirely subject to the decision-maker's control. (In other words, an event carries risk.) Coming from the event fork are branches representing all possible consequences (or outcomes) of the decision. (In this case, the product is either a success or a failure.) At the far right, each branch terminates in an outcome. If the product is successful, the company stands to make $1,000,000. If it fails, the company loses $500,000.

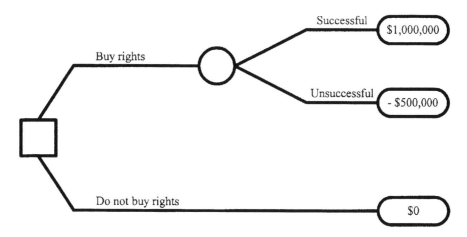

Figure 57.1 A decision tree.

Go back to the act fork. Before the decision is made, the company has an option *not* to buy the rights. Clearly, this decision will cost nothing. There are no consequences associated with this choice, so the outcome is zero whether the product is successful or not.

The oval symbols at the right of the decision tree list all possible outcomes. At this point, a management scientist or decision scientist might associate probabilities with each outcome, compute the expected values, and determine whether or not rights should be purchased.

57.4.2 Nested decisions

Decision trees can also be used to model nested decisions. Assume, for example, that the men's basketball coach wants to look through the student records and produce a list of all full-time male students who are at least 6 feet 5 inches (or 77 inches) tall and who weigh at least 180 pounds. The algorithm consists of a series of four nested questions or decisions (Figure 57.2), each one represented as a box (an act fork).

Start with the first question: Is the student at least 77 inches tall? There are only two possible answers. If the student is less than 77 inches tall, he or she is rejected. If the student is greater than or equal to 77 inches tall, a second question is asked, and so on. Follow each branch on the tree to its logical outcome. Note that a student's name and address are listed only if the student meets all four criteria.

57.4.3 Decision algorithm efficiency

Once a decision tree is drawn, probabilities can be associated with each branch and the expected values of the outcomes computed. The systems

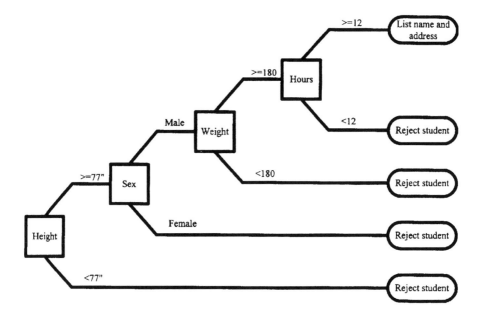

Figure 57.2   A decision tree can be used to model nested decisions.

analyst can take advantage of this idea to improve the efficiency of an algorithm.

Consider, for example, the basketball problem. Rank the tests from most to least discriminating. The height requirement will eliminate all but a handful of the students. Significantly less than half the students will meet the 180-pound requirement. The gender question (male or female) will eliminate roughly half the students. The credit hour question is the least discriminating because, on a residential campus, most students take at least twelve hours, and on a commuter campus, most students do not.

If the height requirement is tested first, only perhaps 5 percent of the records will pass and thus be subject to subsequent tests. If, on the other hand, the credit hour test is conducted first, as many as 90 percent of the students (on a residential campus) might pass the first test and thus be subject to additional tests. In general, performing the most discriminating test first, the second most discriminating test second, and so on results in fewer total tests actually being executed.

57.5   Key terms

Act fork — A point on a decision tree (represented by a box) where a decision is made.

Event — An occurrence that is not entirely subject to the decision-maker's control.

Event fork — A point on a decision tree (represented by a circle) where subsequent branches identify the consequences (or possible outcomes) of a decision.

Outcome — On a decision tree, a final result of a series of decisions and/or outcomes.

57.6   Software

The decision trees in this chapter were prepared using Visio. Other charting programs (such as Micrografx's Flowcharter) can also be used.

57.7   References

1.   Brown, R. V., Kahr, and Peterson, *Decision Analysis for the Manager*, Holt, Rinehart & Winston, New York, 1974.
2.   Davis, W. S., *Systems Analysis and Design: A Structured Approach*, Addison-Wesley, Reading, MA, 1983.

chapter fifty-eight

Decision tables

William S. Davis

Contents

58.1 Purpose

A decision table is a two-dimensional table that shows the action to be taken following a series of related decisions.

58.2 Strengths, weaknesses, and limitations

When an algorithm involves more than two or three nested decisions, a decision table gives a clear and concise picture of the logic. Such algorithms are difficult to describe using logic flowcharts (Chapter 55), Nassi-Shneiderman charts (Chapter 56), pseudocode (Chapter 59), or structured English (Chapter 60). Additionally, decision tables are relatively easy for non-technical users to follow.

Decision tables are not useful for describing non-decision algorithms. They were common in the 1970s and 1980s, but few modern analysts or programmers are familiar with them.

58.3 Inputs and related ideas

Before creating a decision table, the designer must understand the algorithm or procedure. The necessary information might be compiled from direct observation, extracted from existing documentation, or derived from the problem definition (Part II) and/or analysis (Part IV) stages of the system development life cycle.

Other tools for documenting or planning routines or processes include logic flowcharts (Chapter 55), Nassi-Shneiderman charts (Chapter 56), decision trees (Chapter 57), pseudocode (Chapter 59), structured English (Chapter 60), and input/process/output (IPO) charts (Chapter 64). A routine usually exists in the context of a larger program. Tools for documenting or planning program structure include structure charts (Chapter 63) and HIPO (Chapter 64).

58.4 Concepts

Assume that the men's basketball coach wants to look through the student records and produce a list of all full-time male students who are at least 6 feet 5 inches (or 77 inches) tall and who weigh at least 180 pounds.

A decision table for an appropriate algorithm is shown as Figure 58.1. It is divided into four sections: a condition stub at the upper left, a condition entry at the upper right, an action stub at the lower left, and an action entry at the lower right. The questions are listed in the condition stub; note that each question requires a yes/no response. The associated actions are listed in the action stub. The responses (Y or N) are recorded in the condition entry, while the appropriate action is indicated in the action entry.

Condition Stub:	Condition entry:				
Is the student male?	Y	N			
Is the student taking at least 12 hours?	Y		N		
Is the student at least 77 inches tall?	Y			N	
Does the student weigh at least 180 pounds?	Y				N
Action Stub:	Action Entry:				
List the student's name and address	X				
Reject the student		X	X	X	X

Figure 58.1   A decision table.

The easiest way to understand a decision table is to read one. Start with the first question: Is the student male? There are two possible answers: yes (Y) or no (N). If the answer is no, then the student is not male, is not a candidate for the men's basketball team, and can be rejected. Move down the column containing the N and note the X on the action entry line following the action *Reject the student.* If the answer is yes, however, the coach cannot yet make a decision to add the student to the list because the student must first pass three more tests.

Move on to the second question: Is the student taking at least 12 credit hours? Again, there are two possible answers: yes or no. Note how the answers are recorded on Figure 58.1. The second Y is directly under the first one, implying that the answers to both questions (plus two more) must be yes before the action identified by an X in that column's action entry can be taken. If the answer to the second question is no, however, the student can be rejected. Note that any single N, by itself, is enough to reject the student.

Read the rest of the table. It clearly shows that the student's name and address will be listed only if the answers to all four questions are yes, but that the student will be rejected if the answer to any one question is no.

58.5   Key terms

Action entry — The box at the lower right of a decision table where the appropriate action is indicated.

Action stub — The box at the lower left of a decision table where the possible actions are listed.

Condition entry — The box at the upper right of a decision table where the responses (Y or N) to the questions in the condition stub are listed.

Condition stub — The box at the upper left of a decision table where the questions (or decisions) are listed.

Decision table — A two-dimensional table that shows the action to be taken following a set of related decisions.

58.6   Software

Decision tables can conveniently be constructed using a spreadsheet program. The decision tables in this chapter were prepared using Visio. Other charting programs (such as Micrografx's Flowcharter) can also be used.

58.7   References

1. Brown, R. V., Kahr, A. S., and Peterson, C., *Decision Analysis for the Manager,* Holt, Rinehart & Winston, New York, 1974.
2. Davis, W. S., *Systems Analysis and Design: A Structured Approach*, Addison-Wesley, Reading, MA, 1983.

chapter fifty-nine

Pseudocode

William S. Davis

Contents

59.1 Purpose

Pseudocode is a tool for planning, defining, or documenting the contents of a program routine or module. As the name implies, pseudocode is similar to (and often based on) real code.

59.2 Strengths, weaknesses, and limitations

Pseudocode is an excellent tool for planning or designing program logic and computational algorithms. Because it resembles real code, programmers

0-8493-7001-9/99/$0.00+$.50

find it easy to use and to understand. Pseudocode is not a good tool for describing control structures, particularly when several nested decisions are involved. Because pseudocode resembles a programming language, it is not well suited to planning or designing manual procedures.

In part, because pseudocode so closely resembles real code, some designers tend to write (rather than plan or design) the code. Writing the code twice (once in pseudocode and once in real code) is a waste of time. When the designer worries about coding details, crucial design considerations can easily be overlooked. Also, programmers resent such over specification.

Even if the pseudocode is well done, programmers sometimes resent it. Specifying algorithms in what is essentially a high-level language limits the programmer's flexibility. Additionally, the programmer can fail to distinguish between the analyst's coding technique and the analyst's design, and the result may be criticism (even rejection) of a perfectly good design based on inappropriate criteria.

59.3   Inputs and related ideas

Before writing pseudocode, the designer must understand the algorithm or procedure. The necessary information might be compiled from direct observation, extracted from existing documentation, or derived from the problem definition (Part II) and/or analysis (Part IV) stages of the system development life cycle.

Other tools for documenting or planning routines or processes include logic flowcharts (Chapter 55), Nassi-Schneiderman charts (Chapter 56), decision trees (Chapter 57), decision tables (Chapter 58), structured English (Chapter 60), and input/process/output (IPO) charts (Chapter 64). A pseudocode routine usually exists in the context of a larger program. Tools for documenting or planning program structure include structure charts (Chapter 63) and HIPO (Chapter 64). The basic software logic blocks are defined in Chapter 62.

59.4   Concepts

With pseudocode, such details as opening and closing files, initializing counters, and setting flags are explicitly coded, but language-dependent details (such as the distinction between subscripts and indexes or the difference between real and integer numbers) are ignored. The idea is to describe the executable code in a form that a programmer can easily translate into real code.

There is no standard pseudocode; many different versions exist. Most, however, capitalize key words and operations and use indentation to show the logical relationships between blocks of code.

59.4.1   Sequence

Perhaps the easiest way to define sequential logic is by coding an algebra-like expression, for example,

COUNT = 0

or

STOCK = STOCK + QUANTITY

Such details as the sequence of operations and the rules for using parentheses should be consistent with the language to be used for writing the actual code. Data names should be taken from the data dictionary.

Input and output instructions are explicitly defined in pseudocode; for example,

READ data FROM source

and

WRITE data TO destination

where *data* is a list of variables, a data structure, or a record, and *source* and *destination* refer to a file or a database.

59.4.2   Blocks of logic

A block can contain any set of sequence, decision (selection), and/or repetition (iteration) logic. Once defined, the block's instructions can be referenced by coding a PERFORM instruction:

PERFORM block

For example, the instructions

COUNT = 0
ACCUMULATOR = 0

might be assigned the block name INITIALIZE. Subsequently, the instruction

PERFORM INITIALIZE

executes all the instructions in the block.

To distinguish between formal subroutines and internal procedures, some analysts use:

PERFORM block USING list

for a subroutine, where *list* designates a list of variables passed between the calling routine and the subroutine.

59.4.3   Decision or selection

The general form of a decision (selection) block is:

IF condition

    THEN

        PERFORM block-1

    ELSE

        PERFORM block-2

ENDIF

For example,

IF HOURS > 40

    THEN

        PERFORM OVERTIME

    ELSE

        PERFORM REGULAR

ENDIF

By convention, the THEN block is executed if the condition is true and the ELSE block is executed if the condition is false.

Note the ENDIF. A feature of most pseudocodes is that each block of logic is clearly delimited. A decision block always begins with IF and ends with ENDIF, so there is no ambiguity. Note also the use of indentation. It makes the block easy to read.

It is possible to nest decision logic. For example,

IF condition-1

    THEN

        IF condition-2

THEN

    PERFORM block-a

ELSE

    PERFORM block-b

ENDIF

ELSE

    PERFORM block-c

ENDIF

Note how indentation highlights the relationship among these instructions. Note also how IF and ENDIF clearly delimit both decision blocks.

59.4.4   Repetition or iteration

DO WHILE logic tests for the terminal condition at the top of the loop. For example,

WHILE condition DO

    PERFORM block

ENDWHILE

Note the use of indentation and the way WHILE and ENDWHILE delimit the block. The REPEAT UNTIL structure tests for the terminal condition at the bottom of the loop:

REPEAT

    PERFORM block

UNTIL condition

Some analysts use a pseudocode structure much like a DO loop to define a count-controlled loop:

DO index = initial TO limit

    PERFORM block

ENDDO

Again, note the indentation and the ENDDO.

59.4.5 The case structure

A common programming problem involves selecting among several alternative paths. Although nested decision statements could be used to define such logic, the case structure is a better option when nesting goes beyond three or four levels.

The general form of a case structure is:

SELECT variable

    CASE (value-1) block-1

    CASE (value-2) block-2

    .

    .

    .

    DEFAULT CASE block-n

ENDSELECT

The option selected by the case structure depends on the value of the control variable following the keyword SELECT. If the variable contains *value-1*, then *block-1* is executed; if it contains *value-2*, then *block-2* is executed, and so on. The DEFAULT CASE is coded to define the logic to be executed if the control variable contains none of the listed values. A case structure is delimited by ENDSELECT. Once again, indentation makes the structure easy to read.

For example, the following pseudocode routine accepts a code (the TRANSACTION TYPE) and, based on the value of the code, passes control to one of three lower-level routines.

SELECT TRANSACTION TYPE

    CASE (modify)   PERFORM MODIFY STOCK

    CASE (add)   PERFORM ADD RECORD

    CASE (delete)   PERFORM DELETE RECORD

    DEFAULT CASE   PERFORM TRANSACTION ERROR

ENDSELECT

59.5 Key terms

Module — A portion of a larger program that performs a specific task.
Procedure — A set of guidelines, rules, and instructions for performing a task; often, a *manual* procedure.

Pseudocode — A tool for planning, defining, or documenting the contents of a program routine or module that resembles real code.

Routine — A set of instructions that performs a specific, limited task.

59.6 Software

Few software tools are designed to produce pseudocode. Word processors and text editors are sometimes used.

59.7 References

1. Davis, W. S., *Systems Analysis and Design: A Structured Approach*, Addison-Wesley, Reading, MA, 1983.
2. Gane, C. and Sarson, T., *Structured Systems Analysis: Tools and Techniques*, Prentice-Hall, Englewood Cliffs, NJ, 1979.
3. Gillett, W. D. and Pollack, S. V., *An Introduction to Engineered Software*, Holt, Rinehart & Winston, NY, 1982.
4. Peters, L. J., *Software Design: Methods and Techniques*, Yourdon Press, NY, 1981.

chapter sixty

Structured English

William S. Davis

Contents

60.1   Purpose

Structured English is a very limited, highly restricted subset of the English language used to plan, design, or document program routines, modules, and manual procedures.

60.2   Strengths, weaknesses, and limitations

Structured English is useful for planning or designing program routines, modules, and manual procedures. It resembles a programming language, so programmers find it easy to understand. The base for structured English is, of course, English, so users find it easy to follow, too.

0-8493-7001-9/99/$0.00+$.50
©1999 by CRC Press LLC

Structured English is excellent for describing an algorithm, particularly when user communication is essential. If the main concern is communication with the programmers, however, pseudocode may be a better choice. Structured English is not a good choice for describing a high-level control structure or an algorithm in which numerous decisions must be made; logic flowcharts, decision tables, and decision trees are better for such tasks.

60.3   Inputs and related ideas

Before writing structured English, the designer must understand the algorithm or procedure. The necessary information might be compiled from direct observation, extracted from existing documentation, or derived from the problem definition (Part II) and/or analysis (Part IV) stages of the system development life cycle.

Other tools for documenting or planning routines or processes include logic flowcharts (Chapter 55), Nassi-Schneiderman charts (Chapter 56), decision trees (Chapter 57), decision tables (Chapter 58), pseudocode (Chapter 59), and input/process/output (IPO) charts (Chapter 64). A pseudocode routine usually exists in the context of a larger program. Tools for documenting or planning program structure include structure charts (Chapter 63) and HIPO (Chapter 64). The basic software logic blocks are defined in Chapter 62.

60.4   Concepts

There are several variations of structured English, none of which can be considered a standard. Consequently, view this chapter as a guideline.

A good structured English statement reads like a short imperative sentence. By convention, only key words such as IF, THEN, SO, REPEAT, UNTIL, DO, and so on are capitalized; data names and the general English needed to complete a sentence or a phrase are lower case. Many sources recommend that a data name defined in a data dictionary be underlined, and that convention will be followed in the examples shown below.

60.4.1   Sequence

Sequence statements begin with commands such as MOVE, GET, WRITE, READ, or COMPUTE followed by the name or names of the associated data elements or data structures. For example,

COMPUTE gross pay.

ADD 1 to counter.

MULTIPLY hours worked by pay rate to get gross pay.

GET inventory record.

MOVE customer name to invoice.

WRITE invoice.

60.4.2   Blocks of logic

It is often convenient to group several structured English statements into a block, assign a name to the block, and reference the block by coding a single sequence statement. For example, all the instructions required to compute gross pay might be grouped in a block under the name *compute gross pay.* Subsequently, the statement

DO compute gross pay.

references the entire block.

Note that a block can contain any combination of code, including decisions, repetitive logic, and even other blocks. Indentation should always be used to show the relationship between the parts of a block.

60.4.3   Decision or selection

Decision (or selection) logic follows an IF-THEN-ELSE structure:

IF condition

THEN block-1

ELSE (not condition)

SO block-2.

The key word IF is followed by a condition. If the condition is true, the block following THEN is executed. ELSE identifies the negative of the condition. SO precedes the block to be executed if the initial condition is false. For example,

IF stock-on-hand is less than reorder-point

THEN turn on reorder-flag

ELSE (stock-on-hand not less than reorder-point

SO turn off reorder-flag.

Indenting makes the IF-THEN-ELSE logic easier to read. (*Note*: The negative condition following ELSE is often assumed and not explicitly coded.)

Nested decisions are also supported:

IF condition-1

> THEN IF condition-2
>
> > THEN block-a
> >
> > ELSE (not condition-2)
> >
> > SO block-b
>
> ELSE (not condition-1)
>
> SO block-c.

Note that any or all of *block-a*, *block-b*, or *block-c* could contain yet another decision.

60.4.4   Repetition or iteration

Repetitive (or iterative) logic defines a block of structured English that is executed repetitively until a terminal condition is reached. For example, such instructions as:

> REPEAT UNTIL condition-1
>
> > block-1

or

> FOR EACH TRANSACTION
>
> > block-a

imply both repetitive logic and the condition used to terminate that logic.

60.5   Key terms

> **Module** — A portion of a larger program that performs a specific task.
> **Procedure** — A set of guidelines, rules, and instructions for performing a task; often, a *manual* procedure.
> **Routine** — A set of instructions that performs a specific, limited task.
> **Structured English** — A very limited, highly restricted subset of the English language used to plan, design, or document program routines, modules, and manual procedures.

60.6   Software

Few software tools are designed to produce structured English. Word processors and text editors are sometimes used.

60.7 References

1. Davis, W. S., *Systems Analysis and Design: A Structured Approach*, Addison-Wesley, Reading, MA, 1983.
2. Gane, C. and Sarson, T., *Structured Systems Analysis: Tools and Techniques*, Prentice-Hall, Englewood Cliffs, NJ, 1979.

chapter sixty-one

Process design

David C. Yen and William S. Davis

Contents

61.1   Purpose

This chapter briefly discusses several general process design principles and guidelines.

61.2   Strengths, weaknesses, and limitations

Not applicable.

0-8493-7001-9/99/$0.00+$.50
©1999 by CRC Press LLC

61.3   Inputs and related ideas

Processes are designed in the context of a system. The information to support process design is collected during the problem definition (Part II) and analysis (Part IV) stages of the system development life cycle, and the processes are identified during the high-level design stage (Part V). Problem analysis techniques are discussed in Chapter 15. Process design tools and techniques include data flow diagrams (Chapter 24), Warnier-Orr diagrams (Chapter 33), system flowcharts (Chapter 37), logic flowcharts (Chapter 55), Nassi-Shneiderman diagrams (Chapter 56), decision trees (Chapter 57), decision tables (Chapter 58), pseudocode (Chapter 59), structured English (Chapter 60), and structure charts (Chapter 63). Such concepts as decomposition, cohesion, coupling, and span of control are discussed in Chapter 62.

61.4   Concepts

This chapter briefly discusses several general process design principles and guidelines.

61.4.1   Factors that influence process design

Before starting process design, the analyst or designer must carefully consider the process in the context of the system. For example, on-line, batch, and real-time systems (Chapter 73) are inherently different, and process timings must be consistent with system timings.

A complex process might be converted into several smaller and more feasible subprocesses using decomposition techniques (Chapter 15). Numerous, small processes create numerous interfaces that can lead to operational complexity. An option is to merge several subprocesses into one process by using factoring techniques (Chapter 15).

In some cases, abstraction might be used to transform an abstract problem into a form that is more easily understood by the user. Abstraction is a problem-solving technique that focuses on investigating the most critical aspects of a problem and using the results to suggest a solution. Such tools as searching, generate-and-test, and justification building (Chapter 15) can be used to abstract a problem.

Transform-oriented processes create and/or derive new information based on the input data. For example, a payroll process calculates an employee's net income given such input as hours worked, pay rate, federal, state and city income tax rates, and so on. Such processes can usually be divided into input (afferent), output (efferent), and process (transform) modules to form a high-level control structure (Chapter 62).

Transaction-oriented processes transmit or route the right information to the right process and are typically decomposed to form a case structure (Chapter 62). For example, after receiving a customer order, an order routing process might be used to check the order type and then transmit backorders to a back order subprocess, new customer orders to a new customer subprocess, orders from existing customers to a customer verification subprocess, and so on.

The available technology also affects process design. For example, CASE tools, screen, and form generators, and prototyping fundamentally change the process of designing processes. To cite one example, the CASE repository (Chapter 5) might serve as database for designing a new process based on existing similar processes.

61.4.2 Process content

Before starting detailed process design, the analyst or designer must define both static and dynamic information for each process. Static information includes such attributes as the process name, the process number (and other process identifiers), any algorithms or logic associated with the process, the inputs to the process, and the outputs from the process. Dynamic information includes such attributes as the processing cycle (daily, weekly, monthly, quarterly, annually), the nature of the output (query, periodic report), any parameters that vary over time (e.g., the price of gasoline), and any other parameters not subject to the organization's control (e.g., Internal Revenue Service regulations).

61.4.3 Process data

Once the process contents are defined, the analyst or designer must check the process's data flows. Except for constants, input data elements must either flow from a source or a prior process and output data elements must flow to a following process. Any data stores associated with the process must be mapped to a file or a database. A data flow diagram (Chapter 24) is an excellent tool for checking data flows.

61.4.4 Process design guidelines

Listed below are several general process design principles and guidelines.

61.4.4.1 Stepwise refinement

Stepwise refinement is a top-down strategy for dealing with complex or abstract processes. The basic idea is to study the process and define it in a conceptual level, analyze the conceptual knowledge and describe it at a logical level, and transform the logical information into corresponding physical specifications. The structured analysis and design methodology (Chapter 3) utilizes stepwise refinement.

61.4.4.2 Modularization

A complex process is normally implemented as a set of linked, single-task modules (Chapter 62), with a high-level control module calling subordinate modules in the proper order. The control modules and their subordinates must be designed in such a way that they can be easily linked and can share common information. Only those data elements directly relevant to its sub-task should be passed to or returned by a submodule, and a called module should store no global data elements. A called module should always return control to the calling module.

Coupling is a measure of module interdependence. Generally, coupling is a function of the amount of data passed between the calling module and its subordinate, and more data implies tighter coupling. A major objective of process design is to reduce coupling. Structured walkthroughs and inspections (Chapter 23) can help.

Cohesion is a measure of a module's completeness. A well-designed module performs a single, *complete* task. If a module must be decomposed, each submodule should perform a single, complete subtask.

Span of control is another important criterion. Generally, a super-process should control no more than seven subordinate subprocesses.

61.4.4.3 Information hiding

The information hiding principle suggests that all information not directly relevant to a given process should be hidden from that process. Only essential data elements should be passed to a process when the process is called. No subprocess should be allowed to access or modify any global data element that is not explicitly passed to it. If a given process utilizes local data elements, the local data should be known only within that process. A called process should be designed to react only when the correct information is passed to it.

61.5   Key terms

Abstraction — A problem-solving technique that focuses on investigating the most critical aspects of a problem and using the results to suggest a solution.

Afferent process — A process that gathers and prepares input data.

Cohesion — A measure of a module's completeness.

Control structure — A hierarchical model of the flow of control through a program. The control structure resembles a military chain of command or an organization chart. At the top is a main control module that calls secondary control structures. At the bottom are the computational routines, each of which implements a single algorithm.

Coupling — A measure of a module's independence; fewer parameters flowing into or out from a module imply looser coupling.

Decomposition — A problem analysis paradigm that calls for breaking a problem into more manageable subproblems and then attacking the subproblems.

Dynamic information — Time-related parameters, or process information that can change; for example, the processing cycle, the nature of the output, any parameters that vary over time, and any other parameters not subject to the organization's control.

Efferent process — A process that structures and/or transmits output data.

Factoring — Merging several small, isolated, overlapping, or related problems to form a meta-problem.

Functional decomposition — A program design methodology in which the program is broken down (or decomposed) into modules based on the processes or tasks they perform.

Information hiding — A principle that suggests that all information not directly relevant to a given process should be hidden from that process.

Span-of-control (breadth) — A measure of the number of modules directly controlled by a higher-level routine.

Static information — Process information that is not likely to change; for example, the process name, the process number, necessary algorithms, inputs, and outputs.

Stepwise refinement — A top-down strategy for dealing with complex or abstract processes.

Transaction-oriented process — A process that transmits or routes the right information to the right process.

Transform process — A process that converts the input data to output form.

Transform-oriented process — A process that creates and/or derives new information based on the input data.

61.6   *Software*

Not applicable.

61.7   *References*

1. Burch, J. G., *Systems Analysis, Design, and Implementation*, Boyd & Fraser, Boston, MA, 1992.
2. Burd, S. D., *Systems Architecture: Hardware and Software in Business Information Systems*, Boyd & Fraser, Boston, MA, 1994.
3. Dewitz, S. D., *Systems Analysis and Design and The Transition to Objects*, McGraw-Hill, New York, 1996.
4. Hoffer, J. A., George, J. F., and Valacich, J. S., *Modern Systems Analysis and Design*, Benjamin/Cummings, Redwood City, CA, 1996.
5. Pressman, R. S., *Software Engineering: A Practitioner's Approach*, 2nd ed., McGraw-Hill, New York, 1987.

chapter sixty-two

Structured program design

William S. Davis

Contents

0-8493-7001-9/99/$0.00+$.50
©1999 by CRC Press LLC

62.1   Purpose

This chapter discusses the basic principles that underlie structured program design and functional decomposition. The objective of functional decomposition is to design structured programs that are easy to test, debug, and maintain. The basic idea is to break down (or decompose) a program into logically independent modules based on the processes or tasks they perform.

62.2   Strengths, weaknesses, and limitations

Because the detailed computational logic is grouped into independent, single function modules, well-structured programs are easier to test, debug, and maintain than are unstructured programs. Independent modules can be independently coded and tested. The control structure allows the entire program to be tested top down, one module at a time. When an error occurs, it is often possible to quickly isolate the likely cause to a single module. During the maintenance phase, independent modules can be replaced or modified with minimal ripple effects.

Functional decomposition is a process driven methodology. Consequently, although the logic modules are independent, the data are not, and that can lead to ripple effects during testing, debugging, and maintenance.

62.3   Inputs and related ideas

Before starting to design a program using functional decomposition, the necessary logical data structures and the primary processes must be defined during the systems analysis phase (Part IV) of the system development life cycle. Often, the results of analysis are documented in the requirements specification (Chapter 35). Additionally, it is useful to define the physical data structures, file structures, and database structures (Chapters 43, 44, and 45), the required input and output data structures (Chapters 46 through 51), and the algorithms (Chapters 55 through 60) before starting program design.

The design of a structured program is sometimes documented using the HIPO technique (Chapter 64). Structure charts (Chapter 63) are useful planning tools. Such tools as logic flowcharts (Chapter 55), Nassi-Shneiderman charts (Chapter 56), decision trees (Chapter 57), decision tables (Chapter 58), pseudocode (Chapter 59), structured English (Chapter 60), and IPO charts (Chapter 64) are used to document the modules.

62.4   Concepts

Functional decomposition is a popular structured program design methodology. The basic idea is to break down (or decompose) a program into logically independent modules based on the processes or tasks they perform.

62.4.1 The control structure

A well-designed structured program consists of a set of independent, single function modules linked by a control structure that resembles a military chain of command or an organization chart (Figure 62.1). Each module is represented by a rectangle. At the top of the control structure is a single module called the root (or the main control module). All control flows from the root which calls (or invokes) its level-2 child (or son) modules. The level-2 modules, in turn, call their level-3 children, and so on. The calling module (sometimes called the parent) passes data and/or control information to the child and receives data and/or control information back from the child; otherwise, the modules are viewed as independent black boxes. Note that control always returns to the calling module.

A module with no children (a lowest-level module) is called a leaf and often implements a single algorithm. Library modules (e.g., a standard subroutine) are indicated by a rectangle marked with two vertical lines; see the leaf labeled *Library module* in Figure 62.1. Note that a library module can be called by more than one parent.

The modules are often assigned identifying numbers or codes that indicate their relative positions in the hierarchy. For example, the root might be designated module 1.1, the level-2 modules might be designated 2.1, 2.2, 2.3, and so on. Other designers use letters (or even Roman numerals) to

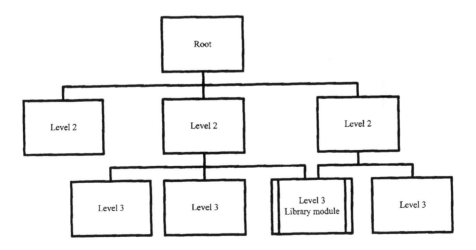

Figure 62.1 A well-designed structured program consists of a set of independent single function modules linked by a control structure.

designate levels; for example, module A.1 is the root, module B.3 is the third module at level 2, module C.6 is the sixth module at level 3, and so on. Sometimes, more complex numbering schemes are used to indicate a path through the hierarchy. The key is consistency.

62.4.2 Designing a control structure

The first step in decomposing a program is to define its high-level control structure. The primary inputs come from the logical models developed during the systems analysis phase (Part IV) and from the requirements specification (Chapter 35). More specifically, the high-level functions to be performed by a given program can often be obtained from the appropriate configuration item's process description.

62.4.2.1 Afferent, transform, and efferent processes

One approach to designing a control structure is to divide the functions (or subprocesses) into three groups (Figure 62.2). The afferent processes gather and prepare input data. The efferent processes structure and transmit output data. In the middle, the transform processes convert the input data to output form. Identifying the afferent, transform, and efferent processes suggests a basic input, process, output control structure.

62.4.2.2 Trigger events

An alternative is to start with the program's trigger event, the event that activates the program or causes it to change from a wait to a run state. Some programs are triggered by an asynchronous event such as the arrival of a transaction or an interrupt. Other applications are clock driven; for example, a batch program might be run at the same time every week, and a scientific data collection routine might take a sample every few seconds. A program's high-level control structure should reference those tasks that are performed in direct response to its trigger event.

62.4.2.3 Data structures

Another technique for designing a high-level control structure is to analyze the data structures. The point of any program is to accept the input data and convert them to the form required for output, so the data actually drive the program design process.

Analyze the output data and determine the order in which the various output substructures are assembled. Then define the input substructures and the algorithms that generate the data elements in a given output substructure. The data structures will, essentially, dictate both the order in which the logical tasks must be performed and the logical structures needed to support those tasks. Generally, sequential data structures call for sequential logic,

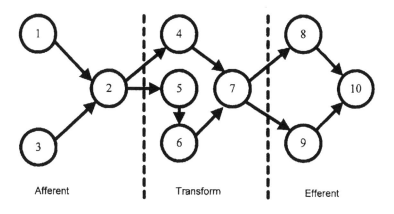

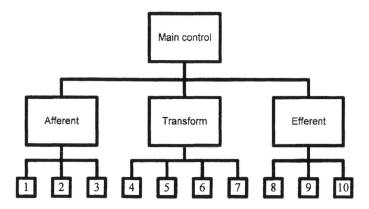

Figure 62.2   Afferent, transform, and efferent processes.

conditional structures call for conditional logic, and repetitive structures call for repetitive logic.

62.4.2.4   Logical access maps

Logical access maps were initially proposed by Martin[4] to help the designer determine the logical execution sequences or access paths through a program. This technique recognizes that each user (or class of users) has a unique logical accessing perspective. For example, a sales associate might start with a customer order and follow the order through order fulfillment, shipping, and so on. In contrast, warehouse personnel might start with the arrival of a shipment from a supplier, track the shipment into inventory, and view a customer order as nothing more than a transaction that deletes individual items from inventory. The point of logical access mapping is to examine the logical accessing sequence of a system's programs and a program's modules from multiple perspectives and to use the consensus view as a design criterion.

62.4.3 Evaluating the control structure

A well-designed control structure exhibits a regular morphology (form, or structure) and achieves a balance between breadth and depth.

62.4.3.1 Morphology

One way to evaluate a control structure's design is to examine its morphology (form or structure). Each module decomposes into several lower-level routines, so the number of modules should increase from level-2 to level-3, perhaps increase again at level-4, and so on. Eventually, however, only some modules require additional decomposition, so the number of routines at each level begins to stabilize and then to decline.

For example, Figure 62.3 shows a control structure for an inventory management program. Figure 62.4 is a simplified version of the control chart that emphasizes the number of modules at each level. Note the shape; some people describe it as a mosque or a cigar. Most good control structures have a similar shape, with the number of modules at each level increasing, then stabilizing, and then decreasing.

Morphology is subjective; over the years, people have noticed that good designs tend to have that characteristic shape. The designer should not consciously try to make the control structure resemble a mosque. Instead, morphology should be checked after the design is complete. If the shape

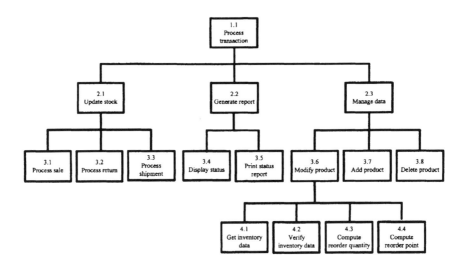

Figure 62.3 A control structure.

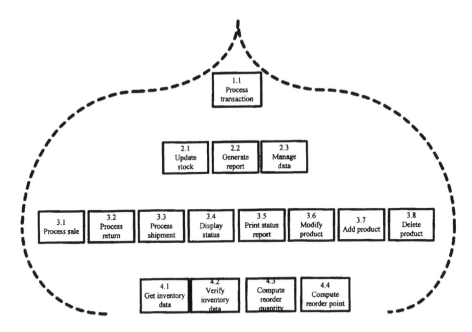

Figure 62.4   The morphology of a good design resembles a mosque or a cigar.

seems reasonable, the design is probably a good one. If the design deviates significantly from the expected shape, it should be restudied.

62.4.3.2   *Depth and breadth*

A well-designed control structure balances two conflicting objectives: depth and breadth. Depth is the number of levels in the control structure. Because each call to a lower level is a potential source of error, shallow structures tend to be better than deep structures. Breadth, or span-of-control, is a measure of the number of modules directly controlled by a higher-level routine. Too many subordinates adds to complexity, so narrow structures tend to be better than broad structures.

Narrow structures are usually deep, so reducing breadth tends to increase depth, and vice versa. One rule-of-thumb for balancing these two parameters suggests that no module should directly control more than seven subordinates. If a given routine has too many subordinate modules, adding a secondary control structure drops some of them to a lower level.

Module size is another useful screen; one page of source code is a common limit. If a module's logic exceeds roughly 50 lines of code, decompose it. If, on the other hand, the logic in a subordinate routine can be merged into its parent without violating the single page rule, merge it. Remember, however, that rules-of- thumb are not absolute. If breaking one means a better design, break it.

62.4.3.3 Structure clash and boundary clash

Structure clash occurs when corresponding elements of two related data structures are incompatible. For example, imagine that customer social security number is the key for an invoice file and customer zip code is the key for a name and address file. Because the files are (presumably) stored in different record sequences and accessed by different keys, it is difficult to design a program to efficiently merge them.

A boundary clash occurs when the physical data structures are incompatible. For example, if a program sets a nonstandard (9 × 12) page size and the printer is loaded with standard (8.5 × 11) paper, the resulting boundary clash produces poorly aligned output.

Structure clashes and boundary clashes lead to errors and inefficiencies. The program designer should carefully evaluate both the logical and physical data structures and change the program design, the data structures, or both to eliminate structure clash and border clash.

62.4.4 Module design

A good module is cohesive and loosely coupled.

62.4.4.1 Cohesion

Cohesion is a measure of a module's completeness. Every statement in the module should relate to the same function, and all of that function's logic should be in the same module. When a module becomes large enough to decompose, each submodule should perform a cohesive subfunction.

The best form of cohesion is called functional cohesion. A functionally cohesive module performs a single logical function, receives and returns no surplus data, and performs only essential logical operations. Functional cohesion is the designer's objective. A module is not considered functionally cohesive if it exhibits other forms of cohesion.

Coincidental cohesion is the weakest type. In a coincidentally cohesive module, there is little or no logical justification for grouping the operations; the instructions are related almost by chance. In a logically cohesive module, all the elements are related to the same logical function; for example, all input operations or all data verification operations might be grouped to form a module. The elements that form a temporally cohesive module are related by time; for example, a setup module might hold all operations that must be performed at setup time.

Procedural cohesion is an intermediate form of cohesion, halfway between coincidental cohesion and functional cohesion. All the elements in a procedurally cohesive module are associated with the same procedural unit, such as a loop or a decision structure. Communicational cohesion groups elements that operate on the same set of input or output data (more generally, on the same data structure). With sequential cohesion, the modules form a chain of transformations, with the output from one module serving as input to the next. The three types of cohesion described in this paragraph often result from viewing the program as a flowchart.

62.4.4.2 Coupling

Coupling is a measure of a module's independence. Perfect independence is impossible because each module must accept data from and return data to its calling routine. Because global data errors can have difficult-to-trace ripple effects, a module should never change the value of any global data element that is not explicitly passed to it. If that rule is enforced, the list of parameters becomes a measure of how tightly the module is linked to the rest of the program. Fewer parameters imply looser coupling.

With data coupling (or input-output coupling), only data move between the modules. Data coupling is necessary if the modules are to communicate. Control coupling involves passing control information (e.g., a switch setting) between the modules. Hybrid coupling is a combination of data coupling and control coupling. For example, if module A modifies an instruction in module B, the operation looks like data coupling to module A and control coupling to module B. Whenever possible, control and hybrid coupling should be eliminated.

With common-environment coupling, two or more modules interact with a common data environment, such as a shared communication region or a shared file. With content coupling, some or all of the contents of one module are included in the other. This problem often occurs when a module is given multiple entry points. Both common-environment and content coupling can lead to severe ripple effects, and should be avoided.

Binding time, the time at which a module's values and identifiers are fixed, is another factor that influences coupling. A module can be fixed (rendered unchangeable) at coding time, at compilation time, at load time, or at execution time. Generally, the later the binding time the better the module.

62.4.4.3 Sequence, selection, and repetition

The modules that form a well-structured program are composed of three basic logical building blocks or constructs: sequence, selection (or decision), and repetition (or iteration). Go to or branch instructions are not permitted.

Sequence (Figure 62.5) implies that the logic is executed in simple sequence, one block after another. Note that each block might represent one or more actual instructions.

Selection (or decision) logic provides alternate paths through the block depending on a run-time condition. With IF-THEN-ELSE logic (Figure 62.6), if the condition is true the logic associated with the THEN branch is executed and the ELSE block is skipped. If the condition is false the ELSE logic is executed and the THEN logic is skipped. A case structure (Figure 62.7) provides more than two logical paths through the block of logic based (usually) on the value of a control variable.

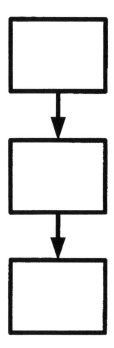

Figure 62.5 Sequence.

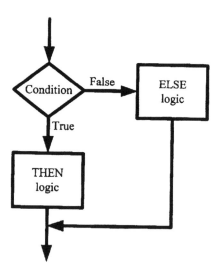

Figure 62.6 Selection.

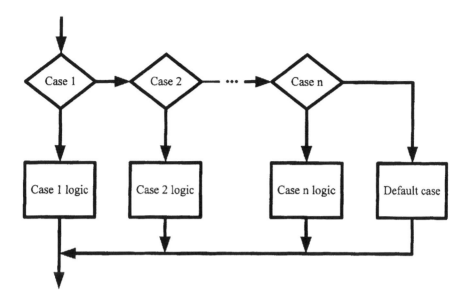

Figure 62.7 A case structure.

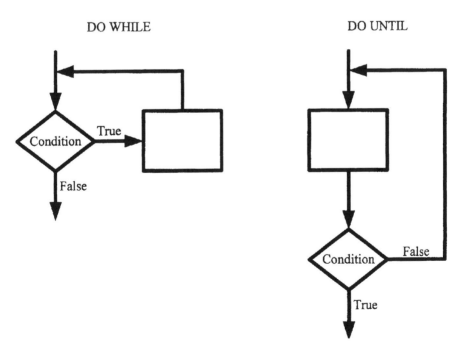

Figure 62.8 Repetition.

There are two basic patterns for showing repetitive logic: DO WHILE and DO UNTIL (Figure 62.8). In a DO WHILE block, the test is performed first and the associated instructions are performed only if (while) the test condition is true. In a DO UNTIL block, the associated instructions are executed first and then the exit condition is tested.

62.5 Key terms

Afferent process — A process that gathers and prepares input data.

Binding time — The time at which a module's values and identifiers are fixed; for example, coding time, compilation time, load time, or execution time.

Breadth (span-of-control) — A measure of the number of modules directly controlled by a higher-level routine.

Case structure — A selection structure with multiple alternative paths; the path through the structure is normally based on the value of a control variable.

Child (son) — An immediate lower-level module in a control structure. Control passes from the parent to the child and then returns to the parent.

Cohesion — A measure of a module's completeness.

Coincidental cohesion — The weakest type of cohesion in which the elements are related almost by chance.

Common-environment coupling — A form of coupling in which two or more modules interact with a common data environment, such as a shared communication region or a shared file.

Communicational cohesion — A form of cohesion that groups elements that operate on the same set of input or output data or on the same data structure.

Configuration item — A functional primitive; above the configuration level are the system's logical, composite elements. Below the configuration level are the system's physical components, including the programs.

Content coupling — A form of coupling in which some or all of the contents of one module are included in the other.

Control coupling — A form of coupling in which control information (e.g., a switch setting) is passed between the modules.

Control structure — A hierarchical model of the flow of control through a program. The control structure resembles a military chain of command or an organization chart. At the top is a main control module that calls secondary control structures. At the bottom are the computational routines, each of which implements a single algorithm.

Coupling — A measure of a module's independence; fewer parameters flowing into or out from a module imply looser coupling.

Data coupling (input-output coupling) — A form of coupling in which only data move between the modules.

Depth — The number of levels in the control structure.

Efferent process — A process that structures and/or transmits output data.

Function cohesion — The strongest type of cohesion in which a given module performs a single logical function, receives and returns no surplus data, and performs only essential logical operations.

Functional decomposition — A program design methodology in which the program is broken down (or decomposed) into modules based on the processes or tasks they perform.

Hybrid coupling — A combination of data coupling and control coupling.

Leaf — A module in a control structure with no lower-level (child) modules.

Logical access map — A program design tool used to help the designer determine the logical execution sequences or access paths through a program.

Logical cohesion — A form of cohesion in which all the elements are related to the same logical function.

Morphology — Form or structure.

Procedural cohesion — A type of cohesion in which all the elements in a module are associated with the same procedural unit, such as a loop or a decision structure.

Repetition (iteration) — A block of logic that is executed repetitively as long as (while) an initial condition holds or until a terminal condition occurs.

Root — The module at the top of a control structure from which all control flows.

Selection (decision) — A block of logic that provides alternate paths through the block depending on a run-time condition.

Sequence — A block of logic in which the instructions are executed in simple sequence, one after another.

Sequential cohesion — A form of cohesion in which the modules form a chain of transformations, with the output from one module serving as input to the next.

Span-of-control (breadth) — A measure of the number of modules directly controlled by a higher-level routine.

Temporal cohesion — A type of cohesion in which the elements are related by time.

Transform process — A process that converts the input data to output form.

Trigger event — The event that activates a program or causes it to change from a wait state to a run state.

62.6 Software

Not applicable.

62.7 References

1. Davis, W. S., *Business Systems Analysis and Design*, Wadsworth, Belmont, CA, 1994.
2. Gane, C. and Sarson, T., *Structured Systems Analysis: Tools and Techniques*, Prentice-Hall, Englewood Cliffs, NJ, 1979.
3. Katzan, H. Jr., *Systems Design and Documentation: An Introduction to the HIPO Method*, Van Nostrand Reinhold, New York, 1976.
4. Martin J., *Information Engineering: Introduction*, Vols. 1–3, Prentice-Hall, Englewood Cliffs, NJ, 1990.
5. Warnier, J.-D., *The Logical Construction of Programs*, Van Nostrand Reinhold, New York, 1976.
6. Yourdon, E. and Constantine, *Structured Design.* Prentice-Hall, Englewood Cliffs, NJ, 1979.

chapter sixty-three

Structure charts

William S. Davis

Contents

63.1 Purpose

A structure chart is a hierarchy chart with arrows showing the flow of data and control information between the modules. Structure charts are used as design tools for functionally decomposing structured programs.

63.2 Strengths, weaknesses, and limitations

A structure chart graphically highlights tightly coupled, excessively dependent modules that can cause debugging and maintenance problems. A structure chart is an extension of a hierarchy chart, so the core of this tool is consistent with other tools. A complete structure chart that shows all the data and control flows for a program can be very difficult to read, however.

63.3   Inputs and related ideas

A structure chart is a functional decomposition tool (Chapter 62) based on a hierarchy chart (Chapters 62 and 64). Before a structure chart is prepared, each module's inputs and outputs must be known. The necessary logical data structures and the program's primary processes are defined during the systems analysis phase (Part IV). Often, the results of analysis are documented in the requirements specification (Chapter 35). Additionally, it is useful to define the physical file and database structures (Chapters 43, 44, and 45), the required input and output data structures (Chapters 46 through 51), and the algorithms (Chapters 55 through 60) before starting to create a structure chart.

63.4   Concepts

A structure chart is a hierarchy chart that shows the data and control information flows between the modules. (Figure 63.1 shows a partial structure chart.) Each module is represented as a rectangle. Each data flow (or data couple) is shown as an arrow with an open circle at the origin end. A control couple (a flow of control information such as a flag or a switch setting) is shown as an arrow with a solid circle at the origin end, see the control couple labeled *Reorder flag* between *Process sale* and *Process transaction* in Figure 63.1. (*Note:* In this program design, *Initiate reorder* is an independent (not shown) level-2 module called by *Process transaction* when the *Reorder flag* is set.) As appropriate, the names of the data elements, data composites, and/or control fields are written alongside the arrows.

A structure chart does not show the program's sequence, selection, or repetitive logical structures; those details are inside the modules, which are viewed as black boxes. However, some designers identify high-level case structures by adding a transaction center to a key control module. For example, the solid diamond (the transaction center symbol) at the bottom of the *Process transaction* module indicates that, based on the transaction type, either *Process sale, Process customer return,* or *Process shipment arrival* is called.

A data couple might list a composite item; for example, *Get data* passes a complete transaction and the associated master record back to *Process transaction*. Higher-level modules generally select substructures or specific data elements from a composite and pass them down to their children. At the bottom of the structure, the detailed computational modules accept and return data elements.

The structured program designer's objective is to define independent, cohesive, loosely coupled modules. Coupling is a function of the amount of data and control information flowing between two modules, and the structure chart graphically shows the data and control flows. An excessive number of data or control flows suggests a poor design or a need for further decomposition.

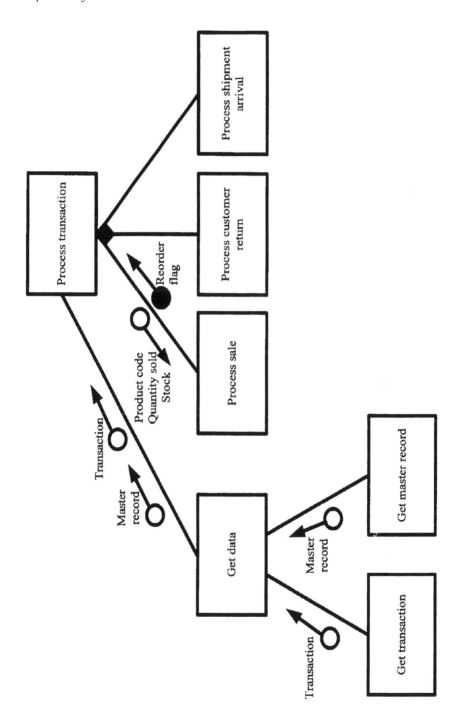

Figure 63.1   A partial structure chart.

63.5   Key terms

Cohesion — A measure of a module's completeness.

Control couple — A flow of control information, such as a flag or a switch setting, between two modules.

Control structure — A hierarchical model of the flow of control through a program. The control structure resembles a military chain of command or an organization chart. At the top is a main control module that calls secondary control structures. At the bottom are the computational routines, each of which implements a single algorithm.

Coupling — A measure of a module's independence. Fewer parameters flowing into or out from a module imply looser coupling.

Data couple — A flow of a data composite and/or data element between two modules.

Functional decomposition — A program design methodology in which the program is broken down (or decomposed) into modules based on the processes or tasks they perform.

Hierarchy chart — A diagram that graphically represents a program's control structure.

Structure chart — A hierarchy chart with arrows showing the flow of data and control information between the modules.

63.6   Software

McDonnell Douglas Automation Company's STRADIS/DRAW is a useful tool for creating and evaluating structure charts. Numerous CASE products support structure charts.

63.7   References

1.   Martin, J. and McClure, C., *Diagramming Techniques for Analysts and Programmers*, Prentice-Hall, Englewood Cliffs, NJ, 1985.
2.   Yourdon, E. and Constantine, *Structured Design*, Prentice-Hall, Englewood Cliffs, NJ: 1979.

chapter sixty-four

HIPO (hierarchy plus input-process-output)

William S. Davis

Contents

64.1 Purpose

The HIPO (Hierarchy plus Input-Process-Output) technique is a tool for planning and/or documenting a computer program. A HIPO model consists of a hierarchy chart that graphically represents the program's control structure and a set of IPO (Input-Process-Output) charts that describe the inputs to, the outputs from, and the functions (or processes) performed by each module on the hierarchy chart.

64.2 Strengths, weaknesses, and limitations

Using the HIPO technique, designers can evaluate and refine a program's design, and correct flaws prior to implementation. Given the graphic nature of HIPO, users and managers can easily follow a program's structure. The hierarchy chart serves as a useful planning and visualization document for managing the program development process. The IPO charts define for the programmer each module's inputs, outputs, and algorithms.

In theory, HIPO provides valuable long-term documentation. However, the "text plus flowchart" nature of the IPO charts makes them difficult to maintain, so the documentation often does not represent the current state of the program.

By its very nature, the HIPO technique is best used to plan and/or document a hierarchically structured program.

64.3 Inputs and related ideas

During the analysis stage of the system life cycle (Part IV), the analyst creates logical models using such tools as data flow diagrams (Chapter 24) and entity-relationship diagrams (Chapter 26). Given those models as a base, the analyst then identifies several alternative solutions during the high-level system design stage (Part V) using such tools as system flow diagrams (Chapter 37) to document them. The alternatives usually identify, at a black box level, one or more programs. HIPO is a tool for planning and/or documenting the programs.

The HIPO technique is often used to plan or document a structured program (Chapter 62). A variety of tools, including pseudocode (Chapter 59) and structured English (Chapter 60), can be used to describe processes on an IPO chart. System flowcharting symbols (Chapter 37) are sometimes used to identify physical input, output, and storage devices on an IPO chart.

64.4 Concepts

A completed HIPO package has two parts. A hierarchy chart is used to represent the top-down structure of the program. For each module depicted on the hierarchy chart, an IPO (Input-Process-Output) chart is used to describe the inputs to, the outputs from, and the process performed by the module.

64.4.1 The hierarchy chart

Table 64.1 summarizes the primary tasks to be performed by an interactive inventory program. Figure 64.1 shows one possible hierarchy chart (or visual table of contents) for that program. Each box represents one module (Chapter 62) that can call its subordinates and return control to its higher-level parent.

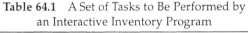

Table 64.1   A Set of Tasks to Be Performed by
an Interactive Inventory Program

1.0 Manage inventory

    2.0 Update stock

        2.1 Process sale

        2.2 Process return

        2.3 Process shipment

    3.0 Generate report

        3.1 Respond to query

        3.2 Display status report

    4.0 Maintain inventory data

        4.1 Modify record

        4.2 Add record

        4.3 Delete record

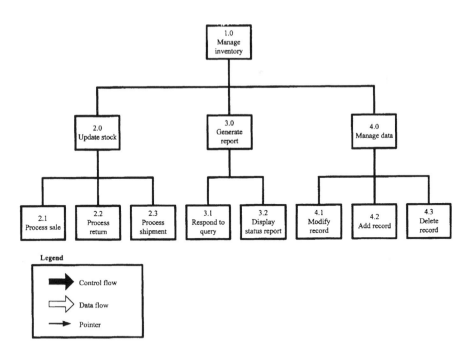

Figure 64.1   A hierarchy chart for an interactive inventory control program.

At the top of Figure 64.1 is the main control module, *Manage inventory* (module 1.0). It accepts a transaction, determines the transaction type, and calls one of its three subordinates (modules 2.0, 3.0, and 4.0).

Lower-level modules are identified relative to their parent modules; for example, modules 2.1, 2.2, and 2.3 are subordinates of module 2.0, modules 2.1.1, 2.1.2, and 2.1.3 are subordinates of 2.1, and so on. The module names consist of an active verb followed by a subject that suggests the module's function.

The objective of the module identifiers is to uniquely identify each module and to indicate its place in the hierarchy. Some designers use Roman numerals (level I, level II) or letters (level A, level B) to designate levels. Others prefer a hierarchical numbering scheme; e.g., 1.0 for the first level; 1.1, 1.2, 1.3 for the second level; and so on. The key is consistency.

The box at the lower-left of Figure 64.1 is a legend that explains how the arrows on the hierarchy chart and the IPO charts are to be interpreted. By default, a wide clear arrow represents a data flow, a wide black arrow represents a control flow, and a narrow arrow indicates a pointer.

64.4.2   The IPO charts

An IPO chart is prepared to document each of the modules on the hierarchy chart.

64.4.2.1   Overview diagrams

An overview diagram is a high-level IPO chart that summarizes the inputs to, processes or tasks performed by, and outputs from a module. For example,

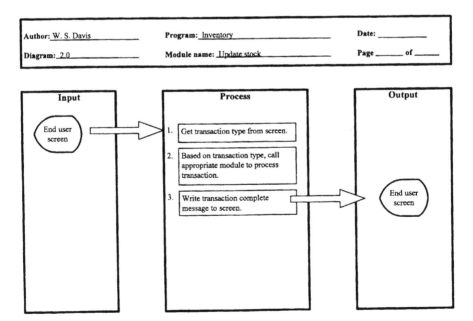

Figure 64.2   An overview diagram for process 2.0.

Figure 64.2 shows an overview diagram for process 2.0, *Update stock*. Where appropriate, system flowcharting symbols (Chapter 37) are used to identify the physical devices that generate the inputs and accept the outputs. The processes are typically described in brief paragraph or sentence form. Arrows show the primary input and output data flows.

Overview diagrams are primarily planning tools. They often do not appear in the completed documentation package.

64.4.2.2 Detail diagrams

A detail diagram is a low-level IPO chart that shows how specific input and output data elements or data structures are linked to specific processes. In effect, the designer integrates a system flowchart into the overview diagram to show the flow of data and control through the module.

Figure 64.3 shows a detail diagram for module 2.0, *Update stock*. The process steps are written in pseudocode. Note that the first step writes a menu to the user screen and input data (the transaction type) flows from that screen to step 2. Step 3 is a case structure. Step 4 writes a *transaction complete* message to the user screen.

The solid black arrows at the top and bottom of the process box show that control flows from module 1.0 and, upon completion, returns to module 1.0. Within the case structure (step 3) are other solid black arrows.

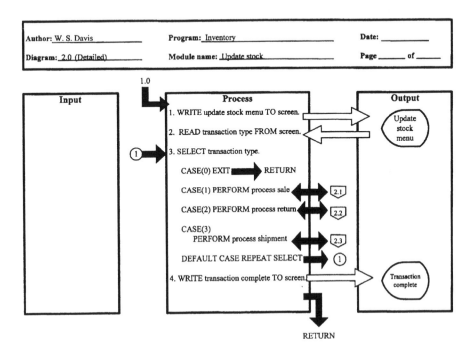

Figure 64.3   A detail diagram for process 2.0.

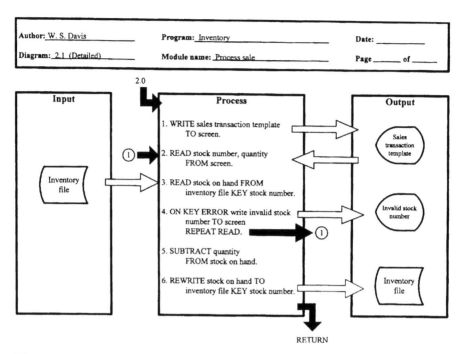

Figure 64.4   A detail diagram for process 2.1.

Following case 0 is a return (to module 1.0). The two-headed black arrows following cases 1, 2, and 3 represent subroutine calls; the off-page connector symbols (the little home plates) identify each subroutine's module number. Note that each subroutine is documented in a separate IPO chart. Following the default case, the arrow points to an on-page connector symbol numbered 1. Note the matching on-page connector symbol pointing to the select structure. On-page connectors are also used to avoid crossing arrows on data flows.

Often, detailed notes and explanations are written on an extended description that is attached to each detail diagram. The notes might specify access methods, data types, and so on.

Figure 64.4 shows a detail diagram for process 2.1. The module writes a template to the user screen, reads a stock number and a quantity from the screen, uses the stock number as a key to access an inventory file, and updates the stock on hand. Note that the logic repeats the data entry process if the stock number does not match an inventory record. A real IPO chart is likely to show the error response process in greater detail.

64.4.2.3   Simplified IPO charts
Some designers simplify the IPO charts by eliminating the arrows and system flowchart symbols and showing only the text. Often, the input and out-

| Author:_____ | Program: _____ | Date: _____ |
| Diagram:_____ | Module name:_____ | Page: ___ of ___ |

Called by:

Calls:

Input

Output

Process

Figure 64.5   A simplified IPO diagram.

put blocks are moved above the process block (Figure 64.5), yielding a form that fits better on a standard 8.5 × 11 (portrait orientation) sheet of paper. Some programmers insert modified IPO charts similar to Figure 64.5 directly into their source code as comments. Because the documentation is closely linked to the code, it is often more reliable than stand-alone HIPO documentation, and more likely to be maintained.

64.5   Key terms

Detail diagram — A low-level IPO chart that shows how specific input and output data elements or data structures are linked to specific processes.

Hierarchy chart — A diagram that graphically represents a program's control structure.

HIPO (Hierarchy plus Input-Process-Output) — A tool for planning and/or documenting a computer program that utilizes a hierarchy chart to graphically represent the program's control structure and a set of IPO (Input-Process-Output) charts to describe the inputs to, the outputs from, and the functions performed by each module on the hierarchy chart.

IPO (Input-Process-Output) chart — A chart that describes or documents the inputs to, the outputs from, and the functions (or processes) performed by a program module.

Overview diagram — A high-level IPO chart that summarizes the inputs to, processes or tasks performed by, and outputs from a module.

Visual Table of Contents (VTOC) — A more formal name for a hierarchy chart.

64.6   Software

In the 1970s and early 1980s, HIPO documentation was typically prepared by hand using a template. Some CASE products and charting programs include HIPO support. Some forms generation programs can be used to generate HIPO forms. The examples in this chapter were prepared using Visio.

64.7   References

1. Gane, C. and Sarson, T., *Structured Systems Analysis: Tools and Techniques*, Prentice-Hall, Englewood Cliffs, NJ, 1979.
2. IBM Corporation, *HIPO—A Design Aid and Documentation Technique*, Publication Number GC20-1851, IBM Corporation, White Plains, NY, 1974.
3. Katzan, H., Jr., *Systems Design and Documentation: An Introduction to the HIPO Method*, Van Nostrand Reinhold, New York, 1976.
4. Peters, L. J., *Software Design: Methods and Techniques*, Yourdon Press, New York, 1981.
5. Yourdon, E. and Constantine, *Structured Design*, Prentice-Hall, Englewood Cliffs, NJ, 1979.

chapter sixty-five

Action diagrams

David C. Yen and William S. Davis

Contents

65.1 Purpose

Action diagrams are used in Martin's information engineering methodology[2] to plan and document both an overview of program logic and the detailed program logic.

65.2 Strengths, weaknesses, and limitations

Action diagrams are relatively easy to draw and require no special tools. Unlike most software design tools, action diagrams can be used to describe both an overview of program logic and the detailed program logic. In addition to documenting logical relationships and structures, action diagrams

0-8493-7001-9/99/$0.00+$.50
©1999 by CRC Press LLC

provide details about tests and conditions. The action diagrams are relatively easy to convert into program code. The structure of an action diagram helps to reduce such errors as infinite loops.

Often, program logic is more easily described by using such tools as pseudocode (Chapter 59) and structured English (Chapter 60). Relatively few analysts or information systems consultants are familiar with action diagrams. Some advanced features require knowledge of data normalization.

65.3   Inputs and related ideas

Programs are designed in the context of a system. The system is planned during the systems analysis stage of the system development life cycle (Part IV). Pseudocode (Chapter 59) or structured English (Chapter 60) are used within the context of an action diagram to describe detailed program logic. The basic logical structures (sequence, selection, and iteration) are discussed in Chapter 62.

Other tools for documenting or planning routines or processes include logic flowcharts (Chapter 55), Nassi-Shneiderman charts (Chapter 56), decision trees (Chapter 57), decision tables (Chapter 58), pseudocode (Chapter 59), structured English (Chapter 60), and input/process/output (IPO) charts (Chapter 64). Tools for documenting or planning program structure include Warnier-Orr diagrams (Chapter 33), structure charts (Chapter 63), and HIPO (Chapter 64).

65.4   Concepts

Action diagrams are used in Martin's information engineering methodology to plan and document both an overview of program logic and the detailed program logic.

65.4.1   Conventions

The basic building block of an action diagram is a bracket that represents a program module. Within the bracket, the module's code is designed using pseudocode, structured English, or fourth-generation language statements. Action diagrams are assembled from sets of brackets. The brackets can be any length, and they can be nested (Figure 65.1).

Figure 65.2 shows the action diagram notation for a simple IF-THEN-ELSE block and for a case structure. Note how horizontal lines are used to partition the bracket into mutually exclusive routines.

Figure 65.3 shows three repetition structures. A double line at the top of the bracket indicates a DO WHILE loop, while a double line at the bottom indicates a DO UNTIL loop. Some designers use an arrow pointing inside the bracket to indicate the next iteration of a loop (Figure 65.3, bottom).

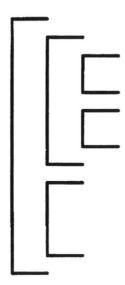

Figure 65.1   The basic building block of an action diagram is a bracket that represents a program module. The brackets can be any length, and they can be nested.

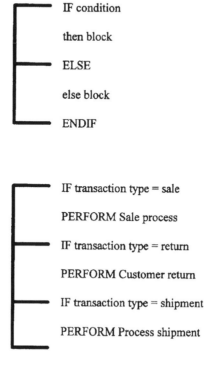

IF condition

then block

ELSE

else block

ENDIF

IF transaction type = sale

PERFORM Sale process

IF transaction type = return

PERFORM Customer return

IF transaction type = shipment

PERFORM Process shipment

Figure 65.2   Decision (or selection) logic.

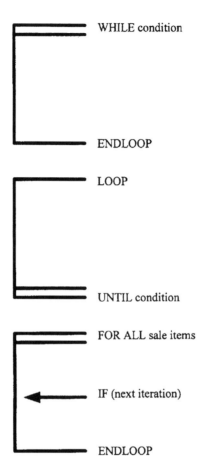

Figure 65.3   Repetition (or iteration) logic.

An arrow drawn through a bracket (or set of brackets) represents a termination action, such as EXIT, QUIT, or BREAK (Figure 65.4). A dotted arrow represents an intentional break such as a GOTO statement.

Subprocesses, subprocedures, subroutines and subsystems are shown by round-cornered rectangles (Figure 65.5). A vertical line near the left of the round-cornered rectangle indicates a common subprocedure (e.g., a square root function). Some designers add a wavy line at the right of the rectangle to indicate a not-yet-designed subprocedure. The detailed logic associated with the subprocedure is documented in a separate action diagram.

65.4.2   Some examples

Figure 65.6 shows an overview action diagram for a sales database maintenance program that documents the primary options available on the program's main menu. Given an overview diagram, the designer decomposes the high-level routine by creating an action diagram for each primary

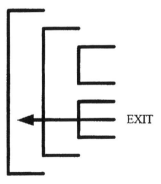

Figure 65.4 An arrow drawn through a bracket (or set of brackets) represents a termination action.

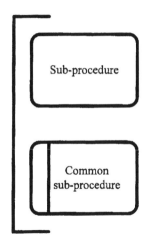

Figure 65.5 Subprocesses are shown by round-cornered rectangles.

function; for example, Figure 65.7 shows the *Maintain customer* function. The subprocesses are documented in lower-level action diagrams.

65.4.3 Input, output, and database operations

Sometimes, a bracket is expanded into a rectangle to show the data entering and leaving a process (Figure 65.8). By convention, input data are noted at the top right and output data are noted at the bottom right of the rectangle.

Simple database actions (e.g., CREATE, READ, UPDATE, or DELETE a single record or transaction) are represented by a rectangular box inside the bracket (Figure 65.9). The type of action is noted to the left of the box, and the record is identified inside the box.

Compound database actions (CREATE, READ, UPDATE, or DELETE a whole file, and such functions as SEARCH, SORT, SELECT, JOIN, PROJECT,

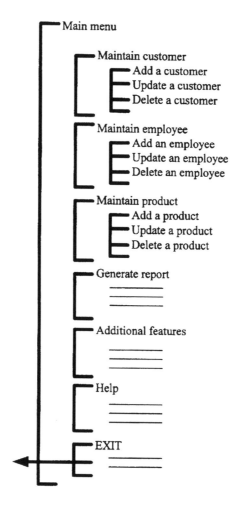

Figure 65.6   An overview action diagram for a sales database maintenance program.

and DUPLICATE) are represented as a double rectangular box (Figure 65.9, bottom). The type of action is noted to the left of the box, the record is identified inside the box, and any conditions are noted to the right of the box.

A concurrency relationship exists between two processes that can be performed concurrently. An arc connecting the two processes' brackets designates a concurrency relationship.

65.5   *Key terms*

Action diagram — A tool used in Martin's information engineering methodology to plan and document both an overview of program logic and the detailed program logic.

Bracket — The basic building block of an action diagram.

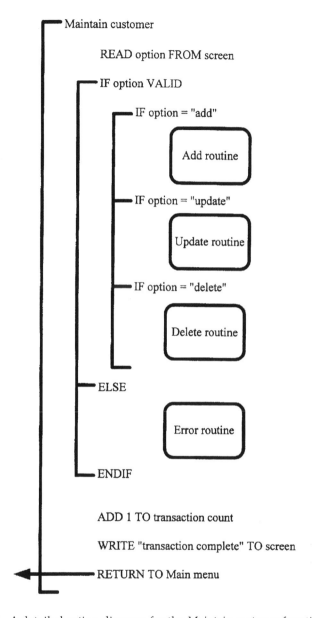

Figure 65.7   A detailed action diagram for the *Maintain customer* function.

Concurrency relationship — A relationship between two (or more) processes that can be performed concurrently.

65.6   *Software*

The action diagrams in this chapter were created using Visio.

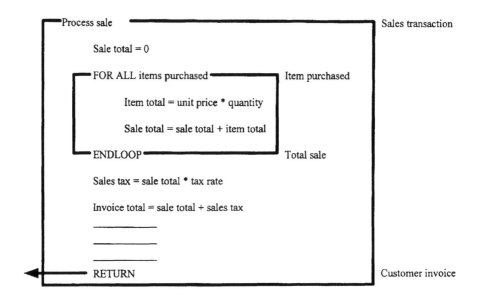

Figure 65.8 A bracket can be expanded into a rectangle to show the data entering and leaving a process.

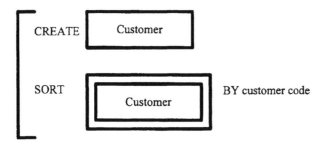

Figure 65.9 Database actions.

65.7 *References*

1. Conner, D., *Information Systems Specification & Design Road Map*, Prentice-Hall, Englewood Cliffs, NJ, 1985.
2. Martin, J., *Information Engineering: Planning and Analysis, Vol. 2*, Prentice-Hall, Englewood Cliffs, NJ, 1990.
3. Martin, J. and McClure, C., *Diagramming Techniques for Analysts and Programmers*, Prentice-Hall, Englewood Cliffs, NJ, 1985.

chapter sixty-six

Object-oriented software design

T. M. Rajkumar
Miami University

Contents

66.1   Purpose

This chapter describes object-oriented design. The purpose of object-oriented design is to transform the object-oriented analysis model into a design class diagram that specifies a software solution.

66.2   Strengths, weaknesses, and limitations

Object-oriented analysis and design is primarily use case driven. The major benefit of the use case approach is traceability. If there is a change in one use case, its ripple effect can be traced into the design. This lessens the impact and risk of changes to the project.

A weakness of use case-driven design is that the use cases may be considered in isolation and the global picture may be missed. Testing the solution across the different use cases helps to ensure that the global picture is not missed. In addition, a use case-driven design may be significantly affected by small changes in user requirements. This problem can be mitigated by selecting a good design architecture and designing for reuse.

Like use cases, object interaction diagrams are useful because they are intuitive and express well the dynamic interaction between objects. Using object interaction diagrams leads to a complete solution and brings to the surface issues that must be resolved at design time. However, like use cases, interaction diagrams depict only one scenario at a time, and a system can consist of hundreds of scenarios under different assumptions. To counter this problem, the designer should start with the interaction diagrams that have the greatest impact on system architecture or that perform key system functions.

Using design patterns means incorporating proven robust design decisions in a system design. Well-chosen and applied design patterns tend to provide clean designs, and patterns also enable designers to communicate their ideas effectively with each other. However, patterns can be misused, particularly if designers strive to force fit a pattern to a problem. Also, if only one designer in a team uses patterns, the result can be miscommunication. In addition, patterns are not a solution to designer incompetence. A designer must be well versed in the standard principles of system design.

66.3   Inputs and related ideas

Object-oriented concepts are covered in Chapter 6. Object-oriented analysis (Chapter 29) focuses on the domain objects and results in use cases and the development of a conceptual model using class diagrams (static modeling). Object-oriented design focuses on defining a solution based on classes. Object interaction diagrams capture the communicational aspect of the objects, but do not provide a convenient picture of its complete behavior.

State transition diagrams (Chapter 30) provide an overview of an object's total behavior.

66.4   Concepts

This chapter concentrates on developing a logical object-oriented design. Logical design is free from implementation considerations and is portable across various interfaces, languages, and computers.

66.4.1   Boundary, control and entity objects

A widely used approach to object-oriented design is to separate the boundary (interface) and control objects from the entity (domain) objects.[1] The main purpose is to develop maintainable systems. Entity objects are objects in the business domain. Boundary objects communicate with the user or with other systems.

Boundary objects are responsible for translating user input into a form that can be used by the system to process the business event and to translate the data from the entity object back to the user. Boundary objects make up the presentation dependent part of the system and isolate the behavior related to user and mechanical interfaces from the entity objects. This ensures that changes in the boundary objects are less likely to affect the core entity objects.

A control object performs use case-specific behavior and contains the application logic or business rules for managing the interaction among multiple entity objects. For example, in an appliance store inventory system, *Store* and *BuyAppliance* are possible control objects. Using control objects leads to a more robust and maintainable system.

Note that boundary, control, and entity objects equate well with the three-tier client server model. Presentation is the responsibility of the client (boundary object). Business logic is the second tier and is the responsibility of the control object. The data layer is the responsibility of the server (entity object).

Typically, one boundary object is allocated for each use case actor or major peripheral device. For example, in an appliance store, the sales representative uses a point-of-sale terminal to enter the details of a sale and a card reader to read the customer's credit card number. Aggregation can sometimes be used for interface objects; for example, a point-of-sale terminal consists of a display unit and a printer (for printing the receipt and the credit card statement). Once the boundary object has been identified, the attributes and operations for that object must be identified. Operations that present information to the external system or request information from external systems (such as requesting credit card approval from a central bank or approval station) are allocated to the boundary object.

Control objects often act as buffers between boundary and entity objects. Initially, define one control object for each use case. After the appropriate responsibilities have been assigned to each entity or boundary object, any remaining behaviors are assigned to the control object. The types of behaviors typically allocated to control objects include behaviors that are unchanged if the surrounding objects change, behaviors that affect multiple entity objects, and state dependent or control logic for a use case. Since control objects are typically used to carry methods that do not fit elsewhere, they generally do not have many attributes.

66.4.2   Identifying operations

An operation provides a service. Whenever a service exists, the object has a responsibility to provide that service to other objects that request it. A method is the implementation of an operation for a specific object class.

66.4.2.1   The CRC technique

One way to find operations is to use the Class, Responsibilities, and Collaborations (CRC) technique.[2] In CRC, a class is a generic specification for an arbitrary number of similar objects. Responsibilities include the knowledge (data) an object maintains and the actions (services) an object can perform. Whenever a service or data is provided by one object to another, there is a client-server relationship. The client object requests a service from the server object, which performs the service or returns data. A given object can be a client at times and a server at other times.

A collaboration is the embodiment of a contract between a client and a server and takes place when a class has a responsibility it cannot fulfill alone and thus requests the necessary service from a server. The pattern of collaboration within the application reveals the flow of information and control during execution. These collaborations represent interaction paths or communication between classes.

To identify responsibilities, start with a class's responsibility and determine if it can fulfill the responsibility itself or must collaborate with another class to acquire what it needs. If collaboration is necessary, start with the class and trace the flow of collaborations until the responsibility is completely fulfilled. Similarly for each class, ask what the class does or knows and identify the other classes that need the result or information. If a class has no interactions with other classes, discard it.

Like use cases, CRC is a responsibility driven technique. Start by identifying the classes, responsibilities, and collaborations that are necessary to support each use case. For each new class, write the class name (singular nouns) on an index card (Figure 66.1). Then partition the index card, writing the responsibilities of the class on the left side and the collaborating classes required to fulfill the responsibility (the servers) on the right side.

The CRC development process is interactive among the analysts and designers. Each individual is assigned a set of index cards and is asked to

Class:	SalesInvoice	
Identifier:	SalesNumber	
Responsibilities		*Collaborating classes*
Know: SalesNumber **Know:** CustomerNumber PrintSale CalculateTotal		 SalesLineItem SalesLineItem

Class:	SalesLineItem	
Identifier:	SalesNumber, LineItemNumber	
Responsibilities		*Collaborating classes*
Know: SalesNumber **Know:** CustomerNumber **Know:** ProductCode **Know:** QuantitySold **Know:** UnitPrice CalculateExtendedPrice PrintLineItem		 Item

Figure 66.1 Two CRC cards.

think like the object he or she is assigned. The individual then acts out the roles the class fulfills when applied to different use cases. The information on the index card is kept to a minimum. Quick iterations encourage searching for classes and the interactions between classes. This is a cheap and highly object-oriented way of identifying the classes and their interactions. It is particularly suited for brainstorming.

An application of this technique to the use case provided in Table 66.1 (a copy of Table 29.2) may yield (among others) the classes *SalesInvoice* and

Table 66.1   An Expanded Level Use Case

Use case	Buy Appliance
Actors	Customer (initiator), Sales Representative
Purpose	Record the sale of an appliance to a customer
Description	A customer, talks to a sales representative about appliances that he/she is interested in buying, and picks the item in consultation with the sales representative. The sales representative then prepares the bill, and the customer makes the payment.

Type	Primary

Normal Course of Events	1. Customer walks up to a sales representative and discusses items to buy.
	2. In consultation, customer decides on item to buy.
	3. Sales representative enters the appliance identifier and the quantity desired into the system.
	4. System responds with the price, and verifies that the appliance is in stock. (Not in stock is not a normal course of events.)
	5. If additional items are to be entered, sales representative does so, and steps 3 and 4 are repeated.
	6. System adds the amounts, calculates tax, and presents the total.
	7. Sales representative informs the customer of the total.
	   * *Assumption:* The normal event is a credit card purchase. Cash purchases are described separately. *
	8. Customer runs his/her credit card through the verification system.
	9. System receives credit approval, and presents credit card transaction form.
	10. Customer signs the credit card transaction form.
	11. System logs the details of the transaction, including sales representative, customer, and item information.
	12. System updates the inventory and closes the transaction.
	13. System generates the receipt.
	14. Receipt is handed by sales representative to customer.
	15. Customer leaves the premises with appliance.
	   Alternative courses: Note errors that can occur and how they are handled can be described here.

SalesLineItem (Figure 66.1). For the *SalesInvoice* class, the operations are *PrintSale* and *CalculateTotal,* and for *SalesLineItem* the operations are *CalculateExtendedPrice* and *PrintLineItem.*

66.4.2.2   Use case object interactions

A second technique used to identify operations is to look at the object inter-action required to support each use case scenario and to prepare an object interaction diagram for each use case. Typically, the developer starts with a normal scenario and then expands the interaction to include alternative courses of events.

From the conceptual model (Chapter 29) for the domain objects, iden-tify the domain objects used in the use case and the control and interface objects (Section 29.4.1) applicable to the use case. Then consider the object interactions required to provide the functionality in each use case by view-ing the system as a black box and, for each actor, identifying the events the actor generates in the use case. These object interactions are events, and each use case is started by an event.

For example, the use case description in Table 66.1 suggests that the salesperson generates events *enterSalesItem, enterPayment,* and *endSale,* and the customer generates the event *scanCard.* Also, it is reasonable to assume that the sales representative interacts with the boundary object *point-of sale terminal* and the customer interacts with the boundary object *card reader.*

For each initial external event, identify the internal events needed to communicate between the objects that support the normal sequence in the use case. Internal events are messages sent from one object to another in order to invoke the operation. For example, the *SalesInvoice* object would raise a *calculateExtendedPrice* on the *SalesLineItem* object.

For each event, identify the operations, the required parameters, the preconditions, and the post conditions. A parameter is information that must be passed so the receiving object can perform the operation. The type of parameters (mandatory or optional) and the possible range of values must be identified. For example, the *enterSalesItem* operation's parameters would include the UPC number and the quantity required. Both parameters are mandatory.

Post conditions include objects that were created, associations that were formed or broken, and any attributes that were modified during an oper-ation. Preconditions include objects that must exist for an event to take place. The *enterSalesItem* operation's post conditions would include the *SalesLineItem* that was created, the *SalesLineItem* that was associated with the *SalesInvoice,* the *SalesLineItem* that was associated with a *ProductSpecification* based on the match on UPC code, the *SalesLineItem* quantity that was set to the quantity required (attribute modification), the *SalesLineItem* that was associated with the *Inventory* based on a match on UPC code, and the reduced quantity on hand (by the quantity purchased). The precondition is that the UPC code must exist in *ProductSpecification.*

66.4.3   Object interaction diagrams

Once the operations are identified, an object interaction diagram is drawn. Object interaction is concerned with identifying how objects work within the system to satisfy the requirements. Interaction diagrams represent objects and show how they communicate with each other in an interaction.

66.4.3.1   Collaboration diagrams

In a collaboration diagram, objects are represented as rectangles with links between objects that interact. Links are instances of associations that are present in the conceptual model. Arrows represent messages, and are labeled with their names and arguments. The message function being sent must exist as an operation (method) of the receiving object. The order of the messages is shown in by a number placed at the head of the the message.

For example, Figure 66.2 shows the representation of a simple collaboration diagram. An object instance A sends a message (M1) to the object instance B. Subsequently, B sends a message (M2) to itself (representing an activity within itself). Finally, B sends a message M3 to object instance C. The colon (inside the box) represents an anonymous object of the specified type (e.g., Faculty as opposed to Rajkumar). An object is an instance of a class, and underlining differentiates an object from a class. For example, :A indicates a generic class and :A indicates a generic object.

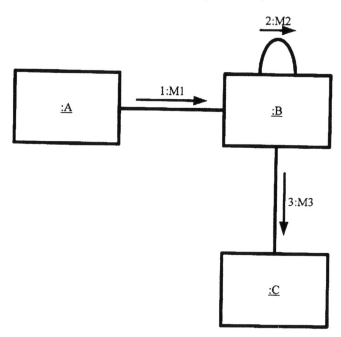

Figure 66.2   The UML notation for a collaboration diagram.

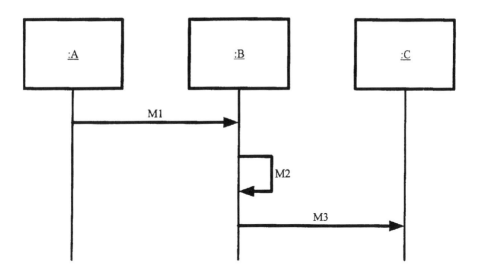

Figure 66.3 The UML notation for a sequence diagram.

66.4.3.2 Sequence diagrams
Figure 66.3 shows an equivalent sequence diagram. Note that the message time line is explicitly represented. A vertical bar represents each object and time elapses from top to bottom, so numbering the messages is optional. Both collaboration diagrams and sequence diagrams show the same information; the choice is a matter of preference.

66.4.3.3 Drawing interaction diagrams
Collaboration (or sequence) diagrams should be drawn for each interaction in the use case. The diagrams for each of the interactions are subsequently merged to create a single collaboration diagram.

For example, Figure 66.4 is a collaboration diagram for *enterSalesItem*. The boundary object is the *POST* object, and other interacting domain objects include *SalesInvoice, SalesLineItem, ProductSpecification*, and *Inventory*. The *POST* boundary object is used by the salesperson to interact with the system and to enter the sale information. The post conditions specify that *enterSalesItem*, is sent to a *SalesInvoice* object, which creates a *SalesLineItem*. The *SalesLineItem* matches the product specification to retrieve the product information, and also reduces the inventory by the quantity purchased.

Before an object can send a message to another object, it must be visible to the object. (In other words, it must be able to see or have a reference to the other object.) Figure 66.4 assumes that the *SalesInvoice* has already been created (and thus is visible) and shows the messages for any additional items purchased. To enable visibility (Figure 66.5), show the creation of the *SalesInvoice* itself via a second message (2.1: *createSalesInvoice*) that is sent to

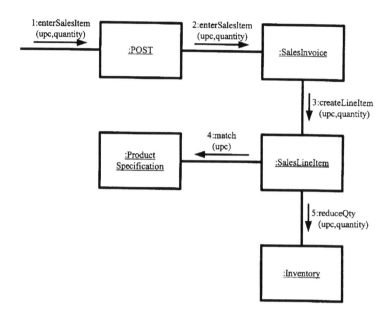

Figure 66.4   A collaboration diagram for *enterSalesItem* interaction.

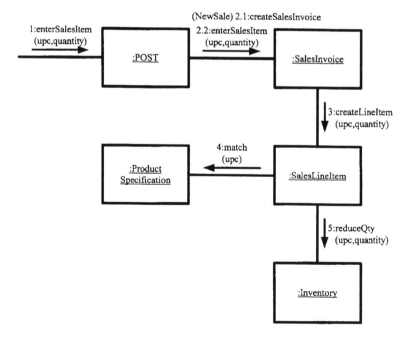

Figure 66.5   A modified collaboration diagram that resolves visibility conditions for *enterSalesItem* interaction.

the *SalesInvoice* object and by modifying the existing message 2 to 2.2: *enterSalesItem.*

Similarly, Figure 66.5 assumes that the *ProductSpecification* and *Inventory* objects have been created by some other initial process. A complete collaboration diagram would establish the visibility of all objects.

66.4.4 Design patterns

Design patterns codify the solutions expert designers use to solve commonly recurring object-oriented design problems and provide guidelines on how to customize the solution. In its simplest sense a pattern describes a problem and (at an abstract level) a solution. Since the solution is a template, using a pattern means tailoring and adapting the solution to the unique needs of the problem. Patterns provide a solution to a problem, are applicable in a variety of domains, are a literary form designed to convey proven solutions based on the wisdom of expert designers, and enable skilled designers to effectively communicate design decisions.

For example, Larman[3] identifies five patterns for assigning responsibilities to classes. The expert pattern suggests that responsibility should be assigned to the class that contains the necessary information. The creator class suggests that the responsibility for creating an instance of A be assigned to the class that contains, has the initializing data for, uses, aggregates, or records A. The controller pattern suggests that a responsibility be assigned to the class responsible for handling a related system event. As the names imply, the objective of the low coupling pattern is to keep coupling low, and the objective of the high cohesion pattern is to keep cohesion high.

These patterns can be used to verify the responsibilities of the object in the collaboration diagram. For example, consider Figure 66.5. Should the *POST* object or some other object create a *SalesInvoice?* The creator pattern states that the object that uses or records the other object is a good choice. Because the *POST* object records a sales invoice, *POST* is the right object to create the *SalesInvoice* instance, and the choice shown in the collaboration diagram is a good one.

The next step might be to evaluate the design and check how the *ProductSpecification* object is created, because it must be visible for the collaboration diagram to work. Using the creator pattern and the controller pattern, it becomes clear that a *Store* object is necessary to create this object. In addition, if the *POST* object is viewed as one instance of a point-of-sale terminal, the *Store* object must create the *POST* object. Taking these modifications into account results in the collaboration diagram shown in Figure 66.6.

In a similar fashion collaboration diagrams should be drawn for each use case and the design refined using the patterns. These steps lead to a robust, and maintainable logical design.

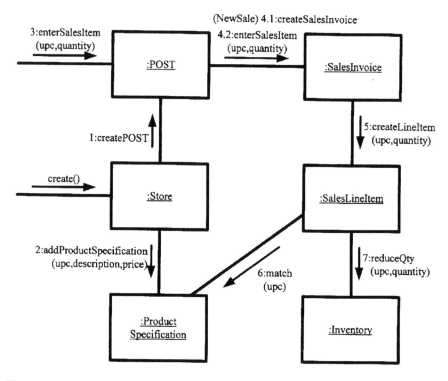

Figure 66.6 A modified collaboration diagram that reflects the application of design patterns for *enterSalesItem* interaction.

66.4.5 *Design class diagrams*

Design class diagrams specify the software classes and interfaces in an application.[3] In general, they include classes, attributes, their operations or methods, and the associations between the classes. Note that the design class diagram represents software entities rather than the conceptual model's conceptual entities.

A design class diagram is drawn by first identifying all the software classes from the interactions (the collaboration diagrams) that participate in the solution. Start with the conceptual model (Figure 66.7, from Chapter 29, Section 29.4.3). Add the attributes to the objects that are similar to the conceptual model. Add the method names by analyzing the interaction diagram. Add associations represented in the conceptual model and shown as links in the collaboration diagrams. Add any other association necessary to maintain visibility. A design class diagram for the appliance store is shown in Figure 66.8; note both the similarities to and the differences from the conceptual model.

Once a design class diagram has been drawn, it must be documented with all information that an implementation team would require to implement the system.

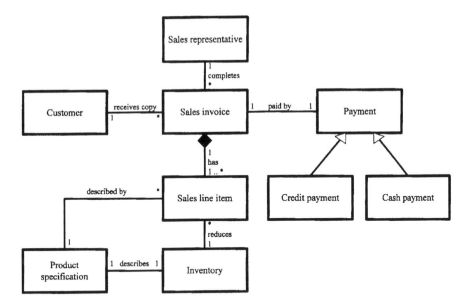

Figure 66.7   The conceptual model (from Chapter 29, Section 29.4.3).

66.5   *Key terms*

Actor — A person or entity external to the system.

Association — A relationship between objects that indicates some meaningful and interesting connection.

Boundary object (interface object) — An object that communicates with the user or with other systems.

Class (object type) — A group of similar objects.

Class, responsibilities, and collaborations (CRC) technique — A technique for identifying operations.

Collaboration — The embodiment of a contract between a client and a server; the interaction that takes place when a class has a responsibility it cannot fulfill alone and thus requests the necessary service from a server.

Collaboration diagram — A diagram that shows the basic message flow between objects and implies the associations between them.

Control object — An object that performs use case-specific behavior and contains the application logic or business rules for managing the interaction among multiple entity objects.

Design class diagram — A diagram that specifies the software classes and interfaces in an application.

Entity object (domain object) — An object in the business domain.

Event — An occurrence that generates a signal.

Method — The implementation of an operation for a specific object class.

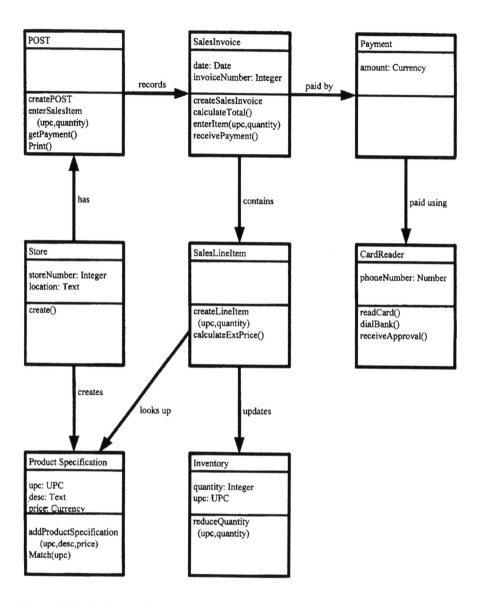

Figure 66.8   A design class diagram.

Object — A thing about which data are stored and manipulated.
Object interaction diagram — A graphical depiction of the way objects interact and collaborate to realize a use case.
Object-oriented analysis — The investigation of a problem by identifying and describing the objects.
Object-oriented design — The logical solution of a problem through a set of interacting objects.

Object type (class) — A group of similar objects.

Operation — A service provided by an object.

Parameter — Information that must be passed so the receiving object can perform the operation.

Pattern — A named problem/solution pair that can be applied in new contexts, along with advice on how to apply it.

Post conditions — Objects that were created, associations that were formed or broken, and any attributes that were modified during an operation.

Preconditions — Objects that must exist for an event to take place.

Responsibility — A contract or obligation of a type or class, including both responsibilities of knowing and responsibilities of doing.

Sequence diagram — A type of interaction diagram, drawn using the UML notation, that depicts the interaction between objects and shows the detailed message flow between objects in a use case; the time axis is directed downwards and the objects are represented in a vertical column.

Signal — A message that allows objects to interact with other objects.

Unified modeling language (UML) — The universal language for object-oriented modeling; its notation forms an object-oriented modeling language and can replace the notation of various object-oriented analysis methods.

Use case — The behaviorally related sequence of transactions that a user performs in a dialogue with the system when he or she uses the system.

Use case diagram — A diagram that depicts the set of use cases for a system, the actors, and the relation between the actors and the use cases.

Visibility — An object has visibility to a second object if it has a reference to the second object.

66.6   Software

CASE (Chapter 5) tools exist to help the designer develop CRC cards, collaboration diagrams, sequence diagrams, and design class diagrams.

66.7   References

66.7.1   Citations

1. Jacobson, I., Christerson, M., Jonsson, P., and Overgaard, G., *Object Oriented Software Engineering: A Use Case Driven Approach*, ACM Press, Reading, MA, 1992.
2. Wirfs-Brock, R., Wilkerson, B., and Weiner, L., *Designing Object Oriented Software*, Prentice-Hall, Englewood Cliffs, NJ, 1990.

3. Larman, C., *Applying UML and Patterns: An Introduction to Object Oriented Analysis and Design*, Prentice-Hall, Upper Saddle River, NJ, 1997.

66.7.2   Suggestions for additional reading

1. Booch, G., *Object Oriented Design with Applications*, Benjamin/Cummings, Redwood City, CA, 1991.
2. Fowler, M., *Analysis Patterns: Reusable Object Models*, Addison-Wesley, Reading, MA, 1997.
3. Gamma, E., Helm, R., Johnson, R., and Vlissides, J., *Design Patterns: Elements of Reusable Object-Oriented Software*, Addison-Wesley, Reading, MA, 1994.
4. IBM Object Oriented Technology Center, *Developing Object Oriented Software: An Experience-Based Approach*, Prentice-Hall, Upper Saddle River, NJ, 1997.
5. Muller, P.-A., *Instant UML*, Wrox Press, Olton, Canada, 1997.
6. Priestley, M., *Practical Object Oriented Design*, McGraw-Hill, London, 1996.
7. Rumbaugh, J., Blaha, M., Premerlani, W., Eddy, F., and Lorenson, W., *Object Oriented Modeling and Design*, Prentice-Hall, Englewood Cliffs, NJ, 1991.
8. UML 1.1 Specification (Rational Software): http://www.rational.com/uml/.
9. Yourdon, E., Whitehead, K., Thomann, J., Oppel, K., and Nevermann, P., *Mainstream Objects: An Analysis and Design Approach for Business*, Yourdon Press, Upper Saddle River, NJ, 1995.

chapter sixty-seven

Knowledge representation

David C. Yen and William S. Davis

Contents

67.1   Purpose

This chapter describes typical expert system applications and briefly describes knowledge representation techniques.

67.2   Strengths, weaknesses, and limitations

The strengths and weaknesses associated with each knowledge representation technique will be discussed in context.

67.3   Inputs and related ideas

Chapter 6 discusses basic object-oriented principles. Chapter 7 discusses expert systems. Chapter 34 discusses expert system problem solving analysis techniques. Chapter 43 discusses data structures.

67.4   Concepts

This chapter discusses typical expert system applications and briefly describes knowledge representation techniques.

67.4.1   Types of expert systems

Interpretation systems are used primarily to explain data by providing appropriate symbolic meanings and describing the situation and/or state that accounts for the data. Applications include surveillance, image analysis, speech understanding, chemical structure analysis, and signal interpretation. For example, PROSPECTOR is a geological expert system, and HEARSAY II is concerned with understanding speech.

Prediction systems are used to infer likely consequences from a given situation. Applications include weather forecasting, demographic predictions, traffic predictions, crop estimates, and military forecasting. For example, SPERIL was developed at Purdue University to analyze structures for possible earthquake damage.

Diagnosis systems are used to relate observed behavioral irregularities with underlying causes. These systems combine knowledge of system design with knowledge of potential design, implementation, or component flaws to diagnose malfunctions or recommend further investigation. Applications are found in medicine and in electronic, mechanical, and software design. For example, DART was developed jointly by Stanford University and IBM to determine computer faults, and MYCIN was developed at Stanford University to diagnosis blood infections.

Design systems construct descriptions of objects in various relationships with each other and verify that the resulting configurations conform to known constraints. These systems often incorporate goal-seeking behavior and attempt to minimize an objective function and accomplish the goal. Applications include circuit design, building design, and budgeting. For example, SYN was developed at MIT to perform electronic circuit analysis.

Monitoring systems compare observations of system behavior to features that seem crucial to successful outcomes. Applications include fiscal management, regulatory enforcement, disease monitoring, and air traffic control. For example, IMS was developed by Carnegie Mellon University to perform automated factory monitoring and CALLISTO was developed by Digital Equipment Corporation to perform project management activities.

Planning systems employ models of agent behavior to infer the results and outcomes of the agent's activities. Applications include automated programming, robotics, routing, data communication, and military planning. For example, PECOS was developed at Stanford to model oil exploration and ISIS-II was developed by Carnegie Mellon University for job shop scheduling.

Debugging systems are used to prescribe remedies for malfunctions and/or failures. Applications include computer programming, software development, text editing, question and answer systems, natural language processing, and computer-aided instruction.

Repair systems develop and execute plans to administer a remedy for some diagnosed problem. Applications include communications networks and computer maintenance. Repair systems are relatively new, and successful implementations are just beginning to emerge.

Instruction systems are used to diagnose and debug system behaviors and to provide the decision-maker with trouble-shooting support. Applications include student instruction and animal behavior explanation systems. For example, GUIDON was developed by Stanford University to provide medical instruction and WUMPUS was developed by MIT to provide athletic coaching instruction.

A control system adaptively governs the overall behavior of a system, repeatedly interpreting the current situation, predicting the future, diagnosing the causes of anticipated problems and/or symptoms, and formulating a plan to monitor execution to ensure success. Air traffic control, business management, battle management, and mission control are possible application areas.

67.4.2 Knowledge representation techniques

The purpose of knowledge representation is to organize the required information into a form that the expert system can readily access for decision making, planning, recognizing objects and situations, analyzing scenes, drawing conclusions, and other cognitive functions.

67.4.2.1 First-order predicate logic

First-order predicate logic is commonly used in mathematics to prove theorems. The idea is to use qualifiers and logical operators to describe objects, properties, situations, and relationships. The process is natural, precise, flexible, and modular, providing simplicity of notation and well-understood formal semantics. On the other hand, this technique lacks organizational principles, has weak manipulation procedures, and does not represent procedural or heuristic knowledge well.

67.4.2.2   Frames and slots

A frame is a complex data structure representing a stereotyped situation, such as an object, an activity, or a person. Slots are frame-like structures for representing stereotyped sequences of events or values. For example, in a frame that describes a bank account, the slots can be used to represent the account number, the account type, and the account balance. Generally, a frame is composed of a concept, one or more slots, one or more values, and one or more attached procedures (Figure 67.1).

Figure 67.2 shows a set of frames that represent information about bank accounts. A bank representative opens the account file for a customer by soliciting, entering, and verifying all the required information. The associated expert system then automatically triggers an attached procedure that asks the representative to select a transaction type (for example, add a new customer, update customer information, delete a customer, and so on). The expert system then responds by triggering the appropriate procedure.

Frame and slots were developed at about the same time object-oriented techniques (Chapter 6) were developed. A frame is similar to an object. A slot holds properties or attributes, a value is an actual instance of a particular property, and an attached procedure is similar to a method.

Using frames and slots facilitates certain predetermined information processing activities (such as add, delete, or update an account) and organizes the knowledge for easy retrieval, reference, and maintenance. Not all real-world situations can be resolved by predetermined logic, however, and new situations (e.g., adding a new feature such as a debit card) are not easily accommodated without major changes to the frames and slots structure.

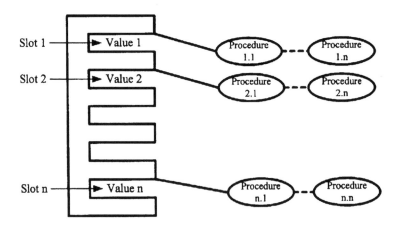

Figure 67.1   Frames and slots.

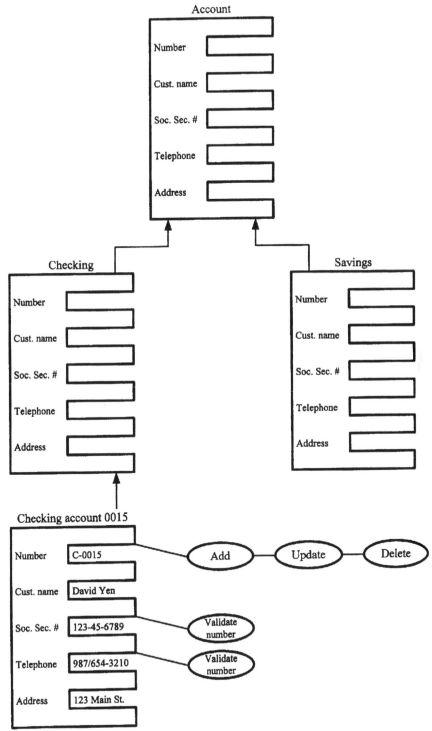

Figure 67.2 A set of frames that represent information about bank accounts.

67.4.2.3   Property lists

The property lists approach uses objects and lists of their properties (or attributes) to describe the state of the world. This method is borrowed from the object-oriented approach (Chapter 6). All appropriate properties for an object are grouped into a list, and lists are easily structured in LISP, a popular expert system programming language. However, property lists are not very effective for inference-oriented operations (Chapter 34).

67.4.2.4   Semantic nets

The semantic net technique describes the state of the world through a collection of nodes that represent objects, object properties, concepts, events, and arcs of links (Figure 67.3); see Chapter 43 for a discussion of the graph

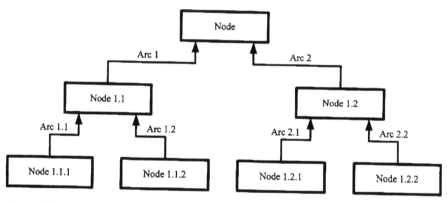

Figure 67.3   A semantic net.

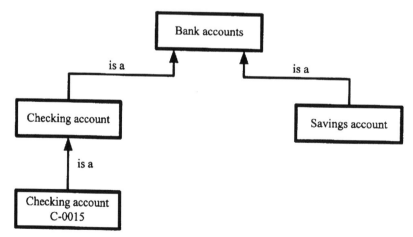

Figure 67.4   A semantic net of bank account information.

data structure. For example, Figure 67.4 shows the bank accounts from Section 67.4.2.2 as a semantic net.

Like an object-oriented class structure, the objects at the bottom of the top-down hierarchy inherit properties from higher-levels but also possess unique properties. For example, an individual checking account inherits such properties as an account number and an account type, but such properties as overdraft protection, minimum balance, and linkages to other accounts can change from account to account.

With a semantic net, important associations and relationships can be described explicitly, and the inheritance hierarchy is easy to understand and revise. Consequently, it is easier to add new situations to a semantic net than to a set of slots and frames. Also, the relevant facts can be found within the hierarchy, so it is not necessary to search through a large database to find specific information. Establishing an inheritance hierarchy is a difficult task, however, and determining the unique (non-inherited) properties for each low-level node calls for (subjective and/or objective) judgment.

67.4.2.5   Direct representation

Direct representation (or analogical representation) is based on analogy. Using direct representation, certain properties of a new situation can be described by reference to a known situation, and the known situation's recommended course of action can be borrowed by an expert system faced with a new but similar situation. For example, to a weather forecasting expert system, the atmospheric conditions (except for the air temperature) that produce a rainstorm and a snowstorm are similar, so once a rainstorm is fully described, many of the parameters associated with a snowstorm are already known.

Direct representation facilitates searching because the important constraints are already known. Also, the known situation provides a base of established information that might prove relevant to the new situation. Direct representation is not suitable for all expert system tasks, however. For example, it is inappropriate when the problem calls for generalizing several specific cases into a generic meta-problem.

67.4.2.6   Procedure/subroutine

In the procedure/subroutine approach, knowledge about the world is contained in procedures, small programs that know how to do specific things (such as proceed in a well-defined situation). This technique is particularly well suited to tasks that require searching a problem domain. In computer program design, this technique views each intelligent routine as an agent that works independently to accomplish a specific task and then passes the results back to the main program (which resolves the meta-problem).

The procedure/subroutine approach is good for representing heuristic knowledge, modeling complex meta-problems, and performing extended logical inferences and reasoning. Procedures and subroutines are difficult to verify or change, however, and the information needed to control the sub-routines can limit or even exclude significant alternatives or information.

67.4.2.7 *Procedural/production system*

In this technique, knowledge is represented by a collection of loosely coupled procedures, which may be organized into sets. For example, imagine a planning or brainstorming session in which numerous participants (multiple independent knowledge sources) nominate ideas that are recorded on a blackboard. Subsequently, the elements of a procedural/production system analyze the contents of the blackboard, locate similarities, distinguish differences, and merge similar ideas to form aggregate categories. Note that the control mechanism is part of an expert system.

Using this technique, information can be easily added, removed, and updated, and it is relatively easy to keep track of changes. Additionally, the procedural/production system technique is consistent with compiler design. Because of the complexity of the logic, program execution is inefficient, however, and the process is constrained by the predetermined control flow imposed by the program.

67.5   *Key terms*

Control system — A type of expert system that adaptively governs the overall behavior of a system, repeatedly interpreting the current situation, predicting the future, diagnosing the causes of anticipated problems and/or symptoms, and formulating a plan to monitor execution to ensure success.

Debugging system — A type of expert system used to prescribe remedies for malfunctions and/or failures.

Design system — A type of expert system that constructs descriptions of objects in various relationships and verifies that the resulting configurations conform to known constraints.

Diagnosis system — A type of expert system used to relate observed behavioral irregularities with underlying causes.

Direct representation (analogical representation) — A technique that allows an expert system to analyze the properties of a new situation and use the course of action for an old situation to deal with it.

Expert system (knowledge-based system) — A computer program that emulates the thought process of a human expert.

First-order predicate logic — The type of logic used in mathematics to prove theorems.

Frame — A complex data structure composed of a concept, one or more slots, one or more values, and one or more attached procedures; a frame represents a stereotyped situation.

Goal — An objective.

Heuristics — General rules derived from experience, common sense, inferences, and intelligent trial and error.

Inference — The act or process of deriving logical conclusions from premises known or assumed to be true.

Instruction system — A type of expert system used to diagnose and debug system behaviors and to provide the decision-maker with trouble-shooting support.

Interpretation system — A type of expert system used to explain data by providing appropriate symbolic meanings and describing the situation and/or state that accounts for the data.

Knowledge — The sum or range of what has been perceived, discovered, or learned; specific information about something.

Language parser — A routine that executes correctly interpreted commands to accomplish the tasks determined by the program.

Lexical analyzer — A component of a compiler that deals with the interpretation and understanding of the commands and related syntax.

Monitoring system — A type of expert system that compares observations of system behavior to features that seem crucial to successful outcomes.

Prediction system — A type of expert system used to infer likely consequences from a given situation.

Procedural/production system — A technique that analyzes information from multiple independent knowledge sources, identifies similarities, distinguishes differences, and merges similar ideas and concepts to form aggregate categories.

Procedure/subroutine approach — An approach to knowledge representation in which knowledge about the world is contained in procedures, small programs that know how to do specific things.

Property lists approach — An approach to knowledge representation that uses objects and lists of their properties (or attributes) to describe the state of the world.

Reasoning — The act of using inference to lead to a conclusion based on existing knowledge and/or data.

Repair system — A type of expert system used to develop and execute plans to administer a remedy for some diagnosed problem.

Rule — A formal specification or description of a unit of knowledge.

Semantic net technique — An approach to knowledge representation that describes the state of the world as a collection of nodes that represent objects, object properties, concepts, events, and arcs of links in a graph.

Slot — A frame-like structure for representing stereotyped sequences of events.

Stereotype — A description that embodies a set image or type; a template.

67.6 Software

Not applicable. However, the chapter did reference LISP, a popular expert system programming language.

67.7 References

1. Awad, E. M., *Building Expert Systems: Principles, Procedures, and Applications,* West, St. Paul, MN, 1996.
2. Durkin, J. and Durkin, J., *Expert Systems: Design and Development,* Macmillan, New York, 1994.
3. Giarratano, J. C. and Riley, G. D., *Expert Systems: Principles and Programming,* 2nd ed., PWS, Boston, MA, 1994.
4. Harmon, P. and King, D., *Expert Systems: Artificial Intelligence in Business,* John Wiley & Sons Inc., New York, 1985.
5. Hayes-Roth, F., Waterman, D., and Lenat, D., *Building Expert Systems,* Addison-Wesley, Reading, MA, 1983.
6. Holsapple, C. W. and Whinston, A. B., *Business Expert Systems,* Richard D. Irwin, Homewood, IL, 1987.
7. Silverman, B. G., *Expert Systems for Business,* Addison-Wesley, Reading, MA, 1991.
8. Waterman, D., *A Guide to Expert Systems,* Addison-Wesley, Reading, MA, 1986.
9. Zahedi, F., *Intelligent Systems for Business: Expert Systems with Neural Networks,* Wadsworth, Belmont, CA, 1993.

chapter sixty-eight

Natural language processing

David C. Yen and William S. Davis

Contents

68.1 Purpose

The ultimate objective of natural language processing is to allow people to communicate with computers in much the same way they communicate with each other. This chapter briefly introduces key natural language processing concepts and terminology.

0-8493-7001-9/99/$0.00+$.50
©1999 by CRC Press LLC

68.2   Strengths, weaknesses, and limitations

Natural language processing removes one of the key obstacles that keeps some people from using computers. More specifically, natural language processing facilitates access to a database or a knowledge base, provides a friendly user interface, facilitates language translation and conversion, and increases user productivity by supporting English-like input.

As of mid-1998 when this chapter was written, natural language processing was not yet capable of supporting true conversational input. Most commercially available software limits the number of different users and/or such parameters as the user's vocabulary, syntax, or speed, and free-form English input must occasionally be supplemented with commands. Most natural language processing software is designed to locate key words first and then interpret the meaning of a sentence or a phrase, which increases programming time and program execution time. Additionally, special equipment is needed to support natural language processing.

68.3   Inputs and related ideas

Natural language processing is a major area of research within the field of artificial intelligence. It is closely related (either as a front end or a user interface) with expert systems (Chapter 7), and shows great promise as a user interface (Chapter 48). State transition diagrams (Chapter 30) are sometimes used to model natural language processing tasks.

68.4   Concepts

The ultimate objective of natural language processing is to allow people to communicate with computers in much the same way they communicate with each other. This chapter briefly introduces key natural language processing concepts and terminology. A detailed discussion of the underlying technology is beyond the scope of this book.

68.4.1   Phases

Natural language processing starts with the input of a string of plain English words (Figure 68.1). The first phase in the process is word recognition. The objective is to restructure the input string as a series of noun phrases, verb phrases, prepositional phrases, adjective phrases, and so on. A state transition diagram (Chapter 30) is sometimes used to model the process.

Next the words and phrases are analyzed to check the integrity of the sentences and to clarify any ambiguities. The knowledge base stores general knowledge (words, linguistic concepts, etc.) and application-specific knowledge. A lexical analyzer is a routine that performs semantic analysis, checking every word in a sentence against the correct spellings stored in the

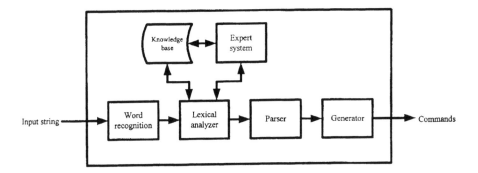

Figure 68.1   Natural language processing.

knowledge base and listing all the possible alternative meanings for the sentence. If necessary, an expert system is consulted to deduce the meanings of ambiguous terms and expressions based on context, questions asked earlier in the session, organization-specific rules, and other factors stored in the knowledge base.

Once the words are properly defined, a parser routine performs syntactic analysis, essentially diagramming the sentence to form a parse tree. Finally, during the natural language implementation phase, a generator outputs one or more commands based on the meaning deduced from the word meanings and the parse tree. For example, a plain English query might be converted to a set of SQL commands. The computer then executes the commands.

68.4.2   The natural language shell

The natural language processing routine is typically visualized as a shell. The user communicates with the shell by entering plain English character strings. The shell translates the plain English strings into the appropriate commands and passes the commands to an application program. Using a common shell makes more sense than duplicating the same complex logic in multiple application programs.

68.4.3   Speech recognition

Speech recognition is an extension of natural language processing. The idea is to use a speech recognition routine (or a chip) to break continuous speech into a string of words, input the string into a natural language processing routine, and then pass the resulting commands to an application program.

One problem with speech recognition is that human language is imprecise and many words have multiple meanings that depend on context. Add multiple languages, dialects, and accents, and the problem becomes very complex. Additionally, few people are skilled at issuing orders or using language with precision.

68.4.4 Other applications

Natural language processing can support several types of translation. Language-to-language systems translate between two languages; English and Chinese, for example. Compiler and interpreter systems convert English-like commands into executable machine or low-level language codes. Code-to-code translators are common in word processing software, supporting conversions between Microsoft Word, ASCII, and WordPerfect formats, for example.

As the term implies, grammar analysis systems are used to check spelling and grammar. For example, the grammar analysis facility in Microsoft Word for Office 97 continuously underlines spelling errors in red and grammatical errors in green as the user types. In addition to highlighting misspellings, commonly misused words, awkward sentence structures, awkward phrases, and incorrect punctuation, a sophisticated grammar analysis system can also provide substitutes for specific words, determine the reading level of a document, and provide status and statistical data for further analysis.

Record management systems read the contents of records (received, stored, and transmitted), analyze the contents, sort the records into proper categories, and add meaningful indexes or key words and phrases for future reference.

A natural language processing system can serve as a user interface to a database system, an expert system, or a specific application. A SQL command generator is a good example of a database system interface. Natural language interfaces show great promise for expert systems, and considerable research has already been done. Other natural language interfaces are used in data communications, manufacturing, and office automation.

Natural language processing will play an important role in future robotic systems. Robotics combines such features as speech recognition, natural language processing, natural language translation, image processing, and pattern recognition, and is beyond the scope of this book.

68.5 Key terms

Expert system (knowledge-based system) — A computer program that emulates the thought process of a human expert.

Generator — A routine that outputs one or more commands that the computer can execute.

Knowledge base — A collection of data, algorithms, and heuristic rules that forms the core of an expert system.

Lexical analyzer — A routine that performs semantic analysis, checking every word in a sentence against the correct spellings stored in the knowledge base and listing all the possible alternative meanings for the sentence.

Natural language processing shell — A natural language processing user interface. The user communicates with the shell by entering plain English character strings. The shell translates the plain English strings into the appropriate commands and passes the commands to an application program.

Parse tree — A hierarchical representation of words (conceptually similar to a diagrammed sentence) arranged in a form that allows a computer program to trace relationships and infer meanings.

Parser — A routine that performs syntactic analysis, essentially diagramming a sentence to form a parse tree.

Semantic analysis — A technique in which the system determines the meaning of each word by looking it up in a dictionary or a knowledge base.

Speech recognition — An extension of natural language processing that uses a speech recognition routine (or a chip) to break continuous speech into a string of words, inputs the string to a natural language processing routine, and then passes the resulting commands to an application program.

Syntactic analysis — A technique that allows a parser routine to, essentially, diagram a sentence to form a parse tree.

Word recognition — The process of restructuring an input string into a series of noun phrases, verb phrases, prepositional phrases, adjective phrases, and so on.

68.6 Software

Dragon Systems' *Naturally Speaking* and IBM's *ViaVoice Gold* are voice recognition software packages that might be used to support a speech recognition system. Other examples include *Intellect* from Artificial Intelligence Corp., *RAMIS II English* from Mathematica, Inc., *Spock* from Frey Associates, Inc., and *NaturalLink* from Texas Instruments.

68.7 References

1. Allen J., *Natural Language Understanding*, Benjamin/Cummings, Redwood City, CA, 1987.
2. Davis, W. S., *Computers and Information Systems: An Introduction*, West, Minneapolis, MN, 1997.
3. O'Shea, T. and Eisenstadt, M., *Artificial Intelligence: Tools, Techniques, and Applications*, Harper & Row, New York, 1984.
4. Rauch-Hindin, W. B., *A Guide to Commercial Artificial Intelligence: Fundamentals and Real World Applications*, Prentice-Hall, Englewood Cliffs, NJ, 1988.
5. Turban E., *Expert Systems and Applied Artificial Intelligence*, Macmillan, New York, 1992.
6. Williamson M., *Artificial Intelligence for Microcomputers: The Guide for Business Decision Makers*, Brady Communications, New York, 1986.
7. Winston, P. H. and Prendergast, K. A., *The AI Business: Commercial Uses of Artificial Intelligence*, MIT Press, Cambridge, MA, 1984.

chapter sixty-nine

Customizing commercial software

Dan Terrio, Miami University
Maria Scott, Software Architects

Contents

69.1   Purpose

Software customization allows for the modification of commercial software in order to meet the unique requirements of an organization. This chapter briefly describes several customization techniques.

69.2   Strengths, weaknesses, and limitations

Utilizing commercial software saves design, programming, and testing time, significantly reduces the time frame for implementing a new system, and significantly reduces system development costs. The software vendor may provide maintenance, support, upgrades, and enhancements, thus reducing maintenance costs. Commercial software is often modular, so the organization can pick the pieces that meet its needs.

Commercial software packages are written to the lowest common denominator. For complex applications, customizing commercial software may be more time consuming and costly than developing and implementing a custom system. Also, because commercial software is widely available, customizing commercial software compromises any competitive advantage the organization may have gained had it developed the application in house.

69.3   Inputs and related ideas

Before choosing between customizing commercial software and building a new system in house, management and information systems personnel must clearly understand the business problem and the system objectives. The necessary understanding is based on the results of the problem definition (Part II) and analysis (Part IV) stages of the system development life cycle. Cost/benefit analysis (Chapter 38) is an important part of the make or buy decision; note that the potential loss of a competitive advantage is a significant intangible cost. Customizing commercial software promotes early user acceptance because prototypes (Chapter 31) are easily created using the software.

One method of customizing commercial software is to create a front end (Chapters 48 and 49) to a database (Chapters 43 and 45). Another approach is to customize the software to match the organization's forms and reports (Chapters 46 and 47). With the growing popularity of the World Wide Web, customization may also include web page design (Chapter 51).

69.4   Concepts

Software customization allows for the modification of commercial software in order to meet the unique requirements of an organization. This chapter briefly describes several customization techniques.

69.4.1   Simple customization

Some customization tools require relatively little technical expertise.

69.4.1.1   Macros

A macro is an instruction (or set of instructions) that performs a series of keystrokes or commands to carry out a specific task. Macros are created to help reduce keystrokes. The user activates the macro feature, performs the target task, and captures the sequence of keystrokes in a file. The macro is subsequently executed by pressing a hot key (or key combination), clicking an icon or a button, or selecting the macro from a menu.

For example, if a Microsoft Word for Office 97 user wants to double-space a block of text, he or she must highlight the text to be double-spaced, open the *Format* menu, select *Paragraph,* select *Line spacing,* and then select *Double.* To create an equivalent macro, the user first highlights the text to be double-spaced and then selects *Macro* from the *Tools* menu. After the user clicks on *Record new macro,* a window opens. In the window, the user gives the macro a name, assigns the macro to a toolbar, the keyboard, or both, and then goes through the steps required to double-space the highlighted text. When the user stops recording (by clicking *Stop recording* on the toolbar), the keystrokes and commands are captured and saved. Once the macro is recorded, the captured steps can be repeated by clicking on the associated toolbar icon or pressing the associated key combination.

The process of creating a macro is similar in other software tools.

69.4.1.2   Styles

A style is a font, a point size, and a set of text formatting rules. For example, a major heading might be centered in 18-point, boldface Arial.

To create a style in Microsoft Word, the user first formats and highlights the target paragraph or block of text, opens the style window (at the left of the tool bar), and types the name of the new style in the style window. An option is to select *Style* from the *Format* menu to open the style window (Figure 69.1) and either select *New* or *Modify* (to change an existing style). Once a style is set, the user can select it by highlighting the affected text and selecting the style by name from the style menu. The process of creating a style is similar in other software tools.

69.4.1.3   Templates

Templates are documents that contain predefined styles and macros. For example, a user might create a template for a memo that includes the company's logo, the date, such headings as TO, FROM, and SUBJECT, and a set of text styles. When the template is opened, the user selects the text to be changed and types the new content. The template defines the document layout, eliminating the need to retype redundant material and ensuring a consistent appearance.

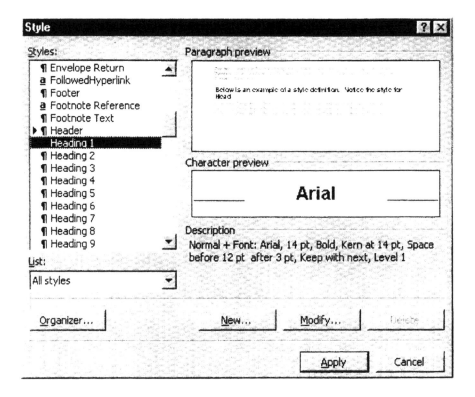

Figure 69.1   The Microsoft Word style window.

To create a template, the user typically enters the initial version of the document and then saves it as (SAVE AS) a template. For example, in Microsoft Word, templates are stored as template files and subsequently accessed by opening the *File* menu, selecting *New,* and then selecting the template by name. Figure 69.2 shows a Microsoft Word memo template for a memo. The process of creating a template is similar in other software tools.

69.4.2   Advanced customization

Such customization techniques as creating a front end for a user to access, query, and/or change a database, or creating a bridge routine to convert the data from the old database to a format the new system can use require more advanced programming skills.

69.4.2.1   Visual basic

The Microsoft suite of packaged software uses the VBA (Visual Basic for Applications) programming language to add custom procedures to a standard program. Other manufacturers support Visual Basic or comparable languages.

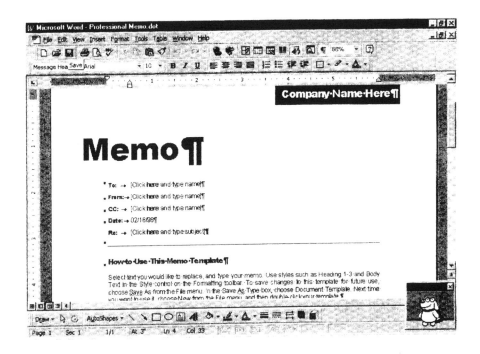

Figure 69.2   A Microsoft Word template for a memo.

69.4.2.2   Forms

Forms (data entry screens with fill-in-the blank or select-an-option windows) are a common type of front end. (Such forms are examples of information-oriented question-answer dialogue, Chapter 49.) A set of forms might be created to allow a user to define queries or add, delete, and edit records in a database. For example, Figure 69.3 shows a form for finding a customer in a Microsoft Access database. Visual Basic is sometimes used to create and execute the forms.

69.4.2.3   Web customization

With the increasing popularity of the World Wide Web, customization often includes web page design (Chapter 51). For example, using a product such as Cold Fusion, a programmer can create custom web pages that allow the user to enter and/or modify data in the organization's database. Web access is platform independent, so a user can browse the web site via any computer platform (e.g. Macintosh, Windows, Unix, and so on), and off-site access to the company's Intranet is possible through any Internet service provider. Security is a major concern, however.

For example, Miami University (Oxford, Ohio) is currently creating web access to parts of its new administrative and student databases. When the system is completed, students will be able to view transcript data and

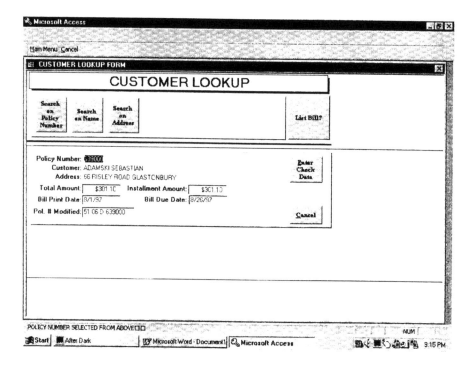

Figure 69.3   A form for finding a customer in a Microsoft Access database.

register for classes through the web. Security will be implemented using encryption techniques.

Java[1] is an object-oriented programming language that was designed for secure use across platforms. A programmer can write a Java applet to implement a form or perform a set of functions within the context of a web page. Another option is to build a search engine to query a database through a web site. Examples include an airfare reservation system and the Library of Congress catalogue search engine (Figure 69.4).

69.5   Key terms

Bridge — A routine that converts the organization's current data to a format that is compatible with the purchased software.

Commercial software package — A set of prewritten application programs that are commercially available for purchase or lease.

Customization — The modification of a software package to meet an organization's unique requirements without destroying the integrity of the package software.

Form — A data entry screen with fill-in-the blank or select-an-option windows.

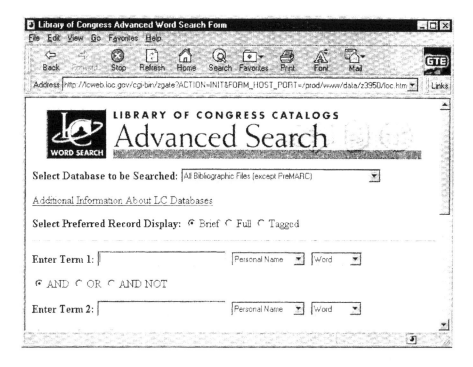

Figure 69.4   The Library of Congress catalogue search engine.

Front end routine — A routine that accepts input data and formats it for a commercial program.

Java — An object-oriented, platform independent programming language from Sun Microsystems.

Macro — An instruction (or set of instructions) that performs a series of keystrokes or commands to carry out a specific task.

Style — A font, a point size, and a set of text formatting rules.

Template — A document that contains predefined styles and macros.

69.6   Software

Below is a list of software tools that can be used to customize commercial software. The list is not exhaustive and does not constitute a recommendation.

Clipper	Java
Cold Fusion	Microsoft Visual Basic
Dbase	Oracle Developer 2000
Delphi	Paradox
Foxpro	PowerBuilder

69.7   References

69.7.1   Web sites

1. Java information can be found at http://sunsite.unc.edu/javafaq/javafaq.html.

69.7.2   Suggestions for additional reading

1. Laudon, K. C. and Laudon, J. P., *Essentials of Management Information Systems: Organization and Technology,* Prentice-Hall, Englewood Cliffs, NJ, 1995.
2. Lin, F., *The Visual Basic Coursebook,* Scott/Jones, El Granada, CA, 1997.
3. Perry, G., *Visual Basic 5 Night School,* QUE (Macmillan Computer Publishing), Indianapolis, IN, 1997.

chapter seventy

Documentation design

David C. Yen and William S. Davis

Contents

0-8493-7001-9/99/$0.00+$.50
©1999 by CRC Press LLC

70.1 Purpose

Documentation consists of the specifications, instructions, tutorials, reference guides, and similar materials that accompany and explain a piece of software or a hardware component. Documentation serves as a communication vehicle, provides a useful reference, and facilitates management's control of the system development process and of system operation. This chapter briefly discusses documentation types and documentation contents and offers several tips for producing good documentation.

70.2 Strengths, weaknesses, and limitations

Documentation serves as a communication vehicle, provides a useful (testing, debugging, maintenance, and operational) reference, enhances productivity, supports user training, and promotes continuity and consistency. Additionally, it facilitates management's control of the system development process and of system operation. Other information system development projects can sometimes borrow components and/or ideas from (or reuse) existing documentation. Details concerning modifications to and versions of an information system are important system validation criteria.

On the negative side, creating and maintaining effective documentation is expensive. However, the benefits almost always outweigh the cost.

70.3 Inputs and related ideas

Documentation is created throughout the system development life cycle. Good documentation is essential during the testing, implementation, and maintenance stages (Parts VII and VIII).

Many of the tools and techniques discussed in this book can be used to generate charts, diagrams, narratives, and other forms of documentation. In particular, see screen and forms design (Chapter 46), report design (Chapter 47), user interface design (Chapter 48), dialogues (Chapter 49), windows design (Chapter 50), web page design (Chapter 51), logic flowcharts (Chapter 55), decision trees (Chapter 57), decision tables (Chapter 58), and HIPO (Chapter 64). A technical inspection (Chapter 23) is an excellent tool for evaluating the quality of the documentation.

70.4 Concepts

The quality of an information system depends not only on such attributes as flexibility, user-friendliness, reliability and performance, but also on the quality of the documentation. In fact, to the user, the documentation and the user interface *are* the system.

Documentation consists of the specifications, instructions, tutorials, reference guides, and similar materials that accompany and explain a piece of software or a hardware component. Good documentation is complete, clear, understandable, current, and reusable.

70.4.1 Documentation types

Internal documentation consists of specifications, records, and manuals that are stored, maintained, and used by technical professionals. (It is "internal" because it is kept within the technical facility.) Examples include system documentation, program documentation, operations manuals, command manuals, input/output specifications, interface specifications and descriptions, sample input/output records and forms, system analysis documentation, system design documentation, and related data descriptions and specifications.

External documentation, in contrast, is kept at the user's location (or some other remote site) and is designed primarily for the user. Examples include user manuals, execution guides, error manuals, assistance manuals, guidelines, operating procedures, and so on.

Command-oriented documentation contains all the commands used by the system and/or the program, usually arranged in alphabetical order. Typically, the syntax, options, formats, attributes, and one or more examples are listed for each command. Operation-oriented documentation groups commands based on the nature of the operation. For example, commands might be grouped into such categories as file, edit, help, tools, and format.

Execution-oriented (or application-based) documentation is designed to support an application. Typically, such details as operating procedures, execution sequence, the rules and privileges associated with accessing a file, and various restrictions associated with the system are documented. On-line help is an example of execution-oriented documentation. Diagnosis-oriented documentation describes the type and the nature of warning messages and error messages and explains the causes of and solutions for each error.

Generally, the systems manual is a combination of command-oriented and diagnosis-oriented documentation. The user manual is often a combination of execution-oriented and operation-oriented documentation.

It is also possible to classify documentation by system development life cycle phase. Requests for proposal (RFP), requests for quotation (RFQ), the requirements specification, various process and data analysis models, and the feasibility study report are examples of analysis documentation. Data flow diagrams, the data dictionary, and other types of data and design specifications are examples of design documentation. Change reports, version control specifications, the system manual, the user manual, and similar manuals and specification are examples of maintenance documentation.

70.4.2 Documentation contents

The precise content of a unit of documentation depends on its intended use. For example, a source code listing might be appropriate for a maintenance programmer, but the end user of that program will need a clear explanation of exactly how to work with the user interface. Form affects content, too; printed documentation and on-line documentation are inherently different.

Documentation is prepared for future reference, so most documentation contains a table of contents and/or an index that makes it easy to find key topics. For example, many on-line help features include a help contents window, an index, and a search facility.

Often, one of the first pages or screens in the documentation is an introduction that explains the purpose of the documentation, identifies the intended audience, and identifies the people responsible for creating the documentation and for answering questions about the documentation. A glossary is often included, too. With the growing acceptance of the Internet and the World Wide Web, some on-line documentation packages now feature key words hyperlinked to a glossary entry.

The detailed contents of the documentation can take many different forms, from pure narrative, to graphics, to interactive dialogue, to hybrid multimedia presentations. Functional narratives are common. For example, a user manual might feature a series of annotated user interface screens with explanations, or an annotated sample report. Play script style features two (or more) columns, with key actions listed in the left column and the associated explanation listed in the right column. See the chapters listed under *Inputs and Related Ideas* for other tools that might be used to prepare documentation.

70.4.3   Documentation tips

Listed below are several tips for creating effective documentation.

70.4.3.1   Write for the user

A basic principle of any kind of writing is to write for the intended audience. Effective documentation begins with a thorough understanding of the user, the user's needs, and the user's technical expertise. Analysis-oriented documentation should be written for the analyst. Detailed program documentation should be written for the programmer. The user manual should be written for the end user.

The principle seems obvious, but it is frequently ignored. All too often, documentation is prepared by technical personnel who either do not understand the user, do not care about the user, or care more about impressing their technical peers than communicating effectively with the user. Documentation that is not written for the intended reader will not be used. Unused documentation is a waste of time and effort.

One final point: Many sources cite ease of use as a primary documentation criterion. Ease of use is a relative concept. The only valid basis for measuring ease of use is the intended user.

70.4.3.2 Never leave the user hanging

Good documentation never leaves the user hanging. All explanations should be written in user terms, using words the user understands. Technical terms should be clearly defined in context or in a glossary. The use of acronyms should be kept to a minimum. When an acronym is used, its meaning should be spelled out on each page where it appears.

70.4.3.3 Design for easy reference

People rarely read documentation from cover to cover. Instead, they use such features as a table of contents, an index, thumb tabs, or a search tool to quickly find a specific answer to a specific question. Effective documentation is designed with such use in mind.

Design the contents to be easy to find. Use a table of contents and/or an index. Put the entries in alphabetical order or group them by function. If the documentation is on line, provide a key word search facility.

Redundancy can be valuable. For example, different users might visualize a document as a page, a form, or a screen. Rather than training everyone to use the same term, it might be better to provide links to the right information from all of those aliases, or from any appropriate starting point. To cite another example, imagine that two topics are closely related. It is unreasonable to assume that a user searching for topic B has previously read topic A, so redundant elements of the explanation should be repeated for both topics.

Not all users need the same amount of detail, so drilldown is another useful principle. For example, each topic might be organized as a pyramid, with general concepts on top, a typical or most likely scenario in the middle, and exceptions or special cases at the bottom. Given such a structure, a given user can "drill down" only as far as necessary to answer his or her question.

70.4.3.4 Be consistent

Consistency is crucial. Consider, for example, the graphic user interface defined by the World Wide Web. Once a user learns how to access and navigate one site, the same point and click operations work on virtually any site. Similarly, if all the elements in a given documentation package are designed with a consistent look and feel, the user's training time is greatly reduced.

Perhaps the best example of a consistent look and feel is the desktop metaphor defined by the Apple Macintosh and Microsoft Windows. A few basic operations (point, click, drag) are used to manipulate a few basic elements (windows, icons, menus) in virtually every application. Consequently, given a little practice, the basic operations and elements become almost intuitive, so the user can effectively ignore them and focus on the task at hand. Similarly, the physical structure of the documentation should make access almost intuitive, and not get in the user's way. In fact, because so many people are already familiar with the metaphors, it often makes sense to design the documentation to resemble a Windows or World Wide Web application.

70.4.3.5   Plan

Good documentation does not just happen; it must be carefully planned. In fact, many software developers view documentation as a discrete phase that is performed concurrently with analysis, design, and implementation, and every organization should (at the very least) have in place a formal documentation process complete with formal procedures and standards.

As a minimum, for each unit of documentation, the content, the organizational structure, the sequence of topics, the intended level of detail, the presentation methods and approaches (print, graphics, interactive, multimedia, etc.), and the users' comprehension level must be clearly defined before detailed writing begins. Additionally, a budget, resource allocations (personnel, equipment), quality standards, timing constraints, and approval procedures must be established for the documentation.

70.4.3.6   Concurrently develop the documentation and the system

Generally, the documentation and the system should be developed concurrently, because if the documentation is viewed as an afterthought, its quality will reflect that point of view. Ideally, the appropriate documentation is a measurable exit criterion from each step in the system development life cycle. In other words, if the documentation is not complete, the step is not complete.

70.4.3.7   Test

The only way to be sure the documentation is good is to test it. The ultimate purpose of the documentation is to support the user. Consequently, the user's opinion is the one that counts, and user involvement in the documentation testing process is essential.

In some organizations, the technical professionals create the documentation, but technical personnel often lack a user prospective and many consider documentation a waste of time. In other organizations, technical writers, subcontractors, temporary workers, and other support personnel create the documentation, but less-technical people often lack technical understanding. A technical inspection (Chapter 23) is an excellent tool for evaluating the quality of the documentation, particularly if the inspection team includes both technical personnel and users.

Standards are important. Some standards are procedural. Start with a plan, have management and the user approve the plan, and conduct regular inspections to enforce the plan. Other standards can be applied to the content. For example, there are several easily computed readability indexes that can be correlated to the reading level of the intended users.

70.4.3.8 Get management committed

People do things they are rewarded (financially or emotionally) for doing and they avoid things they are penalized for doing. If management treats documentation as a necessary evil, rewards those who ignore the documentation in order to get the "real" work done, and penalizes those who insist on doing the job "right" in spite of the schedule, then the documentation will not be done properly. Good documentation is produced by organizations that make good documentation a priority.

70.4.3.9 Learn from what works

Perhaps the best way to improve documentation is to start with documentation that works well, study it carefully to find out why it works, and then use the good documentation as a model.

70.5 Key terms

Command-oriented documentation — Documentation that contains all the commands used by the system and/or the program, usually arranged in alphabetical order.

Diagnosis-oriented documentation — Documentation that describes the type and the nature of warning messages and error messages and explains the causes of and solutions for each error.

Documentation — The specifications, instructions, tutorials, reference guides, and similar materials that accompany and explain a piece of software or a hardware component.

Execution-oriented documentation (application based documentation) — Documentation designed to support an application.

External documentation — Documentation that is kept at the user's location (or some other remote site) and is designed primarily for the user.

Internal documentation — Specifications, records, and manuals that are stored, maintained, and used by technical professionals.

Operation-oriented documentation — Command-oriented documentation that groups commands based on the nature of the operation.

70.6 Software

CASE software is particularly useful for developing analysis and design documentation. Word processing, graphics, and desktop publishing software are also useful. Additionally, many of the tools and techniques discussed in this book produce charts, diagrams, and other materials that can serve as documentation.

70.7   References

1. Birrell, N. D. and Ould, M. A., *A Practical Handbook for Software Development,* Cambridge University Press, Cambridge, U.K., 1986.
2. Hannan, J., Ed., *A Practical Guide to Data Processing Management,* Auerbach Publishers, New York, 1982.
3. Hannan, J., *A Practical Guide to EDP Auditing,* Auerbach Publishers, New York, 1982.
4. Hastings, G. P. and King, K. J., *Creating Effective Documentation for Computer Programs,* Prentice-Hall, Englewood Cliffs, NJ, 1986.
5. Katzin, E., *How to Write a Really Good User's Manual,* Van Nostrand Reinhold, New York, 1985.
6. Saldarini, R. A., *Analysis and Design of Business Information Systems,* Macmillan, New York, 1989.
7. Singer, L. M., *Written Communications for MIS/DP Professionals,* Macmillan, New York, 1986.

chapter seventy-one

Security

David C. Yen and William S. Davis

Contents

71.1 Purpose

The objective of security is to protect the hardware, software, data, and other system resources from unauthorized, illegal, or unwanted access, use, modification, or theft. This chapter describes several information system security risks, outlines some strategies for countering them, and briefly discusses how security is designed into a system.

71.2   Strengths, weaknesses, and limitations

This chapter focuses on concepts and principles. Where appropriate, the strengths and weaknesses of various approaches will be discussed in context.

71.3   Inputs and related ideas

During the problem definition (Part II) and analysis (Part IV) stages of the system development life cycle, the system's security exposures and risks are identified. The costs associated with appropriate countermeasures are a part of the cost/benefit analysis (Chapter 38). At the end of the analysis stage, the necessary security measures are documented in the requirements specification (Chapter 35). Virtually any system component can present a security risk. Consequently, security is an important consideration in the design of almost every system component and is relevant to most of the chapters in Part VI. System controls, including security controls, are discussed in Chapter 77.

71.4   Concepts

The objective of security is to protect the hardware, software, data, and other system resources from unauthorized, illegal, or unwanted access, use, modification, or theft. In a traditional information system constructed around a centralized mainframe the computer and most of its peripherals are locked in a restricted access room. Such lock and key security is not very useful on a modern network, however. The combination of large numbers of users and physically unsecured peripherals, cables, communication lines, and access points make modern network-based systems particularly tempting targets. The Internet complicates the problem.

This chapter describes several information system security risks, outlines some strategies for countering them, and briefly discusses how security is designed into a system.

71.4.1   Security threats

To an expert, an item is considered secure if the cost of breaking security (including the risk of getting caught) exceeds the item's value. To some people, such things as military secrets or a corporation's strategic data are considered priceless. Consequently, perfect information system security may be an impossible goal.

A good way to visualize security threats is to imagine the system as a chain and look for weak links. Exposures can come from people, hardware, and/or software.

71.4.1.1 People

Recently, hackers and crackers have received a great deal of publicity. Originally, a hacker was an expert programmer with a knack for creating elegant software. Today, however, the term is more commonly applied to someone who illegally breaks into computer systems. Within the programming community, hackers are viewed as relatively harmless, while crackers, people who break into computers (generally over a communication line) with malicious intent, are viewed as criminals. In popular usage, hacker (the more common term) is applied to both benign and malicious intruders.

In spite of all the publicity about hackers and crackers, such insiders as employees, former employees, consultants, clients, and customers commit most security violations. Unlike hackers, insiders have relatively free access to the system. Industrial spies have been known to approach insiders with offers of money in exchange for sensitive information or software. Disgruntled information system employees (both current and former) are particularly dangerous.

Even honest insiders can represent a security risk. People are not always careful about protecting their passwords, security codes, telephone numbers, equipment, and work places. For example, hackers have been known to guess casually selected passwords, obtain passwords and other security information by going through paper waste (dumpster diving), or passing themselves off as authorized users and convincing an employee to give them the information they need (social engineering).

71.4.1.2 Hardware

The personal computer or workstation is one of the weakest links in network security. Users upload and download data to and from the Internet, share public domain software, and share common peripherals, any of which can constitute a security threat. Unauthorized access to the server's public access files and peripherals (magnetic tape, printers, plotters, and so on) complicates security.

The physical network is also vulnerable. Intruders have been known to tap a cable or a telephone line or intercept satellite and microwave communications. Dial-in access is particularly difficult to control because an incoming call can originate anywhere. In fact, hackers and crackers sometimes run programs that dial thousands of numbers in sequence and note only the numbers that return a modem tone (power dialing). Those numbers are later used as possible access points to a system.

The theft of laptop computers is a growing problem. In addition to the value of the hardware and software, a laptop's hard disk might hold corporate data, passwords, access codes, and other sensitive information.

71.4.1.3 Software

Execution errors and inaccurate input data generated by both authorized and unauthorized users present a special challenge for network security design because backtracking to the point when the affected information was correct is very difficult given the number of concurrent users and active tasks. Additionally, unauthorized access, whether malicious or benign, makes it difficult to certify the integrity of a database, particularly if there is a chance that the contents were modified.

Other software problems are a bit more dramatic. A time bomb is a program that executes on a particular date or when a particular condition is met. A Trojan horse is a seemingly harmless program that invites an unsuspecting user to try it. Some time bombs and Trojan horses set off logic bombs, programs that (symbolically) blow up in memory, perhaps trashing a hard disk or selected data.

A rabbit is a program that replicates itself until no memory is left and no other programs can run. For example, one well-known rabbit creates two copies of itself and then starts them. A few microseconds later there are four rabbits running. Then eight, then sixteen, and so on until the rabbit is out of control.

A virus is a program that is capable of replicating itself and spreading between computers. Like its biological namesake, a virus is a parasite that attaches itself to another program to survive and propagate. (The boot routine found on every diskette is a common target.) Viruses typically spread to other computers through infected diskettes or downloaded copies of infected programs.

A virus needs a host. A worm, in contrast, is a program that is capable of spreading under its own power. One common technique is to send out small, virus-like scout programs from a source computer. Once the scout is established on the target computer, it sends a message back to the source computer requesting transmission of the rest of the worm.

In addition to the logic needed to replicate and establish itself on a new computer, a virus or worm can also carry a payload that holds a logic bomb, a time bomb, a rabbit, or some other type of destructive code. Viruses and worms have been known to erase disks, crash programs, and modify data.

71.4.2   Counter measures

There are numerous tools and techniques for countering a security threat.

71.4.2.1   Physical Security

Physical security is concerned with denying physical access to the system, preventing the physical destruction of the system, and keeping the system available. For example, mainframe computers are often located in controlled-access rooms and personal computers are sometimes cabled to work tables or placed in locked cabinets when they are not in use. Access to a secure area can be controlled by issuing identification cards, badges, keys, or personal identification numbers (PINs) to authorized personnel, and surveillance cameras are becoming increasingly common. Modern biometric devices can be used to identify an individual via retinal scan, fingerprint analysis, voiceprint, or signature analysis.

The Internet is a significant source of security intrusions. Consequently, many organizations use firewalls (Figure 71.1) to insulate their internal network from the Internet (or from other public networks). A firewall is a set of hardware, software, and data that sits between the internal network and the

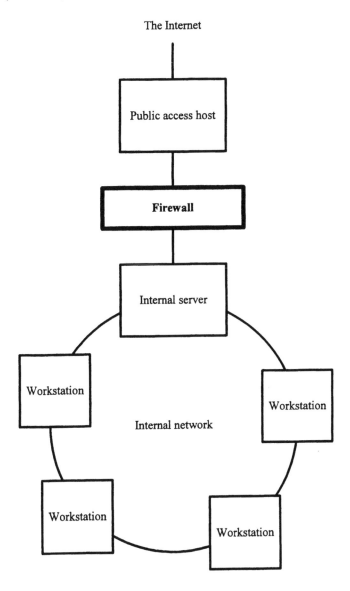

Figure 71.1 A firewall insulates the internal network from the Internet.

Internet, screens all incoming and/or outgoing transactions, and allows only authorized transactions to get through. Often, the firewall is implemented on a physically separate computer, with a public host (the computer that is linked to the Internet) outside the firewall and the internal server inside the firewall. Additionally, critical software can be kernelized, or partitioned to make unauthorized access more difficult.

A disaster plan is essential in the event of such physical threats such as fire, flood, earthquake, or power loss. Environmental controls might be needed to regulate heat, moisture, dust, and so on. Backup copies of all software and data and redundant hardware components are important elements of a recovery plan.

71.4.2.2   *Logical security*

Logical security is implemented by the system as it runs. For example, on most network-based systems, each authorized user is assigned a unique identification code and a password. In some cases, additional passwords are required to access certain critical data or to execute sensitive programs. Often, access privileges are assigned in layers, with most users restricted to read-only access, a smaller group given the authority to change selected data (perhaps subject to independent verification), and only a few people assigned system operator (sysop) status (which implies the authority to access and change anything). Typically, the operating system checks a user profile or an access control matrix to verify a given user's access privileges.

Just having a valid user code and password does not necessarily prove that a user is who he or she claims to be. Authentication, the process of verifying the user's identity, often relies on remembered information (such as a PIN or a mother's maiden name) or variations of the biometric devices described in Section 71.4.2.1.

Callback is another useful authentication tool. After a user logs on from a remote workstation, the host computer verifies the user code and password, breaks the connection (hangs up), looks up the authorized telephone number for that user's workstation, and then redials the workstation.

Viruses can be difficult to detect or remove, so the best defense is prevention. Personnel should not accept "free" software (on diskette, CD-ROM, or via the network) unless the source is known to be clean. Anti-virus software is designed to recognize certain code patterns (called virus signatures) and sound an alarm when a virus is detected. Such software should be used to screen all foreign disks, CD-ROMs, and downloaded software (including software from "legitimate" sources) before they are released for use. On many systems, anti-virus software runs continuously in the background.

Other techniques are intended to provide recovery information or legal documentation when a security breach does occur. A transaction log is a list of all of a system's recent transactions. A comparator is a software routine that compares the contents of a file or a record before and after a transaction and reports any differences. Audit trails and audit procedures can help, too.

71.4.2.3 *Personnel security*

People cause most security problems. Consequently, although they are expensive and sometimes controversial, such personnel controls as pre-employment screens, periodic background checks, and rotating job assignments are necessary. A basic accounting principle suggests that no single individual should ever be allowed to place an order and pay the resulting bill. Similarly, systems are often designed to segregate such related functions as data entry and data verification by assigning the responsibility to different departments.

Standard operating procedures, policies, and/or security manuals are an important part of any security plan, and training is crucial. Employees must understand how to implement the security procedures. Perhaps more important, they must know why a given security procedure is necessary.

For example, given a choice, most people select an easy to remember (and thus easy to guess) password that they never change. Standard procedures can be implemented by the system to force users to change their passwords at regular intervals. The password selection software can be designed to help the user select a better password by rejecting dictionary words, requiring a minimum password length, requiring a combination of letters and digits, and so on. Additionally, explaining why security is necessary and outlining some of the tricks hackers use to guess passwords can help encourage employees to do a better job.

71.4.2.4 *Encryption*

To make sensitive information difficult to read even if a message is intercepted, the data can be encrypted (converted to a secret code), transmitted, and then decrypted at the other end of the line. The U.S. National Bureau of Standards' Data Encryption Standard (DES) is considered very difficult (perhaps impossible) to break. A public/private key system, DES is used for secure government transmissions and for most electronic funds transfers. Another popular public/private key encryption algorithm called PGP (Pretty Good Privacy) was created without government support and is available on the Internet.

As the name implies, a two-key or public/private key system uses two keys. The recipient's public key, which is published or readily available on-line, is used to encrypt the message. Once the message is received, only the secret private key can be used to decrypt it.

71.4.3 *Security design*

Every organization should have established security standards and guidelines that apply to all information systems. Such standards help to ensure that security is not overlooked during the system development process and provide the designer with a security template.

An important element of any set of security standards is the recognition that not all systems, or even all components of the same system, require the same level of security. For example, using retinal scans to control access to a file of press releases is silly, and such inappropriate precautions can destroy the credibility of legitimate security. The standards should identify several levels of security risks and suggest security precautions consistent with the risk.

To an expert, an item is considered secure if the cost of breaking security exceeds the item's value. Consequently, the appropriate level of security for a given system or component is a function of the value of that system or component to those who might be tempted to access or steal it. The objective is to balance cost and risk. During the problem definition and analysis stages of the system development life cycle, the security exposures and risks should be identified. The costs associated with appropriate countermeasures should be a part of the cost/benefit analysis. At the end of the analysis stage, the necessary security measures should be documented in the requirements specification.

Security cannot be added onto a system; it must be designed into the system. A system-wide security plan should be created early in the design process. Once the approach to system security is selected, appropriate security features should be designed into the hardware, the software, the data, and the procedures. Virtually any system component can represent a security risk. Consequently, security is an important consideration in the design of almost every system component.

During the operation and maintenance stage of the system development life cycle, system controls (Chapter 77) play an important role in supporting system security. In addition to the security controls, operational controls, data integrity controls, and auditing controls can provide an early warning of security problems.

71.5   Key terms

Anti-virus software — Software designed to recognize certain code patterns (called virus signatures) and sound an alarm when a virus is detected.

Authentication — The process of verifying the user's identity.

Biometric device — A system component that can identify an individual based on such biological criteria as a retinal scan, a fingerprint analysis, a voice print, or a signature analysis.

Callback — An authentication tool in which the host computer verifies the user code and password, breaks the connection (hangs up), looks up the authorized telephone number for that user's workstation, and then redials the workstation.

Comparator — A software routine that compares the contents of a file or a record before and after a transaction and reports any differences.

Cracker — A person who breaks into computers (generally over a communication line) with malicious intent.

Data encryption standard (DES) — A public/private key encryption system used for secure government transmissions and for most electronic funds transfers.

Dumpster diving — Searching for passwords and other security information by going through paper waste.

Encrypt — To convert to a secret code.

Firewall — A set of hardware, software, and data that sits between the network and the Internet (or other public network), screens all incoming and/or outgoing transactions, and allows only authorized transactions to get through.

Hacker — Originally, an expert programmer with a knack for creating elegant software; today, the term is more commonly applied to someone who illegally breaks into computer systems.

Kernel — A unit of code or a routine that is physically and/or logically isolated from other software and consequently protected.

Logic bomb — A program that (symbolically) blows up in memory.

Logical security — Security features implemented by the system as it runs.

Password — A secret word or string of characters used to uniquely identify a given user.

PGP (pretty good privacy) — A popular public/private key encryption algorithm that was created without government support and is available on the Internet.

Physical security — A set of security features concerned with denying physical access to the system, preventing the physical destruction of the system, and keeping the system available.

Power dialing — Running a program that dials thousands of numbers in sequence and notes only the numbers that return a modem tone.

Public/private key system — An encryption system that uses two keys; the message is encrypted using the published public key and decrypted using the secret private key.

Rabbit — A program that replicates itself until no memory is left and no other programs can run.

Security — Hardware, software, and procedures intended to protect the hardware, software, data, and other system resources from unauthorized, illegal, or unwanted access, use, modification, or theft.

Social engineering — The act of pretending to be an authorized user and attempting to convince an employee or other human source to divulge sensitive information.

Time bomb — A program that executes on a particular date or when a particular condition is met.

Transaction log — A list of a system's transactions.

Trojan horse — A seemingly harmless program that invites an unsuspecting user to try it.

Virus — A program that is capable of replicating itself and spreading between computers by attaching itself to another program.

Worm — A program that is capable of spreading from one computer to another under its own power.

71.6 Software

The following World Wide Web sites are excellent sources of information on various types of security software:

Encryption software	http://www.pgp.com
Firewall software	http://www.sctc.com
Security software products	http://www.datafellows

71.7 References

1. Abrams, M. D. and Podell, H. J., *Tutorial on Computer and Network Security,* IEEE Computer Society Press, Washington, DC, 1987.
2. Cheswick, W. R., Bellovin, S. M., and Cheswick, W., *Firewalls and Internet Security: Repelling the Wiley Hacker,* Addison-Wesley, Reading, MA, 1994.
3. Cross, R. H., III and Yen, D. C., Security in the networking environment, *Journal of Computer Information Systems,* 32(1), 4, 1991.
4. Davis, W. S., *Computers and Information Systems: An Introduction,* West, Minneapolis, MN, 1997.
5. Pipkin, D. L. and Pipkin, D., *Halting the Hacker: A Practical Guide to Computer Security,* Prentice-Hall, Englewood Cliffs, NJ, 1997.
6. White, G. W., Risch, E. A., Pooch, U. W., White, G. B., and Fisch, E. A., *Computer System and Network Security,* CRC Press, Boca Raton, FL, 1995.

chapter seventy-two

General systems design principles

David C. Yen and William S. Davis

Contents

72.1   Purpose

This chapter discusses several general system design topics that are not fully covered in other chapters, including the system life cycle, important factors that affect system design, system attributes, and system design strategies.

72.2   Strengths, weaknesses, and limitations

Where applicable, strengths and weaknesses will be discussed in context.

72.3   Inputs and related ideas

The concepts discussed in this chapter can be applied to most of the methodologies, techniques, and tools in this book. Specifically, this chapter references expert systems (Chapter 7), prototyping (Chapter 31), hardware interface design (Chapter 42), file design (Chapter 44), database design (Chapter 45), report design (Chapter 47), network design (Chapter 52 to 54), program design (Chapter 62), and real-time systems (Chapter 73).

72.4   Concepts

This chapter discusses several general system design topics that are not fully covered in other chapters, including the system life cycle, important factors that affect system design, system attributes, and system design strategies.

72.4.1   The system life cycle

The system life cycle (Figure 72.1) focuses on various stages of system usefulness. In contrast, the system *development* life cycle (Chapter 1) emphases the development stages associated with a new or replacement system.

During the system birth stage, the existing system's problems, errors, and missing features are identified and investigated, and new opportunities suggested by emerging technologies and user requests are examined and evaluated. A systems analysis is then performed, and if the outcome is positive, a new or improved system is developed. This stage encompasses the problem definition, information gathering, and systems analysis stages of the system development life cycle.

During the system development stage, the design, development, conversion, testing, and implementation stages of the system development life cycle are performed.

The growth stage corresponds with the operation and maintenance stages of the system development life cycle. During this stage, usage grows as users become familiar with the new system, and system behavior is adjusted to improve performance and efficiency.

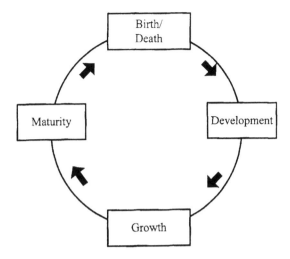

Figure 72.1   The system life cycle.

When the system reaches the maturity stage, its efficiency can no longer be enhanced and performance deficiencies may begin to appear. At this point, such options as upgrading the system, adding new functions, and expanding existing functions must be considered.

During the death stage, the system is investigated to determine if a new system should be developed on a new platform, if a new system should be developed on the existing platform, or if the existing system should be installed on a new platform. Once the platform decision is made, the system birth phase begins for a new system.

72.4.2   Factors that affect system design

Several factors have a broad impact on systems design.

72.4.2.1   The degree of automation

The degree of automation, the extent to which automated or computer-related components are used in a system, affects the design of virtually every system component. At one extreme are manual systems that incorporate few (if any) computer-related components. (Manual systems are not a primary concern of this book). At the other extreme, fully automated systems involve few (if any) human components. Most modern information systems lie between those two extremes.

72.4.2.2   Processing techniques

Batch processing is a transaction-oriented information processing technique in which transactions are accumulated over time and the system's status is updated at the end of a business cycle. Transaction files and master files must be designed, sequential access techniques are often employed, and such reports as transaction listings, master file content listings, exception reports, summary reports, and utility documents (such as paychecks) are typical outputs. Batch processing is still common in banking and financial applications.

On-line processing is the de facto standard in today's business environment. Typically, a transaction is used to update the relevant master file record as soon as it is received. User-friendliness and response time are important considerations, direct (or random) access is usually employed, and query support is at least as important as report generation. Additionally, database and network design are important considerations.

A real-time system responds to events as they occur and (typically) provides immediate feedback to influence or control those events in "real" time. Real-time systems use such tools as probes, sensors, and scanners to get direct input and automatically convert the data to a format that can be processed by the computer. Interrupt handling is particularly important on real-time systems.

72.4.2.3 Management and control

A centralized management philosophy provides integrated top-down control, centralized resource allocation, and good security while minimizing incompatibility problems. The disadvantages include a lack of flexibility, limited local processing power, and localized inefficiency.

Given the pace of information technology development and the growing popularity of microcomputers and networks, a distributed management philosophy is much more common today. Consequently, such topics as networking and hardware interface design have become increasingly important.

72.4.2.4 Information system types

A transaction processing system (TPS) accepts and processes transactions in either batch or on-line mode. The data generated by a transaction processing system are stored in traditional files or databases. Higher-level information systems are constructed on the resulting data platform.

A management information system (MIS) emphasizes report generation. A decision support system (DSS) is more response-oriented and user-controlled. For example, a manager might use a DSS to download a set of data from a central database and then use a fourth-generation language or a spreadsheet program to manipulate the data to generate the information needed to support a decision. A group decision support system (GDSS) adds communication capability and interaction to a DSS. An executive information system (EIS) is designed to support high-level decision-making based (typically) on aggregate and graphic data. An expert system (ES) relies on expertise, a rule base, a control engine, and an expert system shell, and utilizes such development languages as LISP and PROLOG.

72.4.3 System attributes

A system's scope is a sense of its size or magnitude and is often expressed as an estimate of the system's resource implications or cost. Scope is largely a function of the degree of automation, the type of information system, and the complexity of the system.

A system's boundaries define its limits. Boundary-related concerns include interfaces with other systems, the system's ability to be integrated into a super-system, its compatibility with other systems, and any customized routines that might be needed to perform cross-system data conversions.

Common criteria for measuring and evaluating system behavior include throughput, response time, on-line query support, report frequency and timeliness, integration, flexibility, user-friendliness, execution efficiency, fault tolerance, and so on. Note that several of the criteria conflict.

72.4.4 System design strategies

The system design strategies discussed in this section can be applied to virtually any system analysis and design methodology.

72.4.4.1 Top down

Top down-design is goal driven. Basically, the modules (and/or subsystems) at the top of the hierarchy (usually, the broad, control-oriented modules) are designed first and modules at the bottom of the hierarchy (the detailed, computational modules) are designed last. Typically, the designer starts by building a hierarchical structure that defines the links between all the subsystems, modules, subroutines, and/or functions in the proposed system. All the elements at one hierarchical level are then developed before work progresses to the next lower level.

72.4.4.2 Bottom up

Bottom-up design is data driven. Work begins at the lowest level, typically with the detailed, computational modules. When all the modules at one level are completed, work progresses to the next higher level. Bottom-up development is an excellent choice for a project with massive volumes of data.

72.4.4.3 Middle out

As the term suggests, the middle-out approach starts from the middle of the hierarchy. For example, the design of a student database might start with a student file. Subsequently, lower-level files (to hold data about courses, grades, finances, etc.) and higher-level files (to hold data about student organizations, the students enrolled in a given course, athletic teams, etc.) are designed.

72.4.4.4   Evolutionary

The evolutionary (or stepwise refinement) approach is similar to the prototyping methodology described in Chapter 31. The idea is to start with a
small program or subsystem and continuously refine it by adding new functions and/or by modifying features.

72.4.4.5   Incremental

The incremental or sequential increment approach starts with any module,
subroutine, or subsystem. A second module is then developed and those
two modules are integrated before work begins on the third module. This
process continues until all the modules are developed.

72.5.   Key terms

Analysis — To attack a problem by breaking it into subproblems.

Batch processing — A processing technique in which transactions are
    accumulated over time and the system's status is updated at the end
    of a business cycle.

Birth — The system life cycle stage during which the existing system's
    problems, errors, and missing features are identified and investi-
    gated, and new opportunities suggested by emerging technologies
    and user requests are examined and evaluated.

Bottom-up design — A data-driven design strategy in which work
    begins at the lowest level, typically with the detailed, computational
    modules; when all the modules at one level are completed, work pro-
    gresses to the next higher level.

Boundary — An entity that serves to delimit or separate a system from
    its environment.

Centralized management — A management philosophy based on inte-
    grated top-down control.

Data driven — A tool or technique that starts with the data and derives
    the necessary processes.

Death — The system life cycle stage during which the decision is made
    to replace the system.

Decision support system (DSS) — An information system that adds
    response orientation and user control to a management information
    system.

Degree of automation — The extent to which automated or computer-
    related components are used in a system.

Development — The system life cycle stage during which the system is
    designed, developed, tested, and implemented.

Distributed management — A management philosophy that distributes
    responsibility and authority from the top to the bottom levels of the
    organization.

Evolutionary design (stepwise refinement) — A design strategy that starts with a small program or subsystem and continuously refines it by adding new functions and/or modifying features.

Executive information system (EIS) — An information system designed to support high-level decision making based (typically) on aggregate and graphic data.

Expert system (knowledge-based system) — A computer program that emulates the thought process of a human expert.

Goal driven — A method or technique that works through a process until a predefined goal is accomplished.

Group decision support system (GDSS) — An information system that adds communication capability and interaction to a decision-support system.

Growth — The system life cycle stage during which usage grows as users become familiar with the new system, and system behavior is adjusted to improve performance and efficiency.

Incremental design — A design strategy that starts with any module, subroutine, or subsystem; a second module is then developed and those two modules are integrated before work begins on the third module. This process continues until all the modules are developed.

Information system — A set of hardware, software, data, human, and procedural components intended to provide the right data and information to the right person at the right time.

Management information system (MIS) — An information system that emphasizes report generation and combines such attributes as centralized data management, integrated applications, distributed access, and interactive processing to support operational-level decision making.

Maturity — The system life cycle stage during which the system's efficiency can no longer be enhanced and performance deficiencies begin to appear.

Methodology — A body of practices, procedures, and rules used by those who work in a discipline or engage in an inquiry; often implemented as a set of well-defined steps or phases, each of which ends with a clear, measurable set of exit criteria.

Middle out — A design strategy that starts from the middle of the hierarchy.

On-line processing — A processing technique in which a transaction is used to update the relevant master file record as soon as it is received.

Real-time system — A system that responds to events as they occur and provides immediate feedback to influence or control those events in "real" time.

Response time — The elapsed time between a request for service and the delivery of that service.

Scope — A sense of a problem's (or a system's) magnitude; often, a preliminary estimate of the problem's resource implications or cost.

System — A set of interrelated components that function together in a meaningful way.

System development life cycle (SDLC) — A set of steps for solving information system problems; the basis for most systems analysis and design methodologies.

System life cycle — A model that stresses the stages of system usefulness; the stages are birth, development, growth, maturity, and death.

Throughput — A measure of the amount of work going through a computer or a system; often expressed as a percent utilization.

Top-down design — A goal-driven design strategy in which the modules (and/or subsystems) at the top of the hierarchy (usually, the broad, control-oriented modules) are designed first and modules at the bottom of the hierarchy (the detailed, computational modules) are designed last.

Transaction processing system (TPS) — An information system that accepts and processes transactions in either batch or on-line mode.

72.6   Software

Not applicable.

72.7   References

1. Davis, G. B. and Olson M. H., *Management Information Systems: Conceptual Foundations, Structure, and Development,* 2nd ed., McGraw-Hill, New York, 1985.
2. Laudon, K. C. and Laudon, J. P., *Managing Information Systems: A Contemporary Perspective,* 2nd ed., Macmillan, New York, 1991.
3. Rockart, J. F., *Chief executives define their own data needs,* Harv. Bus. Rev., XX, XX, 1979.
4. Rockart, J. F. and Treacy, M. E., *The CEO goes on line,* Harv. Bus. Rev., XX, XX, 1982.
5. Shank, M. E., Boynton, A. C., and Zmud, R. W., *Critical success factor analysis as a methodology for MIS planning,* MIS Q., XX, XX, 1985.
6. Yourdon, E, *Managing the System Life Cycle,* 2nd edition, Prentice-Hall, Englewood Cliffs, NJ, 1988.

chapter seventy-three

Real-time system design

David C. Yen and William S. Davis

Contents

73.1   Purpose

This chapter briefly overviews real-time information processing systems. The technical details associated with real-time systems are beyond the scope

0-8493-7001-9/99/$0.00+$.50
©1999 by CRC Press LLC

of this book. This material is intended as background for systems analysts or information system consultants who must communicate with real-time specialists and/or vendors.

73.2   Strengths, weaknesses, and limitations

A real-time system should be considered when response time requirements are extremely tight. Real-time systems tend to be more expensive to develop and to operate than are online, interactive, and batch systems.

73.3   Inputs and related ideas

Developing a real-time system is much like developing any system. Many of the tools discussed in Parts II, IV, V, and VI are used. State transition diagrams (Chapter 30) are valuable for planning and documenting changes in state. Stacks and queues are explained in Chapter 43. Chapter 78 provides some insight on the process of evaluating computer hardware and peripherals. Chapter 79 discusses queuing theory and bottleneck analysis.

73.4   Concepts

A real-time system responds to events as they occur and (typically) provides feedback to influence or control those events. For example, the system that guides a smart bomb to its target is a real-time system. A production control system that monitors and controls a modern steel mill is another example.

The technical details associated with real-time systems are beyond the scope of this book. The material in this chapter is intended as background for systems analysts or information system consultants who must communicate with real-time specialists and/or vendors. Note that numerous references are listed at the end of this chapter.

73.4.1   Events and states

Most real-time system actions and behaviors are performed in response to asynchronous (hence unpredictable) external events. A given external event triggers a change in state (e.g., a change in value, status, or behavior) and the real-time system reacts by taking a pre-specified action or actions. Consequently, real-time system design is sometimes called event-driven design.

73.4.2   Design considerations

In addition to the problems associated with developing a traditional information system, the analyst or designer of a real-time system faces significant constraints and must consider numerous interrelated hardware, software, and data issues.

73.4.2.1 Constraints

Real-time systems typically operate under very tight time constraints. For example, on a production control system, certain crucial events may require response times of a fraction of a second or the transfer of a certain amount of data between two components in a brief period of time. Additionally, high reliability (as measured by mean time between failures) is often essential. For example, the failure of a production control system can literally put a company out of business.

Concurrency, a measure of the number of tasks the system can process concurrently, is another important criterion. Asynchronous events can (by definition) occur at any time and are not synchronized with other events. Consequently, two or more events can occur concurrently or even simultaneously, and the response time constraint might require a response to both events within a very brief time.

73.4.2.2 Hardware

To achieve rapid response time, most real-time systems are dedicated to a specific realtime application (or set of related applications) and designed to be under-loaded. The designer might analyze all possible events, define worst case scenarios (for example, the maximum possible number of concurrent events), determine the processor and memory configuration needed to provide peak load computing power, and then specify double (or triple, or more) than that level of power. Excess computing power means relatively low percentage utilization, but low utilization means that events rarely wait for the system.

Reliability is usually achieved through redundancy. Fault tolerant computers incorporate redundant circuits and components, and in some cases the entire system (the processor, memory, the database, etc.) is replicated. In the event of a system or component failure, special hardware and software automatically switches control to the backup system or component. Uninterruptable power supplies also contribute to reliability.

To achieve concurrency, a computer must support multi-tasking, the ability to concurrently process several tasks. (A task is a single program or routine in memory and available to be executed.) On many systems, multitasking is implemented by the operating system (Section 73.4.2.3).

A computer with a single processor can execute only one instruction at a time. Such computers implement multi-tasking by quickly switching the processor's attention from one task to another and back again. If the computer is equipped with multiple processors, however, several instructions (one per processor) can be executed simultaneously. The simultaneous execution of two or more instructions on a multiple processor system is called multi-processing or parallel processing.

73.4.2.3   The operating system

Multi-tasking would be impossible without the operating system. A serial batch (or single-stream) operating system supports one program or routine at a time. A multi-programming operating system manages the concurrent execution of multiple tasks on a single processor by switching the processor's attention from task to task. A time-shared operating system manages concurrent execution by assigning the processor to the active task for a brief time slice before moving on to the next task. Multi-processing systems manage the allocation of multiple concurrent or simultaneous tasks to multiple processors.

The operating system routine that manages the processor's time is called the dispatcher. The dispatcher is responsible for managing the tasks that are already in memory. The operating system's queuing and scheduling routines manage pending tasks until the memory and processor resources needed to execute them are available.

Multi-tasking implies multiple tasks in memory and executing. (Generally, only key portions of active programs are physically loaded into memory.) Multiple tasks sharing memory implies, in turn, a need for memory management and memory protection. Common memory management techniques include virtual memory, continuous memory allocation, dynamic memory management, fixed partition memory management, and roll-in/roll-out schemes. The purpose of resource allocation is to prevent (or resolve) the deadlocks that can occur when two concurrent tasks request the same resource (e.g., a peripheral or a record) at the same time.

73.4.2.4   Interrupt handling

On many real-time systems, the external event that triggers a change in state generates an interrupt. An interrupt is an electronic signal that causes the computer to stop what it is doing and activate one of the operating system's interrupt handling routines. The operating system responds to the interrupt signal by activating the routine associated with the particular change in state.

When planning an event-driven real-time system, the designer must specify the status and nature of each interrupt, including the associated state, the address (or name) of the task to be given control, related warnings or error messages, appropriate corrective actions, and so on. After the interrupt is processed, the system must be restored to its original (or pre-interrupt) state. Procedures must also be developed to deal with deviations and/or unexpected actions or behaviors and to log the time, date, precipitating event, and so on for all interrupts. Because interrupts are asynchronous events, the system must also incorporate procedures to deal with concurrent and simultaneous interrupts.

73.4.2.5   *Task synchronization and task sequencing*

Given the asynchronous nature of real-time events and the need for rapid response, task synchronization and task sequencing are important issues. On many systems, when an interrupt occurs the information needed to activate the associated task is placed on a stack or a queue (Chapter 43). If the various tasks (or events) carry significantly different priorities, however, it may be necessary to implement a prioritization scheme (perhaps in the dispatcher) to ensure that the interrupts are processed in the appropriate order. Additionally, some tasks might be linked; for example, it might be necessary to interrupt task A to perform task B because A depends on B.

73.4.2.6   *Event monitoring*

Generally, a log is maintained listing (for each real-time event) the preceding event(s), the following event(s), any dependency relationships between the events, any associations among the events (e.g., merging, diverging, converging), any special requirements (e.g., recursive loops, repetitive loops), and any data required or generated by the event. One use for the data generated by event monitoring is establishing the precise state of the system in the event of system failure. State transition diagrams (Chapter 30) are often used to plan and/or document event monitoring.

73.4.2.7   *Real-time languages*

Such general-purpose third generation languages as C and Pascal have been used to develop real-time systems. Real-time languages (such as Modula-2 and ADA) are preferred, however, because they incorporate embedded real-time features to concurrently handle asynchronous events, an automatic debugger, and such real-time oriented functions as on-line testing and on-line execution simulation.

73.4.2.8   *Real-time databases*

Such features as concurrency control, locking, and time stamps are extremely important in real-time system database design. Concurrency control synchronizes the database and ensures that all copies of a given file contain the same version of the available information. Locking prevents a user from updating or modifying a record while another user is accessing that record. Time stamps allow the system to monitor the access or processing status of a record.

73.4.3   *Developing a real-time system*

Developing a real-time system is much like developing any system, and many of the tools described in Parts II, IV, V, and VI are used. This section outlines some parameters that are unique to real-time systems.

Special attention must be paid to time constraints, events, and other performance factors. Also, the analyst must carefully examine the relationships between the system and its input and output operations, clearly identifying the event that triggers each data movement or change in state.

Performance issues must be investigated thoroughly, too. Workload performance analysis focuses on such criteria as throughput, response time, turnaround time, the frequency and size of transactions, and regular and peak time workloads. System performance analysis focuses on such criteria as processing speed in MIPS (millions of instruction per second) or MFLOPS (millions of floating point operations per second), information access time, data transfer rate, instruction execution time, and so on. Other key performance criteria include mean time between failures (MTBF), the nature and frequency of interrupts, the signals and requirements associated with triggering each event, and so on.

A real-time task can be viewed as a program or routine that is executed in response to an event. System control usually depends on events, the inputs to a particular task, and the current state of the system. Consequently, the designer must decide how to synchronize the tasks and must determine the priority of each task. Given the task synchronization rules and priorities, the relevant triggers, inputs, and states for each task are studied. Finally, a table listing each task, its trigger(s), its related inputs, its preceding and following states, and other control criteria is developed as a logical map for system design. Often, one or more state transition diagrams (Chapter 30) are prepared during this stage.

Monitors are programs or hardware devices that detect and report a real-time system's processing and/or input/output activities. Monitors are used to control, adjust, and/or correct unexpected behaviors in a real-time system. The process of collecting the information needed to define the monitors is called demand analysis. Program profilers are used to track the resources requested and services utilized by a particular program as it executes and, thus, supports utilization analysis. Procedures for incorporating monitors and program profilers into the system must be developed during real-time system design.

73.5   Key terms

Association — A link between two or more events defined by precedence requirements and similar conditions.

Asynchronous event — An event that can occur at any time and is not synchronized with other events.

Concurrency — A measure of the number of tasks a system can process concurrently.

Concurrency control — A database feature that synchronizes the database and ensures that all copies of a given file contain the same version of the available information.

Concurrent — Within the same time period.

Convergence — A process in which several preceding events are combined to form one following event; the opposite of divergence.

Deadlock — A situation that occurs when two tasks each control a resource needed by the other and neither task is willing to relinquish control.

Dependency — A relationship in which the implementation of the following event(s) depends on the completion of the preceding event(s).

Dispatcher — The operating system routine that manages the processor's time.

Divergence — A process in which one preceding event is separated into several following events.

Event — An occurrence.

Event-driven — A system that responds to events.

Fault tolerant computer — A computer that incorporates redundant circuits and components to improve reliability.

Interrupt — An electronic signal that causes the computer to stop what it is doing and activate one of the operating system's interrupt handling routines; generally, the information needed to restore the system to its pre-interrupt state is captured by hardware as part of the interrupt process.

Locking — A technique that prevents a user from updating or modifying a record while another user is accessing that record.

Merge — See convergence.

Monitor — A program or hardware device that detects and reports a real-time system's processing and/or input/output activities.

Multi-processing (parallel processing) — The simultaneous execution of two or more instructions on a multiple processor system.

Multi-programming — Concurrently executing multiple tasks on a single processor by switching the processor's attention from task to task.

Multi-tasking — Concurrently or simultaneously processing several tasks on a single computer.

Program profiler — A routine or device that tracks the resources requested and services utilized by a particular program as it executes.

Real-time system — An information system that responds to events as they occur and (typically) provides feedback to influence or control those events.

Redundancy — The duplication of components to provide backup in case of failure.

Reliability — A measure of the likelihood that a system or a component will function properly over time; often measured by the mean time between failures.

Response time — The elapsed time between a request for service and the delivery of that service.

Simultaneous — At the same instant.

State — A condition; often, the complete set of attribute values and settings that describes the precise condition of a computer system at a specific instant in time.

System performance analysis — A type of analysis that focuses on such criteria as processing speed, information access time, data transfer rate, instruction execution time, and so on.

Task — A single program or routine in memory and available to be executed.

Time-sharing — Concurrently executing multiple tasks by assigning the processor to a given task for a brief time slice before moving on to the next task.

Workload performance analysis — A type of analysis that focuses on such criteria as throughput, response time, turnaround time, the frequency and size of transactions, and regular and peak time workloads.

73.6   Software

Real-time programming languages include Modula-2 and ADA.

73.7   References

1. Aho, A. V., Sethi, R., and Ullman, J. D., *Compilers: Principles, Techniques and Tools*, Addison-Wesley, Reading, MA, 1986.
2. Booch, G., *Software Engineering with ADA*, Benjamin/Cummings, Menlo Park, CA, 1983.
3. Burch, J. G., *Systems Analysis, Design, and Implementation*, Boyd & Fraser, Danvers, MA, 1992.
4. Burd, S. D., *Systems Architecture: Hardware and Software in Business Information Systems*, Boyd & Fraser, Danvers, MA, 1994.
5. Davis, W. S., *Operating Systems: A Systematic View*, 4th ed., Benjamin/Cummings, Redwood City, CA, 1992.
6. Dewitz, S. D., *Systems Analysis and Design and the Transition to Objects*, McGraw-Hill, New York, 1996.
7. Foster, C. C., *Real-Time Programming—Neglected Topics*, Addison-Wesley, Reading, MA, 1981.
8. Gomaa, H., Software development of real-time systems, *CACM*, 27(9), 938, 1984.
9. Hinden, H. J. and Rauch-Hinden, W.B., 1984. Real-time systems, *Electron. Design*, XX, 288, 1983.
10. Keyes, J., *Software Engineering Productivity Handbook*, McGraw-Hill, New York, 1993.
11. Mellichamp, D. A., *Real-Time Computing*, Van Nostrand Reinhold, New York, 1983.
12. Norman, R. J., *Object-Oriented Systems Analysis and Design*, Prentice-Hall, Upper Saddle River, NJ, 1996.
13. Pressman, R. S., *Software Engineering: A Practitioner's Approach*, 2nd ed., McGraw-Hill, New York, 1987.
14. Savitsky, S., *Real-Time Multiprocessor Systems*, Van Nostrand Reinhold, New York, 1985.
15. Steusloff, H. U., Advanced real-time languages for distributed industrial process control, *Computer*, 17(2), 37, 1984.

part seven

Testing and implementation

chapter seventy-four

The test plan

David C. Yen and William S. Davis

Contents

0-8493-7001-9/99/$0.00+$.50
©1999 by CRC Press LLC

74.1   Purpose

The ultimate objective of testing is to ensure that the system performs as designed and, by extension, to ensure that it meets the user's needs. More specifically, testing is the process of exercising the system and its components to locate, investigate, and correct errors and bugs.

74.2   Strengths, weaknesses, and limitations

The strengths and weaknesses of specific techniques will be discussed in context.

74.3   Inputs and related ideas

Chapter 75 discusses test data. Virtually every component described in Part VI must be tested. General system design principles are discussed in Chapter 72. Inspections (Chapter 23) support a form of testing that can be performed on logical components. The joint application design technique (Chapter 14) can be used to develop test procedures. Gantt charts (Chapter 20) and project networks (Chapter 21) can be used to plan, document, and manage a test schedule. The requirements specification (Chapter 35) is an important source of functional and performance requirements, and serves as a base for establishing a test plan. Version controls (Chapter 80) are used to ensure that the appropriate version of the code is tested.

74.4   Concepts

The ultimate objective of testing is to ensure that the system performs as designed and, by extension, to ensure that it meets the user's needs. Consequently, user involvement is crucial in the testing process.

More specifically, testing is the process of exercising the system and its components to locate, investigate, and correct errors and bugs. The goals of testing include ensuring that all system components work properly, finding errors and identifying their causes, revising or modifying the software and other components to eliminate errors, tracking the status of errors, and adjusting system performance and/or operating procedures as appropriate.

74.4.1   The test plan

Effective testing does not just happen; it must be carefully planned. A complete test plan incorporates testing strategies, testing procedures, test data, and a testing schedule. Test data is covered in Chapter 75. The other three elements of a test plan are discussed in this chapter.

Tests are performed on the system's physical components. Consequently, although the logical models and design documentation prepared during the analysis and design stages of the system development life cycle can (and should) be evaluated and inspected, testing does not begin until the implementation stage begins. However, the test plan should be developed in parallel with the design stage of the system development life cycle so it is ready when implementation begins. The requirements specification (Chapter 35) is an important source of functional and performance requirements, and serves as a base for establishing a test plan.

Finally, note that the test plan is constrained by resources (the computing platform, hardware, software, and peripherals), personnel, and time (in the form of the project schedule). The test plan designer's objective is to test the system as thoroughly and as effectively as possible within the constraints.

74.4.2 Testing strategies

Testing can be performed top down, bottom up, and/or middle out. Top-down testing starts at the top (with the broad, control modules) and works through the module hierarchy level by level until the bottom level (the detailed computational modules) is reached. Bottom-up testing starts at the bottom and works up through the hierarchy to the top. The middle-out (or hybrid) approach starts in the middle of the hierarchy and moves bi-directionally toward both the top and the bottom.

With white-box testing, the objective is to directly verify and review the logical structure, flow, and/or sequence of a proposed system by focusing on such internal components as the code. White-box testing is employed when the system is developed internally and the program structure, sequence, and coding are completely understood.

Black-box testing, in contrast, ignores the internal contents of the module, program, subsystem, or system and considers only the inputs and the outputs. Black-box testing is ideal for functional testing or for testing external operations. Often, sophisticated test cases and associated test data sets are designed to support black-box testing.

Gray-box testing is a hybrid approach for testing both the functions and the contents of major programs and/or modules that are likely to be internally maintained, modified, or customized later.

The correct testing strategy is a function of the specific test to be performed. A given test plan might incorporate several different strategies.

74.4.3 Test procedures

Test procedures are needed to define the process for creating the test data, determine the testing sequence, specify test logistics, and document the test results. There is no standard format or style for developing test procedures, although many organizations have implemented broad testing standards and rely on a joint application design (JAD) session to define the specific procedures for a given project.

The individual tests, the test criteria, and the associated test data must be defined. The testing environment and necessary resources must be specified. The people who will conduct each test and the people who will evaluate the results must be identified. (They should be different.) The test scope and test boundaries must be clearly defined, and the tests should overlap to make sure every aspect of the systems is covered. The criteria for passing each test and person or persons responsible for the pass/fail decision must be specified.

Library control procedures are used to create and maintain a test data library and the relevant testing software. Change control procedures are used to record, assess, control, and track all requests for change both during and after the testing process. Typically, when a module or program is changed, the original version, the revised version, and information about the change (the initial proposal, justifications for the change, approvals, the anticipated impact, etc.) are maintained by the change control procedures. Reporting control procedures are used to document all test results. Version controls (Chapter 80) are used to ensure that the appropriate version of the code is tested and passed on to subsequent steps.

74.4.4   Testing levels

Testing occurs throughout the implementation process. Figure 74.1 shows how the various levels of testing build on each other.

74.4.4.1   Scaffolding

Scaffolding is software written specifically to test the system. Scaffolding is generally used to simulate the system environment or to initiate a calling sequence to trigger the execution of selected modules in the proper order.

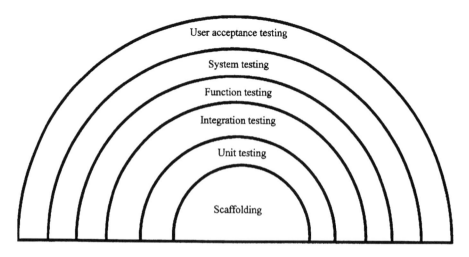

Figure 74.1   Testing levels.

It is not part of the final system. It exists for a limited period of time, and its only purpose is to support testing. Scaffolding software typically contains test drivers (to call modules in the proper order) and stubs (simplified versions of selected modules). Using stubs simplifies system behavior and makes it easier to detect certain types of errors.

74.4.4.2   Unit testing
As the name implies, unit testing (or module testing) is conducted on a single program, a single module, or a single component. The idea is to use test data to check the behavior of a unit without regard for its interfaces or relationships with other units. Unit testing is typically performed at the developer's site by the responsible programmers.

74.4.4.3   Integration testing
Integration testing focuses on two or more individual modules that are grouped to form a partial system. Integration testing uses test data to evaluate the individual units, their interfaces with each other, and their combined behavior. Like unit testing, integration testing is usually performed at the developer's site by the responsible programmers and/or systems analysts.

   Integration testing can be performed top down, bottom up, or middle out. A sequence of related tests can be conducted using a phased, incremental, or evolutionary approach (Chapter 72). Black-box, white-box, and gray-box testing are all possible. Note, however, that no matter which strategy is chosen, integration testing must be performed every time the relevant partial system is changed in any way.

74.4.4.4   Function testing
Function testing is performed on one or more partial systems that have already been integration tested. The objective is to use test data and simulated data (including range constraints, format constraints, etc.) to test a user-defined function. Typically, the function tests are performed at the developer's site by the programmers and/or the systems analysts.

74.4.4.5   System testing
The system test is conducted on the entire system using both test data and real, user supplied data. Generally, the system test is performed at the developer's site using the developer's own hardware and software.

74.4.4.6   User acceptance testing
User acceptance testing is a complete system test performed at the user's site, on the user's hardware/software platform, under the user's control, using real data provided by the user.

   An alpha test is a controlled environment test. Often, the designers demonstrate key system functions, perhaps selected by the users, and the users manipulate the system under developer guidance. Typically, the systems requirements, the general design philosophy, and selected portions of the code and documentation are reviewed.

The purpose of a beta test is to allow real users who are unfamiliar with the technical details to "try out" a preliminary, pre-release beta version of the system. The job of the beta testers is to exercise the system, identify its strengths and weaknesses, document any errors they find, and report their impressions back to the technical experts. Note that a beta test is conducted by (selected) real users who use real hardware, real software, and real (unplanned) data to work on real and imagined problems with any frequency and in any sequence. Often, an automated testing tool or procedure is employed to ensure that all the system's functions and operations are tested and none are ignored.

Gamma testing checks such additional details as the system's compatibility with the old system and the system's performance under peak demand, utilizing such tools as data transform analysis, operator sequence analysis, symbolic manipulation analysis, and so on. Data transform analysis is used to test if the data generated from one platform can be transformed without difficulty as an input to another platform. Operator sequence analysis is used to check if the system can still be operated correctly and reliably when the input sequence of different tasks or jobs is changed. Symbolic manipulation analysis is used to test the ability of the system to operate given different symbolic inputs, such as audio and/or video signals.

74.4.4.7 Regression testing

Regression testing complements unit, integration, function, or system testing and is usually performed by technical personnel. The idea is to use old test cases and test data on an updated or modified version of a system to ensure that the changes have not affected the system's ability to perform its fundamental tasks. Usually, the old system is tested to establish a benchmark, the changes are made, the new system is tested and a new set of benchmark values generated, and the new and old benchmark values are compared.

74.4.4.8 Systems performance testing

Systems performance testing focuses on system behavior. Peak load testing is intended to ensure that the system can handle the stress of a peak load demand. Recovery testing simulates emergency situations such as power failures, equipment malfunctions, database failures, and so on.

74.4.4.9 Audit testing

The purpose of an audit test is to verify that the system is free of errors. The audit is usually conducted by an organization's quality assurance group or by qualified outsiders. The idea is to have objective technical experts with no personal ties to the system conduct an in-depth, white-box evaluation of the system and its components.

74.4.4.10 Testing the hardware and the procedures

Many large organizations employ specialists to test, install, and maintain hardware. A small firm might hire a consultant or rely on the analyst for hardware testing. Some organizations rely on the equipment manufacturer's representatives.

Basic electronic functions are normally tested first. Many hardware components come with their own diagnostic routines, which should be run. Modern electronic equipment is highly reliable; if a component survives the first several hours of operation, it usually continues to work until the end of its useful life. However, start-up failures are common, so many hardware test plans include a burn-in period; for example, a disk drive might be tested by repetitively reading and writing a set of test data for several hours. Stress tests are also a good idea; for example, the system might be run at or near its environmental (temperature and humidity) limits.

Manual procedures, auditing procedures, and security procedures are easily overlooked when the test plan is created. Initially, a draft procedure might be tested in a controlled environment, with technical personnel reading the instructions and doing *exactly* what they say. (The results can be humorous.) Next come controlled user tests, with selected users walking through the procedures and suggesting improvements. Finally come live tests with real users and real data.

74.4.5 The test schedule

The test schedule defines the order in which key tests are performed. Gantt charts (Chapter 20) and project networks (Chapter 21) are useful planning and project management tools. Figure 74.2 summarizes the dependency relationships between the various types of tests, a key factor in planning a test schedule. For example, all unit testing must be completed before the integration test is performed for a given subsystem, and all the subsystems that contribute to performing a given function must be tested before the function is tested.

Finally, remember that testing is part of the system development life cycle. Consequently, the test schedule is a subset of the system development schedule.

74.5 Key terms

Alpha test — A controlled environment test in which the designers demonstrate key system functions, perhaps selected by the users, and the users manipulate the system under developer guidance.

Audit test — An objective, in depth white-box evaluation of the system and its components to verify that the system is free of errors.

Beta test — A test conducted by (selected) real users who use real hardware, real software, and real (unplanned) data to work on real and imagined problems with any frequency and in any sequence.

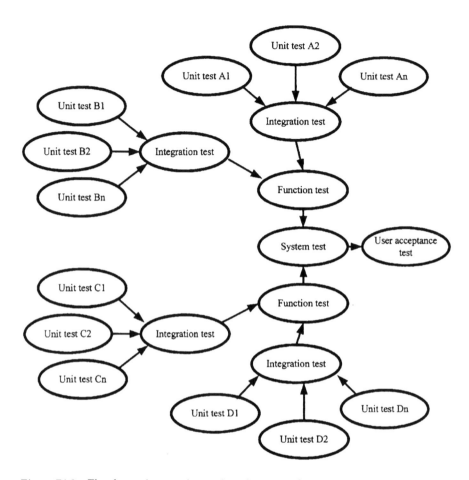

Figure 74.2   The dependency relationships between the various types of tests.

Black-box testing — A testing strategy that ignores the internal contents of the module, program, subsystem, or system and considers only the inputs and the outputs.

Bottom-up testing — A testing strategy that starts at the bottom and works up through the hierarchy to the top.

Burn-in period — An initial period during which a hardware component is run continuously in an attempt to find and eliminate start-up errors.

Change control procedures — A set of procedures for recording, assessing, controlling, and tracking all requests for change both during and after the testing process.

Function test — A test performed on one or more partial systems that have already been integration tested; the objective is to use test data and simulated data to test a user-defined function.

Gamma test — A test of such details as the system's compatibility with the old system and the system's performance under peak demand.

Gray-box testing — A hybrid of white-box and black-box testing in which both the functions and the contents of major programs and/or modules that are likely to be internally maintained, modified, or customized later are tested.

Integration test — A test conducted on an aggregate of two or more components or modules that focuses on the individual units, their interfaces with each other, and their combined behavior.

Library control procedures — A set of procedures for creating and maintaining a test data library and the relevant testing software.

Middle-out testing (hybrid testing) — A testing strategy that starts in the middle of the hierarchy and moves bi-directionally toward both the top and the bottom.

Peak load test — A test designed to ensure that the system can handle the stress of a peak load demand.

Recovery test — A test that simulates emergency situations such as power failures, equipment malfunctions, database failures, and so on.

Regression test — A form of test in which old test cases and test data are applied to a modified version of a system to ensure that the changes have not affected the system's ability to perform its fundamental tasks.

Reporting control procedures — A set of procedures for documenting all test results.

Scaffolding — Software written specifically to support testing.

Stress test — A test conducted under extreme conditions.

System performance test — A test that focuses on system behavior.

System test — A test conducted on the entire system that uses both test data and real, user supplied data.

Test plan — A plan for conducting the necessary tests that incorporates testing strategies, test procedures, test data, and a test schedule.

Testing — A front-end process intended to exercise the system and its components to locate, investigate, and correct errors and bugs.

Top-down testing — A testing strategy that starts at the top (with the broad, control modules) and works through the module hierarchy level by level until the bottom level (the detailed computational modules) is reached.

Unit test (module test) — A test conducted on a single program or a single module.

White-box testing — A testing strategy in which the tester directly verifies and reviews the logical structure, flow, and/or sequence of a proposed system.

74.6   *Software*

Visual Test (Relational Software), ATF (Softbridge), FERRET (Azor Inc.), and QARun (Compuware) support GUI-related testing. Chariot (Ganymede Software), ITE and SDTF (Applied Computer Technology), and FastBench

Agent Tester (NETMANSYS) are communication-related software tools. AdaTEST (IPL), C-Cover (Bullseye Testing Technology), and Code Wizard (Parasoft) are used with C and C++. Web testing tools include Webexam and Webload (Radview Software), WebART (OCLC), and TestWorks/Web (Software Research). Performance-related software tools include Silkperformer (Segue), QAStress (Compuware), Loadrunner and Astra Sitetest (Mercury Interactive Corporation), and Benchmark Factory (Client/Server Solutions Inc.).

74.7   References

1. Beizer, B., *Software Testing and Quality Assurance*, Van Nostrand Reinhold, New York, 1984.

2. Beizer, B., *Software Testing Techniques*, Van Nostrand Reinhold, New York, 1983.

3. Burch, J. G., *Systems Analysis, Design, and Implementation*, Boyd & Fraser, Boston, MA, 1992.

4. Davis, W. S., *Business Systems Analysis and Design*, Wadsworth, Belmont, CA, 1994.

5. Dewitz, S. D., *Systems Analysis and Design and the Transition to Objects*, McGraw-Hill, New York, 1996.

6. Howden, W. E., *Functional Program Testing & Analysis*, McGraw-Hill, New York, 1987.

7. Lamb, D. A., *Software Engineering: Planning for Change*, Prentice-Hall, Englewood Cliffs, NJ, 1988.

8. Norman, R. J., *Object-Oriented Systems Analysis and Design*, Prentice-Hall, Upper Saddle River, NJ, 1996.

9. Power, M. J., Cheney, P. H., and Crow, G., *Structured Systems Development: Analysis, Design, Implementation*, 2nd ed., Boyd & Fraser, Boston, MA, 1990.

10. Pressman, R. S., *Software Engineering: A Practitioner's Approach*, 2nd ed., McGraw-Hill, New York, 1987.

chapter seventy-five

Test data

David C. Yen and William S. Davis

Contents

0-8493-7001-9/99/$0.00+$.50
©1999 by CRC Press LLC

75.1   Purpose

The ultimate objective of testing is to ensure that the system performs as designed and, by extension, to ensure that it meets the user's needs. Test data are developed to support the testing process, locate bugs, and facilitate debugging. This chapter discusses the link between the requirements specification and testing, the types of bugs a system is likely to contain, common testing techniques, some approaches to debugging, and several techniques for generating test data.

75.2   Strengths, weaknesses, and limitations

Where appropriate, the strengths and weaknesses of various techniques will be discussed in context.

75.3   Inputs and related ideas

Chapter 74 discusses the test plan. The requirements specification (Chapter 35) is an important source of functional and performance requirements, and serves as a base for generating test data. Certain test data generation techniques require an understanding of program structure (Chapter 62). State testing applies primarily to real-time systems (Chapter 73). System controls are discussed in Chapter 77.

75.4   Concepts

The ultimate objective of testing is to ensure that the system performs as designed and, by extension, to ensure that it meets the user's needs. Test data are developed to support the testing process, locate bugs, and facilitate debugging. Consequently, the test data designer must understand the system requirements, the types of bugs that are likely to occur, the testing techniques that are likely to be used, and the debugging process.

75.4.1   The system requirements

The system requirements are typically documented in the requirements specification (Chapter 35). Test data must be designed to ensure that each and every system requirement is tested. Additionally, the requirements specify details (such as data types, data ranges, data volumes, data structures, etc.) that can be used to define test data values.

75.4.2   Bugs

Function-related errors are caused by such things as incorrect linkages, incorrect control transfers between a calling and called routine, the inclusion of one or more unnecessary or incorrect functions, and the omission of one or more necessary functions. Such errors are common on menu-based and window-based systems that require frequent transfers of control.

Systems errors are related to input, output, hardware, software, and interfaces. Input errors include human data entry errors and data errors generated by input devices. Output errors result from incompatible or inaccurate data conversion, data compression, and/or data encryption. Hardware errors include data communication errors, data transmission errors, and hardware incompatibilities or failures. Software errors are program bugs and operating system errors. Interface errors, such as loading, customization, and initialization errors, are particularly difficult to debug.

Process errors include computational errors, comparison errors, sequencing errors, and control logic errors. Data errors arise from incorrect data specifications, incorrect formats, and insufficient value representation (e.g., incorrect upper or lower boundary values). Coding errors are also called syntax or command errors.

75.4.3   Testing techniques

Test data must be designed for each of the testing levels described in Chapter 74, Section 74.4.4. Additionally, the testing techniques listed in this section call for specific types of test data.

75.4.3.1   Syntax testing

Test data are needed to find high-level syntax errors that are not flagged by the compiler or language translator. Such errors can cause a program to accept bad data (e.g., non-numeric characters in a numeric field) or misinterpret good data (e.g., inconsistent data formats or data sequences in the parameters lists of the calling and called routines).

Perhaps the best way to test for bad input data is to imagine every data entry mistake the user could possibly make and create test data values to reflect each one. Structured walkthroughs and inspections are useful for identifying inconsistent parameters lists, faulty logic, inefficient control structures, and missing elements. Sets of test data that reflect all possible combinations of variable length input fields can help identify data structure inconsistencies. Some fourth-generation languages incorporate a debugging tool (often embedded in the report or form design utility) that can help with real-time data testing.

75.4.3.2   Logic testing

The point of logic testing is to check the flow of logic through a program. The first step is to physically review (in a walkthrough, an inspection, or a quality assurance review) the program code to make sure it is consistent with the design specifications. Such manual checks are time-consuming, but effective at finding errors of omission that are easily missed by more automated testing procedures.

Path testing is a second step. The idea is to trace the flow of logic through a program and to force the program to follow every logical path. Entrance-exit tests are used to verify that any called routine has only one entry point and one exit point. Loop tests are used to verify the accuracy of a repetition block. Decision tests are applied to case structures and decision logic. Junction testing focuses on points where the control flow merges or diverges.

75.4.3.3   Transaction testing

Transaction testing, also called flow testing or sequence testing, is used to verify the complete logical flow needed to accomplish a task. The idea is to trace the flow of data and logic through the program or routine from the initial input to the final output. Transaction testing is a very effective way to check the consistency and cohesiveness of related components and/or modules in a program or a system.

75.4.3.4   State testing

State testing applies primarily to real-time systems (Chapter 73). Key elements that must be checked include any events that cause a change in state, any recursive loops, any backtracking flows, and the dependency relationships among the states.

75.4.4   Debugging

Testing is a front-end process intended to discover errors and/or problems. Debugging is a back-end process intended to correct errors and/or problems. Testing precedes debugging. The steps in the debugging process include locating the cause of the error or problem, investigating alternative solutions, and correcting the error or problem.

Echo printing (printing or displaying each input value) is a relatively easy way to check for input errors. Stepwise checking involves placing print or write commands throughout the program and using the resulting messages to determine where the program fails or begins producing errors. Backtracking involves tracing backward through the logic from the point where an error is detected until the error's cause is found. Simulated tracing is used to debug selection and repetitive logic by tracing (or following) the program's logical flows. These debugging techniques can be performed manually or by using trace features, step-by-step execution, and other software debugging aids.

75.4.5   Generating test data

A key objective of testing is to try to break the system. Good test data anticipates everything that could possibly go wrong and provides values that potentially cause every conceivable error. Forcing errors during the testing process increases the likelihood that they will be discovered and corrected before the system is released to the user.

The test data should include historical data, hypothetical data, and real data. Historical data (previously processed data) are necessary to check old system and new system compatibility. Hypothetical data, or simulated data, are created specifically for testing purposes. Real data are provided by the user and reflect the system's actual operating environment. Some of the test data should represent normal or typical conditions. Other data should focus on the extremes and incorporate both legal and illegal values.

Listed below are several techniques for generating test data.

75.4.5.1   Value analysis

Value analysis generates test data based on the data values. Range constraint analysis, or boundary analysis, suggests test data to represent such extreme values as upper bounds, lower bounds, and other exceptional values (e.g., a negative number or zero). Typically, both in-range and out-of-range values are included. Format constraint analysis focuses on data type; for example, a zero or a numeric digit might be placed in an alphabetic field, non-digits might be inserted into a numeric field, or a value other than F or M might be recorded in a single-character sex or gender field. Length constraint analysis generates test data with too many or too few characters or digits; this technique is useful for testing such fixed length fields as a social security number or a telephone number.

Value analysis should be performed on the algorithms as well as the input data. For example, a set of test data values might include two out of range parameters (one high and one low) that, taken together, produce an in-range answer. Other algorithm-based test data might reflect all possible extreme (but legal) value combinations; for example, all parameters at the upper limit, all parameters at the lower limit, one high and all others low, and so on.

75.4.5.2   Data analysis

As described in Section 75.4.3.2, path testing, also called branch analysis or loop analysis, is used to check the flow of logic through a program. The idea is to trace the program listing, identify the branch points, and include test data to force the program to follow each path. Generally, this technique relies on data values near the branch values to verify the program logic.

A variation called structured data analysis testing focuses on data structures, the relationships among the data, and such unique data as record keys. For example, structured data analysis testing can be used to evaluate the order of data within a file, a table, or a relation by creating test data with all possible primary and secondary key combinations. A third variation is called data volume analysis. Testing such parameters as response time under peak load conditions calls for large volumes of test data. Data volume can be achieved by replicating and reprocessing test data or by using historical data.

75.4.5.3 Volume analysis

Volume analysis, or control analysis, is intended to check the system's behavior. For example, control totals (Chapter 77) might be checked by processing a set of test data, generating the totals, and then shuffling the transaction order and reprocessing the transactions to see if the same control total is generated.

75.4.5.4 Compatibility analysis

Some applications are designed to access data from multiple versions of a file or a database. For example, imagine a set of old data files developed using the COBOL delimited file format and a new database designed for SQL access. Occasionally, the system might be asked to convert the old data file structure to support a query or to generate a report, and some new transactions might trigger updates to the original file. Test data are needed to force the program to obtain input from and send output to both files.

75.4.5.5 Partition analysis

Partition analysis focuses on aggregate values. The reliability of a database is a function of correctness and completeness. The correctness of each individual transaction can be verified using data analysis techniques (Section 75.4.5.2) with discrete values. Aggregate data are developed to test completeness. For example, a type of aggregate value testing called existence testing might be used to check a database record by simply checking its record number or verifying that the record is referenced in the index.

75.4.5.6 System-dependent test data

Different types of systems call for special test data to test system-specific parameters. For example, symbolic data are essential for testing expert systems, real-time systems require time-varying and environment-dependent data, data communication systems require data to test transmission errors, and so on.

75.5 Key terms

Backtracking — Tracing backward from an error until the error's cause is found.

Branch analysis — A technique for generating test data by checking the flow of logic through a program and providing data to ensure that each logical path is followed; see also *path test, junction test,* and *loop test.*

Bug — An error or malfunction in a module, a program, a procedure, a physical component, or a system.

Coding error — A syntax or command error.

Compatibility analysis — A technique to generate test data to force a program to obtain inputs from or send outputs to multiple versions of a file or a database.

Data error — An error that arises from incorrect data specifications, incorrect formats, or insufficient value representation.

Debugging — The process of removing bugs; a back-end process intended to correct errors and/or problems.

Decision test — A test used to verify a case structure or decision logic.

Echo printing — Printing or displaying each input value.

Entrance-exit test — A test used to verify that any called routine has only one entry point and one exit point.

Format constraint analysis — Generating test data based on data type; for example, a zero or numeric digit might be placed in an alphabetic field, or non-digits might be inserted into a numeric field.

Function-related error — An error caused by such things as incorrect linkages, incorrect control transfers between a calling and a called routine, the inclusion of one or more incorrect or unnecessary functions, and the omission of one or more necessary functions.

Hardware error — A data communication error, a data transmission error, an error caused by hardware incompatibility or failure, and so on.

Historical data — Data previously processed by the old system.

Hypothetical data (simulated data) — Data created specifically for testing purposes.

Input error — A human data entry error or a data error generated by an input device.

Interface error — An error that results from such causes as incorrect loading, customization, or initialization.

Junction test — A test that focuses on points where the control flow merges or diverges.

Length constraint analysis — Generating test data with too many or too few characters or digits.

Logic test — A test of the logical flow through a program.

Loop test — A test used to verify the accuracy of a repetition block.

Output error — An error that results from incompatible or inaccurate data conversion, data compression, or data encryption.

Partition analysis — A technique for testing the completeness of a database using aggregate values.

Path test — A test that traces the flow of logic through a program; typically, test data are provided to make sure each logical path through the program is followed.

Process error — A computational error, a comparison error, a sequencing error, a control logic error, and so on.

Range constraint analysis (boundary analysis) — Generating test data to represent such extreme values as upper bounds, lower bounds, and other exceptional values.

Real data — Data provided by the user that reflect the system's actual operating environment.

Requirements specification — A document that clearly and precisely defines the customer's logical requirements (or needs) in such a way that it is possible to test the finished system to verify that those needs have actually been met.

Simulated tracing — A technique for debugging selection and repetitive logic by tracing the program's logical flows.

Software error — A program bug or an operating system error.

State test — A test that focuses on a real-time system's states.

Stepwise checking — Placing print or write commands throughout a program and using the resulting messages to determine where the program fails or begins producing errors.

Structure analysis testing — A technique for evaluating the order of data within a file, a table, or a relation.

Syntax test — A type of test designed to identify high-level syntax errors that are not flagged by the compiler or language translator; such errors can cause a program to accept bad data or to misinterpret good data.

System error — An error related to input, output, hardware, software, and/or interfaces.

Test data — Data that are developed to support the testing process, locate bugs, and facilitate debugging.

Testing — A front-end process intended to exercise the system and its components to locate, investigate, and correct errors and bugs.

Transaction test (flow test, sequence test) — A test designed to verify the complete logical flow needed to accomplish a task.

Value analysis — Techniques for generating test data based on the data values.

Volume analysis (control analysis) — A technique for generating test data to check the system's behavior.

75.6 Software

Visual Test (Relational Software), ATF (Softbridge), FERRET (Azor Inc.), and QARun (Compuware) support GUI-related testing. Chariot (Ganymede Software), ITE and SDTF (Applied Computer Technology), and FastBench Agent Tester (NETMANSYS) are communication-related software tools. AdaTEST (IPL), C-Cover (Bullseye Testing Technology), and Code Wizard (Parasoft) are used with C and C++. Web testing tools include Webexam and Webload (Radview Software), WebART (OCLC), and TestWorks/Web (Software Research). Performance-related software tools include, Silkperformer (Segue), QAStress (Compuware), Loadrunner and Astra Sitetest (Mercury Interactive Corporation), and Benchmark Factory (Client/Server Solutions Inc.).

75.7   References

1. Beizer, B., *Software Testing and Quality Assurance,* Van Nostrand Reinhold, New York, 1984.
2. Beizer, B., *Software Testing Techniques,* Van Nostrand Reinhold, New York, 1983.
3. Burch, J. G., *Systems Analysis, Design, and Implementation,* Boyd & Fraser, Boston, MA, 1992.
4. Davis, W. S., *Business Systems Analysis and Design,* Wadsworth, Belmont, CA, 1994.
5. Dewitz, S. D., *Systems Analysis and Design and the Transition to Objects,* McGraw-Hill, New York, 1996.
6. Howden, W. E., *Functional Program Testing & Analysis,* McGraw-Hill, New York, 1987.
7. Lamb, D. A., *Software Engineering: Planning for Change,* Prentice-Hall, Englewood Cliffs, NJ, 1988.
8. Norman, R. J., *Object-Oriented Systems Analysis and Design,* Prentice-Hall, Upper Saddle River, NJ, 1996.
9. Power, M. J., Cheney, P. H., and Crow, G., *Structured Systems Development: Analysis, Design, Implementation,* 2nd ed., Boyd & Fraser, Boston, MA, 1990.
10. Pressman, R. S., *Software Engineering: A Practitioner's Approach,* 2nd ed., McGraw-Hill, New York, 1987.

chapter seventy-six

Implementation

David C. Yen and William S. Davis

Contents

76.1 Purpose

Implementation is the process of completing the system and turning it over to the user. This chapter discusses site preparation, documentation preparation, personnel training, system cutover, and system release.

0-8493-7001-9/99/$0.00+$.50
©1999 by CRC Press LLC

76.2   Strengths, weaknesses, and limitations

As appropriate, the strengths and weaknesses associated with various techniques will be discussed in context.

76.3   Inputs and related ideas

Implementation occurs after the system has been analyzed, designed, constructed, and tested. Consequently, the results generated by all the tools and techniques covered in all preceding chapters can be considered inputs to the implementation phase. Additionally, the tasks performed during implementation set the stage for system operation and maintenance (Part VIII).

This chapter references (directly or indirectly) Chapters 31 (prototyping), 32 (rapid application development), 42 (hardware interface design), 67 (knowledge representation), 70 (documentation design), and 71 (security design).

76.4   Concepts

Implementation is the process of completing the system and turning it over to the user. This chapter discusses site preparation, documentation preparation, personnel training, system cutover, and system release.

76.4.1   Site preparation

Site preparation involves preparing the work environment, installing the hardware, and configuring any new equipment to work with existing computers and peripherals. See Chapter 42 for a discussion of hardware interface design.

The work environment must include sufficient space to hold the computer, its peripherals, desks, storage cabinets, printer stands, and other furniture, and to store such supplies as paper, ribbons, disks, backup media, forms, cleaning supplies, documentation, and procedure manuals. Wiring, communication lines, and other physical connections must be installed. A raised floor might be needed. Security features might be required.

A dependable power supply is essential. Large computer systems often require custom-designed power supplies. Although most small computer systems run on standard household current, the equipment can easily tax the limits of existing wiring (particularly in older buildings), so rewiring might be necessary. Surge protectors and an uninterruptable power source (UPS) are recommended for most systems.

Air conditioning is another factor. Computers are heat sensitive, and heat-related problems are difficult to trace. The computer itself generates heat, and that can add to the air conditioning load. The cost of inadequate air conditioning is often measured in excessive downtime and high maintenance costs.

Ergonomic requirements are intended to provide the users with a comfortable working environment. Key parameters include lighting, glare, airflow, noise, temperature, humidity, workspace, and the design of the furniture. Many organizations have implemented ergonomic standards.

76.4.2 Documentation preparation

Documentation consists of the specifications, instructions, tutorials, reference guides, and similar materials that accompany and explain a piece of software or a hardware component. A complete set of user documentation, systems documentation, software documentation, and operations documentation must be available to support the implementation process. In addition to procedures for performing system tasks, preparing paperwork, entering data, and distributing output, documentation for backup, recovery, auditing, and security procedures is also needed. Documentation tells the users how to operate the system, helps to resolve problems and errors, and supports the training process.

76.4.3 Training

Before the system is released, the users, system maintenance personnel, system operators, and other people affected by the system must be trained. The user manual and the written procedures form the core of the training plan. Initially, the analysts and other technical experts should show the users how to perform the various tasks. Gradually, the experts should do less and the users more until the users clearly understand the system. Following the initial intensive training period, the users should begin to work on their own, but the experts should be available to provide quick, accurate technical support. Over time the level of technical support should decline, but facilities for answering user questions (e.g., a help facility) should be maintained for the life of the system.

In addition to the primary users and system support people, back-up personnel must also be trained. Often the primary person trains his or her backup. People retire, resign, suffer injuries and illnesses, and earn promotions, so there will be turnover. Training does not end when the system is released; it is an ongoing activity.

In-house training is suitable when the system is developed internally. The training can be tailored to the system and the organization's environment, touching on the relationship between the new system and existing systems and stressing user interests and needs. Unfortunately, users sometimes undervalue in-house training because they believe the in-house experts will always be available to provide assistance on request.

Third party training includes vendor-supplied training, developer-supplied training, and training from independent outside services. Such training is common when a company lacks in-house information system support or has no on-going training program, or when a third party develops the system.

Some training is done in a traditional classroom environment. In other cases, the trainer goes to the trainee, perhaps providing one-on-one or small group training on specific equipment or in the user's environment. Videoconferencing is an economical training medium for a relatively brief time (hours, days, or weeks). Distance learning (via satellite or other communication media) is effective for longer periods (weeks, months, years). Interactive training software (on tape or CD) is both popular and cost effective. Computer-based training (CBT) utilizes the computer as a training tool; for example, an instruction system is a type of expert system (Chapter 67) that implements computer-based training.

76.4.4　Cutover strategies

System cutover is the process of turning the system over (or releasing the system) to the user. Some experts believe that a system should be released any weekday before Thursday, thus giving the users at least one day (Friday) to experiment and giving the installers the weekend to fix any last-minute problems. Other experts believe that a system should be released on Friday, thus giving the installers three full days to complete the installation before the users begin working with it. Friday conversion is more conservative.

Several cutover strategies are outlined below.

76.4.4.1　Direct cutover

With direct cutover (sometimes called crash cutover, or abrupt cutover), the old system is discontinued on a predefined date (often corresponding to the start of a new accounting period) and the entire organization switches directly to the new system. Direct cutover is risky because, if the new system fails, returning to the old system is virtually impossible. This strategy is relatively inexpensive, however, and it tends to promote user acceptance since there is no old system to serve as a basis for comparison. Direct cutover is often used in response to a government mandate (such as the implementation of new income tax withholding rules) or other legal concerns.

76.4.4.2　Parallel operation

As the term suggests, parallel operation means that the old and the new systems run in parallel for a time. Typically, the source data are processed twice, the results are compared, any discrepancies are carefully analyzed, and appropriate corrections are made. Note that a discrepancy might represent an error in the *old* system.

Parallel operation is less risky than direct cutover, but concurrently running two systems is expensive. Parallel operation tends to be most effective when a computer-based system replaces a manual (or partially manual) system because concurrently running two computer-based systems is very expensive. It is an excellent choice when data accuracy, security, and/or reliability are important concerns. One intangible benefit of parallel operation is the opportunity to build user confidence in the new system (assuming it runs properly, of course) by comparing the new and old systems' results.

76.4.4.3 Gradual cutover

Gradual cutover is a combination of direct and parallel. The idea is to run the new and old systems concurrently and gradually increase the number of transactions handled by the new system. Note that the data are *not* processed twice. Instead, some transactions are processed by the old system, some are processed by the new system, and the percentage sent to the new system gradually increases until the old system fades away.

76.4.4.4 Phased implementation

In a phased implementation, or partial conversion, the new system is released in stages, either by application or by location. For example, new data collection procedures might be implemented first, followed by inventory updating procedures, then new reorder procedures, and so on. Alternatively, the system might be released in one subdivision or location (e.g., a branch office) at a time.

Phased implementation allows for gradual installation and training, reduces user resistance to the new system, and gives the organization considerable flexibility. The installation period is likely to be quite lengthy, however, so phased implementation should not be used when the schedule or the budget is tight.

76.4.4.5 Pilot implementation

In a pilot (or location) implementation, the new system is first released in a single site, such as a branch office or a warehouse, thoroughly tested, and then ported to the other sites. The pilot site is called the beta site. After a pilot implementation, either direct cutover or phased implementation might be used to release the system to the other sites.

Pilot implementation is similar to phased implementation, but the system can be changed based on experiences gained at the pilot site. Pilot implementation is compatible with prototyping (Chapter 31) and rapid application development (Chapter 32). The pilot study gives the developers another opportunity to perfect the system and the rest of the organization is not impacted until the new system (or its prototype) proves its usefulness and reliability. On the other hand, user confidence in the system may be damaged if too many changes are made after the pilot study begins, the results may be biased by the unique characteristics of the pilot site, and system release will be delayed in other parts of the organization.

76.4.5 System release

After the system is installed and stable, it is released, or turned over, to the user. In most cases, the system release or system turnover process includes a formal user sign off that implies user acceptance of the system. If the system was developed in-house, system release marks the end of the developer team's responsibility. If the system was developed by outside contractors or consultants, system release implies successful completion of the contract.

76.4.6 Post-implementation review

A post-implementation (or post-release) review should be scheduled some time after the system is released. During the post-implementation review the developers should investigate any remaining problems and compare the project's objectives, cost estimates, and schedules to the actual outcomes. The idea is not simply to find discrepancies, but to explain them. Knowing why mistakes were made is the key to improving the organization's analysis, design, scheduling, and cost estimating procedures.

During the post-implementation review, such general concepts as the design philosophy and the design strategy should be discussed. The hardware platform, the inputs, the outputs, the interfaces, the dialogues, the processes, the files and databases, and the documentation should all be carefully studied to ensure that the system performs as designed.

76.5 Key terms

Beta site — The pilot site in a pilot implementation.

Cutover — The process of turning the system over to the user; see also *system release*.

Direct cutover (crash cutover, abrupt cutover) — A system release strategy in which the old system is discontinued on a predefined date and the entire organization switches directly to the new system.

Documentation — The specifications, instructions, tutorials, reference guides, and similar materials that accompany and explain a piece of software or a hardware component.

Ergonomics — The study of the relationship between human beings and their workplaces.

Gradual cutover — A system release strategy in which the new and old systems run concurrently and the number of transactions handled by the new system is gradually increased.

Implementation — The process of completing the system and turning it over to the user.

Parallel operation — A system release strategy in which the old and the new systems run in parallel for a time.

Phased implementation (partial conversion) — A system release strategy in which the new system is released in stages.

Pilot implementation (location implementation) — A system release strategy in which the new system is first released in a single site, such as a branch office or a warehouse, thoroughly tested, and then ported to the other sites.

Post-implementation review (post-release review) — A review of the system development process conducted after the system is released.

Site preparation — The process of preparing the work environment, installing the hardware, and configuring any new equipment to work with existing computers and peripherals.

System release — The stage in the system development life cycle when the system is turned over to the user.

Training — Generally, a series of experiences designed to modify behavior; often, a set of activities designed to teach someone how to do something.

76.6 Software

Not applicable.

76.7 References

1. Beizer, B., *Software Testing and Quality Assurance*, Van Nostrand Reinhold, New York, 1984.
2. Beizer, B., *Software Testing Techniques*, Van Nostrand Reinhold, New York, 1983.
3. Burch, J. G., *Systems Analysis, Design, and Implementation*, Boyd & Fraser, Boston, MA, 1992.
4. Capron, H. L., *Systems Analysis and Design*, Benjamin/Cummings, Redwood City, CA, 1986.
5. Davis, W. S., *Business Systems Analysis and Design*, Wadsworth, Belmont, CA, 1994.
6. Dewitz, S. D., *Systems Analysis and Design and the Transition to Objects*, McGraw-Hill, New York, 1996.
7. Fournier, R., *Practical Guide to Structured System Development and Maintenance*, Prentice-Hall, Englewood Cliffs, NJ, 1991.
8. Howden, W. E., *Functional Program Testing & Analysis*, McGraw-Hill, New York, 1987.
9. Hoffer, J. A., George, J. F., and Valacich, J. S., *Modern Systems Analysis and Design*, Benjamin/Cummings, Redwood City, CA, 1996.
10. King, D., *Creating Effective Software: Computer Program Design Using the Jackson Methodology*, Prentice-Hall, Englewood Cliffs, NJ, 1988.
11. Lamb, D. A., *Software Engineering: Planning for Change*, Prentice-Hall, Englewood Cliffs, NJ, 1988.
12. Norman, R. J., *Object-Oriented Systems Analysis and Design*, Prentice-Hall, Upper Saddle River, NJ, 1996.
13. Power, M. J., Cheney, P. H., and Crow, G., *Structured Systems Development: Analysis, Design, Implementation*, 2nd ed., Boyd & Fraser, Boston, MA, 1990.
14. Pressman, R. S., *Software Engineering: A Practitioner's Approach*, 2nd ed., McGraw-Hill, New York, 1987.
15. Saldarini, R. A., *Analysis and Design of Business Information Systems*, Macmillan, New York, 1989.

part eight

Operation and maintenance

chapter seventy-seven

System controls

William S. Davis and David C. Yen

Contents

77.1   Purpose

This chapter discusses several system control tools and techniques that are commonly used in information systems.

0-8493-7001-9/99/$0.00+$.50
©1999 by CRC Press LLC

77.2 Strengths, weaknesses, and limitations

Where appropriate, the strengths and weaknesses associated with specific controls will be discussed in context.

77.3 Inputs and related ideas

General system principles are discussed in Chapters 1 and 72. Key information for defining system controls is documented in the requirements specification (Chapter 35). Effective controls must be designed into a system, so controls are an important consideration throughout the design process (Part VI). Control charts are discussed in Chapter 10. Technical inspections are discussed in Chapter 23. Several techniques for screening input data are described in Chapter 46. Security is discussed in Chapter 71. Configuration management and version controls are discussed in Chapter 80.

77.4 Concepts

In addition to inputs, processes, interfaces, and outputs, a system also includes control and feedback mechanisms that together allow the system to determine if it is achieving its purpose. Feedback is the return of a portion of the system's output to its input. If the feedback suggests a deviation from the expected value (the control), the system reacts by attempting to adjust itself.

This chapter discusses several system control tools and techniques that are commonly used in information systems.

77.4.1 Auditing

An audit is a study of a system or a process designed to ensure that the established procedures and controls are followed. Note that the point of an audit is not to correct errors. For example, a well-conducted audit might not catch an incorrect value input by a data entry clerk, but it should flag an attempt by an unauthorized person to change that value.

One technique used by auditors is to follow an audit trail. Sometimes, the auditor starts with selected input transactions and traces the data through the system until they are eventually output. An option is to start with selected outputs and trace the values back to the source data. Good systems are designed to maintain such audit trails.

Regression testing is a technique that compares the results obtained when the system is being audited to the results obtained under normal condition. Parallel simulation involves testing both the live system and a simulated system with the same data. With both techniques, any discrepancies are analyzed to determine the accuracy and reliability of the system. Finally, experimental design is used to audit system accuracy by building a pilot prototype and testing it using controlled sample data.

In addition to being significant in their own right, audits are an important supplement to virtually all system controls.

77.4.2   Information processing controls

Information processing controls consist of input controls, processing controls, and output controls.

The objective of input controls is to screen out and (if possible) correct bad data before they enter the system. Validity tests are used to ensure that each input field is the right type (numeric, alphabetic), that the value of a given field is within upper and lower bounds, and that fixed-length fields (e.g., social security number, telephone number) are the right length. Exception tests are used to screen such "exceptional" values as a zero (0) in a field that will be used as a divisor. Reasonableness tests are used to screen invalid values (e.g., anything but F or M in a single-character sex or gender field).

Record control is a simple processing control technique that involves counting and verifying the existence of every record in a database. Error controls are used to see if a program or routine can handle an unexpected response or input. Interrupt controls involve intentionally restarting, abandoning, or abnormally terminating a system or program to determine if it is capable of recovering. Transmission controls are used to ensure that there are no missing, incorrectly converted, or wrongly transmitted data. Additionally, audit trails (Section 77.4.1) are valuable processing control tools.

Distribution controls are designed to ensure that all outputs are distributed to the right location at the right time. Quantity controls verify that the correct number of copies is generated. Reconciliation controls are focused on ensuring that the right amount of data is output to support daily statistical analysis and decision-making activities. Finally, control totals (Section 77.4.3) help to detect other types of output exceptions and errors.

77.4.3   Operational controls

The purpose of operational controls is to provide an early warning in the event of system malfunction. The idea is to collect data about system performance (feedback), compare the feedback to established standards (the controls), and sound an alarm if reality differs from expectation.

It is impossible to directly monitor everything that happens on a computer-based information system, but control totals are both effective and relatively easy to generate. A control total is an accumulated sum, a count, or a similar value that summarizes the results of numerous computations or transactions.

For example, consider the process of printing paychecks. In many companies, the necessary computations are performed by the payroll program and stored on disk or magnetic tape. The output from that program also includes such control totals as the number of checks to be printed, the sum of the computed net pays for all those checks, and so on. Later, when the check printing routine runs, it independently computes the same counts and totals. If the control values generated by both programs match, it is reasonable to assume that no one modified the payroll data between the time the computations were made and the checks were printed.

Control totals are sometimes monitored on control charts (Chapter 10). For example, the number of inventory transactions per day might be a useful control total for an inventory system. If the daily count lies between the upper and lower control limits (numbers that should appear in some form on the requirements specification), it is reasonable to assume that the inventory system is functioning as expected. If, however, the transaction count is out of control, management should look for the reason why. Note that the control total does not indicate what is wrong, merely that *something* is wrong.

Inventory controls help to ensure that the necessary software, hardware, and other peripherals are properly maintained and connected for operation. Documentation controls focus on the documentation library. Scheduling controls are used to monitor input or output timings and provide early warning of increasing queue lengths. Service controls measure such parameters as response rate, throughput rate, and turnaround time.

Other operational controls are designed to ensure that backup and recovery (and other operating procedures) are followed; logs and transaction counts are common tools. Finally, audits are used to verify that the correct procedures are followed.

77.4.4 *Personnel controls*

Not all system activities take place on the computer, so personnel controls are essential. One underlying principle is the segregation of functions. For example, at a university, the registrar registers students for classes, the finance department bills the students, and the bursar collects the payments. When functions are segregated, it is relatively easy to design reports and controls that, in essence, allow the different functional groups to check on each other and allow an auditor to verify that the appropriate procedures were followed.

To cite another example, imagine that the requirements for an inventory system specify that the warehouse is responsible for controlling inventory and the shipping department is responsible for delivering the orders to the customers. Given such a structure, comparing daily inventory transactions to daily orders shipped might serve as an effective control on the performance of *both* groups.

77.4.5   Ensuring data integrity

Data integrity is ensured by carefully controlling and managing data entry, data maintenance, and data access from the time the data first enter the system until they are of no further use. The process can be compared to a chain of evidence in a criminal trial. Unless the police can account for a piece of evidence from the instant it is collected to the instant it is presented in court, that evidence is inadmissible. Similarly, unless the system can account for a particular data element from the instant it is captured until the instant it is no longer needed, that data element cannot be trusted.

Only authorized personnel (as defined in the system requirements) should be allowed to enter data, and clear, unambiguous, verifiable, easily monitored data entry procedures are a must. Relatively few individuals should be authorized to modify data, and steps must be taken to verify the identity of anyone who attempts to change a data value. Similar restrictions must be used to limit data access to authorized personnel. The key is building such controls into the system rather than simply adding them on after the system is completed.

Data integrity controls start with data entry, so the input controls described in Section 77.4.2 are an important component. Often, transactions, errors, and corrections are counted and plotted on a control chart, and data entry procedures might be monitored electronically. Ensuring that only authorized personnel enter, access, and modify data is a security function (Section 77.4.6). Detailed logs of all changes to a database allow an auditor to verify that the appropriate change procedures were followed.

77.4.6   Security controls

Security (Chapter 71) involves procedures and other safeguards designed to protect the hardware, software, data, and other system resources from unauthorized access, use, modification, or theft. Once a system's security is breached, the data are particularly vulnerable because they are so easy to copy or change. It is impossible to ensure data integrity if unauthorized people can bypass the normal controls and access the system.

Physical security is concerned with denying physical access to a system. For example, mainframe computers are often located in controlled-access rooms, personal computers are sometimes placed in locked cabinets when they are not in use, and network connections can be deactivated when an office is closed. Typical physical security controls include counting and logging all attempts to access the system or facility. Procedures are needed for tracking keys and entry codes, changing codes regularly, and so on.

Logical security is implemented by the computer itself. Typically, each user is assigned a unique identification code and a password that must be entered each time he or she logs onto the system. On some systems, additional passwords are required to access more secure data or to execute sensitive programs. Logical security controls might include counts of successful and unsuccessful log-ons, detailed records of attempted break-ins, statistics on password changes (on time, late), and so on. Procedures are needed for screening out easy to guess passwords, ensuring that passwords are changed regularly, quickly removing disallowed passwords from the system, and so on. Audits help to verify that the appropriate procedures were followed.

77.4.7   Software development controls

Software development controls are essential. Undocumented or rogue code can cause debugging, testing, and maintenance nightmares. Hackers and crackers routinely exploit Trojan horses, undocumented trap doors, and known bugs to gain access to computer systems, and disgruntled programmers have been known to insert destructive logic into their code.

The first key is insisting that all programmers follow well-defined coding standards. Special software tools can help. For example, a static code analyzer is a program that scans (but does not execute) the code and flags such potential errors as synonyms (different names for the same data element), poor structure, inconsistent usage, dead code (modules that cannot be executed), unreferenced variables, and other deviations from coding standards. A clean code analyzer output is a prerequisite to code approval.

Another key is to conduct technical inspections of all software. A programmer is unlikely to insert unauthorized code into a program if the code is subject to inspection by his or her peers. Inspections can also help to ensure that the programmer does not deviate from the approved design.

Version control (Chapter 80) provides a mechanism for enforcing software development controls. Only the current version of a program is approved for production. Programmers are not permitted to directly access the production version, and all modifications are made to a test version. Before the test version becomes the current version, it must generate a clean compilation and a clean code analysis, pass a technical inspection, pass the appropriate acceptance tests, and be approved by the configuration approval board.

Functional segregation helps, too. For example, in most mainframe environments, computer operators are not allowed to modify software and programmers are not allowed to operate the computer. Unless that standard is enforced, a programmer might be able sit down at the console and make unauthorized changes to a program that cannot be detected by management or by the normal controls. In fact, in many computer centers, banning "via the console" debugging was one of the very first software development controls.

Audits can help to verify that the appropriate procedures are followed.

77.4.8 *Communication controls*

Encryption is a technique for encoding data, transmitting the data, and then decoding the data at the receiving end for processing. Line monitoring involves attaching special circuitry to the communication link to diagnose problems. For example, using loop back analysis, all data received by a destination node are automatically looped back to the transmitting node and compared with the original data.

77.5 *Key terms*

Audit — A study of a system or a process designed to ensure that the established procedures and controls are followed.

Configuration approval board — A committee that reviews change requests and proposed adaptive and perfective maintenance tasks, authorizes work to begin, and schedules the work.

Control — An expected value that can be compared with feedback. If the feedback suggests a deviation from the expected value (the control), the system reacts by attempting to adjust itself.

Control total — An accumulated sum, a count, or a similar value that summarizes the results of numerous computations or transactions.

Data integrity — The state of a database that is protected against loss or contamination; data integrity is ensured by carefully controlling and managing data entry, data maintenance, and data access from the time the data first enter the system until they are of no further use.

Distribution control — An output control designed to ensure that all outputs are distributed to the right location at the right time.

Documentation control — An operational control that focuses on the documentation library.

Encrypt — To convert to a secret code.

Error control — A system control designed to determine if a program or routine can handle an unexpected response or input.

Exception test — A test used to screen such "exceptional" values as a zero (0) in a field that will be used as a divisor.

Experimental design — An auditing technique used to audit system accuracy by building a pilot prototype and testing it using controlled sample data.

Feedback — The return of a portion of the system's output to its input.

Information processing control — An input, processing, or output control.

Input controls — Tests used to screen out and (if possible) correct bad data before they enter the system.

Interrupt control — A control or test to determine if a system or program is capable of recovering after it is intentionally restarted, abandoned, or abnormally terminated.

Inventory control — A type of operational control that helps to ensure that the necessary software, hardware, and other peripherals are properly maintained and connected for operation.

Line monitoring — A communication control technique that involves attaching special circuitry to the communication link to diagnose problems.

Logical security — Security precautions implemented by the computer itself.

Loop back analysis — The process of automatically returning all received messages to the transmitting node where they are compared with the original data.

Operational control — A control intended to provide an early warning in the event of system malfunction.

Parallel simulation — An auditing technique that involves testing both the live system and a simulated system with the same data.

Physical security — Techniques and procedures concerned with denying physical access to a system.

Processing control — A test or technique that measures and controls a processing activity.

Reasonableness test — A test used to screen invalid values (e.g., anything but F or M in a single-character sex or gender field).

Reconciliation control — An output control designed to ensure that the right amount of data is output to support daily statistical analysis and decision-making activities.

Record control — A simple processing control technique that involves counting and verifying the existence of every record in a database.

Regression testing — An auditing technique that compares the results obtained when the system is being audited to the results obtained under normal conditions.

Scheduling control — An operational control that is used to monitor input or output timings and provide an early warning of increasing queue lengths.

Security — Procedures and other safeguards designed to protect the hardware, software, data, and other system resources from unauthorized access, use, modification, or theft.

Service controls — Operational controls that measure such parameters as response rate, throughput rate, and turnaround time.

Software development controls — A set of controls imposed on the software development process. Examples include static code analyzers, technical inspections, version controls, and so on.

Static code analyzer — A program that scans (but does not execute) the code and flags such potential errors as synonyms, poor structure, inconsistent usage, dead code, unreferenced variables, and other deviations from coding standards.

Transmission control — A processing control designed to ensure that there are no missing, incorrectly converted, or wrongly transmitted data.

Validity test — A test used to ensure that each input field is the right type (numeric, alphabetic), that the value of a given field is within upper and lower bounds, that fixed-length fields (e.g., social security number, telephone number) are the right length, and so on.

Version control — A set of tools and procedures used to track and manage multiple versions of the system and its components.

77.6 Software

Not applicable.

77.7 References

1. Davis, G. B. and Olson, M. H., *Management Information Systems: Conceptual Foundations, Structure, and Development*, 2nd ed., McGraw-Hill, New York, 1985.
2. Davis, W. S., *Business Systems Analysis and Design*, Wadsworth, Belmont, CA, 1994.
3. Gilhooley, I., Defining the scope of DP controls, in *A Practical Guide to EDP Auditing*, James Hannon, Ed., Auerbach, New York, 1982, 15.
4. Powers, M. J., Cheney, P. H., and Crow, G., *Structured Systems Development: Analysis, Design, and Implementation*, 2nd ed., Boyd & Fraser, Boston, MA, 1990.
5. Stamper, D. A., *Business Data Communications*, 4th ed., Benjamin/Cummings, Redwood City, CA, 1994.

chapter seventy-eight

Performance analysis

David C. Yen and William S. Davis

Contents

78.1   Purpose

This chapter briefly discusses system evaluation and explains three significant performance criteria: reliability, productivity, and quality.

78.2   Strengths, weaknesses, and limitations

Not applicable.

0-8493-7001-9/99/$0.00+$.50
©1999 by CRC Press LLC

78.3   Inputs and related ideas

Control charts are discussed in Chapter 10. The system requirements against which performance is measured are documented in the requirements specification (Chapter 35). Performance analysis yields valuable information to support future project planning (Part III) and future cost/benefit analysis (Chapter 38). During the system evaluation process, the physical components (as implemented) are compared to the design specifications, so any or all of the design topics discussed in Part VI might be relevant. Performance analysis is closely related to testing (Chapters 74 and 75), implementation (Chapter 76), and to the other chapters in Part VIII.

78.4   Concepts

This chapter briefly discusses system evaluation and explains three significant performance criteria: reliability, productivity, and quality.

78.4.1   System evaluation

After the system is released to the user, it should be evaluated to determine how well it meets the user's needs (as defined in the requirements specification) and conforms to the design specifications. Davis and Olson[1] suggest three categories for system evaluation. Economic evaluation focuses on comparing the project's actual time, cost, and benefits to the estimates prepared after the analysis stage and/or during design. The objective is to improve the estimating process. Technical evaluation deals with the technology and the system design and considers such factors as reliability, productivity, quality, efficiency, and effectiveness. Operational evaluation focuses on such operational elements as system controls, interface design, and security design and considers such factors as integration, flexibility, compatibility, user friendliness, and system efficiency.

Numerous hardware and software tools are available to support system evaluation. IBM's system management facility (SMF) is an example of a job accounting system that can be used to project patterns of growth, manage and plan capacity, and assess system efficiency. A software monitor is a benchmarking program that can be used to measure program efficiency, measure execution performance, keep track of resources used, and so on. System access monitoring can be used to measure such parameters as throughput, turnaround time, access time, and response time. A hardware monitor consists of specially designed circuitry that can be used to measure such parameters as average seek time, rotational delay, arm movement time, and so on.

78.4.2   Reliability

Reliability is the probability that a given component or system will perform as expected (or will *not* fail) for a given period of time. Reliability is typically measured or estimated using probabilities or such statistical parameters as means, modes, and medians. For example, the mean time between failures (MTBF) is the sum of the mean time to fail (the average time between initial use and failure) and the mean time to repair.

There are many mathematically based reliability models[2]. For example, the reliability growth modeling technique expresses cumulative failures as a function of execution time. The reliability cost model describes the relationship between associated costs and failure intensity. System reliability can also be measured by analyzing the relationship between completion date and failure intensity. See Everett and Musa[2] for additional details.

Reliability is an extremely important performance criterion on most computer-based systems, and explicit reliability targets or requirements are often documented in the requirements specification. After the system begins operation, all failures and their associated repair times should be documented in detail. Based on the failure and repair data, the mean time between failures should be computed regularly and compared to the target, perhaps by plotting a control chart. Less than acceptable system performance suggests a need for corrective maintenance and/or system enhancement. An evaluation of the causes of system failure can help to improve the reliability of future systems.

78.4.3 Productivity

Productivity is defined as output per unit of labor, or more generally, output per unit of input. Increased productivity reduces development time and development cost.

The first step in increasing productivity is to measure productivity. After the system is released to the user, all (or most) of the costs and other resources expended on creating the system (the inputs) and all of the system's components, features, and facilities (the outputs) are known. Given the inputs and the outputs, various productivity measures can be computed and compared to similar numbers for other systems.

Software productivity is sometimes measured by computing lines of code per unit of time (for example, lines of code per programmer day). The number of lines of code is taken from the program source listings. Programmer time is taken from the appropriate labor or payroll statistics. Comparing the resulting ratio to the same ratio for other projects can show if the organization's productivity is increasing, decreasing, or staying the same. Explaining discrepancies between projects and linking those discrepancies to other measurable project characteristics (e.g., the computing platform, response time requirements, system type, programming language, etc.) can help to improve the cost estimating process on future projects. Tracking productivity can also help the organization determine if new technology (e.g., a fourth-generation language) really does lead to productivity gains.

Not all system development activities involve code, of course. Other, more general measures of productivity include effort months per user supported, effort months per project or task completed, and reported defects or repairs per user supported.

The distribution of actual costs can also be significant. Assume, for example, that historically 20 percent of post-analysis costs were spent on design, 40 percent were spent on coding, and 40 percent were spent on debugging and testing. On a new project that uses a fourth-generation language, 45 percent of the post-analysis costs were spent on design, 30 percent on coding, and 25 percent on testing and debugging. Assuming that design is language independent, those numbers suggest that fourth-generation languages increase productivity. Additionally, the distribution of costs as a function of language is a useful guide to future cost estimating.

78.4.4   Quality

Quality can be defined (narrowly) as conformance to requirements. In a broader sense, quality implies that the requirements match user needs and that the system meets the requirements. Quality measures are sometimes implemented late in the system development life cycle, but they should be considered during the analysis stage, and specific quality requirements should be documented in the requirements specification.

Quality is often measured by counting defects, where a defect is any failure to meet requirements. The number of defects (perhaps categorized by severity) discovered during testing is a measure of programming and debugging quality. The number of defects discovered after the system is released is a measure of overall system quality. Cost per defect is computed by dividing total debugging or maintenance costs by the total number of defects discovered, and is also used as a measure of productivity. Specific targets (or limits) can be included in the requirements specification and used to define control limits for a control chart. Declining numbers suggest improving quality. Comparing defect statistics for a project developed using traditional programming languages to a project developed using a fourth-generation language will show if the newer technology improves quality.

Quality assurance is a four-step process. The first step, review, involves collecting quality-related information and identifying quality factors. Key quality factors include correctness, reliability, efficiency, integrity, usability, maintainability, testability, flexibility, portability, reusability, and interoperability.[3] During the study phase, a quality framework is identified by selecting and ranking the quality factors and choosing measurable quality attributes for each one. In the implementation step, related quality attributes are grouped (e.g., error tolerance, consistency, accuracy, and simplicity might be grouped under reliability) and conflicting attributes (e.g., execution efficiency and instrumentation, conciseness and completeness) are resolved. During the documentation step, the quality attributes are expressed as measurable system parameters, the appropriate quality information is collected, and quality is tracked. Note that the documentation process can reveal new quality factors, which leads back to the review step. In other words, quality assurance is a continuous process.

78.5   Key terms

Defect — Any failure to meet requirements.

Economic evaluation — A type of system evaluation that focuses on comparing the project's actual time, cost, and benefits to the estimates prepared after the analysis stage and/or during design.

Hardware monitor — Specially designed circuitry that can be used to measure such parameters as average seek time, rotational delay, arm movement time, and so on.

Mean time between failures (MTBF) — A measure of reliability; the sum of the mean time to fail and the mean time to repair.

Operational evaluation — A type of system evaluation that focuses on such operational elements as system controls, interface design, and security design and considers such factors as integration, flexibility, compatibility, user friendliness, and system efficiency.

Productivity — Output per unit of labor; more generally, output per unit of input.

Quality — Conformance to requirements; in a broader sense, quality implies that the requirements match user needs and that the system meets the requirements.

Quality assurance — Goals, procedures, and techniques for measuring and ensuring quality.

Quality factor — A parameter that implies quality, such as correctness, reliability, efficiency, integrity, usability, maintainability, testability, flexibility, portability, reusability, and interoperability.

Reliability — The probability that a given component or system will perform as expected (or will not fail) for a given period of time.

Software monitor — A benchmarking program that can be used to measure program efficiency, measure execution performance, keep track of resources used, and so on.

System access monitoring — Software and hardware used to measure such parameters as throughput, turnaround time, access time, and response time.

Technical evaluation — A type of system evaluation that deals with the technology and the system design and considers such factors as reliability, productivity, quality, efficiency, and effectiveness.

78.6   Software

IBM's system management facility (SMF) is an example of a job accounting system that can be used to project patterns of growth, manage and plan capacity, and assess system efficiency. A software monitor is a benchmarking program that can be used to measure program efficiency, measure execution performance, keep track of resources used, and so on. System access monitoring software can be used to measure such parameters as throughput, turnaround time, access time, and response time.

78.7 References

78.7.1 Citations

1. Davis, G. B., and Olson, M. H., *Management Information Systems: Conceptual Foundation, Structure, and Development,* 2nd ed., McGraw-Hill, New York, 1985.
2. Everett, W. W., and Musa, J. D., Software reliability and productivity, *Software Engineering Productivity Handbook,* Keyes, J., Ed., McGraw-Hill, New York, 1993, chap. 8.
3. McCall, J. A., Richards, P. K., and Walters, G. F., *Factors in Software Quality Assurance: RADC-TR-77-369,* Rome Air Development Center, Rome, Italy, November 1977.

78.7.2 Suggestions for additional reading

1. Burch, J. G., *Systems Analysis, Design, and Implementation,* Boyd & Fraser, Boston, MA, 1992.
2. Davis, W. S., *Business Systems Analysis and Design,* Wadsworth, Belmont, CA, 1994.
3. Dewitz, S. D., *Systems Analysis and Design and the Transition to Objects,* McGraw-Hill, New York, 1996.
4. Hoffer, J. A., George, J. F., and Valacich, J. S., *Modern Systems Analysis and Design,* Benjamin/Cummings, Redwood City, CA, 1996.
5. Keyes J., *Software Engineering Productivity Handbook,* McGraw-Hill, New York, 1993.
6. Lamb, D. A., *Software Engineering: Planning for Change,* Prentice-Hall, Englewood Cliffs, NJ, 1988.
7. Pressman, R. S., *Software Engineering: A Practitioner's Approach,* 2nd ed., McGraw-Hill, New York, 1987.
8. Swanson, E. B., *Information Systems Implementation: Bridging the Gap between Design and Utilization,* Irwin, Homewood, IL, 1988.
9. Vincent, J., Waters, A., and Sinclair, J., *Software Quality Assurance: Practice and Implementation,* Vol. 1, Prentice-Hall, Upper Saddle River, NJ, 1988.
10. Vincent, J., Waters, A., and Sinclair, J., *Software Quality Assurance: A Program Guide,* Vol. III, Prentice-Hall, Upper Saddle River, NJ, 1988.

chapter seventy-nine

Queuing theory

Neil B. Marks
Miami University

Contents

79.1 Purpose

The purpose of this chapter is to provide the fundamental concepts and computations required for the analysis of any system that features a waiting line (queue). Examples of enterprises where these ideas are traditionally applied include grocery stores, airline ticket counters, fast-food restaurants, retail stores, auto license agencies, and banks. Queuing theory may also be used where "customers" are inanimate objects, such as production processes, though sometimes the mathematics becomes quite complex in these situations. In the context of information systems, queuing theory is commonly used to help plan, design, and reconfigure communication networks.

79.2   Strengths, weaknesses, and limitations

Queuing analysis is a mathematical technique for analyzing waiting lines. In a simple waiting line, a customer arrives, joins a queue, is serviced, and leaves. That pattern is consistent with messages flowing through a network, disk access transactions, interrupt processing, and several other activities common to computers. Consequently, queuing theory is an excellent tool for modeling such activities. Given the correct statistical values, a queuing analysis can be completed rapidly using only an electronic calculator or a relatively simple computer-based model.

For some combinations of arrival pattern, service time distribution, and number of servers, measures of performance are limited or unavailable. Queuing theory assumes exponential arrival and service rates and, consequently, should not be used if either rate is clearly not exponential. Other inhibiting factors are prioritization of customers, a service rate that varies by size of the waiting line, a restriction on queue length, and complexity of system design. However, a computer simulation model (Chapter 19) can be constructed easily to produce estimates of system performance measures in most of these situations.

79.3   Inputs and related ideas

Queuing theory is commonly used to support planning, designing, and reconfiguring a network. Relevant network concepts are introduced in Chapters 52, 53, and 54. Hardware interface design is introduced in Chapter 42. Memory queues are described in Chapter 43. Simulation, another mathematical tool used to support similar applications, is discussed in Chapter 19. Performance analysis is discussed in Chapter 78 and system maintenance is discussed in Chapter 81.

79.4   Concepts

The purpose of this chapter is to provide the fundamental concepts and computations required for the analysis of any system that features a waiting line (queue). In a simple waiting line, a customer arrives, joins a queue, is serviced (by a server of some kind), and leaves. Queuing theory uses the arrival rate and the service rate to quickly compute such statistics as the time a customer spends in the queue and in the system, the expected line length, and the expected number of customers in the system.

In the context of information systems, queuing theory is commonly used to help plan, design, and reconfigure communication networks, with each message representing a customer and each server, router, or other device that holds and forwards or otherwise manipulates messages representing a server. Other applications include disk access, printer spooling, interrupt management, process queuing, and so on. In all these activities, messages (customers) arrive at random intervals and are held briefly for processing by a server of some kind.

79.4.1 Bottleneck analysis

One of the more common information system applications of queuing theory is bottleneck analysis, the study of choke points or bottlenecks in a network. Bottleneck analysis is an important network routing tool (Chapter 54).

As messages move from node to node across a network, they are held and forwarded by one or more nodes. As message volume increases, the number of messages waiting for a given server can grow exponentially, creating a bottleneck that slows or even halts traffic. Queuing theory can help predict such bottlenecks by allowing the network analyst to mathematically identify the network nodes most sensitive to message volume. When a bottleneck occurs, the network analyst is typically faced with numerous alternative solutions. Using queuing theory, the analyst can often quickly eliminate all but a few of those alternatives by making the changes mathematically (in a matter of seconds) and studying the impact on queue length and average wait time. Note that queuing theory does not necessary yield *the* answer. Instead, it helps the analyst quickly narrow the set of feasible solutions to a workable number.

79.4.2 Terminology

The fundamental result of a probabilistic experiment is an outcome. Examples in queuing analysis are number of customers in line and interarrival time. The set, or collection, of all possible outcomes is known as a sample space, which may be either finite or infinite according to whether the number of outcomes is countable. If there were a physical or practical limit on queue length, using six as an example, the finite sample space would be comprised of the integers 0, 1, 2, 3, 4, 5, and 6. Interarrival times form an infinite sample space consisting of the positive real numbers since time may be subdivided indefinitely.

An event is a set of outcomes. The probability associated with event A is the ratio of the number of outcomes in A to the number of outcomes in the sample space. The interpretation of probability for the purposes herein is *long run relative frequency*. That is to say, if A denotes "two customers in line" and prob(A) = 0.27, then an observer of the queue over a very long period would see event A occur 27 percent of the time (assuming the process is stable).

A random variable is a symbolic representation of an outcome. Discrete random variables are associated with finite sample spaces, their continuous

**Table 79.1   A Hypothetical
Probability Mass Function**

N_1	prob(N_1)
0	0.05
1	0.18
2	0.27
3	0.20
4	0.14
5	0.10
6	0.06

counterparts with infinite sample spaces. A probability mass function (pmf) is the mathematical relationship between the various values that a discrete random variable may assume and their probabilities of occurrence. A hypothetical probability mass function for the queue length (denoted N_q) example above is shown in Table 79.1. A continuous random variable is defined by a probability density function (pdf) specified on an interval, such as

$$f(x) = (4 - x)/8, \qquad 0 \le x \le 4,$$

$$= 0, \qquad\qquad \text{otherwise.}$$

The probability that x lies on the interval a to b is the definite integral of $f(x)$ evaluated between those numerical values.

The rth percentile of a probability distribution for random variable x is a number x, such that prob$(x \le x_r) = r/100$. In the distribution for N_q above, the 90th percentile is 5 because prob$(N_q \le 5) = 0.94$. [Prob$(N_q \le 4) = 0.84$ makes this queue length incapable of being the 90th percentile.] For the continuous random variable above, the 90th percentile, 2.735, may be obtained by applying the calculus and algebra.

A random variable (call it y) has two important descriptive parameters, $E(y)$ (expected value or mean), a measure of central tendency, and Var(y) (variance), a measure of dispersion about the mean. For the discrete case, the formulas are

$$E(y) = \sum_{\text{all } y} y p(y)$$

$$\text{Var}(y) = \sum_{\text{all } y} [y - E(y)]^2 p(y).$$

Analogous formulas using the calculus exist for continuous random variables. The mean and variance of N_q based on the distribution above are 2.74 and 2.4524, respectively. The continuous random variable x has mean and variance 1.333 and 0.889, respectively.

79.4.3 General ideas

In the simplest of queuing systems, operating characteristics may be derived from knowledge of:

1. The customer arrival process.
2. The service process.
3. The number of servers available.

Some situations featuring greater complexity are discussed briefly in Sections 79.4.5 and 79.4.6, below.

The exponential distribution is of fundamental importance in queuing analysis. Its probability density function is:

$$f(t) = \lambda e^{-\lambda t}, \qquad t > 0,$$
$$= 0, \qquad\qquad \text{otherwise,}$$

where t stands for time and λ is the rate of the process under study. The rate is always specified with reference to a time unit, such as 3 per min, 5 per h, and 12 per d. The mean of an exponential distribution is the reciprocal of λ, and remarkably the variance is precisely the square of the mean. The graph of this distribution (Figure 79.1) is asymmetrical, descending rapidly from a height of λ on the vertical axis, then curving suddenly and moving slowly toward, but never reaching, the horizontal axis. Of the values on an exponential random variable, 63 percent lie below the mean (in contrast to 50 percent for the normal distribution).

Notation for the simplest of queuing systems is of the form $a/b/c$, where a identifies the interarrival time (IAT) distribution, b the service time (ST) distribution, and c the number of servers. In the next section, formulas and an example for the $M/M/1$ queue are given; "M" is the designation for exponential distribution in queuing parlance. The $M/M/1$ designation indicates exponential arrivals, exponential service times, and 1 server.

79.4.4 The M/M/1 Model

In this system, the arrival process draws customers at rate λ from an unlimited population. Customers move from the queue into service via a first come, first served discipline, and the exponential service times have mean $1/\mu$ (implying also rate μ). Note that both the arrival rate (λ) and the service rate (μ) are exponentially distributed. For steady state probabilities to exist, or to ensure that the queue will not grow to infinite length, the traffic intensity $\rho\ (= \lambda/\mu)$ must be less than 1.

Steady state probabilities for the $M/M/1$ model are calculated as follows, where n refers to the number of customers in the system (queue plus service):

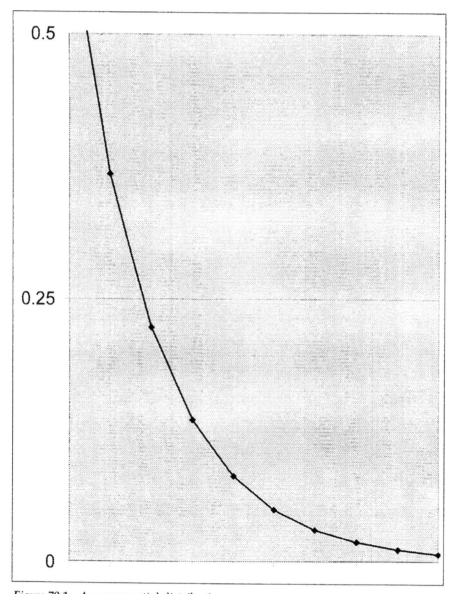

Figure 79.1   An exponential distribution.

$$p_0 = 1 - \rho, \tag{79.1}$$

$$p_n = (1 - \rho)\rho^n, \qquad n = 1, 2, 3, \ldots. \tag{79.2}$$

Important descriptive operating characteristics include the expected time in queue, time in system, line length, and number (of customers) in the system:

$$W_q = E[\text{time in queue}] = \lambda/[\mu(\mu - \lambda)], \tag{79.3}$$

$$W = E[\text{time in system}] = 1/(\mu - \lambda), \tag{79.4}$$

$$L_q = E[\text{line length}] = \lambda^2/[\mu(\mu - \lambda)], \tag{79.5}$$

$$L = E[\text{number in system}] = \lambda/(\mu - \lambda). \tag{79.6}$$

High percentiles (π) for q (time in queue) and w (time in system) may be calculated as follows:

$$\pi_q[90] = W \ln(10\rho), \tag{79.7a}$$

$$\pi q[95] = W \ln(20\rho), \tag{79.7b}$$

$$\pi_w[90] = W \ln 10, \tag{79.8a}$$

$$\pi_w[95] = W \ln 20, \tag{79.8b}$$

where W is expected time in system [e.g., (4)], ln stands for natural logarithm, and ρ is the system's traffic intensity. These percentiles give likelihoods that large waiting times and times in system will occur, knowledge of which is a useful adjunct to means for decision-making purposes.

As an example, consider a single chair barber shop operated by one Harry Schaive. On an ordinary morning, customers arrive at the rate of 4 per h, and the mean time for a haircut is 12 min. Based on extended observation of the shop's operation, Harry's brother, Klaus, an industrial engineer, has concluded that an $M/M/1$ model describes the system adequately.

The information provided show that $\lambda = 4$ per h and $\mu = (1$ per 12 min$) = 5$ per h. With $\rho = 4/5 = 0.8$, the formulas above yield:

$$p_0 = 0.20, \quad p_1 = 0.16, \quad p_2 = 0.128, \quad p_3 = 0.1024,$$

for the probabilities that 0, 1, 2, and 3 people are in the system. Thus Harry is idle (0 people in the queue) 20 percent of the day and an arriving customer has a 0.8 probability of having to wait before having his (or her) hair cut. Note also that prob($n \leq 3$) = 0.5904 (by addition), so there is a substantial chance of finding four or more customers in the shop. The following quatities [equations (3) – (6)] reveal the congested condition of this system:

$$W = 1 \text{ h}, \qquad\qquad W_q = 0.8 \text{ h} = 48 \text{ min},$$

$$L = 4 \text{ customers}, \qquad L_q = 3.2 \text{ customers}.$$

The ratio of mean time in queue to mean service time is four (48/12). Interest in this number is based on the idea that a customer's tolerance for waiting is related to the time already committed to service. A high ratio translates to discontent over the delay involved. Finally, computing the high percentile times in the queue and in the system [equations (7) and (8)]:

$$\pi_q[90] = 2.079\,h = 2\,h\,5\,min,$$

$$\pi_w[90] = 2.303\,h = 2\,h\,18\,min,$$

reveals the astonishing fact that 10 percent of Harry's customers must endure a time in line exceeding 2 h 5 min!

In a network model, the arrival rate (λ) might be several messages per second and the service rate (μ) might be 1000 or more messages per second, but the computations are much the same.

79.4.5   Other models

One solution to the congestion in Harry's shop is to hire another barber for a second chair. This would produce an $M/M/2$ model, a special case of the general $M/M/c$ queuing system. Solving the equations:

$$p_0 = 0.429, \quad p_1 = 0.343, \quad p_2 = 0.137, \quad p_3 = 0.055,$$

$$W = 14.29\,min, \quad W_q = 2.29\,min,$$

$$L = 0.952\ customers \quad Lq = 0.152\ customers,$$

$$\pi_q[90] = 8.27\,min,$$

suggests a vast improvement (at least from the perspective of the customers).

If Harry chooses not to increase his serving capacity, it is possible that customers will start to balk (leave without joining the queue) if the queue is sufficiently long. This would give rise to the $M/M/1/K$ model, where K is the limit on number in system (imposed either by physical operating conditions or by customer behavior). For example, the number of bytes in a memory queue imposes an absolute limit on the length of the queue. The $M/M/1/K/K$ queue is known as the machine repair problem. The population consists of K machines that break down randomly to be repaired by a lone technician. Naturally, there is a limit of K "customers" in this system. Steady-state formulas exist for these models and their multi-server counterparts. The Erlang-k random variable, whose distribution is denoted E_k, is the sum of k identical exponential random variables. Operating characteristics for the commonly observed $M/E_k/1$ and $E_k/M/1$ models can be readily computed.

79.4.6   Ancillary issues

Whether to add a barber in the example above would depend on cost considerations. The following simple formula may be used to determine the total cost (TC) of operating a queuing system:

$$TC = c_w L_q + c_s k, \tag{79.9}$$

where c_w is the cost of one customer's waiting time per hour, c_s is the cost per hour of employing a server, and k equals the number of servers. If it is believed that there is a cost attached to the customer's time in service, then Lq (the mean line length) should be replaced by L (the mean number of customers in the system).

Close examination of equations (3) – (6) reveals the following relationships which apply to all queuing systems:

$$L = \lambda W, \tag{79.10a}$$

$$Lq = \lambda W_q, \tag{79.10b}$$

where λ is the arrival rate, W is the expected time in the system, and W_q is the expected time in the queue. These equations comprise Little's rule, named for the distinguished MIT professor who discovered them. Since $W = W_q + (1/\mu)$, the last term being expected service time, knowledge of λ, μ, and any one of the queue characteristics therein allows computation of the other three.

There are many waiting-line situations that cannot be analyzed using formulas for any particular model. Simulation (Chapter 19) is a methodology capable of handling such problems, as queuing systems in series (unless interarrival time and service time are exponentially distributed), prioritized customers, jockeys (line changes), reneges (departures from the queue without receiving service), bulk arrivals (customers appear in groups of 2, 3, 4, . . .), bulk service, service times dependent on line length, and probabilistic balks.

79.5   Key terms

Arrival rate — The number of arrivals per unit of time.

Balk — To leave without joining the queue.

Bottleneck analysis — The study of choke points or bottlenecks in a network.

Event — A set of outcomes.

Interarrival time — The elapsed time between arrivals of successive customers in a queuing system.

Model — An abstract, mathematical representation of a physical system.

Outcome — The fundamental result of a probabilistic experiment.

Probability mass function (pmf) — The mathematical relationship between the various values that a discrete random variable may assume and their probabilities of occurrence.

Queue — A waiting line.

Random variable — A symbolic representation of an outcome.

Sample space — The set, or collection, of all possible outcomes.

Service rate — The number of customers served per unit of time.

Service time — The time a customer spends receiving service in a queuing system.

Steady state — A condition representative of a system's long run behavior; for example, an assembly line starting without parts in process will be in a transient state until such time that the various stations are being utilized at approximately their expected levels, at which point steady state has been achieved.

Stochastic process — A process organized into states in which movement from state to state is governed by probabilities; examples include the number of customers in a queuing system, levels of inventory on hand, and brands purchased by consumers.

Waiting time — The elapsed time between a customer's arrival and the beginning of service.

79.6   *Software*

SAS, MiniTab, and numerous other statistical programs support queuing theory. The necessary computations can also be performed using spreadsheets and most standard programming languages.

79.7   *References*

1. Allen, A. O., *Probability, Statistics, and Queueing Theory with Computer Science Applications*, 2nd ed., Academic, San Diego, CA, 1990.
2. Gross, D. and Harris, C. M., *Fundamentals of Queueing Theory*, 2nd ed., John Wiley & Sons, New York, 1985.
3. Hall, R. W., *Queueing Methods for Services and Manufacturing*, Prentice-Hall, Englewood Cliffs, NJ, 1991.
4. Hillier, F. S. and Lieberman, G. T., *Introduction to Operations Research*, 6th ed., McGraw-Hill, New York, 1995.

chapter eighty

Configuration management

David C. Yen and William S. Davis

Contents

80.1 Purpose

The purpose of configuration management is to define, manage, control, and audit the changes made to the original system. This chapter considers configuration management personnel and planning, configuration control, and configuration auditing, and reporting.

80.2   Strengths, weaknesses, and limitations

As appropriate, the strengths and weaknesses associated with specific tools or techniques will be discussed in context.

80.3   Inputs and related ideas

System control tools and techniques are covered in Chapter 77. Performance analysis is discussed in Chapter 78, and maintenance is discussed in Chapter 81. Queuing theory (Chapter 79) can be used to perform bottleneck analysis. Virtually all the documentation created during the systems analysis (Part IV), design (Part VI), testing, and implementation (Part VII) stages of the system development life cycle might be relevant to configuration management.

80.4   Concepts

The purpose of configuration management is to define, manage, control, and audit the changes made to the original system. Typical enhancements might include adding new features, adjusting operation procedures, changing execution priorities, fixing bugs, and modifying the original system to accommodate new hardware or software.

80.4.1   Personnel

Many organizations assign change authorization responsibility to a configuration approval board chaired by the chief information officer (or a similar high-level information system manager) and composed of representatives from the user, the developers, the maintainers, and other systems professionals. The board reviews change requests and proposed adaptive and perfective maintenance tasks, authorizes work to begin, and schedules the work. Depending on the project, individual managers, supervisors, or project leaders assign the necessary resources, delegate responsibilities, and monitor progress. The developers and maintainers are responsible for actually performing the work. On some smaller projects, the developers and maintainers perform the management functions.

80.4.2   Planning

The first step in the process is to establish a configuration management plan. The responsible developers and maintainers must be identified and a budget defined. Additionally, steps must be taken to ensure that the appropriate tools and documentation are available.

The configuration items, a set of resources to support configuration management, are collected during this phase. There is no universally accepted standard list; the configuration items are a function of the maintenance project and are subject to time and budget constraints. Typically, system specifications (both generic and detailed), design specifications (logical and physical), manuals (user, operation, command, and system), program code listings, and testing, operation, and execution plans, standards, and procedures are all included. Additionally, such post-release materials as problem and error reports, maintenance requests, change requests, and maintenance standards and procedures might be considered configuration items.

The configuration items are used to define configuration objects, concrete tools that can be used to support the change process. Examples include documents and reports, test cases, input data sets, tools used to build the system, and source code. Also, such parameters as exploded objects, meta-objects, derived objects, imported objects, exported objects, source objects, and detailed processing requirements help to define the relationships between the various configuration entities.

Configuration management standards help to enforce quality, increase productivity, facilitate the management process, and reduce misinterpretation. Three well-known U.S. Government Department of Defense guidelines are MIL-STD-483, DOD-STD-480A, and MIL-STD-1521A. Additionally, software quality assurance standards are applied to configuration management.

80.4.3 Configuration control

A key responsibility of configuration management is to keep track of changes (e.g., new features, upgrades, bug fixes, etc.). A system is composed of numerous interrelated subsystems and/or programs. Each time a subsystem or program is changed, a new version of the system is created. Because the subsystems are interrelated, it is essential that the active version be carefully controlled. For example, a change intended for version 2 may not work or may introduce serious ripple effects if it is incorporated directly into version 3.

80.4.3.1 Establishing a baseline
The term *baseline* comes from surveying. It refers to an initial line that serves as a reference point for all other measurements. In configuration management, the baseline is typically defined as an outcome or milestone of system development; for example, the version of the system on which the final system test is performed might serve as the initial baseline. All changes are made relative to the baseline.

80.4.3.2 Version control
The objective of version control is to track and manage multiple versions of the system and its components. As a minimum, version control should

maintain for each system, subsystem, and/or program a production version, the most recently changed version, and a test version. Additionally, many organizations maintain a repository library of historical versions. The most recently changed version (which presumably worked) serves as back-up in the event of problems with the production version. Changes are made only to the test version. After a change (or set of changes) has been thoroughly tested, the test version becomes the production version and a new test version is initiated.

Often, multiple non-emergency changes are accumulated over time, incorporated in the test version, and released at regular intervals. For example, a university might accumulate changes throughout the first semester, freeze the new version (Section 80.4.3.3) on the day the semester ends, test the new version over the semester break, and release the new version to production at the start of the next semester. Note that once the system is released, no additional changes are permitted to the production version until the next release cycle. The result is a stable, dependable production system. Also, grouping changes makes it easier to identify ripple effects and helps to ensure that the documentation is updated to reflect the changes. Limiting changes to a scheduled release cycle can cause the system to lag behind technological breakthroughs, however.

80.4.3.3   Freezing the system

Before the changes are implemented, the test system is frozen. The freezing process involves archiving the entire system, including the executable programs, data files, source code, and related documentation. The usual practice is to store the archived file on a back-up medium, such as magnetic tape. Should the system fail or become unstable when the changes are made, the archive can be used to reestablish the pre-change version.

80.4.3.4   Benchmarks

At the time the system is frozen, benchmark measurements (execution time, response time, and the like) should be taken for the system. The idea is to establish concrete parameters for measuring baseline performance. Unless the system's pre-change performance is known, there is no way to measure the effect of the change.

80.4.3.5   Regression testing

Once the changes are made, the system must be tested. Unit test all affected programs or components. Then system test the application. Finally, perform regression tests to measure how the change affected response time and other standard performance metrics. The benchmark measurements taken on the baseline is the key to regression testing. The idea is to prove that the old and new versions of the system are functionally equivalent.

80.4.3.6   Establishing a new baseline

After the changes have been implemented and thoroughly tested, the new version is submitted to the configuration approval board. After approval is granted, the production system is frozen, the new version of the test system becomes the production system, and a new baseline (the old production system or the new production system, depending on the configuration management standards in use) is established.

80.4.4   Configuration auditing and reporting

The purpose of configuration auditing is to ensure that the approved changes (and only the approved changes) have been implemented. The auditing process reviews all the changes, investigates any conflicts or ripple effects, and looks for omissions or violations of configuration management standards. An audit can be performed after all changes are implemented, but intermediate audits following important changes are a good idea. The purpose of configuration reporting is to ensure that the changes are broadcast so that everyone involved with the system is aware of the new version.

80.5   Key terms

Adaptive maintenance — Maintenance activities intended to enhance the system by adding features, capabilities, and functions in response to new technology, upgrades, new requirements, or new problems.

Baseline — An initial line that serves as a reference point for all other measurements; an established version of the system that serves as a reference point for future changes.

Benchmark — A set of performance measurements for the baseline.

Configuration approval board — A committee that reviews change requests and proposed adaptive and perfective maintenance tasks, authorizes work to begin, and schedules the work.

Configuration audit — An audit intended to ensure that the approved changes (and only the approved changes) have been implemented.

Configuration item — A resource that supports configuration management.

Configuration management — The process of defining, managing, controlling, and auditing the changes made to the original system.

Configuration object — A concrete tool that can be used to support the change process.

Configuration reporting — The process of broadcasting (or reporting) the changes so that everyone involved with the system is aware of the new version.

Freeze — To archive the entire system, including the executable programs, data files, source code, and related documentation, prior to making a change.

Perfective maintenance — Maintenance activities intended to enhance the system by improving efficiency, reliability, functionality, or maintainability, often in response to user or system personnel requests.

Regression test — A test designed to measure how a change to a system affects response time and other standard performance metrics.

Version control — A set of tools and procedures used to track and manage multiple versions of the system and its components.

80.6 Software

Numerous configuration management and version control software packages are commercially available. Examples include CMVC (Configuration Management Version Control) from IBM, PVCS from Intersolv, SPARCworks/TeamWare from Sun Microsystems, STS/CM (Configuration Management) from Neuma Technology Corporation, VCS-UX Version Control System from Diamond Optimum Systems, Inc., and Visual SourceSafe from Microsoft. QVCS (Quma Version Control System) is a shareware product. This list is by no means complete, nor does it constitute an endorsement.

80.7 References

1. Arthur, L. J., *Software Evolution: The Software Maintenance Challenge,* John Wiley & Sons, New York, 1988.
2. Burch, J. G., *Systems Analysis, Design, and Implementation,* Boyd & Fraser, Boston, MA, 1992.
3. Davis, W. S., *Business Systems Analysis and Design,* Wadsworth, Belmont, CA, 1994.
4. Dewitz, S. D., *Systems Analysis and Design and the Transition to Objects,* McGraw-Hill, New York, 1996.
5. Fournier, R., *Practical Guide to Structured System Development and Maintenance,* Prentice-Hall, Englewood Cliffs, NJ, 1991.
6. Hoffer, J. A., George, J. F., and Valacich, J. S., *Modern Systems Analysis and Design,* Benjamin/Cummings, Reading, MA, 1996.
7. Lamb, D. A., *Software Engineering: Planning for Change,* Prentice Hall, Englewood Cliffs, NJ, 1988.
8. Norman, R. J., *Object-Oriented Systems Analysis and Design,* Prentice-Hall, Upper Saddle River, NJ, 1996.
9. Power, M. J., Cheney, P. H., and Crow, G., *Structured Systems Development: Analysis, Design, Implementation,* 2nd ed., Boyd & Fraser, Boston, MA, 1990.
10. Pressman, R. S., *Software Engineering: A Practitioner's Approach,* 2nd ed., McGraw-Hill, New York, 1987.

chapter eighty-one

Maintenance

William S. Davis and David C. Yen

Contents

0-8493-7001-9/99/$0.00+$.50
©1999 by CRC Press LLC

81.1   Purpose

The objective of the maintenance stage is to keep the system running at an acceptable level. This chapter discusses types of maintenance and techniques for managing maintenance.

81.2   Strengths, weaknesses, and limitations

Where appropriate, the strengths and weaknesses associated with specific maintenance tools and techniques will be discussed in context.

81.3   Inputs and related ideas

Maintenance is the last stage in the system development life cycle and, consequently, is affected by everything that happens in the previous stages. Errors made during the analysis and design stages can significantly impact maintenance. More specifically, maintenance relies on the documentation created during the analysis (Part IV), design (Part VI), testing (Chapters 74 and 75), and implementation (Chapter 76) stages, and the system maintenance life cycle parallels the system development life cycle.

81.4   Concepts

Maintenance begins when the system is released and continues for the life of the system. Over a period of years, it is not unusual for the cost of maintaining a system to significantly exceed the cost of developing it, so a primary objective is controlling maintenance costs. When the cost of maintaining and operating an obsolete or inefficient system exceeds the cost of replacing it, the system life cycle ends and a new life cycle begins.

81.4.1   Development and maintenance

The key to controlling maintenance costs is to design systems that are easy to change, so the link between development and maintenance is very strong. Using such tools as database management software (Chapter 45), data normalization (Chapter 28), program generators, fourth-generation languages, structured techniques (Chapter 62), and object-oriented techniques (Chapters 29 and 66) forces the system designer to create independent modules, to separate the logic from the data, and to avoid programming "tricks." Coding standards can help to enforce a consistent software style that helps to minimize the maintenance programmer's learning time. Walkthroughs and inspections (Chapter 23) are excellent tools for enforcing standards and also help to familiarize personnel with the work of others.

Many of the analysis and design methodologies, tools, and techniques employed during system development can be applied to system maintenance, but there are significant differences between development and maintenance. System development (typically) focuses on new systems and considers such issues such as functional productivity, flexibility, integrity, and user friendliness. Maintenance, in contrast, is concerned with refining and improving the operational efficiency and effectiveness of an existing system and, consequently, is constrained by the existing system's scope, boundaries, and platform, and often must be performed in a short time frame and with a limited budget. Development is a one-time activity, so outsourcing is a viable option. Maintenance is a continuing activity more appropriately performed by in-house personnel. Finally, such resources as test data and test cases, program code, and documentation must be created by the system developers, but are available to the maintenance personnel.

81.4.2   Types of maintenance

There is much more to maintenance than fixing bugs. The categories suggested by Swanson[2] and extended by Reutter[1] are widely accepted.

81.4.2.1   Corrective maintenance

The objective of corrective maintenance is to remove errors or bugs from the software, the procedures, the hardware, the network, the data structures, and the documentation. Corrective maintenance activities include both emergency repairs (fire fighting) and preventive (or corrective) repairs. For example, maintenance programmers are concerned with such tasks as removing residual software bugs, improving the integrity and reliability of the programs, streamlining and tightening data validation routines, correcting invalid processing and reporting, and minimizing downtime.

Maintenance programmers use such traditional debugging tools as static code analyzers, on-line debuggers, and dynamic debugging tools. On-line debuggers are used to trace the order in which modules are executed or to exhibit the names and data values of selected variables as they change. Dynamic debugging tools are used to identify all the possible paths to a given statement, to flag all the statements that modify or access a given data element, or to allow the programmer to determine what happens if the value of a given variable is changed.

In an ideal world, systems and software are so reliable that the need for corrective maintenance does not exist, but that ideal world does not exist and probably never will. However, using such tools as database management software, application development systems, program generators, fourth-generation languages, structured techniques, and object-oriented techniques can significantly improve software reliability.

81.4.2.2   Adaptive maintenance

The point of adaptive maintenance is to enhance the system by adding features, capabilities, and functions in response to new technology, upgrades, new requirements, or new problems. Note that adaptive maintenance is reactive. The idea is to fix the system when the general business climate, competition, growth, new technology, or new regulations make change necessary. The key to minimizing adaptive maintenance costs is to isolate system-dependent features.

81.4.2.3 Perfective maintenance

The point of perfective maintenance is to enhance the system by improving efficiency, reliability, functionality, or maintainability, often in response to user or system personnel requests. Corrective and adaptive maintenance are reactive. Bugs are fixed as they are discovered. An upgrade to an operating system can necessitate a change to application software. Perfective maintenance, in contract, is proactive. The idea is to fix the system *before* it breaks.

Restructuring efforts are aimed at enhancing performance without changing how the system works or what it does. The code might be converted to a more efficient language or run through an optimizing compiler. Code conversion software might be used to reorganize the code or convert the logic to a more structured form. Note that the code is not rewritten, just restructured.

The point of reengineering is to change the system to make it better without affecting its functionality or external behavior. The idea is to gradually "clean up the mess" by doing such things as restructuring files and databases and encasing old code in a wrapper of well-structured or object-oriented code. Reengineered software is easier to reverse engineer or to farm out to subcontractors.

The objective of reverse engineering is to extract an abstract model from the system's physical documentation and then use the model as a base for creating a functionally equivalent system. For example, an analysis of a set of source code might generate a structure chart, a set of data dictionary entries, or an entity-relationship diagram. Reverse engineering has been applied to software almost as long as software has existed. For example, Microsoft might reverse engineer its Excel spreadsheet program to produce equivalent programs to run on different computers or to create an object-oriented version of Excel.

81.4.2.4 Preventive maintenance

Although not explicitly part of the Swanson/Reutter model (except by implication), ongoing preventive maintenance is an important part of any system's standard operating procedures. The objective of preventive maintenance is to anticipate problems and correct them before they occur. Files and databases must be updated, periodically reorganized, and regularly backed up. Control totals must be reset. New software releases must be installed.

System performance monitoring is an important key to preventive maintenance. The idea is to conduct periodic audits and to run regular benchmark tests to determine if the system is continuing to perform to expectations. Both hardware and software are monitored to measure system load and system utilization. The information derived from performance monitoring provides an early warning of potential system problems and often initiates other forms of maintenance.

81.4.3   Managing maintenance

Maintenance is expensive. The elements of a system often interact in unexpected ways, and ripple effects (unexpected bugs or new errors caused by a change intended to fix an initial problem) can be devastating. Sometimes, apparently unrelated maintenance problems are tightly linked. Consequently, maintenance must be carefully managed. Formal maintenance procedures are the key to managing maintenance.

81.4.3.1   The system maintenance life cycle

The system maintenance life cycle is similar to the system development life cycle. Configuration management (Chapter 80), the process of managing and controlling changes to a system, defines a context or methodology, including formal procedures for requesting, evaluating, and implementing changes. Evaluation analysis (a phase that parallels the information gathering and problem definition stage of the system development life cycle) is used to assess the impact of a proposed change. The objective is to identify and document the applications, programs, routines, and other components that must be modified, the likely impact of the change on normal operations, and the time, cost, and other resources required to implement the change. Next, the change is analyzed, designed, coded, and tested. After the work is done, the change is released (Chapter 76).

81.4.3.2   Prioritization

Given the budgetary and resource constraints imposed on the system maintenance process, it is not unusual to have a backlog of change requests. Some organizations rely on simple first-in-first-out or (less frequently) last-in-first-out schemes to prioritize the requests. Other organizations prioritize the requests based on a preliminary evaluation analysis (Section 81.4.3.1). Note that a sound evaluation analysis is the key to deciding if maintenance or new system development is needed to solve the problem.

81.4.3.3   Fire fighting

Some maintenance problems require an immediate response. Following a system crash, a major integrity threat, the release of a new government regulation with a tight deadline, or a similar problem, a fix is needed right now, and formal procedures must wait. Such fire fighting activities are (or should be) relatively rare, however, and emergency patches should be formally incorporated into a subsequent release.

81.4.3.4 Standards and quality assurance

Many system developers (and many maintainers) view all maintenance as fire fighting. Consequently, in their rush to get the job done, they sometimes ignore or disregard quality assurance and other standards. It is important that all changes be made in a consistent manner. Consequently, such standards as code efficiency targets, fault tolerance rates, operational sequence optimization guidelines, and expected performance norms must be established and enforced, and even true fire fighting activities must be brought up to standards after the fact.

81.5 Key terms

Adaptive maintenance — Maintenance activities intended to enhance the system by adding features, capabilities, and functions in response to new technology, upgrades, new requirements, or new problems.

Configuration management — The process of defining, managing, controlling, and auditing the changes made to the original system.

Corrective maintenance — Maintenance activities intended to remove errors or bugs from the software, the procedures, the hardware, the network, the data structures, and the documentation.

Evaluation analysis — A maintenance phase (similar to the problem definition stage in the system development life cycle) during which the impact of a particular change is evaluated.

Fire fighting — Making emergency repairs, often under extreme time pressure.

Maintenance — The final stage of the system development life cycle; a continuing series of activities and costs intended to keep the system running at an acceptable level.

Perfective maintenance — Maintenance activities intended to enhance the system by improving efficiency, reliability, functionality, or maintainability, often in response to user or system personnel requests.

Preventive maintenance — Regularly scheduled maintenance activities; the intent is to anticipate problems and correct them before they occur.

Reengineering — Changing a system to make it better without affecting its functionality or external behavior.

Restructuring — Efforts aimed at enhancing performance without changing how the system works or what it does.

Reverse engineering — Extracting an abstract model from a system's physical documentation and then using the model as a base for creating a functionally equivalent system.

Ripple effects — Unexpected bugs or new errors caused by a change intended to fix an initial problem.

Static code analyzer — A program that scans (but does not execute) the code and flags such potential errors as synonyms, poor structure, inconsistent usage, dead code, unreferenced variables, and other deviations from coding standards.

81.6   Software

Numerous configuration management and version control software packages are commercially available. Examples include CMVC (Configuration Management Version Control) from IBM, PVCS from Intersolv, SPARCworks/TeamWare from Sun Microsystems, STS/CM (Configuration Management) from Neuma Technology Corporation, VCS-UX Version Control System from Diamond Optimum Systems, Inc., and Visual SourceSafe from Microsoft. QVCS (Quma Version Control System) is a shareware product. This list is by no means complete, nor does it constitute an endorsement.

Debugging tools, such as static code analyzers, on-line debuggers, and dynamic debugging tools are found in most software development environments.

81.7   References

81.7.1   Citations

1. Reutter, J., Maintenance is a management problem and a programmer's opportunity, AFIPS Conf. Proc. 1981 Natl. Comput. Conf., Vol. 50, Chicago, May 4 to 7, 1981, 343.
2. Swanson, E., The dimensions of maintenance, 2nd Int. Conf. Software Eng., Proc., San Francisco, October 13 to 15, 1976, 492.

81.7.2   Suggestions for additional reading

1. Arthur, L. J., *Software Evolution: The Software Maintenance Challenge*, John Wiley & Sons, New York, 1988.
2. Birrell, N. D. and Ould, M. A., *A Practical Handbook for Software Development*, Cambridge University Press, Cambridge, UK, 1985.
3. Fournier, R., *Practical Guide to Structured System Development and Maintenance*, Yourdon, Englewood Cliffs, NJ, 1991.
4. Martin, J. and McClure, C., *Software Maintenance. The Problem and Its Solutions*, Prentice-Hall, Englewood Cliffs, NJ, 1983.
5. Parikh, G., *Handbook of Software Maintenance*, John Wiley & Sons, New York, 1985.

chapter eighty-two

Database administration

John "Skip" Benamati
Miami University

Contents

0-8493-7001-9/99/$0.00+$.50
©1999 by CRC Press LLC

82.1   Purpose

The purpose of database administration is to provide reliable, consistent, secure, and available corporate-wide data. This chapter discusses the roles performed by database administration, distinguishes database administration and data administration, and describes several database operation and maintenance issues.

82.2   Strengths, weaknesses, and limitations

Where appropriate, the strengths and weaknesses of various techniques will be discussed in context.

82.3   Inputs and related ideas

Database administration uses such tools as CASE (Chapter 5), the data dictionary (Chapter 25), entity-relationship models (Chapter 26), and data normalization (Chapter 28). Database design is discussed in Chapter 45. System controls are discussed in Chapter 77. Several key data concepts are introduced in Chapters 43 and 44.

82.4   Concepts

The purpose of database administration is to provide reliable, consistent, secure, and available corporate-wide data. This chapter discusses the roles performed by database administration, distinguishes database administration and data administration, and describes several database operation and maintenance issues.

82.4.1   Database administration roles

Although database administration (DBA) means different things to different organizations, the overall objective is to achieve centralization and control of the corporation's data resource.

82.4.1.1   Planning

Database administration is responsible for developing a strategy for the control and use of corporate data and for developing, implementing and supporting standards, guidelines, and tools that are consistent with the strategy. The planning task includes performing strategic planning for managing and centralizing data; evaluating, selecting, and implementing a database management system (DBMS) and related hardware and tools; and ensuring that priorities for application development are consistent with the long range data strategy.

82.4.1.2 Design

Both conceptual and physical database design (Chapter 45) are database administration (DBA) responsibilities. The DBA group provides technical and design support for application developers and controls the conceptual design to ensure that it is consistent with and integrated into the corporate data strategy. Physical database design requires making effective use of the database management system and related tools. Additionally, the DBA group establishes corporate guidelines and standards to ensure data consistency across applications.

82.4.1.3 Operation and control

The database administration group supports existing operational systems and is responsible for data integrity, security, availability, and the performance of the database management system. Database administration also provides education and support for the use of the data standards, guidelines, and tools.

82.4.1.4 Usage

Database administration provides documentation and support for using data by developing and enforcing standards for database content and use. Data dictionaries (Chapter 25) and CASE (Chapter 5) are used to develop documentation, enforce standards, and support design. Tools such as query languages also fall under DBA control. Knowledge, education, and support for all database-related software are other DBA responsibilities.

82.4.2 Data administration

The management side of the database administration group is sometimes called data administration (DA). The data administration people are the policy setters and decision makers responsible for the corporate data. They provide an executive level vision of the corporate data needs. The broader database administration group includes the technicians who implement and enforce the decisions and standards the data administration people put in place.[1] Data administration tends to deal with the conceptual side of the data and database administration deals with the physical side.

Whether or not this break is formalized, database administration calls for a blend of management, technical, and interpersonal skills. Data processing skills are rarely used directly, but the database administration group must have an appreciation for them. Technical skills are required to provide ongoing support for the use of the data model. Interpersonal skills are required because database administration must resolve across functional boundaries any conflicts that concern how the data will be stored and presented. Data administration calls for stronger interpersonal skills to work with the users during logical design.

82.4.3 Operation and maintenance issues

This section covers several database administration operation and maintenance standards, tools, utilities, and methods.

82.4.3.1 Implementation guidelines

Implementation guidelines define how applications will be developed and installed with respect to data. The database administration role is primarily physical database implementation and support, but some of the coding effort may be defined and enforced by the DBA group.

82.4.3.2 Error handling

Database administration is responsible for the error-handling routines that protect the integrity of the database. Techniques for handling errors may require common error routines to ensure databases are rolled back to a point of consistency in the event of an error. Typically, all transactions running in a database management system environment are logged on a transaction log and the database is not permanently altered until the transaction is run to completion or committed. Error handling becomes more complex if more than one database management system is involved in a transaction. Techniques such as two-phase commits may be employed. Two-phase commits synchronize the committing of transaction changes across multiple database management systems to ensure that the transaction is either run to completion or is rolled back on all of the systems.

82.4.3.3 Security

Security is a means of ensuring data integrity and protecting confidential information by controlling who has the authority to view, alter, or delete the data in a database. The ultimate responsibility falls on database administration, but the ability to grant authority can be delegated to other individuals as long as DBA maintains control. Security can be implemented in the database management system itself or controlled at the application level.

82.4.3.4 Backup and recovery

The responsibility for designing and implementing backup and recovery procedures rests with database administration. Data can be lost in many ways, including program errors, hardware failures, incorrect changes, and bad input data. A backup copy is used to restore a table of data to the point in time when the copy was made. Recovery procedures help to ensure that the recovered data are correct.

Backup copies of database tables and transaction log files are the primary inputs for backup and recovery. All changes of any type to the database are stored on the log. With a backup copy of a table and the contents of the log since that copy was made, a table can be recovered to the point where the failure occurred. To avoid recovering "bad" transactions, a well-designed recovery procedure allows the system to be recovered to any point in the log.

Synchronization is an important issue because simply recovering a table does not mean that it is in synch with other related tables in the database. For instance, a given table could contain data that are related to other tables, because deleted data in other tables or the recovered data could contain broken relationships that point to non-existing data. The only way to ensure data integrity is to recover the complete set of relationally connected tables (a referential group) to a consistent or current point.

Points of consistency can be established in two ways. The first is to disable the database and backup the entire referential group. The database must be disabled to ensure that no tables are changed from the time the backup process starts until it is complete. Disabling the database while backups are run is not always acceptable, however, because some applications cannot afford the downtime.

Some database management systems provide a means for establishing a synch point for a set of tables. As transactions are processed against the tables, new transactions are held until the entire set of tables is free from processing. At this time, all the tables are guaranteed to be in synch, and the synch point is recorded on the transaction log. Although the act of establishing a synch point makes the tables unavailable for a time, the duration is very short and, if run during off-peak hours, not noticeable.

Synch points do not eliminate the need for backup; they simply eliminate the need to take the database off-line to back it up. Backup copies should still be taken prior to establishing the synch point. Recovery time will then be short, because only a small piece of the log will be needed.

Another option available on some database management systems is to take incremental backups of tables. An incremental backup copy contains only the data that have changed since the last full or incremental backup. Recovery then starts with the latest full copy, adds any incremental changes, and uses the log from that point.

Note that the log is a finite file with a defined upper limit on its size, so it must periodically be cleared so that changes can continue to be recorded. The existing log information cannot be destroyed unless all the tables in the database have been backed up since the log was previously cleared, but the log may become full at any time. To get around these problems, the existing log file is typically archived or backed up and then reset to empty. Subsequently, the archived log files can be used should recovery become necessary.

The goal is to create a complete backup and recovery plan that . . .minimizes downtime (for taking backups) and also minimizes recovery complexity and time. Backups can be scheduled, perhaps (depending on application requirements) when the application is not running. Recovery however must be performed whenever the need arises (usually at the worst possible time). The issue becomes more complex when the data are centralized and multiple applications access a single, corporate-wide database.

82.4.3.5 Concurrency control

Concurrency issues arise when multiple users can access a database simultaneously. If precautions are not taken, lost updates, uncommitted dependencies, and inconsistent analysis problems can arise, all of which affect database integrity.

82.4.3.5.1 Locking   The solution to these multi-user pitfalls is locking. It is a simple concept. When the data must remain consistent during the entire execution of a transaction, the application routine locks the relevant data, thus denying other transactions the ability to change the data. The transaction can then be processed to completion and concurrency-related problems will be eliminated.[1]

Locking can be performed at many levels or granularities (e.g., the entire database, individual tables, physical pages of data within tables, or individual rows). Higher granularity (i.e., locking a bigger object) implies lower lock maintenance overhead, but it also implies a lower level of concurrency. In other words, granularity and concurrency are tradeoffs. In general, choose the highest level of granularity that will support the required level of concurrency. Some database management systems provide the ability to control the duration that locks are held by transactions, thus allowing the level of concurrency to be increased in some situations.

82.4.3.5.2 Optimistic concurrency   A transaction that maintains locks while information is displayed for update is considered to be a conversational transaction. On such transactions, there is active communication with the database management system and the appropriate locks are maintained for the duration of the transaction. Locking may be the only viable alternative, but it can cause problems.

Consider, for example, the following scenario. A bank teller has just begun updating a customer's address when he or she is interrupted for some reason. The appropriate data have already been accessed, and locks are being held against the data displayed on the screen. If the locking level is coarse (e.g., a page or a table), then locks are also being held against other customers and no information can be updated for those other customers. If the teller is distracted for a long period of time, other tellers and customers will be inconvenienced.

An alternative is to break the transaction into two transactions, one that reads the information and displays it (TRANR) and another that interprets data changes and updates the database (TRANU). An exposure exists between the time the data are displayed and subsequently updated because once the locks are released, another transaction might update the information. This could lead to lost updates when TRANU writes old information over a new change.

The best way to avoid the problem is to determine if the data were updated after the locks were released by TRANR. Typically, all update transactions are required to maintain in the database row-level timestamps indicating the time of the most recent change. Copies of the rows that were displayed by TRANR are maintained in memory. TRANU reads updated timestamps from the rows it wants to change and compares the timestamps to the copies in memory. If the timestamps match the ones in memory, then no changes were made and the updates can be performed. If there is a conflict, then the application must resolve it, possibly by redisplaying the changed row(s) and asking the user to resubmit the changes.

This method of concurrency control, known as optimistic concurrency, adds overhead to the system but greatly improves the concurrency potential. Once again, database administration is faced with a tradeoff, and the method chosen will vary from application to application based on requirements.

82.5   Key terms

Backup and recovery — Logging transactions and database changes, periodically making backup copies of databases, and recovering databases in the event of a failure or loss of data.

Checkpoint — A point at which the database and the transaction logs are physically synchronized.

Concurrency control — Ways of preventing data loss or data corruption when multiple transactions can be updating a database at the same time.

Conversational transaction — A transaction that maintains locks while information is displayed for update.

Data administration (DA) — An administrative function charged with the overall responsibility for data resources in an organization.

Data integrity — The state of a database that is protected against loss or contamination; data integrity is ensured by carefully controlling and managing data entry, data maintenance, and data access from the time the data first enter the system until they are of no further use.

Database administration (DBA) — A technical group charged with the physical functioning of an organization's databases, including backup and recovery, performance, and security enforcement.

Database management system (DBMS) — A software package that provides a means to define, maintain, control, and administer a database and its applications.

Deadlock — A situation that occurs when two or more transactions are waiting for a resource that the other transaction has locked; both transactions will hold their locks waiting for the needed resource to be unlocked.

Granularity — The level of locking; for example, the entire database, individual tables, physical pages of data within tables, or individual rows.

Incremental backup copy — A backup copy that contains only the data that have changed since the last full or incremental back up was performed.

Locking — The process of allocating control over a database resource to a specific transaction to avoid problems associated with concurrent use.

Log — A file containing a record of all database changes.

Optimistic concurrency — Breaking a transaction into two transactions, one that reads the information and displays it, and another that interprets data changes and updates the database, and releases locks between those transactions. The system is optimistic that no other users will change information between the read and update transactions. If another user does change the information, the update transaction is lost.

Referential group — A complete set of relationally connected tables.

Security — Steps taken to protect a database from unauthorized access.

Synch point — A point at which a complete set of relationally connected tables (a referential group) is consistent.

Synchronization — The act of ensuring that a complete set of relationally connected tables (a referential group) is consistent.

Transaction — The sequence of steps required to carry out an event about which data are recorded or processed.

Two-phase commit — A process of committing changes across multiple database management systems. In the first phase each DBMS votes on whether they can commit a transaction. If all vote yes, the transaction is committed on all. If any vote no, the transaction is rolled back on all.

82.6   Software

Many CASE products (Chapter 5), such as Texas Instrument's Information Engineering Facility (IEF), include software to provide integrated support for both database and application design. Other tools such as automated data dictionaries (Chapter 25) provide support as well. Most full functioned database management systems provide a set of utilities or commands that support the creation, maintenance, control, and administration of databases, including back up and recovery. Access, Paradox, dBase, Filemaker Pro, Approach, 4th Dimension, and Alpha Four are popular microcomputer database management programs. Examples of mainframe database software include DB2, IDMS, and ORACLE.

82.7   References

1. Date, C. J., *An Introduction to Database Systems*, Vol. 1, 6th ed., Addison-Wesley, Reading, MA, 1994.

2. Hansen, G. W. and Hansen, J. V., *Database Management and Design,* Prentice-Hall, Upper Saddle River, NJ, 1996.
3. Kroenke, D. M., *Database Processing: Fundamentals, Design, and Implementation,* Prentice-Hall, Upper Saddle River, NJ, 1995.
4. McFadden, F. R. and Hoffer, J. A., *Modern Database Management,* Benjamin/Cummings, Redwood City, CA, 1994.
5. Watson, R. T., *Data Management, an Organizational Perspective,* John Wiley & Sons, New York, 1996.
6. Weldon, J. L., *Data Base Administration,* Plenum Press, New York, 1981.

Glossary

5W analysis — (40) The first step in the business function-task analysis process during which the focus group is asked to answer five key questions (how, where, what, who, and when) about relevant functions, processes, and data elements.

A-specs (system/segment specifications) (SSS) — (35) A hierarchy of requirements specifications that logically defines the system from its high-level objectives down to the configuration item level. (41) A set of specifications that identify major systems and subsystems at a conceptual level; the system/segment specifications define the requirements down to, but not including, the configuration item level; sometimes called the project or mission requirements.

Abrupt cutover (crash cutover, direct cutover) — (76) A system release strategy in which the old system is discontinued on a predefined date and the entire organization switches directly to the new system.

Abstraction — (61) A problem-solving technique that focuses on investigating the most critical aspects of a problem and using the results to suggest a solution.

Access vector — (43) A list of pointers providing access to a set of data items.

Act fork — (57) A point on a decision tree (represented by a box) where a decision is made.

Action diagram — (65) A tool used in James Martin's Information Engineering methodology to plan and document both an overview of program logic and the detailed program logic.

Action entry — (58) The box at the lower right of a decision table where the appropriate action is indicated.

Action-oriented question-answer dialogue — (49) A form of dialogue that requires a single keystroke response to trigger an action.

Action stub — (58) The box at the lower left of a decision table where the possible actions are listed.

Activity — (20, 21, 22) A task to be completed.

Activity (function) — (30) A process or event that moves a system from one state to another.

Actor — (29, 66) A person or entity external to the system.

Adaptability — (42) A measure of the ease of changing or modifying a system, often in response to a technological change.

Adaptive maintenance — (80, 81) Maintenance activities intended to enhance the system by adding features, capabilities, and functions in response to new technology, upgrades, new requirements, or new problems.

Adaptive routing — (54) A distributed routing technique that selects the best route based on such criteria as the speed, capacity, or cost of the link, the utilization rate of a particular node, the failure rate of a particular path, the type of data transmitted, response time, throughput, and so on; also known as dynamic routing.

Afferent process — (61, 62) A process that gathers and prepares input data.

Aggregation — (29) A description of part-of relationships among objects; the higher-level objects are completely described by all of their components.

Algorithm — (43) A rule for arriving at an answer in a finite number of steps.

Alias — (25) An alternate name for a data element.

Alpha test — (74) A controlled environment test in which the designers demonstrate key system functions, perhaps selected by the users, and the users manipulate the system under developer guidance.

Analysis — (1, 72) To attack a problem by breaking it into subproblems; the second step in the system development life cycle (following problem definition) during which the responsible people determine exactly what must be done to solve the problem.

Analytic model — (19) A mathematical equation(s) that will give the value of an output when an input value is specified.

Ancestor — (43) A parent of a parent (or an ancestor).

Anti-virus software — (71) Software designed to recognize certain code patterns (called virus signatures) and sound an alarm when a virus is detected.

Applet — (51) A small application program that performs a single task.

Application analysis — (42) A study of the interactions and relationships between the hardware and software resources; typically, all the required software is installed on a test system and the behavior of the hardware is evaluated as the applications run.

Application based documentation (execution-oriented documentation) — (70) Documentation designed to support an application.

Application entity diagram — (4) An entity diagram that combines all the user entity diagrams and merged entity diagrams for the entire application.

Application generator (generator, program generator) — (31, 32) A program that starts with information in graphical, narrative, list, or some other logical form and generates the appropriate source or executable code.

Arc — (43) An edge on a directed graph.

Archive (history file) — (44) A file that holds already processed transactions or no longer current master records.

Array — (43) An elementary data structure that resembles a table; typically, one data element is stored in each array cell and the cells are distinguished by subscripts.

Arrival rate — (79) The number of arrivals per unit of time.

Assignable cause variation — (10) Variation that is not part of the design of the process; the sources or factors producing assignable cause variation can, by definition, only affect a subset of the output from that process. Assignable cause variation is sometimes referred to as special cause variation.

Assistance dialogue — (49) A form of dialogue designed to provide help with command syntax, error messages, error identification, error symptoms, and so on.

Association — (29, 66) A relationship between objects that indicates some meaningful and interesting connection.

Association — (73) A link between two or more events defined by precedence requirements and similar conditions.

Asynchronous event — (73) An event that can occur at any time and is not synchronized with other events.

Attribute — (25, 26, 27, 28, 43, 44) A property of an entity.

Audit — (77) A study of a system or a process designed to ensure that the established procedures and controls are followed.

Audit test — (74) An objective, in depth white-box evaluation of the system and its components to verify that the system is free of errors.

Authentication — (71) The process of verifying the user's identity.

Author — (23) In an inspection, the person (or the team leader) who prepared the documentation or the code being inspected.

Automation boundary — (36) A line drawn around one or more processes on a data flow diagram, thus grouping them to form a single program or procedure; a set of automation boundaries defines a family of alternative solutions.

Availability requirements analysis — (53) A network analysis process that helps to determine and document the effect of time differences (time zone shifts) between the different geographical areas covered by the network.

B-specs (system/segment design document) (SSDD) — (35) A black-box specification defined for each physical component at (or directly below) the configuration item level; (41) a set of specifications that define, in black-box form, the components that occupy the configuration item level.

Backtracking — (34) Reviewing or checking what has already been done and attempting to find another path or another way to accomplish the goal(s); (75) tracing backward from an error until the error's cause is found.

Backup — (42) A duplicate copy of a set of data, a program, a hardware component, or some other system element that is used to restore the system in the event of failure.

Backup and recovery — (82) Logging transactions and database changes, periodically making backup copies of databases, and recovering databases in the event of a failure or loss of data.

Backup file — (44) A file that holds a copy of a master or transaction file; backup files are used to recover data if disaster strikes.

Backward chaining — (34) A goal-oriented search technique that starts with the desired goal state and works backward to the initial state by applying the inverse operator.

Balance — (24) A characteristic of an exploded data flow diagram in which each input from and output to the parent level is accounted for.

Balk — (79) To leave without joining the queue.

Balking — (19) The act of walking away from a queue; usually occurs when the queue is either too long or at maximum capacity.

Baseline — (80) An initial line that serves as a reference point for all other measurements; an established version of the system that serves as a reference point for future changes.

Batch processing — (72) A processing technique in which transactions are accumulated over time and the system's status is updated at the end of a business cycle.

Behavioral requirement — (35) A requirement that defines something the system does, such as an input, an output, or an algorithm.

Behavior-oriented paradigm — (16) An approach to requirements analysis in which the analyst observes and investigates the problem from the strategic level by focusing on executive decision-making and problem-solving styles.

Benchmark — (42) A standard program, procedure, or set of test data used to measure such performance characteristics as a computer's processing speed; (80) a set of performance measurements for the baseline.

Benefits — (38) Advantages generated by or derived from the system.

Best route algorithm — (54) An adaptive routing technique that uses such parameters as the type of message, the rate of under-utilization or over-utilization of a particular node, and the number of intermediate nodes between the source and the destination.

Beta site — (76) The pilot site in a pilot implementation.

Beta test — (74) A test conducted by (selected) real users who use real hardware, real software, and real (unplanned) data to work on real and imagined problems with any frequency and in any sequence.

Bi-directional flow — (50) A control flow in which the called window can transfer control back to the calling window after execution.

Bias — (9) Any factor that systematically favors some members of the population over others when a sample is drawn.

Binary tree — (43) A special type of tree in which each node has two branches.

Binding time — (62) The time at which a module's values and identifiers are fixed; for example, coding time, compilation time, load time, or execution time.

Biometric device — (71) A system component that can identify an individual based on such biological criteria as a retinal scan, a fingerprint analysis, a voice print, or a signature analysis.

Birth — (72) The system life cycle stage during which the existing system's problems, errors, and missing features are identified and investigated and new opportunities suggested by emerging technologies and user requests are examined and evaluated.

Black box — (35) A routine, module, or component whose inputs and outputs are known, but whose contents are hidden.

Black-box testing — (74) A testing strategy that ignores the internal contents of the module, program, subsystem, or system and considers only the inputs and the outputs.

Blind search — (34) A search technique that visits every node in the search space while following a given solution path no more than once.

Block — (44) Two or more logical records stored together as part of the same physical record.

Bottleneck (choke point) — (53, 54) A place in the network where message flow exceeds capacity, resulting in delays and even lost messages.

Bottleneck analysis — (42) A study of the waiting lines or queues that develop within a system; the objective is to find choke points, or bottlenecks; (79) the study of choke points or bottlenecks in a network.

Bottom-up — (4, 15) A methodology (or an approach to problem solving) that starts with the details and works upward.

Bottom-up design — (72) A data driven design strategy in which work begins at the lowest level, typically with the detailed, computational modules; when all the modules at one level are completed, work progresses to the next higher level.

Bottom-up testing — (74) A testing strategy that starts at the bottom and works up through the hierarchy to the top.

Boundary — (1, 72) An entity that serves to delimit or separate a system from its environment.

Boundary analysis (range constraint analysis) — (75) Generating test data to represent such extreme values as upper bounds, lower bounds, and other exceptional values.

Boundary object (interface object) — (66) An object that communicates with the user or with other systems.

Boyce-Codd normal form — (28) A relation is in Boyce-Codd normal form (BCNF) if and only if every determinant is a candidate key.

Bracket — (65) The basic building block of an action diagram.

Brainstorming — (14) A small-group technique for soliciting and consolidating ideas and thoughts about a problem, a problem's possible causes, system requirements, alternative solutions, and similar issues.

Branch — (43) On a tree, a link between a parent and a child.

Branch analysis — (75) A technique for generating test data by checking the flow of logic through a program and providing data to ensure that each logical path is followed; see also *path test, junction test,* and *loop test.*

Branches — (18) In a cause-and-effect diagram, the factors causing the effect of interest; branches are subdivided into big, medium, small, and tiny branches. When the term fishbone diagram is used, branches are referred to as bones.

Breadth — (51) A measure of the number of items (e.g., menu choices) on a single page.

Breadth (span-of-control) — (61, 62) A measure of the number of modules directly controlled by a higher-level routine.

Breadth search — (7, 34) A blind searching technique that investigates all the nodes at a given level before moving down to the next level.

Bridge — (53) A computer that links two networks with similar protocols; (69) a routine that converts the organization's current data to a format that is compatible with the purchased software.

Broadcast routing — (54) A routing technique in which a header containing the address of the receiving node is added to the message; the message is then transmitted to all the nodes in the network, and the node whose address matches the header reacts to the message.

Browser — (51) A program that converts hyperlinks into the associated URLs, requests pages from the Internet, and displays those pages.

Bug — (75) An error or malfunction in a module, a program, a procedure, a physical component, or a system.

Burn-in period — (74) An initial period during which a hardware component is run continuously in an attempt to find and eliminate start-up errors.

Bus network — (52) A network in which the host computer is located at one end of a common communication line and all the other computers and peripherals in the network are attached to the same line.

Business function-task analysis — (40) A methodology developed by IBM in the 1960s to establish the relationships between an organization's data, processes, and organizational units.

Button bar — (50) A set of buttons that (typically) appears under the menu bar; each button holds a symbol or icon that represents a function and provides a short cut to the function.

Callback — (71) An authentication tool in which the host computer verifies the user code and password, breaks the connection (hangs up), looks up the authorized telephone number for that user's workstation, and then redials the workstation.

Candidate key — (28) A possible key; an attribute or group of attributes that uniquely distinguishes one occurrence of an entity; note that a given entity can have more than one candidate key.

Capability maturity model — (29) A comprehensive framework for describing and evaluating the software development capability of an organization.

Cardinality — (4, 26, 27) A measure of the relative number of occurrences of two entities.

CASE (computer-aided software engineering) — (5, 32) A set of automated tools that assist in the entire software engineering process.

Case structure — (62) A selection structure with multiple alternative paths; the path through the structure is normally based on the value of a control variable.

Census — (9, 17) A set of measurements (or interviews) for every element of a population.

Centralized management — (72) A management philosophy based on integrated top-down control.

Centralized routing — (54) A routing technique in which the central node has super-authority over all the other nodes.

Chaining — (44) Maintaining a linked list of the logical keys of the records in a file.

Change control procedures — (74) A set of procedures for recording, assessing, controlling, and tracking all requests for change both during and after the testing process.

Checkpoint — (82) A point at which the database and the transaction logs are physically synchronized.

Child — (35) A related, lower-level requirement; (43) an immediate lower-level node in a tree; (45) a lower-level record in a hierarchical database structure.

Child (son) — (62) An immediate lower-level module in a control structure; control passes from the parent to the child and then returns to the parent.

Choke point (bottleneck) — (53, 54) A place in the network where message flow exceeds capacity, resulting in delays and even lost messages.

Circular linked list — (43) A linked list in which the last node points back to the first node.

Class (object type) — (6, 66) A group of similar objects.

Class, responsibilities and collaborations (CRC) technique — (66) A technique for identifying operations.

Class structure diagram — (29) A diagram that defines the groups or classes the objects fall into and defines the structural relationships between the groups.

Client — (53) A computer (more generally, a node) that requests a service from a server.

Client/server — (53) A network in which client computers request services from a central server computer.

Client/server computing — (51) A form of networked computing in which a computer that needs a service (the client) requests help from a computer that has the ability to provide the service (the server).

Closed question — (17) A question that requires one of several predetermined choices or that requires a single numerical response.

Code generator — (2) A program that starts with information in graphical, narrative, list, or some other logical form and outputs the appropriate source code; also called a *generator* or *program generator*.

Coding error — (75) A syntax or command error.

Cohesion — (3, 61, 62, 63) A measure of a module's completeness.

Coincidental cohesion — (62) The weakest type of cohesion in which the elements are related almost by chance.

Collaboration — (66) The embodiment of a contract between a client and a server; the interaction that takes place when a class has a responsibility it cannot fulfill alone and thus requests the necessary service from a server.

Collaboration diagram — (66) A diagram that shows the basic message flow between objects and implies the associations between them.

Collision — (44) In data management, an event that occurs when two or more logical keys input to a hashing algorithm yield the same relative address.

Collision detection — (54) A network management technique in which the nodes are allowed to transmit at any time; if two messages collide, the collision is sensed and the messages are retransmitted.

Column header — (47) Documentation at the top of each page or screen that identifies the field displayed in each column.

Command-based interface — (48) A user interface that relies on cryptic commands and/or specific keystrokes to identify the desired action.

Command-oriented documentation — (70) Documentation that contains all the commands used by the system and/or the program, usually arranged in alphabetical order.

Commercial software package — (69) A set of prewritten application programs that are commercially available for purchase or lease.

Common cause variation — (10) Variation that is inherent to a process; common cause variation has the ability to affect all output from a process. All processes are subject to this form of variation.

Common-environment coupling — (62) A form of coupling in which two or more modules interact with a common data environment, such as a shared communication region or a shared file.

Communicational cohesion — (62) A form of cohesion that groups elements that operate on the same set of input or output data or on the same data structure.

Comparator — (71) A software routine that compares the contents of a file or a record before and after a transaction and reports any differences.

Compatibility analysis — (75) A technique to generate test data to force a program to obtain inputs from or send outputs to multiple versions of a file or a database.

Competitive procurement — (41) A set of procedures for subcontracting work through a bidding process.

Complex star network — (52) A network that consists of two or more linked simple star networks.

Composite — (24, 25, 26, 28, 33, 45) A set of related data elements; a data structure.

Composition — (29) A stronger form of aggregation, with the multiplicity at the composite end being at most one.

Compression — (51) Conserving memory, secondary storage space, and data transmission time by removing repetitive or unnecessary bits from data.

Computer-aided software engineering (CASE) — (5, 32) A set of automated tools that assist in the entire software engineering process.

Computer software configuration item (CSCI) — (41) A subsystem that is to be implemented in software.

Concentration point determination — (53) A network analysis process that is concerned with the system's concentration points (or hubs).

Concept — (7) Knowledge in an abstract format that can be used to guide a searching or reasoning process; (29) an object.

Conceptual database design — (45) See *logical database design*.

Conceptual model — (29) A model in which the real-world concepts (i.e., the objects) are explicitly identified, their attributes are documented, and the associations among the objects are specified.

Concurrency — (73) A measure of the number of tasks a system can process concurrently.

Concurrency control — (73) A database feature that synchronizes the database and ensures that all copies of a given file contain the same version of the available information; (82) ways of preventing data loss or data corruption when multiple transactions can be updating a database at the same time.

Concurrency relationship — (65) A relationship between two (or more) processes that can be performed concurrently.

Concurrent — (73) Within the same time period.

Condition entry — (58) The box at the upper right of a decision table where the responses (Y or N) to the questions in the condition stub are listed.

Condition stub — (58) The box at the upper left of a decision table where the questions (or decisions) are listed.

Confidence interval — (9) A range of numbers around an estimate that contains the corresponding population parameter with the stated probability; for example, a 95 percent confidence interval for an estimate of the population mean is a range of numbers that contains the population mean with 95 percent certainty.

Configuration analysis — (42) A study of such system behavior and performance characteristics as response time and reliability.

Configuration approval board — (77, 80) A committee that reviews change requests and proposed adaptive and perfective maintenance tasks, authorizes work to begin, and schedules the work.

Configuration audit — (80) An audit intended to ensure that the approved changes (and only the approved changes) have been implemented.

Configuration item — (24, 41) A functional primitive that appears at the lowest level of decomposition; (35, 62) a composite entity that decomposes into specific hardware and software components; in a data flow diagram, a functional primitive that appears at the lowest level of decomposition; (80) a resource that supports configuration management.

Configuration item level — (24, 35, 41) An imaginary line that links the system's configuration items; a system's physical components lie just below the configuration item level.

Configuration management — (80, 81) The process of defining, managing, controlling, and auditing the changes made to the original system.

Configuration object — (80) A concrete tool that can be used to support the change process.

Configuration reporting — (80) The process of broadcasting (or reporting) the changes so that everyone involved with the system is aware of the new version.

Connection diagram — (53) A diagram that shows the topology, connection points, traffic flows, and patterns of a network.

Connectivity — (42) In a network, the ability of a given hardware or software component to cooperate with other components supplied by other vendors.

Connector — (55) A flowcharting symbol that indicates that the logic is continued at another place on the same page.

Constraint requirement (design requirement) — (35) A requirement that specifies such constraints as physical size and weight, environmental factors, ergonomic standards, and the like.

Construction phase — (32) The rapid application development phase during which a prototype is built, exercised, and modified based on user feedback.

Content coupling — (62) A form of coupling in which some or all of the contents of one module are included in the other.

Context diagram (level 0 data flow diagram) — (24) A data flow diagram that documents the system's boundaries by highlighting its sources and destinations.

Continuous simulation — (19) A simulation model of a system in which changes occur continuously.

Control — (1, 77) An expected value that can be compared with feedback; if the feedback suggests a deviation from the expected value (the control), the system reacts by attempting to adjust itself.

Control analysis (volume analysis) — (75) A technique for generating test data to check the system's behavior.

Control break — (47) A change in the value of a key field.

Control couple — (63) A flow of control information, such as a flag or a switch setting, between two modules.

Control coupling — (62) A form of coupling in which control information (e.g., a switch setting) is passed between the modules.

Control flow — (3) The transfer of control into or out from a module.

Control limits — (10) The upper and lower boundary lines of a control chart; the control limits are typically placed three standard deviations above and below the centerline. The centerline is usually the mean of the statistic being charted.

Control object — (66) An object that performs use case-specific behavior and contains the application logic or business rules for managing the interaction among multiple entity objects.

Control structure — (61, 62, 63) A hierarchical model of the flow of control through a program. The control structure resembles a military chain of command or an organization chart. At the top is a main control module that calls secondary control structures. At the bottom are the computational routines, each of which implements a single algorithm.

Control system — (67) A type of expert system that adaptively governs the overall behavior of a system, repeatedly interpreting the current situation, predicting the future, diagnosing the causes of anticipated problems and/or symptoms, and formulating a plan to monitor execution to ensure success.

Control total — (77) An accumulated sum, a count, or a similar value that summarizes the results of numerous computations or transactions.

Convergence — (73) A process in which several preceding events are combined to form one following event; the opposite of divergence.

Conversational transaction — (82) A transaction that maintains locks while information is displayed for update.

Core page — (51) The highest-level page in a web site's content hierarchy.

Corrective maintenance — (81) Maintenance activities intended to remove errors or bugs from the software, the procedures, the hardware, the network, the data structures, and the documentation.

Count — (11) The number of observations in a category.

Coupling — (3, 61, 62, 63) A measure of a module's independence; fewer parameters flowing into or out from a module imply looser coupling.

CPM (critical path method) — (21, 22) A project management technique based on a project network; the focus of CPM is project planning, with the critical path defining those activities into which additional resources might be poured to accelerate the schedule.

Cracker — (71) A person who breaks into computers (generally over a communication line) with malicious intent.

Crash cutover — **(abrupt cutover, direct cutover)** (76) A system release strategy in which the old system is discontinued on a predefined date and the entire organization switches directly to the new system.

Crash mode — (22) Pouring additional resources into an activity in order to complete the activity in the shortest possible time.

Crash mode analysis — (22) An analysis technique that involves modifying a project network to study time and cost tradeoffs.

CRC (class, responsibilities and collaborations) technique — (66) A technique for identifying operations.

Critical path — (21, 22) The path through a project network that links the critical events that must begin on time and the critical activities that must require no more than their estimated duration if the project is to be completed on time.

Critical path method (CPM) — (21, 22) A project management technique based on a project network; the focus of CPM is project planning, with the critical path defining those activities into which additional resources might be poured to accelerate the schedule.

Critical success factor — (16) A target that must be met or an event that must occur if an organization is to accomplish its strategic goals and objectives.

Critical success factors paradigm — (16) An approach to requirements analysis that starts by identifying and prioritizing corporate-level management information systems goals and objectives and then defining critical success factors for each major functional group within the organization.

Cumulative count — (11) The total number of observations in all the categories up to and including the category of interest; for example, the cumulative count corresponding to the third category is the sum of the counts for categories one, two, and three.

Cumulative percent — (11) The combined percentages of all the categories up to and including the category of interest; the cumulative percent for the last category will always be 100 percent.

Customization — (69) The modification of a software package to meet an organization's unique requirements without destroying the integrity of the package software.

Cutover — (76) The process of turning the system over to the user; see also *system release*.

Cutover phase — (32) The rapid application development phase during which the system is finalized and released to the user.

Cycle — (43) On a graph, a path that leads from a node back to the same node.

Data administration — (45, 82) The administrative function charged with the overall responsibility for data resources in an organization.

Data capture — (46) The process of initially capturing source data.

Data communication — (52, 53) The act of transmitting data from one component to another.

Data couple — (63) A flow of a data composite and/or data element between two modules.

Data coupling (input-output coupling) — (62) A form of coupling in which only data move between the modules.

Data dictionary — (3, 4, 25, 44, 45) A collection of data about a system's data.

Data-driven — (4, 72) A methodology, technique, or tool that starts with the data and derives the processes.

Data element — (25, 26, 27, 28, 33, 43, 44, 45) An attribute that cannot be logically decomposed; the most basic unit of data that has logical meaning.

Data encryption standard (DES) — (71) A public/private key encryption system used for secure government transmissions and for most electronic funds transfers.

Data entry — (46) The process of converting source data into a machine-readable form and entering them into a computer.

Data error — (75) An error that arises from incorrect data specifications, incorrect formats, or insufficient value representation.

Data flow — (3, 24) Data in motion; the transfer of data into or out from a module.

Data flow diagram — (3, 24, 36) A logical model of the flow of data through a system.

Data integrity — (77, 82) The state of a database that is protected against loss or contamination; data integrity is ensured by carefully controlling and managing data entry, data maintenance, and data access from the time the data first enter the system until they are of no further use.

Data model — (2) A logical model that emphasizes or is driven by a system's data.

Data normalization — (2, 28) A formal technique for designing easy-to-maintain, efficient logical data structures (or relations).

Data-oriented — (15) A tool or technique that starts with the data and derives the necessary processes.

Data redundancy — (2) The state that occurs when the same data are stored in two or more different files.

Data store — (24) Data at rest; implies that the data are held between processes.

Data structure — (4, 24, 25, 26, 27, 28, 33, 44, 45) A set of related data elements; a composite; (43) a way of organizing data that considers both the data items and their relationships to each other.

Data symbol — (55) A flowcharting symbol that indicates the input or output of data.

Database — (25, 44) A set of related files; (45) a collection of interrelated and shared data of different types organized into a structure that minimizes redundancies and enhances the manipulation of the data.

Database administration — (45, 82) The technical function charged with physically managing an organization's databases, including such issues as backup and recovery, performance, and security enforcement.

Database integrity — (45) The state of a database that is protected against loss or contamination.

Database management system (DBMS) — (45, 82) A software package that provides the means to define, maintain, control, and administer a database and its applications; a set of software routines that define the rules for creating, accessing, and maintaining a database.

Deadlock — (73, 82) A situation that occurs when two tasks each control a resource needed by the other and neither task is willing to relinquish control.

Death — (72) The system life cycle stage during which the decision is made to replace the system.

Debugging — (75) The process of removing bugs; a back-end process intended to correct errors and/or problems.

Debugging system — (67) A type of expert system used to prescribe remedies for malfunctions and/or failures.

Decision — (55) A point in a program where the logical path is determined by a run-time condition.

Decision (selection) — (62) A block of logic that provides alternate paths through the block depending on a run-time condition.

Decision-support function — (4) A function or operation that supports managerial decision making, often based on responding to "what-if" questions.

Decision-support system (DSS) — (72) An information system that adds a response orientation and user control to a management information system.

Decision table — (58) A two-dimensional table that shows the action to be taken following a set of related decisions.

Decision test — (75) A test used to verify a case structure or decision logic.

Decomposition — (15, 61) A problem analysis paradigm that calls for breaking a problem into more manageable subproblems and then attacking the subproblems.

Defect — (78) Any failure to meet requirements.

Degree of automation — (72) The extent to which automated or computer-related components are used in a system.

Demand report — (47) A report that is created on request.

Demand/utilization analysis — (42) A study that focuses on such utilization issues as throughput, average response time, concurrent incoming messages, simultaneous users, maximum data capacity, the component's ability to deal with peak demand, and so on.

Denormalization — (45) Altering the logical database design to include redundant data.

Dependency — (73) A relationship in which the implementation of the following event(s) depends on the completion of the preceding event(s).

Depth — (51) A measure of the number of levels a user must navigate to reach the desired content; (62) the number of levels in the control structure.

Depth search — (7, 34) A blind searching technique that investigates all lower-level nodes before considering the next node at the same level.

DES (data encryption standard) — (71) A public/private key encryption system used for secure government transmissions and for most electronic funds transfers.

Descendent — (43) A child of a child (or a descendent).

Design — (1) The third step in the system development life cycle (following analysis and preceding development) during which the responsible people determine how the problem will be solved by specifying the system's physical components.

Design class diagram — (66) A diagram that specifies the software classes and interfaces in an application.

Design requirement (constraint requirement) — (35) A requirement that specifies such constraints as physical size and weight, environmental factors, ergonomic standards, and the like.

Design system — (67) A type of expert system that constructs descriptions of objects in various relationships and verifies that the resulting configurations conform to known constraints.

Destination (sink) — (24) A person, organization, or other system that gets data from the target system; a destination defines a system boundary.

Detail diagram — (64) A low-level IPO chart that shows how specific input and output data elements or data structures are linked to specific processes.

Detail line — (47) A single report row that displays the appropriate field values from a single report file record.

Detail report — (47) A report that lists data for each input record or transaction.

Determinant — (28) Usually, a key; the value of the key determines the values of all the non-key attributes because the key defines a unique occurrence of the entity (a unique set of attributes).

Deterministic model — (19) A model having all inputs fixed and known (or assumed known).

Deterministic state transition diagram — (30) A state transition diagram in which a given input function is associated with at most one transition from a given state.

Development — (1) The fourth step in the system development life cycle (following design and preceding testing) during which the system is created; (72) the system life cycle stage during which the system is designed, developed, tested, and implemented.

Development costs — (38) One-time costs that occur before the system is released to the user; they include the labor, hardware, and software costs accumulated from the time the project is initially approved until the system is released to the user.

Diagnosis-oriented documentation — (70) Documentation that describes the type and the nature of warning messages and error messages and explains the causes of and solutions for each error.

Diagnosis system — (67) A type of expert system used to relate observed behavioral irregularities with underlying causes.

Dialogue — (49, 50) The exchange of information between a computer and a user.

Digraph (directed graph) — (43) A graph on which each edge (or arc) has a direction.

Direct access (random access) — (44) Reading records from or writing records to a file in any order.

Direct cutover (abrupt cutover, crash cutover) — (76) A system release strategy in which the old system is discontinued on a predefined date and the entire organization switches directly to the new system.

Direct representation (analogical representation) — (67) A technique that allows an expert system to analyze the properties of a new situation and use the course of action for an old situation to deal with it.

Direct user interface — (48) A user interface through which a user directly accesses a computer (e.g., via a screen and a keyboard).

Directed graph (digraph) — (43) A graph on which each edge (or arc) has a direction.

Directory — (44) A list of the names and addresses of every file stored on a disk (or other secondary storage device).

Discount rate — (38) The interest rate used to discount a sum of money.

Discounting — (38) The act of computing the present value of a future sum of money.

Discrete simulation — (19) A simulation model of a system in which changes occur instantaneously at particular points in time.

Dispatcher — (73) The operating system routine that manages the processor's time.

Distributed database — (54) A database with different subsets of data distributed among several sites that are connected by a network.

Distributed management — (72) A management philosophy that distributes responsibility and authority from the top to the bottom levels of the organization.

Distributed routing — (54) A routing technique that relies on each node to compute its own routing table and build the required connections with its neighbors.

Distributing cable — (53) Generally, a cable that links the computers or nodes on a single floor.

Distribution control — (77) An output control designed to ensure that all outputs are distributed to the right location at the right time.

Diverge — (21) To split a single input path into multiple paths.

Divergence — (73) A process in which one preceding event is separated into several following events.

Documentation — (70, 76) The specifications, instructions, tutorials, reference guides, and similar materials that accompany and explain a piece of software or a hardware component.

Documentation control — (77) An operational control that focuses on the documentation library.

Domain — (7) A possible problem space in which searching or reasoning techniques can be applied.

Domain object (entity object) — (66) An object in the business domain.

Double-barreled question — (17) A question that asks the respondent to answer two questions.

Doubly linked list — (43) A linked list in which each node contains both forward and backward pointers.

Drop-down menu (pull-down menu) — (50) A menu of detailed options that appears when the user clicks or selects a major function on a menu bar.

Dummy activity — (21) An activity that links parallel events but consumes neither time nor resources.

Dumpster diving — (71) Searching for passwords and other security information by going through paper waste.

Duration — (20, 21, 22) The elapsed time required to complete an activity.

Dynamic information — (61) Time-related parameters, or process information that can change; for example, the processing cycle, the nature of the output, any parameters that vary over time, and any other parameters not subject to the organization's control.

Dynamic routing (adaptive routing) — (54) A distributed routing technique that selects the best route based on such criteria as the speed, capacity, or cost of the link, the utilization rate of a particular node, the failure rate of a particular path, the type of data transmitted, response time, throughput, and so on.

Earliest event time (EET) — (21, 22) The earliest time the event can possibly begin.

Echo printing — (75) Printing or displaying each input value.

Economic evaluation — (78) A type of system evaluation that focuses on comparing the project's actual time, cost, and benefits to the estimates prepared after the analysis stage and/or during design.

Economic feasibility — (13) Proof that the likely benefits outweigh the cost of solving the problem; generally demonstrated by a cost/benefit analysis.

Economic requirement — (35) A requirement that specifies such things as performance penalties, limits on development and operating costs, the implementation schedule, and resource restrictions.

Edge — (43) On a graph, a link between two nodes.

Effect of interest — (18) A characteristic or event of a system that the cause-and-effect diagram is meant to study; typically, a problem or undesirable event.

Efferent process — (61, 62) A process that structures and/or transmits output data.

Element analysis — (42) The process of identifying discrete hardware components and required features.

Encapsulation — (6) Hiding implementation details by bundling an object's data and its methods so that the only way to access the data is through the object's own methods.

Encrypt — (71, 77) To convert to a secret code.

End user — (48) Any person who needs the output generated by the computer and/or who interacts with the computer at an operational level.

Entity — (4, 25, 26, 27, 28, 33, 43, 44, 45) A thing or object (a person, group, place, thing, or activity) about which data are stored; (19) a unit, such as a person, part, job, and so on, that flows through a system.

Entity diagram — (4, 33) A simplified entity-relationship diagram that uses bubbles instead of rectangles and ignores cardinality.

Entity object (domain object) — (66) An object in the business domain.

Entity-relationship diagram — (4, 26, 27, 33) A diagram or a model of a system's data that shows how the primary data entities are related.

Entrance-exit test — (75) A test used to verify that any called routine has only one entry point and one exit point.

Entry page — (51) The first page a visitor encounters when accessing a web site.

Entry tunnel (entry chimney) — (51) One or more pages between the entry page and the core page.

Environment — (5) A collection of tools and workbenches that support the entire software process.

Ergonomics — (48, 76) The study of the relationship between human beings and their workplaces.

Error — (9) The difference between the value of a parameter as estimated by a sample and the actual value of that parameter for the entire population.

Error control — (77) A system control designed to determine if a program or routine can handle an unexpected response or input.

Errors of coverage — (17) Errors owing to the sampling frame differing from the target population.

Errors of non-observation — (17) Errors that occur because the elements in the sample are not all of the elements in the target population.

Errors of observation — (17) Errors that occur when the survey data is different from the truth.

Estimate — (9) A value of a parameter determined by a sample.

Evaluation analysis — (81) A maintenance phase (similar to the problem definition stage in the system development life cycle) during which the impact of a particular change is evaluated.

Event — (6, 66, 73) An occurrence that generates a signal; (21, 22) the beginning or end of an activity; (57) an occurrence that is not entirely subject to the decision-maker's control; (79) a set of outcomes.

Event-driven — (73) A system that responds to events.

Event fork — (57) A point on a decision tree (represented by a circle) where subsequent branches identify the consequences (or possible outcomes) of a decision.

Evolutionary approach — (32) An approach to rapid application development in which progressive designs go through multiple, minimum-length cycles in which successive versions of the system under construction are utilized by the end user.

Evolutionary design (stepwise refinement) — (72) A design strategy that starts with a small program or subsystem and continuously refines it by adding new functions and/or modifying features.

Exception report — (47) A report that lists or summarizes only the data for input records that pass a predefined condition or filter.

Exception test — (46, 77) A test used to screen such "exceptional" values as a zero (0) in a field that will be used as a divisor.

Execution-oriented documentation (application-based documentation) — (70) Documentation designed to support an application.

Executive information system (EIS) — (72) An information system designed to support high-level decision making based (typically) on aggregate and graphic data.

Exit page — (51) The last page a visitor encounters just before exiting a web site.

Exit tunnel (exit chimney) — (51) One or more pages between the core page and the exit page.

Expandability — (42) The ability to add components to a system or features to a component.

Expanded use case — (29) A description of the step-by-step events in a process; an expanded use case is more detailed than a high-level use case.

Experimental design — (77) An auditing technique used to audit system accuracy by building a pilot prototype and testing it using controlled sample data.

Expert system (knowledge-based system) — (7, 34, 67, 68, 72) A computer program that emulates the thought process of a human expert.

Expert system interface — (48) A user interface that utilizes natural language processing.

Expert system shell — (7) The user interface to an expert system.

Explanation dialogue — (49) A form of dialogue that performs a glossary function.

Explanation facility — (7) An expert system component that reproduces the logic the inference engine followed to reach its conclusion.

Explode — (24) To decompose a process in a data flow diagram to a lower level.

External documentation — (70) Documentation that is kept at the user's location (or some other remote site) and is designed primarily for the user.

Factoring — (7, 15, 61) A technique for grouping several subproblems into a meta-problem.

Fault tolerant computer — (73) A computer that incorporates redundant circuits and components to improve reliability.

Feasibility study — (13) A compressed, capsule version of the analysis phase of the system development life cycle aimed at determining quickly and at a reasonable cost if the problem can be solved and if it is worth solving.

Feedback — (1, 77) The return of a portion of the system's output to its input; (30) on a state transition diagram, a feedback loop returns the system to a previous state.

Fence diagram — (30) A state transition diagram on which the states are shown as vertical lines and the activities are shown as horizontal arrows.

Field — (25, 43, 44) A data element physically stored on some medium; (47) a data element; a single, logically meaningful unit of data.

Fifth normal form — (28) A fourth normal form relation with all join dependencies removed.

File — (25, 43, 44, 47) A set of related records.

File name — (44) A unique logical identifier assigned to a file (usually by the user).

Filter — (45) A set of logical conditions used to screen records in a query.

Fire fighting — (81) Making emergency repairs, often under extreme time pressure.

Firewall — (71) A set of hardware, software, and data that sits between the network and the Internet (or other public network), screens all incoming and/or outgoing transactions, and allows only authorized transactions to get through.

First normal form — (28) A logical data structure that contains no repeating sets of data elements.

First-order predicate logic — (67) The type of logic used in mathematics to prove theorems.

Fixed routing — (54) A static routing technique that always utilizes a predetermined fixed route when transmitting between a specific pair of nodes.

Flat-file database — (45) A database (more accurately, a file) in which all the data are stored in a single, spreadsheet-like table that is not linked with any other files.

Flow test (sequence test, transaction test) — (75) A test designed to verify the complete logical flow needed to accomplish a task.

Flowdown — (35) A principle that requires each lower level requirement to be linked to a single higher level parent.

Flowline — (55) On a flowchart, a line, often terminating in an arrowhead, that indicates the sequence and direction of the flow between two symbols.

Focus group — (40) A group composed of managers from all the functional units in the entire company that conducts a business function-task analysis.

Foreign key — (25, 28) A key to some other entity stored with the target entity.

Form — (46) A paper document (or a simulated document on a screen) that is used to capture data; (69) a data entry screen with fill-in-the-blank or select-an-option windows.

Format constraint analysis — (75) Generating test data based on data type; for example, a zero or numeric digit might be placed in an alphabetic field, or non-digits might be inserted into a numeric field.

Forward chaining — (34) A data-oriented approach that searches the solution space from an initial state to a final goal state.

Forward engineering — (5) Completely redesigning a system to take advantage of new technologies such as client server computing.

Fourth-generation language — (2) A programming language that allows the programmer to describe (in some way) the logical procedure and then let the language translator determine how to implement it; (31, 32) a non-procedural language that generates the appropriate source or executable code from a programmer's definition or description of a logical operation.

Fourth normal form — (28) A relation is in fourth normal form (4NF) if and only if all existing multi-value dependencies are converted into regular functional dependencies.

Frame — (17) A list of sampling units from which the sample will be selected; (51) a window-like unit that holds and displays the contents of a single html document; (67) a complex data structure composed of a concept, one or more slots, one or more values, and one or more attached procedures; a frame represents a stereotyped situation.

Frameset — (51) A document that defines the relative and/or absolute sizes and positions of several related frames; using the frameset as a guide or framework, the client computer's browser displays each html document in the appropriate frame.

Freeze — (80) To archive the entire system, including the executable programs, data files, source code, and related documentation, prior to making a change.

Front-end routine — (69) A routine that accepts input data and formats it for a commercial program.

Fully connected mesh network — (52) A mesh network in which every computer is directly connected to all the other computers in the network.

Function — (4) A meaningful operation or process that produces a desired result for a proposed system; similar to a process.

Function (activity) — (30) A process or event that moves a system from one state to another.

Function cohesion — (62) The strongest type of cohesion in which a given module performs a single logical function, receives and returns no surplus data, and performs only essential logical operations.

Function-related error — (75) An error caused by such things as incorrect linkages, incorrect control transfers between a calling and a called routine, the inclusion of one or more incorrect or unnecessary functions, and the omission of one or more necessary functions.

Function test (74) A test performed on one or more partial systems that have already been integration tested; the objective is to use test data and simulated data to test a user-defined function.

Functional decomposition — (24) The act of exploding a data flow diagram; (61, 62, 63) a program design methodology in which the program is broken down (or decomposed) into modules based on the processes or tasks they perform.

Functional dependency — (28) A situation that exists when a non-key attribute is fully dependent on the key.

Functional primitive — (24, 35) A process (or transform) that requires no further decomposition.

Functional requirement — (35) A requirement that identifies a task that the system or component must perform.

Future projection analysis — (53) A network analysis process that focuses on parameters that affect capacity planning, storage requirements, transmission speed, connections with the Internet, and so on.

Future value — (38) The value of a sum of money at some future time.

Gamma test — (74) A test of such details as the system's compatibility with the old system and the system's performance under peak demand.

Gantt chart — (20) A chart that shows a project schedule as a series of horizontal lines or bars.

Gateway — (53) A computer that links two or more networks with different protocols.

Generalization — (29) A technique wherein commonality among concepts is identified and a general concept or super-type is defined; subtypes depict "type-of" relationships.

Generate and test — (15) A hierarchical, test-oriented paradigm that starts at the top of a hierarchy with a main problem and continues down the hierarchy through the subproblems, conducting tests of the appropriate criteria and constraints at each level until the bottom is reached and no more testing is necessary.

Generator — (2) A program that starts with information in graphical, narrative, list, or some other logical form and outputs the appropriate source code; also called a *code generator* or *program generator*; (68) a routine that outputs one or more commands that the computer can execute.

Geographical requirements analysis — (53) A preliminary network analysis process that begins with a careful study of the system's geographical locations and focuses on such issues as topology and transmission media.

Gif (graphic interchange format) — (51) A popular compression algorithm for graphic images.

Global data — (24) Data elements or composites that are shared by two or more processes.

Goal — (34, 67) An objective.

Goal driven — (72) A method or technique that works through a process until a predefined goal is accomplished.

Goal-oriented — (15) A method or technique which searches through a process until a predefined goal is accomplished.

Gradual cutover — (76) A system release strategy in which the new and old systems run concurrently and the number of transactions handled by the new system is gradually increased.

Granularity — (82) The level of locking; for example, the entire database, individual tables, physical pages of data within tables, or individual rows.

Graph — (43) A set of nodes (or vertexes) linked by a set of edges.

Graph base — (7) A database with a collection of graphs or graphing tools; for example, most graphic software implements a graph base of customized symbols or pictures.

Graphic input screen (touch screen) — (46) A screen that allows a user to input a command or request information by pointing.

Graphic user interface (GUI) — (48) A user interface that features windows, icons, menus, and pointers; generally, the user points to the desired element and clicks a mouse button to trigger the associated action. The Apple Macintosh and Microsoft Windows interfaces are common examples; sometimes called an *object-oriented interface*.

Graphics display dialogue — (49) A form of dialogue that shows information in graphical form.

Gray-box testing — (74) A hybrid of white-box and black-box testing in which both the functions and the contents of major programs and/or modules that are likely to be internally maintained, modified, or customized later are tested.

Group decision support system (GDSS) — (72) An information system that adds communication capability and interaction to a decision support system.

Growth — (72) The system life cycle stage during which usage grows as users become familiar with the new system, and system behavior is adjusted to improve performance and efficiency.

Hacker — (71) Originally, an expert programmer with a knack for creating elegant software; today, the term is more commonly applied to someone who illegally breaks into computer systems.

Hardware analysis — (53) A network analysis process that helps to define the requirements for the personal computers, workstations, terminals, peripherals, communication interfaces, modems, and other hardware that will be attached to the network and such software as the operating system and communication protocols.

Hardware configuration item (HWCI) — (41) A subsystem that is to be implemented in hardware.

Hardware error — (75) A data communication error, a data transmission error, an error caused by hardware incompatibility or failure, and so on.

Hardware interface design — (42) The process of determining, specifying, evaluating, and acquiring of a set of hardware building blocks and analyzing their relationships with each other.

Hardware monitor — (78) Specially designed circuitry that can be used to measure such parameters as average seek time, rotational delay, arm movement time, and so on.

Hashing — (44) Using an algorithm to convert a logical key to a relative address.

Heuristic rule — (7, 34) A specific rule of thumb or common sense that can be used to restrict a search to a subset of a problem domain.

Heuristic search — (7, 34) A search technique that applies heuristics to reduce the size of a problem domain or search space.

Heuristics — (7, 34, 67) General rules derived from experience, common sense, inferences, and intelligent trial and error.

Hierarchical database — (45) A database in which the file links (or relationships) form a hierarchy.

Hierarchical topology (tree topology) — (52) A hybrid topology that usually consists of two or more linked star or bus networks.

Hierarchy chart — (63, 64) A diagram that graphically represents a program's control structure.

High-level use case — (29) A brief, two or three sentence description of a process.

Highway effect (turnpike effect) — (53, 54) The tendency of users to quickly adopt new technology as soon as it proves its usefulness; because of the highway effect, the demands placed on a system often exceed projections. This term was initially coined in the 1950s when the traffic load on the Pennsylvania Turnpike exceeded the designers' long-term, worst-case projections soon after the road opened.

HIPO (hierarchy plus input-process-output) — (64) A tool for planning and/or documenting a computer program that utilizes a hierarchy chart to graphically represent the program's control structure and a set of IPO (input-process-output) charts to describe the inputs to, the outputs from, and the functions performed by each module on the hierarchy chart.

Historical data — (75) Data previously processed by the old system.

History file (archive) — (44) A file that holds already processed transactions or no longer current master records.

Home page — (51) An initial starting page.

Host — (52, 53) A computer in a wide area network.

Hot key — (50) A key or (more commonly) a combination of keys that triggers a response.

Html (hypertext markup language) — (51) A hypertext language used to tell a browser how to map a page to the screen. When a web page is created, html tags are added to the text, graphics, sounds, and other objects that make up the page. When the browser reads the page, it relies on the html tags to tell it where each object should be placed on the screen, how to format the text, what colors and backgrounds to use, and so on.

Hub — (53) A central controlling device, point, or node in a network.

Hybrid coupling — (62) A combination of data coupling and control coupling.

Hybrid testing (middle-out testing) — (74) A testing strategy that starts in the middle of the hierarchy and moves bi-directionally toward both the top and the bottom.

Hyperlink — (51) On the World Wide Web, a symbolic, logical connection that represents a URL.

Hyperlinked screens — (46) A set of screens connected by hyperlinks; for example, in a slide show presentation, hyperlinks are used to control slide sequence.

Hypothesis space — (7) A mathematical term for a space that is defined abstractly; generally, the subset of a solution space to be considered.

Hypothetical data (simulated data) — (75) Data created specifically for testing purposes.

Icon — (48, 50) A graphic symbol that represents a processing option, a file, or an executable routine.

Icon input screen — (46) An input screen that allows the user to trigger the execution of a related routine by clicking on an icon.

Icon window — (50) A window that displays multiple icons.

Implementation — (1, 76) The sixth step in the system development life cycle (following testing and preceding maintenance) during which the system is installed and released to the user.

In-out diagram — (33) A Warnier-Orr diagram that documents the application's primary inputs and outputs.

Incremental backup copy — (82) A backup copy that contains only the data that have changed since the last full or incremental back-up was performed.

Incremental design — (72) A design strategy that starts with any module, subroutine, or subsystem; a second module is then developed and those two modules are integrated before work begins on the third module. This process continues until all the modules are developed.

Indegree — (43) On a directed graph, the number of arcs entering a given node.

Index — (44, 45) A list of the record keys and the associated physical disk addresses for each record in a file.

Indexed sequential file — (44) A file on which records are stored in key order and an index is maintained, thus allowing the records to be accessed sequentially or randomly.

Indirect user interface — (48) A user interface that does not involve direct computer access; for example, a printed report or a form designed to capture data for subsequent input.

Industry analysis paradigm — (16) An approach to requirements analysis in which the responsible analysts study competitors' information systems and use the resulting information as a primary factor in defining internal information system requirements.

Inference — (34, 67) The act or process of deriving logical conclusions from premises known or assumed to be true.

Inference engine — (7) The component of an expert system that uses input parameters to access the knowledge base, reach a conclusion, and offer expert advice.

Information hiding — (61) A principle that suggests that all information not directly relevant to a given process should be hidden from that process.

Information-oriented paradigm — (16) An approach to requirements analysis that focuses on the information system products actually used by supervisory and middle managers.

Information-oriented question-answer dialogue — (49) A form of dialogue that asks the user to provide information (a sentence, a paragraph, some data) that is generally not used to directly trigger execution.

Information processing control — (77) An input, processing, or output control.

Information system — (1, 72) A set of hardware, software, data, human, and procedural components intended to provide the right data and information to the right person at the right time.

Information systems strategy — (2) High-level information system goals and objectives, often derived from or compatible with corporate goals and objectives.

Inheritance — (6) The principle that allows an object to get attributes and methods from its superclass.

Input control — (46, 77) A test or control, designed to screen out and (if possible) correct bad data before they enter the system.

Input error — (75) A human data entry error or a data error generated by an input device.

Input-output coupling (data coupling) — (62) A form of coupling in which only data move between the modules.

IPO (input-process-output) chart — (64) A chart that describes or documents the inputs to, the outputs from, and the functions (or processes) performed by a program module.

Inspection — (23) A formal review of a set of exit criteria conducted by technical personnel.

Inspector — (23) A technical professional or a skilled user who participates in an inspection.

Instruction dialogue (systems information interface) — (49) Dialogue that provides instructions and other information about the system's operations, functions, and structure.

Instruction system — (67) A type of expert system used to diagnose and debug system behaviors and to provide the decision maker with trouble-shooting support.

Intangible — (39) Difficult to define in concrete, physical (e.g., financial) terms.

Intangible benefits — (38) Benefits that cannot be measured in financial terms, such as improved morale or employee safety.

Integration test — (74) A test conducted on an aggregate of two or more components or modules that focuses on the individual units, their interfaces with each other, and their combined behavior.

Interarrival time — (79) The elapsed time between arrivals of successive customers in a queuing system.

Interest rate — (38) A charge for a loan or a payment for the use of money; usually expressed as a percentage.

Interface — (1) A mechanism or point of interaction between two or more system components.

Interface error — (75) An error that results from such causes as incorrect loading, customization, or initialization.

Interface object (boundary object) — (66) An object that communicates with the user or with other systems.

Interface requirement — (35) A requirement that identifies a link to another system component.

Internal documentation — (70) Specifications, records, and manuals that are stored, maintained, and used by technical professionals.

Internal rate of return — (38) The interest rate that yields a zero (0) net present value.

Internet — (51) A well-known, widely accessed, international network of computers; the set of continuously connected computers that use Transmission Control Protocol/Internet Protocol (TCP/IP).

Interpretation system — (67) A type of expert system used to explain data by providing appropriate symbolic meanings and describing the situation and/or state that accounts for the data.

Interrupt — (73) An electronic signal that causes the computer to stop what it is doing and activate one of the operating system's interrupt handling routines; generally, the information needed to restore the system to its pre-interrupt state is captured by hardware as part of the interrupt process.

Interrupt control — (77) A control or test to determine if a system or program is capable of recovering after it is intentionally restarted, abandoned, or abnormally terminated.

Interview — (8) A face-to-face meeting between two (or more) people in which one person obtains information from another by asking questions.

Inventory control — (77) A type of operational control that helps to ensure that the necessary software, hardware, and other peripherals are properly maintained and connected for operation.

Inverse operator — (34) An operator that works backward from the solution and facts to return to the original state.

Inverted-L chart — (27) A tool for graphically representing a data structure.

Iteration (repetition) — (62) A block of logic that is executed repetitively as long as (while) an initial condition holds or until a terminal condition occurs.

JAD (joint application design) — (14, 32) A technique for quickly determining system requirements in an intensive session attended by a team consisting of major users, managers, and systems analysts.

JAD workbook — (14) A workbook designed to provide JAD team members with necessary information about the project and to facilitate note taking.

Java — (51, 69) A platform independent, object-oriented programming language developed by Sun Microsystems that incorporates excellent security features and has gained wide acceptance on the World Wide Web.

JavaScript — (51) A relatively easy to learn, Java-based scripting language that can be used to perform basic interactive tasks.

Join — (28) The process of consolidating subrelations into one relation.

Join dependency — (28) A type of dependency that is created as a result of a projection or join process.

Joint application design (JAD) — (14, 32) A technique for quickly determining system requirements in an intensive session attended by a team consisting of major users, managers, and systems analysts.

Jpeg (joint photographic experts group) — (51) A popular compression algorithm for photographic images.

Junction test — (75) A test that focuses on points where the control flow merges or diverges.

Justification — (34) Proofs, facts, or reasons/rationales for assumptions.

Kernel — (71) A unit of code or a routine that is physically and/or logically isolated from other software and consequently protected.

Key — (25, 27, 28, 43, 44) The attribute or group of attributes that uniquely distinguishes one occurrence of an entity.

Key indicator report — (47) A form of scheduled report that summarizes critical activities, often on a daily basis.

Knowledge — (34, 67) The sum or range of what has been perceived, discovered, or learned; specific information about something.

Knowledge acquisition facility — (7) A set of software tools for capturing and encoding a human expert's expertise and creating a knowledge base.

Knowledge base — (7, 34, 68) A collection of data, algorithms, and heuristic rules that forms the core of an expert system.

Knowledge-based system (expert system) — (7, 34, 67, 68, 72) A computer program that emulates the thought process of a human expert.

Knowledge engineer — (7) A person who captures and encodes a human expert's expertise and creates a knowledge base.

LAN (local area network) — (52, 53) A network in which the nodes are located in close geographic proximity and are generally linked by direct lines (such as hard wires).

Language parser — (67) A routine that executes correctly interpreted commands to accomplish the tasks determined by the program.

Latest event time (LET) — (21, 22) The latest time an event can occur without impacting the project schedule.

Leaf (leaf node) — (43) On a tree, a node with no branches; (62) a module in a control structure with no lower-level (child) modules.

Length constraint analysis — (75) Generating test data with too many or too few characters or digits.

Level 0 data flow diagram (context diagram) — (24) A data flow diagram that documents the system's boundaries by highlighting its sources and destinations.

Level 1 data flow diagram — (24, 36) A data flow diagram that shows the system's primary processes, data stores, sources, and destinations linked by data flows.

Level 2 data flow diagram — (24, 36) An explosion of a level 1 process.

Lexical analyzer — (67) A component of a compiler that deals with the interpretation and understanding of the commands and related syntax; (68) a routine that performs semantic analysis, checking every word in a sentence against the correct spellings stored in the knowledge base and listing all the possible alternative meanings for the sentence.

Library control procedures — (74) A set of procedures for creating and maintaining a test data library and the relevant testing software.

Life — (38) The number of time periods (usually years) during which the system is expected to be in use.

Line monitoring — (77) A communication control technique that involves attaching special circuitry to the communication link to diagnose problems.

Linked list — (43) A list in which each node contains data plus a pointer to the next node.

List — (43) A series of nodes each of which holds a single data item; the most basic data structure.

Load module — (3) The unit of program logic that is physically loaded and executed on a computer.

Loaded question — (17) A question whose wording suggests what the answer should be.

Local area network (LAN) — (52, 53) A network in which the nodes are located in close geographic proximity and are generally linked by direct lines (such as hard wires).

Local data — (24) Data elements or composites that are known only within one part of the system.

Location connectivity analysis — (54) A network and distributed database design technique used to help control network data flow, determine the status of the sending and receiving nodes, identify the best route to transmit data, reduce transmission delays and related errors, and prevent the overuse of a particular route or node; also known as connectivity analysis or routing analysis.

Location implementation (pilot implementation) — (76) A system release strategy in which the new system is first released in a single site, such as a branch office or a warehouse, thoroughly tested, and then ported to the other sites.

Locking — (73) A technique that prevents a user from updating or modifying a record while another user is accessing that record; (82) the process of allocating control over a database resource to a specific transaction to avoid problems associated with concurrent use.

Log — (82) A file containing a record of all database changes.

Logic bomb — (71) A program that (symbolically) blows up in memory.

Logic flowchart (process flowchart) — (55) A graphical representation of the flow of logic, control, data, or paperwork through a program, a routine, a module, or a process.

Logic test — (75) A test of the logical flow through a program.

Logical access map — (62) A program design tool used to help the designer determine the logical execution sequences or access paths through a program.

Logical cohesion — (62) A form of cohesion in which all the elements are related to the same logical function.

Logical data flow diagram — (24) A data flow diagram that does not suggest physical references but shows the system's components as logical entities.

Logical data structure — (4) A set of related data elements that ignores how the data are physically stored.

Logical database design — (45) The database design stage concerned with defining and documenting the database in user terms.

Logical design phase — (4) The phase in the structured requirements definition methodology during which the system's logical requirements are defined.

Logical model — (2, 3) A model that exists on paper or in an analyst's mind; logical models are easily manipulated; contrast with *physical*.

Logical record — (44) The set of related fields needed to complete a single input/process/output cycle.

Logical security — (71, 77) Security features implemented by the system or the computer as it runs.

Loop back analysis — (77) The process of automatically returning all received messages to the transmitting node where they are compared with the original data.

Loop test — (75) A test used to verify the accuracy of a repetition block.

Lower CASE — (5) A set of tools that support the design, implementation, testing and maintenance phases of the system development life cycle (in general, the back end).

Machine learning — (7) The capacity of a machine (or an expert system) to "learn" from experience.

Macro — (69) An instruction (or set of instructions) that performs a series of keystrokes or commands to carry out a specific task.

Mainline functional flow diagram — (4) A diagram that sequentially links all the processes in a proposed system.

Maintenance — (1) The final step in the system development life cycle (following implementation) intended to keep the system functioning at an acceptable level; (81) a continuing series of activities and costs intended to keep the system running at an acceptable level.

Make-or-buy decision — (2) A decision to purchase or to build internally software (or some other component).

Management definition guide — (14) A portion of the JAD workbook that lists and defines technical terms related to computing platforms, computer technology, and other elements relevant to the problem under study.

Management information system (MIS) — (72) An information system that emphasizes report generation and combines such attributes as centralized data management, integrated applications, distributed access, and interactive processing to support operational-level decision making.

Many-to-many relationship — (26) A relationship in which each occurrence of entity A is associated with one or more occurrences of entity B, and each occurrence of entity B is associated with one or more occurrences of entity A.

Master file — (44) A file that holds permanent data that are accessed over a period of time.

Matrix — (43) A two-dimensional array.

Maturity — (72) The system life cycle stage during which the system's efficiency can no longer be enhanced and performance deficiencies begin to appear.

McCabe statistics — (5) A complexity metric based on a count of the number of decisions in a program; an indicator of the testability and maintainability of software.

Mean — (9) An arithmetic average; the sum of all the observations divided by the number of observations.

Mean time between failures (MTBF) — (78) A measure of reliability; the sum of the mean time to fail and the mean time to repair.

Menu bar (command bar) — (50) A window that (typically) appears at the top of the screen and lists such major functions as file, edit, view, and help. The subcommands related to a particular function are displayed in a pull-down or drop-down menu when the user clicks or selects the function.

Menu interface — (48) A user interface in which the list of the options available to the user is displayed in a table or menu.

Merge — (21) To combine two or more input paths into a single output path; (73) see *convergence*.

Merged entity diagram — (4) An entity diagram that combines the lower-level entity diagrams from two or more major users.

Mesh network — (52) A network that allows any two remote computers to communicate directly.

Message switching — (53) The process of routing a message from its source to its destination; note that sometimes messages are decomposed into packets that reach their destination via different transmission paths.

Meta-data — (25) The contents of the data dictionary.

Meta-problem — (7, 15) A problem that is synthesized or generalized from several lower level sub-problems.

Metaphor — (51) A design element that relies on a familiar object or a familiar pattern of behavior to suggest how the user might interact with a web site.

Method — (6) A process that accesses an object; (66) the implementation of an operation for a specific object class.

Methodology — (1, 72) A body of practices, procedures, and rules used by those who work in a discipline or engage in an inquiry; often implemented as a set of well-defined steps or phases, each of which ends with a clear, measurable set of exit criteria.

Middle-out — (72) A design strategy that starts from the middle of the hierarchy.

Middle-out testing (hybrid testing) — (74) A testing strategy that starts in the middle of the hierarchy and moves bi-directionally toward both the top and the bottom.

Midpoint — (39) The middle or average value from a range of reasonable estimated values for a parameter.

Mini-spec — (24) The process description for a functional primitive.

Minimum spanning tree — (43) Within a graph, a subtree, or spanning tree for which the sum of arc weights is minimal.

Model — (79) An abstract, mathematical representation of a physical system.

Model base — (7) A collection of models that support decision making and/or data analysis; an example is a collection of different forecasting models.

Moderator — (14) The person responsible for conducting a JAD session; (23) the individual who runs an inspection, scheduling all meetings, distributing all necessary documentation, conducting all sessions, and making certain that the inspection is both thorough and fair.

Module — (3, 55, 56, 59, 60) A portion of a larger program that performs a specific task.

Module test (unit test) — (74) A test conducted on a single program or a single module.

Monitor — (73) A program or hardware device that detects and reports a real-time system's processing and/or input/output activities.

Monitoring system — (67) A type of expert system that compares observations of system behavior to features that seem crucial to successful outcomes.

Monte-Carlo simulation — (19) A simulation with one or more random variables where the passage of time plays no substantive role; random numbers are used to generate values from probability distributions.

Morphology — (62) Form or structure.

Multi-determine — (28) Determined (or defined) by more than one attribute; for example, a value that is determined by the key and by some other attribute is multi-determined.

Multi-linked list — (43) A linked list in which each node contains two or more pointers, thus providing access to two or more other nodes.

Multi-processing (parallel processing) — (73) The simultaneous execution of two or more instructions on a multiple processor system.

Multi-programming — (73) Concurrently executing multiple tasks on a single processor by switching the processor's attention from task to task.

Multi-tasking — (73) Concurrently or simultaneously processing several tasks on a single computer.

Multi-value dependency — (28) A situation that exists when one attribute multi-determines (or is multi-determined by) another attribute or attributes.

Multi-way tree — (43) A tree in which each node holds n (two or more) values and can have $(n + 1)$ branches.

Multiplicity — (29) The minimum and maximum number of occurrences of one conceptual object for a single occurrence.

Nassi-Shneiderman chart — (56) An alternative to traditional logic flowcharts that provides a structured, hierarchical, graphical view of the flow of logic through a program, a routine, a module, or a process.

Natural language processing — (7, 48, 68) Hardware and/or software that allows people to communicate with computers in much the same way they communicate with other people.

Natural language processing shell — (68) A natural language processing user interface. The user communicates with the shell by entering plain English character strings. The shell translates the plain English strings into the appropriate commands and passes the commands to an application program.

Navigation — (51) The act of moving from page to page through a web site.

Net benefit — (38) Cost savings or new revenues minus the new cost associated with achieving the benefit.

Net present value — (38) The sum of discounted benefits minus the development costs.

Network — (52, 53, 54) Two or more computers linked by a communication line.

Network (weighted graph) — (43) A graph on which the edges have values.

Network database — (45) A database in which the links or pointers can describe relationships between any two files in any direction, so a child can have many parents.

Network topology — (53) A map of a network; a physical arrangement of the nodes and connections in a network.

Node — (30) A symbol (usually a circle) on a state transition diagram that represents a state; (43) an entry in a list; often, a single data element or a single record; (52, 53, 54) a connection point (computer, workstation, peripheral, concentrator, etc.) in a network.

Non-behavioral requirement — (35) A requirement that defines an attribute of the system, such as speed, frequency, response time, accuracy, precision, portability, reliability, security, or maintainability.

Non-deterministic state transition diagram — (30) A state transition diagram in which a given input function is associated with more than one transition from the state.

Non-response — (17) A type of sampling error that occurs when a sampled element (person, business, etc.) cannot be contacted, when a respondent is not able to answer a question, or when a respondent refuses to answer.

Non-response bias — (9) A form of bias that occurs when one or more members of the selected group are not included or choose not to participate in the sample.

Object — (6, 29, 51, 66) A thing about which data are stored and manipulated.

Object interaction diagram — (66) A graphical depiction of the way objects interact and collaborate to realize a use case.

Object-oriented analysis — (29, 66) The investigation of a problem by identifying and describing the objects.

Object-oriented design — (29, 66) The logical solution of a problem through a set of interacting objects.

Object-oriented interface — (48) A user interface that features windows, icons, menus, and pointers; generally, the user points to the desired element and clicks a mouse button to trigger the associated action; also called an icon-based interface, a *graphic user interface*, or a WIMP interface.

Object type (class) — (6, 66) A group of similar objects.

Objective — (12) A measurable goal which, if met, is likely to contribute to solving the problem.

Occurrence — (25, 26, 28, 43, 44) A single instance of an entity.

Off-page connector — (55) A flowcharting symbol that indicates that the logic is continued on another page.

On-line processing — (72) A processing technique in which a transaction is used to update the relevant master file record as soon as it is received.

One-to-many relationship — (26) A relationship in which each occurrence of entity *A* is associated with one or more occurrences of entity *B*, but each occurrence of entity *B* is associated with only one occurrence of entity *A*.

One-to-one relationship — (26) A relationship in which each occurrence of entity *A* is associated with one occurrence of entity *B* and each occurrence of entity *B* is associated with one occurrence of entity *A*.

Open question — (17) A question for which the respondent is allowed to formulate any answer he or she wishes.

Open systems interconnection (OSI) — (42) An International Standards Organization network model that specifies seven interconnection layers.

Operating costs — (38) Continuing costs that begin after the system is released and last for the life of the system; they include personnel, supplies, maintenance, utilities, insurance, and similar costs.

Operation — (6) An external view of an object that can be accessed by other objects; (66) a service provided by an object.

Operation-oriented documentation — (70) Command-oriented documentation that groups commands based on the nature of the operation.

Operational control — (77) A control intended to provide an early warning in the event of system malfunction.

Operational evaluation — (78) A type of system evaluation that focuses on such operational elements as system controls, interface design, and security design and considers such factors as integration, flexibility, compatibility, user friendliness, and system efficiency.

Operational feasibility — (13) Proof that the problem can be solved in the user's environment.

Optimistic concurrency — (82) Breaking a transaction into two transactions, one that reads the information and displays it and another that interprets data changes and updates the database, and releases locks between those transactions. The system is optimistic that no other user will change the information between the read and the update. If another user does change the information, the update transaction is lost.

Ordered list — (43) A list in which the nodes are stored in data value or key order.

Organizational feasibility — (13) Proof that the proposed system is consistent with the organization's strategic objectives.

Organizational unit-process matrix — (40) A table that identifies the relationships between the organizational units and the processes and shows the degree of involvement of the various units in specific processes.

Outcome — (57) On a decision tree, a final result of a series of decisions and/or outcomes; (79) the fundamental result of a probabilistic experiment.

Outdegree — (43) On a directed graph, the number of arcs exiting from a given node.

Output error — (75) An error that results from incompatible or inaccurate data conversion, data compression, or data encryption.

Output oriented — (4) A methodology or tool that works backward from the output, through the processes, to the input.

Outsourcing — (2) Subcontracting work outside the organization.

Overview diagram — (64) A high-level IPO chart that summarizes the inputs to, processes or tasks performed by, and outputs from a module.

Page — (51) The basic unit of information transferred between a server and a client on the World Wide Web.

Page load time — (51) A measure of the elapsed time between a request for a page and the display of the complete page on the client computer's screen.

Parallel operation — (76) A system release strategy in which the old and the new systems run in parallel for a time.

Parallel processing (multi-processing) — (73) The simultaneous execution of two or more instructions on a multiple processor system.

Parallel simulation — (77) An auditing technique that involves testing both the live system and a simulated system with the same data.

Parameter — (66) Information that must be passed so the receiving object can perform the operation.

Parameter analysis — (42) A study of such factors as the time required to load a test image, the quality and sharpness of a displayed image, or the maximum number of frames required to store a motion picture or display an animation.

Parent — (35) A related, higher-level requirement; (43) the immediate higher-level node in a tree; (45) a higher-level record in a hierarchical database structure.

Pareto principle — (11) In many different situations, the majority of outcomes are the result of a few significant factors. The remainder of the outcomes is owing to a large number of less important factors. This concept is named after the Italian economist Alfredo Pareto who recognized that a large proportion of the wealth in Italy was in the hands of a small number of people.

Parse tree — (68) A hierarchical representation of words (conceptually similar to a diagrammed sentence) arranged in a form that allows a computer program to trace relationships and infer meanings.

Parser — (68) A routine that performs syntactic analysis, essentially diagramming a sentence to form a parse tree.

Partially connected mesh network — (52) A mesh network in which every computer is connected (either directly or via a relay computer) to at least two other computers in the network by more than one path.

Partition — (7) To decompose a large problem into several smaller problems.

Partition analysis — (75) A technique for testing the completeness of a database using aggregate values.

Password — (71) A secret word or string of characters used to uniquely identify a given user.

Path — (43) On a graph, a sequence of edges that links a set of nodes; on a digraph, the path's direction is significant; (54) a group of connected links that allow the transmission of information from a source to destination(s).

Path test — (75) A test that traces the flow of logic through a program; typically, test data are provided to make sure each logical path through the program is followed.

Pattern — (66) A named problem/solution pair that can be applied in new contexts, along with advice on how to apply it.

Payback period — (38) A measure of the time it takes for accumulated benefits to exactly match the development costs.

Payoff — (39) A benefit.

Peak load test — (74) A test designed to ensure that the system can handle the stress of a peak load demand.

Perfective maintenance — (80, 81) Maintenance activities intended to enhance the system by improving efficiency, reliability, functionality, or maintainability, often in response to user or system personnel requests.

Performance requirement — (35) A requirement that specifies such characteristics as speed, frequency, response time, accuracy, precision, portability, reliability, security, and maintainability.

PERT (program evaluation and review technique) — (21) A project management technique based on a project network; with PERT, the critical path is the primary focus of management control and monitoring the critical events provides an early warning if estimates are inaccurate.

PGP (pretty good privacy) — (71) A popular public/private key encryption algorithm that was created without government support and is available on the Internet.

Phased implementation (partial conversion) — (76) A system release strategy in which the new system is released in stages.

Physical — (2, 3) real; actual, operational hardware, software, or data; contrast with *logical*.

Physical data flow diagram — (24) A data flow diagram that identifies the system's physical processes and physical data stores.

Physical data structure — (4) A set of related data elements as they are physically stored.

Physical database design — (45) The database design stage during which a blueprint for physically implementing the database is produced.

Physical design phase — (4) The phase in the structured requirements definition methodology during which the detailed requirements determined by the logical design phase are converted into physical specifications for developing the system.

Physical record — (44) The unit of data that moves between the peripheral device and main memory.

Physical security — (71) A set of security features concerned with denying physical access to the system, preventing the physical destruction of the system, and keeping the system available; (77) techniques and procedures concerned with denying physical access to a system.

Pilot implementation (location implementation) — (76) A system release strategy in which the new system is first released in a single site, such as a branch office or a warehouse, thoroughly tested, and then ported to the other sites.

Pixel — (46) A picture element; a dot on a screen.

Plug-in — (51) A program that plays or displays special files that are beyond the capability of a standard browser.

Pointer — (43) A link to a data item; typically, a key value or an address.

Polymorphism — (6) The property of an operation or method that allows it to produce similar results in different objects or at different levels.

Pop — (43) To remove an entry from the top of a stack.

Population — (9, 17) The entire set of relevant entities or measurements.

Portfolio — (54) A prioritized list of routing decision criteria.

Post conditions — (66) Objects that were created, associations that were formed or broken, and any attributes that were modified during an operation.

Post-implementation review (post-release review) — (76) A review of the system development process conducted after the system is released.

Power dialing — (71) Running a program that dials thousands of numbers in sequence and notes only the numbers that return a modem tone.

Preconditions — (66) Objects that must exist for an event to take place.

Predefined process — (37) On a system flowchart, a high-level process that is more fully documented in a separate, lower-level flowchart; (55) a flowcharting symbol that indicates that the logic is flowcharted in more detail elsewhere.

Prediction system — (67) A type of expert system used to infer likely consequences from a given situation.

Present value — (38) The value of a (current or future) sum of money in today's dollars.

Preventive maintenance — (81) Regularly scheduled maintenance activities; the intent is to anticipate problems and correct them before they occur.

Prime item development specification (PIDS) — (35) A set of high-level design requirements associated with each hardware component defined in (or implied by) a parent system/segment design document; (41) the documentation for a hardware configuration item; a hardware design specification.

Primitive — (3) A process (or transform) that requires no further decomposition; (44) a command that tells a peripheral device to perform one of its basic functions.

Probabilistic model (stochastic model) — (19) A model having some data described by probability distributions.

Probability mass function (pmf) — (79) The mathematical relationship between the various values that a discrete random variable may assume and the probabilities of occurrence.

Problem definition — (1) The first step in the system development life cycle during which the problem is identified, its cause determined, and a strategy for solving it developed.

Problem domain — (34) A collection of all types of knowledge (including common sense and informed guesses), facts, and/or data related to a defined problem.

Problem search space (search space) — (34) In a search-oriented problem-solving technique, a domain with all possible sets of steps and/or alternatives to support comprehensive searching for the completion of a goal or goals.

Problem space (solution space) — (7, 34) A mathematical term for the set of all possible solutions. Solution space is a special type of search space. A desired solution can be obtained by searching all possible problem-solving alternatives in the space.

Problem statement — (12) A written statement that defines a problem by listing its symptoms, identifying a set of objectives for solving the problem, and indicating the problem's scope.

Procedural cohesion — (62) A type of cohesion in which all the elements of a module are associated with the same procedural unit, such as a loop or a decision structure.

Procedural/production system — (67) A technique that analyzes information from multiple independent knowledge sources, identifies similarities, distinguishes differences, and merges similar ideas and concepts to form aggregate categories.

Procedure — (2, 55, 59, 60) Guidelines, rules, and instructions that tell people how to perform a task; often, a *manual* procedure.

Procedure/subroutine approach — (67) An approach to knowledge representation in which knowledge about the world is contained in procedures, small programs that know how to do specific things.

Process — (1) An activity that changes a system in some way; (3, 4) an activity that changes, moves, or manipulates data; (55, 56) a set of steps for performing a task.

Process (transform) — (24) An activity that changes, moves, or otherwise transforms data.

Process-data element matrix — (40) A table that shows the relationships between the data elements and the processes.

Process error — (75) A computational error, a comparison error, a sequencing error, a control logic error, and so on.

Process flowchart (logic flowchart) — (55) A graphical representation of the flow of logic, control, data, or paperwork through a program, a routine, a module, or a process.

Process symbol — (55) A flowcharting symbol that indicates an operation that changes or manipulates data in some way.

Processing control — (77) A test or technique that measures and controls a processing activity.

Productivity — (78) Output per unit of labor; more generally, output per unit of input.

Program generator (application generator, code generator, generator) — (2, 31, 32) A program that starts with information in graphical, narrative, list, or some other logical form and outputs the appropriate source or executable code.

Program profiler — (73) A routine or device that tracks the resources requested and services utilized by a particular program as it executes.

Project dependency — (14) A dependency relationship between two or more subprojects; for example, the input(s) to one subproject are typically output from another subproject.

Project interrelationship — (14) A link or relationship between two or more subprojects; for example, the successful completion of one subproject might be a prerequisite for several other subprojects.

Project network — (21, 22) A bubble chart that graphically depicts activities, their starting and completion times, and their interrelationships.

Project-oriented paradigm — (16) An approach to requirements analysis that focuses on end-user requirements.

Projection — (28) The process of separating one relation into subrelations.

Property lists approach — (67) An approach to knowledge representation that uses objects and lists of their properties (or attributes) to describe the state of the world.

Protocol — (53, 54) A set of rules that governs data communication.

Prototype — (7, 48) A reasonably complete, working model of a system; (31, 32) a preliminary, working, physical model of a system, a subsystem, or a program.

Prototyping — (31, 32) The act of creating a prototype.

Pseudocode — (59) A tool for planning, defining, or documenting the contents of a program routine or module that resembles real code.

Public/private key system — (71) An encryption system that uses two keys; the message is encrypted using the published public key and decrypted using the secret private key.

Pull-down menu (drop-down menu) — (50) A menu of detailed options that appears when the user clicks or selects a major function on a menu bar.

Push — (43) To add an entry to the top of a stack.

Quality — (78) Conformance to requirements; in a broader sense, quality implies that the requirements match user needs and that the system meets the requirements.

Quality assurance — (78) Goals, procedures, and techniques for measuring and ensuring quality.

Quality factor — (78) A parameter that implies quality, such as correctness, reliability, efficiency, integrity, usability, maintainability, testability, flexibility, portability, reusability, and interoperability.

Quality requirement — (35) A requirement that specifies a measure of quality, such as an acceptable error rate, the mean time between failures, or the mean time to repair.

Query — (45) A question; usually, a request for data or information.

Question-answer dialogue — (49) A form of dialogue designed to solicit user input.

Queue — (43) A special type of linked list in which insertions occur at the rear and deletions occur at the front; (79) a waiting line.

Quick-hit approach — (32) An approach to rapid application development that takes advantage of recognized high payoff applications for which a system can be built very quickly.

Quickest route algorithm — (54) An adaptive routing technique that sends the message to the next available neighboring node (other than the sending node) as quickly as possible.

Rabbit — (71) A program that replicates itself until no memory is left and no other programs can run.

RAD (rapid application development) — (32) A system development methodology that employs joint application design, prototyping, CASE technology, application generators, and similar tools to expedite the design process.

Random access (direct access) — (44) Reading records from or writing records to a file in any order.

Random sample — (9) A sample in which each item in the population has the same chance of being selected.

Random variable — (79) A symbolic representation of an outcome.

Range — (9) The difference between the highest value and the lowest value in a set of measurements.

Range constraint analysis (boundary analysis) — (75) Generating test data to represent such extreme values as upper bounds, lower bounds, and other exceptional values.

Rapid application development (RAD) — (32) A system development methodology that employs joint application design, prototyping, CASE technology, application generators, and similar tools to expedite the design process.

Rational subgroup — (10) A sample of measurements taken from a process in such a manner that will maximize the probability that the sample captures common cause variability and that any possible assignable cause variability will occur between rational subgroups; in other words, the variation in the rational subgroup should be the result of common causes of variation only.

Real data — (75) Data provided by the user that reflect the system's actual operating environment.

Real-time system — (30, 72, 73) A system that responds to events as they occur and provides immediate feedback to influence or control those events in "real" time.

Reasonableness test — (46, 77) A test used to screen invalid values (e.g., anything but F or M in a single-character sex or gender field).

Reasoning — (7, 34, 67) The act of using inference to lead to a conclusion based on existing knowledge and/or data.

Reasoning capability — (7) An inference engine feature that reaches a conclusion by applying the rules in the rule base.

Reconciliation control — (77) An output control designed to ensure that the right amount of data is output to support daily statistical analysis and decision-making activities.

Record — (25, 43, 44) The set of fields associated with an occurrence of an entity; (47) a set of related fields.

Record control — (77) A simple processing control technique that involves counting and verifying the existence of every record in a database.

Recovery test — (74) A test that simulates emergency situations such as power failures, equipment malfunctions, database failures, and so on.

Recursion — (30, 43) The ability of a subroutine to call itself; a subroutine initiating a circular chain of calls that returns eventually to itself.

Redundancy — (42) Two (or more) copies of a hardware component; in the event of component failure, the redundant copy provides backup; (73) the duplication of components to provide back up in case of failure.

Reengineering — (2) Rethinking and redesigning business processes; (5) the process of revising application software using a CASE tool; (81) changing a system to make it better without affecting its functionality or external behavior.

Referential group — (82) A complete set of relationally connected tables.

Regression test — (74) A form of test in which old test cases and test data are applied to a modified version of a system to ensure that the changes have not affected the system's ability to perform its fundamental tasks; (80) a test designed to measure how a change to a system affects response time and other standard performance metrics.

Regression testing — (77) An auditing technique that compares the results obtained when the system is being audited to the results obtained under normal conditions.

Relation — (7) An association or link between two objects or entities; (28) an entity in tabular form, with attributes (fields) stored in columns and tuples (records or occurrences of the entity) stored in rows; (45) a table (analogous to a file) in a relational database.

Relational database — (45) A database in which the files (or relations) are visualized as two-dimensional tables with each column holding values of a single field (or attribute) and each row holding a single record (a single occurrence of the entity); the files are linked by pointers or, more generally, relationships.

Relationship — (25, 26, 27, 28, 45) A link between two entities, data structures, or relations.

Relative addressing — (44) Assigning each record (or byte) in a file an address that represents its position relative to the beginning of the file.

Reliability — (73) A measure of the likelihood that a system or a component will function properly over time; often measured by the mean time between failures; (78) the probability that a given component or system will perform as expected (or will *not* fail) for a given period of time.

Reliability requirements analysis — (53) A network analysis process that helps the designer develop a back-up plan or create necessary redundancies.

Repair system — (67) A type of expert system used to develop and execute plans to administer a remedy for some diagnosed problem.

Repetition (iteration) — (62) A block of logic that is executed repetitively as long as (while) an initial condition holds or until a terminal condition occurs.

Report — (47) An organized presentation of data, often printed or displayed in text form.

Report header (report title) — (47) A page, screen, or section that (typically) precedes and identifies the report.

Report summary — (47) One or more lines, a section, or a page that summarizes the entire report.

Reporting control procedures — (74) A set of procedures for documenting all test results.

Repository — (5) An integrated holding area where diagrams, descriptions, specifications, test data, and other items are stored and integrated. The repository is the most critical component in a CASE environment.

Request for proposal (RFP) — (42) A formal (often advertised) request for competitive bids based on a set of requirements.

Requirement — (3, 35) An element (process, data, etc.) that must be part of a system; a user need.

Requirements planning — (32) The rapid application development phase during which the system requirements are defined using joint application design and other tools and techniques; this phase is similar to traditional problem definition and systems analysis.

Requirements specification — (35, 75) A document that clearly and precisely defines the customer's logical requirements (or needs) in such a way that it is possible to test the finished system to verify that those needs have actually been met.

Resolution — (46) The level of detail a screen can show, a function of the number of pixels (or dots) on the screen.

Resource analysis — (42) An evaluation of such hardware component capabilities as mean time between failures, the average number of instruction executed per second, clock speed, multiple processor availability, and expandability.

Response time — (36) The maximum allowable time to complete a process once its trigger event has occurred; (49) traditionally, the interval between the instant a command is issued and the instant the response begins to appear on the screen; dialogue response time includes system response time, the display rate, user scan/read time, user think time, user response time, and error time; (72, 73) the elapsed time between a request for service and the delivery of that service.

Response time analysis — (53) A network analysis process that helps to determine the system's response time requirements (e.g., interactive, store and forward, real-time, etc.).

Responsibility — (66) A contract or obligation of a type or class, including both responsibilities of knowing and responsibilities of doing.

Restructuring — (81) Efforts aimed at enhancing performance without changing how the system works or what it does.

Reuse maturity model — (29) A comprehensive model that measures the extent of reuse of software components, architecture, and processes in an organization.

Reverse engineering — (5) The process of studying the existing application software to understand its design; (81) extracting an abstract model from a system's physical documentation and then using the model as a base for creating a functionally equivalent system.

Ring network — (52) A network that consists of a series of nodes connected to form a ring.

Ripple effects — (81) Unexpected bugs or new errors caused by a change intended to fix an initial problem.

Rising cable — (53) Generally, a cable that runs between two floors in a building.

Risk — (38) The likelihood that an investment will fail to return the expected benefits; (39) a possible negative outcome that can be interpreted, estimated, or quantified by applying past experience.

Risk analysis — (19) An analysis of the potential occurrence of an undesirable outcome when a decision must be taken in the presence of uncertainty.

Root — (62) The module at the top of a control structure from which all control flows.

Root (root node) — (43) A tree's top (or base) node.

Root cause analysis — (18) Identification of the initial factor resulting in an effect of interest; the root cause is usually found in a tiny branch. This initial factor starts a chain reaction of cause-and-effect situations, moving from a tiny branch to a small branch to a medium branch to a big branch, and ultimately resulting in the effect of interest.

Rooted tree network — (52) A tree network with a clearly defined root node that serves as a base for the entire network.

Route — (54) The path(s) or its subset used to actually transmit information from a source to a destination(s).

Router — (53, 54) An intelligent device that provides network connections and performs such services as protocol conversion and message routing.

Routine — (55, 56, 59, 60) A set of instructions that performs a specific, limited task.

Routing — (54) The process of determining the best available path (or path segment) to transmit a message.

Rule — (7, 34, 67) A formal specification or description of a unit of knowledge.

Rule base — (7, 34) A collection of executable rules; in an expert system, the rule base is accessed by the inference engine to support reasoning.

Sample — (9, 17) A selected subset of a population.

Sample space — (79) The set, or collection, of all possible outcomes.

Sampling error — (17) The difference between an estimate based on a sample and the true value of the population parameter being estimated.

Scaffolding — (74) Software written specifically to support testing.

Schedule — (20) A series of events or activities with estimated completion times or target dates.

Scheduled report — (47) A report that is prepared at a predetermined time.

Scheduling control — (77) An operational control that is used to monitor input or output timings and provide an early warning of increasing queue lengths.

Schema — (45) A general description of the entire database that shows all the record types and their relationships.

Scope — (4) In the structured requirements definition methodology, an estimate of input, processing, and output time; (12, 14, 72) more generally, size or magnitude; often, a preliminary estimate of the size or cost of an information system.

Screen — (46) An output device that resembles a television screen.

Screening questions — (17) Questions posed in order to determine whether or not a respondent should answer the main question.

Scribe — (14) During a JAD session, the person responsible for taking notes, recording all discussions, and organizing and compiling the necessary documents.

SDLC (system development life cycle) — (1, 72) A set of steps for solving information system problems; the basis for most systems analysis and design methodologies.

Search space (problem search space) — (34) In a search-oriented problem-solving technique, a domain with all possible sets of steps and/or alternatives to support comprehensive searching for the completion of a goal or goals.

Second normal form — (28) A first normal form relation from which any data elements that depend on only part of a concatenated key have been removed to a separate entity.

Security — (71, 77, 82) Hardware, software, and procedures intended to protect the hardware, software, data, and other system resources from unauthorized, illegal, or unwanted access, use, modification, or theft.

Selection (decision) — (62) A block of logic that provides alternate paths through the block depending on a run-time condition.

Semantic analysis — (68) A technique in which the system determines the meaning of each word by looking it up in a dictionary or a knowledge base.

Semantic net technique — (67) An approach to knowledge representation that describes the state of the world as a collection of nodes that represent objects, object properties, concepts, events, and arcs of links in a graph.

Sequence — (62) A block of logic in which the instructions are executed in simple sequence, one after another.

Sequence diagram — (66) A type of interaction diagram, drawn using the UML notation, that depicts the interaction between objects and shows the detailed message flow between objects in a use case; the time axis is directed downwards and the objects are represented in a vertical column.

Sequence test (flow test, transaction test) — (75) A test designed to verify the complete logical flow needed to accomplish a task.

Sequential access — (44) Reading records from or writing records to a file in key and/or physical storage order.

Sequential cohesion — (62) A form of cohesion in which the modules form a chain of transformations, with the output from one module serving as input to the next.

Server — (53) A computer that holds centralized resources and provides them to clients on request.

Service controls — (77) Operational controls that measure such parameters as response rate, throughput rate, and turnaround time.

Service rate — (79) The number of customers served per unit of time.

Service time — (79) The time a customer spends receiving service in a queuing system.

Siblings — (43) Two or more nodes that share the same level.

Signal — (6, 66) A message that allows objects to interact with other objects.

Simple star network — (52) A network that consists of several computers and/or peripherals, each linked to a central host computer via a dedicated line.

Simulated data (hypothetical data) — (75) Data created specifically for testing purposes.

Simulated tracing — (75) A technique for debugging selection and repetitive logic by tracing the program's logical flows.

Simulation — (19, 42) The use of a mathematical model that behaves in the same manner as the system under study.

Simultaneous — (73) At the same instant.

Singly linked list — (43) A linked list in which each node points only to the next node.

Sink — (43) On a directed graph, a node of outdegree 0.

Sink (destination) — (24) A person, organization, or other system that gets data from the target system; a destination defines a system boundary.

Site preparation — (76) The process of preparing the work environment, installing the hardware, and configuring any new equipment to work with existing computers and peripherals.

Slack — (21) The maximum time an activity can slip without affecting the project schedule.

Slot — (67) A frame-like structure for representing stereotyped sequences of events.

Social engineering — (71) The act of pretending to be an authorized user and attempting to convince an employee or other human source to divulge sensitive information.

Software development controls — (77) A set of controls imposed on the software development process; examples include static code analyzers, technical inspections, version controls, and so on.

Software error — (75) A program bug or an operating system error.

Software monitor — (78) A benchmarking program that can be used to measure program efficiency, measure execution performance, keep track of resources used, and so on.

Software requirements specification (SRS) — (35) A set of high-level design requirements associated with each software component defined in (or implied by) a parent system/segment design document; (41) the documentation for a computer software configuration item; a program design specification.

Solution space (problem space) — (7, 34) A mathematical term for the set of all possible solutions. Solution space is a special type of search space. A desired solution can be obtained by searching all possible problem-solving alternatives in the space.

Source — (24) A person, organization, or other system that supplies data to the target system; a source defines a system boundary; (43) on a directed graph, a node of indegree 0.

Source data — (46) The original data that describe a transaction.

Sources of variability — (18) Many different things can affect the outcomes from systems, including the effects of workers, machines, materials, methods, measurements, and the environment. These six sources of variation are sometimes used as the big branches on a cause-and-effect diagram.

Span-of-control (breadth) — (61, 62) A measure of the number of modules directly controlled by a higher-level routine.

Spanned record — (44) A logical record that extends over two or more physical records.

Spanning tree (subtree) — (43) A tree within a graph; a subset of a tree that is itself a tree.

Specialization — (29) The creation of a subtype from a super-type by refining the super-type; the opposite of generalization.

Speech recognition — (68) An extension of natural language processing that uses a speech recognition routine (or a chip) to break continuous speech into a string of words, inputs the string to a natural language processing routine, and then passes the resulting commands to an application program.

Split screen — (50) A windows technique that allows the user to divide a screen into several subscreens or subwindows.

Stable process — (10) A process that only exhibits common cause variation; in other words, the output from a stable process produces a population of items which has a constant mean and a constant variance. A stable process is predictable and therefore the output from a stable process is predictable. If a stable process is generating output that is undesirable, then the process itself must be redesigned. A stable process is sometimes called an in-control process. If a process is not stable, it is said to be unstable.

Stack — (43) A special type of linked list in which all insertions and deletions occur at the top.

Standard deviation — (9) The square root of the variance.

Star network — (52) A network on which all messages must go through a central computer before they are passed to the destination computer.

State — (6) A set of attribute values for an object; (30) A condition or mode of being, particularly with regard to phase, form, composition, or structure; (73) often, the complete set of attribute values and settings that describes the precise condition of a computer system at a specific instant in time.

State test — (75) A test that focuses on a real-time system's states.

Static code analyzer — (77, 81) A program that scans (but does not execute) the code and flags such potential errors as synonyms, poor structure, inconsistent usage, dead code, unreferenced variables, and other deviations from coding standards.

Static diagram — (29) A model that describes the different kinds of objects that can exist in the system and the possible ways in which the objects can be linked to each other; no methods or responsibilities are shown, as static models do not contain information about how a system behaves.

Static information — (61) Process information that is not likely to change; for example, the process name, the process number, necessary algorithms, inputs, and outputs.

Static routing — (54) A distributed routing technique that establishes routine paths between sending and receiving nodes based on a data flow analysis of historical data.

Steady state — (19) The end of transient state as the system reaches normal operations; (79) a condition representative of a system's long run behavior; for example, an assembly line starting without parts in process will be in a transient state until such time as the various stations are being utilized at approximately their expected levels, at which point steady state has been achieved.

Steering committee — (13) A committee consisting of representatives from various user groups that accepts, rejects, and prioritizes information system proposals.

Stepwise checking — (75) Placing print or write commands throughout a program and using the resulting messages to determine where the program fails or begins producing errors.

Stepwise refinement — (61) A top-down strategy for dealing with complex or abstract processes; (72) a design strategy that starts with a small program or subsystem and continuously refines it by adding new functions and/or modifying features.

Stereotype — (67) A description that embodies a set image or type; a template.

Stochastic model (probabilistic model) — (19) A model having some data described by probability distributions.

Stochastic process — (79) A process organized into states in which movement from state to state is governed by probabilities; examples include the number of customers in a queuing system, the stock levels of inventory on hand, and the brands purchased by consumers.

Strata — (9) The set of subgroups in a stratified random sample.

Stratified random sampling — (9) A random sampling technique in which the population is divided into subgroups called strata such that each element of the population lies in exactly one stratum; samples are taken randomly within each stratum.

Stratum — (9) A single subgroup in a stratified random sample.

Stress test — (74) A test conducted under extreme conditions.

Structure analysis testing — (75) A technique for evaluating the order of data within a file, a table, or a relation.

Structure chart — (3, 63) A hierarchy chart on which the data flows and control flows between modules are traced.

Structured analysis — (3) A set of tools and techniques intended to transform an abstract problem into a feasible logical design.

Structured design — (3) A set of tools and techniques intended to convert a logical design into a concrete information system.

Structured English — (60) A very limited, highly restricted subset of the English language used to plan, design, or document program routines, modules, and manual procedures.

Style — (69) A font, a point size, and a set of text formatting rules.

Sub-problem — (15) A problem that is part of a larger problem.

Subschema — (45) A subset of the schema that includes only those records and relationships needed by a particular user or class of users.

Subtree (spanning tree) — (43) A tree within a graph. A subset of a tree that is itself a tree.

Summary line — (47) On a report, a line (or row) that holds summary information, such as counts or sums; summary lines are typically printed or displayed following a control break.

Summary report — (47) A report that summarizes data accumulated or derived from several input records, often showing *only* the summarized data.

Suprasystem — (1) A system's environment.

Surge protector — (42) A device that protects electronic components against sudden changes in electrical current.

Symbolic reasoning — (7) A technique for performing reasoning or inference with symbolic data such as graph, image, and/or picture.

Symbolic representation — (7) A technique for representing symbolic data or knowledge.

Synch point — (82) A point at which a complete set of relationally connected tables (a referential group) is consistent.

Synchronization — (82) The act of ensuring that a complete set of relationally connected tables (a referential group) is consistent.

Syntactic analysis — (68) A technique that allows a parser routine to, essentially, diagram a sentence to form a parse tree.

Syntax test — (75) A type of test designed to identify high-level syntax errors that are not flagged by the compiler or language translator; such errors can cause a program to accept bad data or to misinterpret good data.

Synthesis — (15) An evolutionary paradigm that starts with a major or influential user's viewpoint and incorporates other users' perspectives until all relevant viewpoints are included.

System — (1, 72) A set of interrelated components that function together in a meaningful way; (19) a set of components (entities, machines, etc.) that interact to perform an operation that is of interest to the modeler.

System access monitoring — (78) Software and hardware used to measure such parameters as throughput, turnaround time, access time, and response time.

System development life cycle (SDLC) — (1, 72) A set of steps for solving information system problems; the basis for most systems analysis and design methodologies.

System error — (75) An error related to input, output, hardware, software, and/or interfaces.

System flowchart — (37) A tool for documenting a physical system in which each component is represented by a symbol that visually suggests its function.

System life cycle — (1, 72) A model that stresses the stages of system usefulness; the stages are birth, development, growth, maturity, and death.

System objective — (4) A desired function of and/or operation performed by a proposed system.

System outputs — (4) The exact data the users need to perform their jobs.

System performance analysis — (73) A type of analysis that focuses on such criteria as processing speed, information access time, data transfer rate, instruction execution time, and so on.

System performance test — (74) A test that focuses on system behavior.

System release — (76) The stage in the system development life cycle when the system is turned over to the user.

System/segment design document (SSDD) (B-specs) — (35) A black-box specification defined for each physical component at (or directly below) the configuration item level; (41) a set of specifications that define, in black-box form, the components that occupy the configuration item level.

System/segment specifications (SSS) (A-specs) — (35) A hierarchy of requirements specifications that logically defines the system from its high-level objectives down to the configuration item level; (41) a set of specifications that identify major systems and subsystems at a conceptual level; the system/segment specifications define the requirements down to, but not including, the configuration item level; sometimes called the project or mission requirements.

System test — (74) A test conducted on the entire system that uses both test data and real, user-supplied data.

Systems information interface (instruction dialogue) — (49) Dialogue that provides instructions and other information about the system's operations, functions, and structure.

Tangible — (39) Easily defined, concrete, physical; for example, payoffs, risks, and uncertainties that can be expressed in financial terms are considered tangible.

Tangible benefits — (38) Benefits that can be measured in financial terms, such as reduced operating costs or enhanced revenues.

Task — (73) A single program or routine in memory and available to be executed.

Technical evaluation — (78) A type of system evaluation that deals with the technology and the system design and considers such factors as reliability, productivity, quality, efficiency, and effectiveness.

Technical feasibility — (13) Proof that the problem can be solved using existing technology.

Template — (69) A document that contains predefined styles and macros.

Temporal cohesion — (62) A type of cohesion in which the elements are related by time.

Temporary file — (44) A file that holds intermediate results and exists for only a brief time.

Terminator — (55) A flowcharting symbol that marks the beginning or end of the flowchart.

Test data — (75) Data that are developed to support the testing process, locate bugs, and facilitate debugging.

Test plan — (74) A plan for conducting the necessary tests that incorporates testing strategies, test procedures, test data, and a test schedule.

Testing — (1) The fifth step in the system development life cycle (following development and preceding implementation) intended to ensure that the system does what it was designed to do; (74, 75) a front-end process intended to exercise the system and its components to locate, investigate, and correct errors and bugs.

Theme — (51) A recurrent idea; on a web page or web site, the consistent use of color, fonts, icons, logos, and sound, a consistent page layout and appearance, and consistent navigational rules.

Third normal form — (28) A relation in which each data element in the relation is a function of the key, the whole key, and nothing but the key. To reach third normal form, all transitive dependencies must be removed from a second normal form relation.

Throughput — (2, 72) The amount of work flowing through a process, a component, or a system; often expressed as a percent utilization.

Time bomb — (71) A program that executes on a particular date or when a particular condition is met.

Time frame factor — (4) A processing cycle; for example, annually, monthly, daily, hourly, on demand, and so on.

Time-sharing — (73) Concurrently executing multiple tasks by assigning the processor to a given task for a brief time slice before moving on to the next task.

Timed-box approach — (29) A project management approach that divides the set of all requirements for a system into subsets, each of which is implemented as a version of the system; the delivery of each new version of the system in a regular and timely fashion is guaranteed by this approach.

Token passing — (52, 53, 54) A network management technique in which an electronic token is passed continuously from node to node around the network and a given node can transmit a message only when it holds the token.

Tool — (5) Software that supports a specific task in the software development process.

Top-down — (15) An approach to problem solving that starts with the high-level control structures and works down to the details.

Top-down design — (72) A goal driven design strategy in which the modules (and/or subsystems) at the top of the hierarchy (usually, the broad, control-oriented modules) are designed first and modules at the bottom of the hierarchy (the detailed, computational modules) are designed last.

Top-down testing — (74) A testing strategy that starts at the top (with the broad, control modules) and works through the module hierarchy level by level until the bottom level (the detailed computational modules) is reached.

Topology — (52, 53, 54) A map of a network; a physical arrangement of the nodes and connections in a network.

Topology determination — (53) A network analysis process that focuses on physically laying out the network using such tools as location connectivity diagrams.

Touch screen (graphic input screen) — (46) A screen that allows a user to input a command or request information by pointing.

Traffic flow pattern analysis — (53) A network analysis process that helps to define the network's topology and connections as well as the message volumes associated with the various data flows.

Traffic load analysis — (53) A network analysis process that helps to determine the required number of communication lines, the maximum required capacity for each line, the time slots during which the communication lines are likely to be busy, and several related network performance parameters.

Training — (76) Generally, a series of experiences designed to modify behavior; often, a set of activities designed to teach someone how to do something.

Transaction — (3) Typically, one occurrence of a business activity; for example, a single customer order or a single shipment from a supplier; an event; (45, 82) the sequence of steps required to carry out an event about which data are recorded or processed.

Transaction analysis — (3) The act of grouping all modules (or processes) triggered by the same transaction to form a transaction center; (45) a study of expected usage levels associated with the various application functions.

Transaction file — (44) A file that holds current data. A transaction file is often used to update (or maintain) a master file.

Transaction log — (71) A list of a system's transactions.

Transaction-oriented process — (61) A process that transmits or routes the right information to the right process.

Transaction processing system (TPS) — (72) An information system that accepts and processes transactions in either batch or on-line mode.

Transaction response time — (49) The sum of the response times for all the screens in the dialogue.

Transaction test (flow test, sequence test) — (75) A test designed to verify the complete logical flow needed to accomplish a task.

Transform (transform process) — (25, 61) A process or operation that modifies data; (62) a process that converts the input data to output form.

Transform analysis — (3) The act of grouping together the modules (or processes) that manipulate a particular set of data or a particular data structure.

Transform-oriented process — (61) A process that creates and/or derives new information based on the input data.

Transient state — (19) The beginning or warm-up period of a model as activity builds up.

Transition — (30) A movement or shift from one state to another.

Transitive dependency — (28) A non-key attribute that depends indirectly (via a third attribute) on the key attribute.

Transmission control — (77) A processing control designed to ensure that there are no missing, incorrectly converted, or wrongly transmitted data.

Tree — (43) A two dimensional, hierarchical data structure; a tree can be defined recursively because each node is the root node of a subtree.

Tree topology (hierarchical topology) — (52) A hybrid topology that usually consists of two or more linked star or bus networks.

Trigger event — (36) The event that activates a process; (62) the event that activates a program or causes it to change from a wait state to a run state.

Trojan horse — (71) A seemingly harmless program that invites an unsuspecting user to try it.

Trunk — (18) The trunk is the central part of a cause-and-effect diagram to which the big branches are attached. When the term fishbone diagram is used, the trunk is referred to as the spine.

Tuple — (28) A row in a relation that holds one occurrence of the entity (or one record).

Turnaround time — (2) The time between a request for a service and the completion of that service.

Turnpike effect (highway effect) — (53, 54) The tendency of users to quickly adopt new technology as soon as it proves its usefulness; because of the highway effect, the demands placed on a system often exceed projections. This term was initially coined in the 1950s when the traffic load on the Pennsylvania Turnpike exceeded the designers' long-term, worst-case projections soon after the road opened.

Two-phase commit — (82) A process of committing changes across multiple database management systems. In the first phase each DBMS votes on whether they can commit a transaction. If all vote yes, the transaction is committed on all. If any vote no, the transaction is rolled back on all.

UML (unified modeling language) — (29, 66) The universal language for object-oriented modeling; its notation forms an object-oriented modeling language and can replace the notation of various object-oriented analysis methods.

Unbiased estimate — (9) An estimate that is high about half the time and low about half the time.

Uncertainty — (39) A possible negative outcome that cannot be interpreted or estimated based on experience because it has never happened before.

Undirected graph — (43) A graph on which the edges have no direction.

Unidirectional flow — (50) A transfer of control from the top-level (calling) window to a lower-level (called) window.

Unified modeling language (UML) — (29, 66) The universal language for object-oriented modeling; its notation forms an object-oriented modeling language and can replace the notation of various object-oriented analysis methods.

Uniform resource locator (URL) — (51) The address of a page on the World Wide Web.

Uninterruptible power supply (UPS) — (42) A device that continues to supply electrical current in the event of a power failure; many uninterruptible power supplies incorporate surge protectors.

Unit test (module test) — (74) A test conducted on a single program or a single module.

Unrooted tree network — (52) A tree network with no clearly defined base root; instead, there are several nodes that act as major hubs to relay messages or perform limited supervisory functions.

Unstable process — (10) A process that exhibits common cause and assignable cause variation; an unstable process is unpredictable and therefore the output from such processes cannot be predicted. Thus, before the true capability of a process can be determined, all assignable causes of variation must be eliminated from the process, in other words, the process must become stable. An unstable process is sometimes called an out-of-control process.

Upper CASE — (5) A set of tools that support the earlier phases (problem definition, analysis, and design) of the system development life cycle.

URL (uniform resource locator) — (51) The address of a page on the World Wide Web.

Use case — (29, 66) The behaviorally-related sequence of transactions that a user performs in a dialogue with the system when he or she uses the system.

Use case diagram — (29, 66) A diagram that depicts the set of use cases for a system, the actors, and the relation between the actors and the use cases.

User design phase — (32) The rapid application development phase during which the joint application design team examines the requirements and transforms them into logical descriptions.

User interface — (48, 49, 50) A point in the system where a human being interacts with a computer.

Validity test — (46, 77) A test used to ensure that each input field is the right type (numeric, alphabetic), that the value of a given field is within upper and lower bounds, that fixed length fields (e.g., social security number, telephone number) are the right length, and so on.

Value analysis — (75) Techniques for generating test data based on the data values.

Variance — (9) The average of the squared differences between the individual population values and the population mean.

Vector — (43) A one-dimensional array.

Version control — (77, 80) A set of tools and procedures used to track and manage multiple versions of the system and its components.

View — (45) A subset of the database that includes only selected fields from the records that meet a set of conditions defined in a logical filter.

Virus — (71) A program that is capable of replicating itself and spreading between computers by attaching itself to another program.

Visibility — (66) An object has visibility to a second object if it has a reference to the second object.

Visual table of contents (VTOC) — (64) A more formal name for a hierarchy chart.

Volume analysis (control analysis) — (75) A technique for generating test data to check the system's behavior.

Waiting time — (79) The elapsed time between a customer's arrival and the beginning of service.

Walkthrough — (23) An informal inspection.

WAN (wide area network) — (52, 53) A network in which the nodes are (usually) geographically disbursed and linked by common carriers.

Warnier-Orr diagram — (33) A diagramming technique that shows a data structure or a logical structure as a horizontal hierarchy with brackets separating the levels.

Web-form interface — (48) A user interface that follows the metaphor established by the Internet and the World Wide Web.

Web site — (51) A collection of related, hyperlinked pages.

Weighted graph (network) — (43) A graph on which the edges have values.

Weighted routing — (54) A static routing technique in which different routing paths are selected for each message based on a predetermined desirable utilization rate.

White-box testing — (74) A testing strategy in which the tester directly verifies and reviews the logical structure, flow, and/or sequence of a proposed system.

White space — (46) Space on a form or a screen that contains no information; empty space.

Wide area network (WAN) — (52, 53) A network in which the nodes are (usually) geographically disbursed and linked by common carriers.

Window — (50) A screen box or a portion of a screen that holds a message, a menu, or some other unit of information.

Window flow analysis — (50) A pre-execution analysis technique used to verify that the sequence of calls to and exits from the various windows is correct.

Window sequence analysis — (50) An analysis technique intended to ensure that each window is properly linked to the next window during execution.

Word recognition — (68) The process of restructuring an input string into a series of noun phrases, verb phrases, prepositional phrases, adjective phrases, and so on.

Workbench — (5) A single application that integrates several tools, providing a consistent user interface, consistent invocation of tools and tool-sets, and access to a common data set from a repository (data integration).

Workload performance analysis — (73) A type of analysis that focuses on such criteria as throughput, response time, turnaround time, the frequency and size of transactions, and regular and peak time workloads.

World Wide Web — (51) A massive, Internet-based, international collection of hyperlinked pages.

Worm — (71) A program that is capable of spreading from one computer to another under its own power.

Trademarks

The following trademarks are referenced in this book.

Company or Organization	Product or Products
ACCPAC International	CA-Clipper
Acius	4th Dimension
Adobe Systems, Inc.	Adobe Acrobat Reader, PDF
Allaire, LLC	Cold Fusion
Alpha Software Corporation	Alpha Four
America OnLine	AOLPress
Apple Corporation	Macintosh, QuickTime Viewer
Applied Business Technology	Project Management Workbench
Applied Computer Technology	ITE, SDTF
Andersen Consulting	Foundation
Arity Corporation	Arity Prolog
Artificial Intelligence Corp.	Intellect
Azor Inc..	FERRET
Borland International	Dbase, Turbo Prolog
Bullseye Testing Technology	C-Cover
Carnegie Mellon University	HEARSAY II, HSRL, KBS, IMS, ISIS-II, OPS83, SRL+
Claris	Filemaker Pro
Client/Server Solutions Inc.	Benchmark Factory
Computer Associates International, Inc.	CA-SuperProject
Compuware Corporation	QARun, QAStress
Consumers Union	Consumer Reports
Control Data Corporation	SCOPE
Corel Corporation	Paradox, Quattro Pro, WordPerfect
Decision Engineering, Inc.	Crystal Ball
Dell Computer Corporation	Dimension
Diamond Optimum Systems, Inc.	VCS-UX
Digital Equipment Corporation	CALLISTO, Cohesion
Dragon Systems	Naturally Speaking

Ganymede Software	Chariot
Expert Systems International	Advisor-2, ESP Advisor, Prolog-2
EXSYS, Inc.	EXSYS Professional
Frey Associates, Inc.	Spock
Goldon Hill Computers	Common Lisp
Helicon, Inc.	Expert-II
Hewlett Packard	Softbench
Imperial College, London	APES
Inference Corporation	ART, ART-IM
Information Builders, Inc.	FOCUS, Level 5
Inset	HiJaak
Integrated Data Management Systems	IDMS
Intellicorp	KEE
Intelligence Environments	Crystal
IntelligenceWare, Inc.	Auto-intelligence
Intelligent Terminal Ltd.	Expert Ease
International Business Machines Corp.	AD/Cycle, CMVC, DART, DB2, ISAM, SMF, ViaVoice Gold, VSAM
International Microcomputer Software, Inc.	Formtool 97
Intersolv	Excelerator II, PVCS
IPL	AdaTEST
Jetform Corporation	Jetform Design
Joint Photographic Experts Group	jpeg
Knowledge Garden, Inc.	KnowledgePro
Learning Company, The	Forms Designer
LogicWorks	BPWIN, ERWIN, OOWIN
Lotus Development Corporation	Approach, Word Pro, Lotus 1-2-3, Lotus Notes
Macromedia	Shockwave Player
Massachusetts Institute of Technology	ARS, SYN, WAMPUS
Mathematica, Inc.	RAMIS II English
McDonnell Douglas Automation Company	STRADIS/DRAW
Mercury Interactive Corporation	Astra Sitetest, Loadrunner
Micrografx	Flowcharter
Microsoft Corporation	Access, Excel, Foxpro, Front Page, Internet Explorer (IE), MS-DOS, Office 97, PowerPoint, Project, Visual Basic (VBA), Visual Modeler, Visual SourceSafe, Windows, Windows 95, Word
Minitab, Inc.	MiniTab
NETMANSYS	FastBench Agent Tester

Netscape Communications Corporation	Netscape
Neuma Technology Corporation	STS/CM
Neuron Data	Nexpert Object
Novell, Inc.	Informs
OCLC	WebART
Oracle Corporation	Designer, Developer 2000, ORACLE
Palisade Corporation	@RISK
Parasoft	Code Wizard
Popkin Software	System Architect
PowerSoft	Powerbuilder, Power-Designer
Primavera Systems, Inc.	Project Manager, Suretrack
Pritsker Corporation	SLAMSYSTEM
Purdue University	SPERIL
Quintus Corporation	Quintus Prolog
Quma Software, Inc.	QVCS
Radian Corporation	RULEMASTER
Radview Software	Webexam, Webload
Rand Corporation	RITA, ROSIE, ROSS
Rational Software Corporation	Rational Rose
RealNetworks	Real Player
Relational Software	Visual Test
Rutgers University	Expert, SEEK, RULEWRITER
SAS Institute, Inc.	SAS
Segue Software Inc.	Silkperformer
Silicon Graphics, Inc.	Cosmo Player
Silogic, Inc.	Knowledge Workbench
Softbridge, Inc.	ATF
Software Publishing Company	Harvard Project Manager
Software Research	TestWorks/Web
SPSS, Inc.	allCLEAR
SRI International	PROSPECTOR
SSI Group, Inc., The	Delphi
Stanford University	DART, GUIDON, MYCIN, PECOS, RLL
Sterling Software	Composer
Sun Microsystems, Inc.	Java, JavaScript, SPARCworks/TeamWare
Texas Instruments	Information Engineering Facility (IEF), NaturalLink
Trellix Corporation	Trellix
University of California, Berkeley	Franz Lisp
University of Edinburgh	Cprolog
University of Illinois	ADVISE
University of Maryland	KMS

University of New South Wales	UNSW Prolog
University of Utah	PSL
Verac Corporation	OPS5
Visio Corporation	Visio
Xerox Corporation	INTERLISP, SMALLTALK

Index

Index

Printed and bound by CPI Group (UK) Ltd, Croydon, CR0 4YY

17/10/2024

01775690-0019